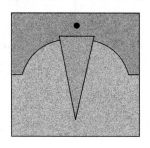

ORGANIZATIONAL BEHAVIOR

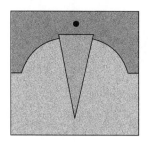

ORGANIZATIONAL BEHAVIOR

Understanding Life at Work

THIRD EDITION

Gary Johns

Concordia University

■ HarperCollins*Publishers*

For my parents, Bill and Jean

Part Opening Photo Credits:
Part One, p. xx, Greg Pease/Tony Stone Worldwide; Part Two,
p. 48, Comstock, Inc.; Part Three, p. 246, Bob Rashid/Tony
Stone Worldwide; Part Four, p. 532, Tony Stone Worldwide

Sponsoring Editor: Melissa Rosati
Development Editor: Lisa Pinto
Project Coordination, Text and Cover Design: York Production
    Services
Cover Art: Copyright 1991 Willem de Kooning/ARS, N.Y. The
    Metropolitan Museum of Art, Rogers Fund, 1956 (S6.205.2).
Photo Researcher: Carol Parden
Production Manager: Michael Weinstein
Compositor: York Graphic Services, Inc.
Printer and Binder: R. R. Donnelley & Sons Company
Cover Printer: The Lehigh Press, Inc.

Organizational Behavior: Understanding Life at Work,
Third Edition

Library of Congress Cataloging-in-Publication Data

Johns, Gary, 1946–
    Organizational behavior : understanding life at
work / Gary Johns.—3rd ed.
        p.   cm.
    Includes bibliographical references and index.
    ISBN 0-673-46550-0 (student ed.).—ISBN 0-673-46552-7
(teacher's ed.)
    1. Organizational behavior.   2. Organization.   3. Management.
I. Title.
HD58.7.J6   1992
658.3—dc20   91-29106
                                                         CIP

    92 93 94 9 8 7 6 5 4 3 2

CONTENTS

*Summary, Key Concepts, Discussion Questions, and References are at the end of every chapter.

PREFACE

In writing this book I have been guided by two goals. First, I wish to convey the genuine excitement inherent in the subject of organizational behavior. Second, I want the presentation of the material to have both academic and practical integrity, acknowledging the debt of the field to both behavioral science research and organizational practice. To put this another way, I wanted to develop a book that would be useful as well as enjoyable to read without oversimplifying key subjects on the premise that this somehow makes them easier to understand.

General Content and Writing Style

Organizational Behavior, Third Edition, is comprehensive; the material included is authoritative and up to date, reflecting current research and practical concerns. Both traditional subjects (such as expectancy theory) and newer topics (such as transformational leadership) are addressed. Balanced treatment is provided to micro topics (covered in the earlier chapters) and macro topics (covered in the later chapters).

Although *Organizational Behavior* is comprehensive, I have avoided the temptation to include too many concepts, theories, and ideas. Rather than comprising a long laundry list of marginally related concepts, each chapter is organized in interlocked topics. The topics are actively interrelated and are treated in enough detail to ensure understanding. Special attention has been devoted to the flow and sequencing of the topics.

The writing style is personal and conversational. Excessive use of jargon is avoided, and important ideas are well defined and illustrated. Special attention has been paid to consistency of terminology throughout the book.

I've tried to foster critical thinking about the concepts under discussion by using devices such as asking the reader questions in the body of the text.

Believing that a well-tailored example can illuminate the most complex concept, I have used examples liberally throughout the text to clarify the points under consideration. The reader is not left wondering how a key idea applies to the world of organizations. The book is illustrated with exhibits, cartoons, and excerpts from the business press such as *Fortune, Business Week,* and the *Wall Street Journal,* to enhance the flow of the material and reinforce the relevance of the examples for the student.

I have treated the subject matter generically, recognizing that organizational behavior occurs in *all* organizations. The reader will find examples, cases, In Focus selections, and You Be the Manager features drawn from a variety of settings, including large and small businesses, high technology firms, social service agencies, hospitals, schools, and the military. In addition, care has been taken to demonstrate that the material covered is relevant to various levels and jobs within these organizations.

Organization

Organizational Behavior is organized in a simple but effective building-block manner. **Part One,** An Introduction, defines organizational behavior, discusses the nature of organizations, and explains how we acquire knowledge about organizational behavior. **Part Two,** Individual Behavior, covers the topics of learning, perception, attribution, attitudes, job satisfaction, and motivation. **Part Three,** Social Behavior and Organizational Processes, discusses groups, socialization, culture, leadership, communication, decision making, power, politics, conflict, and stress. **Part Four,** The Total Organization, considers organizational structure, environment, strategy, technology, change, innovation, and careers.

Some instructors may prefer to revise the order in which particular chapters are read, and this can be accomplished easily. However, Chapter 6, Theories of Work Motivation, should be read before Chapter 7, Motivation in Practice. Also, Chapter 15, Organizational Structure, should be read before Chapter 16, Environment, Strategy, and Technology. The book has been designed to be used in either a quarter or semester course.

New Content Features

A major addition in content to the third edition of *Organizational Behavior* is a strong recognition of the **global aspects of organizational life.** Students must become more comfortable and more competent in dealing with people from other cultures, and the discipline of organizational behavior can be of great assistance in this. I have chosen to integrate material on the international and cross-cultural aspects of organizations into several key points in the text where the research base on these topics is strongest. This integration at several points is designed to encourage students to think naturally and often about cross-cultural issues, rather than seeing this as an isolated topic. Major sections have been integrated in Chapter 5 (cross-cultural values), Chapter 6 (motivation across cultures), and Chapter 11 (cross-cultural communication). In addition, cross-cultural and international coverage can be found among the cases, exercises, You Be the Manager features, and In Focus selections. Among the latter, a special Global Focus logo highlights the selection for students.

Another major addition in content is coverage of the topic of **ethics** in organizations. Since most ethical dilemmas generally result in a decision, I have incorporated a major new section on ethics into Chapter 12, Decision Making. In addition, shorter sections at various points in the text cover research ethics (Chapter 2) and the ethics of organizational politics (Chapter 13). Throughout the text, students should be on the lookout for several Ethical Focus selections, designated by a special logo.

A third major addition in content concerns the related issues of **innovation and technology.** There is growing awareness that organizations will have to be innovative both to compete in the global marketplace and to maintain or improve the quality of life within nations. Chapter 17 includes a major new section on organizational innovation. Much innovation involves the deployment of advanced technology and an appreciation of its impact on employee behavior. Chapter 16 includes a much-expanded discussion of advanced information technology both on the shop floor and in the office.

The third edition also includes new or expanded coverage of procedural fairness (Chapter 5), organizational citizenship behavior (Chapter 5), designing effective work groups (Chapter 8), transformational and charismatic leadership (Chapter 10), strategic alliances (Chapter 16), and resistance to change (Chapter 17).

New Pedagogical Features

Complementing the above changes in content, the third edition also features increased treatment of the applications of the material in actual organizations. This is accomplished with more in-text examples and more In Focus selections.

A major new addition with the same goal is the **You Be the Manager** and **The Manager's Notebook** features. In each chapter, students encounter a You Be the Manager feature that invites them to stop and reflect on the relevance of the material that they are studying to a real problem in a real organization. These problems range from managing workplace diversity (Chapter 1) to ethical concerns (Chapter 12) to environmental issues (Chapter 2). At the end of each chapter, The Manager's Notebook offers some observations about the problem and reveals what the organization actually did.

Each chapter now includes one **Experiential Exercise.** These exercises span individual self-assessment (Chapters 4, 6, 7, 10, 13, 14, and 18), role plays, and group activities (Chapters 1, 3, 5, 8, 9, 11, 12, 15, and 16). To increase confidence in the feedback given to students, the self-assessments generally have a research base.

Finally, a **Glossary** of key concepts is new to the third edition.

Continuing Pedagogical Features

A number of pedagogical features are continued from the previous edition. They are designed to work together to produce an effective text:

- All chapters begin with a short **opening vignette** designed to stimulate interest in the subject matter to be covered. This vignette is carefully analyzed at several points in the chapter to illustrate the ideas under consideration. For example, Chapter 9 begins with a discussion of the corporate culture at the Walt Disney Company. This vignette is then used as an example at eight other points in the chapter, at pages 293, 295, 303, 305, 308, and 315.
- All chapters contain **In Focus** selections to supplement, complement, or illustrate the textual material. These selections are derived from the practicing-management literature (e.g., *Fortune*), the research literature (e.g., the

Academy of Management Journal), and the popular press (e.g., *The New York Times*). They are chosen to exemplify real-world problems and practices as they relate to organizational behavior.

- In addition to the new exercises, each chapter concludes with a **case study,** sixteen of which are new to this edition. The cases are of medium length, thus allowing great flexibility in tailoring the use of them to one's personal instructional style. In general, the cases require active analysis and decision making, not simply passive description. The cases also provide another way to explore some of the important new issues in the field, including the problems of global business (Chapter 11), ethics (Chapters 12 and 13), and managing diversity in the workplace (Chapter 4).
- Each chapter concludes with a **Summary, Key Concepts,** and **Discussion Questions.** Key Concepts are set in boldface type when they are discussed in the body of the text to provide ready reference for students. They are also defined in the Glossary.

Supplements for the Instructor

A comprehensive supplements package is available to adopters of *Organizational Behavior:*

Instructor's Resource Book Written by the text author to ensure close coordination with the book, this extensive manual includes an introduction to the supplements, suggested course syllabi, and audiovisual references. It also includes chapter objectives, a chapter outline, answers to all text questions and cases, supplemental lecture material, and teaching notes for each chapter. In addition, it includes directions for using the study guide's experiential exercises in class and directions on using the computerized interactive cases with the text.

Test Bank Also written by the text author, this bank includes over 1,700 questions, including a mix of factual and application questions. Multiple choice, true-false, and short answer formats are provided.

TestMaster This computer program allows instructors to assemble their own customized tests from the items included in the test bank. If desired, test questions can be viewed on the screen, and test questions can be edited, saved, and printed.

In addition, you can add questions to any test or item bank, or even create your own banks of test questions, which may include graphics.

A real time-saver, it is available for the IBM PC, compatibles, and the Macintosh.

HarperCollins Business Video Library Adopters may select from a variety of original and archival business videos related to the text.

Video Guide This detailed guide ties all applicable videos in the HarperCollins Business Video Library directly to the text. For each applicable video it includes the title, length, teaching objectives, chapters in the text to which the video can be tied, chapter concepts highlighted in the video, a "Video Preview" or brief introduction including what to look for as you watch the video, and a "Video Review." The Video Review includes review questions, an in-class experiential activity, and multiple-choice and other questions on the videos.

Transparency Acetates to Accompany Organizational Behavior A mix of four-color graphics from the text as well as new illustrations from outside sources, this set of 100 acetates is available free to adopters. Reference on using the acetates is in the *Instructor's Resource Book*.

Grades Free to adopters this computerized grade-keeping and classroom management package for use on the IBM PC or compatibles maintains data for up to 200 students.

Supplements for the Student

Study Guide with Experiential Exercises Written by Robert N. Lussier of Springfield College and Lester M. Hirsch of Western New England College, this manual contains for each chapter a self-test section with approximately 75 multiple-choice, true-false, fill-in, and essay questions, an expanded outline, an experiential exercise, and a case analysis section.

Supershell II Micro-Computer Tutorials Written by Robert N. Lussier of Springfield College, this computer-assisted instructional program is designed to help students master the material in the text. The user-friendly program allows students to test their understanding of the text material and receive an individual diagnosis of their performance with suggestions for additional study. The program provides extensive printed output in either glossary form or as printed flash cards. It includes for each chapter a detailed outline, a glossary, and self-test questions.

Interactive Cases in Organizational Behavior Give your students an opportunity to make decisions while sharpening their computer skills with this free interactive program.

Decisions are made in an evolving context on such topics as leadership and motivation. Feedback is provided at each decision point so students can assess their ability to apply the concepts. These timely cases from real company scenarios place students within a variety of corporate environments from pharmaceutical sales to an interior design studio.

Written by Dennis Moberg and David Caldwell of Santa Clara University, each case has been carefully selected to correspond directly with various chapters of *Organizational Behavior*. Detailed instructions on using the cases with the text are in the *Instructor's Resource Book*. Available free to adopters on 3½″ and 5¼″ disks for the IBM PC and compatibles.

Organizational Reality: Reports From the Firing Line, 4/e Written by Peter Frost, Vance Mitchell, and Walter Nord, this popular book includes readings about the "realities" of organizational life. Articles are selected from a variety of popular periodicals such as *Fortune* and *The Wall Street Journal*. It addresses topics of current concern including the environment, ethics, and the global aspects of organizational life. An **instructor's manual** is also available to accompany the reader.

Acknowledgments

Books are not written in a vacuum. In writing *Organizational Behavior*, Third Edition, I have profited from the advice and support of a number of individuals. This is my chance to say thank you.

In preparing the revision, I have received substantial encouragement from my Concordia University Management Department Chair, A. Bakr Ibrahim. I'm also grateful to my other management department colleagues for their interest, support, and ideas. Special thanks to J. Bruce Prince, who authored the careers chapter. Additionally, I'd like to thank my students over the years. In one way or another, many of their questions, comments, challenges, and suggestions are reflected in the book.

A number of colleagues in the field provided informative, thoughtful suggestions for the revision. They include . . .

Allen Bluedorn
University of Missouri-Columbia

Sharon Clinebell
University of Northern Colorado

Patricia A. Fitzgerald
Saint Mary's University

Jeffrey Goldstein
Adelphi University

David B. Greenberger
Ohio State University

Royston Greenwood
University of Alberta

Steven Grover
Indiana University at Bloomington

Eugene H. Hunt
Virginia Commonwealth University

Martha G. Juckett
Monmouth College

Alvin M. Kelly
Langston University

Ron Klocke
Mankato State University

Lissa McRae
Bishop's University

John W. Medcof
McMaster University

Steven B. Moser
University of North Dakota

Gerald Perselay
Winthrop College
Raymond Read
Baylor University
Ben Rosen
University of North Carolina at
Chapel Hill
Elizabeth Ryland
California State University at San
Bernardino
Irwin N. Talbot
Saint Peter's College
Marlene Turner
San Jose State University

Allen J. Schuh
California State University at
Hayward
Yaghoub Shafai
Dalhousie University
Jonathan E. Smith
John Carroll University
Jack W. Wimer
Baylor University
Jeffrey D. Young
Mount Saint Vincent University

Also, thanks to all my colleagues who have taken time to suggest ideas for the book when we have met at professional conferences. Special thanks to Lyman Porter for his ongoing advice and support.

The people at HarperCollins have provided great support for this project. In particular, I thank Melissa Rosati and Anne Smith for keeping the project on track. Also, thanks to Susan Bogle for production assistance.

Finally, thanks to Laurie St. John and the Concordia Academic Support Staff for their patience, efficiency, and good humor.

Gary Johns

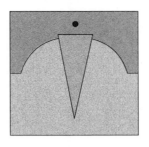

ORGANIZATIONAL BEHAVIOR

PART ONE

AN INTRODUCTION

CHAPTER

1

ORGANIZATIONAL BEHAVIOR AND ORGANIZATIONS

RUSS MICHAELS

One day last winter, Russ Michaels quit his job. Russ had been the news anchorperson for a small New England television station affiliated with one of the major networks. His newscasts had become the most popular in the viewing area during his three years there, and this enabled the station to command premium prices for the commercials aired during these periods. When Russ announced his resignation, the station manager instructed the producer of the news show to "scour the country" for a replacement for Russ. Dozens of long-distance telephone calls were made, and a number of candidates were flown in for auditions. The process cost several thousand dollars. When the replacement broadcaster went on the air, a substantial number of irate viewers called to enquire as to Russ's status and to report that they didn't like the new announcer. In addition, several major advertisers indicated that their commercials should be reduced in frequency or suspended until the acceptability of the new anchor was determined. Two weeks later, the station's newswriter, who had worked very well with Russ, reported that she didn't feel comfortable with the new broadcaster's style and let it be known that she was looking for work in a warmer climate.

This scenario raises some obvious questions. Could Russ's resignation have been anticipated? Why did he resign? Could the resignation have been prevented? In the pages that follow, you will learn that the field of organizational behavior attempts to provide answers to questions such as these. In the chapters that follow, you will learn that it sometimes succeeds.

In this chapter, we will define organizational behavior and discuss why its study is important. We will also discuss the goals of the field of organizational behavior. Then we will define the term organization and discuss some general characteristics of organizations that have implications for the study of organizational behavior. Finally, a framework for the remainder of the book will be presented.

WHAT IS ORGANIZATIONAL BEHAVIOR?

Organizational behavior is a rather general term that refers to the attitudes and behaviors of individuals and groups in organizations. The discipline or **field of organizational behavior** involves the systematic study of these attitudes and behaviors. Thus, the field is concerned with both personal and interpersonal issues in an organizational context. Attitudes of interest might include how organizational members feel about their jobs, co-workers, or pay or how committed they feel to the goals of the organization. Behaviors of interest might include conflict, cooperation, productivity, absence, or resignation.

Why Study Organizational Behavior?

Why should you attempt to read and understand the material in this book? For one thing, like human behavior in general, organizational behavior is *interesting*. You have probably had experiences observing people who were extremely productive or especially unproductive and wondered why such differences exist. Similarly, you might have observed groups whose members worked well together as well as groups riddled with conflict and dissension and wondered what prompted these differences. Although you might have some tentative explanations for these differences, studying organizational behavior should improve your understanding of them.

In addition to the intrinsic interest of its subject matter, the field of organizational behavior is *practical*. To say the least, ours is a highly organized society, and we are all involved with a number of organizations. Most of us are members of organizations, and all of us are consumers of their products and services. In addition, some of us are managers of organizations. Thus, the behavior that occurs in organizations should be of great practical concern. The study of the field should enable you as an organizational member to better understand your own organizational behavior, as well as that of your peers, superiors, and subordinates. This study will suggest what you can do as a manager to increase the effectiveness of your organization and meet the diverse needs of its members. The study of organizational behavior should help you as a consumer to comprehend why some organizations are able to offer their products and services effectively and efficiently while others are not. Such knowledge should make you a wiser consumer of these products and services.

The behavior that occurs in organizations is *important* to their functioning. For example, the story presented earlier demonstrates the profound impact that an apparently routine incident can have. Russ's resignation influenced the work activities of the station manager and the news producer, not to mention the career plans of the newswriter. In addition, it influenced the consumers of the station's services, including the viewing public and the advertisers in the viewing area.

IN FOCUS 1–1

Organizational Behavior: Interesting, Practical, and Important

Chicago's Walkway Woe: It Doesn't Line Up.

In a major snafu, the city and state governments have spent almost $1.9 million on separate sections of an underground walkway only to find that the two do not line up.

Each government built half of the pedestrian tunnel connecting City Hall with the State of Illinois Centre. But the state's segment of the "pedway" is 23 centimetres lower than the city's and 20 cm askew horizontally.

The mistake cost Chicago taxpayers $240,000 to correct and has led to embarrassed finger-pointing. Each government blames the other for the "pedway predicament."

"It's hard to believe this happened," said newly elected Mayor Richard Daley, who ordered an investigation. "It wasn't under my administration."

City hall planners "gave the state an elevation" of 6.8 metres below ground level "and they were supposed to meet it," John Hill, the city's co-ordinating architect, told the Chicago *Sun-Times*, which reported the story yesterday.

"It's very embarrassing," Hill said. "It's like the railroad to nowhere not meeting or a bridge misaligned in midspan because contractors at either end screwed up. Professionals aren't supposed to make mistakes like this."

Frank Conroy, project director for the state, retorted that his people "were right on the money," adding, "If there's a goof, it's on the city's part."

The city did not award the contract for its 36-metre link, most of it under city hall, until September 1987. The mistakes were found about six months later when a city hall basement wall was demolished.

In correcting them, the city changed a ramp into a stairway, added an elevator stop for the disabled and made other modifications.

The walkway should be ready by September, officials said, more than four years later than planned.

Source: Excerpted from "Chicago's Walkway Woe: It Doesn't Line Up" by Bill Peterson, *The Washington Post*, June 3, 1989. © 1989, The Washington Post. Reprinted with permission.

These consequences had obvious short-term costs, and they had the potential to adversely influence the long-term effectiveness of the station. Of course, not all examples of organizational behavior inspire such dramatic consequences. Nevertheless, all of the activities that occur in organizations have the potential to affect how well organizations operate to achieve their own goals and those of society.

Errors in organizations often reveal the importance of organizational behavior, as In Focus 1–1 illustrates.

Goals of the Field

Like any discipline, the field of organizational behavior has a number of commonly agreed upon goals. Chief among these are the *prediction, explanation,* and *control* of the behavior that occurs in organizations. For example, in a later chapter we will discuss the factors that predict which organizational reward systems are most effective in stimulating employee performance. We will then explain the reasons for this differential effectiveness and describe how effective systems can be implemented to enhance performance. As another example, we will discuss the kinds of job characteristics that are predictive of worker satisfaction. We will then explain why these characteristics are satisfying and describe how jobs can be designed to capitalize on these characteristics. Let us now examine the concepts of prediction, explanation, and control in more detail.

Prediction The **prediction** of the behavior of others is an essential requirement of our everyday lives, both inside and outside of organizations. Our lives are made considerably easier by the ability to anticipate when our friends will get angry, when our professors will respond favorably to a finished assignment, and when salespeople and politicians are telling us the truth about a new product or the state of the nation. With regard to organizational behavior, there is considerable interest in predicting the conditions under which people will be productive, or make good decisions, or be absent from work, or be happy with their jobs.

The very regularity of behavior in organizations permits us to make some predictions about the future occurrence of this behavior. If we see enough friendly supervisors with satisfied subordinates, we become pretty skillful at anticipating the reactions of the subordinates of the next friendly supervisor we encounter. However, as we will see in the following chapter, there are several factors that often reduce the accuracy of our casual predictions of organizational behavior. Through systematic study, analysts of organizational behavior seek to improve the accuracy of such predictions in order to reduce the uncertainty with which organizations must cope. Throughout this book, we will discuss matters that should enable you to become more effective in predicting organizational events.

In the story that began the chapter, it would have been advantageous if the station manager had been able to predict Russ's resignation and the events that followed. Minimally, some of the problems that followed the resignation might have been precluded. Under the best of circumstances it might have been possible to prevent the resignation. Of course, being able to predict some behavior does not mean that we will be able to explain the reason for the behavior and develop an effective strategy to control it. This brings us to the second goal of the field of organizational behavior.

Explanation   Another goal of organizational behavior is **explanation** of the events that occur in organizations. Notice that prediction and explanation are not synonymous processes. Primitive societies were certainly capable of predicting the regular setting of the sun, but were unable to explain where it went or why it went there. Similarly, average students may be able to predict with terrible regularity the appearance of C grades on assignments but be unable to explain why their hard work does not result in As. In general, the ability to accurately predict an event precedes the explanation of that event. Thus, the very regularity of the disappearance of the sun at the end of the day gave some clues about why it was disappearing.

In organizational behavior, we are especially interested in determining why people are more or less productive, satisfied, or prone to resign. As the previous paragraph implies, the explanation of these events is much more complicated than their prediction. For one thing, a given behavior may have multiple causes. For example, some individuals may quit an organization because they are dissatisfied with their pay, while others may quit because they dislike the nature of the work they are required to perform. Clearly, an understanding of which of these factors (if either) was motivating Russ's intended resignation would have been extremely helpful for the station manager. Also, the explanation of some event may change over time or circumstances. For example, the reasons people quit organizations may vary greatly from times of full employment to times of high unemployment. Thus, consideration of the current job market for news broadcasters might have given the station manager some clues about the motives for Russ's behavior.

In the next chapter, we will discuss some factors that interfere with the accurate explanation of organizational behavior. In addition, throughout the book you will encounter material that should enhance your understanding of organizational events. The ability to explain these events is a necessary prerequisite for taking action to control them.

Control   The third goal of the field of organizational behavior is the **control** of the behavior that occurs in organizations. It is safe to say that explicit interest in this goal is fairly recent. As it developed, the field was primarily descriptive rather than prescriptive. That is, attempts were made to specify what happens in organizations (prediction) and why it happens (explanation) in order to develop the observational and analytical skills of workers and managers. What *should* be done in response to this information was usually contained in courses in supervision, general management, and personnel management, which were generally more prescriptive. Thus, a knowledge of organizational behavior was seen primarily as a "tool" in the management "tool kit" provided by other courses.

However, as more and more organizational events were described and the accuracy with which behavior in organizations could be predicted and explained increased, it became obvious that such behavior was susceptible to special forms of control. Thus, organizational behavior has developed a number of its own technologies or interventions to supplement those offered by traditional management courses. Clearly, these technologies represent the bottom line for practicing managers and ultimately validate the practicality of our attempts to accurately predict and explain organizational behavior. In the following chapters, you will encounter examples of interventions designed to control the performance, attendance, and job satisfaction of organizational members. These interventions involve changes in reward systems, supervision, and the design of jobs, to name just a few. The important thing to remember is that such interventions should be based on the careful, systematic study of organizational behavior and grounded in previous prediction and explanation. (See the top half of Exhibit 1–1).

Some individuals react negatively to the notion that knowledge of organizational behavior can be used to control the behavior of people at work. Somehow, this use of knowledge smacks of manipulation. However, several factors suggest that such concerns are exaggerated. For one thing, the word *control* is simply a managerial term for affect or influence. Also, every discipline that deals with the management of organizations has implications for the control of behavior. For example, standard accounting practices and procedures, such as budgeting and record keeping, are designed in part to provide performance standards that control the spending behavior of organizational members and units. Finally, it is important to understand that *all* organizations have some kind of reward system, provide some kind of supervision, and provide jobs of a particular design. These factors control the behavior of organizational members, like it or not, and it seems only reasonable to design them to support the effective functioning of the individual and the organization. If this book has a bias, it is that the knowledge

EXHIBIT
1–1

Relationships between goals of the field of organizational behavior and important managerial tasks.

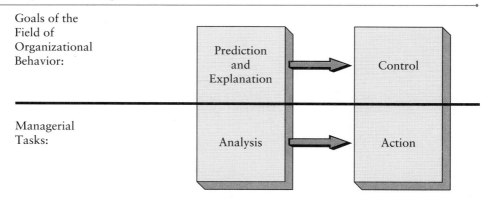

Goals of the Field of Organizational Behavior:

Prediction and Explanation → Control

Managerial Tasks:

Analysis → Action

derived from studying organizational behavior can be used to control behavior in a way that balances the needs of individual employees with the requirements of the larger organization. Achieving this balance is an important determinant of organizational effectiveness (Exhibit 1–2). Clearly, this is an important, practical concern for both the manager who implements control and the recipients of the control. Also, it does not rule out the possibility that employees can effectively control their own behavior via self-management to achieve both personal and organizational goals.

To illustrate this point, let's return to the story of Russ. If the station manager can predict Russ's impending resignation and can truly explain the reason for this behavior, he may be able to act to prevent the resignation, satisfying both the station and the news anchor. Suppose that the manager determines that Russ is not happy with simply broadcasting the news twice a night and wishes to participate in getting the facts behind important local stories. This factor could certainly explain his intention to resign. To control (in this case, prevent) the resignation, the manager might be able to redesign Russ's job to include occasional opportunities to research key stories and go into the field to report on them. As you will discover in a later chapter, this particular intervention is known as job enrichment. Of course, the success of this attempt at control would depend on the adequacy of the manager's explanation for the intended resignation.

EXHIBIT
•————•
1–2

Controlling organizational behavior to balance the needs of individuals with the requirements of the organization.

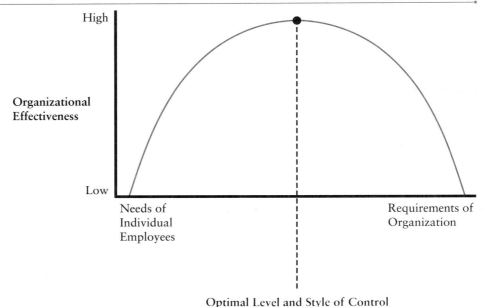

Management Analysis and Action In this section we have said that the goals of the field of organizational behavior involve the prediction, explanation, and control of behavior in organizations. These three goals are closely related to each other. To generate a possible explanation for Russ's impending resignation, the station manager would have to be aware of the cues that might predict resignation. To control this or future resignations, the manager would have to generate an accurate explanation for the behavior.

A clear understanding of how to predict, explain, and control behavior is necessary to effectively accomplish two important managerial tasks: analysis and action. As shown in Exhibit 1–1, prediction and explanation are necessary components for the adequate analysis of organizational problems. With adequate analysis, the manager has a better chance of engaging in actions that will effectively control the behavior in question and deal with the problems. There is a strong tendency for managers to attempt to solve behavioral problems without adequate analysis. I hope this book will improve your analytical abilities and thus improve your attempts to control organizational behavior.

Now that we have considered predicting, explaining, and controlling behavior and have seen how they are related to management, let's apply this knowledge. Read the case about Monsanto in the You Be the Manager feature and answer the questions. At the end of the chapter, find out what Monsanto did in The Manager's Notebook. Be sure to pause and reflect on these applications features as you encounter them in each chapter.

Contingencies in Organizational Behavior

Predicting, explaining, and controlling organizational behavior is not an easy task, partly because human nature is so complex. The admission of this complexity, however, does little to illuminate behavior in general or behavior in organizations. In this book you will find ample evidence that human nature expressed in organizations is indeed complex. Consequently, this is not a "cookbook" of organizational behavior; such a book cannot be written. You will not find formulas to improve performance or job satisfaction with one cup of leadership style and two cups of group dynamics. We have not discovered a simple set of laws or principles of organizational behavior that can be memorized by students and retrieved from the memory bank when necessary to solve any organizational problem.

This does not mean that we are ignorant of the factors that influence what happens in organizations. However, the general answer to many of the questions that will be posed in the following chapters is, "It depends." Which leadership style is most effective? It depends. Will an increase in pay lead to an increase in performance? Again, it depends. These dependencies are often called **contingencies.** Thus, the effectiveness of a particular leadership style is contingent upon the nature of the task being performed, and the consequence of a pay increase is contingent upon how it is administered. Earlier, it was indicated that the reasons for resignation from organizations might be contingent upon the general employment situation. These contingencies reveal the complexity of organizational behavior and provide evidence of the need for its systematic study. Throughout the book we will discuss organizational behavior in a contingency framework.

YOU BE THE MANAGER

Manager

Managing Workplace Diversity at Monsanto

Monsanto Agricultural Company is a St. Louis–based firm that develops and manufactures herbicides and biogenetically advanced products such as hormones that boost the milk production of dairy cows. It has facilities in the United States and in places such as France, Argentina, and South Korea. Monsanto management was concerned about the problems and opportunities of attracting and managing an increasingly diverse work force. On a small scale, international transfers brought culturally diverse people together. Mutual acceptance and cooperation were required despite cultural differences. On a much larger scale, Monsanto was aware of coming labor shortages in science and technology and the changing texture of the U.S. work force. This work force would be composed of more women, members of minorities, and immigrants, who would have to be aggressively recruited and made to feel welcome at Monsanto. At the same time, it was felt that more could be done to move currently employed women and members of minorities into positions of increased responsibility. Monsanto management was looking for a way to meet these challenges of diversity. As a Monsanto manager, what would *you* do?

1. Proper analysis of the Monsanto situation is necessary before any action is taken. What predictions have been made, and what explanations are required to decide on a course of action?

2. What are some actions that might be taken to encourage and manage diversity at Monsanto?

To find out what Monsanto did, see the Manager's Notebook at the end of the chapter.

Source: Adapted from Caudron, S. (1990, November). Monsanto responds to diversity. *Personnel Journal,* 72–80.

WHAT ARE ORGANIZATIONS?

Since this book concerns events in organizations, it might be a good idea to consider briefly the nature of the beast. **Organizations are social inventions for accomplishing goals through group effort.** This fairly simple definition can be dissected to make some important points about organizational behavior and further justify its systematic study.

Social Inventions

The plain and simple fact is that organizations are, by definition, social inventions or contrivances. That is, they basically require the coordinated presence of *people*, not things. This is admittedly a difficult concept, and it is hard to separate the "coordinated presence of people" who work at General Motors from the physical existence of buildings, trucks, and assembly lines. However, if your favorite restaurant or tavern closes its doors because of lack of patronage, it ceases to be an organization, despite the fact that its physical trappings remain behind those doors. Similarly, given our definition, if *everyone* had resigned from the television station and had not been replaced, it would have ceased to be an organization. Of course, none of this should be taken to imply that the material technology of organizations is unimportant. General Motors simply wouldn't *be* General Mo-

Employees of Monsanto Agricultural Company have developed innovative ways of managing a diverse work force. (Courtesy of Monsanto Company)

tors without buildings and assembly lines. Thus, you will learn in Chapter 16 that particular technologies have an important impact on the behavior that occurs in organizations.

This perspective suggests that organizational behavior is pervasive, and that its study is basic to the understanding of any organization. There are organizations (such as neighborhood associations) that exist without balance sheets, capital assets, financial plans, or formal marketing strategies, but not without people. It is worth noting, however, that established organizations do not usually depend upon the presence of *specific* individuals for their existence and continuity. In fact, one of the very reasons that our society supports the formation of organizations is to ensure that "the work gets done," independent of the whim and fancy of specific individuals. That is, organizations are designed to continue achieving their goals even if certain members are replaced. Thus, the television station remained in existence even though Russ, a key member, resigned.

Goal Achievement

Organizations are not random collections of people. Individuals are assembled into organizations for some reason. Thus, the organizations mentioned above have (or had) as one goal the production and sale of cars, the preparation and sale of food, or the transmission of television signals. Nonprofit organizations have goals such as saving souls, curing the sick, or educating people. Two points about these examples of goals are rather obvious. First, they hardly represent the only goals that their respective organizations have. In addition to producing and selling cars, General Motors has the goal of reducing the pollution created by its products and facilities. Similarly, in addition to saving souls, a church seeks to help the needy in its community. Thus, organizations have multiple goals. Second, the goals just cited are general and abstract. Such goals have been referred to as **official goals,** and one finds evidence of their existence in charters, annual reports, and official public pronouncements by organizational representatives.[1] But official goals provide little day-to-day guidance for operating a firm or institution. How are such vague official goals translated to guidelines for organizational activities? It has been proposed that **operative goals** are developed to bridge this gap.[2] These goals, which may reflect the modification or even subversion of official goals by internal interest groups, guide organizational activities by virtue of their specificity. Examples of such goals for an automobile producer might be the development and testing of a diesel-powered passenger car within two years or a decrease of 10 percent in the average fuel consumption of its passenger fleet over three years. A university might resolve to secure funding for a new building to house its school of business administration or to develop a new course registration system. The television station might plan to develop a hard-hitting public affairs show to lure viewers away from competitors.

One important, although often implicit, official goal of virtually all organizations is survival. In fact, it can be argued that most other official organizational goals are ultimately directed toward survival. Thus, when the crippling disease polio was effectively eradicated in the United States during the 1960s, the March of Dimes developed another official goal—the eradication of birth defects. This change in official goals ensured its survival as an organization. In the 1990s, with the easing of East-West tensions, some analysts have predicted that the North Atlantic Treaty Organization (NATO) will add cultural and environmental goals to its military mission to ensure its future role. There are several *behaviors* that appear to be necessary for an organization's survival to be assured:

- Individuals must be induced to join and remain in the organization.
- Members must carry out their assignments reliably.
- Members must occasionally engage in innovative activities that go beyond their usual assignments.[3]

These organizational behaviors are important because they represent a subset of people-related operative goals that help guide organizations in achieving other operative goals (such as developing that diesel car or public affairs show). Some of the operative goals that are of particular concern to the field of organizational behavior include things such as:

- The maintenance of a work environment that is satisfying to present members and attractive to potential members.
- A reasonable level of turnover from the organization.
- A minimal level of absence from work.
- A reasonable level of high-quality performance from both individuals and groups.
- Creative, realistic decision making and problem solving.
- The avoidance or resolution of dysfunctional conflict and other problematic interpersonal behaviors.

Clearly, these (often implicit) people-related operative goals are not separate and independent from official goals. If the television station seeks to survive (official goal), it must produce a profit (official goal). To do this, it might have to develop a hard-hitting public affairs show (operative goal), and the achievement of this outcome depends upon the general attainment of the people-related operative goals listed above. In fact, when we speak of the overall performance or effectiveness of an organization, we are usually referring to how well it achieves such goals.

Group Effort

Organizations achieve their goals with people who operate in some *coordinated* manner. Sometimes this coordination is a matter of efficiency rather than absolute necessity. For example, an artists' cooperative might purchase art supplies and help market its members' work. The members could do these things themselves but find that such things are accomplished more efficiently through group means. On the other hand, Boeing Corporation *must* use group means to design and build products such as the 747 jumbo jet. Though he certainly could have

The General Motors assembly line in Lansing, Michigan is an example of the need for group effort to perform complex tasks.

understood all of the physical and aerodynamic properties of such an aircraft, even Albert Einstein could not have mastered all of the applied skills needed to design one, and he obviously couldn't have built one by himself! Individuals have intellectual and physical limitations that can be overcome only by organized group effort.

The grouping that characterizes organizations is of interest to the field of organizational behavior for several reasons. First, much of the work (both intellectual and physical) done in organizations is quite literally performed by groups, whether they are short-term task forces or formal work groups shown on an organizational chart. We are therefore interested in predicting and explaining the functioning of these groups and controlling them so that they function effectively. You will recall that the two-person newswriting/news reading team was severely disrupted by Russ's resignation. Second, everyone is aware that informal grouping occurs in all organizations. That is, friendships develop and informal alliances are formed to accomplish required work. Such grouping is not prescribed by the organization and is not shown on the chart, but it can have an important impact upon goal achievement. Consequently, we are interested in how such groups form and what their exact impact is. Finally, the field of organizational behavior is concerned with the influence that both formal and informal grouping has on the individuals who enter organizations with their own particular needs and values.

A LOOK AHEAD

Now that we have discussed organizational behavior and the nature of organizations, let's have a look at the "organization" of the book. In Chapter 2 we will examine some sources of information about organizational behavior and suggest that common sense provides a rather limited basis for understanding this behavior. We will then discuss some research methods that behavioral scientists have employed to find out about organizational behavior. This should enable you to see the source of the material discussed in this book.

Part Two (Chapters 3 to 7) is concerned with personal or individual behavior in organizations. These chapters consider how individual characteristics influence organizational behavior and how organizations influence individual members. Most behavior of interest in organizations is learned, and in Chapter 3 we will discuss how this learning occurs and how undesirable behavior can be "unlearned." Since everyone has a somewhat different learning history, it is not surprising that organizational members might have different perceptions of organizational reality. In Chapter 4 we will study the perceptual process as it relates to organizations. In addition, we will examine the process by which people form judgments of the motives, qualifications, and performance of others. Chapter 5 will consider values and attitudes in the work setting, with special emphasis on the causes and consequences of job satisfaction. Chapter 6 presents several theories of motivation in the work setting. Given these theories, Chapter 7 discusses a number of practical strategies to enhance motivation. These strategies are especially clear examples of the *control* goal of the field of organizational behavior.

Part Three (Chapters 8 to 14) is concerned with social or interpersonal behavior and important processes in organizations. As we have already discussed, organizations are social inventions that accomplish goals through group effort, and these chapters will concentrate on groups and the processes that are necessary for goal accomplishment. In Chapter 8 we will examine how and why groups are formed in organizations and what determines their effectiveness. Chapter 9 will discuss how groups influence their members and how people are socialized into groups and organizations. It will also cover the related topic of organizational culture. One important factor in groups is leadership, and all but the most primitive groups have leaders. In Chapter 10 we will see how leadership affects the activities of groups and their members. By definition, communication is an important social process, and we will investigate communication problems and their solutions in Chapter 11. Decision making is one of the key work activities in any organization, and Chapter 12 will consider how organizational decisions are made and how they can be improved. Power, politics, and conflict are natural occurrences in organized life, and these topics will be investigated in Chapter 13. Finally, many of these processes have the potential to generate stress among organizational members, and this is the topic of Chapter 14.

Part Four (Chapters 15 to 18) will view organizational behavior from the perspective of the entire organization. Chapter 15 will consider the topic of organizational structure and the various forms of structure that organizations might exhibit. Chapter 16 will cover environment, strategy, and technology, with special emphasis on the implications of these factors for structure. Chapter 17 is concerned with organizational change and in developing organizations so that they can better achieve their goals. It also considers the important issue of innovation. Finally, Chapter 18 examines careers in organizations from both the organization's perspective and your own perspective as an employee. Exhibit 1–3 shows the relationships among Chapters 3 to 18. As you can see, a reciprocal relationship exists between individual or personal behavior and social behavior and organizational processes. In addition, the structure, strategy, and technology of organizations and organizational change and career paths influence individual behavior, social behavior, and critical processes. For pedagogical purposes, we will move from individual to group to entire organization. However, you should be on the lookout for examples of interrelationships among these levels of analysis.

EXHIBIT 1–3

Relationships among individual behavior, social behavior, organizational processes, and the total organization.

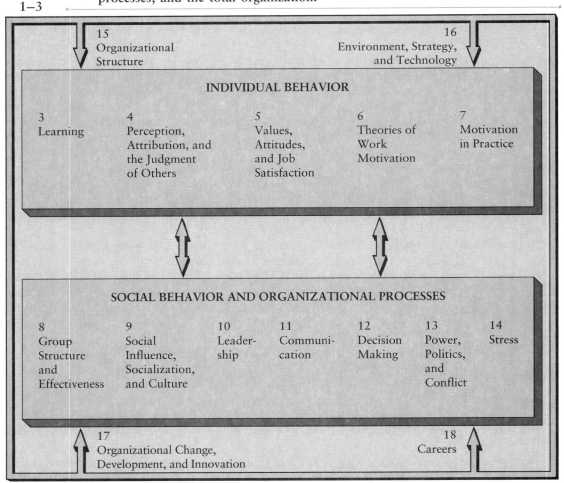

THE MANAGER'S NOTEBOOK

Managing Workplace Diversity at Monsanto

1. In terms of the managerial tasks of analysis and action (Exhibit 1–1), Monsanto has already begun some analysis of the workplace diversity issue. In particular, it has made some critical *predictions* about its future human resources situation. It has recognized that the increasing globalization of business will diversify its work force and, even more significantly, that the changing U.S. labor pool will do the same. Also, it has predicted a shortage of labor in science and technology jobs. Before embarking on a course of action for managing diversity, some *explanation* was needed for how the company culture reacted to diversity. This was accomplished by carrying out an employee survey and by forming a task force that examined subtle means of discrimination in the company. Gradually, this task force changed its role into one of showing managers how to appreciate workplace diversity.

2. The theme of appreciating diversity has been incorporated into one third of the many training courses offered to employees. Both awareness of diversity and skill building in communication are covered. Awareness films and company publications cover the topic for employees who are not scheduled for courses. Company recruiters receive a two-day training session on diversity. The task force on diversity took special pains to get strong management support for these programs.

SUMMARY

- The term *organizational behavior* refers to the attitudes and behaviors of individuals and groups in organizations. The field of organizational behavior involves the systematic study of these attitudes and behaviors.
- The study of organizational behavior is interesting, but it is also practical, because the behavior that occurs in organized settings is an important determinant of how well organizations function. The field of organizational behavior seeks to predict, explain, and control organizational behavior and often deals with contingencies. Contingencies refer to the fact that many of the relationships that exist in organizations depend upon some other factor that must be taken into account.
- Organizations are social inventions for accomplishing goals through group effort. These characteristics have important consequences for the behavior that occurs in organizations. In this book we will move from the study of individuals in organizations to the study of groups to the study of organizations as a whole.

KEY CONCEPTS

Organizational behavior	Explanation	Organizations
Field of organizational behavior	Control	Official goals
Prediction	Contingencies	Operative goals

DISCUSSION QUESTIONS

1. What are your goals in studying organizational behavior? What practical advantages might this study have for you?

2. Consider absence from work as an example of organizational behavior. What are some of the factors that might *predict* who will tend to be absent from work? How might you *explain* absence from work? What are some techniques that organizations use to *control* absence?

3. Consider an organization with which you are familiar. What are some of its official goals? What are some of its operative goals? How do these goals affect the behavior that occurs in the organization?

4. To demonstrate that you grasp the idea of contingencies in organizational behavior, consider how closely managers should supervise the work of their subordinates. What are some factors upon which closeness of supervision might be contingent?

EXPERIENTIAL EXERCISE

Good Job, Bad Job

The purpose of this exercise is to help you get acquainted with some of your classmates by learning something about their experiences with work and organizations. To do this, we will focus on an important and traditional topic in organizational behavior—what makes people satisfied or dissatisfied with their jobs (a topic that we will cover formally in Chapter 5).

_____ 1. Students should break into learning groups of four to six people. Each group should choose a recording secretary.

_____ 2. In each group, members should take turns introducing themselves and then describing to the others either the *best* job or the *worst* job that they have ever had. Take particular care to explain *why* this particular job was either satisfying or dissatisfying. For example, did factors such as pay, co-workers, your boss, or the work itself affect your level of satisfaction? The recording secretary should make a list of the jobs held by group members, noting which were good and which were bad. (15 Minutes)

_____ 3. Using the information generated in Step 2, each group should develop a profile of four or five characteristics that seem to contribute to a dissatisfying job and four or five that contribute to a satisfying job. In other words, are there some common experiences among the group members? (10 Minutes)

_____ 4. Each group should write its "good job" and "bad job" characteristics on the board. (3 Minutes)

_____ 5. The class should reconvene, and each group's recording secretary should report which specific jobs were considered good and bad in his or her group. The instructor will discuss the profiles on the board, noting similarities and differences. Other issues worth probing are behavioral consequences of job attitudes (e.g., quitting) and differences of opinion within the groups (e.g., one person's bad job might have seemed attractive to someone else). (15 Minutes)

CASE STUDY

Dan Dunwoodie's Problem

Up to this point I have been doing very well. At 27 years of age I am chief of an economic analysis branch in the United Automobile Manufacturing Company. I was hired personally by John Roman, my division chief, who interviewed me at the university where I was completing my MBA. John had expressed interest in several of my qualifications: BA in economics from an outstanding university, four years of work experience as an analyst in industry, and a specialty in information systems while working on my MBA.

When I entered on duty three months ago, John gave me guidance as follows: "Economic analysis functions and processing at United need updating. Analysts are substantive experts and do not comprehend the importance of management, nor the possible application of information systems to managerial decision making. They keep insisting that judgmental processes cannot be automated; they resist suggestions that they can augment their activities by using computers. After you have had three to six months to learn your job, you are to come up with recommendations for organizational and procedural changes in your branch. You are to keep in close touch with your peers, the other branch chiefs in the division, all of whom have been with the company for five or more years." (Their responsibilities were almost identical to mine, except each branch had different economic specialties.)

I assumed my responsibilities with great energy and soon saw many possibilities for developing the effectiveness of my branch. I worked evenings and weekends on a new plan. As I developed ideas, I would try them out on each of the other branch chiefs. They were helpful

Source: Lau, J. B., & Shani, A. B. (1988). Dan Dunwoodie's Problem. *Behavior in organizations: An experiential approach* (4th ed.). Copyright © 1988 by Richard D. Irwin, Inc. Homewood, IL: Irwin. Reprinted by permission of J. B. Lau and the publisher.

and responsive. One objection did arise from Carl Carlson, chief of Branch B, who criticized some of the information systems suggestions. (Carl was regarded in the division as the next man in line for John's job. See Exhibit 1.)

At the end of three months with United, I presented my plan to my entire branch in a briefing session, complete with a statement of objectives, charts, and expected results. In response to my request for their reactions, two people spoke up. One was Elsie Eden, who was a contemporary of John and the branch chiefs (I had heard she would have had my job if she had been willing to take an extensive computer training program.) The other was Russ Merrywood, also an old-timer, who had been passed over for advancement (I had also heard that Russ had money and was not too committed to his job, although I find that his work is excellent.) My plan was well thought out, and further clarification of various details appeared to satisfy all questions raised.

On a Wednesday afternoon, I gave the same oral briefing to John (division chief), who showed enthusiasm and pleasure. He promised me an early decision and asked for a copy of my written report for further study. On Thursday afternoon I received the report back with the notation, "Sounds great. Proceed soonest with entire plan with the exception of para. 6, which I wish to study further." (Para. 6 contained an information system suggestion concerning which Carl had expressed disapproval to Dan.)

I spent Friday in meetings with my branch making initial plans for implementing the new program. Over the weekend I continued on my own to make final plans.

Early Monday morning I was asked to come to the division chief's office. I then learned that John had reversed his decision, and no changes were to be put into effect at this time. John appeared rather brisk and said he did not have time to discuss the decision. Later that day, I learned that John had attended a dinner party at Russ's house over the weekend.

EXHIBIT

1

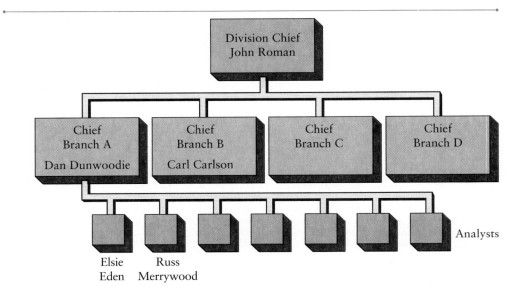

1. In retrospect, which factors in the case might have *predicted* the rejection of Dan's plan?
2. What are some possible *explanations* for the events described in the case? In other words, what are some possible reasons for Dan's problem at United?
3. In retrospect, could Dan have behaved more effectively? How about John Roman? Could a better understanding of the field of organizational behavior have helped both of them?
4. What should Dan do now?

REFERENCES

1. Perrow, C. (1961). The analysis of goals in complex organizations. *American Sociological Review, 26,* 854–866.
2. Perrow, 1961.
3. Katz, D. (1964). The motivational basis of organizational behavior. *Behavioral Science, 9,* 131–146.

CHAPTER

2

FINDING OUT ABOUT ORGANIZATIONAL BEHAVIOR

A QUIZ

Although this is probably your first formal course in organizational behavior, you already have a number of opinions about the subject. To illustrate this, let's begin this chapter with a short quiz. Are the following statements true or false? Please jot down a one-sentence rationale for your answer. There are no tricks involved!

1. Workers who are more satisfied with their jobs tend to be much more productive than those who are less satisfied.
2. Individuals who become organizational leaders tend to possess similar personality traits.
3. Nearly all workers prefer stimulating, challenging jobs.
4. Managers have a very accurate idea about how much their peers and superiors are paid.

Now that you have answered the questions, do one more thing. Assume that the correct answer is opposite to the one you have given. That is, if you answered true to a statement, assume that it is actually false, and vice versa. Now, give a one-sentence rationale why this opposite answer could also be correct.

Each of these statements concerns the behavior of people in organizations. Furthermore, each statement has important implications for the functioning of organizations. If satisfied workers are indeed more productive, organizations might sensibly invest considerable time, energy, and money in fostering satisfaction. Similarly, if most employees prefer stimulating jobs, there are many jobs that could benefit from upgrading. In this book we will investigate the extent to which statements such as these are true or false and why they are true or false. The answers to our brief quiz will be presented shortly.

In this chapter we will examine some of the factors that contribute to our commonsense understanding of organizational behavior and challenge the notion that common sense is the best source of knowledge about organizational behavior. Then, we will examine some research techniques that contribute more accurate knowledge about what happens in organizations.

HOW MUCH DO YOU KNOW ABOUT ORGANIZATIONAL BEHAVIOR?

Let's now return to our quiz. If this were an introductory course in accounting, statistics, computer science, or art appreciation, the reader would likely cry "Foul!" upon encountering such a test. How could one be expected to know that the standard deviation equals the square root of the variance or that Picasso painted his final cubist work in 1921? While we will readily concede ignorance when approaching subjects such as these, our direct and indirect experiences have enabled us to "know" a fair amount about organizational behavior in advance of its formal study. Thus, it is likely that you easily and willingly completed the quiz.

Now to the answers. Substantial research (systematic study) indicates that each of the statements in the quiz is essentially false. There are exceptions, but in general, satisfied workers are not more productive, leaders do not have special personality traits, many people prefer routine jobs, and managers are not well informed about the pay of their peers and superiors. However, you should not jump to unwarranted conclusions based on the inaccuracy of these statements until we determine *why* they tend to be incorrect. There are good reasons for an organization to attempt to satisfy its employees. Also we *can* predict who might assume a leadership role and who might prefer challenging jobs. These issues will be discussed in more detail in later chapters.

Experience indicates that people are amazingly good at giving sensible reasons as to why the same statement is either true or false. Thus, satisfied workers are especially productive because they identify with their work, or they are paying the organization back for providing them with satisfactory employment. Conversely, workers are satisfied because they have developed rewarding social contacts in the workplace, but these relationships interfere with productivity. The ease with which people can generate such contradictory responses suggests that our "common sense" has been developed by the unsystematic and incomplete experiences we have had with organizational behavior.

COMMON SENSE AND ORGANIZATIONAL BEHAVIOR

In case you are wondering, there is a tendency for beginning students of organizational behavior to assume that the statements included in the quiz are true. "After all, it's only common sense. . . . " Where does this **common sense** come from? By the time we reach adulthood we have acquired considerable *direct experience* with behavior, with organizations, and with behavior in organizations. Since birth we have been "behaving" in the informal organization of the family and in formal organizations such as schools, colleges, and places of employment. Most of us have had reasonable success in negotiating the challenges these organizations have presented to us. Furthermore, as consumers of the outputs of organizations, we have had the opportunity to observe those behaviors that seem to lead to efficient performance (e.g., the typical McDonald's restaurant) or inefficient performance (e.g., the typical college course change system). Finally, *indirect experience* is a powerful shaper of our views concerning the nature of work and organizations. When a friend says, "You wouldn't believe what happened to me at work today," or informs us that her bank credit card limit was raised on the same day her loan application was refused, we form implicit assumptions about the nature of behavior in organizations. Similarly, when we follow the progress of a political campaign, a coal strike, or a military action on television or read about the "blue collar blues" in *David Copperfield* or *Newsweek,* we add to our arsenal of knowledge about organizational behavior. Just how systematic this study has been is debatable.

Although we rely on common sense every day, this reliance often results in curious contradictions. For example, in completing a questionnaire concerning the traits of a particular ethnic group, otherwise sensible individuals will report that the group's members are continually attempting to force themselves upon the rest of society. Several questions later, they will agree equally vigorously that the ethnic group sets itself apart and behaves in an excessively clannish manner. In a similar vein, consider the following "wisdom of the ages":
- Look before you leap BUT He who hesitates is lost.
- Better safe than sorry BUT Nothing ventured, nothing gained.
- Absence makes the heart grow fonder BUT Out of sight, out of mind.
- Many hands make light work BUT Too many cooks spoil the broth.
- Two heads are better than one BUT If you want something done, do it yourself.

The common sense provided by these old sayings is certainly common, but is it sensible? These sayings tend to be so abstract that it is impossible to deduce when they are applicable. The last two pairs of sayings have some clear relevance to the design of work groups and to decision making in organizations, but one is hard pressed to know when to implement which advice. The failure of general common sense to provide us with truly useful information suggests that we should carefully differentiate opinions about organizational behavior from actual behavior that occurs in organizations.

WHAT CREATES INACCURATE OPINIONS?

There are a number of reasons for our developing inaccurate opinions about organizational behavior. These reasons stem from the nature and quality of our direct and indirect experiences with organizations.

Overgeneralization

Individuals have a tendency to assume that their experience with a particular organization is typical and general. Thus, the student politician who has acquired considerable expertise in furthering the goals of his constituency in a university setting might find it difficult to translate this expertise to a management trainee job with a bank after graduation. Although both the university and the bank are organizations, and "people are people," the knowledge acquired in one setting might not apply directly to the other. Additionally, people often assume that their own experiences in organizations are shared by other people. Thus, workers who are both satisfied with their jobs and productive assume that other satisfied workers will also be productive. Overgeneralization is often a function of *selective perception,* or seeing what we want to see or expect to see. If we know a couple of executives who are extremely dominant and aggressive, we might tend to perceive these traits in other executives while ignoring contrary instances.

Practice and Media Attention

Some ideas about behavior in organizations have acquired general acceptance simply by virtue of their visibility. This visibility may stem from actual organizational practices or from the exploration of an issue by the media.

Many people think that standard reference checks must be an effective hiring tool based upon the frequency with which they are used: "If organizations use them, then they must work." Likewise, it is often assumed that pay and fringe benefit increases must be an attempt to bolster productivity through increased satisfaction. Such assumptions do not take into account the nonrational actions of organizations, which are more frequent than might be expected. In fact, organizations have exhibited excessive faddishness and a tendency to follow the leader in areas such as the design of pay systems and management training and development.

Media attention can also provide us with oversimplified or sometimes inaccurate ideas about the relationships between people and organizations. Magazine and television portrayals of high-profile organizational people and events (Silicon Valley computer whiz kids, thirty-year-old Wall Street millionaires, Japanese management, and lusty corporate takeovers) surely shape our views about work. However, the critical observer must wonder whether the issue deserves attention or the attention creates the issue. Also, in recent years there has been a phenomenal upsurge of popular books about business and management. Titles such as *In Search of Excellence, A Passion for Excellence, Iacocca,* and *The One Minute Manager* have dominated the best seller lists, reaching a much larger audience than the typical college textbook. Although such books vary tremendously in quality, some do contain valuable insights about organizational behavior. However, it would be a mistake to assume that all such books contain wisdom *because* they are popular. Frequently, popularity stems from catering to what the reader wishes were true rather than what is true. Avid readers of such books might be excused for thinking that some phenomenal advance in organizational behavior research and management occurred sometime around 1982! In fact, research evidence and practical management experience accumulate gradually, by trial and error.

Value Judgments

Our values—our feelings about what is good or bad and right or wrong—often influence our views about what happens or should happen in organizations. These values often differ according to our background and particular position in the social structure. Thus, it is unlikely that managers and unionists would have similar views about the nature of blue-collar work. The values of society and its subgroups also change over time, and this change is reflected in thinking about organizational behavior. It is safe to say that North Americans during the present century have come to value a mildly participative leadership style within organizations—somewhere between rigid authoritarianism and "giving away the shop." Such a change in values was probably prompted by the rise of unionism and observations of the adverse effects of the authoritarianism that led to World War II.

The point, however, is that such value orientations often influence our views about behavior in organizations in spite of the actual consequences of these values. We favor what *we* perceive as "good," even if this goodness is unsupported by evidence or is contrary to the values of others. If we see stimulating, challenging work in a positive light, we expect to encounter such work in organizations. Also, people seem to have an unwarranted tendency to assume that linkages exist between valued phenomena. If we assume that it is good for workers to be satisfied with their jobs and that it is good for workers to be productive, we may tend to assume that these favorable events occur together in some natural relationship—that satisfied workers are productive workers. As was pointed out earlier, this assumption is essentially inaccurate.

The purpose of the preceding discussion has been to differentiate the reality of organizational behavior from opinions about organizational behavior. Our common sense is frequently a product of overgeneralization, media attention, and unwarranted value judgments. However, this does not mean that such opinion is unimportant. On the contrary, it frequently influences our expectations and our behavior. The manager who assumes that people prefer stimulating, challenging work might arrange subordinates' tasks very differently from one who assumes the contrary. The organization whose president thinks that money is an important motivator of productivity might distribute wages and salaries very differently from one whose president does not. So you can see that opinions about organizational behavior affect the practice of management. However, such practice should be based upon informed opinion and systematic study.

RESEARCH IN ORGANIZATIONAL BEHAVIOR

In a general sense, research is a way of finding out about the world by some objective, systematic means of gathering information. The key words here are *objective* and *systematic,* and it is these characteristics that separate the outcomes of the careful study of organizational behavior from opinion and common sense.

We will spend the remainder of this chapter discussing research methods for several reasons. For one thing, you should be aware of the manner in which the information presented in this book was collected. This should increase your confidence in the advantages of systematic study over common sense. Furthermore, you will likely encounter reports in management periodicals and the popular press of interventions designed to improve organizational behavior, such as job redesign or employee development programs. A critical perspective is necessary to differentiate carefully designed and evaluated interventions from useless or even damaging ones. Those backed by good research deserve the greatest confidence. Occasionally, a manager may be called upon to evaluate a research proposal or consultant's intervention to be carried out in his or her own organization. A brief introduction to research methodology should at least enable this person to ask some intelligent questions about such ventures. Research in organizational behavior is carried out by trained behavioral scientists who have backgrounds in management, applied psychology, or applied sociology. While this introduction will not make you a trained behavioral scientist, it should provide some appreciation of the work that goes into generating accurate knowledge about organizational behavior.

Observational Techniques

Observational research techniques are the most straightforward ways of finding out about behavior in organizations and thus come closest to the ways in which we develop commonsense views about such behavior. In this case, *observation* means just what it implies—the researcher proceeds to examine the natural activities of real people in an organizational setting by listening to what they say and watching what they do. The difference between our everyday observations and the formal observations of the trained behavioral scientist is expressed by those key words *systematic* and *objective*. First, the behavioral scientist attempts to keep a careful ongoing record of the events that are observed, either as they occur or as soon as possible afterward. Thus, excessive reliance upon memory is unnecessary. Second, the researcher approaches the setting of interest with extensive training concerning the nature of human behavior and a particular set of questions that the observation is designed to answer. These factors provide a systematic framework for the business of observing. Finally, the behavioral scientist is well informed of the dangers of influencing the behavior of those who are being observed and is trained to draw reasonable, warranted conclusions from his or her observations. These factors help to ensure objectivity. The products of observational research are summarized in a narrative form (sometimes called a *case study*) that specifies the nature of the organization and people studied, the particular role and techniques of the observer, the research questions, and the events observed.

Participant Observation One obvious way for a researcher to find out about organizational behavior is to actively participate in this behavior. In **participant observation** the researcher becomes a functioning member of the organizational unit being studied. At this point you might well respond, "Wait a minute. What about objectivity? What about influencing the behavior of those being studied?" These are clearly legitimate questions, and they might be answered in the following way: In adopting participant observation the researcher is making a conscious bet that the advantages of participation outweigh these problems. It is doubtless true in some cases that "There is no substitute for experience." This is nicely illustrated in George Plimpton's book *Paper Lion*.[1] Plimpton, a journalist and good amateur athlete rather than a behavioral scientist, was permitted to practice with the Detroit Lions football team and act as quarterback in some plays during preseason games. Obviously, being faced with third down and fifteen yards to go in the rain is a very different event when viewed from the stands, and such an experience can be captured only by participation. Another advantage to participant observation is its potential for secrecy—the subjects need not know that they are being observed. There are some clear ethical issues to be confronted in this case, however. One sociologist served as an industrial worker in two plants in England to study the factors that influenced productivity.[2] Although he could have acted in secrecy, he was required to inform management and union officials of his presence to secure records and documents, and he thus felt it unfair not to inform his work mates of his purpose. It should be stressed that his goals were academic, and he was *not* working for the managements of the companies involved. Sometimes, secrecy seems necessary to accomplish a research goal, as the following study of "illegal" industrial behavior shows.

Bensman and Gerver investigated an important organizational problem: What happens when the activities that appear to be required to get a job done conflict with official organizational policy?[3] Examples of such conflicts include the punch press operator who must remove the safety guard from his machine to meet productivity standards, the executive who must deliver corporate money to a political slush fund, or the police officer who can't find time to complete an eight-page report to justify having drawn her revolver on a night patrol. (These examples represent conflicting operative goals or conflicts between operative goals and official goals.)

The behavior of interest to Bensman and Gerver was the unauthorized use of taps by aircraft plant workers. A tap is a hard steel hand tool that is used to cut threads into metal. The possession of this device by aircraft assemblers was strictly forbidden because it could be used to correct sloppy or difficult work such as the misalignment of bolt holes in two pieces of aircraft skin or stripped lock nuts, leading to potential structural weaknesses or maintenance problems. Possession of a tap was a strict violation of company policy, and a worker could be fired on the spot for it. On the other hand, supervisors were under extreme pressure to maintain a high quota of completed work, and the occasional use of a tap to correct a problem could save hours of disassembly and realignment time. How was this conflict resolved? The answer was provided by one of the authors, who served as a participant observer while functioning as an assembler. Put simply, the supervisors and inspectors worked together to encourage the cautious and appropriate use of taps. New workers were gradually introduced to the mysteries of tapping by experienced workers, and the supervisors provided refinement of skills and signals as to when a tap might be used. Taps were not to be used in front of inspectors or to correct chronic sloppy work. If "caught," promiscuous tappers were expected to act truly penitent in response to a chewing out by the supervisors, even if the supervisors themselves had suggested the use of the tap. In short, a *social ritual* was developed to teach and control the use of the tap to facilitate getting the work out without endangering the continued presence of the crucial tool. Clearly, this is the kind of information about organizational behavior that would be extremely difficult to obtain except by participant observation.

Direct Observation This research technique involves observation without participation in the activity being observed. There are a number of reasons why one

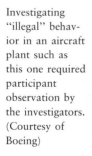

Investigating "illegal" behavior in an aircraft plant such as this one required participant observation by the investigators. (Courtesy of Boeing)

might choose **direct observation** over participant observation. First, there are many situations in which the injection of a new person into an existing work setting would severely disrupt and change the nature of the activities in that setting. These are cases in which the "influence" criticism of participant observation is especially true. Second, there are many tasks that a trained behavioral scientist could not be expected to learn for research purposes. For example, it seems unreasonable to expect a person to spend years acquiring the skills of a pilot or banker in order to be able to investigate what happens in the cockpit of an airliner or in a boardroom. Finally, participant observation places rather severe limitations upon the observers' opportunity to record information. Existence of these conditions suggests the use of direct observation. In theory, such observation could be carried out covertly, but there are few studies of organizational behavior in which the presence of the direct observer was not known and explained to those being observed.

An excellent example of the use of direct observation is provided by Mintzberg's study of the work performed by chief executives of two manufacturing companies, a hospital, a school system, and a consulting firm.[4] At first glance, this might appear to be an inane thing to investigate. After all, everybody knows that managers plan, organize, lead, and control, or some similar combination of words. In fact, as Mintzberg forcefully argues, we actually know very little about the routine, everyday behavior managers enact to achieve these vague goals. Furthermore, if we ask managers what they do (in an interview or questionnaire), they usually respond with a variation of the plan-organize-lead-control theme.

Mintzberg spent a week with each of his five executives, watching them at their desks, attending meetings with them, listening to their phone calls, and inspecting their mail. He kept detailed records of these events and gradually developed a classification scheme to make sense of them. What Mintzberg found belies the commonsense view that some hold of managers: They sit behind a large desk, reflecting on the state of affairs of their organizations or affixing their signatures to impressive documents all day. In fact, Mintzberg found that his managers performed a terrific amount of work and had little time for reflection. On an average day they examined thirty-six pieces of mail, engaged in five telephone discussions, attended eight meetings, and made one tour of their facilities. Work-related reading encroached upon home lives. The activities managers engaged in were varied, unpatterned, and of short duration. Half of the activities lasted less than nine minutes, and 90 percent less than one hour. Furthermore, these activities tended to be directed toward current, specific issues rather than historical, general issues. Finally, the managers revealed an extensive preference for verbal communications, by either telephone or unscheduled face-to-face meetings, and two thirds of their contacts were of this nature. In contrast, they generated an average of only one piece of mail a day.

In summary, both observational techniques capture the depth, breadth, richness, spontaneity, and realism of organizational behavior. However, they also involve some weaknesses. One of these weaknesses is a lack of control over the environment in which the study is being conducted. Thus, Mintzberg could not ensure that unusual or atypical events would not occur to affect the behavior of the executives he observed. Also, the small number of observers and situations in the typical observational study is problematic. With only one observer (measuring instrument) there is a strong potential for selective perceptions and interpretations of observed events. Since only a few situations are analyzed, the extent to which the observed behaviors can be generalized to other settings is limited. (Do most executives behave like the five Mintzberg studied?) It is probably safe to say that observational techniques are best used to make an initial examination of some organizational event on which we have little information and to generate ideas for further investigation with the more refined techniques we will now discuss.

Correlational Techniques

Correlational research sacrifices some of the breadth and richness of the observational techniques for more precision of measurement and greater control. It necessarily involves some abstraction of the real event that is the focus of observation in order to accomplish this precision and control. More specifically, correlational approaches differ from observational approaches in terms of the nature of the data collected and the issues investigated.

The data of observational studies is most frequently notes made by the observer. We hope that it exhibits **reliability**; that is, we hope that other observers would see the same thing, and that any one observer would report seeing the same thing if it occurred again tomorrow. We also hope that this data exhibits **validity**; that is, we hope that it is a true reflection of what was actually observed or that it measures what it is supposed to measure. Unfortunately, because observations are generally the products of a single individual viewing a unique event, we have very little basis on which to judge their reliability and validity.

The data of correlational studies involves interviews and questionnaires as well as existing data. Existing data comes from organizational records and includes productivity, absence, and biographical information (age, sex, etc.). Variables often measured by questionnaires and interviews involve things like:

- subordinates' perceptions of how their supervisors behave on the job,
- the extent to which employees are satisfied with their jobs,
- reports by employees about how much freedom of action they have on their jobs.

It is possible to determine in advance of our research the extent to which such measures are reliable and valid. Thus, when constructing a questionnaire to measure job satisfaction, we can check its reliability by repeatedly administering it to a group of workers over a period of time. If individual responses remain fairly stable, we have evidence of reliability. Evidence of the validity of our questionnaire might come from its ability to predict who would quit the organization for work elsewhere. It seems reasonable that dissatisfied employees would be more likely to quit, and such an effect is partial evidence of the validity of our satisfaction measure. The point here is that in doing correlational research we can choose to use measurement instruments with known reliability and validity.

In addition to the nature of the data collected, it was pointed out that correlational studies differ from observational studies in terms of the kinds of events they investigate. Although the questions investigated by observational research appear fairly specific (What maintains an "illegal" behavior such as tapping? What do executives do?), virtually any event deemed relevant to the question is fair game for observation. Thus, such studies are extremely broad based. Correlational research sacrifices this broadness to investigate the relationship (correlation) between specific, well-defined variables. The relationship between the variables of interest is usually stated as a **hypothesis**, which is a prediction about the way in which variables are expected to be connected. Using the variables mentioned above, we can construct three sample hypotheses and describe how they would be tested:

- Employees who are satisfied with their jobs will tend to be more productive than those who are less satisfied. (To test this, we might administer a reliable, valid questionnaire concerning satisfaction and obtain production data from company records.)
- Employees who perceive their supervisor as friendly and considerate will be more satisfied with their jobs then those who do not. (To test this, we might use reliable, valid questionnaires or interview measures of both variables.)
- Older employees will be absent less than younger employees. (To test this, we might obtain data concerning the age of employees and their absenteeism from organizational personnel records.)

In each case, our interest lies in a very specific set of variables, and we take pains to measure them precisely.

A good example of a simple correlational study is reported by Waters, Roach, and Waters.[5] They were interested in the relative ability of biographical variables, job satisfaction, and intent to remain with the organization to predict turnover among female clerks in an insurance company. Based on some previous research, they hypothesized that intent to remain would be the best predictor. This intention was measured in a questionnaire, as were several dimensions of job satisfaction (pay, promotions, co-workers, supervision, and work). In this case, biographical information (age, marital status, job grade, and tenure) was also obtained in the questionnaire. Two years later, company records were examined to determine who had quit. Useful predictors of turnover included intent, dissatisfaction with the work itself, and three of the biographical variables. Specifically, older employees, those with more tenure, and those with higher job grades were less likely to have quit. Intent to remain was the best predictor, with 78 percent of those who claimed they would stay remaining and 76 percent of those who reported that they would leave quitting. The researchers suggested the inclusion of such an intentions measure in attitude surveys to aid in personnel planning.

A final important point should be made about correlational studies. Suppose we hypothesize that friendly, considerate supervisors will have more productive subordinates than unfriendly, inconsiderate supervisors. In this case, we might have some subordinates describe the friendliness of their supervisors on a reliable, valid questionnaire designed to measure this variable and obtain subordinates' productivity levels from company records. The results of our hypothetical study are plotted in Exhibit 2–1, where each dot represents a subordinate's response to the questionnaire in conjunction with his or her productivity. In general, it would appear that our hypothesis is confirmed—that is, subordinates who describe their supervisor as friendly tend to be more productive than those who describe him or her as unfriendly. Because of this study, should an organization attempt to select friendly supervisors or perhaps train existing supervisors to be more friendly in order to facilitate productivity? The answer is *no*. The training and selection proposal assumes that friendly supervisors *cause* their subordinates to be productive, and this might not be the case. Put simply, supervisors might be friendly *if* their subordinates are productive. This is hardly an impossible interpretation of our data, and such an interpretation does not suggest selection or training to make supervisors friendly. This line of argument should not be unfamiliar to you: Heavy smokers and cigarette company lobbyists like to claim that smoking is related to the incidence of lung cancer because cancer proneness prompts smok-

EXHIBIT 2–1

Hypothetical data from a correlational study of the relationship between supervisory friendliness and subordinate productivity.

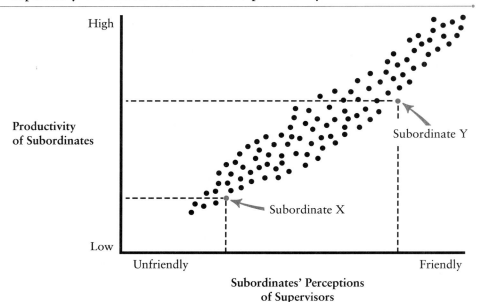

ing, rather than vice versa. The point here is that *correlation does not imply causation.* How can we find out which factors cause certain organizational behaviors? The answer is to perform an experiment.

Experimental Techniques

If observational research involves observing nature, and correlational research involves measuring nature, **experimental research** *manipulates* nature. In an experiment, some variable is manipulated or changed under controlled conditions, and the consequence of this manipulation for some other variable is measured. If we have truly controlled all other conditions, and a change in the second variable follows the change that we have introduced in the first variable, we can infer that the first change caused the second change. In experimental language the variable that the researcher manipulates or changes is called the **independent variable.** The variable that the independent variable is expected to affect is called the **dependent variable.** Consider the following hypothesis: The introduction of recorded music into the work setting will lead to increased productivity. In this hypothesis, the independent variable is music, which is expected to affect productivity, the dependent variable. Consider another hypothesis: Stimulating, challenging jobs will increase the satisfaction of the work force. Here, the design of the job is the independent variable and satisfaction is the dependent variable.

Let's return to our hypothesis that friendly, considerate supervisors will tend to have more productive subordinates. If we wish to determine whether friendly supervision causes (leads to, contributes to) subordinate productivity, the nature

EXHIBIT

2–2

Hypothetical data from an experiment concerning human relations training.

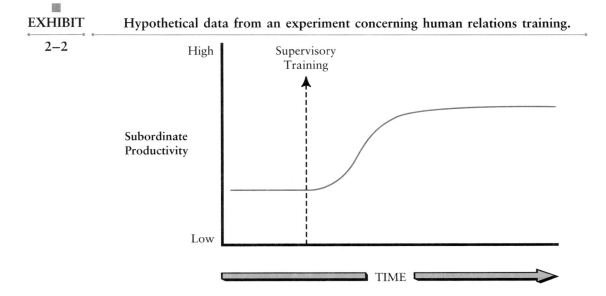

Source: T. Haggerty/The New Yorker Magazine, Inc.

You won't be needing those, sir, you're in the control group.

of supervision becomes our independent variable, and productivity becomes our dependent variable. This means that we must manipulate or change the friendliness of some supervisors and observe what happens to the productivity of their subordinates. In practice, this would probably be accomplished by exposing the bosses to some form of human relations training designed to teach them to be more considerate and personable toward their workers.

Exhibit 2–2 shows the results of such a hypothetical experiment. The line on the graph represents the average productivity of a number of subordinates whose supervisors have received our training. It can be seen that this productivity increased and remained higher following the introduction of the training. Does this mean that friendliness indeed increases productivity and that we should proceed to train all of our supervisors in this manner? The answer is again no. We cannot be sure that *something else* didn't occur at the time of the training to influence productivity (such as a change in equipment or job insecurity prompted by rumored layoffs). To control this possibility, we need a **control group** of supervisors who are not exposed to the training, and we need productivity data for their subordinates (see the cartoon). Ideally, these supervisors would be as similar as possible in experience and background to those who receive the training, and their subordinates would be performing at the same level. The results of our improved experiment are shown in Exhibit 2–3. Here, we see that the productivity of the subordinates whose supervisors were trained increases following training, while that of the control supervisors remains constant. We can thus infer that the friendliness acquired by training affected subordinate productivity.

Ivancevich and Lyon conducted an interesting experiment concerning the effects of a shortened workweek on the operative employees of a company that manufactures food-packaging equipment.[6] The independent variable was the length of the workweek (4 days, 40 hours versus 5 days, 40 hours). Two of the company's divisions were converted to a 4-40 week from a 5-40 week. A third division, remaining on the 5-40 schedule, served as a control group. Workers in the control division were similar to those in the other divisions in terms of age, seniority, education, and salary. The dependent variables (measured one month before the conversion and several times after) included questionnaire responses concerning job satisfaction and stress, absence data from company records, and performance as rated by supervisors. After twelve months, several aspects of satisfaction and performance showed a marked improvement for the 4-40 workers when compared with the 5-40 workers. However, at twenty-five months this edge existed for only one aspect of satisfaction. The authors concluded that benefits that have been proposed for the 4-40 workweek might be of short-term duration.

A Continuum of Research Techniques

You might reasonably wonder which of the research techniques just discussed is best. As shown in Exhibit 2–4, the methods that we have been discussing can be placed on a continuum ranging from rich, broad based, and loosely controlled

EXHIBIT 2–3

Hypothetical data from an improved experiment concerning human relations training.

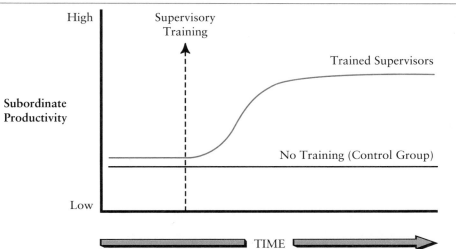

(observation) to specific, precise, and rigorous (experimentation). The position on this continuum at which we choose to investigate organizational behavior should be dictated by the nature of the problem that interests us. In the writing of this section of the chapter, special pains were taken to choose examples of problems that were well suited to the research techniques employed to investigate them. Bensman and Gerver, as well as Mintzberg, were interested in variables that were not well defined. The variables were thus not easy to isolate and measure precisely, and observation was the appropriate technique. Furthermore, "tapping" was a delicate issue, and considerable trust would have had to be developed to investigate it with questionnaires or formal interviews. Similarly, Mintzberg insists that such instruments have failed to tell us what executives do. The researchers who were concerned with predicting turnover were interested in a specific set of variables that were relatively easily measured. On the other hand, experimentally manipulating "intent to stay" would seem unethical, even if we knew how to do it. Ivancevich and Lyon were also interested in a specific set of variables, and they conducted their research on the shortened workweek in a situation in which it was both possible and ethical to manipulate the workweek. In all of these cases the research technique chosen was substantially better than dependence on common sense or opinion.

Research techniques can often be used in combination to better understand behavior. For an example, see In Focus 2–1.

Now that we have compared the various research techniques, why not try out your knowledge on an actual management problem? Please consult You Be the Manager on page 39.

Issues in Organizational Research

In every field of study there are particular issues that confront the researcher, and the field of organizational behavior is no exception. To conclude this chapter, we will consider three issues that have concerned researchers in organizational behavior: sampling, Hawthorne effects, and ethical issues.

EXHIBIT
2–4

Continuum of research techniques.

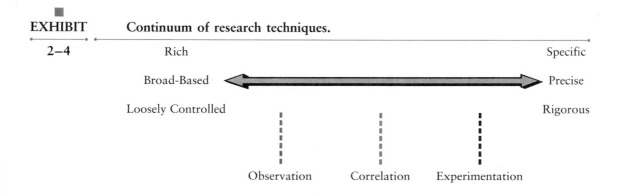

IN FOCUS 2–1

Friendly Store Employees Reduce Sales!?

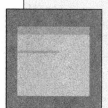

Robert I. Sutton and Anat Rafaeli tested what might seem to be an obvious hypothesis—that friendly, pleasant behavior on the part of sales clerks would be positively associated with store sales. Obvious as this might be, it would be a good idea to confirm it before spending thousands of dollars on human relations training for clerks. The study used both correlational and observational methods. In the quantitative, correlational part of the study, teams of researchers entered each of 576 convenience stores of a large North American chain and, posing as shoppers, rated the friendliness of the sales clerks on rating scales. Other factors, such as the length of the line at the register, were also recorded. Existing data from company records provided the total annual sales recorded by each store. When the data were analyzed, the results were surprising—the "unfriendly" stores tended to chalk up higher sales!

To understand this unexpected result, the authors resorted to qualitative, observational research techniques. Specifically, each spent extensive time in many of the convenience stores directly observing transactions between customers and clerks. In addition, each spent time as a participant observer, actually doing the sales clerk job. This observation resolved the mystery. They found that when stores were busy, the sales clerks tended to bear down, stop the small talk, and process customers as quickly as possible. This behavior corresponded to customers' expectations for fast service in a convenience store. When business was slow, clerks tended to be friendly and engage in small talk to relieve boredom. Since the busier stores tended to have higher sales, it is not surprising that their clerks tended to express fewer friendly emotions. In fact, further analysis of the correlational data showed that clerks were less friendly when the lines were longer.

This study illustrates how two research techniques can complement each other. It also shows that correlation does not imply causation. Here, volume of sales affected the expression of friendliness, not the other way around. Of course, these results would probably not generalize to sales settings in which customers expect more personal attention.

Source: Excerpted from Sutton, R. I., & Rafaeli, A. (1988). Untangling the relationship between displayed emotions and organizational sales: The case of convenience stores. *Academy of Management Journal, 31,* 461–487. Reprinted by permission of the Academy of Management and Professor R. I. Sutton.

Sampling If we wish to generalize the results of our research beyond the particular setting being studied, we can have the greatest confidence in results that are based on large, random samples. Large samples ensure that the results obtained are truly representative of the individuals, groups, or organizations being studied and not merely the product of an extreme case or two. Similarly, random samples that ensure that all relevant individuals, groups, or organizations have an equal probability of being studied also give confidence in the generality of findings. As was noted earlier, observational studies usually involve small samples, and they are seldom randomized. Thus, generalizing from such studies in a problem. However, a well-designed observational study that answers important questions is surely superior to a large-sample, randomized correlational study that enables us to generalize about a trivial hypothesis.

In experimental research, randomization means randomly assigning subjects to experimental and control conditions. To illustrate the importance of this, we can return to our hypothetical study of the effects of human relations training. Suppose that, instead of assigning supervisors to the experimental and control groups randomly, we have managers nominate supervisors for training. Suppose further that to "reward" them for their long service, more experienced supervisors are nominated for the training. This results in an experimental group of more experienced supervisors and a control group of less experienced supervisors. If supervisory experience promotes subordinate productivity, we might erroneously conclude that it was the *human relations training* that led to any improved results and that our hypothesis is confirmed. Poor sampling has biased the results in favor of our hypothesis. To be sure that randomization has been achieved, it would be a good idea to ascertain that the subordinates of the experimental and control supervisors were equally productive *before* the training began.

Hawthorne Effects The term *Hawthorne effect* stems from a series of studies conducted at the Hawthorne plant of the Western Electric Company near Chicago many years ago. These studies were designed to examine the effects of independent variables such as rest pauses, lighting intensity, and pay incentives on the productivity of assemblers of electrical components.[7] In a couple of these loosely controlled experiments, unusual results occurred (see In Focus 2–2 on page 41). In the illumination study, both experimental and control workers improved their productivity. In another study, productivity increased and remained high despite the introduction and withdrawal of factors such as rest pauses, shortened workdays, and so on. These results gave rise to the **Hawthorne effect,** which might be defined as a favorable response on the part of subjects in an organizational experiment that is due to some factor other than the independent variable being manipulated. This "other factor" is generally thought to be psychological in nature, although it is not well understood.[8] Likely candidates include reactions to being given special attention, including feelings of prestige, heightened morale, and so on. The point is that the researcher might misinterpret the true reason for any observed change in behavior.

YOU BE THE MANAGER

Netherlands Postal and Telecommunications Services

The Netherlands Postal and Telecommunications Services (PTT) is responsible for mail delivery and telephone services throughout the Netherlands. Management had become concerned about the high level of gasoline consumption of its postal delivery vans. Not only is such consumption environmentally unsound, but the price of gasoline in Europe is particularly high, thus adding greatly to operating expenses. A survey showed that many drivers were unaware of how their driving habits affected fuel economy. Some had the incorrect idea that shifting gears at high engine speeds (a fuel-wasting practice) kept the engine in better tune. Many reported that they were unaware of their shifting practices because the trucks had no tachometers to report engine speed. In general, the impact of acceleration, shifting, and speed on fuel economy was not appreciated. Neither postal supervisors nor drivers discussed driving style or thought of energy saving as an important part of their jobs.

PTT decided on a trial program, to be initiated in some local post offices, to motivate energy-saving driving behavior. A goal of 5 percent reduction in fuel consumption was put in place, and a training film showing fuel efficient driving practices was shown. Performance feedback was provided in two primary ways. Gas flow meters and tachometers (to report engine speed) were installed in many trucks to make drivers more aware of their driving habits. Also, weekly figures on gasoline consumption for each postal office were posted in a prominent location.

PTT wished to rigorously evaluate the impact of the program on fuel consumption and employee attitudes. How would *you* do this?

1. Design an experiment to evaluate the PTT economy program.
2. Comment on the use of observational or correlational methods for this problem.

To find out what PTT did, see The Manager's Notebook at the end of the chapter.

Source: Adapted from Siero, S., Boon, M., Kok, G., & Siero, F. (1989). Modification of driving behavior in a large transport organization: A field experiment. *Journal of Applied Psychology, 74*, 417–423.

To return to the human relations training experiment, a Hawthorne effect might occur if the experimental subjects are grateful to management for selecting them for this special training and resolve to work harder back on the job. These supervisors might put in longer hours thinking up ways to improve productivity that have nothing to do with the training they received. However, the researcher could easily conclude that the human relations training itself had improved productivity.

It is very difficult to prevent Hawthorne effects. However, it is possible, if expensive, to see whether they have occurred. This is usually done by establishing a second experimental group that receives special treatment and attention but is not exposed to the key independent variable. In the human relations experiment, this might involve training that is not expected to increase productivity. If the productivity of the subordinates of the subjects in both experimental groups increases equally, the Hawthorne effect is probably operating. If productivity increases only in the human relations training condition, it is unlikely to be due to the Hawthorne effect.

Ethics Researchers in organizational behavior, no matter who employs them, have an ethical obligation to do rigorous research and to report that research accurately. In all cases, the psychological (and physical) well-being of the research subjects is of prime importance. In general, ethical researchers avoid unnecessary deception, inform participants about the general purpose of their research, and protect the anonymity of research subjects. For example, in a correlational study involving the use of questionnaires, the general reason for the research should be

The Netherlands Postal and Telecommunications Service is experimenting with ways to motivate energy-saving behavior among its employees. (Peter Vadnai/ The Stock Market)

IN FOCUS 2–2

▼
....
The Hawthorne Effect

Placed in separate enclosures, control subjects received a constant illumination of 10 foot-candles while the illumination for experimental subjects, begun at this level, was decreased in 1-foot-candle steps in successive work periods. Throughout the experiment, both sets of subjects increased their performance, slowly but steadily. It was not until illumination in the experimental room reached 3 foot-candles that subjects started to complain that they could hardly see what they were doing, and productivity finally started to decline. Something other than level of illumination was affecting productivity. . . . In one instance the illumination was reduced to .06 of a foot-candle, the level of ordinary moonlight, and yet efficiency was maintained!

The Hawthorne effect probably owes its existence to a second experiment, called the Relay Assembly Test Room Study. Five female employees who spent each work day assembling relays, were separated from their large department and placed into a special test room where all relevant variables could be better controlled or evaluated. The study was designed to explore the optimal cycle of rest and work periods. However, to make the subjects independent of influences from their former department and sensitive to experimental manipulations, the investigators began by changing the method of determining wages. During the experiment the investigators also manipulated, on different occasions and sometimes concurrently, the length and timing of rest periods, the length of the work week, the length of the work day, and whether or not the company provided lunch and/or beverage. Productivity seemed to increase regardless of the manipulation introduced. Finally, well into the second year the investigators decided to discontinue all treatments and to return the workers to full work days and weeks without breaks or lunches. Unexpectedly, rather than dropping to preexperiment levels, productivity was maintained.

Before the experiment had begun, the investigators had feared that workers taken from their regular work to be placed in a test room would be negative and resistant to the experiment. To overcome this anticipated negative set supervision was removed, special privileges were allowed, and considerable interest and attention was expressed toward the worker, all changes intended to provide for a controlled experiment. However, it was these unintentional manipulations, researchers were forced to conclude, that had caused the subjects to improve their overall productivity and that had given birth to the Hawthorne effect.

Source: Excerpted from Adair, J. G. (1984). The Hawthorne effect: A reconsideration of the methodological artifact. *Journal of Applied Psychology, 69,* 334–345, pp. 336–337.

explained, and potential subjects should be afforded the opportunity not to participate. If names or company identification numbers are required to match responses with data in personnel files (e.g., absenteeism or subsequent turnover), guarantees must be given and honored that responses of individuals will not be made public. In some observation studies and experiments, subjects may be unaware that their behavior is under formal study. Here, researchers have special obligations to prevent negative consequences for subjects. Ethical research has a practical side as well as a moral side. Good cooperation from research subjects is necessary to do good research. Such cooperation is easier to obtain when people are confident that ethical procedures are the rule, not the exception.

THE MANAGER'S NOTEBOOK

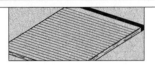

Netherlands Postal and Telecommunications Services

1. The Netherlands Postal and Telecommunications Services (PTT) actually did an experiment to test the success of its economy program. One postal district, with several offices, was used as an experimental district. The program, which is the independent variable, was installed there. Another district that did not experience the program served as a control group. Dependent variables were fuel consumption (measured objectively) and questionnaire responses about driving habits, attitudes toward economy, and so on. They were measured both before and after the program was instituted. The results actually exceeded management expectations, with a 7.3 percent decline in gasoline use in the experimental district. Driving habits and attitudes also changed favorably.

2. Evaluating the results of the program solely with observation would not be sensible, since there were many drivers, and they were "on the move." However, observation did suggest that local management instruction and pep talks contributed to program success. Correlational research was actually used in a pilot study that led to the economy program. In questionnaire responses, drivers who claimed to use thrifty driving habits tended to have correct beliefs about the impact of driving on economy.

SUMMARY

- Common sense provides a somewhat limited basis for understanding organizational behavior. This is because knowledge derived from common sense is often a function of overgeneralization and value judgments. In addition, we frequently assume that actual organizational practices or media presentations of them yield correct pictures of organizational behavior.
- The systematic study of organizational behavior, using carefully designed research, represents a useful alternative to reliance only on common sense. Observational research techniques are closest to commonsense methods for finding out about organizational behavior, in that they involve one or a few observers assessing one or a few instances of the activity in question. In participant observation the observer actually takes part in the activity being observed. In direct observation the assessment occurs without the active participation of the researcher.

- Compared with observation, correlational research techniques attempt to measure the variables in question more precisely by using questionnaires, interviews, and existing data. One problem with correlational research is its inability to reveal which variables cause other variables. Experiments are used to overcome this problem.
- In experimental research the investigator actually manipulates some factor in the organizational setting and measures the effect that this manipulation has. Each of the three basic research techniques is useful for answering certain kinds of questions about behavior in organizations.
- Proper sampling, attention to Hawthorne effects, and ethical considerations are all components of good organizational research.

KEY CONCEPTS

Common sense	Reliability	Independent variable
Observational research	Validity	Dependent variable
Participant observation	Hypothesis	Control group
Direct observation	Experimental research	Hawthorne effect
Correlational research		

DISCUSSION QUESTIONS

1. Describe the assumptions about organizational behavior that are reflected in television shows such as situation comedies and police dramas. How accurate are these portrayals? Do they influence our thinking about what occurs in organizations?

2. Discuss an example in which an inaccurate assumption about organizational behavior caused you a problem.

3. State three very specific hypotheses about behavior in organizations and describe how you would test them.

4. Review the comparative strengths and weaknesses of experimental research, correlational research, and observational research.

5. A researcher finds that superior ratings of subordinate performance are reliable but not valid. What does this mean?

6. A company introduces a complicated new bonus plan for its factory workers. To explain how it works, it holds a number of meetings, puts up posters, and prepares a video information campaign. After the bonus plan is introduced, productivity increases for a while and then reverts to preplan levels. Interpret what happened in terms of the Hawthorne effect.

■

EXPERIENTIAL EXERCISE

OB on TV

In the first part of the chapter we examined various unsystematic sources of knowledge about organizational behavior. The purpose of this exercise is to explore in greater detail one of these sources: the portrayal of organizational behavior on television. Most experts on the function of TV as a communication medium agree on two points. First, although TV may present an inaccurate or distorted view of many specific events, the overall content of TV programming *does* accurately reflect the general values and concerns of society. Second, it is generally agreed that TV has the power to *shape* the attitudes and expectations of viewers. If this is so, we should pay some attention to the portrayal of work and organizational behavior on TV.

This exercise is to be prepared before its assigned class:

_____ 1. Choose a prime time TV show that interests you. (This means a show that begins between 8 P.M. and 10 P.M. in your viewing area. If your schedule prohibits this, choose another time.) The show in question could be a comedy, a drama, or a documentary. Your instructor may give you some more specific instructions about what to watch.

_____ 2. On a piece of paper, list the name of the program and its date and time of broadcast. Write the answers to the following questions during or immediately following the broadcast:

a. What industry is the primary focus of the program? Use the following list to categorize your answer: Agriculture; Mining; Construction; Manufacturing; Transportation; Communication; Wholesale trade; Retail trade; Finance; Service; Public administration. (Examples of service industries include hotel, health, legal, education, newspaper, amusement, and private investigation. Examples of public administration include justice, police work, and national security.)

b. What industries or occupations are of secondary focus in the program?

c. What exact job categories or occupational roles are played by the main characters in the program? Use this list to categorize your answers: Managerial; Clerical; Professional; Sales; Service; Craftsperson; Machine Operator; Laborer; Lawbreaker; Military personnel; Customer/patient/client; Housework.

d. Write several paragraphs describing how organizational life is portrayed in the program. For example, is it fun or boring? Does it involve conflict or cooperation? Are people treated fairly? Do they seem motivated? Is work life stressful?

e. What aspects of the TV portrayal of organizational behavior do you think were realistic? Which were unrealistic?

_____ 3. Be prepared to discuss your findings in class. Your instructor will have some research information about how organizational life has actually been portrayed on TV over the years.

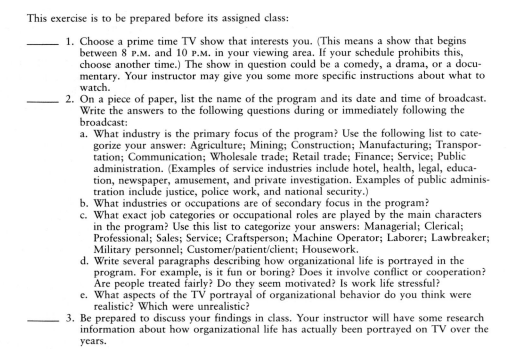

Source: Inspired by the research of Leah Vande Berg and Nick Trujillo as reported in Vande Berg, L., & Trujillo, N. (1989). *Organizational life on television*. Norwood, NJ: Ablex. Reprinted by permission of the publisher.

Electric City

Twenty-five years ago, Ollie Grayson had a good idea. Over the years the fruits of that idea provided him with a lot of personal satisfaction and made him a lot of money. At the time, Ollie owned a modest appliance store on the main street of a medium-sized southern city. Ollie's store prospered by selling stoves, refrigerators, washers, dryers, and televisions to the good citizens of that city. Ollie's main competitors were two large chain department stores located on the same street. However, a combination of lower overhead and more personalized selling techniques enabled Ollie's store to more than hold its own against the department stores.

During this period, Ollie accurately foresaw several trends that were to radically reshape American retailing. One of these was the rise in popularity of large suburban shopping malls located on relatively low-priced land outside of city centers. Another was a boom in the home appliance and consumer electronics market. Electric dishwashers and trash compactors were coming onto the market already, and Ollie knew that microwave ovens for home use were not far behind. And the home entertainment market had nowhere to go but up, as his increased sales of color televisions were already showing. Ollie was a great fan of classical music, and he had recently purchased a sophisticated, expensive component stereo system from a very small specialist music shop. His own store did not carry such equipment, only low-priced one-unit record player systems and overpriced (he thought) console versions of the same thing. But Ollie read all the electronics trade magazines, and he foresaw the day when most American homes would have component sound systems. And Ollie felt that when the market for such sound systems was saturated, new devices such as video recorders or even home computers might come along to take up the slack.

What Ollie saw was space in the marketplace for a new kind of store that wasn't a department store, a specialist shop, or even a traditional appliance store like his own. Rather, it was predicated on selling large volumes of appliances and electronic gear at very competitive prices—a "warehouse-type operation" Ollie called it at the time. Ollie predicted that when the big department stores moved to the malls, they would think twice about devoting much floor space to bulky, low-turnover items like appliances. And he felt that they would not attract the sales talent to do a good job of selling the more sophisticated electronic equipment. On the other hand, he felt that as the mystique disappeared from sound systems, price—not esoteric music knowledge—would be key to sales. This would make the small specialist shops less competitive.

When he heard rumors of a large mall development just outside of town, Ollie jumped into action. He took an option on a piece of property on the main road between the city and the proposed mall, and he began to turn his dream into a reality. Ollie named his new store Electric City, and it was immediately successful. As he says today, "I let the glitzy shopping mall attract the customers, and I peddled them low-cost appliances and electronics gear from my rather spartan premises."

Over the years, using basically the same tactics, Ollie repeated his success, gradually opening eighteen Electric City stores throughout the South. All the stores are profitable, although this varies according to store location. The average store employs twenty-five people, most of whom are sales personnel, and none of whom are unionized. Nowadays, Ollie spends most of his time touring his stores and "managing by walking around." He visits each store at least three times a year and is well-liked and respected by almost all personnel. For relaxation, Ollie listens to classical music on a top-of-the-line compact disc system that is readily available in any Electric City outlet.

In the late 1980s, Ollie became aware that the profitability of the Electric City chain was gradually leveling off. In response he called in a consulting firm that he had employed successfully in the past and asked them to do a thorough analysis of the situation. The consultants examined financial data, visited Electric City stores, talked to store managers and personnel, and visited competing electronics and appliance outlets. The partner who headed the consulting project summarized the results for Ollie:

"Mr. Grayson, you have prime store locations, a good selection of merchandise, a good pricing policy, and an efficient distribution system. What we think you need to do is pursue a more aggressive selling policy in the stores. Competition has increased tremendously in your market sector, and clinching sales on the premises seems to be the key to continued success. We recommend a two-part strategy. First, we think you need to institute a formal sales training program for your personnel. This may cover some product knowledge, but they seem pretty good there. What they need more is some advanced sales skills training. To reinforce your concern with sales, we also recommend that you replace your current hourly pay plan for sales personnel with a system based partly on hourly pay and partly on commission. Here, let me show you some projected figures. . . . "

Ollie Grayson pondered the consultant's recommendations. It was true that Electric City had never used formal sales training. Sales personnel had been viewed more as order takers in the warehouse-type operation. Sales training was expensive. Would it be effective? Ollie also debated the question of commissions. How would the sales staff react? How would the nonsales staff react?

Electric City stores had always had good labor relations, and Ollie didn't want this to change. And how would customers react to all this? Would the sales staff become overly aggressive? Could training be used without the commission scheme, or vice versa? Ollie just wasn't sure.

1. Construct a research design to help Ollie Grayson solve his dilemmas. Justify the logic behind your choice of research techniques, and state the hypotheses being tested.
2. Discuss the issue of measurement in your proposed research design. What should be measured, how should it be measured, and when should it be measured?
3. Discuss any problems that might occur in performing the research you propose.
4. Could the Hawthorne effect come into play in your research study?

REFERENCES

1. Plimpton, G. (1966). *Paper lion.* New York: Harper & Row.
2. Lupton, T. (1963). *On the shop floor.* Oxford: Pergamon.
3. Bensman, J., & Gerver, I. (1963). Crime and punishment in the factory: The function of deviancy in maintaining the social system. *American Sociological Review, 28,* 588–598.
4. Mintzberg, H. (1973). *The nature of managerial work.* New York: Harper & Row.
5. Waters, L. K., Roach, D., & Waters, C. W. (1976). Estimates of future tenure, satisfaction, and biographical variables as predictors of termination. *Personnel Psychology, 29,* 57–60.
6. Ivancevich, J. M., & Lyon, H. L. (1977). The shortened workweek: A field experiment. *Journal of Applied Psychology, 62,* 34–37.
7. Roethlisberger, F. J., & Dickson, W. J. (1939). *Management and the worker.* Cambridge, MA: Harvard University Press; Greenwood, R. G., & Wrege, C. D. (1986). The Hawthorne studies. In D. A. Wren & J. A. Pearce II. *Papers dedicated to the development of modern management.* The Academy of Management.
8. Adair, J. G. (1984). The Hawthorne effect: A reconsideration of the methodological artifact. *Journal of Applied Psychology, 69,* 334–345.

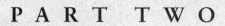

PART TWO

INDIVIDUAL BEHAVIOR

LEARNING

ELLEN WILDER

Ellen Wilder had just been promoted to supervisor of the Accounts Payable department of a large urban department store. Anxious to perform her new job well, she paid particular attention to the supervisory techniques of her counterpart in Accounts Receivable, Gail Marcus. Gail was a very experienced supervisor and was generally conceded to be one of the best in the company. Over a period of a couple of weeks, Ellen noticed that Gail frequently praised her subordinates to acknowledge good performance. This appeared logical enough to Ellen, but there seemed to be some inconsistency in the way Gail used praise. Some subordinates were the object of frequent and immediate praise, while others were praised much less frequently, even though they were performing just as well. Once, Gail had actually interrupted a conversation with Ellen to go over and praise a new teller who had just done a good job of handling a very irate customer. On the other hand, Ellen had seen Gail delay praising some subordinates for work well done until the end of the week. Gail also had some curious habits regarding the way she criticized ineffective behavior. Some undesirable activities, such as disruptive shouting and quarreling among the staff, were actually ignored. Ellen wondered why Gail resisted the temptation to jump in and straighten these incidents out. This is not to say that Gail never criticized her subordinates. In fact, she had the reputation for giving a very harsh dressing down in the privacy of her office or after working hours. Ellen wondered why Gail didn't offer criticism in front of the rest of the staff to make an example of the offender.

After several months, Ellen had her first performance review since becoming Accounts Payable supervisor. In the review, Ellen's boss was especially complimentary of how she dealt with her subordinates. Ellen smiled and thought to herself, "I just did everything Gail did."

You may have some of the same questions about Gail's supervisory style that Ellen had. Why did Gail praise some subordinates frequently and immediately while delaying the praise given to others? Why did Gail ignore some instances of ineffective performance and refuse to "make an example" of poor performers? In this chapter you will discover that Gail Marcus is a good learning theorist and practitioner. She knows what to say to whom (and when) in order to aid her subordinates in learning effective organizational behavior, and Ellen was able to acquire her skill by observing her closely.

To some important degree, people *learn* to show up for work, to be motivated on the job, to be good leaders, and to create conflict in organizations. In the following pages we will define learning and discuss the learning process. We will examine how the work environment can be managed to encourage the learning of effective organizational behavior and the errors that organizations sometimes make in trying to do this. In addition, we will investigate how the environment can be managed to terminate unwanted organizational behavior.

WHAT IS LEARNING?

Learning occurs when practice or experience leads to a relatively permanent change in behavior potential. The words *practice or experience* rule out viewing changes in behavior caused by factors like drug intake or biological maturation as learning. One does not learn to be relaxed after taking a tranquilizer, and a boy does not suddenly learn to be a bass singer at the age of fourteen. The practice or experience that prompts learning stems from an environment that gives feedback concerning the consequences of behavior. Gail's praise and criticism provided such experience for her subordinates.

When we say that learning indicates a change in *behavior potential,* we mean that what is learned might not always be reflected in performance. The word *learning* is psychological shorthand for a process that cannot be observed directly. We assume that learning has occurred when we see a change in an individual's behavior or performance. While learning and performance are usually correlated, there are cases in which this might not be true. Consider the bright new business administration graduate who accepts a management trainee position. His corporation requires trainees to rotate through several departments to acquire a feel for the organization. Such an individual might not perform up to his potential while in these departments because of the boredom of a series of short-term, disconnected assignments. In this case, learning is not reflected in performance.

OPERANT LEARNING AND SOCIAL LEARNING

In the 1930s the psychologist B. F. Skinner investigated the behavior of rats that were confined in a box containing a lever that delivered food pellets when pulled.

Initially, the rats ignored the lever, but at some point they would accidently operate it and a pellet would appear. Over time, the rats gradually acquired the lever-pulling response as a means of obtaining food. In other words, they *learned* to pull the lever. The term **operant learning** has been used to describe the kind of learning studied by Skinner, because the organism learns to operate on the environment to achieve certain consequences. The rats learned to operate the lever to achieve food. Notice that operantly learned behavior is controlled by the consequences that follow it. These consequences are usually contingent upon (depend upon) the behavior, and this connection is what is learned. For example, salespeople have learned effective sales techniques to achieve commissions and to avoid criticism from the sales manager. The consequences of commissions and criticism depend upon which sales behaviors are exhibited.

Besides experiencing consequences directly, humans can learn by observing the behavior of others. This form of learning is called **social learning.** Generally, social learning involves examining the behavior of others, seeing what consequences they experience, and thinking about what might happen if we act the same way. If we expect favorable consequences, we might imitate the behavior. For example, the rookie salesperson might be required to make calls with a seasoned sales veteran. By simply observing the veteran in action, the rookie might begin to acquire considerable skill without yet having personally made a sale. Obviously, operant learning theory and social learning theory complement each other in explaining organizational behavior.[1]

INCREASING THE PROBABILITY OF BEHAVIOR

One of the most important consequences that promotes behavior is called reinforcement. **Reinforcement** is the process by which stimuli strengthen behaviors. Thus, a *reinforcer* is a stimulus that follows some behavior and increases or maintains the probability of that behavior. The sales commissions and criticism mentioned above are reinforcers. In each case, reinforcement serves to strengthen behaviors of interest to the organization (proper sales techniques). In general, organizations are interested in maintaining or increasing the probability of behaviors such as correct performance, prompt attendance, and accurate decision making. As we shall see, some reinforcers work by their application *to* a situation, while others work by their removal *from* a situation.

Positive Reinforcement

Positive reinforcement increases or maintains the probability of some behavior by the *application* or *addition* of a stimulus to the situation in question. Such a stimulus is called a positive reinforcer. In the basic Skinnerian learning situation described earlier, we can assume that reinforcement occurred because the probability of lever operation increased over time. We can further assume that the food pellets were positive reinforcers because they were applied to or injected into the situation after the lever was pulled.

Imagine a new telephone operator who has been instructed in the proper language and demeanor to use when answering the telephone and whose performance is being monitored by a supervisor. Suppose the supervisor praises each correct handling of a call and remains silent when errors are made. Over time, if the operator's performance improves, we can assume that the praise offered by the supervisor served as a positive reinforcer for this performance. In fact, returning to the story that began the chapter, it would appear that Gail Marcus used praise to positively reinforce the good performance of her subordinates. Similarly, consider the experienced securities analyst who tends to read a particular set of financial newspapers regularly. If we had been able to observe the development of this reading habit, we might have found that it occurred as the result of a series of successful business decisions. That is, the analyst has learned to scan those papers whose reading has been positively reinforced by subsequent successful decisions. In these examples, something has been added to the situation (praise, favorable decisions) that has increased the probability of certain behaviors (correct telephone performance, selective reading). Also, in both cases, the appearance of the reinforcer is dependent or contingent upon the occurrence of those behaviors.

In general, positive reinforcers tend to be pleasant stimuli such as food, praise, or business success. However, the intrinsic character of stimuli do not determine whether they are positive reinforcers, and pleasant stimuli are not positive reinforcers when considered in the abstract. Whether or not something is a positive reinforcer depends only upon whether it increases or maintains the occurrence of some behavior by its application. Thus, it is improbable that the Christmas turkey given to all the employees of a manufacturing plant positively reinforces anything. The only behavior upon which receipt of the turkey is contingent is being employed by the company during the third week of December. It is unlikely that the turkey increases the probability that employees will remain for another year or work harder. On the other hand, stimuli that most of us find unpleasant might serve as positive reinforcers for the behavior of masochists, who seek pain. Reinforcers are designated by what they do and how they do it, not by their surface appearance.

Negative Reinforcement

Negative reinforcement increases or maintains the probability of some behavior by the *removal* of a stimulus from the situation in question. Also, negative reinforcement occurs when a response *prevents* some event or stimulus from occurring. In each case, the removed or prevented stimulus is called a *negative reinforcer*. Negative reinforcers are usually aversive or unpleasant stimuli, and it stands to reason that we will learn to repeat behaviors that remove or prevent these stimuli.

Let's repeat this point, because it frequently confuses students of learning: Negative reinforcers *increase* the probability of behavior. Suppose we rig a cage with an electrified floor so that it provides a mild shock to its inhabitant. In addition, we install a lever that will turn off the electricity. On the first few trials, a rat put in the cage will become very upset when shocked. Sooner or later, however, it will accidently operate the lever and turn off the current. Gradually, the rat will learn to operate the lever as soon as the shock is felt. The shock serves as a negative reinforcer for the lever pulling, increasing the probability of the behavior by its removal.

Managers who continuously nag their subordinates unless they work hard are attempting to use negative reinforcement. The only way subordinates can stop the aversive nagging is to work hard and "toe the line." The nagging maintains the probability of productive responses by its removal. In this situation, subordinates often get pretty good at anticipating the onset of nagging by the look on the boss's face. This look serves as a signal that nagging can be avoided altogether if they work harder.

Mechanics are often guided in correct work performance by negative reinforcement. Suppose that a loud squeaking or grinding noise indicates the improper functioning of a machine. The maintenance person who is assigned to correct this problem knows that repairs have been properly performed when the noise goes away. Thus, the noise increases the probability of proper repairs in the future when it is removed. It has functioned as a negative reinforcer.

Negative reinforcers generally tend to be unpleasant stimuli such as shock, threat, nagging, or nasty noises. Again, however, negative reinforcers are defined only by what they do and how they work, not by their unpleasantness. Above, we indicated that nagging could serve as a negative reinforcer to increase the probability of productive responses. However, nagging could also serve as a positive reinforcer to increase the probability of unproductive responses if a subordinate has a need for attention and nagging is the only attention provided by the manager. In the first case, nagging was a negative reinforcer—it was terminated following productive responses. In the second case, nagging was a positive reinforcer, because it was applied following unproductive responses. In both cases, the responses increased in probability.

ORGANIZATIONAL ERRORS INVOLVING REINFORCEMENT

Now that we have established the basic dynamics of reinforcement, we can consider some of the more interesting implications of the concept for behavior in organizations. It is, of course, not surprising that people tend to repeat behaviors that lead to valued outcomes or terminate unfavorable states of affairs. However, a learning analysis can sometimes reveal effects that are not revealed by casual observation. Such analyses show that organizations frequently commit errors when attempting to implement reinforcement.

Confusing Rewards With Reinforcers

Organizations and individual managers frequently "reward" workers with things such as pay, promotions, fringe benefits, paid vacations, overtime work, and the opportunity to perform special tasks. Such rewards can fail to serve as reinforcers, however, because they are not made contingent upon specific behaviors that are of interest to the organization, such as attendance, punctuality, or productivity. For example, many organizations assign overtime work on the basis of seniority, rather than performance or good attendance, even when not required to do so by union contract. Although the opportunity to earn extra money might have strong potential as a reinforcer, it is seldom made contingent upon some desired behavior.

For another instance of a "lost" reinforcer, take an advertising manager whose graphic artist has trouble meeting deadlines for the completion of projects. When the artist completed his work on an especially crucial sales presentation well before the deadline, the manager waited until a slack period two weeks later to reward him with an afternoon off work. Not only did the manager fail to specify why she was granting the time off, but during the two-week interval the artist failed to complete two other projects on time! The long period of time between the good performance and the reward destroyed any contingent reinforcing effects, and one might suspect that, if anything, the tardy completions were more likely reinforced.

Neglecting Individual Preferences for Reinforcers

Organizations often fail to appreciate individual differences in preferences for reinforcers. In this case, even if rewards are administered after a desired behavior, they might fail to have a reinforcing effect. Intuitively, it seems questionable to reinforce a workaholic's extra effort with time off from work, yet such a strategy is fairly common. A more appropriate reinforcer might be the assignment of some special preferred task, such as work on a very demanding key project. Some labor contracts include clauses that dictate that overtime be assigned to the workers who have the greatest seniority. Not surprisingly, high-seniority workers are often the best paid and the least in need of the extra pay available through overtime. Even if it is administered so that the best-performing high-seniority workers get the overtime, such a strategy might not prove reinforcing—the usual time off might be preferred over extra money.

Managers should carefully explore the possible range of stimuli under their control (such as task assignment and time off from work) for their applicability as reinforcers for particular subordinates. Furthermore, organizations should attempt to administer their formal rewards (such as pay and promotions) to capitalize upon their reinforcing effects for various individuals.

Neglecting Important Sources of Reinforcement

There are many reinforcers of organizational behavior that are not especially obvious. While concentrating upon potential reinforcers of a formal nature, such as pay or promotions, organizations and their managers often neglect those which are administered by co-workers or intrinsic to the jobs being performed. Many managers cannot understand why a worker would persist in potentially dangerous horseplay despite threats of a pay penalty or dismissal. Frequently, such activity is positively reinforced by the attention provided by the joker's co-workers. In fact, on a particularly boring job, even such threats might act as positive reinforcers for horseplay by relieving the boredom, especially if the threats are never carried out.

One very important source of reinforcement that is often ignored is that which accompanies the successful performance of tasks. This reinforcement is available on jobs that provide *feedback* concerning the adequacy of performance. On some jobs, feedback contingent upon performance is readily available. Doctors can observe the success of their treatment by observing the progress of their patients' health, and mechanics can take the cars they repair for a test drive. In other cases, some special feedback mechanism must be designed into the job. Consultant

Using feedback as reinforcement, the management at Emery Air Freight motivated its employees to load containers fully to prevent waste. (Nubar Alexanian/Stock Boston)

Edward J. Feeney, former vice-president of Emery Air Freight, has described that company's experience in providing such a system. Emery's profits were highly dependent upon the use of large containers to forward smaller pieces of freight to a common destination. Costs soared when these containers were not fully utilized. For this reason, warehouse workers and their supervisors were carefully trained to use the containers when possible, and both parties felt that they were achieving around 90 percent utilization. In fact, a performance audit indicated a rate of 45 percent. The change in the job implemented by Feeney was very simple. Workers had to keep a checklist to provide themselves with feedback concerning container utilization. This feedback so reinforced correct performance that utilization jumped to 95 percent within a very short time. Emery estimated that this simple change saved $650,000 in one year.[2]

A similar feedback system is in place at Fleming Foods, a large wholesaler headquartered in Oklahoma City:

> Fleming is getting workers to make themselves more productive. Each warehouse worker about to start a task inserts a card into a computer terminal that tells him how long management thinks a job should take. When the job is done, the worker reinserts the card. If he beats the clock, the screen flashes "good job." If he doesn't, the screen tells him how far below capacity he's working.[3]

REINFORCEMENT STRATEGIES AND THEIR EFFECTS

What is the best way to administer reinforcers? Should we apply a reinforcer immediately after the behavior of interest occurs, or should we wait for some period of time? Should we reinforce every correct behavior, or should we reinforce only a portion of correct responses? You will recall that Ellen Wilder was confused by Gail Marcus's differential use of these strategies in praising her subordinates. Obviously, pragmatic factors sometimes dictate the answer to these questions. The busy manager who wishes to use praise or nagging to reinforce performance or attendance might find it physically impossible to immediately and continuously reinforce each and every desired response of subordinates. On the other hand, it should be equally apparent that some responses are well enough learned that they do not have to be reinforced quickly or even every time they occur.

To obtain the *fast acquisition* of some response, **continuous** and **immediate reinforcement** should be used—that is, the reinforcer should be applied every time the behavior of interest occurs, and it should be applied without delay after each occurrence. Many conditions exist in which the fast acquisition of responses is desirable. These include correcting the behavior of "problem" employees, training employees for emergency operations, and dealing with unsafe work behaviors. Consider the otherwise excellent performer who tends to be late for work.

Under pressure to demote or fire this good worker, the boss might sensibly attempt to positively reinforce instances of prompt attendance with compliments and encouragement. To modify the subordinate's behavior as quickly as possible, the supervisor might station herself near the office door each morning to supply these reinforcers regularly and immediately.

You might wonder when one would *not* want to use a continuous, immediate reinforcement strategy to mold organizational behavior. Put simply, behavior learned under such conditions tends not to persist when reinforcement is made less frequent or stopped. Intuitively, this should not be surprising. For example, under normal conditions, operating the power switch on your stereo system is continuously and immediately reinforced by music. If the system develops a short circuit and fails to produce music, your switch-operating behavior will extinguish very quickly. In the example in the preceding paragraph, the use of continuous, immediate reinforcement was justified by the need for fast learning. Under more typical circumstances, we would hope that prompt attendance could occur without such close attention.

Behavior tends to be *persistent* when it is learned under conditions of **partial** and **delayed reinforcement.** That is, it will tend to persist under reduced or terminated reinforcement when not every instance of the behavior is reinforced during learning or when some time period elapses between its enactment and reinforcement. In most cases, the supervisor who wishes to reinforce prompt attendance knows that he will not be able to stand by the shop door every morning to compliment his crew's timely entry. Given this constraint, the supervisor should compliment prompt attendance occasionally, perhaps later in the day. This should increase the persistence of promptness and reduce the subordinates' reliance on the boss's monitoring.

To repeat, fast learning is facilitated by continuous, immediate reinforcement, and persistent learning is facilitated by delayed, partial reinforcement (Exhibit 3–1). There are two important implications here. First, it is impossible to maxi-

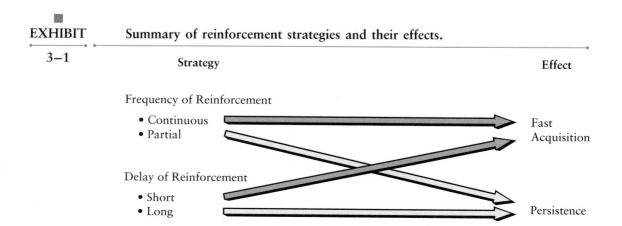

EXHIBIT

3–1

Summary of reinforcement strategies and their effects.

Strategy   **Effect**

Frequency of Reinforcement

• Continuous   Fast
• Partial   Acquisition

Delay of Reinforcement

• Short
• Long   Persistence

mize both speed and persistence with a single reinforcement strategy. Second, many responses in our everyday lives cannot be continuously and immediately reinforced, so in many cases it pays to sacrifice some speed in learning to prepare the learner for this fact of life. The "spoiled brat" has been continuously and immediately reinforced for correct behavior. When such a child finds that the world outside his or her home does not provide such reinforcement, this correct behavior might extinguish rapidly.

All of this suggests that reinforcement strategies have to be tailored to the needs of the situation. Often, this means that they must be altered over time to achieve effective learning and maintenance of behavior. For example, the manager breaking in a new subordinate should probably use a reinforcement strategy that is fairly continuous and immediate (whatever the reinforcer). "Looking over the subordinate's shoulder" to obtain the fast acquisition of behavior is appropriate. Gradually, however, the supervisor should probably reduce the frequency of reinforcement and perhaps build some delay into its presentation to reduce the subordinate's dependency upon his or her attention. Since the manager has other subordinates to attend to, and since it is desirable to build long-term persistence into the subordinate's behavior, such a strategy seems reasonable. In addition, as the subordinate learns the job, other sources of reinforcement (feedback from co-workers, customers, and the job itself) will come into play.

This should clarify the rationale for Gail Marcus's seemingly inconsistent use of praise as a reinforcer. Gail was quick to provide immediate, on-the-spot reinforcement for her new teller on the presumption that her good performance was not well learned and was thus in special need of attention. Furthermore, we can assume that Gail provided less frequent and delayed praise for experienced workers whose correct work behaviors were better established.

SCHEDULES OF PARTIAL REINFORCEMENT

Earlier, it was indicated that many responses in everyday circumstances are only partially reinforced—not every response that occurs is followed by reinforcement. In this section we will consider the different ways this partial reinforcement might be scheduled and the particular effects that these schedules have upon behavior. This topic is important for two reasons. First, a consideration of reinforcement schedules enables us to explain many natural variations in behavior that appear somewhat puzzling at first glance. Second, reinforcers are often expensive and time-consuming to administer, and we need to know which schedules will enable us to achieve most efficiently the behaviors we desire.

One kind of reinforcement schedule that we will consider is called an *interval* schedule. Under interval schedules, some *time period* must elapse after a reinforced response before another reinforcement is available. In this case, the number of responses following a reinforcement is irrelevant to how quickly the next reinforcement becomes available, since interval schedules are time-dependent. (Of course, responses must be made for reinforcement to occur.) The other kind of schedule to be examined is called a *ratio* schedule. Under ratio schedules, some *number of responses* must occur after a reinforced response before another reinforcement is available. Here, the responses following a reinforcement determine how quickly the next reinforcement becomes available. In other words, "fast work equals more reinforcement" under ratio schedules, which are response-dependent. Each of these types of schedules has two subtypes, which we will discuss below.

Fixed Interval

Under a **fixed interval schedule,** some *fixed* time period occurs between a reinforced response and the availability of the next reinforcement. Under ideal conditions, mail is delivered according to this schedule—every twenty-four hours your mailbox-checking activity is reinforced by the mail carrier's visit. Similarly, if you have three equally spaced announced tests during the semester in your organizational behavior class, you can see a fixed interval schedule at work. Your studying behavior is reinforced by the opportunity to demonstrate your knowledge and receive a grade. Notice the kind of behavior that this schedule induces (Exhibit 3–2). The individual in question learns to anticipate when reinforcement is avail-

■
EXHIBIT
•————•
3–2

Idealized response curves for reinforcement schedules. The steeper the curve, the higher the rate of response. Reinforcements are indicated by short diagonal lines.

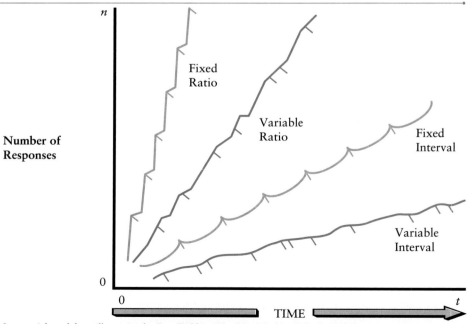

Number of Responses

able and tends to respond more rapidly as this time approaches. After reinforcement, the behavior subsides because the individual has learned that no further reinforcement will occur for awhile. If you are expecting an important letter and the mail is habitually delivered at 10:00 A.M., you might check the mailbox at 9:15, 9:30, and 9:45 in anticipation. If the mail finally comes at 10:00 and does not include your letter, it is unlikely that you will look again at 10:15. Similarly, the fixed interval exam schedule often leads to "cramming" behavior on the part of students in advance of "E day," followed by a moratorium on studying until the next exam approaches.

Organizations abound with examples of fixed interval schedules. Yearly performance reviews are arranged in this manner. On a certain date, or on an employee's anniversary date with the firm, his or her supervisor sits down and discusses the employee's previous year's performance. In advance of this reinforcement, many managers have observed a tendency for performance to improve as the date for the review draws near. Again, the individual learns to anticipate the reinforcing event. Similarly, considering pay as a reinforcer for performance and attendance, organizational records often reveal that the best attendance occurs on paydays and falls off afterwards.

Variable Interval

Under this schedule, some *variable* time period occurs between a reinforced response and the chance for the next reinforcement. As shown in Exhibit 3–2, **variable interval schedules** lead to a slow, steady rate of response, because the individual cannot anticipate when a reinforcement will occur and cannot influence its occurrence by responding faster. A random "pop quiz" system, in which the students do not know when they will be examined during the semester, is an example of a variable interval schedule. Not surprisingly, such a system makes "cramming" impossible and tends to distribute study time more evenly over the semester. For obvious reasons, bank examiners tend to schedule their visits to banks according to a variable interval schedule, arranged around some average number of inspections per year. By the same token, some managers have learned to overcome the deficiencies of the formal yearly performance appraisal system by providing unannounced informal reviews during the year.

Fixed Ratio

Under **fixed ratio schedules,** after a reinforced response, some *fixed* number of responses must be made before another reinforcement becomes available. Hand-operated water pumps work according to a fixed ratio schedule. A given number of pumping movements is necessary before the water flows. As shown in Exhibit 3–2, this schedule leads to a high rate of response followed by a short pause after reinforcement. The loading dock supervisor who permits his workers to take a rest break after they stack a hundred crates is implementing a fixed ratio schedule. He is assuming that the break will serve as a reinforcer for high performance when coupled with a specific, known performance goal of a hundred crates. The firm that gives its office workers an extra vacation day for every forty working days they complete without being absent is applying a fixed ratio schedule to reinforce attendance.

Variable Ratio

With this schedule, some *variable* number of responses is necessary after a reinforcement before another reinforcement is offered. As shown in Exhibit 3–2, **variable ratio schedules** typically lead to a very high response rate with little or no pause after reinforcement. Slot machines are programmed according to a variable ratio schedule, paying off after some variable number of attempts by the players. The ratio of payoffs to plays is designed around some average that nets the casino a handsome profit. (You should consider why the other three schedules are inappropriate for slot machines.) Door-to-door salespeople are reinforced by sales according to a variable ratio schedule. The more houses they call on, the more likely they are to make a sale, but the number of houses called on between sales varies. Lower-level managers have their suggestions accepted by top management according to this schedule. The more suggestions offered, the greater the chance of having one approved, although the number of ideas generated between approvals varies. People who enjoy fishing know the power of the variable ratio schedule.

Pay as a Scheduled Reinforcer

The pay offered to employees is a reward for work behaviors that are of interest to the organization. The potential reinforcing effects of this reward depend upon exactly how it is administered. An hourly pay scheme is an example of a fixed interval reinforcement schedule. In theory, employees are paid at the end of each hour they work (although they are typically paid at the end of the workweek). Just what is being reinforced under an hourly pay schedule? Hourly pay is contingent upon putting in time on the job and performing at the minimal acceptable level. Thus, these are the behaviors that the hourly schedule reinforces. Hourly pay can be contrasted with a piecerate scheme. Under piecerate, workers are paid a certain amount of money for producing a particular number of objects, or pieces. For example, sewing machine operators might be paid one dollar for every two jackets they stitch. It can be seen that piecerate pay represents a fixed ratio schedule of reinforcement—a certain number of responses are necessary for payment to occur. Under this pay scheme, *productivity* is reinforced because pay is contingent upon performance of the job; that is, more work equals more pay. The information presented earlier indicated that fixed ratio schedules lead to higher response rates than fixed interval schedules, and such is the case here. In general, studies reveal that piecerate pay leads to greater productivity than hourly pay.[4]

(There are a number of exceptions to this rule, and there are certain problems involved in the introduction of piecerate pay systems. We will discuss these matters in Chapter 7.)

ORGANIZATIONAL BEHAVIOR MODIFICATION

From what has been said thus far, it should be clear to you that much of the behavior that occurs in organizations is the product of reinforcement. Most of this reinforcement occurs naturally, rather than as the result of a conscious attempt to control behavior. However, the description of the feedback procedure instituted at Emery Air Freight is an example of **organizational behavior modification,** the systematic use of learning principles to influence organizational behavior. The results achieved at Emery have been essentially anecdotal. In this section we will report several attempts to scientifically monitor practical applications of organizational behavior modification. In each case, an attempt was made to positively reinforce employee behaviors that were of interest to the organization. In general, research supports the effectiveness of such programs.[5]

Reinforcing Punctuality

The first situation involves a manufacturing firm that was having trouble with workers reporting for work after the scheduled starting time. Such behavior is disruptive to production scheduling, and it occurred in spite of the fact that the company had devised a yearly bonus for the workers with the best attendance and punctuality records. Clearly, the reinforcing properties of such a bonus are questionable because its very long delay characteristic obscured the contingency between any instance of punctuality and the subsequent achievement of money. In fact, the bonus probably rewarded workers who would have been prompt even without such a scheme while having no effect on problem employees. Researchers suggested a behavior modification plan in which chronically tardy workers received a small bonus for every day they arrived at work on time. You will recall that such a continuous, low-delay reinforcement strategy is especially effective for teaching proper organizational behavior because it clarifies the contingency between the reinforcer and the behavior. The plan was implemented by having the gate guard give each chronically tardy person in the experimental group a credit slip when he or she arrived on time. Compared with a control group of chronic tardies who did not receive this treatment, the experimental subjects showed a clear increase in on-time arrival. Thus, the company used money (in the guise of credit slips) as a continuous, immediate reinforcer of punctual arrival at the workplace.[6]

Reinforcing Attendance

In the previous study, the major concern was punctuality, although workers obviously had to show up for work to be on time. In another study, the organization in question was primarily interested in attendance, although punctuality was also reinforced. Workers in four sections served as control subjects, while those in another section were confronted with the following behavior modification plan:

> Each day an employee comes to work on time, he is allowed to choose a card from a deck of playing cards. At the end of the five-day week, he will have five cards or a normal poker hand. The highest hand wins $20. There will be eight winners, one for approximately each department.[7]

Supervisors were in charge of monitoring attendance, passing out the cards, and posting on a large chart the poker hands held by subordinates as the week progressed. Over four months, the attendance rate increased by 18 percent for workers exposed to the behavior modification plan, while the attendance rate for control workers actually decreased somewhat. Notice that at least two reinforcers were probably responsible for this success. First, the $20 that could be won evidently worked according to a variable ratio schedule. That is, more instances of prompt attendance increased the probability of winning $20, but a certain level of attendance did not guarantee reinforcement in any given week. Second, the cards themselves and the attendant discussion concerning the progress of the week's hands as revealed on the chart probably acquired continuous and immediate reinforcing properties. These reinforcers were available even for those who did not win the $20.

Reinforcing Safe Work Practices

A final example of the use of organizational behavior modification involves the reinforcement of safe working behavior in a food-manufacturing plant. At first glance, accidents appear to be chance events or wholly under the control of factors such as equipment failures. However, the researchers felt that accidents could be reduced if specific safe working practices could be identified and reinforced. These practices were identified with the help of past accident reports and advice from supervisors. Systematic observation of working behavior indicated that safe practices were being followed only about 74 percent of the time. A brief slide show was prepared to illustrate safe versus unsafe job behaviors. Then, two reinforcers of safe practices were introduced into the workplace. The first consisted of a feedback chart that was conspicuously posted in the workplace to indicate the percentage of safe behaviors noted by observers. This chart included the percentages achieved in observational sessions before the slide show, as well as those achieved every three days after the slide show. This approximated a fixed interval schedule of reinforcement. In addition, supervisors were encouraged to praise instances of safe performance that they observed, approximating a variable interval schedule. These interventions were successful in raising the percentage of safe working practices to around 97 percent almost immediately. When the reinforcers were terminated, the percentage of safe practices quickly returned to the level exhibited before the reinforcement was introduced. (See Exhibit 3–3.)[8]

MODELING

Organizational behavior modification programs involve the conscious use of reinforcement to manage organizational behavior. However, it has perhaps occurred to you that much learning can occur in organizations without the conscious control of positive and negative reinforcers by managers. Often, effective (or ineffective) behavior seems to occur "automatically," without the benefit of gradual shaping through trial and error and selective reinforcement. For instance, after experiencing just a couple of executive committee meetings, a newly promoted vice-president might look like an "old pro," bringing appropriate materials to the meeting, asking questions in an approved style, and so on.

How are we to account for such learning? One important factor is **modeling,** the process of imitating the behavior of others. With modeling, learning occurs by observing or imagining the behavior of others, rather than through direct personal experience.[9] Thus, the new vice-president doubtless modeled his behavior

EXHIBIT
3–3

Percentage of safe working practices achieved with and without reinforcement.

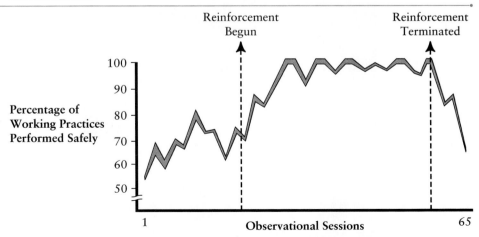

Source: Adapted from Komaki, J., et al. (1978, August). A behavioral approach to occupational safety: Pinpointing and reinforcing safe performance in a food manufacturing plant. *Journal of Applied Psychology,* 63(4), 439. Copyright © 1978 by American Psychological Association. Adapted by permission.

on that of his more experienced peers on the executive committee. Also, in the story that began the chapter, Ellen Wilder evidently modeled her supervisory style on that of Gail Marcus. But has reinforcement occurred here? It is probably *self*-reinforcement that occurs in the modeling process. For one thing, it is reinforcing to acquire an understanding of others who are viewed positively. In addition, we are able to imagine the reinforcers that the model experiences coming our way when we imitate his or her behavior. Surely this is why children imitate the behavior of sports heroes. In any event, modeling is an aspect of what we earlier called social learning.

What kinds of models are likely to provoke the greatest degree of imitation? In general, attractive, credible, competent, high-status people stand a good chance of being imitated. Gail Marcus fulfilled this role in the department store. In addition, it is important that the model's behavior provoke consequences that are seen as positive and successful to the observer. Finally, it helps if the model's behavior is vivid and memorable—bores do not make good models.[10] In business schools, it is not unusual to find students who have developed philosophies or approaches that are modeled on credible, successful, high-profile business leaders. Current examples include Microsoft's Bill Gates and Next Computer's Steven Jobs, both of whom have been the object of extensive coverage in the business and popular press.

Bill Gates of Microsoft is a role model for many in the software industry. (Nubar Alexanian/ Woodfin Camp & Associates)

The extent of modeling as a means of learning in organizations suggests that managers should pay more attention to the process. For one thing, managers who operate on a principle of "do as I say, not as I do" will find that what is done is more likely to be imitated, including undesirable behaviors such as expense account abuse. Also, in the absence of credible management models, workers might imitate dysfunctional peer behavior if peers meet the criteria for strong models. On a more positive note, well-designed performance evaluation and reward systems permit organizations to publicize the kind of organizational behavior that should be imitated.

Now that you have studied reinforcement, organizational behavior modification, and modeling, let's see how you apply this knowledge. Please consult You Be the Manager.

REDUCING THE PROBABILITY OF BEHAVIOR

Thus far in our discussion of learning, we have been interested in *increasing* the probability of various work behaviors, such as attendance or good performance. Both positive and negative reinforcement can be used to accomplish this goal. However, in many cases we encounter learned behaviors that we wish to *stop* from occurring. Such behaviors are detrimental to the operation of the organiza-

Scandinavian Airlines used learning theory to turn its reservation personnel into effective salespeople. (The Photographers' Library/ Uniphoto)

YOU BE THE MANAGER

M anager

SAS Airline Reservation Personnel

The management of Scandinavian Airlines (SAS) had a brainstorm. By airline industry tradition, advertising and flight scheduling were considered to be the factors that had the greatest impact upon sales. Reservation agents were seen as people who provided information and took orders rather than as active salespeople who could have a decided impact on company profit. This view was so ingrained that the standard computerized booking system used by the major airlines could not even total a specific agent's sales for a day or a week. Thus, neither management nor employees knew which agents achieved the highest sales. Rather, the sole individual performance indicator was the number of calls taken by an agent. If agents could truly have an impact on sales, the system was clearly focusing on the wrong behavior. The major incentive for agents was to avoid taking so few calls that they stood out from their peers.

A pilot study showed that agents specifically offered to book a flight on only 34 percent of calls. Of course, if a flight isn't booked, sales from add-on flights, hotel reservations, and rental car reservations may also be missed. In addition, the study revealed that many agents lacked standard sales skills such as relaxing callers, determining their exact needs, and making travel suggestions.

SAS management was convinced that the sales performance of its reservations agents could be improved by using sound learning principles. What do *you* think?

1. Use learning theory to analyze the reservation agent job. What behaviors are being reinforced, and what is the reinforcer?

2. Design an organizational behavior modification program to stimulate selling among the reservation agents.

To find out what SAS did, see The Manager's Notebook at the end of the chapter.

Source: Adapted from Feeney, E. J., Staelin, J. R., O'Brien, R. M., & Dickinson, A. M. (1982). Increasing sales performance among airline reservation personnel. In R. M. O'Brien, A. M. Dickinson, & M. P. Rosnow (Eds.), *Industrial behavior modification: A management handbook*. New York: Pergamon.

tion and could be detrimental to the health or safety of the individual worker. There are two strategies that can be used to reduce the probability of learned responses. One is called extinction, and the other is called punishment.

Extinction

The process of **extinction** simply involves doing away with the reinforcer that is maintaining some unwanted behavior. If the behavior is not reinforced, it will gradually dissipate or be extinguished. In a large university, the heads of the accounts and records departments were upset by the tendency for their employees to leave their job stations on paydays to pick up their paychecks halfway across campus. This resulted in a twenty-minute absence during the working day, which was often disruptive. In response to this problem, the department heads arranged with the treasurer's office to have the checks delivered to the departments for direct distribution. After this, the reinforcer for leaving the job station was removed, and the dysfunctional behavior stopped.

As another example of the extinction process, consider the case of a bright young marketing expert who was headed for the "fast track" in his organization. Although he was being considered for a promotion by his boss, the vice-president of marketing, he had developed a very disruptive habit—the tendency to play comedian during department meetings. The vice-president observed that this wisecracking was reinforced by the appreciative laughs of two other department members. He proceeded to enlist their aid to extinguish the joking. After having the problem explained to them, they agreed to ignore the disruptive one-liners and puns. At the same time, the vice-president took special pains to positively reinforce constructive comments by the young marketer. Very quickly, joking was extinguished, and the young man's future with the company improved.[11]

The preceding example illustrates that extinction works best when coupled with the reinforcement of some desired substitute behavior. It should be noted that behaviors that have been learned under delayed or partial reinforcement schedules are more difficult to extinguish than those learned under continuous, immediate reinforcement. Ironically, it would be harder to extinguish the joke-telling of a partially successful committee member than of one who was always successful at getting a laugh.

Punishment

The process of **punishment** involves following an unwanted behavior with some unpleasant, aversive stimulus. In theory, this should reduce the probability of the response when the actor learns that the behavior leads to unwanted consequences. Notice the difference between punishment and negative reinforcement. In negative reinforcement a nasty stimulus is *removed* following some behavior, increasing the probability of that behavior. With punishment, a nasty stimulus is *applied* after some behavior, *decreasing* the probability of the behavior. If a boss yells at her secretary after seeing the office phone used for personal calls, we expect to see less of this activity in the future.

The word *punishment* has a rather negative connotation. It is important to understand, however, that many of our everyday activities are controlled by punishing consequences. Losing a golf game because you hooked a shot or failing an exam because you studied the wrong material represents a negative consequence that influences your future golfing or studying behavior. While we readily accept the operation of punishment in these natural circumstances, we tend to feel uncomfortable when discussing the use of punishment in organizations. One reason for this discomfort is the fact that punishment is difficult to administer effectively and fairly. We will discuss some of the reasons for this difficulty shortly.

There is consensus that organizations and individual managers rely rather heavily upon punishment to control behavior.[12] Why is this so? After all, we have discussed techniques for influencing behavior (positive reinforcement and extinction) that do not have the negative connotations of punishment. First, there are some cases in which dangerous behaviors must be terminated immediately. For example, one cannot hope that smoking in an area where combustible chemicals are kept will somehow extinguish through boredom. For safety's sake, immediate attention is necessary to stop this activity. Second, many lower-level managers do not have a wide range of formal organizational rewards (such as money and promotional opportunities) under their control for use as positive reinforcers. Thus, they feel that punishment is the only tool available to control behavior.[13] Finally, busy managers have some tendency to notice problematic behaviors while ignoring instances of correct performance. For example, instead of positively reinforcing prompt attendance, they develop a strategy of punishing lateness and absence. While such an approach might save time in the short run, its long-term consequences may be less than successful.

Exhibit 3–4 compares punishment with reinforcement and extinction.

Using Punishment Effectively

In theory, punishment should be useful for eliminating unwanted behavior. After all, it seems unreasonable to repeat actions that cause us trouble. Unfortunately, punishment has some special characteristics that often limit its effectiveness in stopping unwanted activity. First of all, while punishment provides a clear signal as to which activities are inappropriate, it does not by itself demonstrate which activities should *replace* the punished response. Reconsider the executive who chastises her secretary for making personal calls at the office. If the secretary makes personal calls only when she has caught up on her work, she might legitimately wonder what she is supposed to be doing during her occasional free time. If the boss fails to provide substitute activities, the message contained in the punishment might be lost.

Both positive and negative reinforcers specify which behaviors are appropriate. Punishment indicates only what is not appropriate. This has some important consequences. Since no reinforced substitute behavior is provided, punishment only temporarily suppresses the unwanted response. When surveillance is removed, the response will tend to recur. Constant monitoring is very time-consuming, and individuals become amazingly adept at learning when they can get away with the forbidden activity. The secretary will soon learn when personal calls can be made without detection. The moral here is clear: *Provide an acceptable alternative for the punished response.*

EXHIBIT 3–4   **Summary of learning effects.**

Probability of Behavior	Consequence Following Behavior	Learning Effect	Example
Increasing or Being Maintained	Positive Stimulus Added	POSITIVE REINFORCEMENT	An apprentice machinist learns to operate a lathe correctly as the master machinist praises his performance over time.
	Negative Stimulus Removed	NEGATIVE REINFORCEMENT	A shipping clerk whose boss is a chronic nagger learns that she has filled an order properly when the boss stops nagging.
Decreasing	Negative Stimulus Added	PUNISHMENT	An engineer stops providing suggestions for ways to cut costs because her boss always criticizes the suggestions harshly.
	None (Reinforcer Terminated)	EXTINCTION	A salesperson stops calling on an established customer after making ten visits without a sale.

A second difficulty with punishment is that it has a tendency to provoke a strong emotional reaction on the part of the punished individual.[14] This is especially likely when the punishment is delivered in anger or perceived to be unfair. (See In Focus 3–1.) Managers who try overly hard to be patient with subordinates and then finally blow up risk overemotional reactions. So do those who tolerate unwanted behavior on the part of their subordinates and then impulsively decide to make an example of one individual by punishing him or her. At best, emotional reactions to punishment may interfere with the learning of acceptable alternative behavior. The worker who is "chewed out" for the unsafe operation of his machine might be so angered and humiliated that he fails to hear the valuable safety instructions that the boss proceeds to provide. At worst, emotional reactions might lead to acts of revenge or sabotage. To avoid such reactions, managers should be sure that their own emotions are under control before punishing, and punishment in front of observers should be avoided. Because of the emotional problems involved in the use of punishment, some organizations, such as Tampa Electric Company and Union Carbide, have downplayed its use in discipline systems.

In addition to providing correct alternative responses and limiting the emotions involved in punishment, there are several other principles that can increase the effectiveness of punishment:

- *Make sure the chosen punishment is truly aversive.* Organizations frequently "punish" chronically absent employees by making them take several days off work. Managers sometimes "punish" ineffective performers by requiring them to work overtime, which allows them to earn extra pay. In both cases, the presumed punishment might actually act as a positive reinforcer for the unwanted behavior.
- *Punish immediately and intensely.* Managers frequently overlook early instances of rules violations or ineffective performance, hoping that things will "work out."[15] This only allows these behaviors to gain strength through repetition. In addition, many organizational disciplinary programs start off with mild punishment for some offense (a note in the person's file) and proceed to stronger punishment (perhaps firing) if the offense continues.[16] Ironically, there is evidence that responses acquired in the presence of mild punishment may become especially persistent. Thus, the mild early warnings might have an effect opposite to that which is intended. Sometimes immediate punishment is difficult to apply because of the presence of observers. In this case, the manager should delay action until a more appropriate time and then reinstate the circumstances surrounding the problem behavior. For example, the bank manager who observes inappropriate behaviors by one of her tellers might ask this person to remain after work. She should then carry out punishment at the teller's window rather than in her office, perhaps demonstrating correct procedures and role-playing a customer to allow the subordinate to practice them. Of course, such delay

▼
....

Fines Punish Bad Writing at *Success* Magazine

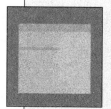

If I worked for Scott DiGarmo, this sentnce alone, would cost me at least $550. That's $25 for garbling "sentence," $25 for the extraneous comma after "alone" and $500 for fumbling the guy's name.

Mr. DeGarmo—that's correct now; I checked it twice—is pulling his purse strings tight on lazy writing. At Success, the magazine he runs, Mr. DeGarmo recently began fining senior editors for approving articles containing typographical and grammatical mistakes. He charges $25 for misused commas and hyphens after "ly" words (as in "hastily-conceived"). Most typos also cost $25, but the price for misspelling the name of the main person in a story is $500—minimum.

"This seems lenient to me, perhaps because on my first newspaper job anyone who made such an error was automatically fired," a memo from Mr. DeGarmo says. Another missive warns that lapses may bring nonmonetary penalties, too: "I will come tearing at you like a raging bull, a shrieking harpy, a Mad Dog from Hell."

The fines are deducted from next year's pay raises for the six affected staffers, Mr. DeGarmo says. He adds that he tried "all the nice, positive things"—gently citing mistakes and lauding perfect copy—but simply tired of editors saying they couldn't spell. "Believe me," Mr. DeGarmo says, "if they're motivated, they'll learn."

Maybe so. Mistakes have dwindled in the six weeks since the penalties started—but not before costing staffers $625 for three misspellings, two "ly" glitches and one maimed name.

"We probably didn't check things as carefully as we should have," says Michael Maren, who confesses to handling the story that cost all but $25 of the fines. Though he plans to check copy more thoroughly from now on, Mr. Maren doesn't consider the penalties unreasonable. "It's probably one of the least outrageous things that happens around here," he adds.

Some don't need to know any more. "I wouldn't work for Success on any basis," says Stephen D. Isaacs, academic dean at Columbia University's journalism school. "Here's a person penalizing people for human frailties. It's crazy."

Mr. DeGarmo softened briefly last week, letting two errors go by without penalty; but then he changed his mind. "Now that I'm talking to you, I realize I'm so right that I really shouldn't be doing anything that suggests I'm not 100% behind this whole approach."

Vancouver Sun/©
Punch/Rothco

"I realize these days it is only money, Miss Debbett, but in the interest of tidiness, could we try not to spill?"

tactics must be balanced with the seriousness of the infraction. (See the accompanying cartoon for an example of a punishment dilemma!)

- *Do not reward unwanted behaviors before or after punishment.* Many supervisors join in horseplay with their subordinates until they feel it's time to get some work done. Then, unexpectedly, they do an about-face and punish those who are "goofing around." Sometimes, managers feel guilty about punishing their subordinates for some rule infraction and then quickly attempt to make up with displays of good-natured sympathy or affection. For example, the boss who criticizes her secretary for personal calls might show up an hour later with a gift of flowers. Such actions present subordinates with extremely confusing signals about how they should behave, since the manager could be inadvertently reinforcing the very response that he or she wants to terminate.

- *Do not inadvertently punish desirable behavior.* This happens commonly in organizations. Managers who do not use all of their capital budget for a given fiscal year might have their budget for the next year reduced, punishing their prudence. Government employees who "blow the whistle" on wasteful or inefficient practices might find themselves demoted.[17] University professors who are considered excellent teachers might be assigned to onerous, time-consuming duty on a curriculum committee, cutting into their class preparation time.

In summary, punishment can be an effective means of stopping undesirable behavior. However, it must be applied very carefully and deliberately in order for this effectiveness to be achieved. In general, reinforcing correct behaviors and extinguishing unwanted responses may be safer strategies for the practicing manager than the frequent use of punishment.

SELF-MANAGEMENT

Much of this chapter has been concerned with how organizations and individual managers can use learning principles to manage the behavior of organizational members. However, employees can use learning principles to manage their *own* behavior, making the use of external control less necessary. This process is called **self-management**.[18] In many respects, it is economical for the organization while building trust and self-confidence among employees.

How can self-management occur? You will recall that our discussion of social learning and modeling involved factors such as observation, imagination, imitation, and self-reinforcement. Advocates of self-management argue that these and similar techniques can be used in an intentional way to control one's own behavior. The basic process involves observing one's own behavior, comparing the behavior with a standard, and rewarding oneself if the behavior meets the standard.[19]

To illustrate some specific self-management techniques, consider the executive who finds that he is taking too much work home to do in the evenings and over weekends. While his peers seem to have most evenings and weekends free, his own family is ready to disown him due to lack of attention! What can he do?[20]

- *Collect self-observation data.* This involves collecting objective data about one's own behavior. For example, the executive might keep a log of phone calls and other interruptions for a few days if he suspects that these contribute to his inefficiency.
- *Observe models.* The executive might examine the time-management skills of his peers to find someone successful to imitate.
- *Goal setting.* The executive might set specific short-term goals to reduce telephone interruptions and unscheduled personal visits, enlisting the aid of his secretary and using self-observation data to monitor his progress. Longer-term goals might involve four free nights a week and no more than four hours of work on weekends. (We will examine goal setting in some detail in Chapter 7.)
- *Rehearsal.* The executive might anticipate that his co-workers will have to be educated about his reduced availability. So as not to offend them, he might practice explaining the reason for his revised accessibility.

- *Self-reinforcement.* The executive might promise himself a weekend at the beach with his family the first time he gets his take-home workload down to his target level.

As you can see, self-management involves a package of interrelated processes. Managers can encourage their subordinates to practice self-management by doing it themselves and by reinforcing attempts at self-management. Also, unnecessary rules, regulations, and procedures do not provide a conducive climate for self-management. In Focus 3–2 illustrates a successful self-management program.

IN FOCUS 3–2

▼
....
Self-Management Improves Attendance

Colette Frayne and Gary Latham developed a self-management program to improve work attendance among unionized maintenance employees in a state government. Employees who had used over half of their sick leave were invited by the personnel department to participate in an eight-week program with the following features:

- Discussion of general reasons for use of sick leave. High on the list were transportation problems, family difficulties, and problems with supervisors and co-workers.
- Self-assessment of personal reasons for absence and development of personal coping strategies.
- Goal setting to engage in behaviors that should improve attendance (short-term goals) and to improve attendance by a specific amount (long-term goal).
- Self-monitoring using charts and diaries. Employees recorded their own attendance, reasons for missing work, and steps taken to get to work.
- Identification of specific reinforcers and punishers to be self-administered for reaching or not reaching goals.
- Discussion of the possibility of a relapse and how to deal with it.

Compared to a control group, the employees who were exposed to the program posted a significant improvement in attendance, and they also felt more confident that they would be able to come to work when confronted with various obstacles to attendance. These effects persisted over a nine-month follow-up.

Source: Frayne, C., & Latham, G. (1987). Application of social learning theory to employee self-management of attendance. *Journal of Applied Psychology, 72,* 387–392, Washington, DC: APA; Latham, G., & Frayne, C. (1989). Self-management training for increasing job attendance: A follow-up and a replication. *Journal of Applied Psychology, 74,* 411–416, Washington, DC: APA.

THE MANAGER'S NOTEBOOK

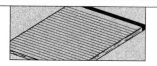

SAS Airline
Reservation Personnel

1. The system that SAS had in place for its reservation agents was essentially one of negative reinforcement. Taking calls was what was reinforced. The reinforcer was the chance of a reprimand if one didn't take enough calls. Notice the side effects of this system. It encouraged agents to take a *large volume* of *short-duration* calls. This is not the best strategy for a service industry. The shorter the call, the less likely that some active selling can occur.

2. SAS called in consultant Edward J. Feeney, noted in the chapter for his work with Emery Air Freight. His firm designed an organizational behavior modification program to stimulate selling. It began with paper forms that agents could use to record their sales activities, including offering to book and actually booking flight segments, hotels, and so on. This performance data was summarized weekly and averaged to represent the performance of small sales teams. Thus, each agent could compare his or her weekly performance with that of the team without public embarrassment. This feedback mechanism positively reinforced good sales performance and also stimulated some competition among the teams. Detailed training was provided on how to talk to customers. Periodically, supervisors sat in with agents as they took calls, and they positively reinforced proper phone behavior with compliments. They also modeled correct behavior when improvements were necessary. Criticism of improper technique was avoided. The program boosted offers to book from 34 to 84 percent and increased the actual number of flight segments booked, thus substantially increasing revenues.

SUMMARY

- Learning occurs when practice or experience leads to a relatively permanent change in behavior potential. Operant learning occurs as a function of the consequences of behavior. Social learning occurs by observing the behavior of others.
- If some behavior is occurring regularly or increasing in probability, you can assume that it is being reinforced. The consequence that is maintaining the behavior is the reinforcer. If the reinforcer is added to the situation following the behavior, it is a positive reinforcer. These are usually pleasant consequences. If the reinforcer is removed from the situation following the behavior, it is a negative reinforcer. These are typically unpleasant stimuli.
- Organizations and managers often confuse rewards with reinforcers, neglect individual preferences for reinforcers, and neglect important sources of reinforcement.
- Behavior is learned quickly when it is reinforced immediately and continuously. Behavior tends to be persistent under reduced or terminated reinforcement when it is learned under conditions of delayed and/or partial reinforcement. Partial reinforcement can be administered under interval or ratio schedules. The former are time dependent, and the latter are response dependent. Ratio schedules usually lead to higher response rates, because the individual can increase the frequency of reinforcement by responding faster.
- Organizational behavior modification is the systematic use of learning principles to influence organizational behavior. It has been used successfully to improve punctuality and attendance and to reinforce safe work practices.

- Modeling, an example of social learning, is the process of imitating others. Models are most likely to be imitated when they are high in status, attractive, competent, credible, successful, and vivid.
- If some behavior decreases in probability, you can assume that it is being either extinguished or punished. If the behavior is followed by no observable consequence, it is being extinguished. That is, some reinforcer that was maintaining the behavior has been terminated. If the behavior is followed by the application of some unpleasant consequence, it is being punished.
- Self-management occurs when workers use learning principles to manage their own behavior, thus reducing the need for external control. Aspects of self-management include collecting self-observation data, observing models, goal setting, rehearsal, and self-reinforcement.

KEY CONCEPTS

Learning
Operant learning
Social learning
Reinforcement
Positive reinforcement
Negative reinforcement
Continuous versus partial reinforcement

Immediate versus delayed reinforcement
Fixed interval schedule
Variable interval schedule
Fixed ratio schedule
Variable ratio schedule

Organizational behavior modification
Modeling
Extinction
Punishment
Self-management

DISCUSSION QUESTIONS

1. Consider some examples of behavior that you repeat fairly regularly (such as studying or going to work every morning). What are the positive and negative reinforcers that maintain this behavior?

2. It was pointed out that managers frequently resort to punishing ineffective behavior. What are some of the practical demands of the typical manager's job that lead to this state of affairs?

3. Discuss a situation that you have observed in which the use of punishment was ineffective in terminating some unwanted behavior. Why was punishment ineffective in this case?

4. Describe a situation in which you think organizational behavior modification could be used to improve or correct employee behavior. Can you anticipate any dangers in using this approach?

5. A supervisor in a textile factory observes that one of her subordinates is violating a safety rule that could result in severe injury. What combination of reinforcement, punishment, extinction, and modeling could she use to correct this behavior?

6. Contrast the reinforcement strategies that a supervisor might use to manage the work behavior of an experienced versus an inexperienced subordinate. Be sure to consider the issue of self-management.

■

EXPERIENTIAL EXERCISE

The Expense Account

General Instructions

This is a role-playing exercise. DO NOT READ THE ROLES GIVEN BELOW UNTIL ASSIGNED TO DO SO BY YOUR INSTRUCTOR! In this exercise, you might play a sales manager or a sales representative. In role-playing, assume the attitudes and facts supplied by the role. When things arise that are not covered in the role, act the way you feel and the way things might actually happen at work. It is best to read the role carefully and then not consult it during role-playing.

_____ 1. Break into groups of four to six students.
_____ 2. Have one student in each group assume the role of Marla and one assume the role of Rick. The other students, serving as observers, can read both roles if they wish.
_____ 3. Role-play for ten minutes. Marla will begin the discussion.
_____ 4. Following the role-playing, see the Further Instructions below.

Role for Marla Scott, Sales Manager

You are the sales manager for a large company that manufactures industrial products. You have twenty-two sales representatives reporting to you. Over the past few months, a problem has developed that you now feel that you have to deal with. One of your sales reps, Rick Ackroyd, has consistently exceeded his allotted monthly expenses by a fairly large amount. The accounting department reimburses the sales reps directly for these expenses, which include transportation, hotel costs, and restaurant bills, some of which may be incurred in entertaining current and prospective customers. You get a monthly report from accounting that lists the expenses paid to each rep. Unless a particular expense is completely outrageous, accounting pays it and expects you to monitor the expenses against what is allowed. Because this allowance varies according to the nature of the sales territory covered, accounting has resisted installing a system to "cut off" reps who go over the allowance in a given month.

You know that most of Rick's excessive expenses are devoted to meals in fine eating establishments. Rick is something of a bon vivant and has gourmet tastes. In fact, during breaks at sales meetings you've heard Rick describing some of his gourmet experiences to the younger sales reps, and their expenses have been climbing recently as well.

You have called a meeting with Rick to discuss his expenses. It will be difficult, since Rick is your best sales rep, grossing about 20 percent more sales than your next best salesperson. This is why you've put off the meeting until now.

Role for Rick Ackroyd, Sales Rep

You are an experienced sales representative for a large company that manufactures industrial products. You really like your job, and you get along well with your sales manager, Marla Scott. You enjoy the independence that sales offers, being out "on the road" drumming up new customers and touching base with established ones. After a hard day of work, you enjoy nothing better than a good meal, and over the years you have become acquainted with the finest restaurants in your territory. If you are alone, you often grab breakfast or lunch "on the run," even forgetting a receipt, but at night, you like a proper dinner. Also, you know that customers or potential customers appreciate a good meal, and you can't count the number of deals that have been cemented over a gourmet lunch or dinner.

Marla Scott has asked you to meet with her to discuss your expense account. You don't generally pay much attention to expenses. You just submit your receipts to accounting, and they pay them. You feel that you're pretty close to your expense allowance. Besides, you are the highest-grossing sales rep in the company by a considerable margin. What's a few good meals against all the sales you generate?

Further Instructions

The role-play presents both parties with the difficult but common dilemma of a good performer who has developed some behavior that management considers undesirable. Following the role-play, each group should do the following:

_____ 1. *General discussion.* What themes ran through the interaction? How did Marla and Rick feel? (5 minutes)
_____ 2. *Focused discussion.* How does the material covered in the chapter relate to this situation? Be sure to consider reinforcement, feedback, modeling, and punishment. (10 minutes)
_____ 3. *Self-management.* The group should develop a self-management program for Rick to improve his expense performance. Be specific. (10 minutes)
_____ 4. *Class reconvenes.* The instructor will review the ideas from the focused discussion and ask each group to report its self-management program. A Marla and a Rick can role-play the discussion of one program if desired. (10 minutes)

CASE STUDY

Mr. P., The Philippine Manager

Mr. P., a promising young manager in a multinational corporation, was placed in charge of one section of a large Philippine manufacturing plant. His section was one of four identical sections producing the same product; each section had the same physical set-up, used the same work method, and had the same number of workers. All four section managers were informed of the total daily output of each section.

When Mr. P. was first given the position of section manager, he learned that his section output was lower than the output of the other three sections: 360 units per day versus approximately 400 units output in the other three sections. The executive over him encouraged him to "think of something to raise productivity."

Mr. P. (an eager fellow who brims with enthusiasm and good will), had had a management training course when he had been originally hired in the multinational corporation. He had learned about positive reinforcement as a well-substantiated method of motivation to increase production. He considered the kinds of positive reinforcement he could give to the workers. Because of organizational policies, he could not offer raises, promotions, or fringe benefits. The number of workers in his section was too large for him to offer "individual praise." He hit on the idea of offering the workers the privilege of stopping work one minute early each day for each seven units of increased group production (over the base figure of 360 units). He figured that if they could look forward to stopping early, he could get them to increase daily output.

First thing the next morning, he assembled his workers and enthusiastically presented his idea. He

Source: Elbing, C. J. (1984, November-December). "'Yes, but . . .': Hidden criteria for judging managerial innovations." *Business Horizons,* 10–14. Copyright © 1984 by the Foundation for the School of Business at Indiana University. Used with permission.

explained, however, that if they produced more and therefore stopped early, they could not leave the plant because they were getting paid by the hour. However, they could talk and have a soft drink and relax.

To his delight, worker production quickly went up to the point where workers got thirty-three minutes free at the end of the day. This meant that output was up from 360 to 590 units! During that half hour at the end of the day, workers sat around talking and smoking. They were enthusiastic about the new arrangement. They indicated that the boring work was not quite so boring with a goal to look forward to. Besides, they liked getting acquainted.

Over a period of about two months, they gradually improved their speed even more. Finally, they reached a level of efficiency where they earned the right to a full hour off at the end of each day. The hour off had a party atmosphere. Their morale was high. They were pleased with the new rules of the game, they were pleased with the social time, and they were proud of their performance.

Mr. P. was just as pleased and proud. His section was now producing 800 units per day, *twice* the production output of each of the other units. The managing director of the plant phoned and congratulated him. He announced that he had recommended Mr. P. to be sent to a fast-track corporate management program at the Executive and Environment Center in Switzerland.

But before Mr. P. could leave for Switzerland, disaster struck. The managing director decided to take a plant tour. He arrived at the young manager's "super section" one hour before closing time. The workers, having produced their 800 units, had already quit working. They were lounging about, smoking, drinking sodas, and talking and laughing.

Mr. P. was immediately called to the managing director's office, where he was confronted with angry indignation. The managing director threatened to fire the young manager on the spot. Why was he allowing the workers to loaf?

Mr. P. explained his ingenious incentive system. The managing director's angry retort was that if the workers could produce 800 units in seven hours, they could produce 900 units if they worked one more hour!

The young manager explained in vain. The managing director stated, in no uncertain terms, that if Mr. P.'s unit was caught loafing again, he would be fired. The managing director proclaimed that the workers were being paid to work, and work the whole time, and that workers should obey authority. It would be shocking if "anyone" found out that employees at this plant could get away with loafing.

Sadly, Mr. P informed his workers the next morning that the incentive system was over. The workers went back to working to the very end of the day, and production gradually slipped back to that of the other units.

The managing director of the plant scolded the

workers for their fall in production and suggested Mr. P do the same. But production did not rise, and interestingly enough, Mr. P. was never reprimanded for that.

1. What was the precise problem that Mr. P. faced when he assumed his job as section manager?

2. In learning theory terms, describe precisely the system that Mr. P. implemented. What reinforcers were used, and how were they scheduled?

3. Evaluate the effectiveness of Mr. P.'s system. What were its good points and bad points?

4. Can you think of any alternative solutions to Mr. P.'s problem that would satisfy the managing director?

REFERENCES

1. For a presentation of operant learning theory, see Honig, W. K., & Staddon, J. E. R. (Eds.), (1977). *Handbook of operant behavior*. Englewood Cliffs, NJ: Prentice-Hall. For a presentation of social learning theory, see Bandura, A. (1986). *Social foundations of thought and action*. Englewood Cliffs NJ: Prentice-Hall.

2. (1972). Performance audit, feedback, and positive reinforcement. *Training and Development Journal*, 26, 8–13; (1973, Winter). At Emery Air Freight: Positive reinforcement boosts performance. *Organizational Dynamics*, 41–50.

3. Dumaine, B. (1985, January 21). Fleming's fast rise in wholesale foods. *Fortune*, 54.

4. Lawler, E. E., III (1971). *Pay and organizational effectiveness: A psychological view*. New York: McGraw-Hill; Locke, E. A., Feren, D. B., McCaleb, V. M., Shaw, K. N., & Denny, A. T. (1980). The relative effectiveness of four methods of motivating performance. In K. D. Duncan, M. M. Gruneberg, & D. Wallis (Eds.). *Changes in working life*. London: Wiley & Sons.

5. O'Hara, K., Johnson, C. M., & Beehr, T. A. (1985). Organizational behavior management in the private sector: A review of empirical research and recommendations for further investigation. *Academy of Management Review*, 10, 848–864.

6. Hermann, J. A., De Montes, A. I., Dominguez, B., Montes, F., & Hopkins, B. L. (1973). Effects of

bonuses for punctuality on the tardiness of industrial workers. *Journal of Applied Behavior Analysis*, 6, 563–570.

7. Pedalino, E., & Gamboa, V. U. (1974). Behavior modification and absenteeism: Intervention in one industrial setting. *Journal of Applied Psychology*, 59, 694–698.

8. Komaki, J., Barwick, K. D., & Scott, L. R. (1978). A behavioral approach to occupational safety: Pinpointing and reinforcing safe performance in a food manufacturing plant. *Journal of Applied Psychology*, 63, 434–445. For a similar study, see Haynes, R. S., Pine, R. C., & Fitch, H. G. (1982). Reducing accident rates with organizational behavior modification. *Academy of Management Journal*, 25, 407–416.

9. Luthans, F., & Kreitner, R. (1985). *Organizational behavior modification and beyond: An operant and social learning approach*. Glenview, IL: Scott, Foresman; Manz, C. C., & Sims, H. P., Jr. (1981). Vicarious learning: The influence of modeling on organizational behavior. *Academy of Management Review*, 6, 105–113.

10. Bandura, 1986; Goldstein, A. P., & Sorcher, M. (1974). *Changing supervisor behavior*. New York: Pergamon.

11. Luthans, F., & Kreitner, R. (1975). *Organizational behavior modification*. Glenview, IL: Scott, Foresman.

12. Luthans, F., & Kreitner, R. (1972). The role of punishment in organizational behavior modification (o.b.mod.). *Public Personnel Management, 2,* 156–161.

13. Ashour, A. S., & Johns, G. (1983). Leader influence through operant principles: A theoretical and methodological framework. *Human Relations, 36,* 603–626.

14. However, more research is necessary to establish the extent of this in organizations. See Arvey, R. D., & Ivancevich, J. M. (1980). Punishment in organizations: A review, propositions, and research suggestions. *Academy of Management Review, 5,* 123–132.

15. Organ, D. W., & Hamner, W. C. (1982). *Organizational behavior: An applied psychological approach* (Revised ed.). Plano, TX: Business Publications.

16. Organ & Hamner, 1982.

17. See Parmerlee, M. A., Near, J. P., & Jensen, T. C. (1982). Correlates of whistle-blowers' perceptions of organizational retaliation. *Administrative Science Quarterly, 27,* 17–34.

18. Manz, C. C., & Sims, H. P., Jr. (1980). Self-management as a substitute for leadership: A social learning theory perspective. *Academy of Management Review, 5,* 361–367; Hackman, J. R. (1986). The psychology of self-management in organizations. In M. S. Pollack & R. Perloff (Eds.), *Psychology and work.* Washington, D.C.: American Psychological Association.

19. Kanfer, F. H. (1980). Self-management methods. In F. H. Kanfer & A. P. Goldstein (Eds.), *Helping people change: A textbook of methods* (2nd ed.). New York: Pergamon.

20. Luthans & Kreitner, 1985; Manz & Sims, 1980.

CHAPTER	**PERCEPTION,**
4	**ATTRIBUTION,**
	AND THE
	JUDGMENT
	OF OTHERS

ZACK THOMAS

It was 9:10 when Zack Thomas rolled his Corvette into the staff parking lot at First Seaway National Bank. Zack, branch accountant at First Seaway, had a 9:00 appointment with his boss, branch manager Henry Pellan. The purpose of the appointment was to discuss Pellan's review of Zack's past year's performance at the bank. Zack had begun his job there exactly one year before, and according to bank policy, this was his first yearly performance review.

Fighting his way over the congested Narrows Bridge, Zack had had mixed feelings about the upcoming performance review session. On the one hand, Zack knew that he had experienced a good year. Several changes in procedure that he had suggested had saved dozens of hours a week in clerical time. In addition, some dedicated detective work on his part had uncovered a case of embezzlement at the head office and led to the apprehension of a particularly troublesome bad check writer. Although such activities required a lot of uncompensated overtime, Zack felt good about his performance. On the other hand, he was not exactly looking forward to sitting down with Henry Pellan. Zack wasn't sure why, but he and the branch manager had never hit it off very well, right from the start. However, Zack felt that he got along great with the assistant manager and the tellers.

After exchanging formalities and describing the bank's performance appraisal philosophy, Henry Pellan handed Zack the rating form he had completed. Zack did a double take, as if he didn't believe his eyes.

"Mr. Pellan, I don't understand this. You've rated me below average on quality of work, quantity of work, promptness, and initiative. This doesn't make sense!"

"Zack, I just don't think you've exhibited a strong sense of commitment to the bank and dedication to your job. I'm not sure you fit in well here."

"Look, sir, what possible evidence do you have for that statement?" Zack said desperately.

"Zack, you were fifteen minutes late for work a year ago today—your first day on the job! And you've been late often ever since. That's no example to set for the others."

Zack remembered that first day with a mixture of exasperation and embarrassment. There had been an accident on the Narrows Bridge, and the traffic had been unbelievable.

"Look, Mr. Pellan, other people around here are late too, and I live in Roxboro. You know the traffic across the bridge is absolutely unpredictable."

"Our other employees are very seldom late, Zack. In fact, if I remember correctly, you were late for the bank's awards dinner and for our golf tournament too. And you know how furious I was when Gravitz was down here from the head office and you didn't get in until 10:30!"

Zack knew, all right. The Corvette had broken down on the way to work. Zack had shown Pellan the towing bill, but Pellan was so angry that it hadn't seemed to register.

"My car broke down," Zack said quietly.

"Speaking of that car, Zack, are you sure a Corvette is appropriate transportation for a branch accountant? I'm certain the female tellers like it, but what image does it convey?"

Zack was flabbergasted. "Mr. Pellan, that Corvette is an eight-year-old, secondhand car. I'm happily married, and I have a kid. What about the clerical procedures I instituted? What about the bad check artist I helped nail?"

Zack left Pellan's office depressed and irritated. How could two people see things so differently? Zack resolved to cool off and enlist the help of the assistant manager in dealing with his problem.

How *could* two people see things so differently? Why did Pellan place so much emphasis on Zack's tardiness to the exclusion of his achievements? How did he form his overall impression of Zack? Was Zack just inventing excuses for his behavior? These are the kinds of questions that we will attempt to answer in this chapter. First, we will define perception and examine how various aspects of the perceiver, the object or person being perceived, and the situation influence perception. Following this, a model of the perceptual process will be presented, and we will consider some of the perceptual tendencies that we employ in forming impressions of people and attributing causes to their behavior. Finally, we will examine the perceptual problems of employment interview and performance evaluation situations. In general, you will learn that perception and attribution influence who gets into organizations, how they are treated as members, and how they interpret this treatment.

WHAT IS PERCEPTION?

Perception is the process of interpreting the messages of our senses to provide order and meaning to the environment. The world is a complex place, and perception helps us sort out and organize the input received by our senses of sight, smell, touch, taste, and hearing. The key word in this definition is *interpreting*. Mr. Pellan interpreted Zack's lateness as a lack of dedication. People frequently base their actions on the interpretation of reality provided by their perceptual system, rather than the reality itself. If you perceive your pay to be very low, you might seek employment in another firm. The reality—that you are the best-paid person in your department—will not matter if you are unaware of the fact. However, to go a step further, you might be aware that you are the best-paid person and *still* perceive your pay as low in comparison to that of the company president or your ostentatious next-door neighbor. Again, this perception might prompt you to look for work elsewhere.

Some of the most important perceptions that influence organizational behavior are the perceptions that organizational members have of each other. Such perceptions have strong potential to influence the interactions between members, as the case that began the chapter indicates. Because person perception is such an important aspect of organizational behavior, we will concentrate on person perception in this chapter.

COMPONENTS OF PERCEPTUAL EVENTS

Any perceptual event has three components—a perceiver, a target that is being perceived, and some situational context in which the perception is occurring. Each of these components influences the perceiver's impression or interpretation of the target.

The Perceiver

The perceiver's experience, motives, and emotions can affect his or her perceptions. Let's explore each of these more closely.

Experience   One of the most important characteristics of the perceiver that influences his or her impressions of a target is experience. Past experiences lead us to develop expectations, and these expectations affect current perceptions. In Mr. Pellan's experience, responsible bankers did not drive Corvettes, and people who did were perceived with vague distrust.

An interesting example of the influence of experience upon perceptions is revealed by the responses of executives in a development seminar who were required to read a case study regarding the operation of a steel company.[1] They were asked to specify the company's most pressing problem. Not only did their perceptions of the key problem differ, but they tended to differ according to the executives' specialties. That is, sales executives tended to see marketing problems, the industrial relations specialist identified human relations problems, and so on. As you might imagine, such differences in perceptions due to experience can sometimes lead to communication problems and conflict within organizations.

Motivational State   In addition to experience, a major characteristic of the perceiver that influences his or her perceptions is motivational state. Motivational state refers to the particular needs that an individual has at any given point in time. These might be needs for things such as water, food, affection, or money. Frequently, our motivational state has an unconscious influence on our perceptions by causing us to perceive what we wish to perceive. Research has demonstrated that perceivers who have been deprived of food will tend to "see" more edible things in ambiguous pictures than will well-fed observers. Similarly, lonely university students might misperceive the most innocent actions of members of the opposite sex as indicating interest in them.

Consider the case of a sales representative who was puzzled by the actions of his colleagues. These sales reps worked on an incentive system, in which the individual who achieved the best sales every month was awarded a prize. What surprised the representative was the attention that the current prize was receiving—a trip to Mexico with the company president. The trip was the talk of the office. In contrast, the previous month's prize, a very expensive diamond ring, had provoked little interest. The sales rep knew that, in fact, the ring was worth about three times as much as the trip. However, it was as if the sales representatives *perceived* the trip as being more valuable. It is probable that this phenomenon was caused by the motivational state of the workers. In short, they were very well paid, and it would appear that the dollar value of the trip was less important to them than its symbolic value. The chance to "hobnob" with the company president in Mexico matched their evident need for prestige and recognition, which appeared to be stronger than their current need for a diamond ring.

Emotional State   Emotional state refers to the particular emotions that an individual is experiencing at any given point in time. Emotions such as anger, happiness, or fear can influence our perceptions. We have all had the experience of misperceiving the innocent comment of a friend or acquaintance when we were angry. For example, a worker who is upset about not getting a promotion might perceive the consolation provided by a co-worker as gloating condescension. On the other hand, consider the worker who does get a promotion. He is so happy that he fails to notice how upset his co-worker is because she wasn't the one promoted. Mr. Pellan was so upset with one of Zack's lateness episodes that he failed to register Zack's excuse.

In some cases, our perceptual system serves to defend us against unpleasant emotions. This phenomenon is known as **perceptual defense.** We have all experienced cases in which we "see what we want to see" or "hear what we want to hear." In many of these instances, our perceptual system is working to ensure that we don't see or hear things that are threatening. For example, some executives fail to perceive signals that their organization is in financial trouble because they cannot handle the emotions aroused by this knowledge. Such defensiveness can have serious consequences. One writer has made a detailed study of the planning of the disastrous Cuban Bay of Pigs invasion by President John Kennedy and his advisors. Evidence suggests that there were plenty of signals to indicate that such an invasion would fail. However, Kennedy and his planners evidently misperceived these signals because they couldn't face up to the unpleasant message that they contained.[2]

The Target

In addition to the experience, motivational state, and emotional state of the perceiver, perceptions are affected by characteristics of the target. Two of the most important characteristics are the degree of ambiguity of the target and the target's social status.

Ambiguity Theoretically, an ambiguous target should not present problems for a perceiver. Its characteristics or motives should simply be perceived as unclear, and that should be that. However, if you have been reading carefully, you realize how naive this viewpoint is. Perception involves interpretation and the addition of meaning to the target, and ambiguous targets are especially susceptible to interpretation and addition. Perceivers seem to have some need to resolve such ambiguities. Psychotherapists sometimes ask their clients to report what they see in ink blots. The assumption behind this is that the client's interpretation of the ambiguous blots will reveal something about the inner workings of the personality.

A word of warning should be offered about ambiguous targets. You might be tempted to believe that providing more information about the target will necessarily improve perceptual accuracy. Unfortunately, this is not always the case. Writing clearer memos might not always get the message across. Similarly, assigning minority workers to a prejudiced manager will not always improve his or her perceptions of their true abilities. As we shall see shortly, the perceiver does not or cannot always use all of the information provided by the target. In these cases a reduction in ambiguity might not be accompanied by greater accuracy. Just ask the executive who has a hundred pages of detailed computer printout on plant operations to guide his or her next decision!

Social Status In the case of person perception, another factor that influences our perceptions of the target is the target's social status. Social status refers to the person's position in society and is generally determined by factors such as income, occupation, location of residence, and so on. At a simple level, status can influence our perceptions of physical characteristics. An individual was introduced to several groups of Australian students as a visitor to their university. Although he was always portrayed as coming from Cambridge University, his social status was varied by changing his academic standing (professor, senior lecturer, laboratory assistant, student). The students were then asked to estimate the height of their visitor. Perceptions of height were neatly correlated with academic standing, and the "professor" was seen as being two-and-a-half inches taller than the "student"![3]

The status of the target also affects our perceptions of what the target says. If a co-worker warned you about your attendance or work habits, you would probably perceive it differently than a warning from your boss. Organizations frequently use their high-status members to make important pronouncements to enhance perceptions of the validity of these statements. Several years ago, when poisoned bottles of the headache remedy Tylenol turned up on drugstore shelves, Johnson & Johnson's chief executive officer personally represented the company's position on *Donahue* and *60 Minutes*. Although a subordinate could have made a technically accurate presentation, it was assumed that the presentation would be more believable when it came from a high-status organizational member.

The Situation

Thus far we have discussed certain characteristics of the perceiver and certain characteristics of the target that affect the former's perception of the latter. In addition, every instance of perception occurs in some situational context, and this context can affect what is perceived. The most important effect that the situation can have is to add information about the target. Imagine a casual critical comment about your performance from your boss the week before she is to decide whether or not you will be promoted. You will likely perceive this comment very differently than you would if you were not up for promotion. Also, a worker might perceive a racial joke overheard on the job very differently before and after racial strife has occurred in the plant. In both of these examples, the perceiver and the target are the same, but the perception of the target changes with the situation. Again, perception involves interpreting or adding meaning to a target, and the situation can serve to influence this interpretation and addition.

Exhibit 4–1 summarizes the factors that influence perception.

EXHIBIT
4–1

Factors that influence perception.

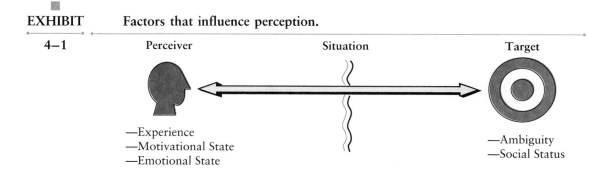

Perceiver

Situation

Target

—Experience
—Motivational State
—Emotional State

—Ambiguity
—Social Status

A MODEL OF THE PERCEPTUAL PROCESS

In the previous section we discussed the way the perceiver, the target, and the situation influence perception. In this section we will consider exactly how the perceiver goes about putting together the information contained in the target and the situation to form a picture of the target. In other words, how does the perceiver form his or her perceptions?

Psychologist Jerome Bruner has developed a model of the perceptual process that can provide a useful framework for our discussion.[4] A key concept in this model is cue. Cues are nothing more than the bits and pieces of information contained in the target and the situation that we use (or ignore) in forming our perceptions of the target. In the story at the beginning of the chapter, Zack's tardiness, his car, and his style with tellers were cues that Mr. Pellan used in developing perceptions of him. The bigoted manager who underrates the performance of her minority subordinates might ignore the cues contained in their work behavior and concentrate on the cues provided by their skin color.

According to Bruner, when we encounter an unfamiliar target, we are very open to the cues contained in the target and the situation surrounding it. In this unfamiliar state, we are "hard up" for information upon which to base our perceptions of the target, and we will actively seek out cues to resolve this ambiguity. Gradually, we will encounter some familiar cues (note the role of the perceiver's experience here) that enable us to crudely categorize the target in some manner. At this point, our cue search becomes less open and more selective. We begin to search out cues that confirm our categorization of the target. As this categorization becomes stronger, we tend to actively ignore or even distort cues that violate our initial perceptions. (See the left side of Exhibit 4–2.) This does not mean that

EXHIBIT 4–2   **Bruner's model of the perceptual process and an example.**

Model	Example
Unfamiliar target encountered	New co-worker
⇓	⇓
Openness to target cues	Observation; search for information
⇓	⇓
Familiar cues encountered	Co-worker is Stanford graduate with good grades
⇓	⇓
Target categorized	Co-worker is "good man" with "great potential"
⇓	⇓
Cue selectivity	Co-worker's poor performance ignored or distorted
⇓	⇓
Categorization strengthened	Co-worker is still "good man" with "great potential"

Bruner, J. S. (1957) On Perceptual Readiness. *Psychological Review, 64*, 123–152.

our early categorization can't be changed. It does mean, however, that it will take a good many contradictory cues before we recategorize the target, and that these cues will have to overcome the expectations that we have developed.

Let's clarify your understanding of Bruner's perceptual model with an example, shown on the right side of Exhibit 4–2. Imagine that a woman who works as an engineer for a large aircraft company is trying to size up a newly hired co-worker. Since he is an unfamiliar target, she will probably be especially open to any cues that might provide information about him. In the course of her cue search, she discovers that he has a Master's degree in aeronautical engineering from Stanford University and that he graduated with top grades. These are familiar cues because she knows that Stanford is a top school in the field, and she has worked with many excellent Stanford graduates. She then proceeds to categorize her new co-worker as a "good man" with "great potential." With these perceptions, she takes a special interest in observing his performance, which is good for several months. This increases the strength of her initial categorization. Gradually, however, the engineer's performance deteriorates for some reason, and his work becomes less and less satisfactory. This is clear to everyone except the other engineer, who continues to see him as adequate and excuses his most obvious errors as stemming from external factors beyond his control.

Several aspects of this example and Bruner's general model deserve elaboration. You will notice that selectivity is often exhibited in perception. Not all of the available cues are used, and those that are used are thus given special emphasis. The established engineer was especially interested in the new recruit's academic credentials and his job performance. A different observer might be interested in different cues but would doubtless be just as selective in forming an impression of the target. This selectivity means that our perception is efficient, and this efficiency can both aid and hinder our perceptual accuracy. The interviewer screening applicants for a sales job will sensibly pay more attention to a candidate's social skills than whether the person is wearing designer clothes. Of course, the efficiency provided by selectivity can also hurt perceptual accuracy. The engineer in the above example, in concentrating upon her new co-worker's academic background, probably ignored other cues that might have predicted the subsequent performance problem. Similarly, an interviewer who concentrates upon an applicant's sex or race at the expense of the person's past achievements will likely provide inaccurate recommendations.

Bruner's model and the accompanying example also illustrate that our perceptual system works to paint a constant and consistent picture of the target. Perceptual *constancy* refers to the tendency for the target to be perceived in the same way over time or across situations. We have all had the experience of "getting off on the wrong foot" with a teacher or a boss and finding it difficult to change their constant perception of us. The engineer's image of the new co-worker's performance remained constant despite objective reality. Perceptual *consistency* refers to the tendency to select, ignore, and distort cues in such a manner that they fit together to form a homogeneous image of the target. We strive for consistency in our perception of people. We do not tend to see the same person as both good and bad or dependable and untrustworthy. For the engineer, consistency demanded that a Stanford graduate be a good performer. Often, cues that are discrepant with our general image of a person are distorted to make them consistent with this image. An individual who has a generally good impression of an executive might perceive some of her actions as indicative of confidence. Another observer with an unfavorable image might see the same actions as evidence of conceit.

In summary, Bruner's model suggests that our perceptual system works selectively and efficiently, if not always accurately, to present us with a constant and consistent image of the target. In the next section we will consider some specific perceptual biases that contribute to selectivity, constancy, and consistency in our perception of people.

BASIC BIASES IN PERSON PERCEPTION

For accuracy's sake, it would be convenient if we could encounter others under laboratory conditions, in a vacuum or a test tube, as it were. Because the real world lacks such ideal conditions, the impressions that we form of others are susceptible to a number of perceptual biases.

Primacy and Recency Effects

Given the examples of person perception that have been discussed thus far, you might gather that we form our impressions of others fairly quickly. One reason for this fast impression formation is our tendency to rely on the cues that we encounter early in a relationship. This reliance on early cues is known as the **primacy effect.** First impressions due to primacy often have a lasting impact. Thus, the worker who can favorably impress his or her boss in the first days on the job is in an advantageous position due to primacy. Similarly, the labor negotiator who comes across as "tough" on the first day of contract talks might find this image difficult to shake as the talks wear on. Primacy is a form of selectivity, and its lasting effects illustrate the operation of constancy. Sometimes, a **recency effect** occurs in which cues encountered most recently are given undue weight. Landing a big contract today might be perceived as excusing a whole year's bad sales performance. In the story that began the chapter, Zack Thomas might have been the victim of both primacy and recency. He was late the first day of work and the very day of his performance review.

Reliance on Central Traits

Even though perceivers tend to rely upon early information when developing their perceptions, these early cues do not receive equal weight. There is evidence that people tend to organize their perceptions around the presence of certain traits or characteristics that are of interest to them. In developing her perceptions of her new co-worker, the experienced engineer seemed to organize her impressions around his intellectual capacity. For her, this was a **central trait** that influenced her overall image of him. The centrality of traits depends upon the perceiver's interests and the situation. Thus, not all engineers would organize their perceptions of the new worker around his intellectual abilities, and the established engineer might not use this trait as a central factor in forming impressions of the people she meets at a party. Central traits often have a very powerful influence on our perceptions of others. Researchers presented groups of English university students with contrived newspaper stories about a soccer club manager and a local police officer. There were two forms of each story. In one form of the soccer story, the manager was described by the team captain as "warm-hearted." In the other, he was called "a cold fish at times." The officer was alternately described as "humane" and "ruthless." These traits were mixed with a number of others that remained constant across stories. Evidently, the varied traits were central to the impressions that the students formed of the manager and the officer because they strongly influenced their descriptions of the targets on other dimensions. For example, the ruthless police officer was seen as more self-centered, blunt, irritable, and evasive than the humane officer.[5] Thus, it would appear that central traits are a basis for the development of consistent perceptions. Clearly, tardiness was a central trait around which Mr. Pellan organized his perceptions.

Implicit Personality Theory

In the previous example, how was it that the ruthless police officer was also seen as blunt, irritable, and evasive when no information about these characteristics was presented in the newspaper stories? It has been suggested that each of us has an implicit personal "theory" about which personality characteristics go together. Thus, the students saw ruthlessness as indicative of other traits, even though they had no objective cues to this effect. Perhaps you expect hard-working people to also be honest. Perhaps you feel that people of average intelligence tend to be most friendly. These assumed connections are examples of **implicit personality theories.** To the extent that such theories are inaccurate, they provide a basis for misunderstanding.[6] The worker who assumes that her dominant boss is also insensitive might be reluctant to discuss a work-related problem with him that could be solved fairly easily. Mr. Pellan, the bank manager, seemed to hold an implicit personality theory that tied together lateness, lack of commitment, and flirtatious behavior.

Projection

In the absence of information to the contrary, and sometimes in spite of it, people often assume that others are like themselves. This tendency to attribute one's own characteristics and feelings to others is called **projection.** In some cases, projection is an efficient and sensible perceptual strategy. After all, people with similar backgrounds or interests often *do* think and feel similarly. Thus, it is not unreasonable for a capitalistic businessperson to assume that other businesspeople favor the free enterprise system and disapprove of government intervention in this system. However, projection can also lead to perceptual difficulties. The chairperson who feels that an issue has been resolved and perceives committee members to feel the same way might be very surprised when a vote is taken. The honest warehouse manager who perceives others as honest might find stock disappearing. In the case of threatening or undesirable characteristics, projection can serve as a form of perceptual defense. The dishonest worker might say, "Sure I steal from the company, but so does everyone else." Such perceptions can be used to justify the perceiver's thievery. In the story that began the chapter, Zack projected his own tardiness onto his co-workers to justify his behavior.

Stereotyping

One way to form a consistent impression of other people is simply to assume that they have certain characteristics by virtue of some category that they fall into. This perceptual tendency is known as **stereotyping,** and the categories upon which a stereotype might be based include race, age, sex, ethnic background, social class, occupation, and so on. There are actually three specific aspects to stereotyping.[7]

- We distinguish some category of people (College professors).
- We assume that the individuals in this category have certain traits (absent-minded, disorganized, ivory tower mentality).
- We perceive that everyone in this category possesses these traits ("All of my professors this year will be absent-minded, disorganized, and have an ivory tower mentality.").

People can evoke stereotypes with incredibly little information. In one study, students were asked to describe the traits of a number of ethnic groups, including several fictional ones. Although the students had never met a Danerian, a Pirenian, or a Wallonian, this did not inhibit them from assigning traits, and those assigned were usually unfavorable.[8] Of course, not all stereotypes are unfavorable. You probably hold favorable stereotypes of the social categories of which you are a member, such as student. However, it is worth noting that these stereotypes might be less well developed and less rigid than others you hold. Stereotypes help us develop impressions of ambiguous targets, and we are usually pretty familiar with the people in our own groups. In addition, this contact helps us appreciate individual differences among group members, and such differences work against the development of stereotypes. It is worth noting that the language can be easily twisted to turn neutral or even favorable information into a basis for unfavorable stereotypes. For example, if British people do tend to be reserved, it is fairly easy to interpret this reserve as snobbishness. Similarly, if women who achieve executive positions have had to be aggressive, it is easy to interpret this aggressiveness as pushiness.

On the average, not all stereotypes are inaccurate. You probably hold fairly correct stereotypes about the educational level of the typical college professor and the on-the-job demeanor of the typical telephone operator. These accurate stereotypes ease the task of developing perceptions of others. However, it is probably safe to say that most stereotypes are inaccurate, especially when we use them to develop perceptions of specific individuals. This follows from the fact that stereotypes are most likely to develop when we don't have good information about a particular group.

This raises an interesting question: If many stereotypes are inaccurate, why do they persist? After all, reliance upon inaccurate information to develop our perceptions would seem to be punishing in the long run. In fact, it would appear that a couple of factors work to *reinforce* inaccurate stereotypes. For one thing, even incorrect stereotypes help us process information about others quickly and efficiently. Sometimes, it is easier for the perceiver to rely on an inaccurate stereotype than it is to discover the true nature of the target. The male manager who is required to recommend one of his twenty subordinates for a promotion might find it easier to automatically rule out promoting a woman than to carefully evaluate all of his subordinates, regardless of sex. Also, inaccurate stereotypes are often reinforced by selective perception and the selective application of language that was discussed above. The black worker who stereotypes all white managers as unfair might be on the lookout for behaviors to confirm these stereotypes and fail to notice examples of fair and friendly treatment. If such treatment *is* noticed, it might be perceived as patronizing rather than helpful.

Occupational Stereotypes Knowing a person's occupation or field of study, we often make assumptions about his or her behavior and personality. Accountants might be stereotyped as compulsive, precise, and one-dimensional, while engineers might be perceived as cold and calculating. Reflect on your own stereotypes of psychology or computer science students. Labor and management representatives often hold stereotypic views of each other. One study asked union and management people to "analyze the personalities" of men shown in photographs. Each picture included a fictional description of the history of the man, who was incidentally said to be a plant manager or union official. These descriptions were manipulated so that the same picture with the same history was sometimes portrayed as a manager and sometimes as a unionist. When actual managers or unionists saw their "opposites" in the pictures, they responded with negative stereotypes—the person portrayed was seen as undependable and intellectually, emotionally, and interpersonally deficient. This occurred despite the fact that both had viewed the same photograph with the same history, except for the manipulated group membership of the portrayed person.[9] Mr. Pellan had a stereotype of bank accountants that Zack Thomas did not match. For a violation of accountant stereotypes, see the cartoon!

Sex Stereotypes One of the most problematic stereotypes for organizations is the sex stereotype. Considering their numbers in the work force, women are severely underrepresented in managerial and administrative jobs. There is evidence that sex stereotypes are partially responsible for this state of affairs, discouraging

Accountant street gangs

women from business careers and blocking their ascent to managerial positions. It would appear that this happens because stereotypes of women do not correspond especially well with stereotypes of businesspeople or managers.

What is the nature of sex stereotypes? A series of studies has had managers describe men in general, women in general, and typical "successful middle managers." These studies have determined that successful middle managers are perceived as having traits and attitudes that are more similar to those generally ascribed to men.[10] That is, successful managers are seen as more similar to men in factors such as leadership ability, competitiveness, self-confidence, ambitiousness, and objectivity. Thus, stereotypes of successful middle managers do not correspond to stereotypes of women. The trend over time in the results of these studies contains some bad news and some good news. The bad news is that *male* managers today hold the same dysfunctional stereotypes about women and management that they held in the early 1970s when the first of these studies was done. At that time, women managers held the same stereotypes as the men. The good news is that the recent research shows a shift by the women—they now see successful middle managers as possessing attitudes and characteristics that describe *both* men and women in general.[11]

Granting that sex stereotypes exist, do they lead to biased personnel decisions? The answer would appear to be yes. In a typical study, male bank supervisors were asked to make hypothetical personnel decisions about workers who were described equivalently except for sex.[12] Women were discriminated against for promotion to a branch manager position. They were also discriminated against when they requested to attend a professional development conference. In addition, female supervisors were less likely than males to receive support for their request that a problem employee be fired. In one case, bias worked to *favor* women. The bank supervisors were more likely to approve a request for a leave of absence to care for one's children when it came from a female. This finding is similar to others that show that sex stereotypes tend to favor women when they are being considered for "women's" jobs (such as editorial assistant) or for "women's" tasks (such as supervising other women).[13]

In general, research suggests that the above findings are fairly typical. Women suffer from a sex stereotype that is detrimental to their hiring, starting salaries, development, and promotion. However, the picture is not entirely bleak. There is growing evidence that the detrimental effects of sex stereotypes are reduced or removed when decision makers have good information about the qualifications and performance of particular women and an accurate picture of the job that they are applying for or seeking promotion into.[14] In particular, several field studies reveal convincingly that women do not suffer from sex stereotypes in *performance evaluations* provided by their supervisors.[15] This is not altogether surprising. Stereotypes help us process information in ambiguous situations. To the extent that we have good information upon which to base our perceptions of people, reliance on stereotypes is less necessary. Day-to-day performance is often fairly easy to observe, and sex stereotypes do not intrude on evaluations. On the

Do you have a stereotype of female executives? What do you think it would be like to work for this person? (COMSTOCK INC.)

other hand, hiring and promotion decisions might confront managers with ambiguous targets or situations and prompt them to resort to sex stereotypes in forming impressions.

Age Stereotypes Another kind of stereotype that presents problems for organizations is the age stereotype. Knowing that a person falls into a certain age range, we have a tendency to make certain assumptions about the person's physical, psychological, and intellectual capabilities. Again, it would appear that such stereotypes might be partially responsible for unfair treatment of older workers. In one four-year period, state and federal age discrimination complaints rocketed from around 5,000 to over 19,000, showing the increasing sensitivity of this issue.[16]

What is the nature of age stereotypes that are relevant to organizational behavior? Older workers are seen as having less *capacity for performance*. They tend to be viewed as less productive, creative, logical, and capable of performing under pressure than younger workers. In addition, older workers are seen as having less *potential for development*. Compared with younger workers, they are considered more rigid and dogmatic and less adaptable. Not all stereotypes of older workers are negative, however. They tend to be perceived as more honest, dependable, and trustworthy (in short, more *stable*). In general, these stereotypes are held by both younger and older individuals. In addition, it is worth noting that there is evidence that these stereotypes are essentially inaccurate.[17]

Again, the relevant question arises: Do age stereotypes affect personnel decisions? It would appear that such stereotypes can affect decisions regarding hiring, promotion, and skills development. In one study, university students were required to make hypothetical recommendations regarding younger and older male workers. An older man was less likely to be hired for a finance job that required rapid, high-risk decisions. An older man was considered less promotable for a marketing position that required creative solutions to difficult problems. Finally, an older worker was less likely to be permitted to attend a conference on advanced production systems.[18] These decisions reflect the stereotypes of the older worker depicted above. Again, however, it should be recognized that age stereotypes may have less impact upon personnel decisions when managers have good information about the capacities of the particular worker in question.

In summary, the accurate perception of others is difficult and subject to bias. Primacy, recency, central traits, implicit personality theories, projection, and stereotypes may all reduce the accuracy of impression formation.

Did biased perception damage Ann Hopkins' career? Please pause and consider You Be the Manager (see page 99).

ATTRIBUTION: PERCEIVING CAUSES AND MOTIVES

Thus far we have considered a general model of perception and discussed some specific perceptual tendencies that operate as we form impressions of others. We

YOU BE THE MANAGER

anager

Price Waterhouse and Ann Hopkins

Price Waterhouse is one of the country's largest public accounting and management consulting firms. Currently, it has around 900 partners, twenty-seven of whom are women.

Several years ago, Ann Hopkins took a job as a manager in the firm's management consulting operation. During the following five years she proceeded to bring in $40 million in new business. Finally, she was nominated for partnership in the firm, along with eighty-seven other employees, all of them men. Among the eighty-eight nominees, Hopkins ranked number one in generating new business. This is one of the chief roles of a partner and a very important consideration for partnership in accounting and consulting firms.

Opposition to Ann Hopkins' partnership quickly surfaced. Most of it centered on her interpersonal skills, which were said to be aggressive and abrasive. Some partners claimed that she was "too macho" and needed to enroll in a "charm school." Others complained about her swearing. Even one of the supporters of her nomination advised her to walk, talk, and dress in a more feminine manner.

About half of the nominees would achieve partnership status. Would Ann Hopkins be one of them? *You* be the manager.

1. What biases in person perception are relevant to the events in the case?
2. Imagine that you are a Price Waterhouse partner. What are the considerations that should influence the Hopkins partnership decision?

To find out what happened to Ann Hopkins, see The Manager's Notebook at the end of the chapter.

Source: Adapted from Lewin, T. (1990, May 16). Partnership in firm awarded to victim of sex bias. *The New York Times*, pp. A1, A20; Youngstrom, N. (1990, July). Hopkins wins lawsuit against ex-employer. *APA Monitor*, p. 34.

will now consider a further aspect of impression formation—how we perceive people's motives. This process is called attribution. **Attribution** is the process by which we assign causes or motives to people's behavior. The attribution process is important because many rewards and punishments in our society are based upon judgments about what really caused a target person to behave in a certain way.

In making attributions about behavior, an important goal is to determine whether the behavior is caused by dispositional or situational factors. **Dispositional attributions** suggest that some personality characteristic "inside the person" is responsible for the behavior, and that the behavior thus reflects the "true person." If we explain a behavior as a function of intelligence, greed, friendliness, or laziness we are making dispositional attributions. **Situational attributions** suggest that the external situation or environment in which the target person exists was responsible for the behavior, and that the person might have had little control over the behavior. If we explain behavior as a function of bad weather, good luck, proper tools, or poor advice, we are making situational attributions. In the story that began the chapter, Zack Thomas explained his lateness in situational terms (the Narrows Bridge bottleneck), while Mr. Pellan attributed it to dispositional factors (Zack lacked commitment and dedication). In general, the business press attributed the turnaround of the Chrysler Corporation to Lee Iacocca's leadership skills and market savvy, not to government loan guarantees or an improving economy.

Obviously, it would be nice to be able to read minds in order to understand people's motives. Since we can't do this, we are forced to rely on external cues and make inferences from these cues. Research indicates that as we gain experience with the behavior of a target person, three implicit questions guide our decisions as to whether the behavior should be attributed to dispositional or situational causes:[19]

- Does the person engage in the behavior regularly and consistently? (**Consistency cues**)
- Do most people engage in the behavior, or is it unique to this person? (**Consensus cues**)
- Does the person engage in the behavior in many situations, or is it distinctive to one situation? (**Distinctiveness cues**)

Let's examine consistency, consensus, and distinctiveness cues in more detail.

Consistency Cues

Unless we see clear evidence of the operation of external constraints, we tend to perceive behavior that is performed regularly as indicative of a person's true motives. In other words, high consistency leads to dispositional attributions. Thus, one might assume that the professor who has generous office hours and is always there for consultation really cares about students. Similarly, we are likely to make dispositional attributions about workers who are consistently good or poor performers, perhaps perceiving the former as "dedicated" and the latter as "lazy." When behavior occurs inconsistently, we begin to consider situational attributions. For example, if a person's performance cycles between mediocre and excellent, we might look to variations in workload to explain the cycles.

Consensus Cues

In general, acts that deviate from social expectations provide us with more information about the actor's motives than conforming behaviors do. Thus, unusual, low-consensus behavior leads to more dispositional attributions than typical, high-consensus behavior. The person who acts differently from the majority is seen as revealing more of his or her true motives. In a department in which the norm is not to keep regular office hours, the professor who is available is seen as especially concerned with students. The informational effects of low-consensus behavior are magnified when the actor is expected to suffer negative consequences because of the deviance. Consider the job applicant who makes favorable statements about the role of big business in society while being interviewed for a job at General Motors. Such statements are so predictable in this situation that the interviewer can place little confidence in what they really indicate about the candidate's true feelings and motives. On the other hand, imagine an applicant who makes critical comments about big business in the same situation. Such comments are hardly expected, and could clearly lead to rejection. In this case, the interviewer would be more confident about the applicant's true disposition re-

The business press attributed Lee Iacocca's success at Chrysler to disposition—his leadership qualities—rather than to the situation—government loan guarantees and an improving economy. (Natsuko Utsumi/ Gamma-Liaison)

garding big business. A corollary to this would suggest that we place more emphasis upon people's private actions than their public actions when assessing their motives.[20] When our actions are not open to public scrutiny, we are more likely to act out our genuine motives and feelings. Thus, we place more emphasis upon a co-worker's private statements about his boss than we do on his public relations with the boss.

Distinctiveness Cues

When a behavior occurs across a variety of situations, it lacks distinctiveness, and the observer is prone to provide a dispositional attribution about its cause. We reason that the behavior reflects a person's true motives if it "stands up" in a variety of environments. Thus, the professor who has generous office hours, stays after class to talk to students, and attends student functions is seen as truly student-oriented. The worker whose performance was good in his first job as well as several subsequent jobs is perceived as having real ability. When a behavior is highly distinctive, in that it occurs in only one situation, we are likely to assume that some aspect of the situation caused the behavior. If the only student-oriented behavior that we observe is generous office hours, we assume that they are dictated by department policy. If a worker performed well on only one job, back in 1975, we suspect that his uncle owned the company!

Attribution in Action

Frequently, observers of real life behavior have information at hand about consistency, consensus, *and* distinctiveness. Let's take an example that shows how the observer puts such information together in forming attributions. At the same time, the example will serve to review the previous discussion. Imagine that Smith, Jones, and Kelley are employees who work in separate firms. Each is absent from work today, and an organizational observer must develop an attribution about the cause in order to decide which personnel action is warranted.

- *Smith*—Smith is absent a lot, his peers are seldom absent, and he was absent a lot in his previous job.
- *Jones*—Jones is absent a lot, her peers are also absent a lot, but she was almost never absent in her previous job.
- *Kelley*—Kelley is seldom absent, his co-workers are seldom absent, and he was seldom absent in his previous job.

Just what kind of attributions are likely to be made regarding the absences exhibited by Smith, Jones, and Kelley? Smith's absence is highly consistent, it is a low-consensus behavior, and it is not distinctive, since he was absent in his previous job. As shown in Exhibit 4–3, this combination of cues is very likely to prompt a dispositional explanation, perhaps that Smith is lazy or irresponsible. Jones is also absent consistently, but the behavior is high-consensus in that her

EXHIBIT
4–3

Cue combinations and resulting attributions.

	Consistency	Consensus	Distinctiveness	Likely attribution
Smith	High	Low	Low	Disposition
Jones	High	High	High	Situation
Kelley	Low	High	Low	Temporary situation

peers also exhibit absence. In addition, the behavior is highly distinctive—she is absent only on this job. As indicated, this combination of cues will usually result in a situational attribution, perhaps that working conditions are terrible or that the boss is nasty. Finally, Kelley's absence is inconsistent. In addition, it is similar to that of co-workers and not distinctive, in that he was inconsistently absent on his previous job as well. As shown, this combination of cues suggests that some temporary, short-term situational factor causes his absence. It is possible that a sick child occasionally requires him to stay home.

In the story that began the chapter, Mr. Pellan perceived Zack's lateness as highly consistent and a low-consensus behavior, in that he felt that Zack's co-workers were seldom late. In addition, the lateness was not seen as distinctive to the work setting because Zack was also late for activities away from work. Thus, Mr. Pellan developed the dispositional attribution that Zack's lateness stemmed from lack of dedication and commitment.

Biases in Attribution

As the preceding section indicates, observers often operate in a rational, logical manner in forming attributions about behavior. The various cue combinations and the resulting attributions have a sensible appearance. This does not mean that such attributions are always correct, but that they do represent good bets about why some behavior occurred. This having been said, it would be naive to assume that attributions are always free from bias or error. Earlier, a number of very basic perceptual biases were noted, and it stands to reason that the complex task of attribution would be open to further problems. Let's consider three attribution biases.[21]

Fundamental Attribution Error   Suppose you make a mistake in attributing a cause to someone else's behavior. Would you be likely to err on the side of a dispositional cause or a situational cause? Substantial evidence indicates that when we make judgments about the behavior of people other than ourselves, we tend to overemphasize dispositional explanations at the expense of situational

ETHICAL FOCUS 4–1

▼
....
Attribution and Unethical Business Practices

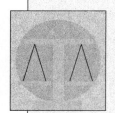

James A. Waters studied a number of cases of unethical or illegal organizational practices, such as price fixing and the bribery of government officials. Waters argues that the public, as well as organizational observers, frequently assume that the involved executives are intrinsically immoral and dishonest. Such a position is reflected in media coverage implying that formerly respected pillars of the business community were really crooks deep down. This corresponds to the proposition that observers tend to explain the behavior of others dispositionally, via personality characteristics. However, Waters presents testimony from congressional hearings that suggests that those convicted of such activities saw themselves at the mercy of situational forces. This corresponds to the proposition that people are more likely to explain their own behavior in situational, rather than dispositional, terms. Situational factors that Waters identifies as contributing to illegal and unethical business activities include respected higher-status organizational members or more experienced peers serving as models and severe group pressure.

Jeffrey Sonnenfeld conducted interviews with executives in the folding carton industry shortly after twenty-two companies were convicted of a massive price-fixing conspiracy. Sonnenfeld found that top corporate executives explained the price fixing differently from divisional executives. Corporate executives, removed from the day-to-day demands of the marketplace, adopted the perspective of an external observer and attributed price fixing to dispositional factors such as low intelligence or weak morals. One said:

> There seem to be pretty low standards in the folding carton industry and a lot of stupid people there. Now we hear them cry, but we thought it didn't mean us. You begin to wonder about the intelligence of these people. Either they don't listen or they're just plain stupid.

Sonnenfeld found that divisional executives, closer to "the line of fire" of falling demand and tough competition, were more likely to identify with the situational constraints faced by the price fixers. One reported:

> The financial pressures are very strong. We are hurting for investment due to our bad earnings record. With declining demand and no new capital, price level is crucial. The drive to stay alive has led to price collusion.

Source: Waters, J. A. (1978, Spring). Catch 20.5. Corporate morality as an organizational phenomenon. *Organizational Dynamics*, 2–19, American Management Association, New York. All rights reserved; and Sonnenfeld, J. (1981). Executive apologies for price fixing: Role biased perceptions of causality. *Academy of Management Journal, 24*, (1), 192–198. Reprinted by permission of the Academy of Management and Jeffrey Sonnenfeld.

explanations. This is called the **fundamental attribution error.**[22] For example, Marine Corps recruits see their gruff and demanding drill sergeant as a cold, uncaring person and discount the fact that the philosophy of the Marine training program (a situational factor) causes his behavior.

Why does the fundamental attribution error occur? For one thing, we often discount the strong effects that social roles can have on behavior. We might see bankers as truly conservative people because we ignore the fact that their occupational role and their employer dictate that they act conservatively. Second, many people whom we observe are seen in rather constrained, constant situations (at work, at school, etc.) that reduce our appreciation of how their behavior can vary in other situations. Thus, we fail to realize that the observed behavior is distinctive to a particular situation. That conservative banker might actually be a weekend skydiver!

The fundamental attribution error can lead to problems for the managers of poorly performing subordinates. It suggests that dispositional explanations for the poor performance will sometimes be invoked even when situational factors are the true cause. Laziness or low aptitude might be cited, while poor training or a bad sales territory are ignored. However, this is less likely when the manager has had actual experience in performing the subordinate's job and is thus aware of situational roadblocks to good performance.[23]

Actor-Observer Effect   It is not surprising that actors and observers often view the causes for the actor's behavior very differently. Recall that Zack Thomas and Mr. Pellan viewed Zack's lateness from very different perspectives. This difference in attributional perspectives is called the **actor-observer effect.**[24] Specifically, while the observer might be busy committing the fundamental attribution error, the actor might be emphasizing the role of the situation in explaining his or her own behavior. Thus, as actors, we are often particularly sensitive to those environmental events that led us to be late or absent. As observers of the same behavior in others, we are more likely to invoke dispositional causes. (See Ethical Focus 4–1 on page 104.)

Why are actors prone to attribute much of their own behavior to situational causes? First, they might be more aware than observers of the constraints and advantages that the environment offered. At the same time they are aware of their private thoughts, feelings, and intentions regarding the behavior, all of which might be unknown to the observer. Thus, I might know that I sincerely wanted to get to the meeting on time, that I left home extra early, and that the accident that delayed me was truly unusual. My boss might be unaware of all of this information.

Self-Serving Bias   It has probably already occurred to you that certain forms of attributions have the capacity to make us feel good or bad about ourselves. In fact, people have a tendency to take credit and responsibility for successful outcomes of their behavior and to deny credit and responsibility for failures.[25] This tendency is called **self-serving bias,** and it is interesting because it suggests that the very same behavior will be explained differently on the basis of events that happened *after* the behavior occurred. If the vice-president of marketing champions a product that turns out to be a sales success, she might attribute this to her retailing savvy. If the very same marketing process leads to failure, she might attribute this to poor performance by the marketing research firm that she used. Notice that the self-serving bias can overcome the tendency for actors to attribute their behavior to situational factors. In this example, the vice-president invokes a dispositional explanation ("I'm an intelligent, competent person") when the behavior is successful.

Much self-serving bias might represent intentional self-promotion or excuse-making. However, again, it is possible that it reflects unique information on the part of the actor. Especially when behavior has negative consequences, the actor might scan the environment and find situational causes for the failure. (See In Focus 4–2.)[26]

IN FOCUS 4–2

Attribution in Corporate Annual Reports

At first blush, it seems unlikely that attribution bias could creep into corporate annual reports, the glossy booklets prepared by corporations to communicate with investors, banks, and brokers. After all, these reports are open to close scrutiny by the financial community, and they are prepared with the assistance of dozens of people who should serve as checks and balances. James R. Bettman and Barton A. Weitz analyzed 181 annual reports to see how organizations explained their successes and failures. What they found was an expected self-serving pattern. When organizations performed well or scored some advantages, they were likely to cite an internal cause such as management strategy, good research and development, or a committed workforce. When organizations performed poorly, they were more likely to cite external environmental factors such as inflation, bad weather, or strong competition. Some of these attributions appeared to be defensively motivated, while others seemed to represent genuine beliefs given the information that was available. Other researchers have subsequently found similar trends in corporate annual reports.

To review the basics of the attribution process, people often use consistency, consensus, and distinctiveness cues in a sensible and rational manner when trying to explain some observed behavior. However, the fundamental attribution error suggests that observers are often overly ready to invoke dispositional explanations for the behavior of actors. The actor-observer effect suggests that the actor is more ready to attribute his or her own behavior to situational factors. According to the self-serving bias, this is especially likely if the behavior is unsuccessful.

THE ACCURACY OF PERSON PERCEPTION IN ORGANIZATIONS

How accurate are our perceptions of others? Given the attribution process just discussed, you might predict that they are not especially accurate. In fact, this would appear to be correct, especially when the perceptual task increases in complexity. To illustrate this, let's consider two complex perceptual tasks that are common to all organizations: the employment interview and performance evaluation.

Interviewers' Perceptions of Job Applicants

You have probably had the pleasure (or displeasure!) of sitting through one or more job interviews in your life. After all, the interview is one of the most common organizational selection devices, applied with equal opportunity to applicants for everything from the janitorial staff to the executive suite. With our futures on the line, we would like to think that the interview is a fair and accurate selection device, but is it? Research shows that the interview is a valid selection device, although it is far from perfectly accurate, especially when it is conducted in an unstructured, free-form format. Validity improves whenever interviewers use a guide to order and organize their questions and impressions.[27]

What factors threaten the validity of the interview? To consider the most obvious problem first, applicants are usually motivated to present an especially favorable impression of themselves. As our discussion of the perception of people implies, it is difficult enough to gain a clear picture of another individual without having to cope with active deception! A couple of the perceptual tendencies that we have already discussed have also been shown to operate in the interview context. For one thing, there is evidence that interviewers compare applicants with a stereotype of the ideal applicant.[28] In and of itself, this is not a bad thing. However, this ideal stereotype must be accurate, and this requires a clear understanding of the nature of the job in question and the kind of person who can do well in this job. This is a tall order, especially for the interviewer who is hiring applicants for a wide variety of jobs. Second, interviewers have a tendency to exhibit primacy reactions.[29] Minimally, this means that information acquired early in the interview will have an undue impact on the final decision. However, it also means that information obtained *before* the interview (for instance, by scanning an application form or résumé) can have exaggerated influence on the interview outcome.

A couple of perceptual tendencies not discussed earlier have also been observed in interviews. First, interviewers have a tendency to *underweight positive information* about the applicant.[30] This means that negative information has undue impact on the decision.[31] This might occur because interviewers get more feedback about unsuccessful hiring than successful hiring ("Why did you send me that idiot?"). It might also happen because positive information isn't perceived as telling the interviewer much, since the candidate is motivated to put up a good front. In addition, **contrast effects** sometimes occur in the interview.[32] This means that the applicants who have been interviewed previously affect the interviewer's perception of a current applicant. For example, if the interviewer has seen two excellent candidates and then encounters an average candidate, she might rate this person lower than if he had been preceded by two average applicants. (See Exhibit 4–4.) It should be noted that this is an example of the impact of the situation upon perception.

It is clear that the interview constitutes a fairly difficult setting in which to form accurate impressions about others. It is of short duration, a lot of information is generated, and the applicant is motivated to present a favorable image. Thus, interviewers often adopt "perceptual crutches" that hinder accurate perception. Earlier, it was noted that unstructured interviews are less valid than

EXHIBIT
4–4

Two examples of contrast effects.

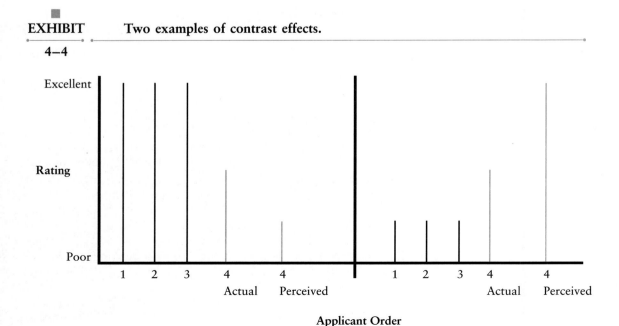

Applicant Order

structured interviews, in which the interviewer scores the applicant's responses to a predetermined series of questions. This form of interview probably reduces information overload and ensures that applicants can be more easily compared, since they have all responded to an identical sequence of questions.[33]

Observers' Perceptions of Job Performance

Once a person is hired, however imperfectly, further perceptual tasks confront organization members. Specifically, the organization will want some index of the person's job performance for decisions regarding pay raises, promotions, transfers, and training needs. Measures of job performance are also useful for evaluating the impact of changing factors like job design or pay plans.

Objective and Subjective Measures It is possible to find objective measures of performance for certain aspects of some jobs. These are measures that do not involve a substantial degree of human judgment. Accurate attendance records are examples of objective performance measures. So are the dollar sales achieved by salespeople or the number of defect-free pieces turned out by machine operators. Unfortunately, objective performance measures have many problems associated with them. In general, as we move up the organizational hierarchy, it becomes more difficult to find objective indicators of performance. Thus, it is often hard to find countable evidence of a manager's success or failure. When objective indicators of performance do exist, they are often contaminated by situational factors. For example, it might be very difficult to compare the dollar sales of a snowmobile salesperson whose territory covers Maryland and Virginia with one whose territory is Minnesota and Wisconsin. Also, objective performance measures for a given job might not cover all the relevant areas of performance. While dollar sales might be a good indicator of current sales performance, they might say little about a person's capacity for sales management. Thus, dollar sales might be a weak foundation on which to base a promotion to district sales manager.

Because of the difficulties that objective performance indicators present, organizations must often rely upon subjective measures of effectiveness. Thus, perceptual judgments of performance are made by observers of the job incumbents. These observers are usually the workers' direct superiors, and they typically report their judgments on rating scales designed to tap several dimensions of effectiveness (e.g., quantity of work, quality of work, leadership capacity, etc.). Compared with the employment interviewer, the performance evaluator should be in a better perceptual position. After all, such a person should have ample opportunity to observe examples of real performance over an extended period of time. However, the performance evaluator is also confronted by a number of perceptual roadblocks. The evaluator might not be in a position to observe many instances of effective and ineffective performance. This is especially likely when the subordinate's job activities cannot be monitored directly by the boss. For example, a police sergeant cannot ride around in six squad cars at the same time, and a telephone company supervisor cannot visit customers' homes or climb telephone poles with all of his or her installers. Such situations mean that the target (the subordinate's performance) is frequently ambiguous, and we have seen that the perceptual system resolves ambiguities in an efficient but often inaccurate manner. Even when performance is observable, performers often alter their behavior to look good when the boss is around.

Rater Errors Subjective performance evaluation is surely susceptible to some of the perceptual biases discussed earlier, including primacy and stereotypes. In addition, a number of other perceptual tendencies occur in performance evaluation. One class of these tendencies includes leniency, harshness, and central tendency (Exhibit 4–5). **Leniency** refers to the tendency to perceive the performance of one's ratees as especially good, while **harshness** is the tendency to see their performance as especially ineffective. Lenient raters tend to give "good" ratings, and harsh raters tend to give "bad" ratings. Professors with reputations as easy graders or tough graders exemplify these types of raters. **Central tendency** involves assigning most ratees to a middle-range performance category—the extremes of the rating categories are not used. The professor who assigns 80 percent of her students Cs is committing this error. Each of these three rating tendencies is probably partially a function of the rater's personal experiences. For example, the manager who has had an especially good group of subordinates might respond with special harshness when transferred to supervise a group of slightly less able workers. It is worth noting that not all instances of leniency, harshness, and central tendency represent perceptual errors. In some cases, raters intentionally commit these errors, even though they have accurate perceptions of workers'

EXHIBIT

4–5

Leniency, harshness, and central tendency rater errors.

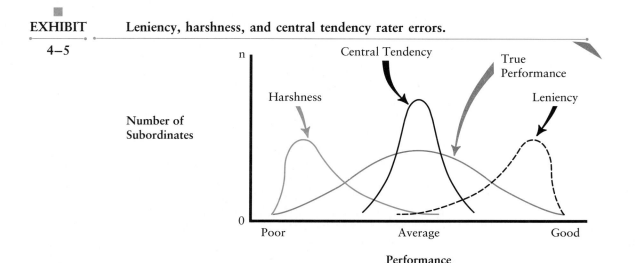

performance. For example, a manager might use leniency or central tendency in performance reviews so that his subordinates do not react negatively to his evaluation.

Another perceptual error that is frequently committed by performance raters is called **halo**.[34] The halo effect occurs when the observer allows the rating of an individual on one trait or characteristic to color ratings on other traits or characteristics. For example, in a teacher evaluation system, a student might perceive his instructor as a nice person, and this might favorably influence his perception of the instructor's knowledge of the material and speed in returning exams and papers. Similarly, a manager might rate a subordinate as frequently late for work, and this might in turn lead her to devalue the subordinate's productivity and quality of work, as Mr. Pellan did in the story that began the chapter. As these examples illustrate, halo can work either for or against the ratee. In both cases, the rater fails to perceive differences *within* ratees. It is proably safe to assume that halo tends to be organized around central traits that the rater considers important. The student feels that being nice is an especially important quality, while the manager places special emphasis upon promptness. Ratings on these characteristics then affect the rater's perceptions of other characteristics.

The **similar-to-me effect** is an additional rater error that may in part reflect perceptual bias. The rater tends to give more favorable evaluations to people who are similar to the rater in terms of background or attitudes. For example, the

Does the similar-to-me effect reduce employee diversity? (Melanie Carr/Uniphoto)

manager with an M.B.A. degree who comes from an upper middle class family might perceive a similar subordinate as a good performer even though the person is only average. Similarly, a rater might overestimate the performance of an individual who holds similar religious and political views. Such reactions probably stem from a tendency to view our own performance, attitudes, and background as "good." We then tend to generalize this evaluation to others who are to some degree similar to us.

A final rater error that may often be perceptual in nature is called **knowledge of predictor bias.** This unusual name refers to cases in which the rater gains knowledge of some factor that might predict the success of the ratee and then rates the subordinate to confirm this prediction. For example, there is a large retail food chain that puts certain store employees through a series of exercises and tests designed to predict promotability to managerial positions. The superiors of the employees are made aware of their subordinates' scores on these tests and exercises. Promotions are based upon these scores and on subsequent ratings of managerial potential made by the superiors. Not surprisingly, the managers always see the high-scoring subordinates as most promotable! This is probably a partial function of selective perception. Knowing which subordinates are *supposed* to be most promotable (from their test and exercise scores), the superiors tend to see their effective behaviors and miss their ineffective behaviors. Thus, the high scorers are invariably perceived as promotable and are given good ratings by the boss. The same effect can occur in other settings. A friend whose judgment you trust might tell you that Professor Bloggs is an excellent teacher. When you take Bloggs's class, you might be predisposed to notice his good aspects and deemphasize his bad characteristics. As we said earlier, expectations held by the perceiver influence his or her perception of the target.

Given all of these problems, it should be clear that it is difficult to get good subjective evaluations of employee performance. Because of this, personnel specialists have explored various techniques for reducing perceptual errors and biases. Obviously, knowledge of predictor bias can be controlled by being sure that predictors of performance are unavailable to the performance rater. Halo can be reduced by requiring the rater to evaluate all ratees on a given performance characteristic before going to the next characteristic, rather than rating one person on all characteristics before turning to the next person. In recent years, there has been a tendency to attempt to reduce rater errors by going to rating scales with more specific behavioral labels. The assumption here is that giving specific examples of effective and ineffective performance will facilitate the rater's perceptual processes and recall. Exhibit 4–6 shows a traditional rating scale that could be used to measure police patrol officer performance on the dimension of judgment. Clearly, such a scale is open to most of the perceptual errors discussed above. It simply does little to help the rater avoid these errors. Exhibit 4–7 shows a behaviorally anchored rating scale that gives very specific behavioral examples of good, average, and poor judgment. With such an aid, the rater might be less likely to succumb to perceptual errors when completing the rating task, although the evidence for this is mixed.[35]

EXHIBIT 4–6

Traditional rating scale that might be used to evaluate a police officer's judgment.

This Officer's Judgment Is:

1	2	3	4	5
Poor		Average		Excellent

EXHIBIT 4–7

Behaviorally anchored scale for rating police officer judgment.

High

Calls for assistance and clears the area of bystanders before confronting a barricaded, heavily-armed suspect.

Notices potentially dangerous situations before anything actually occurs.

Radios in his position and discontinues a high-speed chase before entering areas of high vehicle and pedestrian traffic, such as school areas.

Average

Issues warnings instead of tickets for traffic violations that occur at particularly confusing intersections for motorists.

Permits traffic violators to explain why they violated the law and then decides whether or not to issue a citation.

Does not leave a mother and daughter in the middle of a fight just because no law is being violated.

Low

Enters a building with a broken door window instead of guarding the exits and calling for a backup unit.

Does nothing in response to a complaint about a woman cursing loudly in a restaurant.

Continues to write a traffic violation when he hears a report of a nearby robbery in progress.

Judgment—Observation and assessment of the situation and taking appropriate action.

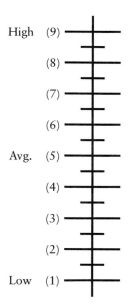

The rater observes the examples to the left in order to understand instances of high, average, and poor judgment. The rater then marks the scale with a circle to indicate the officer's level of performance on judgment.

Source: From Landy, F. J., & Farr, J. L. (1975). *(A)* Performance Description Scales and *(B)* Instructions and Examples for Performance Description Scales. *Supervisor.* Reprinted by permission.

In conclusion, the perceptual task confronting the performance evaluator is difficult but subject to improvement. Such improvements are necessary to provide the organization with accurate information on which to base decisions regarding pay, promotions, and training needs.

THE MANAGER'S NOTEBOOK

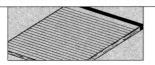

Price Waterhouse and Ann Hopkins

Ann Hopkins was passed over for partnership at Price Waterhouse. When she failed to be nominated the next year, she resigned her job. She subsequently filed a suit claiming sex discrimination under Title VII of the Civil Rights Act. A U.S. District Court ruled that Hopkins had been a victim of sex discrimination. The court ordered that she receive partial back pay, and, in a very unusual decision, ruled that Hopkins be admitted into partnership at Price Waterhouse.

1. In rendering its verdict, the court explicitly recognized that Hopkins had been the victim of a sex stereotype by failing to conform to stereotyped expectations of how a woman should act. It is also probable that occupational stereotypes about the proper demeanor of managers and accounting firm partners contributed to Hopkins' partnership veto.

2. An important consideration in the case would obviously involve being fair to Hopkins. Minimally, this would include placing great weight on her skill at bringing in new business and placing no weight on factors that are not relevant to her performance. Another consideration might be ensuring that more women are represented in the partnership ranks. A final consideration might be protecting the overall reputation of the firm. Evidently, some partners thought that they were doing this in rejecting her nomination, but they did not foresee the results of the subsequent lawsuit and ensuing publicity.

SUMMARY

- Perception involves interpreting the input from our senses to provide meaning to our environment, and any instance of perception involves a perceiver, a target, and a situational context. The experience, motivational state, and emotional state of the perceiver affect perception, as do the ambiguity and social status of the target.
- Bruner's model of the perceptual process suggests that we are very receptive to cues provided by the target and the situation when we encounter an unfamiliar target. However, as we discover familiar cues, we quickly categorize the target and process other cues to maintain a consistent and constant picture of the target. When the target is a person, this drive for constancy and consistency is revealed in a number of specific perceptual biases, including primacy, recency, implicit personality theory, reliance on central traits, projection, and stereotyping. Sex and age stereotypes are especially problematic for organizations.

- Attribution is the process of assigning causes or motives to people's behavior. The observer is often interested in determining whether the behavior is due to dispositional (internal) or situational (external) causes. Behavior is likely to be attributed to the disposition of the actor when the behavior (1) is performed consistently, (2) differs from that exhibited by other people, and (3) occurs in a variety of situations or environments. An opposite set of cues will prompt a situational attribution. Observers are biased toward making dispositional attributions, while actors are more likely to explain their own behavior in situational terms, especially when its outcomes are unfavorable.
- Judging the suitability of job applicants in an interview and evaluating job performance are especially difficult perceptual tasks, in part because the target is motivated to convey a good impression. In addition, interviewers and performance raters exhibit a number of perceptual tendencies that are reflected in inaccurate judgments.

KEY CONCEPTS

Perception	Attribution	Self-serving bias
Perceptual defense	Dispositional attributions	Contrast effects
Primacy effect	Situational attributions	Leniency
Recency effect	Consistency cues	Harshness
Central trait	Consensus cues	Central tendency
Implicit personality theory	Distinctiveness cues	Halo
Projection	Fundamental attribution error	Similar-to-me effect
Stereotyping	Actor-observer effect	Knowledge of predictor bias

DISCUSSION QUESTIONS

1. Discuss how differences in the experiences of students and professors might affect their perceptions of students' written work and class comments.

2. Discuss the occupational stereotypes that you hold of computer programmers, the clergy, truck drivers, bartenders, and bankers. How do you think these stereotypes have developed? Has an occupational stereotype ever caused you to commit a socially embarrassing error when meeting someone for the first time?

3. Use Bruner's perceptual model (Exhibit 4–2) to explain why performance evaluation and interviewers' judgments are frequently inaccurate.

4. Discuss the assertion that "the perception of reality is more important than reality itself" in the context of organizations.

5. Suppose an employee does a particularly poor job on an assigned project. Discuss the attribution process that this person's manager will use to form judgments about this poor performance. Be sure to discuss how consistency, consensus, and distinctiveness cues will be used.

6. A study of small business failures found that owners generally cited factors such as economic depression or strong competition as causes. However, creditors of these failed businesses were much more likely to cite ineffective management. What attribution bias is indicated by these findings? Why do you think the difference in attribution occurs?

7. Discuss the factors that make it difficult for employment interviewers to form accurate perceptions of interviewees.

8. Using the material in the chapter, explain why managers and subordinates often differ in their perceptions of subordinate performance.

■

EXPERIENTIAL EXERCISE

Women in Business

The following items are an attempt to assess the attitudes people have about women in business. The statements cover many different and opposing points of view; you may find yourself agreeing strongly with some of the statements, disagreeing just as strongly with others, and perhaps uncertain about others.

Using the numbers from 1 to 7 on the rating scale, mark your personal opinion about each statement in the blank that immediately precedes it. Remember, give your *personal opinion* according to how much you agree or disagree with each item.

1 = Strongly Disagree

2 = Disagree

3 = Slightly Disagree

4 = Neither Disagree nor Agree

5 = Slightly Agree

6 = Agree

7 = Strongly Agree

_____ 1. It is less desirable for women than men to have a job that requires responsibility.

_____ 2. Women have the objectivity required to evaluate business situations properly.

_____ 3. Challenging work is more important to men than it is to women.

_____ 4. Men and women should be given equal opportunity for participation in management training programs.

_____ 5. Women have the capability to acquire the necessary skills to be successful managers.

_____ 6. On the average, women managers are less capable of contributing to an organization's overall goals than are men.

_____ 7. It is not acceptable for women to assume leadership roles as often as men.

_____ 8. The business community should someday accept women in key managerial positions.

_____ 9. Society should regard work by female managers as valuable as work by male managers.

_____ 10. It is acceptable for women to compete with men for top executive positions.

_____ 11. The possibility of pregnancy does not make women less desirable employees than men.

_____ 12. Women would no more allow their emotions to influence their managerial behavior than would men.

_____ 13. Problems associated with menstruation should not make women less desirable than men as employees.

_____ 14. To be a successful executive, a woman does not have to sacrifice some of her femininity.

_____ 15. On the average, a woman who stays at home all the time with her children is a better mother than a woman who works outside the home at least half time.

_____ 16. Women are less capable of learning mathematical and mechanical skills than are men.

_____ 17. Women are not ambitious enough to be successful in the business world.

_____ 18. Women cannot be assertive in business situations that demand it.

_____ 19. Women possess the self-confidence required of a good leader.

_____ 20. Women are not competitive enough to be successful in the business world.

_____ 21. Women cannot be aggressive in business situations that demand it.

Scoring and Interpretation

The scale you have just completed is called the Women as Managers Scale (WAMS). It measures your attitudes toward women assuming managerial roles. To score your WAMS, subtract your responses to each of the following items from 8: 1, 3, 6, 7, 15, 16, 17, 18, 20, 21. For example, if you put 3 for item 1, give yourself a 5 (8 minus 3). Then, simply add up your resulting responses to all 21 items. Your score should fall somewhere between 21 and 147. The higher the score, the more favorable are your attitudes toward women as managers. One study of 1,014 university business students and 602 managers reported the following WAMS averages: Male managers = 111; female managers = 128; male students = 103; female students = 130.[36]

To facilitate discussion, the instructor might have students write their WAMS score and their sex on pieces of paper. Working in groups and using calculators, the class can compute the class average, the male average, and the female average. Also, a distribution of the scores might be posted on the board.

■

Source: Peters, L. H., Terborg, J. R., & Taynor, J. (1974). Women as managers scale (WAMS): A measure of attitudes toward women in management positions. *JSAS Catalog of Selected Documents in Psychology,* Ms. No. 585.

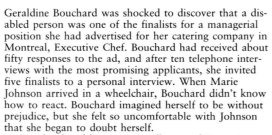

CASE STUDY

Willing and Able

Geraldine Bouchard was shocked to discover that a disabled person was one of the finalists for a managerial position she had advertised for her catering company in Montreal, Executive Chef. Bouchard had received about fifty responses to the ad, and after ten telephone interviews with the most promising applicants, she invited five finalists to a personal interview. When Marie Johnson arrived in a wheelchair, Bouchard didn't know how to react. Bouchard imagined herself to be without prejudice, but she felt so uncomfortable with Johnson that she began to doubt herself.

Bouchard and her sister Lucille started Executive Chef two years ago as a small catering service operating out of Bouchard's home. While working as a private secretary to the president of a large financial investment company, Bouchard had realized there was a market for catering business meetings with gourmet food. After several months of planning with her sister, who was also a corporate secretary, Bouchard felt confident that with their connections, they could develop a large enough client list to make their business profitable. They were both excellent cooks, having learned from their father who had served as a master chef in some of Montreal's top restaurants. Each borrowed $25,000 from her bank to purchase equipment and supplies and pay for advertising. Within six months they had so much business they had to rent a large office and hire several staff.

By the end of two years, Executive Chef had ten employees and annual sales of approximately $600,000. The task of running the office had become Geraldine's primary responsibility, while Lucille was in charge of the kitchen. Geraldine had left her secretarial job to escape what she considered the drudgery of paperwork and administration. As the business prospered, however, she found herself immersed in activities she disliked. When she told Lucille of her frustration, her sister suggested

they hire a manager to run the office, allowing Geraldine to spend more of her time promoting the company.

All of the finalists for the position had comparable levels of experience and excellent references. The decision, Bouchard knew, would come down to which person could fit best into the existing office environment. Although Johnson had impressed her to a certain extent, Bouchard did not really have a clear picture of her as a person. This was as a result of Bouchard's discomfort during the interview. While the conversation flowed easily with the others, it was much more distant and formal with Johnson. Bouchard was so afraid of saying the wrong thing that she didn't allow the interview to proceed beyond a superficial level. One question she wanted to ask was how Johnson had become disabled, but she was concerned that it might embarrass Johnson or violate her human rights. As the interview progressed, Bouchard had trouble listening to some of the answers because of the emotional stress she was experiencing.

In addition, Bouchard failed to address some practical questions she had about Johnson's disability. Had Johnson found it difficult to get into the building? Would she be able to use the existing washroom? If not, did that disqualify her from the job, or is it Bouchard's responsibility to provide a solution?

As she reflected on the experience, Bouchard knew that she hadn't interviewed Johnson fairly. Bouchard had never dealt with a person in a wheelchair before. What made it even more difficult was Johnson's appearance and manner. Johnson was very attractive, well-dressed, and aggressive. This ran counter to how Bouchard imagined a disabled person would be.

Bouchard wondered what to do. She knew that at least two of the other candidates would make excellent employees. It would be easy to select one and end the matter there. But she felt guilty about her reaction to Johnson. She considered that, all things being equal, she had an obligation to hire a disabled person because of the difficulties many of them have in finding employment.

Source: Excerpted from McLaughlin, P. (1989, February). Willing and able. *Canadian Business*, 117–119. Reprinted by permission of the author.

1. Apply Bruner's model of the perceptual process (Exhibit 4–2) to the events in the case.

2. How did Geraldine's experience, motivational state, and emotional state affect her perceptions of Marie?

3. What biases in person perception colored Geraldine Bouchard's view of Marie Johnson?

4. What aspects of attribution theory apply to the case?

5. What does the case say about using the employment interview as a selection device?

6. What should Geraldine do now?

REFERENCES

1. Dearborn, D. C., & Simon, H. A. (1958). Selective perception: A note on the departmental identification of executives. *Sociometry, 21,* 140–144. For a study that did not find this effect (using much shorter cases), see Walsh, J. P. (1988). Selectivity and selective perception: An investigation of managers' belief structures and information processing. *Academy of Management Journal, 31,* 873–896.

2. Janis, I. (1982). *Groupthink: Psychological studies of policy decisions and fiascoes.* Boston: Houghton Mifflin.

3. Wilson, P. R. (1968). The perceptual distortion of height as a function of ascribed academic status. *Journal of Social Psychology, 74,* 97–102.

4. Bruner, J. S. (1957). On perceptual readiness. *Psychological Review, 64,* 123–152.

5. Warr, P. B., & Knapper, C. (1968). *The perception of people and events.* London: Wiley.

6. See Krzystofiak, F., Cardy, R., & Newman, J. E. (1988). Implicit personality and performance appraisal: The influence of trait inferences on evaluations of behavior. *Journal of Applied Psychology, 73,* 515–521.

7. Secord, P. F., Backman, C. W., & Slavitt, D. R. (1976). *Understanding social life: An introduction to social psychology.* New York: McGraw-Hill. For elaboration, see Wilder, D. A. (1986). Social categorization: Implications for creation and reduction of intergroup bias. *Advances in Experimental Social Psychology, 19,* 291–349.

8. Hartley, E. L. (1946). *Problems in prejudice.* New York: King's Crown Press.

9. Haire, M. (1955). Role-perceptions in labor-management relations: An experimental approach. *Industrial and Labor Relations Review, 8,* 204–216.

10. Schein, V. E. (1975). Relationships between sex role stereotypes and requisite management characteristics among female managers. *Journal of Applied Psychology, 60,* 340–344; Brenner, O. C., Tomkiewicz, J., & Schein, V. E. (1989). The relationship between sex role stereotypes and requisite management characteristics revisited. *Academy of Management Journal, 32,* 662–669; Heilman, M. E., Block, C. J., Martell, R. F., & Simon, M. C. (1989). Has anything changed? Current characterizations of men, women, and managers. *Journal of Applied Psychology, 74,* 935–942.

11. Brenner et al., 1989.

12. Rosen, B., & Jerdee, T. H. (1974). Influence of sex role stereotypes on personnel decisions. *Journal of Applied Psychology, 59,* 9–14.

13. Cohen, S. L., & Bunker, K. A. (1975). Subtle effects of sex role stereotypes on recruiters' hiring decisions. *Journal of Applied Psychology, 60,* 566–572. See also Rose, G. L., & Andiappan, P. (1978). Sex effects on managerial hiring decisions. *Academy of Management Journal, 21,* 104–112.

14. Tosi, H. L., & Einbender, S. W. (1985). The effects of the type and amount of information in sex discrimination research: A meta-analysis. *Academy of Management Journal, 28,* 712–723.

15. For a review, see Dipboye, R. L. (1985). Some neglected variables in research on discrimination in appraisals. *Academy of Management Review, 10,* 116–127. For a representative study, see Pulakos, E. D., White, L. A., Oppler, S. A., & Borman, W. C. (1989). Examination of race and sex effects on performance ratings. *Journal of Applied Psychology, 74,* 770–780.

16. Faley, R. H., Kleiman, L. S., & Lengnick-Hall, M. L. (1984). Age discrimination and personnel

psychology: A review and synthesis of the legal literature with implications for future research. *Personnel Psychology, 37,* 327–350.

17. Rosen, B., & Jerdee, T. H. (1976). The nature of job-related age stereotypes. *Journal of Applied Psychology, 61,* 180–183. For a more complete review of age-related characteristics, see Rhodes, S. R. (1983). Age-related differences in work attitudes and behavior. *Psychological Bulletin, 93,* 328–367. For a review of the age-performance relationship, see McEvoy, G. M., & Cascio, W. F. (1989). Cumulative evidence of the relationship between employee age and job performance. *Journal of Applied Psychology, 74,* 11–17.

18. Rosen, B., & Jerdee, T. H. (1976). The influence of age stereotypes on managerial decisions. *Journal of Applied Psychology, 61,* 428–432. Also see Cleveland, J. N., & Landy, F. J. (1983). The effects of person and job stereotypes on two personnel decisions. *Journal of Applied Psychology, 68,* 609–619.

19. Kelley, H. H. (1972). Attribution in social interaction. In E. E. Jones et al. (Eds.), *Attribution: Perceiving the causes of behavior.* Morristown, NJ: General Learning Press. For a recent integrative attribution model, see Medcof, J. W. (1990). PEAT: An integrative model of attribution processes. *Advances in Experimental Social Psychology, 23,* 111–209.

20. Baron, R. A., Byrne, D., & Griffitt, W. (1974). *Social psychology: Understanding human interaction.* Boston: Allyn and Bacon.

21. This discussion of attribution biases draws upon Fiske, S. T., & Taylor, S. E. (1984). *Social cognition.* Reading, MA: Addison-Wesley.

22. Ross, L. (1977). The intuitive psychologist and his shortcomings: Distortions in the attribution process. *Advances in Experimental Social Psychology, 10,* 173–220; Jones, E. E. (1979). The rocky road from acts to dispositions. *American Psychologist, 34,* 107–117.

23. Mitchell, T. R., & Kalb, L. S. (1982). Effects of job experience on supervisor attributions for a subordinate's poor performance. *Journal of Applied Psychology, 67,* 181–188.

24. Watson, D. (1982). The actor and the observer: How are their perceptions of causality divergent? *Psychological Bulletin, 92,* 682–700.

25. Greenwald, A. G. (1980). The totalitarian ego:

Fabrication and revision of personal history. *American Psychologist, 35,* 603–618.

26. Pyszczynski, T., & Greenberg, J. (1987). Toward an integration of cognitive and motivational perspectives on social inference: A biased hypothesis-testing model. *Advances in Experimental Social Psychology, 20,* 197–340.

27. Wiesner, W. H., & Cronshaw, S. F. (1988). A meta-analytic investigation of the impact of interview format and degree of structure on the validity of the employment interview. *Journal of Occupational Psychology, 61,* 275–290.

28. Hakel, M. D. (1982). Employment interviewing. In K. M. Rowland & G. R. Ferris (Eds.), *Personnel management.* Boston: Allyn and Bacon.

29. Hakel, 1982; Dipboye, R. L. (1989). Threats to the incremental validity of interviewer judgments. In R. W. Eder & G. R. Ferris (Eds.), *The employment interview: Theory, research, and practice.* Newbury Park, CA: Sage.

30. Hollmann, T. D. (1972). Employment interviewers' errors in processing positive and negative information. *Journal of Applied Psychology, 56,* 130–134.

31. Rowe, P. M. (1989). Unfavorable information in interview decisions. In R. W. Eder & G. R. Ferris (Eds.), *The employment interview: Theory, research, and practice.* Newbury Park, CA: Sage.

32. Schmitt, N. (1976). Social and situational determinants of interview decisions: Implications for the employment interview. *Personnel Psychology, 29,* 70–101.

33. For other reasons and a review of the recent interview literature, see Harris, M. M. (1989). Reconsidering the employment interview: A review of recent literature and suggestions for future research. *Personnel Psychology, 42,* 691–726.

34. Cooper, W. H. (1981). Ubiquitous halo. *Psychological Bulletin, 90,* 218–244.

35. Kingstrom, P. D., & Bass, A. R. (1981). A critical analysis of studies comparing behaviorally anchored rating scales (BARS) and other rating formats. *Personnel Psychology, 34,* 263–289; Landy, F. J., & Farr, J. L. (1983). *The measurement of work performance.* New York: Academic Press.

36. Crino, M. D., White, M. C., & De Sanctis, G. L. (1981). A comment on the dimensionality and reliability of the women as managers scale (WAMS). *Academy of Management Journal, 24,* 866–876.

CHAPTER
5

VALUES, ATTITUDES, AND JOB SATISFACTION

Candice Rowe and Mike Sherrill landed what were generally considered by their M.B.A. graduating class to be the "plum" jobs of the year. Both were corporate planning jobs in the large conglomerate United Products. United had a reputation for offering good salaries and job security. However, new M.B.A.s usually began their jobs "in the trenches" in one of the firms held by United and gradually worked their way up to a headquarters posting. Candice's and Mike's planning jobs were already at headquarters. By most standards, the jobs paid well and offered some interesting opportunities for expense account travel. Candice and Mike were the envy of their classmates when they received their offers from United. Thus, most were amazed to learn that Mike had quit his job only seven months after being hired. Mike's boss was also surprised, since his performance had been fine during the seven months.

The person who wasn't surprised about Mike's quitting was Candice. Between trips, they had frequently compared notes on the jobs they held, jobs that were essentially identical except for the specific project each was working on. Early on, Mike began to indicate that he was less than happy with what he had gotten himself into.

"This travel is really getting to me, Candice. My wife and kids look at me like I'm a deserter when I tell them I've got another business trip coming up."

Candice, who was single, responded, "Yes, I guess it's tough when you have a family. It's funny, though, I really like the travel. It's like a fringe benefit for me, getting to see so many places."

"Also," continued Mike, "the extra hours I'm putting in here when I'm not traveling are causing the same problem. I'm often working until seven every night. When I was an engineer, we'd get paid overtime for doing that!"

Candice looked thoughtful and then said, "I guess I don't mind putting in the extra hours because everyone else here is doing it. If others were taking off early, I'm sure I'd change my tune."

On another occasion, Mike and Candice had discussed the actual kind of work done in corporate planning. Candice said, "I'm glad this is a staff job. I'm good at digging out information, doing financial projections, and writing reports. I don't think I'd be very good at line management—telling people what to do."

Mike laughed. "I got out of engineering and took an M.B.A. so I *could* tell people what to do. Somehow, though, I've landed another staff position here at United, and I don't have any slaves at my beck and call!"

Shortly after this discussion, Mike told Candice that he had landed a management position back at his old engineering firm and that he would be leaving United in two weeks.

Candice marveled at how two people could view the same job so differently.

This scenario raises some interesting issues. How do attitudes toward the job develop, and how can two employees exhibit such different attitudes toward the same job? How important are such attitudes to individuals and organizations? And why didn't Mike's performance suffer because of his unhappiness? In this chapter, we will attempt to answer questions of this kind. First, we will examine the nature of values, beliefs, and attitudes. Then we will discuss techniques that organizations attempt to use to change employee attitudes and the factors that contribute to the success of these endeavors. Finally, we will consider job satisfaction, an attitude of special interest to organizations. Both its causes and its consequences will be examined.

WHAT ARE VALUES?

We might define **values** as "a broad tendency to prefer certain states of affairs over others."[1] The *preference* aspect of this definition means that values have to do with feelings and emotions, with what we consider good and bad. The feelings or emotions inherent in values are motivational, since they signal the attractive aspects of our environment that should be sought out and the unattractive aspects that should be avoided or changed. The words *broad tendency* in this definition mean that values are very general emotional orientations, and that they don't predict behavior in specific situations very well. Knowing that a person generally embraces the values that support capitalism doesn't tell us much about how he or she will respond to a beggar on the street this afternoon.

It is useful to classify values into several categories: intellectual, economic, aesthetic, social, political, and religious.[2] Not everyone holds the same values. Managers might value high productivity (an economic value), while union officials might be more concerned with enlightened supervision and full employment (social values). Similarly, professors probably value clear, accurate writing (an intellectual value) more than illiterates do. Of course, individuals might value the same factor for different reasons. Economically oriented students might value clear, accurate writing because it enables them to do well in school and ultimately obtain a good job, not because such writing furthers knowledge per se. Values are learned by the processes discussed in Chapter 3. Most are socially reinforced by parents, teachers, and representatives of religions. In fact, our entire social system is designed to teach and reinforce the values that our society has decided are appropriate. In the story that began the chapter, Mike expressed some values that had to do with family life and with directing the work of others.

To firm up your understanding of values and their impact on organizational behavior, let's examine some occupational differences in values and how work values differ across cultures.

Occupational Differences in Values

Values are not randomly distributed across the population. Of particular interest is the fact that members of different occupational groups espouse different values. A research program showed that university professors, city police officers, oil company salespeople, and operators of small businesses had values that distinguished them as groups from the general population.[3] For example, the professors valued "equal opportunity for all" more highly than the average American. On the other hand, the salespeople and business proprietors ranked social values (peace, equality, freedom) lower than the average American. Value differences such as these might be partially responsible for the occupational stereotypes that we discussed in Chapter 4. Also, such differences might be responsible for conflict between organizations and within organizations when members of different occupations are required to interact with each other. For instance, the evidence cited above indicates that police officers and professors differ rather radically in the value they place on equal opportunity. This suggests that the average professor who is asked to serve as a consultant in developing a community relations program for a police force might encounter a severe case of value conflict. The same kind of problem can exist within an organization. Doctors frequently report that their social values are at odds with the economic values of hospital administrators. Do differences in occupational values develop after a person enters an occupation, or do such differences cause people to gravitate to certain occupations? Given the fact that values are relatively stable and that many values are acquired early in life, it would appear that people choose occupations that correspond to their values.

Work Values Across Cultures

It is by now a cliché to observe that business has become global in its scope—Japanese cars dot American roads; Mickey Mouse invades Japan and France; McDonald's opens in Moscow; Wall Street devotes intense interest to the Tokyo stock exchange; Europe unites as a trading block. All of this activity and evident success tends to obscure just how difficult it can be to forge business links across cultures. For example, research has shown that anywhere from 16 to 40 percent of managers who are given foreign assignments terminate them early because they perform poorly or don't adjust to the culture.[4] Similarly, there is a lengthy history of failed business negotiations attributable to cross-cultural differences. At the root of many of these problems might be a lack of appreciation of basic differences in work-related values across cultures.

Work Centrality   To begin at the beginning, work itself is valued differently across cultures. One large-scale survey of over 8,000 individuals in seven nations found marked cross-national differences in the extent to which work was perceived as a central life interest.[5] As shown in Exhibit 5–1 on page 125, Japan topped the list, with very high work centrality. Belgians and Americans exhibited average work centrality; the British scored low.

One question in the survey asked respondents whether they would continue working if they won a large amount of money in a lottery. As you might imagine, those with more central interest in work were more likely to report that they would continue working despite new-found wealth.

The survey also found that people for whom work was a central life interest tended to work longer hours. This illustrates how cross-cultural differences in work centrality can lead to adjustment problems for foreign employees and managers. Imagine the unprepared British executive who is posted to Japan only to find that Japanese managers commonly work late and then socialize with co-workers or customers long into the night. In Japan, this is all part of the job, often to the chagrin of the lonely spouse. On the other hand, consider the Japanese executive posted to Britain who finds out that an evening at the pub is *not* viewed as an extension of the day at the office and not a place to continue talking business.

Hofstede's Study   In one of the most ambitious survey programs ever, Dutch social scientist Geert Hofstede questioned over 116,000 IBM employees located in forty countries about their work-related values.[6] (Twenty different language versions of the questionnaire were needed.) Virtually everyone in the corporation participated, from blue-collar workers to top executives. When Hofstede analyzed the results, he discovered four basic dimensions along which work-related values differed across cultures:

- *Power distance.* Power distance refers to the extent to which the unequal distribution of power is accepted by society members, including those who hold more power and those who hold less. In small power distance cultures, inequality is minimized, superiors are accessible, and power differences are downplayed. In large power distance societies, inequality is accepted as natural, superiors are inaccessible, and power differences are highlighted. Small power distance societies include Denmark, New Zealand, Israel, and

Austria. Large power distance societies include the Philippines, Venezuela, and Mexico. Out of forty societies, Canada and the United States rank 14 and 15, falling on the low power distance side of the average.

- *Uncertainty avoidance.* Uncertainty avoidance refers to the extent to which the society is uncomfortable with uncertain and ambiguous situations. Strong uncertainty avoidance cultures stress rules and regulations, hard

EXHIBIT

5–1

Work centrality across cultures.

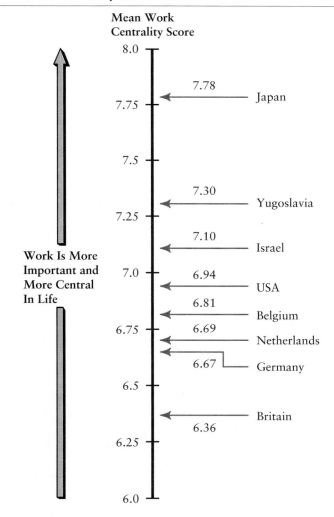

Mean Work
Centrality Score

Work Is More
Important and
More Central
In Life

8.0

7.78 Japan
7.75

7.5

7.30 Yugoslavia
7.25

7.10 Israel

7.0
6.94 USA

6.81 Belgium
6.75
6.69 Netherlands

6.67 Germany

6.5

Britain
6.36

6.25

6.0

Note: **Scores can range from 2 to 10.**

Source: MOW International Research Team (1987). *The Meaning of work.* London: Academic Press: London, p. 83. Reprinted by permission of the publisher and Dr. P. J. D. Drenth.

work, conformity, and security. Cultures with weak uncertainty avoidance are less concerned with rules, conformity, and security, and hard work is not seen as a virtue. However, risk taking is valued. Strong uncertainty avoidance cultures include Japan, Greece, and Portugal. Weak uncertainty avoidance cultures include Singapore, Denmark, and Sweden. On uncertainty avoidance, the United States and Canada are well below average, ranking 9 and 10 out of 40.

- *Masculinity/feminity.* More masculine cultures clearly differentiate sex roles, support the dominance of men, and stress economic performance. More feminine cultures accept fluid sex roles, stress sexual equality, and stress quality of life. In Hofstede's research, Japan is the most masculine society, followed by Austria, Mexico, and Venezuela. The Scandinavian countries are the most feminine. Canada ranks about mid-pack, and the United States is fairly masculine, falling about halfway between Canada and Japan.

- *Individualism/collectivism.* More individualistic societies tend to stress independence, individual initiative, and privacy. More collective cultures favor interdependence and loyalty to one's family or clan. The United States, Australia, Great Britain, and Canada are among the most individualistic societies. Venezuela, Columbia, and Pakistan are among the most collective, with Japan falling about mid-pack.

In Japan, socializing with colleagues is often part of the job, reflecting the high centrality of work in Japanese values. (Gerd Ludwig/ Woodfin Camp & Associates)

Hofstede has produced a number of interesting "cultural maps" that show how countries and regions cluster together on pairs of cultural dimensions. The map in Exhibit 5–2 shows the relationship between power distance and degree of individualism. As you can see, these two values tend to be related. Cultures that are more individualistic tend to downplay power differences, while those that are more collectivistic tend to accentuate power differences.

The most important general message to be taken from the cross-cultural study of work values is that organizational behavior theories, principles, and research from North America might not translate well to other societies, even the one located just south of Texas.[7] The basic questions (How should I lead? How should we make this decision?) remain the same. It is just the *answers* that differ. For example, North American managers tend to encourage a moderate degree of participation in work decisions by subordinates. This corresponds to the fairly low degree of power distance valued here. Trying to translate this leadership style to cultures that value high power distance might prove unwise. In these cultures, people might be more comfortable deferring to the boss's decision. Similarly, in individualistic North America, calling attention to one's accomplishments is expected and often rewarded in organizations. In more collective cultures, individual success might be devalued and it might make sense to reward groups rather than individuals (see Global Focus 5–1). Finally, in extremely masculine cultures, integrating women into management positions might require special sensitivity and timing.

As you proceed through the text, you will encounter further discussion about the impact of cultural values on organizational behavior. Now, let's examine attitudes and see how they are related to values.

WHAT ARE ATTITUDES?

Although your conception of the meaning of the term *attitude* might be vague, you are probably aware that you hold attitudes toward many people and things in your environment. Thus, you might have attitudes regarding the Middle East situation, Mexican food, your job, your boss, and your organizational behavior instructor.

An **attitude** is a fairly stable emotional tendency to respond consistently to some specific object, situation, person, or category of people. First, notice that attitudes involve *emotions* directed toward *specific* targets. If I inquire about your attitude toward your boss, you will probably tell me something about how well you *like* him or her. This illustrates the emotional aspect of attitudes. Notice also that attitudes are much less general than values, which dictate only broad preferences.

The definition states that attitudes are *relatively stable*. Under normal circumstances, if you truly dislike Mexican food and your boss today, you will probably

EXHIBIT

5–2

Power distance and individualism values for various countries and regions.

Power Distance

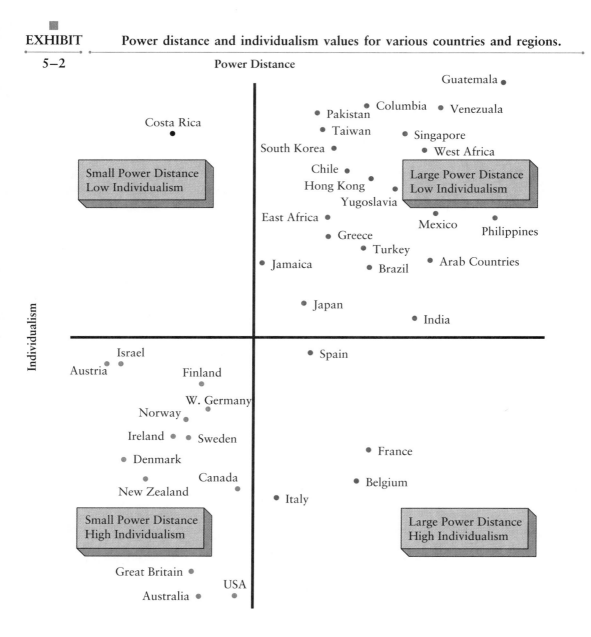

Source: Adapted from Hofstede, G. (1984). The cultural relativity of the quality of life concept. *Academy of Management Review, 9,* 389–398, p. 391. Reprinted by permission of the Academy of Management and the author.

GLOBAL FOCUS 5–1

▼
....
Business Courage, Japanese Style

When I asked a group of 51 Japanese managers about business courage, I came up with a cultural problem. Like the Americans in my study, these Japanese managers were mostly well-educated, male, and middle-aged. What made them different was that in business, as in Japanese society as a whole, people express their identity mainly through the group.

The Japanese view individualistic behavior, even when it involves the introduction of a new idea or approach, as selfish or inconsiderate. New ideas in Japanese business are normally discussed in a series of meetings designed to take the initiative away from an individual and give credit to the group.

In the "kaigi" system, someone presents a report, the boss nods and everyone provides modest support in a modest way. Then someone else offers an "afterthought," making it clear that the idea is just a suggestion and not an attempt to refute what had been brought up earlier. The meeting proceeds this way, with others offering ideas but no one attacking or defending a proposal vigorously. Because of the process, no one person can claim credit for the final plan; the group is responsible. By the same token, no one person is blamed for an idea that fails. Individuals are rewarded by nurturance from the group rather than praised for their individual effort.

Perhaps because of these and other cultural differences, 40 percent of the Japanese managers said they had never acted courageously in their entire career, compared to only 15 percent of American managers. Further, 22 percent of the Japanese managers who said they had acted courageously and had ideas accepted wound up resigning from the organization. They were not fired, but they felt they had to leave. One said his behavior was "embarrassing." Another felt his idea had caused "disruption." No American manager resigned because his or her idea had succeeded.

These different procedures and different attitudes toward managerial courage are another reminder that, while we can learn from Japanese business techniques, we shouldn't simply mimic them. The Japanese approach both reflects and benefits from the country's culture. The kaigi system, for example, works well in Japan. But any attempt to exactly replicate its use in this country would probably fail. It would lessen displays of managerial courage by discouraging individualism without providing the support offered by the Japanese tradition of group nurturance and group success.

Source: Hornstein, H. A. (1986). When corporate courage counts. *Psychology Today*, 56–60, p. 60. Reprinted with permission. Copyright © 1986 by Sussex Publishers, Inc.

dislike them tomorrow. Of course, some attitudes are less strongly held than others and are thus more open to change. If your negative attitude toward Mexican cuisine stems only from a couple of fast food experiences, I might be able to improve it greatly by exposing you to a home-cooked Mexican meal. This provides you with some new information.

Our definition indicates that attitudes are *tendencies to respond* to the target of the attitude. Thus, attitudes often influence our behavior toward some object, situation, person, or group:

$$ATTITUDE \rightsquigarrow BEHAVIOR$$

This is hardly surprising. If you truly dislike Mexican food, I would not expect to see you eating it. By the same token, if you like your boss, it would not be surprising to hear you speaking well of him:

$$DISLIKE\ MEXICAN\ FOOD \rightsquigarrow DON'T\ EAT\ MEXICAN\ FOOD$$
$$LIKE\ BOSS \rightsquigarrow PRAISE\ BOSS$$

Of course, not everyone who likes the boss goes around praising him in public for fear of charges of brown-nosing. Similarly, people who dislike the boss don't always engage in public criticism for fear of retaliation. These examples indicate that attitudes are not always consistent with behavior, and that attitudes provide useful information over and above the actions that we can observe.

The story that began the chapter illustrates the attitudes of Candice and Mike toward their jobs at United Products. Both were emotionally disposed toward the travel required and the nature of the work that the planning job involved. Over the seven months, these attitudes revealed some stability and consistency. In one sense, Mike's behavior corresponded to his unfavorable attitudes, since he quit his job. Notice, however, that his performance had not deteriorated. The attitudes exhibited by Candice and Mike are called job satisfaction. We shall examine these attitudes in detail later in the chapter.

ATTITUDE FORMATION

Where do attitudes come from? Put simply, attitudes are a function of what we think and what we feel. These thoughts are called beliefs, and these feelings are called values, which we studied earlier in the chapter.

Beliefs

Beliefs are assumed facts or statements about the nature of the world that do not involve evaluation. As such, they merely describe how certain concepts or ideas are perceived to fit together. Some examples of beliefs might include the following:

- My boss consults me about many work decisions.

- The four-day workweek improves job satisfaction.
- Close, directive supervision leads to high productivity.

You will notice that beliefs do indeed reveal relationships between concepts (e.g., length of workweek and satisfaction). Beliefs are learned by the processes that we discussed in Chapter 3. Reinforcers might involve direct experience or indirect social reinforcement, which is often very potent. Thus, you probably believe that obtaining a college degree will enhance your earning power because someone whose opinion you respect has told you that this is the case.

What is the relationship between beliefs and attitudes? In a sense, our beliefs set the stage for the development of attitudes. If you have absolutely no beliefs about phargs (whatever they are), it is unlikely that you will develop attitudes concerning phargs. Beliefs contribute to the development of attitudes when some emotion or feeling is attached to one of the components of the belief. If you think that your boss is highly consultative and involves you in many decisions, your attitude toward your boss will depend in part on how you feel about such consultation—is it good, bad or indifferent? This emotional or feeling aspect of attitudes is captured by your values, in this case perhaps the degree to which you value large or small power distance between yourself and the boss.

Belief + Value = Attitude

Attitudes are the product of a related belief and value. If you believe that your boss is consultative, and you value consultation, we can assume that you might have a favorable attitude toward the boss. We can represent this relationship in the form of a simple syllogism:[8]

> If the boss is consultative, (Belief)
>
> And consultation is good, (Value)
>
> Then the boss is good. (Attitude)

Given this point of view, we can now expand the attitude model presented earlier to include the thinking and feeling aspects of attitudes represented by beliefs and values:

$$\begin{matrix} \text{BELIEF} \\ + \\ \text{VALUE} \end{matrix} \Rightarrow \text{ATTITUDE} \rightsquigarrow \text{BEHAVIOR}$$

Thus, we can imagine the following sequence of ideas in the case of the dissatisfied corporate planner Mike Sherrill:

> "My job is interfering with my family life." (Belief)
>
> "I dislike anything that hurts my family." (Value)
>
> "I dislike my job." (Attitude)
>
> "I'll search for another job." (Behavior)

In attempting to understand attitudes, it is important to distinguish between their belief components and their value components. For example, consider the manager of a manufacturing plant that is plagued by low productivity. Working backward through our attitude model, the manager might assume that low productivity (a behavior) is caused by "poor attitudes" toward performance on the part of the work force. Are such "poor attitudes" likely to stem from the employees' values or their beliefs about performance? Either might be true. First, the work force might *value* high performance but *believe* that such performance is impossible to achieve. Beliefs of this nature might include: "My performance depends on the performance of my work group." "My equipment is unreliable." On the other hand, the work force might *believe* that it can perform at a high level but not *value* high performance: "I value a lack of fatigue more than I value making a buck for the company." "I value social interaction on the job more than I value working hard."

Behavioral scientists have not developed the concepts of beliefs, values, and attitudes as an exercise in semantics. To understand the employees' attitudes toward performance, the manager must understand both their belief and value systems. Knowledge of only one system can lead to inaccurate conclusions about what is limiting performance. Also, the kind of administrative action that might be necessary to change the work force's attitudes toward performance depends upon the accurate assessment of these beliefs and values. For example, if the beliefs listed above appear to limit performance, management will have to carefully explore the basis for these beliefs (Is the organization of work into groups limiting productivity? Is equipment really unreliable?). On the other hand, if values appear to be the problem, a different intervention might be called for (such as attempting to hire workers whose value systems correspond more closely to those desired by the organization).

CHANGING ATTITUDES

In our everyday lives, we frequently try to change other people's attitudes. By presenting ourselves in a favorable light (putting our best foot forward), we attempt to get others to develop favorable attitudes toward us. By arguing the case for some attitude we hold, we attempt to get others to embrace this attitude. Thus, it should not surprise us that organizations are also involved in the modification and management of attitudes. Some examples of cases in which attitude change might be desired include the following:

- Managers' attitudes toward racial minorities, women, or older workers
- Managers' attitudes on how to praise or discipline subordinates
- Attitudes toward anticipated changes, such as the introduction of a four-day workweek or new technology
- Attitudes toward safety practices and the use of safety equipment

Most attempts at attitude change are initiated by a communicator who tries to use persuasion of some form to modify the beliefs or values of an audience that supports a currently held attitude. For example, a seminar might be held to persuade managers to modify discriminatory attitudes, or a training program might be developed to change attitudes toward the praise and discipline of subordinates. An information campaign might be implemented in the company newsletter to change attitudes toward conversion to a shortened workweek. Demonstrations and poster messages might be used to persuade workers of the advantages of safety practices and equipment. Persuasion that is designed to modify or emphasize certain values is usually emotionally oriented. A safety message that concentrates upon a dead worker's weeping, destitute family exemplifies this approach. Persuasion that is slanted toward modifying certain beliefs is usually rationally oriented. A safety message that tries to convince workers that hard hats and safety glasses are not uncomfortable to wear reveals this angle. You have probably seen both of these approaches used in seat belt and antismoking campaigns.

What factors influence the extent to which persuasion will actually change attitudes? To answer this question, we must investigate the answers to two other questions. First, who should do the persuading? Second, which techniques should the persuader use? Some answers to these questions have been provided by a large number of experiments that were begun at Yale University.[9]

The Communicator

Who would be most able to change the beliefs or values that support a currently held attitude? Research indicates that **communicators** who are perceived as *believable* are most effective at inducing attitude change. In general, we tend to perceive others as believable when they are seen as expert, unbiased, and likable. To induce attitude change, experts must be perceived as having special skills and knowledge relevant to the *subject at hand*. Thus, an experienced line manager might be an especially credible trainer in a program designed to change new supervisors' attitudes toward praising and disciplining subordinates. In fact, many organizations have begun to use such individuals to do such training exactly because outside experts lack credibility as trainers. On the other hand, such a manager would probably not be perceived as an expert on the ramifications of introducing a shortened workweek and would be unlikely to induce much attitude change concerning this subject.

Besides having expertise, the communicator who wishes to change attitudes must also be seen as unbiased. A safety campaign initiated by a union safety officer is probably more convincing than one initiated by the company's accident insurance carriers. The former will probably be seen as caring for the health and welfare of the work force, while the latter might be seen as attempting to reduce claims costs. This might occur in spite of the fact that both parties are perceived as equally expert in matters of safety. By the same token, union support for a shortened workweek will probably induce more favorable attitudes than will exhortations from the company president, who might be perceived as seeing increased productivity as the main goal of the change.

Finally, likeable communicators will usually be able to induce more attitude change than disliked individuals. It is easy to imagine the thoughts of an audience confronted by a disliked persuader: "If a jerk like this supports a four-day work-week, there must be something wrong with the idea." Not surprisingly, cagey managers often attempt to effect attitude changes among subordinates by converting a well-liked subordinate to their cause.

Persuasion Techniques

There are many **persuasion techniques** used to effect attitude change. Face-to-face persuasion is more likely to change attitudes than indirect communication by memo, newsletter, or posters. This probably occurs because such persuasion is flexible, demands attention, and gives the audience the opportunity to be surer about the credibility of the source. Written communications such as posters and newsletters cannot offer active counterarguments or demand attention, and they might be of ambiguous origin (who knows whether the union or the insurance company supplied that safety poster?).

How much attitude change should the communicator try to induce? It is usually best to stick with arguments that are moderately discrepant with the audience's viewpoint. Positions that are especially "soft" or "hard" are less likely to induce change. For example, consider a seminar leader who is attempting to change the attitudes of male managers regarding the evaluation and promotion of females. Attitudes that females are not cut out for business, and especially for managerial positions, are often strongly ingrained by years of social stereotyping. Thus, the seminar leader would probably hit pretty hard at the inconsistent belief and value system supporting these attitudes. However, it is possible to hit too hard and induce backlash on the part of the audience. Thus, it would probably be wise for the leader to stick to job-related issues of performance and promotion rather than trying to change the managers' attitudes toward women in general.

Finally, should the communicator attempt to present the audience with both sides of the attitude change argument or just stick to the side in favor of change? Presenting only the case for change is effective if the audience is basically receptive and unlikely to generate counterarguments or hear them from others. However, when the audience is not especially receptive and knows (or will be exposed to) counterarguments against change, the communicator should present both points of view. For example, arguments that safety equipment is cumbersome or uncomfortable should be raised and discussed by the communicator. Similarly, the seminar leader should probably acknowledge that in the past, many women have been inadequately prepared for business careers.

Cognitive Dissonance Theory

When communicators are successful in changing attitudes, exactly why are they successful? The **theory of cognitive dissonance** provides an explanation for many instances of attitude changes.[10] Cognitions are simply thoughts or knowledge that people have about their own beliefs, values, attitudes, and behavior. Dissonance refers to a feeling of tension that is experienced when certain cognitions are contradictory or inconsistent with each other (i.e., dissonant). For example, knowing that you have spent a great deal of money on a car that has turned out to be a "lemon" involves inconsistent cognitions that should arouse dissonance. Also, seeing that a workmate's shattered safety glasses protected her eyes in an accident is inconsistent with your having a negative attitude toward wearing your glasses. Again, dissonance should be felt. These examples suggest that dissonance is an unpleasant feeling, and individuals are usually motivated to reduce this feeling.

There are several ways by which dissonance might be reduced. One of them is to downplay the importance of the inconsistency ("I have more important things to worry about than my car"). Another is to marshal additional cognitions that can reduce the dissonance ("At least the car looks classy and prestigious—it impresses my friends"). For our purposes, however, the most interesting way to reduce dissonance is to *change* one of the dissonant cognitions to bring it in line with the other and reduce the tension-producing inconsistency ("My car really isn't so bad"). Notice that this example illustrates a *change in attitude* toward the car that now corresponds to the belief that one paid a lot for it. Similarly, one obvious way to reduce the dissonance between the belief that safety glasses saved a co-worker's eyesight and your own negative attitude toward safety glasses is to change your attitude to a favorable one. Thus, it can be argued that communicators attempt to change attitudes by stressing beliefs and values that are inconsistent with currently held attitudes. It is hoped that this will arouse dissonance, which will be reduced by changing one's attitudes to correspond to the new cognitions.

Changing Behavior to Change Attitudes

You will observe that in our discussion of using persuasion to change attitudes, we have been moving from left to right in our attitude model:

CHANGED BELIEFS AND/OR VALUES →
CHANGED ATTITUDES → CHANGED BEHAVIOR

Indeed, this is the traditional way most organizational attitude change programs are designed. However, our discussion of dissonance theory suggests an alternative approach. Specifically, would it be sensible to change a person's behavior *first,* with the assumption that the person would realign his or her attitudes to support this behavior? Dissonance theory suggests that engaging in behavior that is not supported by our attitudes might indeed lead us to change our attitudes to reduce the tension produced by inconsistency. Such effects have been observed in studies in which people were required to role-play behaviors that were inconsistent with their attitudes. For example, heavy smokers were required to role-play lung cancer victims, and prejudiced whites were required to advocate pro-black

positions. Evidence indicated that attitude change in the expected direction followed the role-playing—the smokers smoked less and the whites became less
negative toward blacks.[11]

In an excellent book, Goldstein and Sorcher argue that the traditional view of
attitude change has not proven very effective in business and industry (Exhibit
5–3).[12] They suggest that attempts to use persuasion to change beliefs and values
often fail to lead to attitude change because the audience is unable to see how the
new beliefs or values will be applicable to their on-the-job behavior. For example,

EXHIBIT

5–3

Models of attitude change.

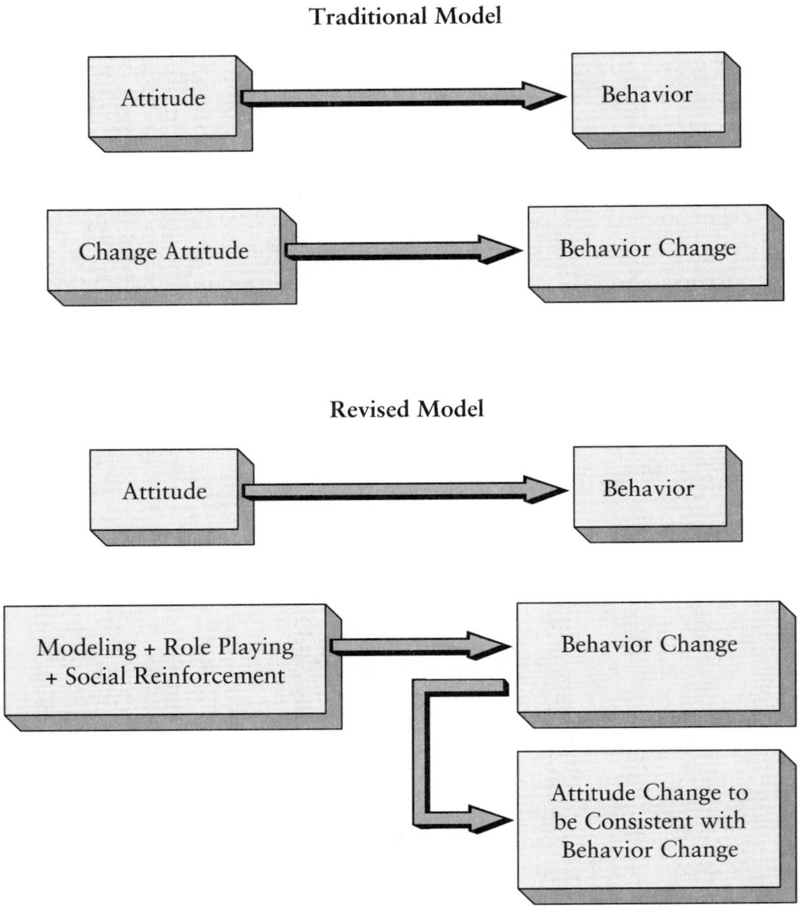

Traditional Model

Attitude → Behavior

Change Attitude → Behavior Change

Revised Model

Attitude → Behavior

Modeling + Role Playing + Social Reinforcement → Behavior Change

→ Attitude Change to be Consistent with Behavior Change

Source: Reprinted with permission from Goldstein, A. P., & Sorcher, M. (1974). *Changing supervisor behavior.*
New York: Pergamon Books Ltd.

trainees might learn that women can be good performers and that they have been discriminated against but not understand how to apply this knowledge to dealing with women on the job. To deal with this problem, Goldstein and Sorcher suggest that individuals should be taught specific *behaviors* that they can apply on the job that correspond to the desired attitude change. When the trainees find out that these behaviors are successful in carrying out their daily activities, dissonance theory suggests that attitudes will change to correspond to the newly learned behaviors. To teach the new behaviors, Goldstein and Sorcher recommend three techniques:

- Modeling of correct behaviors. Videotape is usually employed for this purpose.
- Role-playing of correct behaviors by those being trained. In this phase, trainees get a chance to actually *practice* the desired behaviors.
- Social reinforcement of role-played behaviors. Trainers and fellow trainees provide reinforcement for correct role-playing performance.

The revised model of attitude change suggested by Goldstein and Sorcher is shown in the lower portion of Exhibit 5–3. These techniques have been applied with apparent success by organizations such as Agway, AT&T, IBM, and General Electric.[13]

WHAT IS JOB SATISFACTION?

Recall the story about the corporate planners that began the chapter. The attitudes that they revealed about their jobs are examples of job satisfaction. Job satisfaction is such an important attitude that we will spend the remainder of the chapter discussing it. Exactly what does this term mean? **Job satisfaction** refers to a collection of attitudes that workers have about their jobs. At least two aspects of satisfaction can be differentiated. The first of these is called facet satisfaction, the tendency for an employee to be more or less satisfied with various facets of the job. The notion of facet satisfaction is especially obvious when we hear someone say "I love my work but hate my boss" or "This place pays lousy, but the people I work with are great." Both of these statements represent different attitudes toward separate facets of the speakers' jobs. In theory, one can conceive of literally hundreds of facets that might provoke more or less favorable attitudes, ranging from the size of the parking spaces in the company lot to the color scheme of the cafeteria. In fact, however, research suggests that the most relevant attitudes toward jobs are contained in a rather small group of facets: the work itself, pay, promotions, recognition, benefits, working conditions, supervision, co-workers, and organizational policy.[14]

In addition to facet satisfaction, we can also conceive of overall satisfaction, an overall or summary indicator of a person's attitude toward his or her job that cuts across the various facets. The statement, "On the whole, I really like my job, although a couple of aspects could stand some improvement," is indicative of the nature of overall satisfaction. In a sense, overall satisfaction is an average or total of the attitudes held toward various facets of the job. Thus, two workers might express the same level of overall satisfaction for different reasons. Specifically, they would have offsetting attitudes toward various facets of the job.

To provide you with a better understanding of what we actually mean when referring to job satisfaction, it will be useful to discuss briefly how this attitude is typically measured. The most popular measure of job satisfaction is the *Job Descriptive Index* (JDI).[15] This questionnaire is designed around five facets of satisfaction. Employees are asked to respond "yes," "no," or "?" (Can't decide) in describing whether or not a particular word or phrase is descriptive of particular facets of their jobs. Some sample JDI items under each facet, shown scored in the "satisfied" direction, are shown in Exhibit 5–4. A scoring system is available to provide an index of satisfaction for each facet. In addition, an overall measure of satisfaction can be calculated by adding the separate facet indexes.

Another carefully constructed measure of satisfaction, developed around a somewhat different set of facets, is the *Minnesota Satisfaction Questionnaire*

EXHIBIT
5–4

Sample items from the Job Descriptive Index with "satisfied" responses indicated.

Work

N   Routine
Y   Creative
N   Tiresome
Y   Gives sense of accomplishment

People

Y   Stimulating
Y   Ambitious
N   Talk too much
N   Hard to meet

Promotions

Y   Good opportunity for advancement
Y   Promotion on ability
N   Dead-end job
N   Unfair promotion policy

Supervision

Y   Asks my advice
Y   Praises good work
N   Doesn't supervise enough
Y   Tells me where I stand

Pay

Y   Income adequate for normal expenses
N   Bad
N   Less than I deserve
Y   Highly paid

Source: The Job Descriptive Index, revised 1985, is copyrighted by Bowling Green State University. The complete forms, scoring key, instructions, and norms can be obtained from the Department of Psychology, Bowling Green State University, Bowling Green, Ohio, 43404. Reprinted with permission.

(MSQ).[16] On this measure, respondents are asked to indicate how happy they are with various aspects of their job on a scale ranging from "very satisfied" to "very dissatisfied." Sample items from the short form of the MSQ include:

- The chance to work alone on the job
- The competence of my supervisor in making decisions
- The way my job provides for steady employment
- The chance to do things for other people
- My pay and the amount of work I do

The responses of these items can be scored to provide an index of overall satisfaction and to measure satisfaction on the facets on which the MSQ is based.

WHAT DETERMINES JOB SATISFACTION?

When the JDI or the MSQ is completed by workers on a variety of jobs, we often find differences in the average scores across the jobs. Of course, this could almost be expected. The various jobs might differ objectively in the facets that contribute to satisfaction. Thus, you would not be astonished to learn that a corporate vice-president was more satisfied with her job than a janitor in the same company. Of even greater interest is the fact that we frequently find decided differences in job satisfaction expressed by individuals performing the same job in a given organization. For example, two nurses who work side by side might indicate radically different satisfaction in response to the MSQ item "The chance to do things for other people." In fact, Candice and Mike, the planners who were described at the beginning of the chapter, had decidedly different attitudes toward the same job. How does such a state of affairs occur?

Discrepancy

You will recall that attitudes such as job satisfaction are the product of associated beliefs and values. It would appear that these two factors operate to cause differences in job satisfaction even when jobs are identical. First, workers might differ in their beliefs about the job in question. That is, they might differ in their *perceptions* concerning the actual nature of the job. Given our detailed discussion of perception in Chapter 4, this should not surprise you. For example, one of the nurses might perceive that most of her working time is devoted to direct patient care, while the other might perceive that most of her time is spent on administrative functions. To the extent that they both value patient care, the former nurse should be more satisfied with this aspect of the job than the latter nurse. Second, even if individuals perceive their jobs as equivalent, they might differ in what they *want* from the jobs. Such desires are preferences that are dictated in part by the workers' value systems. Thus, if the two nurses perceive their opportunities to engage in direct patient care as high, the one who values this activity more should be more satisfied with the patient care aspect of work. This point of view concerning the causes of job satisfaction is sometimes called a **discrepancy theory** of satisfaction.[17] This theory holds that satisfaction is a function of the discrepancy between the job outcomes a person wants and the outcomes that are perceived to be obtained. The individual who desires a job entailing interaction with the public but who is required to sit alone in an office should be dissatisfied with this aspect of the job. Similarly, the person who is especially concerned with having a pleasant supervisor might be very dissatisfied with one who is cold and distant. In general, employees who have more of their job-related desires met will report more overall job satisfaction.

Fairness

In addition to a discrepancy between received and desired outcomes, the other factor that determines job satisfaction is fairness. Issues of fairness affect both what people want from their jobs and how they react to the inevitable discrepancies of organizational life. As we will see, there are two basic kinds of fairness. One has to do with the level of outcomes we receive, and the other with the process that led to those outcomes.

Distributive Fairness   **Distributive fairness** (often called distributive justice) occurs when we get from our job what we think we deserve. That is, it involves the ultimate *distribution* of work rewards and resources. Above, we indicated that what people want from their jobs is a partial function of their value systems. In fact, however, there are practical limitations to this notion. You might value money and the luxurious lifestyle that it can buy very highly, but this does not suggest that you expect to receive a salary of $200,000 a year. In the case of many job facets, individuals probably want "what's fair." And how do we develop our conception of what is fair? **Equity theory** suggests that the inputs that we perceive ourselves as investing in our job and the outcomes that the job provides for us are compared against the inputs and outcomes of some other relevant person or group.[18] Equity will be perceived when the following distribution ratios exist:

$$\frac{\text{My outcomes}}{\text{My inputs}} = \frac{\text{Other's outcomes}}{\text{Other's inputs}}$$

Inputs consist of anything that individuals consider relevant to their exchange with the organization, anything that they give up, offer, or trade to the organization. These might include factors such as education, training, seniority, hard work, high-quality work, and so on. **Outcomes** are those factors that the organization distributes in return for the inputs. The most relevant outcomes are represented by the job facets discussed earlier—things such as pay, promotions, supervision, the nature of the work, and so on. The "other" might be a co-worker performing the same job, a number of co-workers, or even one's conception of all the individuals in one's occupation. For example, the president of the Ford Motor

Company probably compares his outcome/input ratio with those that he assumes exist for the presidents of General Motors and Chrysler. You probably compare your outcome/input ratio in your organizational behavior class with that of one or more fellow students.

Equity theory has important implications for job satisfaction. First, inequity itself is a dissatisfying state of affairs, especially when we ourselves are on the "short end of the stick." For example, suppose you see the hours spent studying as your main input to your organizational behavior class and the final grade as an important outcome. Imagine that a friend in the class is your comparison person. Under these conditions, the following situations appear equitable and should not provoke dissatisfaction on your part:

$$\frac{\text{YOU}}{\text{C grade}} = \frac{\text{FRIEND}}{\text{A grade}} \qquad or \qquad \frac{\text{YOU}}{\text{A grade}} = \frac{\text{FRIEND}}{\text{C grade}}$$

$$\frac{\text{C grade}}{50 \text{ hours}} = \frac{\text{A grade}}{100 \text{ hours}} \qquad or \qquad \frac{\text{A grade}}{60 \text{ hours}} = \frac{\text{C grade}}{30 \text{ hours}}$$

In each of these cases, a "fair" relationship seems to exist between study time and grades distributed. Now consider the following relationships:

$$\frac{\text{YOU}}{\frac{\text{C grade}}{100 \text{ hours}}} \neq \frac{\text{FRIEND}}{\frac{\text{A grade}}{50 \text{ hours}}} \qquad or \qquad \frac{\text{YOU}}{\frac{\text{A grade}}{30 \text{ hours}}} \neq \frac{\text{FRIEND}}{\frac{\text{C grade}}{60 \text{ hours}}}$$

In each of these situations, an unfair connection appears to exist between study time and grades received, and you should perceive inequity. However, the situation on the left, in which you put in more work for a lower grade, should be most likely to prompt dissatisfaction. This is a "short end of the stick" situation. Conditions such as this often lead to dissatisfaction in organizational life. For example, the employee who frequently remains on the job after regular hours (input) and receives no special praise or extra pay (outcome) might perceive inequity and feel dissatisfied. Similarly, the teacher who obtains a Master's degree (input) and receives no extra compensation (outcome) might react the same way if others have been rewarded for achieving extra education. Equity considerations also have an indirect effect on job satisfaction by influencing what people want from their jobs. If you study 100 hours while the rest of the students average 50 hours, you will expect a higher grade than the class average. By the same token, in a school system that usually provides higher pay for extra education, the teacher who receives a Master's degree will demand a raise.

In summary, the equitable distribution of work outcomes contributes to job satisfaction by providing for feelings of distributive fairness. However, let's remember our earlier discussion of cross-cultural differences in values. The equity concept suggests that outcomes should be tied to individual contributions or inputs. This corresponds well with the individualistic North American culture. In more collective cultures, *equality* of outcomes might produce more feeling of distributive fairness. In more feminine cultures, allocating outcomes according to *need* (rather than performance) might provide for distributive fairness.

Procedural Fairness **Procedural fairness** (often called procedural justice) occurs when the *process* used to determine outcomes is seen as fair. That is, rather than involving the actual distribution of resources or rewards, it is concerned with how these outcomes are decided and allocated. An example will illustrate the difference between distributive and procedural fairness: Out of the blue, Alan's boss tells him that she has completed his performance evaluation and that he will be given a healthy pay raise starting next month. Alan has been working very hard, and he is pleased with the pay raise (distributive fairness). However, he is vaguely unhappy about the fact that all of this occurred without his participation. Where he used to work, the subordinate and the boss would complete independent performance evaluation forms and then sit down and discuss their differences. This provided good feedback for the subordinate. Alan wonders how his peers who got less generous raises are reacting to the boss's style.

Procedural fairness is particularly relevant to outcomes such as performance evaluations, pay raises, promotions, layoffs, and work assignments. In allocating such outcomes, the following factors contribute to perceptions of procedural fairness:[19]

- Adequate reasons are given for decisions taken.
- The allocator follows consistent procedures over time and across people.
- The allocator uses accurate information and appears to be unbiased.
- Two-way communication can occur during the allocation process.
- Appeals of the procedure or allocation are welcome.

As you might imagine, procedural fairness seems especially likely to provoke dissatisfaction when distributive fairness is also seen to be low.[20] One view notes that dissatisfaction will be "maximized when people believe that they *would* have obtained better outcomes if the decision maker had used other procedures that *should* have been implemented."[21] (Students who receive lower grades than their friends will recognize the wisdom of this observation!) Thus, Alan, mentioned above, will probably not react too badly to the lack of consultation, while his peers who didn't receive large raises might strongly resent the process that was used.

A Model of Satisfaction

Exhibit 5–5 summarizes what has been said thus far about the determinants of job satisfaction. To recapitulate, satisfaction is a function of the discrepancy between the job outcomes a person wants and the outcomes that are perceived to be received. More specifically, greater satisfaction will be experienced to the extent that these outcomes are met or exceeded, they are perceived as equitable compared to the outcomes others receive, and they are determined by fair procedures. The outcomes that people want from a job are a function of their personal value systems, moderated by equity considerations. The outcomes that people perceive themselves as receiving from the job represent their beliefs about the nature of

EXHIBIT
5–5

How discrepancy and fairness affect job satisfaction.

that job. Again, we note that job satisfaction represents a set of attitudes about the job stemming from the beliefs and values of the worker.

In the story that began the chapter, Mike Sherrill encountered a discrepancy between what he wanted from his job and what it offered. He desired a chance to spend some time with his family and the opportunity to supervise others, and the job offered neither. For Candice Rowe, the requirement to travel and the lack of supervisory responsibilities corresponded to what she wanted from a job. In addition, Mike felt inequity because the extra hours that he put in on the job were unpaid. In this regard, he chose to compare his situation with that of his ex-colleagues in his old engineering job. Candice did not experience inequity, since she compared her inputs and outcomes with those of her co-workers who were also putting in unpaid overtime. Thus, Candice was more satisfied with the United job than Mike.

Let's apply your understanding of job satisfaction to this point by considering the You Be the Manager feature.

Key Contributors to Job Satisfaction

From what has been said thus far, you might expect that job satisfaction is a highly personal experience. While this is essentially true, we can make some general statements about the facets that seem to contribute the most to feelings of job satisfaction for most North American workers.[22]

YOU BE THE MANAGER

Job Satisfaction at Steelcase, Inc.

Steelcase, Inc., located in Grand Rapids, Michigan, is a prominent producer of office furniture. It employs around 8,000 people. To remain competitive, Steelcase management had several specific goals pertaining to its human resources:

- Attract the best work force possible
- Keep turnover at a low level
- Fiercely control costs
- Retain nonunion status

   Management was aware that maintaining a high level of employee job satisfaction would be critical in achieving these goals. However, this was complicated by the fact that different employees have different needs and desires. For example, older workers might be especially interested in retirement benefits, while younger workers with families might be most concerned about a dental plan. And a costly benefits plan might not be a source of satisfaction at all for a person who is already covered by a spouse's plan elsewhere. Also, consider working hours, a particular concern for working mothers. A number of office workers found the usual fixed schedule inconvenient, and a number of otherwise excellent job candidates didn't have a full forty hours a week to devote to working. Management was convinced that job satisfaction could be boosted and that it could achieve its human resources goals. What do *you* think?

1. Use the discrepancy theory of job satisfaction to explain the general problem facing Steelcase.

2. What would you do to boost job satisfaction, given the specific issues noted above?

To find out what Steelcase did, see The Manager's Notebook at the end of the chapter.

Source: Adapted from Cohn, B. (1988, August 1). A glimpse of the 'flex' future. *Newsweek*, 38–39.

Mentally Challenging Work This is work that tests employees' skills and abilities and allows them to set their own working pace. Such work is usually perceived as personally involving and important and provides the worker with clear feedback regarding performance. Of course, some types of work can be too challenging, and this can result in feelings of failure and reduced satisfaction. In addition, some employees seem to prefer repetitive, unchallenging work that makes few demands on them.

High Pay It should not surprise you that pay and satisfaction are positively related. However, not everyone is equally desirous of money, and some workers are certainly willing to accept less physically demanding work, less responsibility, or fewer working hours for lower pay. Individual differences in preferences for pay are especially obvious in the case of employee reactions to overtime work. In most companies, one finds a group of employees who are especially anxious to earn extra money through overtime and another group that actively avoids overtime work.

Promotions The ready availability of promotions administered according to a fair system contributes to job satisfaction. Ample opportunity for promotion is an important contributor to job satisfaction because promotions contain a number of valued signals about a person's self-worth. Some of these signals may be mate-

Steelcase, Inc. uses innovative strategies to increase job satisfaction. (James Schnepf/Woodfin Camp & Associates)

Friendly
co-workers can
be an important
source of job
satisfaction,
especially in
non-management
jobs. (Jim Har-
rison/Stock
Boston)

rial (such as an accompanying raise), while others are of a social nature (recognition within the organization and increased prestige in the community). Of course,
there are cultural and individual differences in what is seen to constitute a fair
promotion system. Some employees might prefer a strict seniority system, while
others might wish for a system based strictly upon job performance. In addition,
some people are more concerned with the opportunity for promotions than others. It is these people for whom fair and ample opportunities will contribute most
to job satisfaction. Individuals who are unwilling or unable to accept the extra
work or responsibility that accompanies promotion will probably be less concerned with opportunities and fairness, and these factors will exert less influence
on their job satisfaction.

People It should not surprise you that friendly, considerate, good-natured superiors and co-workers contribute to job satisfaction. Individuals have a need to
affiliate with others, and this affiliation is most rewarding when these others are
"nice" people. In this case, our criterion for job satisfaction is similar to our
criterion for satisfaction in off-the-job relationships—we enjoy people who are
easy to be around. There is, however, another aspect to interpersonal relation-

ships on the job that contributes to job satisfaction. Specifically, we tend to be satisfied in the presence of people who help us attain job outcomes that we value. Such outcomes might include doing our work better or more easily, attaining a raise or promotion, or even staying alive. For example, a company of soldiers in battle might be less concerned with how friendly their commanding officer is than with how competently he is able to act to keep them from being overrun by the enemy. Similarly, an aggressive young executive might like a considerate boss but prefer even more a boss who can clarify her work objectives and see that she is rewarded for attaining them. Similar analyses can be made in cases in which co-workers help us achieve our goals. The friendliness aspect of interpersonal relationships seems most important in lower-level jobs with clear duties and various dead-end jobs. As jobs become more complex, pay becomes tied to performance, or promotion opportunities increase, the ability of others to help us do our work well begins to contribute more to job satisfaction.

THE CONSEQUENCES OF JOB DISSATISFACTION

If you have to spend eight hours a day five days a week on the job, it would obviously be worthwhile for you to have favorable attitudes toward that job. Thus, job satisfaction is an attitude worthy of interest in and of itself. However, job satisfaction also has important personal and organizational consequences beyond mere happiness with the job. In this section we shall explore the nature of these consequences.

Mental Health and Off-the-Job Satisfaction

Can your job drive you crazy? Phrased more formally, can job dissatisfaction promote psychological disturbance? The opportunity to participate in satisfying work is often thought to contribute to psychological well-being. In fact, psychologists and psychiatrists frequently use the ability to attain and hold meaningful work as one criterion of adequate psychological adjustment. Although this question has not been very well researched, it would appear that more satisfied workers do tend to be psychologically healthier.[23] In addition, positive attitudes toward one's job are often associated with positive attitudes toward one's life in general.[24] That is, satisfied workers tend to report satisfaction with various nonwork aspects of their lives. Of course, the actual causality in these findings can be ambiguous. For example, it is not difficult to conceive of an individual who becomes psychologically disturbed because of off-the-job factors and *then* encounters problems on the job due to this disturbance, leading to dissatisfaction. However, to the extent that job satisfaction does contribute to mental health and general life satisfaction, this probably happens because of self-esteem. That is, people feel a sense of accomplishment and worth in performing a satisfying job, and this feeling spills over into their off-job life.

Absence from Work

Abseenteeism is an expensive behavior in North America. One estimate pegs the annual U.S. cost at $30 billion and the Canadian cost at $8 billion.[25] On a smaller scale, one expert cites $1 million annually for a 1,000-employee firm with a 5 percent absence rate.[26] Such costs are attributable to "sick" pay, lost productivity, chronic overstaffing to compensate for absentees, and so on. Many more days are lost to absenteeism than to strikes and other industrial disputes.

Is some of this absenteeism the product of job dissatisfaction? The research literature is fairly firm in the following conclusions:[27]

- Speaking generally, the association between job satisfaction and absenteeism is fairly small.
- The satisfaction facet that is the best predictor of absenteeism is the content of the work itself.
- Job satisfaction is a better predictor of how *often* employees are absent rather than how many *days* they are absent. In other words, it is associated more with frequency of absenteeism than with time lost.

Why is the relationship between absenteeism and job satisfaction not stronger? After all, as we noted in Chapter 3, actions with unpleasant consequences are unlikely to be repeated. Thus, it seems that employees who dislike their jobs would be motivated to skip a lot of work. Earlier in the present chapter, it was pointed out that the link between attitudes and behavior is not always strong, and the relationship between satisfaction and absence is an example of this. Several factors probably constrain the ability of many workers to convert their like or dislike of work into corresponding attendance patterns.

- Some absence is simply unavoidable because of illness, weather conditions, or other pressing matters. Thus, some very happy workers will occasionally be absent owing to circumstances beyond their control.
- Opportunities for off-the-job satisfaction on a missed day may vary. Thus, you might love your job but love skiing or sailing even more. In this case, you might skip work while a dissatisfied worker who has nothing better to do shows up.
- Some organizations have attendance control policies that can influence absence more than satisfaction does. In a company that refuses to pay workers for missed days (typical of many hourly paid situations), absence may be more related to economic needs than to dissatisfaction. The unhappy worker who absolutely needs money will probably show up for work. By the same token, dissatisfied and satisfied workers might be equally responsive to threats of dismissal and to threats of visits from the company nurse if they are absent. These various forms of pressure represent attempts to get employees to come to work whether or not they are satisfied.
- On many jobs, it might be unclear to workers how much absenteeism is reasonable or sensible. With a lack of company guidelines, workers might look to the behavior of their peers for a norm to guide their behavior. This

norm and its corresponding "absence culture" might have a stronger effect than the individual employee's satisfaction with his or her job.[28]

The high level of absenteeism in Sweden (Global Focus 5–2) is unlikely to be due to extreme job dissatisfaction. Rather, it is probably a product of lack of organizational controls and a national absence culture that is tolerant of the behavior. Liberal attitudes toward absence itself have developed.

Research regarding the connection between job satisfaction and absence has some interesting implications for managing absenteeism. For one thing, general increases in job satisfaction will probably have little effect on absence levels unless this satisfaction stems mainly from a revision in job content (a topic that we will consider in Chapter 7). In addition, a high frequency of short-term absence spells is probably a better indicator of an "attitude problem" than a few long spells of time lost. The latter pattern is more likely to reflect medical problems or family demands than job dissatisfaction.

Turnover

As used here, *turnover* refers to voluntary resignation from an organization. Turnover can be incredibly expensive for organizations. For example, it costs several thousand dollars to replace a nurse or a bank teller who resigns. As we move up the organizational hierarchy, or into technologically complex jobs, such costs escalate dramatically. For example, it costs hundreds of thousands of dollars to hire and train a single military fighter pilot. Thus, it is no wonder that turnover (failure to reenlist) has become an especially important problem for the armed forces. Estimates of turnover costs usually include the price of hiring, training, and developing to proficiency a replacement employee. Such figures probably underestimate the true costs of turnover, however, because they do not include intangible factors such as work group disruption or the loss of employees who informally acquire special skills and knowledge over time on a job. All of this would not be so bad if turnover were concentrated among poorer performers. Unfortunately, this is not always the case. In one study, 23 percent of scientists and engineers who left an organization were among the top 10 percent of performers.[29]

What is the relationship between job satisfaction and turnover? Research indicates a moderately strong connection.[30] That is, less satisfied workers are more likely to quit. Thus, you are probably more likely to withdraw from a disliked course than from one you enjoy. However, the relationship between the attitude (job satisfaction) and the behavior in question (turnover) is far from perfect. This is because a number of steps intervene between being dissatisfied and actually leaving (Exhibit 5–6). At each of these steps, the dissatisfied individual might decide that it is too much trouble to proceed further or that resignation would be an unwise move. A few comments on some of the steps in the model shown in Exhibit 5–6 seem appropriate:[31]

GLOBAL FOCUS 5-2

▼
....
Absenteeism Crisis in Sweden

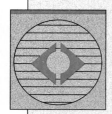

Absenteeism because of sickness is rapidly turning into a national crisis for Sweden. Employers fear it will undermine their international competitiveness by pushing up labor costs and slowing down an already sluggish rate of productivity. It seems that Swedes at work are growing sicker by the year, though their life expectancy remains among the highest in the world. Last year, the average worker collected 23.4 days of sick pay compared with 18.4 days five years ago. By contrast, the average British worker takes 10 days a year off sick. In Canada, illness and injury cost only about 6.4 lost days.

Swedish workers suffer no monetary loss if they stay away from work claiming to be sick. Under a change in the law in May, 1988, they receive benefits equal to their net income, and for the past two years have been able to claim it from the first day.

It would be wrong to deduce from the country's high sick rate that Sweden has a particularly oppressive and dangerous industrial system by international standards. In fact, few countries have better working conditions.

The engineering industry has been particularly badly hit. Last year the average Swedish engineering worker was absent on grounds of sickness for 29 days. In Britain the figure was 11 days and in West Germany 18 days. In 1988, a worker in the Swedish engineering industry worked 1,496 hours, compared with 1,839 hours in Britain and 1,576 hours in West Germany.

The public services sector has enormous levels of sickness absenteeism as well. A recent study in Stockholm county council found that cleaning ladies had 83 days off sick a year, while telephone operators and caretakers were absent 60 days on average because of sickness.

What is being done about this national malaise? The main employers' organization, SAF, pins much of the blame on the 1987 reform in sickness benefit rules. It is proposing that no worker should be able to claim sickness benefits for the first day off work, and it wants Sweden's companies—not the public social insurance system—to be responsible for sick pay for the first two weeks of a worker's illness. Such a change would give companies an incentive to crack down on any abuse of the system. It might also put greater pressure on doctors not to rubber stamp their patients' claims. Companies are looking at ways of increasing commitment to work through productivity bonuses, loans, and profit-sharing schemes, though this conflicts with the traditional Swedish union commitment to wage equality among all workers.

Source: Abridged from Taylor, R. (1989, August 30). Absentees now crisis in Sweden. *Financial Times*. Reprinted by permission of the Financial Times Syndication, London.

EXHIBIT

5–6

Decision process between job dissatisfaction and turnover.

1. Job dissatisfaction experienced

↓

2. Think of quitting

↓

3. Evaluation of expected usefulness of searching for new job and cost of quitting

↓

4. Intention to search for alternatives

↓

5. Search for alternatives

↓

6. Evaluation of alternatives

↓

7. Comparison of alternatives vs. present job

↓

8. Intention to quit or stay

↓

9. Quit or stay

Source: From Mobley, W. H. (1977, April). Intermediate linkages in the relationship between job satisfaction and employee turnover. *Journal of Applied Psychology, 62*(2). Copyright 1977 by the American Psychological Association. Adapted by permission of the author.

Step 2: Certain individuals might be highly dissatisfied with their jobs but do not even think of quitting. Bad experiences with previous job searches or a poor self-image might not even permit *fantasies* about quitting.

Step 3: One key factor affecting this step is the labor market situation.[32] Under conditions of high unemployment, the dissatisfied worker might evaluate the chances of finding another decent job at nearly zero. The cost of quitting also receives serious consideration here. Consider the senior professor who says, "I make too much money here to take another job elsewhere." You might hate a certain class but have to remain in it because it is required for graduation.

Step 7: It is probably safe to assume that comparisons of alternative jobs with one's present job involve equity considerations. That is, the job seeker compares the inputs and outcomes of his or her present job with those that are anticipated on alternative jobs. If the comparison favors the alternative, the person will intend to resign.

Step 8: Substantial research indicates that stated intentions to quit are better predictors of turnover than is job satisfaction.[33] You will recall that one such study was described in Chapter 2. The reason for this should be clear from the process depicted in the model. Put simply, intentions to quit are "closer" to an actual behavior—quitting—than is job satisfaction. Such intentions take into account a number of factors that do not influence satisfaction, and they represent very specific attitudes about *quitting* rather than more general attitudes about the job.

Performance

For many years, the literature targeted at practicing managers was filled with articles extolling the virtues of the human relations approach. In a nutshell, this approach suggested that considerate, humane supervision and a stated interest in the personal needs of employees were useful ways to manage. Such a management style was not advocated on sheerly humanitarian grounds, however. Each article usually indicated that such a style would pay off with increased performance on the part of the work force. Thus, human relations were seen as a good motivational strategy. For our purposes, the fact that this period of management history emphasized human relations (rather than designing more challenging work, for instance) is less important than its assumption about the relationship between satisfaction and performance. Specifically, the writers of that period suggested the following sequence:

GOOD HUMAN RELATIONS → JOB SATISFACTION → PERFORMANCE

That is, it was assumed that good human relations would lead to job satisfaction and that satisfaction would in turn stimulate high performance. In discussing the causes of job satisfaction, we have pointed out that certain human relations practices do lead to increased satisfaction. But, does satisfaction (however achieved) lead to high performance?

With reference to the quiz presented in Chapter 2, you will recall that satisfied workers are not generally much more productive than dissatisfied workers. In fact, a large body of research shows that the relationship between satisfaction and performance is positive but usually very low and often inconsistent.[34] Why is this correlation between job attitudes and job behavior so low? Intuition suggests that we might work harder to pay back the organization for a satisfying job. However, intuition also suggests that we might be so busy enjoying our satisfying job that we have little *time* to be productive. For example, satisfying co-workers and a pleasant superior might lead us to devote more time to social interactions than to work. These contradictory intuitions provoke suspicion that the **"satisfaction causes performance" hypothesis** might be incorrect.

In recent years, the "satisfaction causes performance" hypothesis has been replaced by the so-called **"performance causes satisfaction" hypothesis.**[35] On the face of it, this viewpoint seems rather curious. How does performance lead to satisfaction? Specifically, performance would seem to lead to satisfaction when the performance is *followed by rewards*. That is:

PERFORMANCE → REWARDS → JOB SATISFACTION

For example, if you study hard for a midterm exam and are rewarded with a good grade, you should be satisfied with at least some aspects of the course. In this case your performance would be related to your satisfaction because the performance was rewarded. Similarly, if a supermarket manager increases his store's sales by 30 percent (performance) and is then promoted to district manager (reward), this should increase his job satisfaction. Again, in cases like this, performance and satisfaction should be fairly closely related. Now for a final crucial question: If performance does cause satisfaction, why do so many studies show a very low relationship between the two variables? Put very simply, many organizations do not do a very good job of tying rewards to performance. In many cases, especially high productivity is not followed by a promotion, extra pay, or assignment to a more interesting task. For example, you have probably experienced doing what you thought was a good job in a course only to receive a mediocre grade. It is doubtful that such an outcome will cause you to be happy with the course. In Chapters 6 and 7 we will consider in greater detail why organizations should attempt to link rewards to performance and why it is often difficult to do so. For the moment, it is sufficient to understand that simply increasing employees' satisfaction should not cause them to perform better.

Organizational Citizenship Behavior

Despite your author's best efforts in the previous section, you might well be saying to yourself, "Wait a minute. Somehow, some way, job satisfaction has to have some impact on the extent to which employees will 'go the extra mile,' the extent to which they'll cooperate to get the job done." In fact, you could be correct. Recent theory and research suggests that although job satisfaction is not closely related to formal performance measures, it is more strongly related to the informal "citizenship" aspects of organizational membership. **Organizational citizenship behavior** (OCB) is voluntary, informal behavior that contributes to organizational effectiveness.[36] In many cases, it does not get detected and rewarded by the formal performance evaluation system.

An example of OCB should clarify the concept. You are struggling to master a particularly difficult piece of software and making the attendant noises of discouragement. A colleague at the next desk, busy on her own rush job, comes over and offers assistance. Irritated with the software, you aren't even very grateful at first, but within ten minutes you've solved the problem with her help. Notice the defining characteristics of this example of OCB:

- The behavior is voluntary. It is not included in her job description.
- The behavior is spontaneous. It wasn't ordered or suggested by someone.
- The behavior contributes to organizational effectiveness. It extends beyond simply doing you a personal favor.
- The behavior is unlikely to be explicitly picked up and rewarded by the performance evaluation system, especially since it isn't part of the job description.

What are the various forms that OCB might take? As the software example indicates, one prominent form is *helping* behavior, offering assistance to others. Another might be *conscientiousness* to the details of work, including getting in on the snowiest day of the year and not wasting organizational resources. A third form of OCB involves being a *good sport* when the inevitable frustrations of organizational life crop up—not everyone can have the best office or the best parking spot. A final form of OCB is *courtesy and cooperation*.[37] Examples might include warning the word processing pool about a big job that is on the way or delaying one's own work to assist a colleague on a rush job.

Just how does job satisfaction contribute to OCB? Tentative evidence suggests that fairness, and especially equity, considerations are the key.[38] If one feels unfairly treated by the organization, especially with regard to pay, it might be difficult to lower one's formal performance for fear of dire consequences. It might be much easier to withdraw the less visible, informal activities that comprise OCB. On the other hand, fair treatment and its resulting satisfaction might be reciprocated with OCB, a truly personalized input.

USING ATTITUDE SURVEYS TO MEASURE JOB SATISFACTION AND EMPLOYEE CONCERNS

A good understanding of the determinants and consequences of job satisfaction can assist individual managers in improving the effectiveness of their work units. However, the potential financial impact of job dissatisfaction (in terms of health care costs, turnover costs, and poor labor relations) has prompted some organizations to take a formal interest in measuring and monitoring employee attitudes on a regular basis. Thus, the intuition of individual managers is supplemented with systematic data about the state of employee satisfaction. For most companies, "regular basis" usually means every couple of years, although greater frequency might be advisable. Printed questionnaires are the most common medium for such surveys, which can be prepackaged or custom tailored. Responses are anonymous, but employees are asked to provide enough information to summarize results by level, job, department, and so on. It is universally agreed that feedback of the results to employees is critical for gaining credibility (see Chapters 11 and 17).

To what uses can attitude surveys be put? One use is diagnosis of existing problems. For example, a survey might suggest that high turnover among engineers is due to boring work rather than low pay. Second, trends in repeated surveys can be used to predict future events such as increased turnover or unionization campaigns. Finally, repeated surveys can be used to evaluate the effectiveness of changes that have been made with the goal of increasing employee satisfaction.

A recent study asked human resources executives in the insurance industry their opinions about the use of attitude surveys.[39] The executives were in general agreement about the value of such surveys. However, only 16 percent of the insurance firms surveyed attitudes regularly! Perhaps concerns about survey interpretation or concentration on negative factors are responsible. Perhaps the human resources executives were unable to convince executives in other parts of their organizations of the value of surveys. Employee surveys have been used extensively by firms such as Sears and Maryland's Preston Trucking.

THE MANAGER'S NOTEBOOK

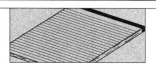

Job Satisfaction
at Steelcase, Inc.

The office furniture manufacturer Steelcase has managed to attract and retain a good work force by putting in place flexible human resource practices that meet employees' varied needs.

1. According to discrepancy theory, people will be satisfied with their jobs when there is little gap between the job outcomes that they want and those that they receive. The problem faced by Steelcase was that its diverse work force had different wants or needs. Thus, a fixed system of benefits and work scheduling was suboptimal in generating job satisfaction.

2. Steelcase uses a flexible "cafeteria-style" benefits package that offers a choice of several medical plans, dental plans, life and disability options, and retirement funds. Employees can also take unused benefits in cash, an attractive strategy for those who are already covered by a spouse's benefits plan. Steelcase also has many of its office workers on flex-time that allows them to participate in setting their own work hours (a topic that we'll cover in detail in Chapter 7). In addition, it has experimented (with mixed success) with job sharing, in which one job is performed by two people who work half-time. These alternative work schedules are particularly attractive to working mothers. Some evidence of the success of the company's flexible practices can be found in its very low 3 percent turnover rate.

SUMMARY

- In this chapter we have discussed the importance of values and attitudes and the impact that they have on organizational behavior. Attitudes are a function of what we think about the world (our beliefs) and how we feel about the world (our values). The fact that individuals have different learning histories means that they may develop different belief and value systems and hence different attitudes. In theory, attitudes are especially important because they influence how we behave, although we have discussed several factors that reduce the correspondence between our attitudes and behaviors.
- One method of attitude change is to attempt to change individuals' beliefs and values through persuasion. In general, this procedure works best when a credible, believable communicator requests a moderate degree of change from an audience. Cognitive dissonance theory suggests that attitude change occurs in cases such as this because the newly learned cognitions are inconsistent with previously held attitudes. Dissonance theory also suggests that attitudes can be changed by getting people to enact desired behaviors that are incompatible with their attitudes.
- Job satisfaction is an especially important attitude for organizations. Satisfaction is a function of the discrepancy between what individuals want from their jobs and what they perceive that they obtain, taking into account distributive and procedural fairness. Factors such as challenging work, high pay, promotion opportunities, and friendly, helpful co-workers contribute to job satisfaction. Job satisfaction is important because it may promote mental health and reduce expensive turnover. Satisfied workers are not necessarily much better performers, since good performance might not lead to the acquisition of satisfying rewards. However, they might be better organizational citizens. Regular attitude surveys can enable organizations to monitor employee satisfaction.

KEY CONCEPTS

Values	Job satisfaction	Procedural fairness
Attitudes	Discrepancy theory	"Satisfaction causes performance"
Beliefs	Distributive fairness	hypothesis
Communicators	Equity theory	"Performance causes satisfaction"
Persuasion techniques	Inputs	hypothesis
Theory of cognitive dissonance	Outcomes	Organizational citizenship behavior

DISCUSSION QUESTIONS

1. State several of your attitudes regarding school or work. What are the beliefs and values that underlie these attitudes? What are some of the behavioral outcomes of these attitudes? Are any of your behaviors inconsistent with these attitudes? Why?

2. The U.S. armed forces have been concerned with changing the attitudes of service personnel toward various racial and ethnic groups in order to improve working relationships. Given our discussion of attitude change, which factors would improve the success of such efforts at persuasion? How might the armed forces implement a behavior change program to foster attitude change?

3. Discuss the pros and cons of the argument, "Orga-

nizations should do everything they can to enhance the job satisfaction of their employees."

4. Using the model of the turnover process shown in Exhibit 5–6, explain why a very dissatisfied worker might not quit his or her job.

5. Use equity theory to explain why a dentist who earns $60,000 a year might be more dissatisfied with her job than a factory worker who earns $20,000.

6. Explain why workers who are very satisfied with their jobs might not be better performers than those who are less satisfied.

7. Discuss the pros and cons of using regular attitude surveys to monitor employee job satisfaction.

8. Describe some job aspects that might contribute to job satisfaction for a person in a more collective culture. Do the same for a person in a more individualistic culture.

9. Give an example of an employee who is experienc-

ing distributive fairness but not procedural fairness. Give an example of an employee who is experiencing procedural fairness but not distributive fairness.

10. Give an example of value conflict between two occupations.

EXPERIENTIAL EXERCISE

Unfairness at Work

The purpose of this exercise is to explore the dynamics of procedural and distributive fairness at work and to examine how they contribute to job satisfaction.

Working alone, students should prepare a brief paragraph in response to each of the following instructions:

_____ 1. Describe an incident at work (or school) in which you experienced *procedural* unfairness. That is, describe a situation in which the process used to allocate rewards or other outcomes was unfair (even though things might have worked out well for you). Why was the process unfair?

_____ 2. Describe an incident at work (or school) in which you experienced *distributive* unfairness. That is, describe a situation of inequity in which your ratio of inputs to outcomes put you at a disadvantage in comparison to someone else. Be sure to be explicit about the inputs, outcomes, and comparison person or group. How did you react?

Students should divide into learning groups of three to five individuals. Half of the groups should be assigned to discuss their examples of procedural unfairness, and the remaining groups should discuss their examples of distributive unfairness. (If enough time is available, each group can discuss both forms of unfairness.)

Similarities and differences in the stories within the groups should be of interest. Groups discussing procedural unfairness should be prepared to report to the class as a whole on (1) the major issues (e.g., work assignments) that prompt unfairness and (2) the key factors that make procedures seem unfair. Groups discussing distributive unfairness should be prepared to report on the (1) inputs, (2) outcomes, (3) comparison persons, and (4) reactions to inequity that were most common.

Michael Simpson

Michael Simpson is one of the most outstanding managers in the management consulting division of Avery McNeil and Co. (Avery McNeil is primarily an accounting firm that has two divisions besides accounting: tax and management consulting.) A highly qualified individual with a deep sense of responsibility, Simpson had obtained his M.B.A. two years ago from one of the leading northeastern schools. Before graduating from business school, Simpson had interviewed a number of consulting firms and decided that the consulting division of Avery McNeil offered the greatest potential for rapid advancement.

Simpson had recently been promoted to manager, making him the youngest individual at this level in the consulting group. Two years with the firm was an exceptionally short period of time in which to achieve this promotion. Although the promotions had been announced, Simpson had not yet been informed of his new salary. Despite the fact that his career had progressed well, he was concerned that his salary would be somewhat lower than the current market value that a headhunter had recently quoted him.

Simpson's wife, Diane, soon would be receiving her M.B.A. One night over dinner, Simpson was amazed to hear the salaries being offered to new M.B.A.s. Simpson commented to Diane,

> I certainly hope I get a substantial raise this time. I mean, it just wouldn't be fair to be making the same amount as recent graduates when I've been at the company now for over two years! I'd like to buy a house soon, but with housing costs rising and inflation following, that will depend on my pay raise.

Several days later, Simpson was working at his desk

when Dave Barton, a friend and colleague, came across to Simpson's office. Barton had been hired at the same time as Simpson and had also been promoted recently. Barton told Simpson, "Hey, Mike, look at this! I was walking past Jane's desk and saw this memo from the personnel manager lying there. She obviously forgot to put it away. Her boss would kill her if he found out!"

The memo showed the proposed salaries for all the individuals in the consulting group that year. Simpson looked at the list and was amazed by what he saw. He said, "I can't believe this, Dave! Walt and Rich will be getting $2,000 more than I am."

Walt Gresham and Rich Watson had been hired within the past year. Before coming to Avery McNeil they had both worked one year at another consulting firm. Barton spoke angrily:

> Mike, I knew the firm had to pay them an awful lot to attract them, but to pay them more than people above them is ridiculous!

> *Simpson:* You know, if I hadn't seen Walt and Rich's salaries, I would think I was getting a reasonable raise. Hey listen, Dave, let's get out of here. I've had enough of this place for one day.

> *Barton:* Okay, Mike, just let me return this memo. Look, it's not that bad; after all, you are getting the largest raise.

On his way home, Simpson tried to think about the situation more objectively. He knew that there were a number of pressures on the compensation structure in the consulting division.

If the division wished to continue attracting M.B.A.s from top schools, it would have to offer competitive salaries. Starting salaries had increased about $3,500 during the last two years. As a result, some of the less experienced M.B.A.s were earning nearly the same amounts as others who had been with the firm several

Source: Nadler, D. A., Tushman, M. L., & Hatvany, N. G. (1982). *Managing organizations: Readings and cases.* Boston: Little, Brown. Reprinted by permission of the author.

years but had come in at lower starting salaries, even though their pay had been gradually increasing over time.

Furthermore, because of expanding business, the division had found it necessary to hire consultants from other firms. In order to do so effectively, Avery McNeil had found it necessary to upgrade the salaries they offered.

The firm as a whole was having problems meeting the federally regulated Equal Opportunity Employment goals and was trying especially hard to recruit women and minorities.

One of Simpson's colleagues, Martha Lohman, had been working in the consulting division of Avery McNeil and Company until three months ago, when she was offered a job at another consulting firm. She had become disappointed with her new job and on returning to her previous position at Avery McNeil was rehired at a salary considerably higher than her former level. Simpson had noticed on the memo that she was earning more than he was, even though she was not given nearly the same level of responsibility as he was. Simpson also realized that the firm attempted to maintain some parity between salaries in the auditing and consulting divisions.

When Simpson arrived home, he discussed the situation with his wife:

> Diane, I know I'm getting a good raise, but I am still earning below my market value—$3,000 less than that headhunter told me last week. And the fact that those two guys from the other consulting firm are getting more than I shows the firm is prepared to pay competitive rates.

> *Diane:* I know it's unfair, Mike, but what can you do? You know your boss won't negotiate salaries after they have been approved by the compensation committee, but it wouldn't hurt to at least talk to him about your dissatisfaction. I don't think you should let a few thousand dollars a year bother you. You will catch up eventually, and the main thing is that you really enjoy what you are doing.

Simpson: Yes I do enjoy what I'm doing, but that is not to say that I wouldn't enjoy it elsewhere. I really just have to sit down and think about all the pros and cons in my working for Avery McNeil. First of all, I took this job because I felt that I could work my way up quickly. I think that I have demonstrated this, and the firm has also shown that they are willing to help me achieve this goal. If I left this job for a better-paying one, I might not get the opportunity to work on the exciting jobs that I am currently working on. Furthermore, this company has time and money invested in me. I'm the only one at Avery that can work on certain jobs, and the company has several lined up. If I left the company now, they would not only lose me, but they would probably lose some of their billings as well. I really don't know what to do at this point, Diane. I can either stay with Avery McNeil or look for a higher-paying job elsewhere; however, there is no guarantee that my new job would be a "fast track" one like it is at Avery. One big plus at Avery is that the people there already know me and the kind of work I produce. If I went elsewhere, I'd essentially have to start all over again. What do you think I should do, Diane?

1. Use discrepancy theory concepts to explain Michael Simpson's feelings.
2. Use equity theory to explain Michael's feelings. Provide details about inputs, outcomes, and likely comparison people.
3. Comment on Mike's likely perceptions about procedural fairness at Avery McNeil and Co.
4. Speculate on the likely consequences of Mike's dissatisfaction if he does not quit the firm.
5. What should Mike do now?

REFERENCES

1. Hofstede, G. (1980). *Culture's Consequences: International differences in work-related values.* Beverly Hills, CA: Sage, p. 19.

2. Spranger, E. (1928). *Types of men.* New York: Stechat.

3. Rokeach, M. (1973). *The nature of human values.* New York: Free Press.

4. Black, J. S., & Mendenhall, M. (1990). Cross-cultural training effectiveness: A review and theoretical framework for future research. *Academy of Management Review, 15,* 113–136.

5. MOW International Research Team. (1987). *The meaning of working.* London: Academic Press.

6. Hofstede, 1980. For a critique of this work, see

Dorfman, P. W., & Howell, J. P. (1989). Dimensions of national culture and effective leadership patterns: Hofstede revisited. *Advances in International Comparative Management, 3,* 127–150.

7. Hofstede, G. (1984). The cultural relativity of the quality of life concept. *Academy of Management Review, 9,* 389–398; Hofstede, G. (1980, Summer). Motivation, leadership, and organization: Do American theories apply abroad? *Organizational Dynamics,* 42–63.

8. Jones, E. E., & Gerard, H. B. (1967). *Foundations of social psychology.* New York: Wiley.

9. Accessible summaries of this work can be found in Middlebrook, P. N. (1974). *Social psychology and modern life.* New York: Knopf; Zimbardo, P. G., Ebbesen, E. B., & Maslach, C. (1972). *Influencing attitudes and changing behavior* (2nd ed.). Reading, MA: Addison-Wesley.

10. Festinger, L. (1957). *A theory of cognitive dissonance.* Stanford, CA: Stanford University Press.

11. Janis, I. L., & Mann, L. (1965). Effectiveness of emotional role-playing in modifying smoking habits and attitudes. *Journal of Experimental Research in Personality, 1,* 84–90; Culbertson, F. M. (1957). Modification of an emotionally held attitude through role-playing. *Journal of Abnormal and Social Psychology, 54,* 230–233.

12. Goldstein, A. P., & Sorcher, M. (1974). *Changing supervisor behavior.* New York: Pergamon.

13. For a review and critique, see Mayer, S. J., & Russell, J. S. (1987). Behavior modeling training in organizations: Concerns and conclusions. *Journal of Management, 13,* 21–40.

14. Locke, E. A. (1976). The nature and causes of job satisfaction. In M. D. Dunnette (Ed.), *Handbook of industrial and organizational psychology.* Chicago: Rand McNally.

15. Smith, P. C., Kendall, L. M., & Hulin, C. L. (1969). *The measurement of satisfaction in work and retirement.* Chicago: Rand McNally; Smith, P. C., Kendall, L. M., & Hulin, C. L. (1985). *The job descriptive index* (Rev. ed.). Bowling Green, OH: Department of Psychology, Bowling Green State University.

16. Weiss, D. J., Dawis, R. V., England, G. W., & Lofquist, L. H. (1967). *Manual for the Minnesota satisfaction questionnaire: Minnesota studies in vocational rehabilitation.* Minneapolis: Vocational Psychology Research, University of Minnesota.

17. Locke, E. A. (1969). What is job satisfaction? *Organizational Behavior and Human Performance, 4,* 309–336; Rice, R. W., McFarlin, D. B., & Bennett, D. E. (1989). Standards of comparison and job satisfaction. *Journal of Applied Psychology, 74,* 591–598.

18. Adams, J. S. (1973). Toward an understanding of inequity. *Journal of Abnormal and Social Psychology, 67,* 422–436. For a review, see Greenberg, J., & Cohen, R. L. (Eds.) (1982). *Equity and justice in social behavior.* New York: Academic Press.

19. Greenberg, J. (1987). A taxonomy of organizational justice theories. *Academy of Management Review, 12,* 9–22.

20. Greenberg, J. (1987). Reactions to procedural injustice in payment distributions: Do the means justify the ends? *Journal of Applied Psychology, 72,* 55–61.

21. Cropanzano, R., & Folger, R. (1989). Referent cognitions and task decision autonomy: Beyond equity theory. *Journal of Applied Psychology, 74,* 293–299, p. 293. See also Folger, R. (1987). Reformulating the preconditions of resentment: A referent cognitions model. In J. C. Masters & W. P. Smith (Eds.), *Social comparison, justice, and relative deprivation: Theoretical, empirical, and policy perspectives.* Hillsdale, NJ: Erlbaum.

22. This material draws upon Locke, 1976.

23. Warr, P. B. (1987). *Work, unemployment, and mental health.* Oxford: Oxford University Press; Jamal, M., & Mitchell, V. F. (1980). Work, nonwork, and mental health: A model and a test. *Industrial Relations, 19,* 88–93.

24. Tait, M., Padgett, M. Y., & Baldwin, T. T. (1989). Job and life satisfaction: A reevaluation of the strength of the relationship and gender effects as a function of the date of the study. *Journal of Applied Psychology, 74,* 502–507.

25. Steers, R. M., & Rhodes, S. R. (1984). Knowledge and speculation about absenteeism. In P. S. Goodman & R. S. Atkin (Eds.), *Absenteeism: New approaches to understanding, measuring, and managing employee absence.* San Francisco: Jossey-Bass.

26. Kempen, R. W. (1982). Absenteeism and tardiness. In L. W. Frederiksen (Ed.), *Handbook of organizational behavior management.* New York: Wiley.

27. Hackett, R. D., & Guion, R. M. (1985). A reevaluation of the absenteeism–job satisfaction relationship. *Organizational Behavior and Human Decision Processes, 35,* 340–381; Scott, D. D., & Taylor, G. S. (1985). An examination of conflicting findings on the relationship between job satisfaction and absenteeism: A meta-analysis. *Academy of Management Journal, 28,* 599–612; McShane, S. L. (1984). Job satisfaction and absenteeism: A meta-analytic re-examination. *Canadian Journal of Administrative Sciences, 1*(1), 61–77.

28. Nicholson, N., & Johns, G. (1985). The absence culture and the psychological contract—Who's in control of absence? *Academy of Management Review, 10,* 397–407.

29. Farris, G. F. (1971). A predictive study of turn-over. *Personnel Psychology, 24,* 311–328. However, the more general relationship between performance and voluntary turnover is weakly negative, as shown by Bycio, P., Hackett, R. D., & Alvares, K. M. (1990). Job performance and turnover: A review and meta-analysis. *Applied Psychology: An International Review, 39,* 47–76.

30. Steel, R. P., & Ovalle, N. K., 2d. (1984). A review and meta-analysis of research on the relationship between behavioral intentions and employee turnover. *Journal of Applied Psychology, 69,* 673–686.

31. In general, tests of aspects of the Mobley turnover model have been very supportive. See, for example, Mowday, R. T., Koberg, C. S., & McArthur, A. W. (1984). The psychology of the withdrawal process: A cross-validation test of Mobley's intermediate linkages model of turnover in two samples. *Academy of Management Journal, 27,* 79–94; Michaels, C. E., & Spector, P. E. (1982). Causes of employee turnover: A test of the Mobley, Griffeth, Hand, and Meglino model. *Journal of Applied Psychology, 67,* 53–59.

32. Carsten, J. M., & Spector, P. E. (1987). Unemployment, job satisfaction, and employee turnover: A meta-analytic test of the Muchinsky model. *Journal of Applied Psychology, 72,* 374–381.

33. Steel & Ovalle, 1984.

34. Iaffaldano, M. T., & Muchinsky, P. M. (1985). Job satisfaction and job performance: A meta-analysis. *Psychological Bulletin, 97,* 251–273.

35. Lawler, E. E., III (1973). *Motivation in organizations.* Monterey, CA: Brooks/Cole.

36. Organ, D. W. (1988). *Organizational citizenship behavior: The good soldier syndrome.* Lexington, MA: Lexington Books.

37. Organ, 1988.

38. Organ, 1988; Organ, D. W., & Konovsky, M. (1989). Cognitive versus affective determinants of organizational citizenship behavior. *Journal of Applied Psychology, 74,* 157–164.

39. Neiner, A. G. (1985). Employee attitude surveys: Opinions and experiences of human resources executives. *The Industrial/Organizational Psychologist, 22*(3), 44–48.

THEORIES OF WORK MOTIVATION

WHY DO *YOU* WORK?

Fred, Al, Tom, and Marilyn met for their usual Friday afternoon drinks at an establishment on Michigan Avenue near the Ford River Rouge plant in Dearborn, Michigan. Although they worked in different parts of the giant Ford complex, they had become friends. As usual, Fred began complaining, this time about his job.

"Man, I *hate* working. It's a good thing the assembly line keeps moving and the bosses are always on my tail, or I'd never get anything done. Been that way all my life. Give me a beer and a shade tree over any kind of work any time. If I could get me a little welfare, I'd quit in a minute. Too bad people have to work."

"Ah, you single guys," responded Tom, who was also on the line. "I've *gotta* work. I've got a wife and three kids to support. I admit I work for *money,* pure and simple. My philosophy is more work for more pay, and I'll take any job that provides the green stuff. Here's hoping the union gets us a good increase this time around," he said.

"Wait a minute," said Al. "I *like* my job. I have a real sense of accomplishment at the end of the day. Don't tell the company, but I'd even take a pay cut to keep doing the same kind of work. That job makes me feel good about myself, and I'll keep hustling for any company that gives me the chance to do it."

Tom and Fred protested in unison. Tom said, "Easy for you to say. You've got a trade, you're a machinist, and you're making a ton of money." Fred simply mumbled that anyone who *liked* work must be crazy.

Finally, Marilyn responded. "Fred, I don't see how you could sit around all day doing nothing. That would drive me batty! Sure, good pay and interesting work are nice, but I took this job to make some new friends. My husband makes a good salary, and I don't have to work, but I'd go insane cooped up at home all day. Working gives me an opportunity to get out and meet people."

Another round of drinks was ordered, and the debate continued.

Explicitly, the preceding discussion has to do with why the four Ford employees work. Implicitly, it also involves some notions about motivation on the job, that is, what makes people work "harder" or "better." As you can see, there is considerable variation in the philosophies of work held by the four employees. How correct are these philosophies? How useful are they for explaining work motivation? These are some of the questions that this chapter will explore.

First, we will examine some commonsense notions about why people work. Then we will define motivation and distinguish it from performance. After this, several popular theories of work motivation will be described and contrasted. Then a model that links motivation, performance, and job satisfaction will be presented. Finally, we will briefly explore a controversy about the compatibility of various forms of motivation.

WHY DO PEOPLE WORK?

Before we begin our formal discussion of motivation, we can profit from an exploration of a very basic issue—why do people work? An examination of some responses to this question will illustrate some themes that have concerned researchers who are interested in motivation at work. At the same time, the inconsistency of these responses should convince you of the need to develop and test comprehensive theories of work motivation.

At first glance, the answer to the question posed above may seem obvious to you: People work because _____. In place of this blank, you have probably inserted a phrase such as "they have to," "they like to," "they want to earn money," "they want to meet people," and so on. In fact, these are the respective work philosophies espoused by Fred, Al, Tom, and Marilyn in the story that began the chapter. Let's examine some of the themes that are inherent in these commonsense explanations about why people work.

The "people work because they have to work" notion is illustrated by the Theory X view of people described by Douglas McGregor.[1] McGregor was a psychologist whose career spanned both private industry and the presidency of Antioch College. According to McGregor, **Theory X** (an arbitrarily coined label) includes assumptions that people generally dislike work, lack ambition, and will avoid responsibility if possible.

There are two prominent motivational themes underlying the assumption that people work because they have to work, as embodied in Theory X. One is that punishment, threat, and close supervision might be necessary to motivate individuals. Recall, for example, that in the story presented earlier, Fred said that he performed to the extent that the bosses were "on his tail." A second motivational theme underlying the notion that people work because they have to do so is that positive reinforcement (in the form of money) can serve as a powerful motivator. Thus, whether or not people like working, they can be induced to do so without explicit threat or punishment. Tom, the family man, voiced this point of view.

Notice that both of these motivational themes assume that motivation is something that is "applied" to workers.

There is obviously a degree of truth in both themes. For example, the Nazis were able to make concentration camp prisoners contribute to the German war effort through force and intimidation. However, punishment and threat do little to explain why people continue to work after they are eligible for retirement, why people work for voluntary community organizations, or why entrepreneurs start their own businesses. Similarly, if people work primarily for money, one is hard-pressed to explain why some people continue working after having won a lucrative lottery or why some millionaires continue to put in twelve-hour days at the office. These contradictory observations suggest that the notion that people work because they have to work provides an incomplete basis for building a comprehensive theory of work motivation.

Now let's turn to the notion that "people work because they like to work," which seems diametrically opposed to the assumption that people work because they "have" to do so. This notion is illustrated by the Theory Y view of people, also described by Douglas McGregor.[2] **Theory Y** assumes that work is as natural as rest or play, and that workers will accept responsibility when self-control can be used to pursue valued objectives.

Like Theory X, Theory Y includes a theme that has relevance for work motivation. In assuming that work is as "natural" as rest or play, McGregor is arguing that work can be *inherently* motivating. That is, he assumes that people can apply their own motivators in the work setting, which may be just as powerful as the close supervision or money that are applied by agents of the organization. This is seen in the use of the term *self*-control.

Obviously, there are some people, like Al in the story presented earlier, who are motivated by the fact that they really like their work. Perhaps the lottery winners and millionaires who continue to work fall into this category. However, if work is really as natural as rest or play, we would expect a substantial proportion of individuals to report that work is a central factor in their lives. In fact, this does not appear to be the case. Rather consistently, North American surveys indicate that individuals are more concerned about their health, their family life, and their standard of living than they are about their job.[3] In addition, it would appear that many jobs in our society do not offer the self-control and valued objectives that McGregor associates with such a concern. Thus, once again, we see that the assumption that people work because they like to work is an inadequate basis for a comprehensive theory of work motivation.

Doubtless, some people work only because they have to do so, and some work because they enjoy working. However, both everyday experience and research evidence suggest that both of these simple commonsense explanations are incomplete and in some sense inaccurate. Thus, comprehensive theories of work motivation are needed to guide our understanding of the complexity of work motives. The commonsense notions suggest some themes that such theories must confront. For example, any useful theory of motivation should have something to say about those circumstances in which motivators are "applied to" workers, as well as those cases in which workers appear to be self-motivated. In addition, such a theory should attempt to specify the *conditions* under which either form of motivation might be more effective or more likely to occur.

WHAT IS MOTIVATION?

The term *motivation* is not easy to define. However, from an organization's perspective, when we speak of a person as being motivated, we usually mean that the person works "hard," "keeps at" his or her work, and directs his or her behavior toward appropriate outcomes.

Basic Characteristics of Motivation

We can formalize the notions presented above into three basic characteristics of motivation.[4]

Effort The first aspect of motivation refers to the strength of the person's work-related behavior or the amount of *effort* the person exhibits on the job. Clearly, this involves different kinds of activities on different kinds of jobs. A loading dock worker might exhibit greater effort by carrying heavier crates, while a researcher might reveal greater effort by searching out an article in some obscure foreign technical journal. Both are exerting effort in a manner appropriate to their jobs.

Persistence The second characteristic of motivation refers to the *persistence* that individuals exhibit in applying effort to their work tasks. The organization would not be likely to think of the loading dock worker who stacks the heaviest crates for two hours and then goofs off for six hours as especially highly motivated. Similarly, the researcher who makes an important discovery early in her career and then rests on her laurels for five years would not be considered especially highly motivated. In each case, workers have not been persistent in the application of their effort.

Direction Effort and persistence refer mainly to the quantity of work an individual produces. Of equal importance is the quality of a person's work. Thus, the third characteristic of motivation refers to the *direction* of the person's work-related behavior. In other words, do workers channel persistent effort in a direction that benefits the organization? From the employer's point of view, motivated stockbrokers are expected to advise their clients of good investment opportunities, and motivated quality control inspectors are expected to discover defects and approve acceptable work. These correct decisions increase the probability that persistent effort is actually translated into accepted organizational outcomes.

To simplify matters, the preceding discussion has been presented from an organizational perspective, assuming that motivated individuals act to enhance organizational objectives. Of course, you are aware that employees can be motivated to engage in many activities that are contrary to the objectives of the organization. Thus, we can formally define **motivation** as the extent to which persistent effort is directed toward a goal. Such goals might include productivity, attendance, or creative job behaviors. Notice, however, that some goals need not be good outcomes for the organization as a whole. Workers might be motivated to be absent, engage in strikes, or provoke sabotage. In these cases, they are channeling their persistent effort in directions that are dysfunctional for the organization.

Extrinsic and Intrinsic Motivation

In our discussion of commonsense views about why people work, a distinction was noted concerning the source of motivation. Some views hold that workers are motivated by factors in the external environment (such as close supervision or pay), while others hold that people can in some sense be self-motivated without the application of these external factors. You might have experienced this distinction. As a worker, you might recall tasks that you enthusiastically performed simply for the sake of doing them and others that you performed only to keep your job or placate your boss.

Experts in organizational behavior have seen fit to distinguish between intrinsic and extrinsic motivation. At the outset, it should be emphasized that there is only weak consensus concerning the exact definitions of these concepts and even weaker agreement about whether specific motivators should be labeled intrinsic or extrinsic.[5] However, the following definitions and examples seem to capture the distinction fairly well.

Intrinsic motivation stems from the direct relationship between the worker and the task and is usually self-applied. Feelings of achievement, accomplishment, challenge, and competence derived from performing one's job are examples of intrinsic motivators, as is sheer interest in the job itself.

Extrinsic motivation stems from the work environment external to the task and is usually applied by someone other than the person being motivated. Pay, fringe benefits, company policies, and various forms of supervision are examples of extrinsic motivators (see the cartoon!).

Obviously, not all conceivable motivators can be packaged as neatly as these definitions suggest. For example, a promotion or a compliment might be applied by the boss but might also be a clear signal of achievement and competence. Thus, some potential motivators have both extrinsic and intrinsic qualities.

Despite the fact that the distinction between intrinsic and extrinsic motivation is fuzzy, many theories of motivation seem to make the distinction. This will be demonstrated shortly.

Motivation and Performance

At this point, you might well be saying, "Wait a minute, I know many people who are 'highly motivated' but just don't seem to perform well. They work long and hard, but they just don't measure up." This is certainly a sensible observation,

Source: Leo
Cullum, *Harvard
Business Review.*
The New Yorker
Magazine, Inc.

"TELL THE COURT..... IS THIS, OR IS THIS NOT, THE CARROT YOUR EMPLOYER DANGLED IN FRONT OF YOU ?"

and it points to the important distinction between motivation and performance. **Performance** can be defined as the extent to which an organizational member contributes to achieving the objectives of the organization.

Some of the factors that contribute to individual performance in organizations are shown in Exhibit 6–1.[6] Notice that while motivation clearly contributes to performance, the relationship is not one to one because a number of other factors intervene. Thus, it is certainly possible for performance to be low even when a person is highly motivated—low aptitude, weak skills, poor understanding of the task, or chance can damage the performance of the most highly motivated individual. Of course, an opposite effect is also conceivable. An individual with rather marginal motivation might "know the ropes" (understand the task) so well that some compensation occurs—what little effort the individual makes is expended very efficiently in terms of goal accomplishment. Also, a person with weak motivation might perform well because of some luck or chance factor that boosts performance. Thus, it is no wonder that workers sometimes complain that they receive lower performance ratings than colleagues who "don't work as hard."

In this chapter we will concentrate on the motivational components of performance, rather than the other determinants shown in Exhibit 6–1. However, the moral here should be clear: Motivation cannot be considered in isolation, and

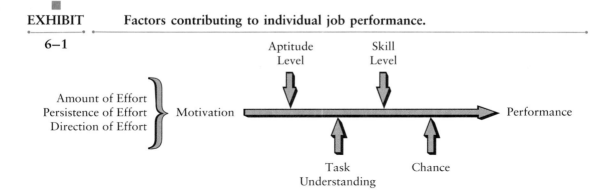

high motivation will not result in high performance if workers lack basic aptitudes and skills, don't understand their jobs, or encounter unavoidable obstacles
over which they have no control.

NEED THEORIES OF WORK MOTIVATION

The first three theories of motivation to be considered are called **need theories.**
These theories attempt to specify the kinds of needs people have and the conditions under which they will be motivated to satisfy these needs in an organizationally useful manner. Needs are physiological and psychological wants or desires
that can be satisfied by acquiring certain incentives or achieving particular goals.
It is the behavior stimulated by this acquisition process that reveals the motivational character of needs:

NEEDS → BEHAVIOR → INCENTIVES AND GOALS

Notice that need theories are concerned with *what* motivates workers (needs
and their associated incentives or goals). They can be contrasted with *process
theories,* which are concerned with exactly *how* various factors motivate people.
Need and process theories are complementary rather than contradictory. Thus, a
need theory might contend that money can be an important motivator (what),
and a process theory might explain the actual mechanics by which money motivates (how).[7]

In this section we will examine three prominent need theories of motivation
and then explore their research support and managerial implications. In a following section we will consider two process theories.

Maslow's Hierarchy of Needs

Abraham Maslow was a psychologist who, over a number of years, developed and refined a general theory of human motivation.[8] According to Maslow, humans have five sets of needs that are arranged in a hierarchy, beginning with the most basic and compelling needs (see the left side of Exhibit 6–2):

1. *Physiological needs.* These include the needs that must be satisfied for the person to survive, including food, water, oxygen, shelter, and so on. Organizational factors that might satisfy these needs include the minimum pay necessary for survival and working conditions that promote existence.

2. *Safety needs.* These include needs for security, stability, freedom from anxiety, and a structured and ordered environment. Organizational conditions that might meet these needs include safe working conditions, fair and sensible rules and regulations, job security, a comfortable work environment, pension and insurance plans, pay above the minimum needed for survival, freedom to unionize, and so on.

3. *Belongingness needs.* These include needs for social interaction, affection, love, companionship, and friendship. Organizational factors that might meet these needs include the opportunity to interact with others on the job, friendly and supportive supervision, opportunity for teamwork, opportunity to develop new social relationships, and so on.

EXHIBIT
6–2

Relationship between Maslow and Alderfer need theories.

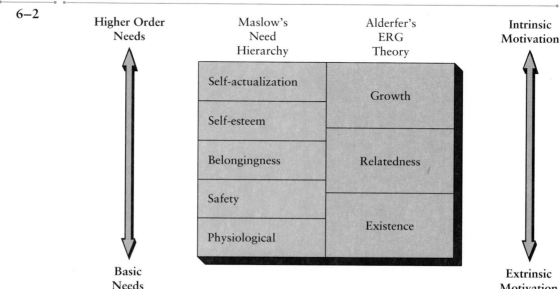

Higher Order Needs · Maslow's Need Hierarchy · Alderfer's ERG Theory · Intrinsic Motivation · Self-actualization · Growth · Self-esteem · Belongingness · Relatedness · Safety · Physiological · Existence · Basic Needs · Extrinsic Motivation

4. *Esteem needs.* These include needs for feelings of adequacy, competence, independence, strength, and confidence, and the *deserved* appreciation and recognition of these characteristics by others. Organizational factors that might satisfy these needs include the opportunity to master tasks leading to feelings of achievement and responsibility. Also, awards, promotions, prestigious job titles, professional recognition, and the like might satisfy these needs when they are felt to be truly deserved.

5. *Self-actualization needs.* These needs are the most difficult to define. They involve the desire to develop one's true potential as an individual to the fullest extent and to express one's skills, talents, and emotions in a manner that is most personally fulfilling. Maslow suggests that self-actualizing people have clear perceptions of reality, accept themselves and others, and are independent, creative, and appreciative of the world around them. Organizational conditions that might provide self-actualization include absorbing jobs with the potential for creativity and growth as well as a relaxation of structure to permit self-development and personal progression.

Given the fact that individuals may harbor these needs, in what sense do they form the basis of a theory of motivation? That is, what exactly is the motivational premise of **Maslow's hierarchy of needs?** Put simply, the lowest-level unsatisfied need category has the greatest motivating potential. Thus, none of the needs is a "best" motivator; motivation depends upon the worker's position in the need hierarchy. According to Maslow, individuals are motivated to satisfy their physiological needs before they reveal an interest in safety needs, and safety must be satisfied before social needs become motivational, and so on. When a need is unsatisfied, it exerts a powerful effect on the individual's thinking and behavior, and this is the sense in which needs are motivational. However, when needs at a particular level of the hierarchy are satisfied, the individual turns his or her attention to the next higher level. Notice the clear implication here that a *satisfied need is no longer an effective motivator.* Once one has adequate physiological resources and feels safe and secure, one doesn't seek more of the factors that met these needs but looks elsewhere for gratification. According to Maslow, the single exception to this rule involves self-actualization needs. He felt that these were "growth" needs that become stronger as they are gratified.

Individuals who are in the lower-level need categories (physiological, safety, and belongingness) seem to be most susceptible to extrinsic motivation, its exact form corresponding to the need that is most pressing. Notice, for example, that extrinsic threat and punishment might even prove to be effective stimuli for individuals who are fighting to satisfy their basic physiological needs. Such people should show little interest in pleasant social relationships or interesting work if they are fighting to survive and might endure strict control in exchange for the basics that are necessary for existence. As further evidence of the role of extrinsic motivation at lower levels of the need hierarchy, also observe that money and money substitutes (e.g., insurance and pension plans) figure heavily here. However, as individuals progress up the hierarchy, and higher-order needs (esteem and self-actualization) become prominent, intrinsic motivation comes into play. Here, organizational conditions must be arranged to permit individuals to "motivate themselves."

Alderfer's ERG Theory

Clayton Alderfer has developed another need-based theory, called **ERG theory**.[9] It involves a streamlining of Maslow's need classifications and some different assumptions about the relationship between needs and motivation. The name ERG stems from Alderfer's compression of Maslow's five-category need system into three categories—existence, relatedness, and growth needs:

1. *Existence needs*. These are needs that are satisfied by some material substance or condition. As such, they correspond closely to Maslow's physiological needs and to those safety needs that are satisfied by material conditions rather than interpersonal relations. These include the need for food, shelter, pay, and safe working conditions.

2. *Relatedness needs*. These are needs that are satisfied by open communication and the exchange of thoughts and feelings with other organizational members. They correspond fairly closely to Maslow's belongingness needs and to those esteem needs that involve feedback from others. However, Alderfer stresses that relatedness needs are satisfied by open, accurate, honest interaction rather than by uncritical pleasantness.

3. *Growth needs*. These are needs that are fulfilled by strong personal involvement in the work setting. They involve the full utilization of one's skills and abilities and the creative development of new skills and abilities. Growth needs correspond to Maslow's need for self-actualization and some aspects of his esteem needs.

As you can see in Exhibit 6–2, Alderfer's need classification system does not represent a radical departure from that of Maslow. In addition, Alderfer agrees with Maslow that as lower-level needs are satisfied, the desire to have higher-level needs satisfied will increase. Thus, as existence needs are fulfilled, relatedness needs gain motivational power. Alderfer explains this by arguing that as more "concrete" needs are satisfied, energy can be directed toward satisfying less concrete needs. Finally, Alderfer agrees with Maslow that the least concrete needs—growth needs—become *more* compelling and *more* desired as they are fulfilled.

It is, of course, the differences between ERG theory and the need hierarchy that represent Alderfer's contribution to the understanding of motivation. First, unlike the need hierarchy, ERG theory does not assume that a lower-level need *must* be gratified before a less concrete need becomes operative. Thus, ERG theory does not involve a rigid hierarchy of needs, and some individuals, owing to background and experience, might seek relatedness or growth even though their existence needs are ungratified. Hence, ERG theory seems to account for a wide variety of individual differences in motive structure. Second, ERG theory assumes that if the higher-level needs are ungratified, individuals will increase their desire for the gratification of lower-level needs. Notice that this represents a *radical* departure from Maslow. According to Maslow, if esteem needs are strong but ungratified, a person will not revert to an interest in belongingness needs because these have necessarily already been gratified. (Remember, he argues that satisfied needs are not motivational.) According to Alderfer, however, the frustration of higher-order needs will lead workers to regress to a more concrete need category. For example, the office worker who is unable to establish rewarding social relationships with superiors or co-workers might increase his interest in fulfilling existence needs, perhaps by seeking a pay increase. Thus, according to Alderfer, an apparently satisfied need can act as a motivator by substituting for an unsatisfied need.

Given the preceding description of ERG theory, we can identify its two major motivational premises as follows: *The more lower-level needs are gratified, the more higher-level need satisfaction is desired; and the less higher-level needs are gratified, the more lower-level need satisfaction is desired.*

ERG theory is particularly interesting in its implications for extrinsic and intrinsic motivation. Obviously, extrinsic motivators are especially likely to satisfy existence and relatedness needs, while intrinsic motivators are especially likely to satisfy growth needs. Notice, however, that Alderfer contends that all three need categories can be operative at the same time. Thus, the opportunity to satisfy growth needs through stimulating and challenging work might prove motivational even though existence needs are not fully gratified. Similarly, extrinsic motivators can sometimes serve as substitutes for intrinsic motivators. For example, the person who is denied a job that provides for the satisfaction of growth needs might respond to an open, trusting, helpful supervisor.

McClelland's Theory of Needs

Psychologist David McClelland has spent several decades studying the human need structure and its implications for motivation. According to McClelland, needs reflect relatively stable personality characteristics that are acquired through early life experiences and exposure to selected aspects of one's society. Unlike Maslow and Alderfer, McClelland has not been interested in specifying a hierarchical relationship among needs. Rather, he has been more concerned with the specific behavioral consequences of needs. In other words, under what conditions are certain needs likely to result in certain patterns of motivation? The three needs that have been most studied by McClelland have special relevance for organizational behavioral—needs for achievement, affiliation, and power.[10]

Individuals who are high in **need for achievement** (*n* Ach) have a special desire to perform challenging tasks well. More specifically, they exhibit the following characteristics:

- *A preference for situations in which personal responsibility can be taken for outcomes.* Those high in *n* Ach do not prefer situations in which outcomes are determined by chance because success in such situations does not provide an experience of achievement.

- *A tendency to set moderately difficult goals that provide for calculated risks.* Success with easy goals will provide little sense of achievement, while extremely difficult goals might never be reached. The calculation of successful risks is stimulating to the high *n* Ach person.
- *A desire for performance feedback.* Such feedback permits individuals with high *n* Ach to modify their goal attainment strategies to ensure success and signals them when success has been reached.[11]

People who are high in *n* Ach are concerned with bettering their own performance or that of others. They are often concerned with innovation and long-term goal involvement. However, these things are not done to please others or to damage the interests of others. Rather, they are done because they are *intrinsically* satisfying. Thus, *n* Ach would appear to be an example of a growth or self-actualization need.

People who are high in **need for affiliation** (*n* Aff) have a special desire to establish and maintain friendly, compatible interpersonal relationships. In other words, they like to like others, and they want others to like them! More specifically, they have an ability to learn social networks quickly and a tendency to communicate frequently with others, either face to face, by telephone, or by letter. Also, they prefer to avoid conflict and competition with others, and they sometimes exhibit strong conformity to the wishes of their friends. The *n* Aff motive is obviously an example of a belongingness or relatedness need.

People who are high in **need for power** (*n* Pow) desire to have a strong influence over others. In other words, they wish to make a significant impact or impression on them. People who are high in *n* Pow seek out social settings in which they can be influential. When in small groups, they act in a "high-profile" manner. There is some tendency for those who are high in *n* Pow to advocate risky positions. Also, some people who are high in *n* Pow show a strong concern for personal prestige. The need for power is a complex need because power can be used in a variety of ways, some of which serve the power-seeker and some of which serve other people or the organization. However, *n* Pow seems to correspond most closely to Maslow's self-esteem need.

McClelland predicts that people should be motivated to seek out and perform well in jobs that match their needs. Thus, people with high *n* Ach should be strongly motivated by sales jobs or entrepreneurial positions, such as running a small business. Such jobs offer the feedback, personal responsibility, and opportunity to set goals noted above. People who are high in *n* Aff should be motivated by jobs such as social work or employee relations because these jobs have as a primary task the establishment of good relations with others. Finally, high *n* Pow should result in high motivation on jobs that enable one to have a strong impact on others, jobs such as journalism and management. In fact, McClelland has found that the most effective managers have a low need for affiliation, a high need for power, and the ability to direct power toward organizational goals.[12] (We will study this further in Chapter 13.)

McClelland is careful to point out that there is not a one-to-one correspondence between a person's need structure and his or her behavior. Needs are only one determinant of behavior, and the person's values, habits, and skills, as well as environmental opportunities, are also influential. Thus, a person with high n Ach will not always exhibit higher motivation than a person with another need structure. For example, a person with high n Aff might perform better than a person with high n Ach on a group task in which high performance is the norm and friendship is contingent on good teamwork. Here, the need achiever's desire to set individual goals and take personal responsibility is constrained by the demands of the task.

Research Support for Need Theories

Measuring peoples' needs and the extent to which these needs are fulfilled has proven to be a difficult task. Thus, the need theories are not especially easy to test. Nevertheless, we can draw some tentative conclusions about their usefulness.

Maslow's need hierarchy suggests two main hypotheses. First, various specific needs should cluster into the five main need categories that Maslow proposes. Second, as the needs in a given category are satisfied, they should become less important, while the needs in the adjacent higher need category should become more important. This second hypothesis captures the hierarchical and dynamic aspects of the theory. In general, research support for both of these hypotheses is weak or negative. This is probably a function of the rigidity of the theory, which suggests that most people experience the same needs in the same hierarchical order. However, in this research, there is fair support for a simpler two-level need hierarchy comprising the needs toward the top and the bottom of Maslow's hierarchy.[13]

This latter finding provides some indirect encouragement for the compressed need hierarchy found in Alderfer's ERG theory. Several tests indicate fairly good support for many of the predictions generated by the theory, including its dynamic aspects. Particularly interesting is confirmation that the frustration of relatedness needs increases the strength of existence needs.[14] When it comes to hierarchies, the simplicity and flexibility of ERG theory seem to capture the human need structure better than the greater complexity and rigidity of Maslow's theory.

McClelland's need theory has generated a wealth of predictions about many aspects of human motivation. Recently, more and more of these predictions have been tested in organizational settings, and the results are generally supportive of the idea that particular needs are motivational when the work setting permits the satisfaction of these needs.[15]

Managerial Implications of Need Theories

The need theories have some important things to say about managerial attempts to motivate workers.

The lack of support for the fairly rigid need hierarchy suggests that managers must be adept at evaluating the needs of individual employees and offering incentives or goals that correspond to these needs. Unfounded stereotypes about the needs of the "typical" worker and naive assumptions about the universality of need satisfaction are bound to reduce the effectiveness of chosen motivational strategies. Recall the story that began the chapter. Marilyn was interested in a job that provided her with a feeling of belongingness and enabled her to affiliate with others. Al, the machinist, was motivated by the opportunity to do a challenging job that enhanced his self-esteem and feelings of achievement. Observing these needs, it seems inadvisable to try to motivate Marilyn by promoting her to a job in which she is socially isolated or to transfer Al to a higher-paying but boring job. Unfortunately, inattention to the needs of individual employees often leads to these kinds of motivational errors. The best salesperson might not make the best sales manager!

The need theories also serve the valuable function of calling to the attention of managers the existence of higher-order needs (whatever specific label we apply to them). The recognition of these needs in many employees is important for two key reasons. First, you will recall from Chapter 1 that one of the basic conditions for organizational survival is the expression of some creative and innovative behavior on the part of members. Such behavior seems most likely to occur during the pursuit of higher-order need fulfillment, and ignorance of this factor can cause the demotivation of the members who have the most to offer the organization. Second, observation and research evidence support Alderfer's idea that the frustration of higher-order needs prompts demands for greater satisfaction of lower-order needs. This can lead to a vicious motivational circle. That is, because the factors that gratify lower-level needs are fairly easy to administer (e.g., pay and fringe benefits), management has grown to rely on them to motivate employees. In turn, some employees, deprived of higher-order need gratification, come to expect more and more of these extrinsic factors in exchange for their services. Thus, a circle of deprivation, regression, and temporary gratification continues at great cost to the organization.[16]

How can organizations take advantage of the intrinsic motivation that is inherent in strong higher-order needs? First, such needs will fail to develop for most employees unless lower-level needs are reasonably well gratified.[17] Thus, very poor pay, job insecurity, and unsafe working conditions will preoccupy most workers at the expense of higher-order outcomes. Second, if basic needs are met, jobs can be "enriched" to be more stimulating and challenging and to provide feelings of responsibility and achievement. This will be discussed fully in the next chapter. Finally, organizations could pay more attention to designing career paths that enable interested workers to progress through a series of jobs that continue to challenge their higher-order needs. In a similar vein, individual managers could assign tasks to subordinates with this goal in mind.

PROCESS THEORIES OF WORK MOTIVATION

In contrast to need theories of motivation, which concentrate upon *what* motivates persons, **process theories** concentrate upon *how* motivation occurs. In this section we will examine two important process theories, expectancy theory and equity theory.

Expectancy Theory

The basic idea underlying **expectancy theory** is the belief that motivation is determined by the outcomes that people expect to occur as a result of their actions on the job. Psychologist Victor Vroom is usually credited with developing the first complete version of expectancy theory to be applied to the work setting.[18] The basic components of Vroom's theory are shown in Exhibit 6–3:

- *Outcomes* are the consequences that may follow certain work behaviors. *First-level* outcomes are of particular interest to the organization, for example, high productivity versus average productivity (illustrated in Exhibit 6–3) or good attendance versus poor attendance. Expectancy theory is concerned with specifying how an employee might attempt to choose one first-level outcome instead of another. *Second-level* outcomes are consequences that follow the attainment of a particular first-level outcome. Contrasted with first-level outcomes, second-level outcomes are most personally relevant to the individual worker and might involve amount of pay, sense of accomplishment, acceptance by peers, fatigue, and so on.
- **Instrumentality** is the probability that a particular first-level outcome (such as high productivity) will be followed by a particular second-level outcome (such as pay). For example, a bank teller might figure that the odds are 50-50 (instrumentality = .5) that a good performance rating will result in a pay raise.
- **Valence** is the expected value of outcomes, the extent to which they are attractive or unattractive to the individual. Thus, good pay, peer acceptance, the chance of being fired, or any other second-level outcome might be more or less attractive to particular workers. The valence of first-level outcomes is said by Vroom to be the sum of products of the associated second-level outcomes and their instrumentalities. That is, *the valence of a particular first-level outcome = Σ instrumentalities $\times$ second-level valences*. In other words, the valence of a first-level outcome depends upon the extent to which it leads to favorable second-level outcomes.

EXHIBIT

6–3

A hypothetical expectancy model (E = Expectancy, I = Instrumentality,
V = Valence).

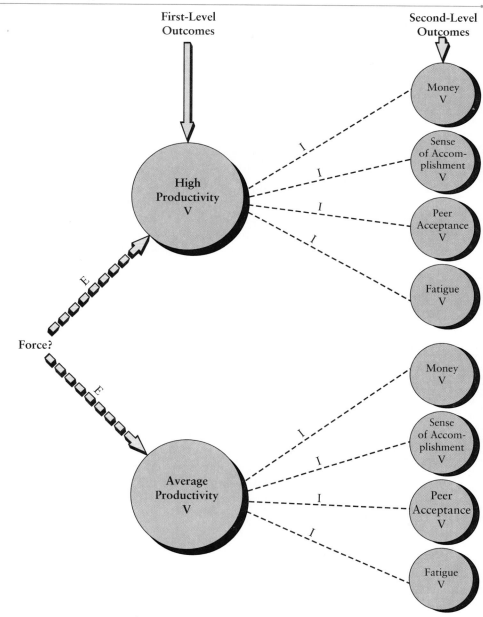

- **Expectancy** is the probability that the worker can actually achieve a particular first-level outcome. For example, a machinist might be absolutely certain (expectancy = 1.0) that she can perform at an average level (producing 15 units a day) but less certain (expectancy = .6) that she can perform at a high level (producing 20 units a day).
- *Force* is the end-product of the other components of the theory. It represents the relative degree of effort that will be directed toward various first-level outcomes. According to Vroom, the force directed toward a first-level outcome is a product of the valence of that outcome and the expectancy that it can be achieved. Thus, *force = first-level valence × expectancy.* An individual's effort can be expected to be directed toward the first-level outcome that has the largest force product. Notice that no matter how valent a particular first-level outcome might be, a person will not be motivated to achieve it if the expectancy of accomplishment approaches zero.

Believe it or not, the mechanics of expectancy theory can be distilled into a couple of simple sentences! In fact, these sentences nicely capture the premises of the theory: *People will be motivated to engage in those work activities that they find attractive and that they feel they can accomplish. The attractiveness of various work activities depends upon the extent to which they lead to favorable personal consequences.*

It is extremely important to understand that expectancy theory is based on the perceptual perspective of the individual worker. Thus, expectancies, valences, instrumentalities, and relevant second-level outcomes depend upon the perceptual system of the person whose motivation is being analyzed. For example, two workers performing the same job might attach different valences to money, differ in their perceptions of the instrumentality of performance for obtaining high pay, and differ in their expectations of being able to perform at a high level. Therefore, they would likely exhibit different patterns of motivation.

Although expectancy theory does not concern itself directly with the distinction between extrinsic and intrinsic motivators, it can handle any form of second-level outcome that has relevance for the person in question. Thus, some people might find second-level outcomes of an intrinsic nature, such as feeling good about performing a task well, positively valent. Others might find extrinsic outcomes such as high pay positively valent. Either intrinsic or extrinsic motivators should enhance motivation to the extent that they are highly valent and to the extent that they reliably follow first-level outcomes that the individual feels able to achieve.

An Example To firm up your understanding of expectancy theory, consider Tony Angelas, a middle manager in a firm that operates a chain of retail stores (Exhibit 6–4). Second-level outcomes that are relevant to him include the opportunity to obtain a raise and the chance to receive a promotion. The promotion is more highly valent to Tony than the raise (7 versus 5 on a scale of 10) because the promotion means more money *and* increased prestige. Tony figures that if he can perform at a very high level in the next few months, the odds are six in ten that he will receive a raise. Thus, the instrumentality of high performance for obtaining a raise is .6. Promotions are harder to come by, and Tony figures the odds at .3 if he performs well. The instrumentality of average performance for achieving these

EXHIBIT

6–4

Expectancy model for Tony Angelas (E = Expectancy, I = Instrumentality, V = Valence).

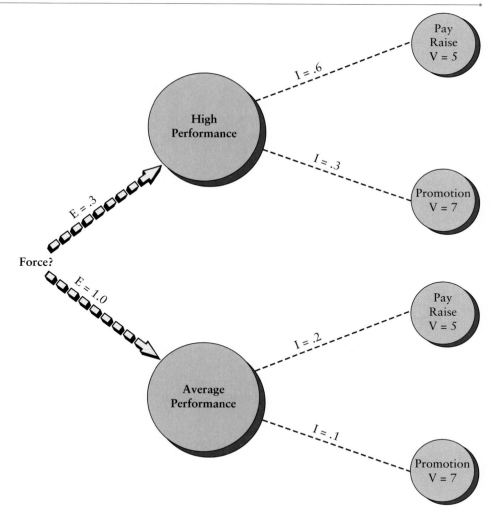

favorable second-level outcomes is a good bit lower (.2 for the raise and only .1 for the promotion). Recall that the valence of a first-level outcome is the sum of the products of second-level outcomes and their instrumentalities. Thus, the valence of high performance for Tony is $(5 \times .6) + (7 \times .3) = 5.1$. Similarly, the valence of average performance is $(5 \times .2) + (7 \times .1) = 1.7$. We can conclude that high performance is more valent for Tony than average performance.

Does this mean that Tony will necessarily try to perform at a high level in the next few months? To determine this, we must take into account his expectancy that he can actually achieve the competing first-level outcomes. As shown in Exhibit 6–4, Tony is absolutely certain that he can perform at an average level (expectancy = 1.0) but much less certain (.3) that he can sustain high performance. Force is a product of these expectancies and the valence of their respective first-level outcomes. Thus, the force associated with high performance is $.3 \times 5.1 = 1.53$, while that associated with average performance is $1.0 \times 1.7 = 1.70$. As a result, although high performance is attractive to Tony, he will probably perform at an average level.

With all this complicated figuring, you might be thinking "Look, would Tony really do all this calculation to decide his motivational strategy? Do people actually think this way?" The answer to these questions is probably no. Rather, the argument is that people *implicitly* take expectancy, valence, and instrumentality into account as they go about their daily business of being motivated. If you reflect for a moment on your behavior at work or school, you will realize that you have certain expectancies about what you can accomplish, the chances that these accomplishments will lead to certain other outcomes, and the value of these outcomes for you.

Research Support Research tests of expectancy theory usually involve asking people in work settings to estimate the expectancy that they have of achieving various first-level outcomes. In addition, they are requested to estimate the instrumentality connections between first- and second-level outcomes and to report the valence that various second-level outcomes have for them. Then, these estimates are combined as dictated by the theory to determine the extent to which they explain some behavior, such as effort expended on the job.

In brief, such tests have provided moderately favorable support for expectancy theory.[19] In particular, there is especially good evidence that the valence of first-level outcomes depends upon the extent to which they lead to favorable second-level consequences. It must be recognized, however, that the sheer complicatedness of expectancy theory makes it difficult to test. For example, we have already suggested that people are not used to *thinking* in expectancy terminology. Thus, some research studies show that individuals have a difficult time discriminating between instrumentalities and second-level valences. Despite this and other technical problems, expectancy theory is generally well accepted by experts in motivation.

Managerial Implications The motivational practices suggested by expectancy theory involve "juggling the numbers" that individuals attach to expectancies, instrumentalities, and valences. One of the most basic things managers can do is ensure that their subordinates *expect* to be able to achieve first-level outcomes that are of interest to the organization. No matter how positively valent high productivity or good attendance might be, the force equation suggests that workers will not pursue these goals if expectancy is low. Low expectancies can take many forms, but a few examples will suffice to make the point:

- Employees might feel that poor equipment, poor tools, or lazy co-workers impeded their work progress.
- Employees might not understand what is considered good performance or see how it can be achieved.
- If performance is evaluated by a subjective supervisory rating, employees might see the process as capricious and arbitrary, not understanding how to obtain a good rating.

Although the specific solutions to these problems vary, expectancies can usually be enhanced by providing proper equipment and work facilities, demonstrating correct work procedures, carefully explaining how performance is evaluated, and listening to employee performance problems. The point of all this is to clarify the path to beneficial first-level outcomes.

Managers should also attempt to ensure that the paths between first- and second-level outcomes are clear. Employees should be convinced that first-level outcomes desired by the organization are clearly *instrumental* to obtaining positively valent second-level outcomes and avoiding negatively valent outcomes. If a manager has a policy of recommending good performers for promotion, this policy should be spelled out. Similarly, if regular attendance is desired, the consequences of good and poor attendance should be clarified. To ensure that instrumentalities are strongly established, they should be clearly stated and then acted upon by the manager. Managers should also attempt to provide stimulating, challenging tasks for workers who appear to be interested in such work. On such tasks, the instrumentality of good performance for feelings of achievement, accomplishment, and competence is almost necessarily high. The ready availability of intrinsic motivation in this case might reduce the need for the manager to constantly monitor and clarify instrumentalities.[20]

Obviously, it might be difficult for managers to change the valences that subordinates attach to second-level outcomes. Individual preferences for high pay, promotion, interesting work, and so on are the product of a long history of development and unlikely to change rapidly. However, managers would do well to analyze the preferences of particular subordinates and attempt to design individualized "motivational packages" to meet their needs. Of course, such packages must be perceived to be fair by all concerned. Let's examine another process theory that is concerned specifically with the motivational consequences of fairness.

Equity Theory

In Chapter 5 we discussed the role of **equity theory** in explaining job satisfaction. To review, the theory asserts that workers compare the inputs that they invest in their jobs and the outcomes that they receive against the inputs and outcomes of some other relevant person or group. When these ratios are equal, the worker should feel that a fair and equitable exchange exists with the employing organization. Such fair exchange should contribute to job satisfaction. When the ratios are unequal, inequity is perceived to exist, and job dissatisfaction should be experienced, at least if the exchange puts the worker at a disadvantage vis-à-vis others.

But in what sense is equity theory a theory of motivation? Put simply, *individuals should be motivated to maintain an equitable exchange relationship*. Inequity is unpleasant and tension-producing, and people should devote considerable energy to reducing inequity and achieving equity. What tactics can be used to do this? Psychologist J. Stacey Adams has suggested the following possibilities:

- Perceptually distort one's own inputs or outcomes
- Perceptually distort the inputs or outcomes of the comparison person or of the group
- Choose another comparison person or group
- Alter one's inputs or alter one's outcomes
- Leave the exchange relationship[21]

Notice that the first three tactics for reducing inequity are essentially psychological, while the later two involve overt behavior.

An Example To clarify the motivational implications of equity theory, consider Terry, a middle manager in a consumer products company. He has five years work experience and an M.B.A. degree and considers himself a good performer. His salary is $35,000 a year. Terry finds out that Maxine, a co-worker with whom he identifies closely, makes the same salary he does. However, she has only a Bachelor's degree and one year of experience, and he sees her performance as average rather than good. Thus, from Terry's perspective, the following outcome/input ratios exist:

$$\frac{\text{TERRY} \quad \$35,000}{\substack{\text{Good performance,} \\ \text{M.B.A., 5 years}}} \neq \frac{\text{MAXINE} \quad \$35,000}{\substack{\text{Average performance,} \\ \text{Bachelors, 1 year}}}$$

In Terry's view, he is underpaid and should be experiencing inequity. What might he do to resolve this inequity? Psychologically, he might distort the outcomes that he is receiving, rationalizing that he is due for a certain promotion that will bring his pay into line with his inputs. Behaviorally, he might try to increase his outcomes (by seeking an immediate raise) or reduce his inputs. Input reduction could include a decrease in work effort or perhaps excessive absenteeism. Finally, Terry might resign from the organization to take a more equitable job somewhere else.

Let's reverse the coin and assume that Maxine views the exchange relationship identically to Terry—same inputs, same outcomes, and so on. Notice that she too should be experiencing inequity, this time from relative overpayment. It doesn't take a genius to understand that Maxine would be unlikely to seek equity by marching into the boss's office and demanding a pay cut. However, she might well attempt to increase her inputs by working harder or enrolling in an M.B.A. program. Alternatively, she might distort her view of Terry's performance to make it seem closer to her own.

As this example implies, equity theory is somewhat vague about just when various inequity reduction strategies will be employed. However, it handles both intrinsic and extrinsic outcomes equally well when they are viewed as relevant to the exchange. In Focus 6–1 shows how equity considerations can affect motivation.

Research Support. Most research on equity theory has been restricted to economic outcomes and has concentrated on the alteration of inputs and outcomes as a means of reducing inequity. In general, this research is very supportive of the theory when inequity occurs because of *underpayment*.[22] For example, when workers are underpaid on an hourly basis, they tend to lower their inputs by producing less work. This brings inputs into line with (low) outcomes. Also, when workers are underpaid on a piecerate basis (e.g., paid $1 for each interview conducted), they tend to produce a high volume of low-quality work. This enables them to raise their outcomes to achieve equity. Finally, there is also evidence that underpayment inequity leads to resignation. Presumably, some underpaid workers thus seek equity in another organizational setting.

The theory's predictions regarding *overpayment* inequity have received less support.[23] The theory suggests that such inequity can be reduced behaviorally by increasing inputs or by reducing one's outcomes. The weak support for these strategies suggests either that people tolerate overpayment more than underpayment or that they use perceptual distortion to reduce overpayment inequity.

Managerial Implications The most straightforward implication of equity theory is that perceived underpayment will have a variety of negative motivational consequences for the organization, including low productivity, low quality, and/or turnover. (See In Focus 6–2.) On the other hand, attempting to solve organizational problems through overpayment (disguised bribery) might not have the intended motivational effect. The trick here is to strike an equitable balance.

But how can such a balance be struck? Managers must understand that feelings about equity stem from a *perceptual* social comparison process in which the worker "controls the equation." That is, employees decide what are considered relevant inputs, outcomes, and comparison persons, and management must be sensitive to these decisions. For example, offering the outcome of more interesting work might not redress inequity if pay is considered a more relevant outcome.

Similarly, basing pay only on performance might not be perceived as equitable if employees consider seniority an important job input.

Understanding the role of comparison people is especially crucial. The fact that the best engineer in the design department earns $2000 more than anyone else in the department might still lead to feelings of inequity if he compares his salary with that of more prosperous colleagues in *other* companies. Similarly, blue-

IN FOCUS 6–1

▼
....
Office Assignments Provoke Inequity, Affect Motivation

Many employees consider status symbols an important outcome of their jobs. Although not all might like to admit it, status enhancers such as company cars, expense accounts, or fancy offices can under certain circumstances be an important part of the motivational equation. What would happen if your work status were "accidentally" increased or decreased even though the job itself and your pay remained the same? According to equity theory, if you consider status an important job outcome, you might respond to increased status with more inputs—enhanced performance. On the other hand, a decrease in status should lead to decreased performance.

Organizational psychologist Jerald Greenberg was actually able to study these predictions in an insurance company. Because of renovations, some underwriters were required to occupy other offices for a two-week period. Greenberg arranged to have some employees assigned to offices that were either one or two status levels above their own offices. Other employees were assigned to offices that were one or two status levels below their usual offices. Higher-status offices had larger desks, they were more private, and they provided more occupant space. Just as equity theory predicts, underwriters assigned to higher-status offices increased their performance during the move, while those assigned to lower-status offices decreased their performance. Also in line with equity research, "underpayment" (reduced status) had a stronger effect than "overpayment" (enhanced status). When the employees returned to their usual offices, performance returned to normal levels. Who says status isn't motivational?

Source: Greenberg, J. (1988). Equity and workplace status: A field experiment. *Journal of Applied Psychology,* 73, 606–613.

collar workers might experience inequity when they hear about the fantastic salaries being paid in exotic locations such as remote mining sites or the oil fields of the Middle East. However, they often ignore the inputs that might be mandated to achieve these high outcomes, such as separation from the family or high housing expenses. Awareness of the comparison people chosen by workers might suggest strategies for reducing felt inequity. Perhaps the company will have to pay even more to retain its star engineer. Perhaps a detailed article in the company

---

IN FOCUS 6–2

Two-Tier Wage Contracts: Institutionalized Inequity?

"Equal pay for equal work" has long been a principle of labor contract negotiations endorsed by unions and generally conceded by employers. For both parties, the principle reflects an implicit understanding of equity theory—that workers who exhibit equivalent work inputs ("equal work") will expect equivalent work outcomes ("equal pay"). However, beginning in the 1980s, following several years of recession, many labor contracts were signed that squarely violated the "equal work for equal pay" principle. In essence, these contracts provide new employees with a much less lucrative salary structure than that enjoyed by existing employees. Thus, under a two-tier contract, new employees generally begin at a lower rate than their predecessors began at. In some cases, new employees can gradually achieve parity with experienced workers. In other cases, the wage discrepancy is permanent. *Fortune* cites Lockheed, Boeing, and American Airlines (pilots, mechanics, and flight attendants) as examples of companies that have introduced two-tier systems. Supermarket chains such as Kroger, Safeway, and Giant Food have gone the same route.

Equity theory predicts job dissatisfaction, lowered inputs, and turnover among employees on the lower tier, who are likely to compare themselves with those on the upper tier. Indeed, there is anecdotal evidence of these reactions in some of the companies mentioned above.

James Martin and Melanie Peterson did a formal study of reactions to a two-tier wage structure among retail store employees. They found that employees on the lower tier reported lower pay equity than those on the higher tier. Lower-tier employees also saw the union as being less effective in achieving fair pay.

Source: Martin, J. E., & Peterson, M. M. (1987). Two-tier wage structures: Implications for equity theory. *Academy of Management Journal, 30,* 297–315; Ross, I. (1985, April 29). Employers win big in the move to two-tier contracts. *Fortune,* 82–92.

newsletter about remote employment will reduce felt inequity for the blue-collar workers.

Having covered the various motivation theories, let's use them to evaluate an actual motivation program. Please consult You Be the Manager.

DO MOTIVATION THEORIES TRANSLATE ACROSS CULTURES?

Are the motivation theories that we have been considering in this chapter culture-bound? That is, do they apply only to North America, where they were developed? The answer to this question is important for North American organizations that wish to understand motivational patterns in their international operations. It is also important to foreign managers, who are often exposed to North American theory and practice as part of their training and development.

It is safe to assume that most theories that revolve around human needs will come up against cultural limitations to their generality. For example, both Maslow and Alderfer suggest that people pass through a social stage (belongingness, relatedness) on their way to a higher-level personal growth or self-actualization stage. However, as discussed in the previous chapter, it is well established that there are cross-national differences in the extent to which societies value a more

"The American Airlines two-tier wage scale pays people doing the same job at different rates. What would equity theory predict about their reactions? See also In Focus 6–1 and In Focus 6–2. (Courtesy American Airlines)

YOU BE THE MANAGER

Manager

DuPont's Achievement Sharing Program

Facing stiff domestic and global competition, DuPont's largest division, the fibers division, determined that a radical change in strategy and structure was necessary. This was begun by reducing the work force from 27,000 to 20,000. In turn, as in many contemporary "downsized" organizations, employees were required to learn new skills. These skills were to be employed in self-directed teams.

Management was especially concerned with developing a new compensation system that would reinforce the team spirit and concentrate employee attention squarely on the business strategy of improved competitiveness. To this end, it developed the Achievement Sharing Program, a program that tied employee pay to fibers division profits and losses. A specific goal of 4 percent growth in profits each year was set. Gradually, through a reduction in regular raises, base pay in the division was to be reduced 6 percent compared to other DuPont divisions. If the profit goal was achieved, fibers employees would get back the 6 percent as a bonus. If 80 percent of the goal was achieved, they would get 3 percent; less than 80 percent would result in no bonus. On the other hand, 150 percent of the goal would result in a 12 percent bonus. A worker who had been earning $30,000 would now earn between $28,200 and $33,600, depending on the fibers division's yearly profit picture.

Use the questions below to frame *your* opinion about the motivational effectiveness of the Achievement Sharing Program.

1. Use expectancy theory to evaluate the strengths and weaknesses of the program.
2. How could equity considerations influence employee receptiveness to the program?

For some commentary on DuPont's program, see The Manager's Notebook at the end of the chapter.

Source: Adapted from Ost, E. J. (1990, Spring). Team-based pay: New wave strategic incentives. *Sloan Management Review*, 19–27; Hays, L. (1988, December 5). All eyes on DuPont's incentive-pay plan. *The Wall Street Journal*, p. B1; Santora, J. E. (1991, February). DuPont returns to the drawing board. *Personnel Journal*, 34–36.

collective or a more individualistic approach to life.[24] In individualistic societies (e.g., the United States, Canada, Great Britain, Australia), people tend to value individual initiative, privacy, and taking care of oneself. In more collective societies (e.g., Mexico, Singapore, Pakistan), more closely knit social bonds are observed in which members of one's in-group (family, clan, organization) are expected to take care of each other in exchange for strong loyalty to the in-group.[25] This suggests that there might be no hierarchical superiority to self-actualization as a motive in more collective cultures. In some cases, for example, appealing to employee loyalty might prove more motivational than the opportunity for self-expression because it relates to strong belongingness needs that stem from cultural values. Also, cultures differ in the extent to which they value need for achievement, and conceptions of achievement might be more group-oriented in collective cultures than in individualistic North America. Similarly, the whole concept of intrinsic motivation might be more relevant to wealthy societies than to third-world societies.

Turning to equity theory, we noted that people should be appropriately motivated when outcomes received "match" job inputs. Thus, higher producers are

Do the motivation theories learned in one culture prepare managers to motivate workers from another culture? An American executive talks with colleagues at a construction site in Kuwait. (James Willis/ Tony Stone Worldwide)

likely to expect superior outcomes compared to lower producers. This is only one way to allocate rewards, however, and it is one that is most likely to be endorsed in individualistic cultures. In collective cultures there is a tendency to favor reward allocation based on equality rather than equity.[26] In other words, everyone should receive the same outcomes despite individual differences in productivity, and group solidarity is a dominant motive. Trying to motivate employees with a "fair" reward system might backfire if your definition of fairness is equity and theirs is equality.

Finally, because of its flexibility, expectancy theory comes off pretty well when considered cross-culturally. The theory allows for the possibility that there may be cross-cultural differences in the expectancy that effort will result in high performance. It also allows for the fact that work outcomes (such as social acceptance versus individual recognition) may have different valences across cultures.[27]

One observer has exemplified how cultural blinders often lead to motivational errors:

> International management literature is replete with examples of overgeneralization, due to the dominance of American reward structures. For example, . . . raising the salaries of a particular group of Mexican workers motivated them to work *fewer,* not more, hours. As the Mexicans explained, "We can now make enough money to live and enjoy life [one of their primary values] in less time than previously. Now, we do not have to work so many hours." In another example, an expatriate manager in Japan decided to promote one of his Japanese sales representatives to manager (a status reward). To the surprise of the expatriate boss, the promotion diminished the new Japanese manager's performance. Why? Japanese have a high need for harmony—to fit in with their work colleagues. The promotion, an individualistic reward, separated the new manager from his colleagues, embarrassed him, and therefore diminished his motivation to work.[28]

PUTTING IT ALL TOGETHER: THE PORTER-LAWLER MODEL

In this chapter, we have presented several theories of work motivation and attempted to distinguish between motivation and performance. In Chapter 5 we discussed the relationship between job performance and job satisfaction. At this point, it seems appropriate to review just how all of these concepts fit together. Psychologists Lyman Porter and Edward Lawler have devised an excellent model to portray these relationships (Exhibit 6–5).[29] Boxes 1 through 3 are simply a restatement of the expectancy theory of motivation. *Value of Reward* (Box 1) refers to the valence of second-level outcomes, while *Perceived Effort → Reward Probability* (Box 2) refers to perceptions of expectancy and instrumentality. Thus, an individual will exert effort on the job to the extent that this effort is expected to be followed by valued rewards.

Boxes 3 through 6 illustrate that high effort will be translated into good performance *if* the worker has traits and abilities relevant to the job and *if* the worker understands his or her role in the organization (especially with regard to what the organization considers good performance). If these conditions are not met, high effort will not result in good performance. For example, consider a hospital nurse who exhibits tremendous effort but lacks compassion, doesn't know how to use a syringe properly, and is confused about the respective responsibilities of nurses, doctors, and attendants. Clearly, such an individual will perform poorly in spite of high effort. It is at the link between effort and performance that observers frequently make judgments about the motivation of workers. Thus, our nurse

EXHIBIT   **The Porter-Lawler model.**

6–5

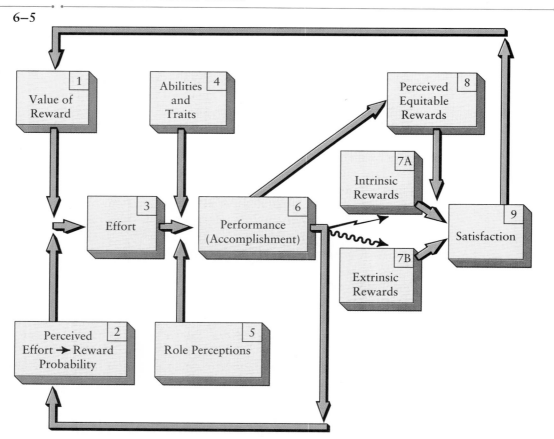

Source: Porter, L. W. & Lawler, E. E. *Managerial Attitudes and Performances*, 165. Copyright © 1968 by Richard D. Irwin, Inc. Reprinted by permission.

might be judged by the head nurse as having "high" but "misdirected" motivation because the nurse is directing persistent effort in a way that doesn't help the hospital achieve its goals. You will see that this portion of the Porter-Lawler model is essentially a simplification of the relationships shown in Exhibit 6–1.

A particular level of performance (Box 6) will be followed by certain outcomes. To the extent that these are positively valent second-level outcomes, they can be considered *rewards* for good performance (Boxes 7A and 7B). In general, the connection between performance and the occurrence of *intrinsic* rewards should be strong and reliable because such rewards are self-administered. For example, the nurse who assists several very sick patients back to health is almost certain to feel a sense of competence and achievement because such feelings stem directly from the job. On the other hand, the connection between performance and *extrinsic* rewards might be much less reliable (note the wavy line in Exhibit 6–5) because the occurrence of such rewards depends on the actions of some organizational agent. Thus, the head nurse might or might not recommend attendance at a nursing conference (an extrinsic fringe benefit) for the good performance.

The availability of intrinsic and extrinsic rewards affects job satisfaction (Box 9) to the extent that these rewards are seen as equitable (Box 8). You will recall that this relationship between job outcomes, equity, and job satisfaction was discussed in Chapter 5. Also recall that in Chapter 5 it was emphasized that job satisfaction does not lead to good performance. Rather, it was argued that *good performance leads to job satisfaction if that performance is rewarded.*

The feedback loop in the lower portion of the model indicates that the worker's actual experience with the connection between performance and rewards influences *future* expectations of the probability that effort will lead to reward. Thus, the worker whose effort is eventually rewarded uses this information to guide future effort expenditure. The feedback loop in the upper portion of the model suggests that the satisfaction derived from job rewards can influence the valence (anticipated value) of these rewards in the future. Sometimes, satisfaction might decrease the valence of a reward. For example, the person who is highly paid, and thus financially satisfied, might not see extra pay that can be achieved through overtime work as highly valent. On the other hand, satisfaction might increase the valence of some rewards. For example, Maslow argued that self-actualization is a growth need. This suggests that as the self-actualization need is satisfied, it should become more highly valent.

In summary, the Porter-Lawler model provides an excellent picture of the motivational process. It is entirely consistent with the process theories of motivation and the concept of job satisfaction presented in Chapter 5.

A FOOTNOTE: DO EXTRINSIC REWARDS DECREASE INTRINSIC MOTIVATION?

Frequently, when students are asked what kind of job they would like to achieve following graduation, they respond, "Give me an interesting job that pays well."

Indeed, this might be the most commonly held stereotype of a good job, and people who desire such a job would probably report that they would be motivated to perform the job especially well. Notice that there is an implicit assumption operating here—intrinsic motivators (in this case, interesting work) and extrinsic motivators (in this case, pay) "add up" to enhance motivation. Thus, from a motivational standpoint, a "Superjob" would be one that is especially high on both intrinsic and extrinsic motivation. Thus far in the chapter, little has been said about the possible **relationship between extrinsic and intrinsic motivation.** However, expectancy theory and the Porter-Lawler model suggest that if intrinsic outcomes and extrinsic outcomes are both highly valent, they should contribute to motivation in an additive fashion.

In recent years, a number of research studies have reached the conclusion that the availability of extrinsic motivators can reduce the intrinsic motivation stemming from the task itself.[30] At first, this might seem counterintuitive to you. However, many parents have observed that linking a monetary allowance to the completion of household chores leads their children to denigrate work that was once enthusiastically performed. Similarly, many professors have noticed that a strong emphasis on grades seems to reduce students' motivation to engage in learning for its own sake. The notion here, then, is that when extrinsic rewards depend upon performance, the valence of intrinsic rewards decreases. Proponents of this view have suggested that making extrinsic rewards contingent upon performance makes individuals feel less competent and less in control of their own behavior.[31] That is, they come to believe that their performance is controlled by the environment and that they perform well only because of the money. Thus, intrinsic motivation suffers.

Research tests of the effects of extrinsic rewards on intrinsic motivation have produced very mixed results—sometimes intrinsic motivation is reduced, and sometimes it is not. Many of these tests have used students as subjects, and most have relied on rather artificial short-term tasks. One review concludes that intrinsic motivation is likely to suffer under these highly restrictive conditions. However, in more realistic settings in which extrinsic rewards are seen as symbols of success and as signals of what to do to achieve future rewards, the hypothesis is less likely to be confirmed.[32] Thus, it is probably safe to assume that both kinds of rewards are compatible in enhancing motivation in actual work settings.

THE MANAGER'S NOTEBOOK

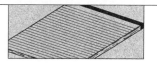

DuPont's Achievement Sharing Program

DuPont's Achievement Sharing Program was unusual in that it built a real element of risk into pay—employees could effectively *lose* money as well as *gain* it. The program was discontinued after two years in the face of two problems: Individual employees wanted to choose the amount of their pay that was put at risk (note how our need theories would explain this). Because of a provision of Securities Act of 1933, such variable compensation would have required the company to disclose detailed competitive financial information about the fibers division. Also, the company was not anywhere near to achieving its profit goal for the second year.

Let's put the Achievement Sharing Program through a motivation theory audit.

1. In expectancy theory terms, the 4 percent division profit growth was a first-level outcome, and the bonus was a second-level outcome. The bonus was clearly large enough to get employees' attention (up to 12 percent of base pay), and it should thus have been highly valent. Also, the instrumentality connection between profit and the bonus was clear and obvious, being spelled out by a formula. Potential problems centered on the *expectancy* that employees would be able to achieve the earnings goal. Outstanding management support would be necessary, as would true teamwork. Also, factors beyond the employees' control could adversely affect profit growth and thus damage expectancy. A weak economy did just that.

2. A couple of potential equity problems could have led to reduced motivation, and they center on comparison people. First, employees in the fibers division might have felt inequity in comparison to other DuPont employees. After all, they would have to contribute more inputs just to get back to par with the 6 percent base pay disadvantage. Also, feelings of inequity could have cropped up within the fibers division if some individuals or units felt that others had performed poorly and were threatening the bonus. Some conflict about this was reported.

SUMMARY

- Commonsense views about why people work were discussed, and it was concluded that such views provide an incomplete basis for a comprehensive theory of motivation. Motivation is the extent to which persistent effort is directed toward a goal. Intrinsic motivation stems from the direct relationship between the worker and the task and is usually self-applied. Extrinsic motivation stems from the environment surrounding the task and is applied by others. Performance is the extent to which an organization member contributes to achieving the objectives of the organization. It is influenced by motivation but also by aptitudes, skills, task understanding, and chance factors.
- Need theories propose that motivation will occur when employee behavior can be directed toward goals or incentives that satisfy personal wants or desires. The three need theories discussed were Maslow's need hierarchy, Alderfer's ERG theory, and McClelland's theory of needs for achievement, affiliation, and power. Maslow and Alderfer have concentrated on the hierarchical arrangement of needs and the distinction between intrinsic and extrinsic motivation. McClelland has focused on the conditions under which particular need patterns stimulate high motivation.
- Process theories attempt to explain how motivation occurs rather than what specific factors are motivational. Expectancy theory argues that people will be motivated to engage in work activities that they find attractive and that they feel they can accomplish. The attractiveness of these activities depends upon the extent to which they lead to favorable personal consequences. Equity theory states that workers compare the inputs that they apply to their jobs and the outcomes that they achieve from their jobs with the inputs and outcomes of others. When these outcome/input ratios are unequal, inequity exists, and workers will be motivated to restore equity. The Porter-Lawler model summarizes the relationships among the process theory variables and performance, rewards, and job satisfaction.

KEY CONCEPTS

Theory X versus Theory Y
Motivation
Intrinsic motivation
Extrinsic motivation
Performance
Need theories

Maslow's hierarchy of needs
ERG theory
Need for achievement
Need for affiliation
Need for power
Process theories

Expectancy theory
Instrumentality
Valence
Expectancy
Equity theory
Intrinsic/extrinsic relationship

DISCUSSION QUESTIONS

1. Many millionaires continue to work long, hard hours, sometimes even beyond the usual age of retirement. Use the ideas developed in the chapter to speculate about the reasons for this motivational pattern. Is the acquisition of wealth still a motivator for these individuals?

2. Discuss a time when you were highly motivated to perform well (at work, at school, in a sports contest) but performed poorly in spite of your high motivation. How do you know that your motivation was really high? What factors interfered with good performance? What did you learn from this experience?

3. Use Maslow's hierarchy of needs and Alderfer's ERG theory to explain why assembly line workers and executive vice-presidents might be susceptible to different forms of motivation.

4. Do you feel that unions are more concerned with obtaining extrinsic rewards or intrinsic rewards for their members? What does ERG theory say about this?

5. Describe in detail a specific job in which a person with high need for affiliation would be more motivated and perform better than a person with high need for achievement.

6. Colleen is high in need for achievement, Eugene is high in need for power, and Max is high in need for affiliation. They are thinking about starting a business partnership. To maximize the motivation

of each, what business should they go into, and who should assume which roles or jobs?

7. Reconsider the case of Tony Angelas, which was used to illustrate expectancy theory. Imagine that you are Tony's boss and you think that he can be motivated to perform at a high level. Suppose you cannot modify second-level outcomes or their valences, but you can affect expectancies and instrumentalities. What would you do to motivate Tony? Prove that you have succeeded by recalculating the force equations to demonstrate that Tony will now perform at a high level.

8. Set up a hypothetical outcome/input equation that reveals inequity. Review the methods that might be used to reduce this particular case of inequity.

9. Using the Porter-Lawler model as a guide, design an ideal motivational system for a chain of food supermarkets. What would be the role of the supermarket managers in this system? What practical constraints would interfere with the operation of this ideal system?

10. Discuss the following assertion: Many organizations simply lack the time and resources to maximize the motivation of their employees. In many cases, energy could be better devoted to developing a new marketing plan or investing in better equipment rather than trying to motivate individual workers.

EXPERIENTIAL EXERCISE

Attitudes Toward Achievement

The purpose of this exercise is to measure your attitudes toward the achievement of others. Using the following scale, place the number that best expresses your opinion in front of each of the twenty questions.

7 = I agree very much
6 = I agree on the whole
5 = I agree a little
3 = I disagree a little
2 = I disagree on the whole
1 = I disagree very much

_____ 1. People who are very successful deserve all the rewards they get for their achievements
_____ 2. It's good to see very successful people fail occasionally
_____ 3. Very successful people often get too big for their boots
_____ 4. People who are very successful in what they do are usually friendly and helpful to others
_____ 5. At school it's probably better for students to be near the middle of the class than the very top student
_____ 6. People shouldn't criticise or knock the very successful
_____ 7. Very successful people who fall from the top usually deserve their fall from grace
_____ 8. Those who are very successful ought to come down off their pedestals and be like other people
_____ 9. The very successful person should receive public recognition for his/her accomplishments
_____ 10. People who are "tall poppies" (very successful) should be cut down to size
_____ 11. One should always respect the person at the top
_____ 12. One ought to be sympathetic to very successful people when they experience failure and fall from their very high positions
_____ 13. Very successful people sometimes need to be brought back a peg or two, even if they have done nothing wrong
_____ 14. Society needs a lot of very high achievers
_____ 15. People who always do a lot better than others need to learn what it's like to fail
_____ 16. People who are right at the top usually deserve their high position
_____ 17. It's very important for society to support and encourage people who are very successful
_____ 18. People who are very successful get too full of their own importance
_____ 19. Very successful people usually succeed at the expense of other people
_____ 20. Very successful people who are at the top of their field are usually fun to be with

Scoring and Interpretation

This questionnaire is called the Tall Poppy Scale. It was developed by Professor Norman T. Feather of Flinders University in Australia to measure attitudes toward the success and achievement of others. The term "tall poppy" is commonly used in Australia to describe a person who is conspicuously successful. Although Australians value achievement as much as North Americans, they are very ambivalent about its public expression, and they are known to take delight in seeing tall poppies cut down to size and lose status.

To score your Tall Poppy Scale, add your responses to the following ten items: 2, 3, 5, 7, 8, 10, 13, 15, 18, 19. The higher your score (which should range between 10 and 70), the more you favor seeing a tall poppy *fall*. Now add your responses to the remaining ten items. The higher your score (again, the range is 10 to 70), the more you favor the *reward* of tall poppies for their success. In a sample of Australian adults, the average *fall* score was 38, and the average *reward* score was 45. Speaking generally, those who were more favorably disposed toward tall poppies valued achievement more highly, had higher self-esteem, were more politically conservative, and held higher-status jobs.

Source: Tall Poppy Scale from Feather, N.T. (1989). Attitudes toward the high achiever: The fall of the tall poppy. *Australian Journal of Psychology, 41,* 239–267. Reprinted by permission of the author.

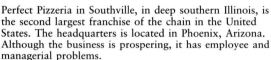

Perfect Pizzeria

Perfect Pizzeria in Southville, in deep southern Illinois, is the second largest franchise of the chain in the United States. The headquarters is located in Phoenix, Arizona. Although the business is prospering, it has employee and managerial problems.

Each operation has one manager, an assistant manager, and from two to five night managers. The managers of each pizzeria work under an area supervisor. There are no systematic criteria for being a manager or becoming a manager trainee. The franchise has no formalized training period for the manager. No college education is required. The managers for whom the case observer worked during a four-year period were relatively young (ages 24 to 27), and only one had completed college. They came from the ranks of night managers or assistant managers, or both. The night managers were chosen for their ability to perform the duties of the regular employees. The assistant managers worked a two-hour shift during the luncheon period five days a week to gain knowledge about bookkeeping and management. Those becoming managers remained at that level unless they expressed interest in investing in the business.

The employees were mostly college students, with a few high school students performing the less challenging jobs. Since Perfect Pizzeria was located in an area with few job opportunities, it had a relatively easy task of filling its employee quotas. All the employees, with the exception of the manager, were employed part-time. Consequently, they worked for less than the minimum wage.

The Perfect Pizzeria system is devised so that food and beverage costs and profits are set up according to a percentage. If the percentage of food unsold or damaged in any way is very low, the manager gets a bonus. If the percentage is high, the manager does not receive a bonus; rather, he or she receives only his or her normal salary.

There are many ways in which the percentage can fluctuate. Since the manager cannot be in the store 24 hours a day, some employees make up for their paychecks by helping themselves to the food. When a friend comes in to order a pizza, extra ingredients are put on the friend's pizza. Occasional nibbles by 18 to 20 employees throughout the day at the meal table also raise the percentage figure. An occasional bucket of sauce may be spilled or a pizza accidentally burned. Sometimes the wrong size of pizza may be made.

In the event of an employee mistake or a burned pizza by the oven man, the expense is supposed to come from the individual. Because of peer pressure, the night manager seldom writes up a bill for the erring employee. Instead, the establishment takes the loss, and the error goes unnoticed until the end of the month when the inventory is taken. That's when the manager finds out that the percentage is high and that there will be no bonus.

In the present instance, the manager took retaliatory measures. Previously, each employee was entitled to a free pizza, salad, and all the soft drinks he or she could drink for every 6 hours of work. The manager raised this figure from 6 to 12 hours of work. However, the employees had received these 6-hour benefits for a long time. Therefore, they simply took advantage of the situation whenever the manager or the assistant was not in the building. Though the night manager theoretically had complete control of the operation in the evenings, he did not command the respect that the manager or assistant manager did. That was because he received the same pay as the regular employees; he could not reprimand other employees; and he was basically the same age or sometimes even younger than the other employees.

Thus, apathy grew within the pizzeria. There seemed to be a further separation between the manager and his workers, who started out to be a closely knit group. The manager made no attempt to alleviate the problem, because he felt it would iron itself out. Either the

Source: Prepared by Lee Neely for Professor J. G. Hunt. From Dittrich, J. E., & Zawacki, R. A. (1981). *People and organizations*. Plano, TX: Business Publications. Copyright © 1981 by Business Publications. Reprinted by permission of Richard D. Irwin, Inc.

employees that were dissatisfied would quit or they would be content to put up with the new regulations. As it turned out, there was a rash of employee dismissals. The manager had no problem in filling the vacancies with new workers, but the loss of key personnel was costly to the business.

With the large turnover, the manager found he had to spend more time in the building, supervising and sometimes taking the place of inexperienced workers. This was in direct violation of the franchise regulation, which stated that a manager would act as a supervisor and at no time take part in the actual food preparation. Employees were not placed under strict supervision with the manager working alongside them. The operation no longer worked smoothly because of differences between the remaining experienced workers and the manager concerning the way in which a particular function should be performed.

Within a two-month period, the manager was again free to go back to his office and leave his subordinates in charge of the entire operation. During this two-month period, the percentage had returned to the previous low level, and the manager received a bonus each month. The manager felt that his problems had been resolved and that conditions would remain the same, since the new personnel had been properly trained.

It didn't take long for the new employees to become influenced by the other employees. Immediately after the manager returned to his supervisory role, the percentage began to rise. This time the manager took a bolder step. He cut out any benefits that the employees had—no free pizzas, salads, or drinks. With the job market at an even lower ebb than usual, most employees were forced to stay. The appointment of a new area supervisor made it impossible for the manager to "work behind the counter," since the supervisor was centrally located in Southville.

The manager tried still another approach to alleviate the rising percentage problem and maintain his bonus. He placed a notice on the bulletin board, stating that if the percentage remained at a high level, a lie detector test would be given to all employees. All those found guilty of taking or purposefully wasting food or drinks would be immediately terminated. This did not have the desired effect on the employees, because they knew if they were all subjected to the test, all would be found guilty, and the manager would have to dismiss all of them. This would leave him in a worse situation than ever.

Even before the following month's percentage was calculated, the manager knew it would be high. He had evidently received information from one of the night managers about the employees' feelings toward the notice. What he did not expect was that the percentage would reach an all-time high. That is the state of affairs at the present time.

1. Use any relevant material in the chapter to describe the "formal" motivation system (such as it is!) that was in place at Perfect Pizzeria at the beginning of the case.

2. Describe the likely need structure of the majority of the employees at Perfect Pizzeria. How does this contribute to the events in the case?

3. Use expectancy theory to explain the persistence of employee behavior that the manager considers dysfunctional.

4. How do equity considerations influence employee behavior at Perfect Pizzeria?

5. How does the case illustrate the distinction between motivation and performance?

6. If you were a new manager, how would you try to get things under control and improve performance at Perfect Pizzeria?

REFERENCES

1. McGregor, D. (1960). *The human side of enterprise.* New York: McGraw-Hill.

2. McGregor, 1960.

3. Kasl, S. (1978). Epidemiological contributions to the study of work stress. In C. L. Cooper & R. Payne (Eds.), *Stress at work.* New York: Wiley. Also see Dubin, R., Hedley, R. A., & Taveggia, T. C. (1976). Attachment to work. In R. Dubin (Ed.), *Handbook of work, organization, and society.* Chicago: Rand McNally. However, the centrality of work varies cross-culturally. See MOW International Research Team. (1987). *The meaning of working.* London: Academic Press.

4. Campbell, J. P., Dunnette, M. D., Lawler, E. E., III, & Weick, K. E., Jr. (1970). *Managerial behavior, performance, and effectiveness.* New York: McGraw-Hill. Also see Katerberg, R., & Blau, G. (1983). An examination of level and direction of effort and job performance. *Academy of Management Journal, 26,* 249–257.

5. Dyer, L., & Parker, D. F. (1975). Classifying outcomes in work motivation research: An examination of the intrinsic-extrinsic dichotomy. *Journal of Applied Psychology, 60,* 455–458; Kanungo, R. N., & Hartwick, J. (1987). An alternative to the intrinsic-extrinsic dichotomy of work rewards.

Journal of Management, 13, 751–766. Also see Brief, A. P., & Aldag, R. J. (1977). The intrinsic-extrinsic dichotomy: Toward conceptual clarity. *Academy of Management Review, 2,* 496–500.

6. Based on Campbell, J. P., & Pritchard, R. D. (1976). Motivation theory in industrial and organizational psychology. In M. D. Dunnette (Ed.), *Handbook of industrial and organizational psychology.* Chicago: Rand McNally.

7. The distinction between need (content) and process theories was first made by Campbell et al., 1970.

8. Maslow, A. H. (1970). *Motivation and personality* (2nd ed.). New York: Harper & Row.

9. Alderfer, C. P. (1969). An empirical test of a new theory of human needs. *Organizational Behavior and Human Performance, 4,* 142–175. Also see Alderfer, C. P. (1972). *Existence, relatedness, and growth: Human needs in organizational settings.* New York: The Free Press.

10. McClelland, D. C. (1985). *Human motivation.* Glenview, IL: Scott, Foresman.

11. McClelland, D. C., & Winter, D. G. (1969). *Motivating economic achievement.* New York: The Free Press, pp. 50–52.

12. McClelland, D. C., & Boyatzis, R. E. (1982). Leadership motive pattern and long-term success in management. *Journal of Applied Psychology, 67,* 737–743; McClelland, D. C., & Burnham, D. (1976, March–April). Power is the great motivator. *Harvard Business Review,* 159–166. However, need for power might not be the best motive pattern for managers of technical and professional people. See Cornelius, E. T., III, & Lane, F. B. (1984). The power motive and managerial success in a professionally oriented service industry organization. *Journal of Applied Psychology, 69,* 32–39.

13. Wahba, M. A., & Bridwell, L. G. (1976). Maslow reconsidered: A review of research on the need hierarchy theory. *Organizational Behavior and Human Performance, 15,* 212–240.

14. Schneider, B., & Alderfer, C. P. (1973). Three studies of measures of need satisfaction in organizations. *Administrative Science Quarterly, 18,* 498–505. Also see Alderfer, C. P., Kaplan, R. E., & Smith, K. K. (1974). The effect of relatedness need satisfaction on relatedness desires. *Administrative Science Quarterly, 19,* 507–532. For a disconfirming test, see Rauschenberger, J., Schmitt, N., & Hunter, J. E. (1980). A test of the need hierarchy concept by a Markov model of change in need strength. *Administrative Science Quarterly, 25,* 654–670.

15. McClelland, 1985.

16. Herzberg, F. (1966). *Work and the nature of man.* Cleveland: World Publishing.

17. Lawler, E. E., III. (1973). *Motivation in work organizations.* Monterey, CA: Brooks/Cole.

18. Vroom, V. H. (1964). *Work and motivation.* New York: Wiley.

19. Mitchell, T. R. (1974). Expectancy models of job satisfaction, occupational preference, and effort: A theoretical, methodological, and empirical appraisal. *Psychological Bulletin, 81,* 1053–1077. Also see Pinder, C. C. (1984). *Work motivation:* Theory, issues, and applications. Glenview, IL: Scott, Foresman. For some recent refinements, see Miller, L. E., & Grush, J. E. (1988). Improving predictions in expectancy theory research: Effects of personality, expectancies, and norms. *Academy of Management Journal, 31,* 107–122.

20. A good discussion of how managers can strengthen expectancy and instrumentality relationships is presented by Strauss, G. (1977). Managerial practices. In J. R. Hackman & J. L. Suttle (Eds.), *Improving life at work: Behavioral science approaches to organizational change.* Glenview, IL: Scott, Foresman.

21. Adams, J. S. (1965). Injustice in social exchange. *Advances in Experimental Social Psychology, 2,* 267–299.

22. Carrell, M. R., & Dittrich, J. E. (1978). Equity theory: The recent literature, methodological considerations, and new directions. *Academy of Management Review, 3,* 202–210; Mowday, R. T. (1987). Equity theory predictions of behavior in organizations. In R. M. Steers & L. W. Porter (Eds.), *Motivation and work behavior* (4th ed.). New York: McGraw-Hill.

23. Carrell & Dittrich, 1978; Mowday, 1987.

24. Kagitcibasi, C., & Berry, J. W. (1989). Cross-cultural psychology: Current research and trends. *Annual Review of Psychology, 40,* 493–531.

25. Hofstede, G. (1980). *Culture's consequences: International differences in work-related values.* Beverly Hills, CA: Sage.

26. For a review, see Kagitcibasi & Berry, 1989.

27. Adler, N. J. (1986). *International dimensions of organizational behavior.* Boston: Kent.

28. Adler, 1986, pp. 132–133.

29. Porter, L. W., & Lawler, E. E., III. (1968). *Managerial attitudes and performance.* Homewood, IL: Dorsey.

30. Deci, E. L., & Ryan, R. M. (1985). *Intrinsic motivation and self-determination in human behavior.* New York: Plenum.

31. Deci & Ryan, 1985. For another explanation, see Mawhinney, T. C. (1979). Intrinsic × extrinsic work motivation: Perspectives from behaviorism. *Organizational Behavior and Human Performance, 24,* 411–440.

32. Guzzo, R. A. (1979). Types of rewards, cognitions, and work motivation. *Academy of Management Review, 4,* 75–86.

MOTIVATION IN PRACTICE

Quad/Graphics is one of the largest magazine printers in the country. The company prints more than 100 magazines and catalogues, including *Newsweek, Playboy* and *Harper's.* Its president, Harry Quadracci, founded the company in 1972 with 10 others and a 20,000-square-foot plant with one press in Pewaukee, Wisconsin. It now boasts more than 1,800 employees, more than a million square feet in floor space, and new operations in Wisconsin and on the East Coast. The company has maintained a compound sales growth rate of 30–40 percent a year, though the industry average is less than 10 percent. Quad/Graphics makes its own ink and has a self-supporting trucking fleet.

Quad/Graphics' employees own 37 percent of the company through the Employee Stock Ownership Plan. But this is only the beginning of Quad/Graphics' efforts to make employees feel and act like owners. New workers have a mentor to school them in company culture. Performance is the key to success, they are told, and success is defined in terms of both job performance and personal satisfaction.

Each spring, Quadracci puts his managerial philosophy, his employees, and his company to the test. During the "Spring Fling," all managers take one day off for a special management retreat, leaving the company in the hands of the rank and file. Anything could go wrong, from a misplaced advertisement to a miscalculated ink hue on millions of magazine covers. The risk is worth it. "Responsibility should be shared," Quadracci says. "Our people shouldn't need me or anyone else to tell them what to do." This is "Theory Q"—management by walking away. Theory Q trains employees to be owners of the company.

Theory Q also trains managers to manage. Quadracci believes that the managerial function at any level is to coordinate, not control. Since Quadracci feels that "managers should be virtually indistinguishable from those they manage," Quad/Graphics has only three reporting levels.

The workweek at Quad/Graphics is short: just 36 hours in three days. Two shifts keep the presses going 24 hours a day. Institution of the three-day workweek increased productivity 20 percent and saved tremendous amounts in overtime pay.

These and other innovative management practices have earned Quad/Graphics numerous awards, including a spot in *The 100 Best Companies to Work for in America.* For Quad/Graphics' employee-partners, working at the company is its own reward, both financially and personally.

Source: Rosen, C., Klein, K. J., & Young, K. M. (1986, January). When employees share the profits. *Psychology Today*, 30–36, p. 34.

Notice the motivational strategies employed at Quad/Graphics—an economic incentive through stock ownership, job design that provides considerable independence, and a very unusual work schedule. In this chapter we will discuss four motivational techniques—money, job enrichment, goal setting, and alternative working schedules. In each case, we will consider the practical problems that are involved in implementation. Also, we will be concerned with the impact of the motivational techniques on the **quality of working life** of organizational members; that is, to what extent do these techniques make the work experience more rewarding and fulfilling while avoiding stress and other negative personal consequences?

Harry Quadracci of Quad/Graphics, performing at a company party. (Courtesy of Quad/Graphics)

MONEY AS A MOTIVATOR

The money that employees receive in exchange for organizational membership is in reality a package made up of pay and various fringe benefits that have dollar values, such as insurance plans, sick leave, and vacation time. In this section, we shall be concerned with the motivational characteristics of pay for both production workers and white-collar personnel.

First, however, let us briefly consider what various motivation theories would suggest about the motivational properties of pay. According to Maslow and Alderfer, pay should prove especially motivational to those individuals who are characterized by strong lower-level needs. For these people, pay can be exchanged for food, shelter, and other necessities of life. However, suppose you receive a healthy pay raise. Doubtless, this raise will enable you to purchase food and shelter, but it might also demonstrate that your boss cares about you, give you prestige among friends and family, and signal your competence as a worker. Thus, using need hierarchy terminology, pay can also function to satisfy social, esteem, and self-actualization needs. If pay has this capacity to fulfill a variety of needs, then it should have especially good potential to serve as a motivator. How can this potential be realized? Expectancy theory provides the clearest answer to this question. According to expectancy theory, if pay can satisfy a variety of needs, it should be highly valent, and it should prove to be a good motivator to the extent that *good performance is instrumental to obtaining it.*

Linking Pay to Performance on Production Jobs

The prototype of all schemes to link pay to performance on production jobs is piecerate. In its pure form, **piecerate** is set up so that individual workers are paid a certain sum of money for each unit of production completed. For example, sewing machine operators might be paid one dollar for each dress stitched together, or punch press operators might be paid a few cents for each piece of metal fabricated. Even more common than pure piecerate is a system whereby workers are paid a basic hourly wage and paid a piecerate differential on top of this hourly wage. For example, a forge operator might be paid four dollars an hour plus ten cents for each unit produced. In some cases, of course, it is very difficult to measure the productivity of an individual worker because of the nature of the production process. Under these circumstances, group incentives are sometimes employed. For example, workers in a steel mill might be paid an hourly wage and a monthly bonus for each ton of steel produced over some minimum quota. These various schemes to link pay to performance on production jobs are called **wage incentive plans.**

Compared with straight hourly pay, the introduction of wage incentives is usually accompanied by substantial increases in productivity.[1] One review reports a median productivity improvement of 30 percent following the installation of piecerate pay, an increase that is not matched by goal setting or job enrichment.[2]

Also, a study of four hundred manufacturing companies found that those with wage incentive plans achieved 43 to 64 percent greater productivity than those without such plans.[3] Successful firms that make extensive use of wage incentives include Cleveland's Lincoln Electric Company (producer of electric welders and motors) and Steelcase, the Michigan manufacturer of office furniture. In fact, however, only about 26 percent of the U.S. manufacturing work force is operating under some form of wage incentive.[4] What problems account for this relatively low utilization of a motivational system that has proven results?

Problems with Wage Incentives   It is sometimes argued that wage incentives can increase productivity at the expense of quality. While this may in some cases be true, it does not require particular ingenuity to devise a system to monitor and maintain quality. A more serious technical threat to the establishment of wage incentives exists when workers have differential opportunities to produce at a high level. If the supply of raw materials or the quality of production equipment varies from workplace to workplace, some workers will be at an unfair disadvantage under an incentive system (in expectancy theory terminology, workers will differ in the expectancy that they can produce at a high level). In addition, wage incentives that reward individual productivity might decrease cooperation among workers. For example, to maintain a high wage rate, machinists might hoard raw materials or refuse to engage in peripheral tasks such as keeping the shop clean or unloading supplies. Consider what happened when Solar Press, an Illinois printing and packaging company, installed a team wage incentive:

> It wasn't long before both managers and employees began to spot problems. Because of the pressure to produce, teams didn't perform regular maintenance on the equipment, so machines broke down more often than before. When people found better or faster ways to do things, some hoarded them from fellow employees for fear of reducing the amount of their own payments. Others grumbled that work assignments weren't fairly distributed, that some jobs demanded more work than others. They did, but the system didn't take this into account.[5]

In some cases, the manner in which jobs are designed can make it very difficult to install wage incentives. On an assembly line, it is almost impossible to identify and reward individual contributions to productivity. As pointed out above, wage incentive systems can be designed to reward team productivity in such a circumstance. However, as the size of the team *increases,* the relationship between any individual's productivity and his or her pay *decreases.* For example, the impact of your productivity in a team of two is much greater than the impact of this productivity in a team of ten—as team size increases, the linkage between your performance and your pay is erased, removing the intended incentive effect.

A chief psychological impediment to the use of wage incentives might be the tendency for workers to restrict productivity under such systems (see the car-

Source: Norris, Len
(1984). *The best of
Norris.* Toronto,
Ontario: McClelland
and Stewart Limited.
(© Punch/Rothco)

"YOU NEW ON THE JOB?"

toon). This restriction is illustrated graphically in Exhibit 7–1. Under normal
circumstances, without wage incentives, we can often expect productivity to be
distributed in a "bell-shaped" manner—a few workers are especially low producers, a few are especially high producers, and most produce in the middle range.
When wage incentives are introduced, however, workers sometimes come to an
informal agreement about what constitutes a fair day's work and artificially limit
their output accordingly. In many cases, this **restriction of productivity** can decrease the expected benefits of the incentive system, as shown in Exhibit 7–1.

Why does restriction often occur under wage incentive systems? Sometimes, it
happens because workers feel that increased productivity due to the incentive will
lead to reductions in the work force. More frequently, however, employees fear
that if they produce at an especially high level, the rate of payment will be reduced
to cut labor costs. In the early days of industrialization, when unions were nonexistent or weak, this was especially likely to happen. Workers were studied under
normal circumstances by engineers, and a payment rate for each unit of productivity was set by management. When the incentive system was introduced, workers employed various legitimate shortcuts that they had learned on the job to
produce at a higher rate than expected. In response to this, management simply
changed the rate to require more output for a given amount of pay! Stories of
such rate-cutting are often passed down from one generation of workers to another in support of restricting output under incentive systems. As you might
expect, restriction seems less likely when a climate of trust and a history of good
relations exist between employees and management.

EXHIBIT

7–1

Hypothetical productivity distributions, with and without wage incentives, when incentives promote restriction.

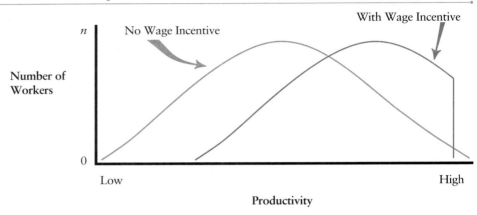

Gain Sharing Many of the dysfunctional aspects of wage incentive systems stem from their concentration on individual-level performance as the basis for payment. In effect, workers become more concerned with their individual productivity (and pay) than they are with the overall performance of their department or unit. As a result, a number of group-level incentive plans have been proposed. In general, these plans are based on the assumption that the practical benefits of increased cooperation can offset the theoretical benefits of paying for individual performance. Profit sharing and stock ownership plans are examples of group incentives. However, their motivational impact may be limited because factors that control profit or stock prices (such as the condition of the general economy) might not be under the control of employees.

Gain-sharing plans are group incentive plans that are based on measurable cost reductions that are under the control of the work force—factors such as the cost of labor or materials and supplies used.[6] When measured costs decrease, a monthly bonus is paid according to a predetermined formula that shares this "gain" between employees and the firm. Gain-sharing plans have usually been installed by using committees that include the participation of the work force. This builds commitment for the formulas that are used to convert gains into bonuses. Also, most plans include all members of the work unit, including production people, managers, and support staff.

The most common gain-sharing plan is the Scanlon Plan, developed by union leader Joe Scanlon in the 1930s.[7] It has been used with apparent success by many small family-owned manufacturing firms. However, in recent years, many large corporations (e.g., General Electric, Motorola, Carrier, Dana) have installed Scanlon-like gain-sharing plans in some manufacturing plants.[8] In general, productivity improvements following the introduction of Scanlon-type plans support the motivational impact of this group wage incentive (see In Focus 7–1).

Quality of Working Life We have established that wage incentive plans may serve as effective motivators, but what is their impact on the quality of working life of the individuals who operate under them? First, it should be obvious that a wage incentive plan that has any of the difficulties discussed above could promote feelings of inequity and induce conflict among organizational members. Second, North American unions have generally been opposed to wage incentive plans that are based on individual performance, although they sometimes support group-based plans. Unionists often argue that plans such as piecerate promote unhealthy competition among workers, lead to fatigue and accidents, and disadvantage older or less fit workers. Of course, individual incentives might undermine the notions of worker equality and the importance of seniority, which are the very foundation of unionism. In summary, wage incentive systems must operate smoothly and be perceived as equitable by all relevant parties if they are not to have negative impact.

Linking Pay to Performance on White-Collar Jobs

Compared with production jobs, white-collar jobs (including clerical, professional, and managerial) frequently offer fewer objective performance criteria with which pay can be associated. To be sure, company presidents are often paid annual bonuses that are tied to the profitability of the firm, and salespeople are frequently paid commissions on sales. However, trustworthy objective indicators of individual performance for the majority of white-collar jobs are often difficult to find. For this reason (as pointed out in our discussion of perception), performance in many such jobs must be evaluated by the subjective judgment of the performer's superior.

Attempts to link pay to performance on white-collar jobs are often called **merit pay plans.** Just as straight piecerate is the prototype for most wage incentive plans, there is also a prototype for most merit pay plans: Periodically (usually yearly), managers are required to evaluate the performance of subordinates on some form of rating scales (such as those shown in Chapter 4) or by means of a written description of performance. Using these evaluations, the managers then recommend that some amount of merit pay be awarded to individuals over and above their basic salaries. This pay is usually incorporated into the subsequent year's salary checks.[9] Since the indicators of good performance can be unclear on some white-collar jobs (especially managerial jobs), merit pay can provide an especially tangible signal that an employee's performance is considered to be "on track" by the organization.

There is good evidence that individuals who see a strong link between rewards and performance tend to be better performers.[10] In addition, white-collar workers (especially managers) are particularly supportive of the notion that performance should be an important determinant of pay.[11] Thus, it should not be

IN FOCUS 7–1

▼
....

Gain Sharing at Fraser Inc.

Incentives may be filtering down through management hierarchies, but just try putting your local union shop on a bonus plan. "Sure, buddy," they'll say, "but give me my base pay increase first." With a little arm-twisting and a lot of cooperation, however, some companies make incentive pay work in a union shop. Take the case of New Brunswick-based pulp and paper producer Fraser Inc.

Since last July, the 1,132 workers at Fraser's Madawaska, Me., paper mill have been splitting with management the financial gains from any productivity improvements they make. The deal is that workers get 50% of the gains as long as profits don't dip below 90% of Fraser's operating forecast for the mill; below that, the company's share goes up to 75%. Known as productivity gain sharing, the plan is, in the words of Fraser's vice-president of human resources, Regal McLean, an incentive "to better use all resources—capital, manpower and brains."

So far everyone is winning. Workers turned up US$2 million in cost savings in the first six months of the plan. Fraser kept half and paid out the rest in two quarterly bonuses of US$280 and US$637 per employee.

In designing the plans with management, the union's stance was "trust but verify." UPIU [United Paperworkers International Union] representatives had an equal voice in selecting the 11 productivity measures that make up the bonus formula. "If employees don't have a say in the formula, then you might as well not have it," says [union rep Lucien] Deschaine. They made sure that every measure of productivity (such as man-hours per ton of paper produced, or waste through sewer losses) was something workers or automation could realistically improve.

Indeed, one of the reasons that companies choose productivity gain sharing over profit sharing is that it links bonuses with measures employees can control. With a plan linked to profit, on the other hand, a hoped-for bonus can go up in smoke the minute energy costs soar or selling prices get hit by a sudden surplus on the other side of the world. This is not much of an incentive for someone supporting a family on $30,000 a year, particularly when they've been counting on that bonus in lieu of a wage increase. That's why Fraser's bonus formula tracks defective paper returned to the plant, but not the price that paper fetches on the international market. And that's why the formula includes steam used per ton of paper produced, but not the cost of generating that steam. Says McLean: "All items are ones the employees have control over. That's important."

Source: Abridged from Davis, V. (1989, April). Eyes on the prize. *Canadian Business*, 93–106, p. 96. Reprinted by permission of the author.

surprising that merit pay plans are employed with a much greater frequency than wage incentive plans. For example, a survey of 493 major companies revealed that 87 percent used some form of merit pay plan for salaried workers.[12]

At this point, we encounter a curiosity. Despite the facts that merit pay can stimulate effective performance, that substantial support exists for the idea of merit pay, and that most organizations claim to provide merit pay, it would appear that many such systems now in use are *ineffective*. Many individuals who supposedly work under such plans do not perceive a link between their job performance and their pay. Evidently, this is not simply the result of some perceptual aberration; there is also evidence to suggest that pay is in fact *not* related to performance under some merit plans.[13] Adding more evidence of ineffectiveness are studies that track pay increases over time. For example, one study of managers showed that pay increases received in a given year were often uncorrelated with pay increases received in adjacent years.[14] From what we know about the consistency of human performance, such a result seems unlikely if organizations are truly tying pay to performance. It would seem that, in most organizations, seniority and job level account for more variation in pay than does performance. Of course, some organizations do hold the line. HBO, Inc., the entertainment company, is one firm that seriously tries to maintain the link between pay and performance. So does the Bank of America.

Problems with Merit Pay Plans   One reason that many merit pay plans fail to achieve their intended effect is that managers might be unable or unwilling to discriminate between good performers and poor performers. In Chapter 4 it was pointed out that subjective evaluations of performance can be difficult to make and are often distorted by a number of perceptual errors. In the absence of performance rating systems designed to control these problems, managers might feel that the only fair response is to rate most employees as equal performers. Good rating systems are, evidently, rarely employed. In a survey of management performance evaluation systems, only 10 percent of the responding personnel executives deemed their systems effective.[15] Even when managers feel capable of clearly discriminating between good and poor performers, they might be reluctant to do so. If the performance evaluation system does not assist the manager in giving feedback about his or her decisions to subordinates, the equalization strategy might be employed to prevent conflicts with them or among them. If there are true performance differences among subordinates, equalization overrewards poorer performers and underrewards better performers.

A second threat to the effectiveness of merit pay plans exists when merit increases are simply too small to be effective motivators. In this case, even if rewards are carefully tied to performance and managers do a good job of discriminating between more and less effective performers, the intended motivational effects of pay increases might not be realized. Ironically, some firms all but abandon merit when inflation soars or when they encounter economic difficulties. Just when high motivation is needed, the motivational impact of merit pay is removed. When merit pay makes up a substantial portion of the compensation package, however, extreme care has to be taken to ensure that the merit pay is tied to performance criteria that truly benefit the organization. Otherwise, employees could be motivated to earn their yearly bonus at the expense of long-term organizational goals (see In Focus 7–2).

A final threat to the effectiveness of merit pay plans is the extreme secrecy that surrounds salaries in most organizations. It has long been a principle of personnel management that salaries are confidential information, and employees who receive merit increases are frequently implored not to discuss these increases with their co-workers. Notice the implication of such secrecy for merit pay plans: Even if merit pay is administered fairly, contingent on performance, and generous, employees might remain ignorant of these facts because they have no way of comparing their own merit treatment with the treatment of others. In consequence, the motivational impact of a well-designed merit plan might be severely damaged. Rather incredibly, the great majority of organizations fail to inform employees about the average raise received by those doing similar work and fail to differentiate between merit pay and cost-of-living increases![16]

Given this extreme secrecy, you might expect that workers would profess profound ignorance about the salaries of other organizational members. In fact, this does not appear to be the case—in the absence of better information, employees are inclined to "invent" salaries for other members. Unfortunately, this invention seems to reduce both satisfaction and motivation. Specifically, several studies

Steven J. Ross, CEO of Time Warner. Ross made $39 million in 1990. How well does high performance translate into high pay? See In Focus 7–2. (Peter C. Borsari/ Gamma-Liaison)

▼
....

Reebok CEO's Pay Increases—To $14 Million

Paul Fireman, CEO of the sports and leisure shoe company Reebok International, enjoyed quite a pay increase in 1989. That year he earned over $14 million, up from $11 million the previous year. Fireman's base salary of around $350,000 is not high by CEO standards; the balance of his compensation was a bonus based on a percentage of Reebok profits. Fireman is obviously a highly capable executive. However, it is instructive to compare his pay with that of another outstanding CEO, David Glass of Wal-Mart Stores. The same year Fireman earned $14 million, Glass earned $840,000, a figure that is small by comparison!

This case of two outstanding executives receiving radically different levels of pay illustrates what researchers have known for a long time—that CEO pay is not closely related to performance. A similar point can be made by cross-national comparisons. In general, North American executives are paid *much* more than their European and Asian counterparts. For example, the year that Chrysler CEO Lee Iacocca was paid over $17 million, France's Jacques Calvet, head of the equally profitable Peugeot firm, was paid $250,000! However, with the increasing globalization of business, foreign executives are expected to profit from North American pressure.

What are the causes and consequences of very high pay levels that are made up of a very substantial bonus? Do they make motivational sense? *Fortune* explains that the pay package for top executives is constructed by a compensation committee from the board of directors. This committee relies heavily on salary surveys commissioned by the vice-president of personnel and on the advice of outside consultants. However, the chief executive is a member of the board, and the vice-president reports to the chief executive. In addition, the consulting firm is interested in maintaining a good relationship with the chief executive. The result is that the chief executive often exerts a fair amount of indirect control over the design of his or her own compensation package. Frequently, such packages define performance in terms of earnings per share of stock, a measure that can be manipulated in the short term.

To deal with these problems, Louis J. Brindisi, Jr., of the consulting firm Booz Allen & Hamilton, advocates tying executive pay to achieving longer-term strategic objectives and to return on equity, a firmer measure of shareholder value. He also advocates that a larger portion of the compensation package be devoted to long-term compensation and less to yearly bonuses.

Source: Crystal, G. S. (1990, June 18). The great CEO pay sweepstakes. *Fortune*, 94–102; Tully, S. (1988, November 7). American bosses are overpaid . . . *Fortune*, 121–136; Williams, M. J. (1985, April 1). Why chief executives' pay keeps rising. *Fortune*, 66–76; Brindisi, L. J., Jr. (1985, September). Shareholder value and executive compensation. *Planning Review*, 14–17.

have shown that managers have a tendency to overestimate the pay of their subordinates and their peers and underestimate the pay of their superiors (see Exhibit 7–2).[17] In general, these tendencies will reduce satisfaction with pay, damage perceptions of the linkage between performance and rewards, and reduce the valence of promotion to a higher level of management.

An interesting experiment examined the effects of pay disclosure on the performance and satisfaction of pharmaceutical salespeople who operated under a merit pay system:

> At the time of a regularly scheduled district sales meeting, each of the 14 managers in the experimental group presented to his subordinates the new open salary administration program. The salesmen were given the individual low, overall average, and individual high merit raise amounts for the previous year. The raises ranged from no raise

■
EXHIBIT   **Managers' estimates of pay earned by boss, peers, and subordinates.**

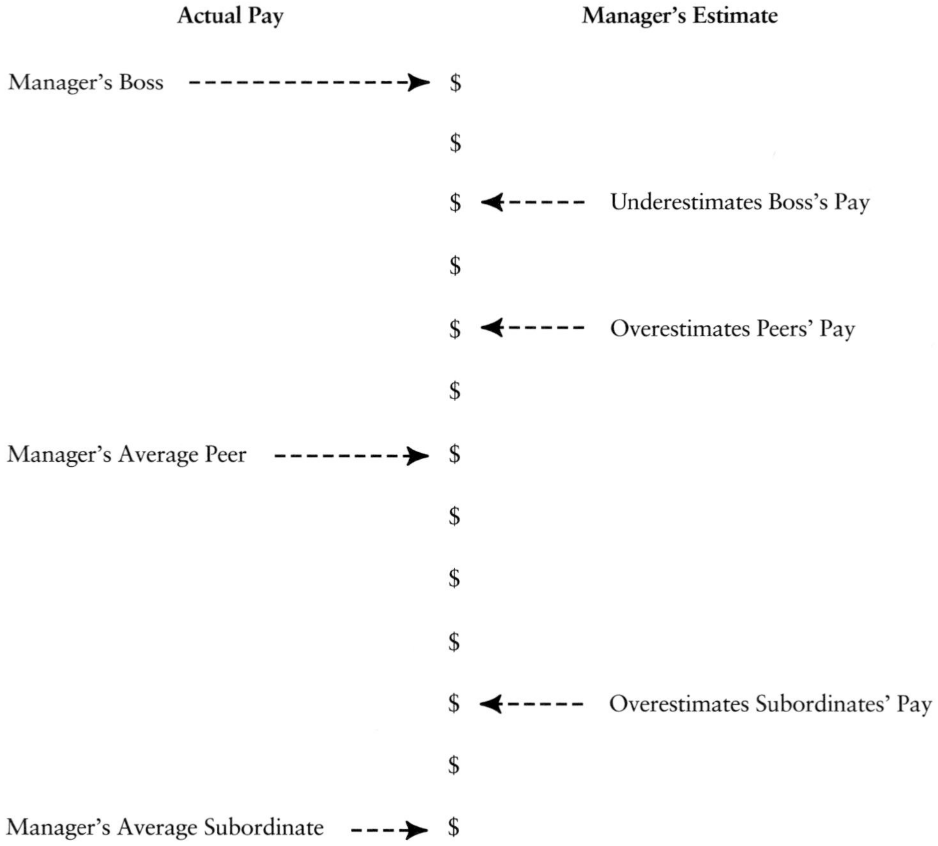

7–2   **Actual Pay**   **Manager's Estimate**

Manager's Boss   – – – – – – – – – – –▶ $

$

$ ◀ – – – – –   Underestimates Boss's Pay

$

$ ◀ – – – – –   Overestimates Peers' Pay

$

Manager's Average Peer   – – – – – – –▶ $

$

$

$

$ ◀ – – – – –   Overestimates Subordinates' Pay

$

Manager's Average Subordinate   – – –▶ $

to $75 a month, with a company average of $43. Raises were classified according to district, region, and company increases in pay. Likewise, salary levels (low, average, and high) were given for salesmen on the basis of their years with the company (1 to 5; 5 to 10; 10 to 20; and more than 20 years). Specific individual names and base salaries were not disclosed to the salesmen. However, this information could be obtained from the supervisor. Each salesman's performance evaluation was also made available by the district manager for review by his other salesmen.[18]

After the pay disclosure was implemented, salespeople in the experimental group revealed significant increases in performance and satisfaction with pay. However, since performance consisted of supervisory ratings, it is possible that supervisors felt pressured to give better ratings under the open pay system, in which their actions were open to scrutiny. This, of course, raises an important point. If performance evaluation systems are inadequate and poorly justified, a more open pay policy will simply expose the inadequacy of the merit system and lead managers to evaluate performance in a manner that is designed to reduce conflict. Unfortunately, this might be why most organizations maintain relative secrecy concerning pay. One exception is Steven Jobs's Next Computers, which has a completely open salary system. Although many public and civil service jobs have open pay systems, most make little pretense of paying for performance.

Quality of Working Life There is ample evidence to suggest that *well-conceived and implemented* merit pay plans could contribute to the quality of working life

At Next Computers, Steven Jobs has introduced an open salary system. There is no secret about who is paid what. (Shahn Kermani/Gamma-Liaison)

of white-collar personnel. As pointed out earlier, there is general support at this level for the notion that pay should be tied to performance. Also, there is evidence that individuals who see a reliable connection between pay and performance tend to be satisfied with their pay.[19] In a properly designed merit pay system, the Porter-Lawler model suggests that the following connections will be strong and reliable: Performance → reward → satisfaction. As a result of this connection, good performers should experience a sense of recognition and satisfaction, which will encourage them to pursue their careers within the organization rather than seeking work elsewhere. Poor performers should experience dissatisfaction, which could prompt them to seek work in an organization in which they can more properly apply their skills. However, an effective merit pay system should provide some poor performers with the feedback necessary to correct their behavior and increase their performance. Overall, these conditions seem conducive to a high-quality work experience.

JOB DESIGN AS A MOTIVATOR

If the use of money as a motivator is primarily an attempt to capitalize on extrinsic motivation, current approaches to using job design as a motivator represent an attempt to capitalize on intrinsic motivation. Certainly, some tasks *seem* more intrinsically motivating than others. For example, an assembly line worker in an automobile plant who is poorly motivated on the job might go home and spend many highly motivated hours preparing his own racing car. Intrinsic motivation is apparent here. In essence, the current goal of job design is to discover the characteristics that make some tasks more motivating than others and to capture these characteristics in the design of jobs.

Traditional Views of Job Design

From the advent of the Industrial Revolution until the 1960s, the prevailing philosophy regarding the design of most nonmanagerial jobs was job simplification. The historical roots of job simplification are found in social, economic, and technological forces that existed even before the Industrial Revolution. This preindustrial period was characterized by increasing urbanization and the growth of a free market economy, which prompted a demand for manufactured goods. Thus, a division of labor within society occurred, and specialized industrial concerns, using newly developed machinery, emerged to meet this demand. With complex machinery and an uneducated, untrained work force, these organizations recognized that *specialization* was the key to efficient productivity. If the production of an object could be broken down into very basic, simple steps, even an uneducated and minimally trained worker could contribute his or her share by mastering one of these steps.

The zenith of job simplification occurred in the early 1900s when industrial engineer Frederick Winslow Taylor presented the industrial community with his principles of **Scientific Management.**[20] Rather than traditional "rules of thumb" for the design of jobs, Taylor advocated the use of careful study to determine the optimum degree of specialization and standardization. Also, he supported the development of written instructions to clearly define work procedures, and he encouraged supervisors to standardize workers' movements and rest pauses for maximum efficiency. Taylor even extended Scientific Management to the boss's job, advocating "functional foremanship," whereby foremen would specialize in particular functions. For example, one foreman might become a specialist in training workers, while another might fulfill the role of a disciplinarian.

Intuitively, jobs designed according to the principles of Scientific Management do not seem intrinsically motivating. However, during the period sketched above, most managers' philosophies about why people work were probably confined to the assumption that "people work because they have to work." Thus, it is not surprising that the motivational strategies used during this period consisted of close supervision and the use of piecerate pay. It would be a historical disservice to conclude that job simplification was unwelcomed by workers, who were mostly nonunionized, uneducated, and fighting to fulfill their basic needs. Such simplification helped them to achieve a reasonable standard of living. However, in recent years, with a better-educated work force whose basic needs are fairly well met, behavioral scientists have begun to question the impact of job simplification on both performance and the quality of working life.

Job Scope and Motivation

Job scope can be defined as the breadth and depth of a job.[21] Breadth refers to the number of different activities performed on the job, while depth refers to the degree of discretion or control the worker has over how these tasks are performed. "Broad" jobs require workers to *do* a number of different tasks, while "deep" jobs emphasize freedom in *planning* how to do the work.

As shown in Exhibit 7–3, jobs that have great breadth *and* depth can be called high-scope jobs. The professor's job is a good example of a high-scope job. It is broad because it involves the performance of a number of different tasks, such as teaching, grading, doing research, writing, and participating in committees. It is also deep because there is considerable discretion in how these tasks are performed. In general, professors have a fair amount of freedom to choose a particular teaching style, grading format, and research area. Similarly, management jobs are high-scope jobs. Managers perform a wide variety of activities (supervision, training, performance evaluation, report writing, etc.) and have some discretion over how these activities are accomplished.

The classic example of a low-scope job is the traditional assembly line job. This job is both "shallow" and "narrow" in the sense that a single task (such as bolting on car wheels) is performed repetitively and ritually, with no discretion as to method. Traditional views of job design were attempts to construct low-scope jobs in which workers specialized in a single task.

Occasionally, jobs are encountered that involve high breadth but little depth or vice versa. For motivational purposes, these jobs can also be considered relatively low in scope. For example, a utility worker on an assembly line fills in for absent workers on various parts of the line. While this job involves the performance of a number of tasks, it involves little discretion as to when or how the tasks are performed. On the other hand, some jobs involve a fair amount of discretion over a single, narrowly defined task. For example, quality control inspectors perform a single, repetitive task, but they might be required to exercise a fair degree of judgment in performing this task. Similarly, workers who monitor the performance of equipment (such as in a nuclear power plant) might perform a single task but again be required to exercise considerable discretion when a problem arises.

The motivational theories discussed in the previous chapter suggest that high-scope jobs (*both* broad and deep) should provide more intrinsic motivation than low-scope jobs. Maslow's need hierarchy and the ERG theory both seem to indicate that higher-order needs can be fulfilled by the opportunity to perform high-scope jobs. Expectancy theory suggests that high-scope jobs can provide intrinsic motivation *if* the outcomes derived from such jobs are positively valent. This is an important qualification. As we shall see shortly, not everyone is enthusiastic about high-scope jobs.

EXHIBIT

7–3

Job scope as a function of job depth and job breadth.

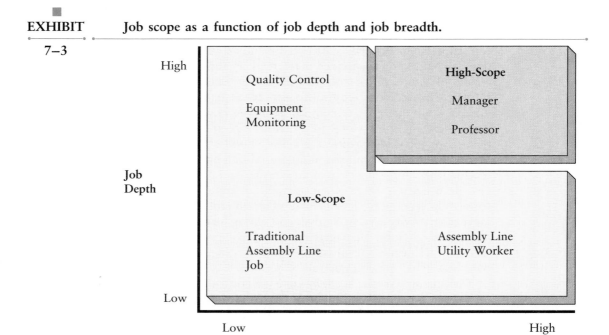

The Job Characteristics Model

The concept of job scope provides an easy-to-understand introduction to why some jobs seem more intrinsically motivating than others. However, the concepts of breadth and depth are more descriptive than scientific. A more rigorous delineation of the motivational properties of jobs is found in the Job Characteristics Model developed by J. Richard Hackman and Greg Oldham (Exhibit 7–4).[22] As you can observe, the Job Characteristics Model proposes that there are several "core" job characteristics that have a certain psychological impact upon workers. In turn, the psychological states induced by the nature of the job lead to certain outcomes that are relevant to the worker and the organization. Finally, several other factors (moderators) influence the extent to which these relationships hold true.

Let's look more closely at the major parts of this model.

EXHIBIT 7–4 The Job Characteristics Model.

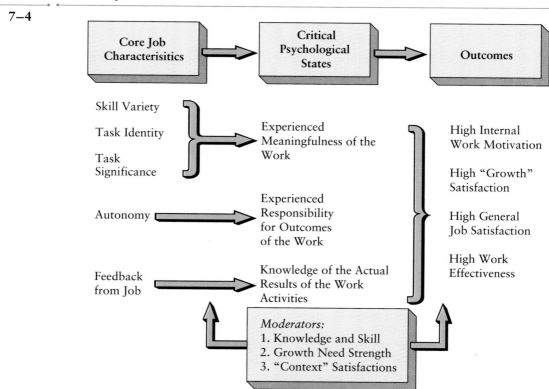

Source: Hackman, J. R., & Oldham, G. R. (1980). *Work redesign.* Reading, MA: Addison-Wesley. Copyright © 1980 by Addison-Wesley Publishing Company. Figure 4.6. Reprinted with permission of the publisher.

Core Job Characteristics The Job Characteristics Model shows that there are five core job characteristics that have particularly strong potential to affect worker motivation: skill variety, task identity, task significance, autonomy, and job feedback. These characteristics are defined in Exhibit 7–5. In general, higher levels of

---

EXHIBIT

7–5

Core job characteristics and examples.

1. **Skill variety:** The degree to which a job requires a variety of different activities in carrying out the work, involving the use of a number of different skills and talents of the person.
   High variety: The owner-operator of a garage who does electrical repair, rebuilds engines, does body work, and interacts with customers.
   Low variety: A body shop worker who sprays paint eight hours a day.

2. **Task identity:** The degree to which a job requires completion of a "whole" and identifiable piece of work, that is, doing a job from beginning to end with a visible outcome.
   High identity: A cabinet maker who designs a piece of furniture, selects the wood, builds the object, and finishes it to perfection.
   Low identity: A worker in a furniture factory who operates a lathe solely to make table legs.

3. **Task significance:** The degree to which the job has a substantial impact on the lives of other people, whether those people are in the immediate organization or in the world at large.
   High significance: Nursing the sick in a hospital intensive care unit.
   Low significance: Sweeping hospital floors.

4. **Autonomy:** The degree to which the job provides substantial freedom, independence, and discretion to the individual in scheduling the work and in determining the procedures to be used in carrying it out.
   High autonomy: A telephone installer who schedules his or her own work for the day, makes visits without supervision, and decides on the most effective techniques for a particular installation.
   Low autonomy: A telephone operator who must handle calls as they come according to a routine, highly specified procedure.

5. **Job feedback:** The degree to which carrying out the work activities required by the job provides the individual with direct and clear information about the effectiveness of his or her performance.
   High feedback: An electronics factory worker who assembles a radio and then tests it to determine if it operates properly.
   Low feedback: An electronics factory worker who assembles a radio and then routes it to a quality control inspector who tests it for proper operation and makes needed adjustments.

Source: Definitions from Hackman, J. R., & Oldham, G. R. (1980). The properties of motivating jobs. *Work redesign*. Reading, MA: Addison-Wesley. Copyright © 1980 by Addison-Wesley Publishing Company, Reading, Massachusetts. Reprinted by permission of the publisher.

these characteristics should lead to the favorable outcomes shown in Exhibit 7–4. Notice that **skill variety** corresponds fairly closely to the notion of job breadth discussed earlier, while **autonomy** corresponds to job depth. However, Hackman and Oldham recognized that one could have a high degree of control over a variety of skills that were perceived as meaningless or fragmented. Thus, the concepts of **task significance** and **task identity** are introduced. In addition, they recognized that **feedback** regarding one's performance is also essential for high intrinsic motivation.

Hackman and Oldham have developed a questionnaire called the Job Diagnostic Survey (JDS) to measure the core characteristics of jobs. The JDS requires job incumbents to report the amount of the various core characteristics contained in their jobs. From these reports, profiles can be constructed to compare the motivational properties of various jobs. For example, Exhibit 7–6 shows JDS profiles for lower-level managers in a certain company (collected by your author) and those for keypunchers in another firm (reported by Hackman and Oldham). While the managers perform a full range of managerial duties, the keypunchers perform a highly regulated job—anonymous work from various departments is assigned to them by a supervisor, and their output is verified for accuracy by others. Not surprisingly, the JDS profiles reveal that the managerial jobs are consistently higher on the core characteristics than the keypunching jobs.

EXHIBIT 7–6

Levels of core job characteristics for managers and keypunchers.

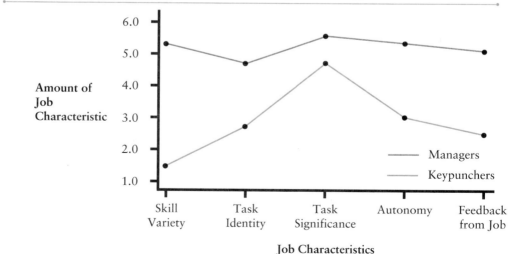

Source: Hackman, J. R., & Oldham, G. R. (1980). *Work redesign*. Reading, MA: Addison-Wesley. Copyright © 1980 by Addison-Wesley Publishing Company. Figure 6.2. Reprinted with permission of the publisher. (Managers' data collected by the author.)

According to Hackman and Oldham, an overall measure of the **motivating potential** of a job can be calculated by the following formula:

$$\text{Motivating potential score} = \left[\frac{\text{Skill variety} + \text{Task identity} + \text{Task significance}}{3} \right] \times \text{Autonomy} \times \text{Job feedback}$$

Since the JDS measures the job characteristics on seven-point scales, a motivating potential score could theoretically range from 1 to 343. For example, the motivating potential score for the keypunchers' jobs shown in Exhibit 7–6 is 20, while that for the managers' jobs is 159. The average motivating potential score for 6930 employees on 876 jobs has been calculated at 128.[23]

Critical Psychological States Why should jobs that are higher on the core characteristics be intrinsically motivating? What is their psychological impact? Hackman and Oldham argue that work will be intrinsically motivating when it is perceived as *meaningful,* when the worker feels *responsible* for the outcomes of the work, and when the worker has *knowledge* about his or her work progress. As shown in Exhibit 7–4, the Job Characteristics Model proposes that the core job characteristics affect meaningfulness, responsibility, and knowledge of results in a systematic manner. When an individual uses a variety of skills to do a "whole" job that is perceived as significant to others, the work should be perceived as meaningful. When a person has autonomy to organize and perform the job as he or she sees fit, the person should feel personally responsible for the outcome of the work. Finally, when the job provides feedback about performance, the worker will have knowledge of the results of this opportunity to exercise responsibility.

Outcomes The presence of the critical psychological states should lead to a number of outcomes that are relevant to both the individual and the organization. Chief among these is high intrinsic motivation. When the worker is truly in control of a challenging job that provides good feedback about performance, the key prerequisites for intrinsic motivation are present. The relationship between work and the worker is emphasized, and the worker is able to draw motivation from the job itself. This should result in high-quality productivity. By the same token, such a state of affairs should lead workers to report satisfaction with higher-order needs (growth needs) and general satisfaction with the job itself. This might lead to reduced absenteeism and turnover.

Moderators Hackman and Oldham recognize that jobs that are high in motivating potential do not *always* lead to favorable outcomes. Thus, as shown in Exhibit 7–4, they propose certain moderator or contingency variables (Chapter 1) that intervene between job characteristics and outcomes. One of these is the job-relevant knowledge and skill of the worker. Put simply, workers with weak knowledge and skills should not respond favorably to jobs that are high in motivating potential, since such jobs will prove too demanding. Another proposed moderator is **growth need strength,** which refers to the extent to which workers desire to achieve higher-order need satisfaction by performing their jobs. It is argued that those with high growth needs should be most responsive to challenging work. Finally, Hackman and Oldham argue that workers who are dissatisfied with the **context factors** surrounding the job (such as pay, supervision, and company policy) will be less responsive to challenging work than those who are reasonably satisfied with context factors.

Research Support Tests of the Job Characteristics Model have usually required workers to describe their jobs by means of the Job Diagnostic Survey and then measured their reactions to these jobs via a variety of techniques. Although there is some discrepancy regarding the relative importance of the various core characteristics, these tests have generally been very supportive of the basic prediction of the model—workers tend to respond more favorably to jobs that are higher in motivating potential. Also as predicted by the model, workers who are high in growth need strength appear to respond most favorably.[24] However, there is contradictory evidence regarding the role of context satisfaction in influencing reactions to job characteristics.[25]

Job Enrichment

Job enrichment is the attempt to design jobs to enhance intrinsic motivation and the quality of working life. In general, enrichment involves increasing the motivating potential of jobs via the arrangement of their core characteristics. There are no hard and fast rules for the enrichment of jobs. Specific enrichment procedures depend upon a careful diagnosis of the work to be accomplished, the available technology, and the organizational context in which enrichment is to take place. However, many job enrichment schemes involve one or more of the following techniques:[26]

- *Combining tasks.* This involves assigning tasks that might be performed by different workers to a single individual. For example, in a furniture factory a lathe operator, an assembler, a sander, and a stainer might become four "chair makers"; each worker would then do all four tasks. Such a strategy should increase the variety of skills employed and might contribute to task identity as each worker approaches doing a unified job from start to finish.
- *Establishing external client relationships.* This involves putting employees in touch with people outside the organization who depend upon their products or services. Such a strategy might involve the use of new (interpersonal) skills, increase the identity and significance of the job, and increase feedback about one's performance. Consider this example:

  At the Duncan Hines angel food cake factory in Jackson, Tennessee, the line workers are given letters from customers who have problems with the product. One factory hand called up a customer whose angel food cake didn't rise, and helped figure out why by asking such questions as "How long did you beat the mix?" and "At what temperature did you bake it?" Says [Procter & Gamble CEO John] Smale: "What we've said to the workers is, this is the only place we make angel food cake, and you're responsible for it, and if you want to talk to the consumer, we'd like you to talk to the consumer."[27]

Establishing external relationships works particularly well when it is part of an overall culture that stresses good customer service. For example, employees of Lexus, Toyota's new luxury car division, are required to call several customers each month to find out how their cars are performing. Lexus must give obsessive attention to quality and satisfaction if it is to compete with better-established luxury makes such as BMW and Mercedes.

- *Establishing internal client relationships.* This involves putting employees in touch with people who depend upon their products or services within the organization. For example, billers and expediters in a manufacturing firm might be assigned permanently to certain salespeople, rather than working on any salesperson's order as it comes in. The advantages are similar to those mentioned for establishing external client relationships.
- *Reducing supervision or reliance on others.* The goal here is to increase autonomy and control over one's own work. For example, clerical employees might be permitted to check their own work for errors instead of having someone else do it. Similarly, workers might be allowed to order needed supplies or contract for outside services up to some dollar amount without obtaining permission.
- *Forming work teams.* This can be used as an alternative to a sequence of "small" jobs performed by individual workers when a product or service is too large or complex for one person to complete alone. For example, social workers with particular skills might operate as a true team to assist a particular client, rather than passing the client from person to person. Similarly, stable teams can be formed to construct an entire product, such as a car or boat, in lieu of an assembly-line approach. Such approaches should lead to the formal and informal development of a variety of skills and increase the identity of the job.
- *Making feedback more direct.* This technique is usually used in conjunction with other job design aspects that permit workers to be identified with their "own" product or service. For example, an electronics firm might have assemblers "sign" their output on a tag that includes an address and toll-free phone number. If problems are encountered, customers contact the assembler directly. In Sweden, workers who build trucks by team assembly are responsible for service and warranty work on "their" trucks that are sold locally. For another example of a job with enhanced feedback, see Global Focus 7–3.

In the next sections we will explore some actual applications of job enrichment and then look at some problems associated with the technique.

Examples of Job Enrichment

As pointed out earlier, the exact techniques that are used to enrich jobs vary with the nature of the organization and its particular products or services. Thus, in this

---

GLOBAL FOCUS 7–3

▼
....
Work Teams Have Own Planes, Direct Feedback at Japan Air Lines

Japan Air Lines suffered the worst air accident in history in 1985, when a Boeing 747 slammed into a mountain and killed 520 people. Seven years earlier Boeing engineers had improperly repaired the pressure bulkhead at the rear of the passenger cabin. JAL inspectors failed to find the defect—a missing line of rivets—in five heavy inspections.

Before the 1985 crash, JAL's maintenance teams looked after jets the way American mechanics do, seeing dozens of planes in the course of a year. Since then the company has assigned its work teams to specific aircraft. Today a typical 15-man team of mechanics and engineers at Haneda airport near Tokyo oversees a 747 and a DC-10. The team members sign their names on a special plaque inside the passenger cabin. After a major repair, the team leader is expected to fly on the plane.

Satoru Totoki, JAL managing director and senior vice president, compares the system to using a family doctor instead of a clinic. He points out that in English the teams are called "dedicated maintenance crews," in the sense of being assigned to specific planes. But in Japanese, they are called *kizuki,* or "plane crazy." One August day in 1986, a JAL plane was laid over in Thailand with engine trouble. JAL's Bangkok maintenance staff took care of the problem without informing the team leader in Tokyo about "his" plane. The leader, on vacation that day, somehow found out and got the next flight to Bangkok to verify that the repair had been done properly.

The *kizuki* approach is expensive. Government-owned for many years and only recently privatized, JAL has just 96 planes and lavishes 51 maintenance people—including specialists in hydraulics and electronics—on each one. That's almost double the number for a typical U.S. carrier.

Source: Ramirez, A. (1989, May 22). How safe are you in the air? *Fortune,* 75–88, p. 88. Copyright © 1989 by Fortune. Reprinted by permission.

section we will examine enrichment exercises that were carried out in two very different organizational environments—one involving the mass production of automobiles in Sweden and the other office jobs in the United States.

Volvo Volvo is a large Swedish producer of cars, buses, trucks, and industrial equipment. In the late 1960s, Volvo was beset by serious labor problems—wildcat strikes occurred, turnover was running about 40 percent a year, 20 percent of the work force was absent on a given day, and recruiting was very difficult. With the encouragement of a new president, Pehr Gyllenhammar, Volvo decided to build a new car assembly plant at Kalmar designed around enriched jobs. There is no assembly line at Kalmar. Rather, partially assembled cars move around the plant on self-propelled electric carriers, guided by a central computer and an electric track.

Cars at Kalmar are assembled by twenty-five permanent groups of about fifteen workers. Each group is responsible for installing all of a particular assembly, such as the electrical system, the interior, or wheel and brake units. The group is free to decide how to divide up and schedule its work, as along as it completes so many assemblies each day. When a car arrives at the group's permanent "workshop," the computer can be overridden and the carrier stopped. If any group detects a problem, such as scratched paint, it can automatically send the car back to the appropriate work station for corrections. The group also inspects its own work. After about every three workshops, more sophisticated quality control procedures are performed. A computer immediately informs the group when a problem has been detected, and its memory system tells the group how the problem was solved in the past. In addition, the computer informs the group when error-free performance is occurring. Each assembly group is responsible for initiating the contacts necessary to secure its own supplies and parts from a storage core.

Notice the techniques that have been implemented to enrich the assembly jobs at Kalmar: Permanent *work teams* perform a *combined series of tasks* that have a logical identity. Since the teams plan, organize, and inspect their own work, *supervision and reliance on others are reduced*. Obtaining their own parts and supplies *enhances internal client relationships*. Finally, self-inspection and the more sophisticated computer inspection *make feedback more direct*.

The Kalmar plant represents a remarkable achievement in enriching jobs that might seem to lack the potential for such treatment. Attitude surveys indicate that workers have responded very favorably to Kalmar. Absence and turnover are reported to be lower than at conventional plants, while productivity is equivalent.[28]

Originally, the new General Motors Saturn plant in Spring Hill, Tennessee, was slated to have an electric track and job design similar to Kalmar's. Finally, GM decided on a more conventional assembly line with jobs that are richer than average but probably not as stimulating as those at Kalmar. We will look at the entire Saturn project in Chapter 16.

AT&T American Telephone and Telegraph and its former associated companies in the Bell System have shown that job enrichment can also work on this side of the Atlantic. These organizations have been involved in an ongoing series of enrichment exercises.

The first job to be enriched was that of stockholder correspondent in the AT&T Treasury Department. This job involves dealing with queries and complaints from AT&T stockholders by mail or telephone. Since many of these issues can be quite complex, the work force consisted mostly of college graduates. Ironically, although interactions with stockholders are important and sensitive, the correspondent's job had been designed as a glorified clerical job—after correspondents had researched the problem in question, they composed a form letter response, which was verified and signed by their supervisors. Job dissatisfaction was high among the correspondents, and this dissatisfaction was reflected in a high rate of costly turnover. In addition, quality measures indicated an unacceptable level of errors and delays in responses. Gradually, a number of changes were introduced to the correspondent's job with the goal of enhancing its motivating potential. As you can see, these changes involved combining tasks, increasing teamwork, reducing supervision, and indirectly enhancing the external client relationship:

- *Subject-matter experts were appointed within each unit for other members of the unit to consult with before seeking supervisory help.*
- *Correspondents were told to sign their own names to letters from the very first day on the job after training.*
- *The work of the more experienced correspondents was looked over less frequently by supervisors, and this was done at each correspondent's desk.*
- *Production was discussed, but only in general terms: "A full day's work is expected," for example.*
- *Outgoing work went directly to the mail room without crossing the supervisor's desk.*
- *All correspondents were told they would be held fully accountable for quality of work.*
- *Correspondents were encouraged to answer letters in a more personalized way, avoiding the previous form letter approach.*[29]

In general, these changes would seem to affect each of the five core job characteristics, and the results were highly favorable. Compared with control groups, job satisfaction increased, while absence and turnover decreased.[30] In addition, the quality of performance rose, and more promotions were made from among the correspondents whose jobs had been enriched, presumably because they were now better able to demonstrate their skills and responsibility to management.

Numerous other enrichment attempts were made by AT&T and the former Bell System on jobs as diverse as service representatives, toll and information operators, telephone installers, keypunchers, and equipment engineers. While some of these attempts were more successful than others, AT&T, like Volvo, has shown strong commitment to the goal of making work more challenging and rewarding.

Problems with Job Enrichment

Despite the theoretical attractiveness of job enrichment as a motivational strategy, and despite the fact that many organizations have experimented with such schemes, practical attempts at enrichment can encounter a number of difficult problems.

First, put simply, some workers do not *desire* enriched jobs. Almost by definition, enrichment places greater demands upon workers, and some might not relish this extra responsibility. In such cases, enrichment should lead to nothing but trouble. Finding out who is ready for enrichment could be accomplished by measuring the growth need strength of the work force with a questionnaire (such as the one in the exercise at the end of the chapter). Also, some research suggests that organizations might do well to simply ask workers directly whether they would prefer to participate in job enrichment.[31] The results of this approach will be most trustworthy when workers feel absolutely free to decline the invitation and when they have a clear picture of what an enriched job will be like.

Even when workers have no basic objections to enrichment in theory, they might lack the skills and competence necessary to perform enriched jobs effectively. Thus, for some poorly educated work forces, enrichment might entail substantial training costs. In addition, it might be very difficult to train workers in certain skills required by enriched jobs, such as social skills. For example, part of the job enrichment scheme at a Philips television manufacturing plant in Holland required TV assemblers to initiate contacts with high-status staff members in other departments when problems were encountered. This is an example of the establishment of an internal client relationship, and many workers found this job requirement threatening.[32]

Occasionally, workers who experience job enrichment ask that greater extrinsic rewards, such as pay, accompany their redesigned jobs. Most frequently, this desire is probably prompted by the fact that such jobs require the development of new skills and entail greater responsibility. For example, one enrichment exercise for clerical jobs in a U.S. government agency encountered this reaction.[33] Sometimes, such requests are motivated by the wish to share in the financial benefits of a successful enrichment exercise. In one documented case, workers with radically enriched jobs in a General Foods dog food plant in Topeka sought a financial bonus that they based on the system's success.[34]

Generally, it is safe to say that North American unions have been less than enthusiastic about job enrichment. As one union leader has said:

> If you want to enrich the job, enrich the paycheck. . . . If you want
> to enrich the job, do something about the nerve-shattering noise, the

heat, the fumes. . . . Worker dissatisfaction diminishes with age. And that's because older workers have accrued more of the kinds of job enrichment that unions have fought for—better wages, shorter hours, vested pensions, a right to have a say in their working conditions, the right to be promoted on the basis of seniority, and all the rest. That's the kind of job enrichment that unions believe in.[35]

While this statement might represent an extreme position, it is certain that interesting work has not been one of the traditional union bargaining issues. In fact, almost all attempts at job redesign must confront labor contracts that segment and specialize work. This is ironic, since unionists have seldom been fans of Taylor's Scientific Management!

Another problem with job enrichment can occur when it is effected without a careful diagnosis of the needs of the organization and the particular jobs in question. Some enrichment attempts might be half-hearted tactical exercises that really don't increase the motivating potential of the job adequately. An especially likely error here is increasing job breadth (variety) while leaving the other crucial core characteristics unchanged. Thus, workers are simply given *more* boring, fragmented, routine tasks to do, such as bolting intake manifolds *and* carburetors onto engines. On the other side of the coin, in their zeal to use enrichment as a cure-all, organizations might attempt to enrich jobs that are already perceived as "too rich" by their incumbents:

> "When I read this stuff on job enrichment it makes me shake my head. My job is already too enriched for me or anyone else. Every day I'm being called on to make decisions I'm not prepared to make. I don't have enough time and I've got too many things to do. It's frustrating to be spread so thin."[36]

Even when enrichment schemes are carefully implemented to truly enhance the motivating potential of deserving jobs, they might fail because of their unanticipated impact on other jobs or other parts of the organizational system. A key problem here might involve the supervisors of the workers whose jobs have been enriched. By definition, enrichment involves increasing the autonomy of employees. Unfortunately, such a change might "disenrich" the boss's job, a consequence that is hardly calculated to facilitate the smooth implementation of the job redesign. Some organizations have responded to this problem by effectively doing away with direct supervision of workers performing enriched jobs. More likely, however, is the use of the supervisor as a trainer and developer of individuals on enriched jobs. Enrichment increases the need for this supervisory function in most cases.

In summary, although job enrichment has the potential to increase motivation and enhance the quality of working life, there are many obstacles to the effective implementation of enrichment. It is simply not a strategy that can be casually adopted and expected to take care of itself.

GOAL SETTING AS A MOTIVATOR

As pointed out in Chapter 1, one of the basic characteristics of all organizations is that they have goals. In Chapter 6, individual performance was defined as the extent to which a member contributes to the attainment of these goals or objectives. Thus, if acceptable performance is to be achieved by employees, some method of translating organizational goals into individual goals must be implemented.

Unfortunately, there is ample reason to believe that personal performance goals are vague or nonexistent for many organizational members. Employees frequently report that their role in the organization is unclear or that they don't really know what their boss expects of them. Even in cases in which performance goals would seem to be obvious because of the nature of the task (e.g., filling packing crates to the maximum to avoid excessive freight charges), employees might be ignorant of their current performance. This suggests that the implicit performance goals simply aren't making an impression.

The notion of **goal setting** as a motivator has been around for a long time. However, theoretical developments and some very practical research demonstrations have begun to suggest just when and how goal setting can be effective.[37]

What Kinds of Goals are Motivational?

A large body of evidence suggests that goals are most motivational when they are *specific, challenging,* and *accepted* by organizational members. In addition, *feedback* about progress toward goal attainment should be provided.[38] Let's examine each of these characteristics in turn.

Specific goals are goals that specify an exact level of achievement to be accomplished in a particular time frame. For example, "I will enroll in five courses next semester and achieve a *B* or better in each course" is a specific goal. Similarly, "I will increase my net sales by 20 percent in the coming business quarter" is a specific goal. On the other hand, "I will do my best" is not a specific goal, since level of achievement and time frame are both vague.

Obviously, specific goals will not motivate effective performance if the goals are especially easy to achieve. However, goal challenge is a much more personal matter than goal specificity, since it depends upon the experience and basic skills of the organizational member. One thing is certain, however—when goals become so difficult that they are perceived as *impossible* to achieve, the goals will lose their potential to motivate. Thus, goal challenge is best when it is pegged to the competence of individual workers and increased as the particular task is mastered. One practical way to do this is to base initial goals upon past performance. For example, an academic counselor might encourage a *D* student to set a goal of achieving *C*s in the coming semester and encourage a *C* student to set a goal of achieving *B*s. Similarly, a sales manager might ask a new salesperson to try to increase his sales by 5 percent in the next quarter and ask an experienced salesperson to try to increase her sales by 10 percent.

Finally, specific, challenging goals must be accepted by the individual if the goals are to have effective motivational properties. In a sense, goals really aren't goals unless they are consciously accepted. In the next section we will discuss some factors that affect goal acceptance.

Just why should specific, challenging, accepted goals, in and of themselves, serve as effective motivators? First, in expectancy theory terms, goal specificity should strengthen both expectancy and instrumentality connections. The individual now has a clear picture of a first-level outcome to which effort should be directed and greater certainty about the consequences of achieving this outcome. Turning to goal challenge, the need theories of motivation suggest that feelings of achievement, competence, and esteem should accompany the mastery of a challenging goal. In addition, certain motivational side effects might accompany goal setting. For one thing, workers might compete with their own "best record" and set even higher goals. For example, the typist who sets and achieves a goal of typing thirty pages on Monday might set a goal of thirty-two pages on Tuesday. In addition, in some goal-setting situations, workers might informally compete among themselves to outdo each other. Again, this might stimulate individual workers to set more challenging personal goals.

Specific, challenging, accepted goals have the most beneficial effect when they are accompanied by ongoing feedback that enables the person to compare current performance with the goal. Having set a goal, the typist who keeps a running log of pages typed should perform better than one who is unaware of his or her progress.

Enhancing Goal Acceptance

It has probably not escaped you that the requirements for goal challenge and goal acceptance seem potentially incompatible. After all, you might be quite amenable to accepting an easy goal but balk at accepting a "toughie." Thus, it is important to consider some of the factors that might affect the acceptance of challenging, specific goals.

It seems reasonable that organizational members should be more accepting of goals that are set with their participation than of those simply handed down from their superior. Sensible as this sounds, the research evidence on the effects of participation is very mixed—sometimes participation in goal setting increases performance, and sometimes it doesn't.[39] If goal acceptance is a potential *problem*, participation might prove beneficial.[40] When a climate of distrust between superiors and subordinates exists, or when participation provides information that assists in the establishment of fair, realistic goals, then it should facilitate performance. On the other hand, when subordinates trust their boss, and when the boss has a good understanding of the capability of the subordinates, participation might be quite unnecessary for acceptance.[41] It is interesting to note that participation has been shown to increase performance by increasing the *difficulty* of the goals that are adopted.[42] This might occur because participation induces competition or a feeling of team spirit among members of the work unit that leads them to exceed the goal expectations of the supervisor.

Will the promise of extrinsic rewards (such as money) for goal accomplishment increase the acceptance of goals? Probably, although there is little field research on this issue. However, there is plenty of evidence that goal setting has led to performance increases *without* the introduction of monetary incentives for goal accomplishment. One reason for this might be the fact that many "ambitious" goals involve no more than doing the job as it was designed to be done in the first place. For example, encouraging employees to pack crates or load trucks to within 5 percent of their maximum capacity doesn't really involve a greater expenditure of effort or more work. It simply requires more attention to detail. Finally, goal setting should be compatible with any systems to tie pay to performance that already exist for the job in question, such as wage incentives, commissions, or merit pay.

There is considerable agreement about one factor that will *reduce* the acceptance of specific, challenging performance goals. When supervisors behave in a coercive manner to encourage goal accomplishment, commitment to the goal should be badly damaged. For goal setting to work properly, supervisors must demonstrate a desire to assist employees in goal accomplishment and behave supportively if failure occurs, even adjusting the goal downward if it proves to be unrealistically high. Threat and punishment in response to failure will be extremely counterproductive.[43]

Goal setting has led to increased performance on a wide variety of tasks, including servicing drink machines, keypunching, selling, cutting trees, and typing. Studies reveal that the positive results of goal setting are not a "flash in the pan"—they persist over a long enough time to have practical value.[44] However, the performance impact of goal setting is strongest for simpler jobs rather than more complex jobs, such as scientific and engineering work.[45]

Before continuing, let's apply what you've been reading by considering the You Be the Manager feature.

Management by Objectives

In the bare-bones form presented above, goal setting is just that—a specific, challenging goal is established to solve a particular performance problem. In this basic form, goal setting is rather lacking in the potential to assist in employee development over time. No particular provisions are made for counseling employees in goal accomplishment or for changing goals in some systematic manner as the need arises. It might also occur to you that certain jobs require the simultaneous accomplishment of *several* goals and that superiors and subordinates might differ in the importance that they attach to these goals or disagree about how goal accomplishment can be evaluated. This is particularly likely in the more complex jobs that exist at higher levels in the organization, such as management jobs and staff jobs (e.g., the personnel department or the research and development department).

YOU BE THE MANAGER

 anager

The Weyerhaeuser Truck Drivers

Weyerhaeuser Company is a large forest products firm headquartered in Tacoma, Washington. Weyerhaeuser faced a problem that commonly crops up in production operations—the underutilization of expensive resources. The problem centered on truck drivers who hauled logs from the forest to a company sawmill. The drivers, who also loaded the trucks, were unionized and hourly paid. Management determined that the trucks were averaging only about 60 percent of their legal weight capacity. This extreme underloading was very undesirable, because extra trucks, extra drivers, and extra diesel fuel were necessary to transport a given amount of timber.

Management was convinced that the situation could be improved if drivers could be motivated to pay more attention to their loading procedures. Because logs differ in diameter and length, a full load could vary between 60 and 120 logs. Thus, judgment had to be exercised in the loading process. Although a scale was available at the loading point, drivers didn't seem to be making good use of it.

As a manager, what would *you* do to improve truck utilization? Remember, you don't want to encourage loading *over* the legal limit.

1. What are the pros and cons of using a monetary incentive to improve the loading process?

2. What are the pros and cons of using goal setting to improve the loading process?

To find out what Weyerhaeuser did, see The Manager's Notebook at the end of the chapter.

Source: Adapted from Latham, G. P., & Locke, E. (1979, Autumn). Goal setting—a motivational technique that works. *Organizational Dynamics*, 68–80; Latham, G. P., & Baldes, J. J. (1975). The "practical significance" of Locke's theory of goal setting. *Journal of Applied Psychology, 60*, 122–124.

Management by Objectives (MBO) is an elaborate, systematic, ongoing management program that is designed to facilitate goal establishment, goal accomplishment, and employee development.[46] The objectives in MBO are simply another label for goals. In a well-designed MBO program, objectives for the organization as a whole are developed by top management and diffused down through the organization by the MBO process. In this manner, organizational objectives are translated into specific behavioral objectives for individual members. Our primary focus here is with the nature of the interaction between superiors and individual subordinates in an MBO program. Although there are many variations on the MBO theme, most superior-subordinate interactions share the following similarities:

1. The superior meets with individual subordinates to develop and agree upon subordinate objectives for the coming months. These objectives usually involve both current job performance and personal development that may prepare the subordinate to perform other tasks or seek promotion. The objectives are made as specific as possible and quantified, if feasible, to assist in subsequent evaluation of accomplishment. Time frames for accomplishment are specified, and the objectives may be given priority according to their agreed-upon importance. The methods to be used to achieve the objectives might or might not be discussed. Objectives, time frames, and priorities are put in writing.

2. Periodic meetings are held to monitor subordinate progress in achieving objectives. During these meetings, objectives can be modified if new needs or problems are encountered.

3. An appraisal meeting is held to evaluate the extent to which the agreed-upon objectives have been achieved. Special emphasis is placed upon diagnosing the reasons for success or failure so that the meeting serves as a learning experience for both parties.

4. The MBO cycle is repeated.

An example of a simple MBO objectives form is shown in Exhibit 7–7. Plant manager John Atkins has met with company president F. W. Crawford and agreed upon eight objectives for the coming months. Notice that these objectives are specific and in most cases quantified. Objectives 7 and 8 are personal development objectives, while the others are performance objectives. The objectives have been given "A" priority or "B" priority (column 2), and a specific deadline for accomplishment (column 3). In his own role as a manager, Atkins would probably use some of these objectives as a basis for establishing the objectives of *his* subordinates. Thus, objectives 1 through 6 would become the basis of even more specific goals for the production manager, the shipping manager, and the personnel manager who report to Atkins. In this manner, the MBO program diffuses a "goal mentality" throughout the organization.

Although many organizations have implemented MBO programs, careful tests of the impact of these exercises on employee performance have been rare. Further, the more sophisticated research studies tend to be less complimentary of the effectiveness of MBO. Still, the weight of the evidence seems to indicate that when MBO programs are properly established and administered, they can have a positive effect on performance.[47]

Experience and research indicate that a number of factors might be associated with the failure of MBO programs. For one thing, MBO is an elaborate, difficult, time-consuming process, and its implementation must have the full support of top management. If such support is absent, managers at lower levels simply go through the motions of practicing MBO. At the very least, this reaction will lead

EXHIBIT

7–7

A simple format for recording objectives in an MBO program.

		Manager's job title	
John Atkins Prepared by the Manager	7/2 Date	PLANT MANAGER Managerial Job Objectives	
F. W. Crawford Reviewed by Supervisor	7/2 Date	PRESIDENT Supervisor's Job Title	
Statement of Objectives	Priority	Deadline	Outcomes or Results
1. To Increase Deliveries to 98% of All Scheduled Delivery Dates	A	6/31	
2. To Reduce Waste and Spoilage to 3% of All Raw Materials Used	A	6/31	
3. To Reduce Lost Time Due to Accidents to 100 Person-Days/Year	B	2/1	
4. To Reduce Operating Cost to 10% Below Budget	A	1/15	
5. To Install a Quality Control Radioisotope System at a Cost of Less Than $53,000	A	3/15	
6. To Improve Production Scheduling and Preventative Maintenance so as to Increase Machine Utilization Time to 95% of Capacity	B	10/1	
7. To Complete the UCLA Executive Program This Year	A	6/31	
8. To Teach a Production Management Course in University Extension	B	6/31	

Source: Adapted from Raia, A. P. (1974). *Managing by objectives.* Glenview, IL: Scott, Foresman, © 1974, p. 60. Reprinted by permission.

to the haphazard specification of objectives and thus subvert the very core of MBO, goal setting. A frequent symptom of this degeneration is the complaint that MBO is "just a bunch of paperwork." Indeed, at this stage, it is! Even with the best of intentions, setting specific, quantified objectives can be a difficult process. This might lead to an overemphasis on measurable objectives at the expense of more qualitative objectives. For example, it might be much easier to agree on production goals than on goals that involve subordinate development, although both might be equally important. Finally, even if reasonable objectives are established, MBO can still be subverted if the performance review becomes an exercise in browbeating or punishing subordinates for failure to achieve objectives.[48]

Goal Setting and Quality of Working Life

By now, you should be able to anticipate the argument—goal-setting exercises, whether simple or elaborate, have the potential to enhance the quality of working life if they are *properly managed*. Clear, specific performance goals should reduce role ambiguity and stress and thus promote a high-quality work experience. By the same token, achieving challenging goals should promote feelings of competence and self-reliance among many employees. It should be clear, however, that goal-setting programs place very special demands upon supervisory personnel. Even in simple goal-setting exercises, a proper level of challenge must be identified, unavoidable obstacles to performance must be recognized, and the necessity for subordinate participation must be accurately gauged. More elaborate programs, such as MBO, compound these demands. If employees perceive that goals are too difficult, arbitrary, or unachievable through no fault of their own, they will experience dissatisfaction and resentment.

ALTERNATIVE WORKING SCHEDULES AS MOTIVATORS

Most North Americans work a five-day, forty-hour week. Furthermore, they are usually required to do this work within a fixed set of hours—e.g., the "nine-to-five grind." Recently, some organizations have begun to experiment with modifications of these traditional working schedules. Although sometimes prompted in part by general social concerns (such as saving energy or reducing traffic during rush hours), these experiments are primarily of interest because of their potential impact on motivation and the quality of working life.

One alternative to traditional working schedules is **flex-time,** which was first introduced on a large scale in Europe. In its most simple and common form, workers are required to report for work on each working day and work a given number of hours. However, the times at which they arrive and leave are flexible, as long as they are present during certain core times. For example, employees might be permitted to begin their day anytime after 7 A.M. and work until 6 P.M., as long as they put in eight hours and are present during the core times of 9:15

until noon and 2 until 4:15 (Exhibit 7–8). Other systems permit employees to tally hours on a weekly or monthly basis, although they are still usually required to be present during the core time of each working day.[49]

A second alternative to traditional working schedules is the **compressed work-week.** This system compresses the hours worked each week into fewer days. The most common compressed workweek is the 4-40 system, in which employees work four ten-hour days each week rather than the traditional five eight-hour days. Thus, the organization or department might operate Monday through Thursday or Tuesday through Friday, although rotation schemes that keep the organization open five days a week are also employed.[50]

It should be obvious that there are certain technical constraints to the implementation of modified working schedules. When jobs are highly interdependent, such as on an assembly line, flex-time becomes an unlikely strategy. To cite an even more extreme example, we simply can't have members of a hospital operating room team showing up for work whenever it suits them! In addition, flex-time

EXHIBIT

7–8

An example of a flex-time schedule.

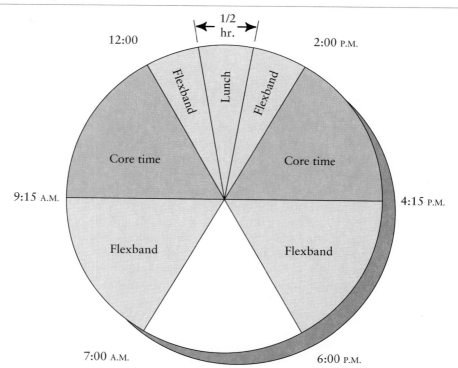

Source: Adapted from Ronen, S. (1981). *Flexible working hours: An innovation in the quality of work life.* New York: McGraw-Hill, p. 42. Reprinted by permission.

might lead to problems in achieving adequate supervisory coverage. For these reasons, it should not surprise you that flex-time has been implemented most frequently in office environments. For instance, in a bank, the core hours might be when the bank is open to the public.

Technical roadblocks to the implementation of the 4-40 workweek include the possibility of reduced customer service and the negative effects of fatigue that can accompany longer working days. The latter problem is likely to be especially acute when the work is strenuous.

Despite these technical limitations, what are the supposed advantages of modified working times? First, it should be clear that the theories of motivation discussed in the last chapter would suggest few *direct* performance benefits. That is, simply manipulating the hours of work should not motivate employees to produce more work or higher-quality work. However, modified working hours might have both direct and indirect effects upon other work behaviors and on the quality of working life of employees. For example, both flex-time and the 4-40 workweek might reduce absenteeism because they permit workers greater freedom to take care of personal business or family matters during what had been working time. In addition, the 4-40 schedule reduces commuting costs by 20 percent, while flexible working hours might connote a degree of prestige and trust that is usually reserved for executives and professionals. Such consequences might increase job satisfaction, reducing turnover and making it easier to recruit new employees.

Although flex-time has generally been limited to white-collar personnel, it has been applied in a variety of organizations, including insurance companies (Prudential), financial institutions (Canada Trust, Boston's State Street Bank), and government offices (many U.S. states, Canadian and U.S. civil service). Although the quality of the research on flex-time varies, a number of conclusions can be drawn.[51] First, employees who work under flex-time almost always prefer the system to fixed hours. In addition, work attitudes generally become more positive, and employers report minimal abuse of the arrangement. When measured, absenteeism and tardiness have often shown decreases following the introduction of flex-time, and first-line supervisors and managers are usually positively inclined toward the system. Interestingly, slight productivity gains are often reported under flex-time, probably due to better use of scarce resources or equipment rather than to increased motivation. As an extreme example, a computer-programming group that shared a computer system increased its productivity 24 percent following the introduction of flex-time (a clear improvement over several control groups). Flex-time evidently gave more programmers more access time to the computer each workday.[52]

While solid evidence regarding the effects of the four-day week is rare, a couple of tentative conclusions stand out.[53] First, workers who have experienced the four-day system seem to *like* it. Sometimes this liking is accompanied by increased job satisfaction, but the effect might be short-lived.[54] In many cases, the impact of the compressed workweek might be better for family life than for work life. Second, workers have often reported an increase in fatigue following the introduction of the compressed week. This might be responsible for the uneven impact of the system on absenteeism, sometimes decreasing it and sometimes not. Potential gains in attendance might be nullified as workers take an occasional day off to recuperate from fatigue.[55] Finally, the more sophisticated research studies do not report lasting changes in productivity due to the short workweek.[56]

In conclusion, research has shown some positive outcomes and very few negative attitudinal or motivational effects stemming from flex-time or the compressed workweek. Furthermore, their general popularity among the work force makes the systems good recruiting tools for attracting competent workers.

THE MANAGER'S NOTEBOOK

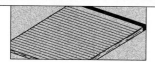

The Weyerhaeuser Truck Drivers

1. In theory, a monetary incentive could certainly get the drivers' attention and motivate them to haul heavier loads. In practice, however, unions have not shown great enthusiasm for such incentives (especially when they are given individually), and management might balk at paying drivers extra for what they should already be doing. Also, a financial incentive could encourage overloading, and it will require an expensive system to record weights and calculate bonuses.

2. Weyerhaeuser chose goal setting. With the union's cooperation, drivers were assigned a specific, challenging performance goal of loading their trucks to 94 percent of legal weight capacity. Before this goal was set, drivers had simply been asked to do their best to maximize their weight. The results? Over the first several weeks, load capacity gradually increased to over 90 percent and remained at this high level for *seven years*! In the first nine months alone, company accountants conservatively estimated the savings at $250,000. These results were achieved without driver participation in setting the goal and without monetary incentives for goal accomplishment. Drivers evidently found the 94 percent goal motivating in and of itself; they frequently recorded their weights in informal competition with other drivers.

SUMMARY

- In this chapter we have discussed four strategies that have been employed to increase the motivation of organizational members. Money should be most effective as a motivator when it is made contingent upon performance. Schemes to link pay to performance on production jobs are called wage incentive plans. Piecerate, in which workers are paid a certain amount of money for each item produced, is the prototype of all wage incentive plans. In general, wage incentives have been shown to increase productivity, but their introduction can be accompanied by a number of problems, one of which is the restriction of production. Attempts to link pay to performance on white-collar jobs are called merit pay plans. Evidence suggests that many merit pay plans are less effective than they could be because merit pay is inadequate, performance ratings are mistrusted, or extreme secrecy about pay levels prevails.

- Recent views advocate increasing the scope (breadth and depth) of jobs to capitalize on their inherent motivational properties, as opposed to the job simplification of the past. The Job Characteristics Model, proposed by Hackman and Oldham, suggests that jobs have five core characteristics that affect their motivating potential: skill variety, task identity, task significance, autonomy, and feedback. When jobs are high in these characteristics, favorable motivational and attitudinal consequences should occur. Job enrichment involves designing jobs to enhance intrinsic motivation and the quality of working life. Some specific enrichment techniques include combining tasks, establishing client relationships, reducing supervision and reliance on others, forming work teams, and making feedback more direct.
- Goal setting can be an effective motivator when goals are specific, challenging, and acceptable to workers. In some cases, acceptance might be facilitated by participation in goal setting and by financial incentives for goal attainment, but freedom from coercion and punishment seems to be the key factor in achieving goal acceptance. Management by Objectives (MBO) is an elaborate goal-setting and evaluation process that is typically used for management jobs.
- Some organizations have adopted alternative working schedules such as flex-time or the compressed workweek with expectations of motivational benefits. Although these schemes should have little effect on productivity, they have the potential to reduce absence and turnover and enhance the quality of working life. Where adopted, both schemes have usually proved acceptable to workers and management.

KEY CONCEPTS

Quality of working life	Task identify	Context factors
Piecerate	Feedback	Job enrichment
Wage incentive plans	Motivating potential	Goal setting
Restriction of productivity	Gain-sharing plans	Management by Objectives (MBO)
Skill variety	Merit pay plans	Flex-time
Autonomy	Scientific Management	Compressed workweek
Task significance	Growth need strength	

DISCUSSION QUESTIONS

1. Describe some jobs for which you think it would be difficult to link pay to performance. What is there about these jobs that provokes this difficulty?

2. Imagine two insurance companies that have merit pay plans for salaried white-collar personnel. In one organization the plan truly rewards good performers, while in the other it does not. Both companies decide to make salaries completely public. What will be the consequences of such a change for each company? (Be specific, using concepts such as expectancy, instrumentality, job satisfaction, and turnover.)

3. You are, of course, familiar with the annual lists of the world's ten worst-dressed women or the ten worst movies. Here's a new one: A job enrichment consultant has developed a list of the ten worst jobs, which includes a highway toll collector, pool

typist, bank guard, and automatic elevator operator. Use the five core job characteristics to describe each of these jobs. Could any of these jobs be enriched? How? Which should be completely automated? Can you add some jobs to the list?

4. Hackman and Oldham state that context dissatisfaction may detract from the motivational properties of an enriched job. Use Maslow's Need Hierarchy to explain this statement.

5. Some observers have argued that the jobs of the President of the United States and the Prime Minister of Canada are "too big" for one person to perform adequately. This probably means that the jobs are perceived as having too much scope or being too enriched. Use the Job Characteristics Model to explore the accuracy of this contention.

6. Debate the following statements: Of all the motiva-

tional techniques discussed in this chapter, goal setting is the simplest to implement. Goal setting is no more than doing what a good manager should be doing anyway.

7. Imagine an office setting in which a change to either a four-day week or flex-time would appear to be equally feasible to introduce. What would be the pros and cons of each system? How would factors

such as the nature of the business, the age of the work force, and the average commuting distance affect the choice of systems?

8. Debate the following proposition: The motivational strategies discussed in this chapter are manipulative and unethical, and they put too much pressure on the work force.

EXPERIENTIAL EXERCISE

Choose Your Job

People differ in the kinds of jobs they prefer. The following questions give you a chance to consider just what it is about a job that is most important to *you*. For each question, indicate the extent to which you would prefer Job A or Job B if you had to make a choice between them. In answering, assume that everything else about the two jobs is the same except the characteristics being compared. There are no "correct" answers. Just give your personal choice.

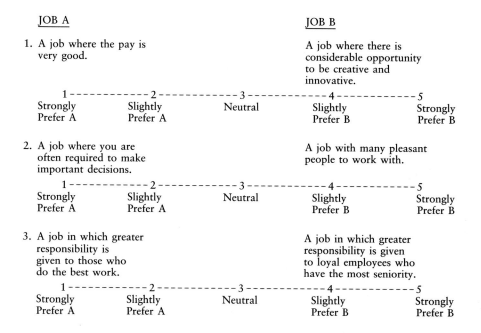

JOB A

1. A job where the pay is very good.

JOB B

A job where there is considerable opportunity to be creative and innovative.

```
1 ----------- 2 ------------ 3 ------------ 4 ----------- 5
Strongly        Slightly        Neutral        Slightly       Strongly
Prefer A        Prefer A                       Prefer B       Prefer B
```

2. A job where you are often required to make important decisions.

A job with many pleasant people to work with.

```
1 ----------- 2 ------------ 3 ------------ 4 ----------- 5
Strongly        Slightly        Neutral        Slightly       Strongly
Prefer A        Prefer A                       Prefer B       Prefer B
```

3. A job in which greater responsibility is given to those who do the best work.

A job in which greater responsibility is given to loyal employees who have the most seniority.

```
1 ----------- 2 ------------ 3 ------------ 4 ----------- 5
Strongly        Slightly        Neutral        Slightly       Strongly
Prefer A        Prefer A                       Prefer B       Prefer B
```

JOB A   JOB B

4. A job in an organization   A job in which you are
which is in financial   not allowed to have any
trouble—and might have   say whatever in how your
to close down within the   work is scheduled, or in
year.   the procedures to be used
                                     in carrying it out.

1------------2------------3------------4------------5
Strongly   Slightly   Neutral   Slightly   Strongly
Prefer A   Prefer A   Prefer B   Prefer B

5. A very routine job.   A job where your co-workers
                                     are not very friendly.

1------------2------------3------------4------------5
Strongly   Slightly   Neutral   Slightly   Strongly
Prefer A   Prefer A   Prefer B   Prefer B

6. A job with a supervisor who   A job which prevents you
is often very critical of   from using a number of
you and your work in front   skills that you worked
of other people.   hard to develop.

1------------2------------3------------4------------5
Strongly   Slightly   Neutral   Slightly   Strongly
Prefer A   Prefer A   Prefer B   Prefer B

7. A job with a supervisor   A job which provides
who respects you   constant opportunities
and treats you fairly.   for you to learn new
                                     and interesting things.

1------------2------------3------------4------------5
Strongly   Slightly   Neutral   Slightly   Strongly
Prefer A   Prefer A   Prefer B   Prefer B

8. A job where there is a   A job with very little
real chance you could   chance to do challenging
be laid off.   work.

1------------2------------3------------4------------5
Strongly   Slightly   Neutral   Slightly   Strongly
Prefer A   Prefer A   Prefer B   Prefer B

9. A job in which there is   A job which provides
a real chance for you to   lots of vacation time
develop new skills and   and an excellent fringe
advance in the organization.   benefit package.

1------------2------------3------------4------------5
Strongly   Slightly   Neutral   Slightly   Strongly
Prefer A   Prefer A   Prefer B   Prefer B

10. A job with little freedom   A job where the working
and independence to do   conditions are poor.
your work in the way you
think best.

1------------2------------3------------4------------5
Strongly   Slightly   Neutral   Slightly   Strongly
Prefer A   Prefer A   Prefer B   Prefer B

JOB A   JOB B

11. A job with very   A job which allows you
    satisfying team-work.   to use your skills and
                                                               abilities to the fullest
                                                               extent.

1 ----------- 2 ----------- 3 ----------- 4 ----------- 5
Strongly   Slightly   Neutral   Slightly   Strongly
Prefer A   Prefer A   Prefer B   Prefer B

12. A job which offers   A job which requires you
    little or no challenge.   to be completely isolated
                                                               from co-workers.

1 ----------- 2 ----------- 3 ----------- 4 ----------- 5
Strongly   Slightly   Neutral   Slightly   Strongly
Prefer A   Prefer A   Prefer B   Prefer B

Scoring and Interpretation

These questions make up the Growth Need Strength measure from J. Richard Hackman and
Greg Oldham's Job Diagnostic Survey. To determine your own growth need strength, first subtract your responses on items 2, 3, 4, 6, 8, and 9 from six. Then, add up the resulting scores on
all twelve items and divide the total by twelve. This is your growth need strength score. It should
fall somewhere between 1 and 5.

People with high growth needs have a strong desire to obtain growth satisfaction from their
jobs. They have some tendency to respond better to enriched, high scope jobs than those with
lower growth needs. The average growth score for thousands of individuals employed in a wide
variety of jobs is 4.23. Here are some other growth need norms based on occupation, education,
and age:[57]

4.46 White collar   4.13 Machine trades
4.00 Blue collar   4.16 Construction
4.92 Middle managers   4.02 High school graduates
4.62 First line managers   4.72 University graduates
4.76 Professional and technical   4.01 Under age 20
4.18 Clerical   4.25 Ages 20–29
4.92 Sales

Source: Hackman, J. R., & Oldham, G. R. (1980). The Job Diagnostic Survey: An instrument for the diagnosis
of jobs and the evaluation of job redesign projects. *Work Redesign.* Yale University Department of Administrative Sciences Technical Report No. 4. Addison-Wesley: Reading, MA. Reprinted by permission.

FAB Sweets Limited

Organizational Setting

FAB Sweets Limited is a manufacturer of high quality sweets [candies]. The company is a medium-sized, family-owned, partially unionized and highly successful confectionery producer in the north of England. The case study is set within a single department in the factory where acute problems were experienced.

Background to the Case

The department (hereafter called 'HB') produces and packs over 40 lines of hard-boiled sweets on a batch-production system. It is organized in two adjacent areas, one for production staffed by men and one for packing staffed by women. The areas are separated by a physical barrier, allowing the packing room to be air conditioned and protected from the humidity resulting from production. Management believed this was necessary to stop the sweets from sweating (thus sticking to their wrappers) during storage. Each room has a chargehand and a supervisor who reports to the departmental manager, who himself is responsible to the factory manager. In total 37 people work in the department (25 in production, 12 in packing), the majority of whom are skilled employees. Training takes place on the job, and it normally takes two years to acquire the skills necessary to complete all the production tasks. Exhibit 1 presents an outline of the physical layout of the department and the work flow.

The production process is essentially quite simple. Raw materials, principally sugar, are boiled to a set temperature, with 'cooking time' varying from line to

Source: Case prepared by Clegg, C., Kemp, N., & Wall, T. (1985). In Clegg, C., Kemp, N., & Legge, K. (Eds), *Case studies in organizational behaviour*. London: Harper & Row. Copyright © 1985 by Harper & Row, Publishers, Inc. Reprinted by permission.

line. The resulting batches are worked on by employees who fold and manipulate them so as to create the required texture, while adding coloring and favorings ('slabbing' and 'mixing'). Different batches are molded together to create the flavor mixes and patterns required ('make up'). The batch, which by now is quite cool, is then extruded through a machine which cuts it into sweets of individual size. Some products at this stage are automatically wrapped and then passed by conveyor belt to the packing room where they are inspected, bagged, and boxed ready for dispatch to retail and wholesale outlets. Other products progress unwrapped into the packing room where they are fed into a wrapping machine, inspected, bagged and dispatched. Several different product lines can be produced at the same time. The most skilled and critical tasks occur early in the process; these include 'cooking' mixtures for different products and 'make up' (e.g., for striped mints). These skills are gradually learned until the operator is able to 'feel' the correct finish for each of the 40 lines. All the tasks are highly interdependent such that any one individual's performance affects the ease with which the next person down the line can successfully achieve his/her part of the production process. Although the work appears quite simple and the management of the process straightforward, the department nevertheless experienced acute problems. These are outlined below.

The Problem

In objective terms the problems in HB were manifest in a high level of labor turnover, six new managers in eight years, production which consistently fell below targets based on work study standards, and high levels of scrap. The department was known as the worst in the factory and its problems were variously characterized in terms of 'attitude,' 'atmosphere' and 'climate.' Moreover, employees had few decision-making responsibilities, low motivation, low job satisfaction, and received little information

EXHIBIT 1

The HB department: physical layout and work flow.

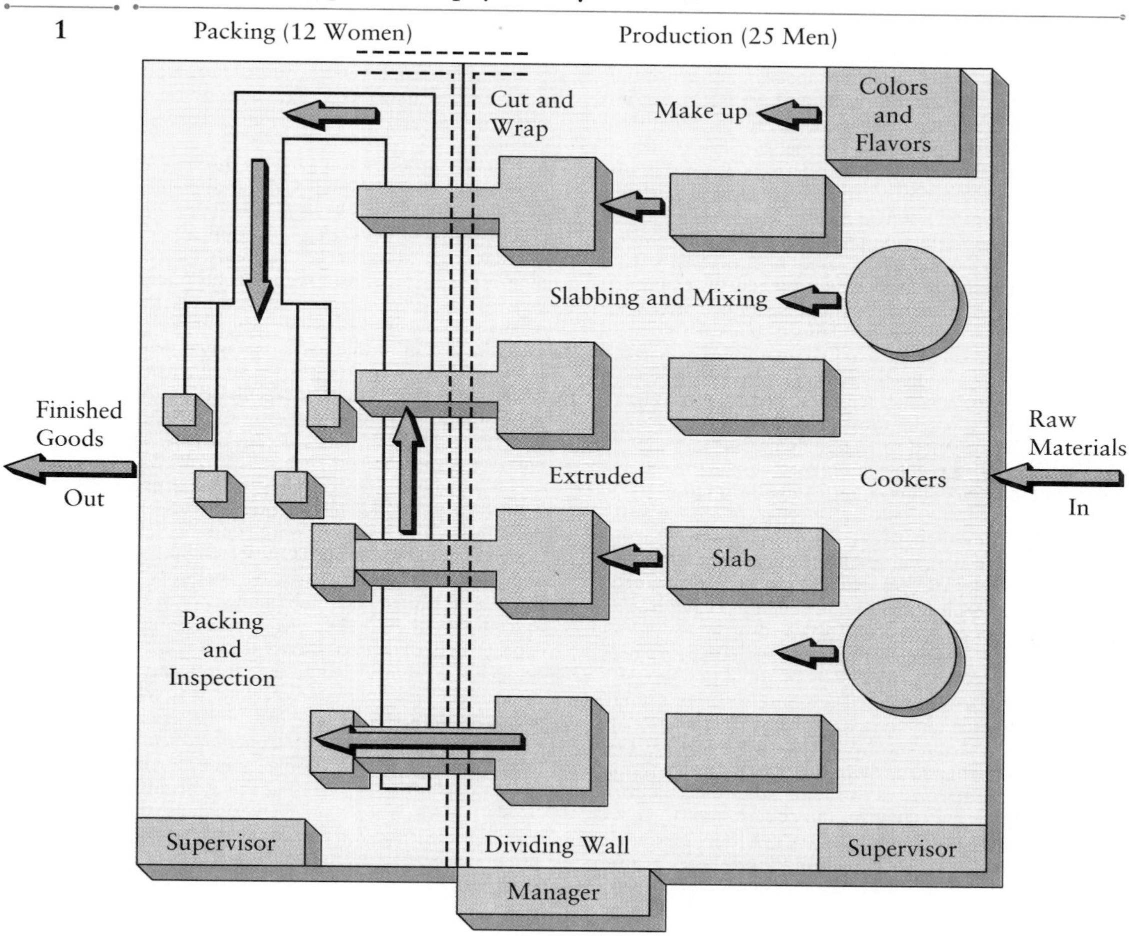

Packing (12 Women)   Production (25 Men)

Colors and Flavors

Make up

Cut and Wrap

Slabbing and Mixing

Finished Goods Out

Extruded

Raw Materials In

Slab

Cookers

Packing and Inspection

Supervisor

Dividing Wall

Supervisor

Manager

on their performance. Finally there were interpersonal problems between the employees in the production and packing rooms, between the two supervisors, and also among the operators, and there were a number of dissatisfactions relating to grading and payment levels.

Experience of the Method of Working

To understand how HB works and how people experienced their work it is necessary to recognize the strong drive throughout the organization for production. Departmental managers are judged primarily in terms of their production levels (against targets) and the efficiency

(against work study standards) at which they perform. In HB this pressure was transmitted to the two supervisors. In practice, production levels were the number of batches of sweets processed, and efficiency was the ratio of batches produced to hours used by direct labor.

The production supervisor responded to the pressure for production in a number of ways. First, in an attempt to maximize production, he always allocated people to the jobs at which they performed best. He also determined the cooker speeds. In effect, this set the pace of work for both production and packing. Buffer stocks were not possible in production because the sweets needed processing before they cooled down. If he was falling behind his target, the supervisor responded by speeding up the pace of work. In addition, he regarded his job purely in terms of processing batches, and ignored problems in the packing room which may in fact have resulted directly from his actions or from those of his staff. The supervisory role thus involved allocating people to tasks, setting machine speeds (and hence the pace of work), organizing reliefs and breaks, monitoring hygiene, safety and quality standards, maintaining discipline and recording data for the management information systems. The chargehand undertook these responsibilities in the absence of a supervisor, spending the rest of his time on production.

The men in production complained that they were bored with always doing the same jobs, especially as some were physically harder than others (for example, 'slabbing' involved manual manipulation of batches of up to 50 kilograms). Several claimed that their greater efforts should receive financial recognition. Furthermore, this rigidity of task allocation was in direct conflict with the grading system which was designed to encourage flexibility. To be on the top rate of pay in the department, an operator had to be capable of performing all the skills for all the lines, and hence be able to cover any job. Training schedules matched this. In practice, however, people rarely used more than one or two of their skills. The others decayed through disuse. All the staff recognized that the grading system was at odds with how the department actually worked and tended to be dissatisfied with both. The production supervisor's strict control over the pace of work also proved suboptimal in other ways. For example, he sometimes pushed the pace to a level regarded as impossible by the staff. Whether this was true or self-fulfilling is a moot point— the net result was an increase in the level of scrap. Also he ignored the wishes of the staff to work less hard in the afternoon when they were tired: again scrap resulted. In addition the feeling was widespread among the men in production that management and supervision organized the work badly and would do better if they took advice from the shop floor. Their own perceived lack of control over the job led them to abrogate responsibility when things went wrong ("We told them so!!"). And finally, although the processes of production were highly interdependent, operators adopted an insular perspective and the necessary cooperation between workers was rarely evident, and then only on the basis of personal favors between friends.

The equivalent pressure on the packing supervisor was to pack the sweets efficiently. As her section could pack no more than was produced, her only manipulable variable was hours worked. Thus to increase her efficiency she could only transfer the packers to 'other work' within her room (e.g. cleaning) or to another department.

The packers for their part resented being asked to work flat out when HB was busy, only to be moved elsewhere when things were slacker. As described above, their own work flow was basically controlled by the speed at which the men were producing. When in difficulty, direct appeals to the men to slow down were unsuccessful and so they channeled their complaints through their supervisor. Because of the insular perspective adopted by the production supervisor (in rational support of his own targets), her approaches were usually ignored ("It's my job to produce sweets"), and the resulting intersupervisory conflict took up much of the departmental manager's time. In addition the packing room was very crowded and interpersonal conflicts were common.

Finally, production problems throughout the factory were created by seasonal peaks and troughs in the market demand for sweets. These 'busy' and 'slack' periods differed between production departments. In order to cope with market demands the production planning department transferred staff, on a temporary basis, between production departments. In HB this typically meant that, when they were busy, 'unskilled' employees were drafted in to help, whereas when demand was low HB employees were transferred to other departments where they were usually given the worst jobs. Both of these solutions were resented by the employees in HB.

This description of the department is completed when one recognizes the complications involved in scheduling over 40 product lines through complex machinery, all of it over 10 years old. In fact breakdowns and interruptions to smooth working were common. The effects of these on the possible levels of production were poorly understood and in any case few operators were aware of their targets or of their subsequent performance. More immediately the breakdowns were a source of continual conflict between the department and the maintenance engineers responsible to an engineering manager. The department laid the blame on poor maintenance, the engineers on abuse or lack of care by production workers in handling the machinery. Much management time was spent in negotiating 'blame' for breakdowns and time allowances resulting since this affected efficiency figures. Not surprisingly, perhaps, the factory-wide image of the department was very poor on almost all counts, and its status was low.

Participants' Diagnoses of the Problems

Shopfloor employees, chargehands, supervisors, the department manager and senior management were agreed that much was wrong in HB. However, there was no coherent view of the causes and what should be done to make improvements. Many shopfloor employees placed the blame on supervision and management for their lack of technical and planning expertise, and their low consideration for subordinates. The production supervisor favored a solution in terms of "getting rid of the trouble-makers," by transferring or sacking his nominated culprits. The department manager wanted to introduce a senior supervisor to handle the conflicts between the production and packing supervisors and further support the pressure for production. The factory manager thought the way work was organized and managed might be at the core of the difficulties.

1. Use expectancy theory and equity theory (Chapter 6) to analyze the general motivational climate in the HB department.
2. Discuss the specific roles of money, job design, and goal setting as they relate to the problems experienced in the HB department.
3. What should be done by management to improve the motivation and quality of working life in the HB department? Be specific, and cover major issues as well as supporting details.
4. In light of the above, evaluate the solutions proposed by the shopfloor employees, the production supervisor, the department manager, and the factory manager.

REFERENCES

1. For reviews, see Lawler, E. E., III. (1971). *Pay and organizational effectiveness: A psychological view.* New York: McGraw-Hill; Chung, K. H. (1977). *Motivational theories and practices.* Columbus, OH: Grid. For a recent careful study, see Wagner, J. A., III, Rubin, P. A., & Callahan, T. J. (1988). Incentive payment and nonmanagerial productivity: An interrupted time series analysis of magnitude and trend. *Organizational Behavior and Human Decision Processes, 42,* 47–74.

2. Locke, E. A., Feren, D. B., McCaleb, V. M., Shaw, K. N., & Denny, A. T. (1980). The relative effectiveness of four methods of motivating employee performance. In K. D. Duncan, M. M. Gruneberg, & D. Wallis (Eds.), *Changes in working life.* London: Wiley.

3. Fein, M. (1973, September). Work measurement and wage incentives. *Industrial Engineering,* 49–51.

4. Fein, M. (1976). Motivation for work. In R. Dubin (Ed.), *Handbook of work, organization, and society.* Chicago: Rand McNally.

5. Posner, B. G. (1989, May). If at first you don't succeed. *Inc.,* 132–134, p. 132.

6. Lawler, E. E., III, (1981). *Pay and organizational development.* Reading, MA: Addison-Wesley; Miller, C. S., & Shuster, M. H. (1987, Summer). Gainsharing plans: A comparative analysis. *Organizational Dynamics,* 44–67.

7. Lesieur, F. G. (Ed.). (1958). *The Scanlon plan.* Cambridge, MA: M.I.T. Press.

8. Lawler, E. E. (1984). Whatever happened to incentive pay? *New Management, 1*(4), 37–41; Perry, N.J. (1988, December 19). Here come richer, riskier pay plans. *Fortune,* 50–58.

9. Bureau of National Affairs (1974). *Management performance appraisal programs.* BNA Personnel Policies Forum survey no. 104.

10. Lawler, 1971.

11. Lawler, 1971; Nash, A., & Carrol, S. (1975). *The management of compensation.* Monterey, CA: Brooks/Cole.

12. Weeks, D. A. (1976). *Compensating employees: Lessons of the 1970's.* New York: The Conference Board.

13. Lawler, 1971; Ungson, G. R., & Steers, R. M. (1984). Motivation and politics in executive compensation. *Academy of Management Review, 9,* 313–323; Tosi, H. L., & Gomez-Mejia, L. R. (1989). The decoupling of CEO pay and performance: An agency theory perspective. *Administrative Science Quarterly, 34,* 169–189.

14. Haire, M., Ghiselli, E. E., & Gordon, M. E. (1967). A psychological study of pay. *Journal of Applied Psychology Monograph, 51,* (Whole No. 636).

15. Bureau of National Affairs, 1974. Also see De Vries, D. L., & McCall, M. W., Jr. (1976, January). *Performance appraisal: Is it tax time again?* Paper presented at the Center for Creative Leadership, Greensboro, NC.

16. Weeks, 1976.

17. Lawler, E. E., III, (1972). Secrecy and the need to know. In H. L. Tosi, R. J. House, & M. D. Dunnette (Eds.), *Managerial motivation and compensation.* East Lansing, MI: Michigan State University Press.

18. Futrell, C. M., & Jenkins, O. C. (1978). Pay secrecy versus pay disclosure for salesmen: A longitudinal study. *Journal of Marketing Research, 15,* 214–219, p. 215.

19. Penner, D. D. (1966). *A study of the causes and consequences of salary satisfaction.* Crotonville, NY: General Electric Behavioral Research Service; Lawler, E. E. (1966). Managers' attitudes toward how their pay is and should be determined. *Journal of Applied Psychology, 50,* 273–279.

20. Taylor, F. W. (1967). *The principles of scientific management.* New York: Norton.

21. This discussion draws upon Gibson, J. L., Ivancevich, J. M., & Donnelly, J. H., Jr. (1985). *Organizations* (5th ed.). Plano, TX: Business Publications.

22. Hackman, J. R., & Oldham, G. R. (1980). *Work redesign.* Reading, MA: Addison-Wesley.

23. Oldham, G. R., Hackman, J. R., & Stepina, L. P. (1979). Norms for the job diagnostic survey. *JSAS Catalog of Selected Documents in Psychology, 9,* 14. (Ms. No. 1819).

24. Three separate meta-analyses find some support for growth need moderation. However, they differ in their conclusions about the scope and location of the effects. See Loher, B. T., Noe, R. A., Moeller, N. L., & Fitzgerald, M. P. (1985). A meta-analysis of the relation of job characteristics to job satisfaction. *Journal of Applied Psychology, 70,* 280–289; Spector, P. E. (1985). Higher-order need strength as a moderator of the job scope-employee outcome relationship: A meta-analysis. *Journal of Occupational Psychology, 58,* 119–127; Fried, Y., & Ferris, G. R. (1987). The validity of the job characteristics model: A review and meta-analysis. *Personnel Psychology, 40,* 287–322.

25. For a supporting study, see Oldham, G. R., Hackman, J. R., & Pearce, J. L. (1976). Conditions under which employees respond favorably to enriched work. *Journal of Applied Psychology, 61,* 395–403. For negative evidence, see Katerberg, R., Jr., Hom, P. W., & Hulin, C. L. (1979). Effects of job complexity on the reactions of part-time employees. *Organizational Behavior and Human Performance, 24,* 317–332.

26. This section draws in part on Hackman & Oldham, 1980.

27. Dumaine, B. (1989, November 6). P & G rewrites the marketing rules. *Fortune,* 34–48, p. 46.

28. The description of Volvo's job enrichment efforts draws on Dowling, W. F. (1973, Autumn). Job redesign on the assembly line: Farewell to the blue-collar blues? *Organizational Dynamics,* 51–67; Gyllenhammar, P. G. (1977). *People at work.* Reading, MA: Addison-Wesley; Walton, R. E. (1977). Successful strategies for diffusing work innovations. *Journal of Contemporary Business, 6,* 1–22.

29. Ford, R. N. (1969). *Motivation through the work itself.* New York: American Management Association, pp. 29–30. Other description in this section also relies upon Ford.

30. Job enrichment has proven fairly effective in reducing turnover. See McEvoy, G., & Cascio, W. F. (1985). Strategies for reducing employee turnover: A meta-analysis. *Journal of Applied Psychology, 70,* 342–353.

31. Cherrington, D. J., & England, J. L. (1980). The desire for an enriched job as a moderator of the enrichment satisfaction relationship. *Organizational Behavior and Human Performance, 25,* 139–159.

32. Dowling, 1973.

33. Locke, E. A., Sirota, D., & Wolfson, A. D. (1976). An experimental case study of the successes and failure of job enrichment in a government agency. *Journal of Applied Psychology, 61,* 701–711.

34. Stonewalling plant democracy (1977, March 28). *Business Week.*

35. Winpisinger, W. (1973, February). Job satisfaction: A union response. *AFL-CIO American Federationist,* pp. 8–10.

36. Cherrington & England, 1980, p. 156.

37. The best-developed theoretical position is that of Locke, E. A. (1968). Toward a theory of task motivation and incentives. *Organizational Behavior and Human Performance, 3,* 157–189.

38. Mento, A. J., Steel, R. P., & Kasser, R. J. (1987). A meta-analytic study of the effects of goal setting on task performance: 1966–1984. *Organizational Behavior and Human Decision Processes, 39,* 52–83; Tubbs, M. E. (1986). Goal setting: A meta-analytic examination of the empirical evidence. *Journal of Applied Psychology, 71,* 474–483.

39. Mento et al., 1987; Locke, E. A., Latham, G. P., & Erez, M. (1988). The determinants of goal commitment. *Academy of Management Review, 13,* 23–39.

40. See Erez, M., Earley, P. C., & Hulin, C. L. (1985). The impact of participation on goal acceptance and performance: A two-step model. *Academy of Management Journal, 28,* 50–66.

41. Latham, G. P., Erez, M., & Locke, E. A. (1988). Resolving scientific disputes by the joint design of crucial experiments by the antagonists: Application to the Erez-Latham dispute regarding participation in goal setting. *Journal of Applied Psychology, 73,* 753–772.

42. Latham, G. P., Mitchell, T. R., & Dosset, D. L. (1978). The importance of participative goal setting and anticipated rewards on goal difficulty and job performance. *Journal of Applied Psychology, 63,* 163–171; Saari, L. M., & Latham, G. P. (1979). The effects of holding goal difficulty constant on assigned and participatively set goals. *Academy of Management Journal, 22,* 163–168.

43. For a discussion of this issue, see Saari & Latham, 1979.

44. Latham, G. P., & Locke, E. A. (1979, Autumn). Goal setting—A motivational technique that works. *Organizational Dynamics,* 68–80.

45. Wood, R. E., Mento, A. J., & Locke, E. A. (1987). Task complexity as a moderator of goal effects: A meta-analysis. *Journal of Applied Psychology, 72,* 416–425. See also Earley, P. C., Connolly, T., & Ekegren, G. (1989). Goals, strategy development, and task performance: Some limits on the efficacy of goal setting. *Journal of Applied Psychology, 74,* 24–33.

46. Good descriptions of MBO programs can be found in Raia, A. P. (1974). *Managing by objectives.* Glenview, IL: Scott, Foresman; Odione, G. S. (1965). *Management by objectives.* New York: Pitman; Mali, P. (1986). *MBO updated: A handbook of practices and techniques for managing by objectives.* New York: Wiley.

47. Kondrasuk, J. N. (1981). Studies in MBO effectiveness. *Academy of Management Review, 6,* 419–430.

48. For discussions of these and other problems with MBO, see Pringle, C. D., & Longenecker, J. G. (1982). The ethics of MBO. *Academy of Management Review, 7,* 305–312; Levinson, H. (1979, July–August). Management by whose objectives. *Harvard Business Review,* 125–134; McConkey, D. D. (1972, October). 20 ways to kill management by objectives. *Management Review,* 4–13.

49. See Ronen, S. (1984). *Alternative work schedules: Selecting, implementing, and evaluating.* Homewood, IL: Dow Jones-Irwin; Ronen, S. (1981). *Flexible working hours: An innovation in the qual-* *ity of work life.* New York: McGraw-Hill; Nollen, S. D. (1982). *New work schedules in practice: Managing time in a changing society.* New York: Van Nostrand Reinhold.

50. See Ronen, 1984; Nollen, 1982.

51. Ronen, 1981 and 1984; Golembiewski, R. T., & Proehl, C. W. (1978). A survey of the empirical literature on flexible workhours: Character and consequences of a major innovation. *Academy of Management Review, 3,* 837–853.

52. Ralston, D. A., Anthony, W. P., & Gustafson, D. J. (1985). Employees may love flextime, but what does it do to the organization's productivity? *Journal of Applied Psychology, 70,* 272–279.

53. Ronen, 1984; Ronen, S., & Primps, S. B. (1981). The compressed workweek as organizational change: Behavioral and attitudinal outcomes. *Academy of Management Review, 6,* 61–74.

54. Ivancevich, J. M., & Lyon, H. L. (1977). The shortened workweek: A field experiment. *Journal of Applied Psychology, 62,* 34–37.

55. Johns, G. (1987). Understanding and managing absence from work. In S. L. Dolan & R. S. Schuler (Eds.), *Canadian readings in personnel and human resource management.* St. Paul, MN: West.

56. Ivancevich & Lyon, 1977; Calvasina, E. J., & Boxx, W. R. (1975). Efficiency of workers on the four-day workweek. *Academy of Management Journal, 18,* 604–610; Goodale, J. G., & Aagaard, A. K. (1975). Factors relating to varying reactions to the 4-day workweek. *Journal of Applied Psychology, 60,* 33–38.

57. Oldham et al., 1979.

PART THREE

SOCIAL BEHAVIOR AND ORGANIZATIONAL PROCESSES

GROUP STRUCTURE AND EFFECTIVENESS

TRITON COMPUTERS

Like many small computers of the time, the first Triton was designed and constructed in a California garage. The brainchild of three young engineers, Triton succeeded where many others had failed. Although Triton never became an Apple or an IBM, it became a strong factor in the burgeoning personal computer market of the 1980s.

The first Triton was a crude device, really just a circuit board for the growing ranks of dedicated computer hobbyists. The three engineers, Max Bart, Ali Sharma, and Wayne Griggs, were employed full time by established electronics and computer firms. Over many evenings and weekends in Max Bart's garage, they managed to design and build the first Triton prototype. The work was difficult and frustrating, but the men worked as a closely knit team to solve the problems they encountered. With the prototype, Bart scoured the mushrooming electronics and computer stores of the region and finally obtained orders for one hundred of the Triton computers. After much difficulty, financing was secured, and Max, Ali, and Wayne built the hundred computers in record time on a crude "assembly line" in the garage. They felt just great.

Over the next several months, Max, Ali, and Wayne set about designing a prototype for a real personal computer. At the same time, plans had been laid for establishing a real company. Finally, the men quit their jobs, pooled their personal savings, and with the help of some venture capital, acquired small premises in a local industrial park. Several other computer experts and technicians were hired, and work began in earnest.

The atmosphere at Triton was informal and exciting. Although there were no set working hours, most of the people put in 12- to 14-hour days and could be found at Triton well into the evening. There were no formal job descriptions, and everyone was welcome to contribute ideas and labor to the various aspects of the project. A couple of new employees found this lack of structure not to their liking and quit, but they were replaced by people who functioned well. Everyone dressed casually in jeans and

T-shirts, and there were no private offices, just a "bull pen" of terminals and drawing boards that were decorated with posters and cartoons.

As the design of the Triton personal computer was finalized, things at Triton began to change. An M.B.A. was brought in to handle finance, and another was brought in to assist Max Bart, who had now assumed the role of marketer and outside spokesperson. Bart was seen more frequently in a suit, and a separate office was designed so that he could entertain visitors in a more formal atmosphere. A production crew was hired, and Wayne Griggs took over their management. Ali Sharma was formally named head of design, and he set to work with his staff fine-tuning future models of the personal computer.

A year after the successful introduction of the Triton personal computer, Max Bart was interviewed about the company's future.

"A key problem is maintaining a team spirit in design and in production," Bart said. "As you get bigger, that's hard to do. In design, a lot of what we do now involves developing the existing product. Some people don't find that challenging. In production, we've got a large staff, and it's hard to get such a large group excited about shipping computers. In the old days, we were all equals here. Now, some are more equal than others, and that can't be helped. Maybe it was more fun slaving away back in the garage."

Shortly after this interview, Wayne Griggs quit his job at Triton to take a design job at a small start-up computer firm. "I just decided I'm a computer designer, not a production manager," he told Bart and Sharma.

■

The Triton Computer story illustrates how a small group of dedicated entrepreneurs developed into an organization made up of several larger groups. What accounted for the enthusiasm and success of the initial group of three, and why does Max Bart fear for future enthusiasm and success? Was the division of labor and status among Triton members as inevitable as Bart suggests? What happens when groups make incompatible demands on people? These are some of the questions we will try to answer in this chapter.

First, we will define the term *group* and discuss the nature of formal groups and informal groups in organizations. After this, the reasons for group formation will be presented. Then, we will consider how groups differ from one another structurally and explore the consequences of these differences. Finally, we will examine how to design effective work groups.

WHAT IS A GROUP?

The word *group* is used rather casually in everyday discourse—special-interest group, ethnic group, and so on. However, for behavioral scientists, a **group** consists of two or more people interacting interdependently to achieve a common goal.

Interaction is the most basic aspect of a group—it suggests to us who is in the group and who is not. The interaction of group members need not be face-to-face, and it need not be verbal. For example, astronauts in a space shuttle and Mission Control personnel in Houston form a group by virtue of radio communication, even though they are separated by thousands of miles of space. Also, the impromptu group that forms to pass water buckets to fight a fire need not speak to meet the requirement of interaction. Interdependence simply means that group members rely to some degree upon each other to accomplish goals. Ten individuals who independently throw buckets of water on a fire do not constitute a true group. Finally, all groups have one or more goals that their members seek to achieve. These goals can range from having fun to marketing a new product to achieving world peace.

Group memberships are very important for two reasons. First, groups exert a tremendous influence *upon us*. They are the social mechanisms by which we acquire many beliefs, values, attitudes, and behaviors. Group membership is also important because groups provide a context in which *we* are able to exert influence upon *others*.

Let's have a look at how groups form in organizations.

GROUP FORMATION

For the purposes of organizational behavior, groups can be characterized most usefully as formal and informal. **Formal work groups** are groups that are established by the organization to facilitate the achievement of organizational goals. They are intentionally designed to channel individual effort in an appropriate direction. The most common formal group consists of a superior and the subordinates who report to that superior. In a manufacturing company, one such group might consist of a production manager and the six shift supervisors who report to him. In turn, the shift supervisors head work groups composed of themselves and their respective subordinates. Thus, the hierarchy of most organizations is a series of formal interlocked work groups.

Other types of formal work groups include task forces and committees. Task forces are temporary groups that are formed to achieve particular goals or to solve particular problems, such as suggesting productivity improvements. Committees are usually permanent groups that handle recurrent assignments outside of the usual work group structures. For example, a firm might have a standing committee on equal employment opportunity.

It is safe to say that early writers about management and organization felt that their work was done when they had described an organization's formal groups. After all, such groups had management's seal of approval and could be illustrated in black and white on an organizational chart. What more was there to say about grouping? In fact, you probably recognize how incomplete this view is. In addition to formal groups sanctioned by management to achieve organizational goals, informal grouping occurs in all organizations. **Informal groups** are groups that emerge naturally in response to the common interests of organizational members. They are seldom sanctioned by the organization, and their membership often cuts across formal groups. Informal groups can either help or hurt the organization, depending on their norms. We will consider this in detail later.[1]

To orient ourselves to the role of groups, it is useful to consider the factors that lead to group formation. In the case of informal groups, we are concerned with the factors that prompt their emergence in the formal work setting. In the case of formal groups, we are interested in the factors that lead organizations to form such groups and the ease with which the groups can be maintained and managed.

One obvious prerequisite for group formation is *opportunity for interaction*. When people are able to interact with one another, they are able to recognize that they might have common goals that can be achieved through dependence on each other.[2] For example, "inside" employees (such as headquarters technical advisors) often develop more informal solidarity than "outside" employees (such as technicians who visit clients) because they are in more constant interaction. Similarly, organizations are adept at using open-plan offices, face-to-face meetings, and electronic networks to bolster formal work groups.

Potential for goal accomplishment is another factor that contributes to group formation and maintenance. Physical goals (such as building a bridge) or intellectual goals (such as designing a bridge) are often accomplished most efficiently by the careful division of labor among groups. Groups can also achieve social-emotional goals such as esteem and security. Informally, strangers might band together during a natural disaster, or employees might band together to protest the firing of a co-worker. Formally, organizations might use decision-making groups to spread the risk associated with a tough decision.

Finally, *personal characteristics* can influence group formation and maintenance. When it comes to attitudes, there is plenty of evidence that "birds of a feather flock together." That is, people with similar attitudes (such as satisfaction with their job) tend to gravitate together.[3] When it comes to personality characteristics, similar people are often attracted to each other, but opposites sometimes attract.[4] For example, dominant people might seek the company of submissive people. We are speaking here mainly of informal attraction and grouping. When organizations staff formal working groups, they often assign people with different but complementary skills, attitudes, or personalities to the group. A tight-fisted, practical accountant might be included to offset an impulsive, creative marketer. We shall have more to say about this when we discuss how to design effective work groups.

GROUP STRUCTURE AND ITS CONSEQUENCES

As a member of at least several groups, you are no doubt aware that groups frequently seem to differ from one another. The differences that are most obvious might include the way members interact with one another, how members feel about the group, and how the group performs. It is often possible to trace these differences in interaction, feelings, and performance back to how the group is organized.

Group structure refers to the characteristics of the stable social organization of groups. As such, it refers to the way a group "looks" to a behavioral scientist or the way the group is "put together." The most basic structural characteristic along which groups vary is size. Other structural characteristics involve the expectations that members have about each other's behavior (norms), agreements about "who does what" in the group (roles), the rewards and prestige allocated to various group members (status), and how attractive the group is to its members (cohesiveness).

Group Size

Of one thing we can be certain—the smallest possible group consists of two people, such as that made up of a superior and a particular subordinate. It is possible to engage in a lot of theoretical nit-picking about just what constitutes an upper limit on group size. However, given the definition of *group* presented earlier, it would seem that congressional or parliamentary size (three to four hundred members) is somewhere close to this limit. In practice, most work groups, including task forces and committees, usually have between three and twenty members.

Size and Participation   As group size increases, the time available for verbal participation by each member decreases. (See the cartoon for an example!) For example, assuming equal participation, a two-person task force that meets for one hour allows each member one half hour of input. If this task force were composed of four members, each would only have fifteen minutes of input. This analysis assumes ideal conditions. In fact, as groups get larger, time for participation is lessened even more by the sheer mechanics of deciding "who should participate when about what." In addition, there is evidence that *inhibition* regarding participation increases among many group members as group size increases.[5] As you may know, popular surveys show that fears about speaking in front of groups frequently top the fear list. Thus, the assumption of equal participation becomes less valid as group size gets bigger.

Size and Satisfaction   The more the merrier? In theory, yes. On an informal level, larger groups provide more opportunities for members to encounter friends who share their attitudes or meet their social needs. For example, in a three-person work group, each member is confronted with two friendship possibilities, while in a seven-person work group, six such possibilities exist. In fact, however, members of larger groups rather consistently report less satisfaction with group membership than those who find themselves in smaller groups.[6] What accounts for this apparent contradiction?

For one thing, as opportunities for friendship increase, the chance to work on and develop these opportunities might decrease owing to the sheer time and en-

"I believe the gentleman over there had his hand up first."

ergy required. In addition, larger groups, in incorporating more members with different viewpoints, might prompt conflict and dissension, which work against member satisfaction. Turning to formal task requirements, we have already pointed out that participation decreases with size. To the extent that such participation is valued, dissatisfaction should again be the outcome. Finally, in larger groups, individual members can identify less easily with the success and accomplishments of the group. For example, a particular member of a four-person cancer research team should be able to identify *his* or *her* contributions to a research breakthrough more easily than can a member of a twenty-person team.

Size and Performance Participation and satisfaction aside, do large groups perform tasks better than small groups? This question has great relevance to practical organizational decisions: How many people should a bank assign to evaluate loan applications? How many carpenters should a construction company assign to build a garage? If a school system decides to implement team teaching, how big should the teams be? The answers to these and similar questions depend upon the exact task to be accomplished and upon just what we mean by good performance.[7]

Some tasks are **additive tasks.** This means that potential performance can be predicted by adding the performances of individual group members together. For example, moving a heavy stone is an additive task, and the potential productivity of a group of laborers can be estimated by summing the forces that they are able to exert. Similarly, building a garage is an additive task, and potential speed of construction can be estimated by adding the efforts of individual carpenters. Thus, for additive tasks, the potential performance of the group increases with group size.

Some tasks are **disjunctive.** This means that the potential performance of the group depends on the performance of its *best member*. For example, suppose that a research team is looking for a single error in a complicated computer program. In this case, the performance of the team might hinge upon its containing at least one bright, attentive, logical individual. Obviously, the potential performance of groups doing disjunctive tasks also increases with group size because the probability that the group includes a superior performer is greater.

The term "potential performance" is used consistently in the preceding two paragraphs for the following reason: As groups performing tasks get bigger, they tend to suffer from *process losses*.[8] Process losses involve performance difficulties that stem from the problems of organizing and coordinating larger groups. For one thing, in larger groups, members might feel more anonymous and less responsible. In this case, they might feel more freedom to "goof off" and "let Joe do it." Also, even with good intentions, problems of communication and decision making increase with size—imagine fifty carpenters trying to build a house. Thus, actual performance = potential performance − process losses. These points are summarized in Exhibit 8–1. As you can see in part (a), both potential performance and process losses increase with group size for additive and disjunctive tasks. The net effect is shown in part (b), which demonstrates that actual performance increases with size up to a point and then falls off. Part (c) shows that the *average* performance of group members decreases as size gets bigger. Thus, up to a point, larger groups might perform better as groups, but their individual members should be less efficient.

One other kind of task should be noted. **Conjunctive tasks** are those in which the performance of the group is limited by its *poorest performer*. For example, an assembly line operation is limited by its weakest link. Also, if team teaching is employed to train workers how to perform a complicated, sequential job, one poor teacher in the sequence will severely damage the effectiveness of the team. Both the potential and actual performance of conjunctive tasks should decrease as group size increases because the probability of including a weak link in the group goes up.

In summary, for additive and disjunctive tasks, larger groups might perform better up to a point, but at increasing costs to the efficiency of individual members. By any standard, performance on purely conjunctive tasks should decrease as group size increases. At Triton Computers, Max Bart feared the negative impact of increasing group size.

EXHIBIT
8–1

Relationships among group size, productivity, and process losses.

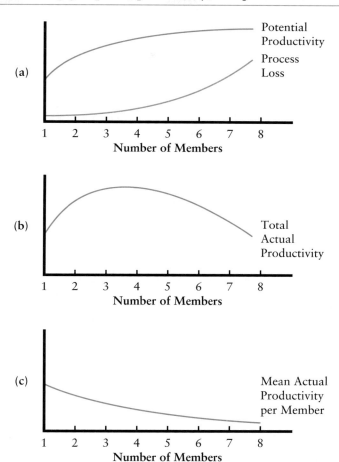

Source: From Steiner, I. D. (1972). *Group process and productivity.* New York: Academic Press, p. 96. Copyright © 1972, by Harcourt Brace Jovanovich, Inc., reprinted by permission of the publisher and the author.

Group Norms

Social **norms** are expectations that members of social units have regarding the behavior of others. As such, they are codes of conduct that specify what ought and ought not to be done or standards against which the appropriateness of behavior is evaluated. Some norms are supported by society as a whole ("Thou shalt not kill"), while others are peculiar to particular portions of society (e.g., the white middle class) or to individual small groups (e.g., the billing office staff at XYZ Company).

It is impossible to overestimate the pervasiveness with which norms regulate our behavior. Many habits that we have acquired, such as brushing our teeth x times a day, are in fact the product of social norms. As this example indicates, much normative influence is unconscious, and we are often aware of such influence only in special circumstances, such as when we see children struggling to master adult norms or foreigners sparring with the norms of our culture. We also become conscious of norms when we encounter ones that seem to conflict ("Get ahead," but "Don't step on others") or when we enter new social situations. For instance, the first day on a new job, workers frequently search for cues about what is considered proper office etiquette: Should I call the boss "mister"? Can I smoke in the presence of clients?

Norm Development *Why* do norms develop? The most important function served by norms is to provide regularity and predictability to behavior. This consistency provides important psychological security and permits us to carry out our daily business with minimal disruption.

What do norms develop *about*? Norms are developed to regular behaviors that are considered at least marginally important to their supporters. For example, managers are more likely to adopt norms regarding the performance and attendance of subordinates than norms concerning how offices are personalized and decorated. In general, less deviation is accepted from norms that concern more important behaviors. Stealing from a co-worker's locker will probably result in ostracism, while failing to assist her on the job might not. Some norms involve behaviors that are considered so important that they are stated as formal rules and/or backed by laws that specify penalties for violation. For example, the law specifies strict penalties for violating the "thou shalt not kill" norm. However, formal rules and laws should not be confused with social norms. Alcohol prohibition and the 55-mile-an-hour speed limit are examples of laws that have had little normative support among the public.

How do norms develop? In short, a norm develops from the shared attitudes of at least some of its supporters (Exhibit 8–2).[9] As we discussed in Chapter 5, individuals develop attitudes as a function of a related belief and value. In many cases, their attitudes affect their behavior. When the members of a group *share* related beliefs and values, we can expect them to share consequent attitudes. These shared attitudes then form the basis for norms. For example, the sequence for a work group performing under piecerate might go something like this:

"If we produce too much, management will cut the pay rate." *(Shared belief)*

"Economic loss is bad." *(Shared value)*

"Therefore, high production is bad." *(Shared attitude)*

"We should limit productivity." *(Norm)*

Productivity is limited. *(Behavior)*

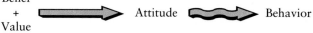

EXHIBIT

8–2

Individual attitude development and social norm development.

Individual Level

Belief
+
Value
⟹ Attitude ⟹ Behavior

Social Level

Shared Belief
+
Shared Value

⟹ Shared Attitude ⟹ Norm ⟹ Behavior

Recall that individuals can hold personal, idiosyncratic attitudes toward some person or activity. On the other hand, it really doesn't make sense to talk about "my personal norm." Norms are *collectively* held expectations, depending upon two or more people for their existence. However, norms can be targeted at a single individual. For example, work groups frequently develop agreed-upon expectations about how their bosses should behave.

Why do individuals tend to comply with norms? Much compliance occurs simply because the norm corresponds to privately held attitudes. This is the case with true supporters of the norm. In addition, even when norms support trivial social niceties (such as when to shake hands or when to look serious), they often save time and prevent social confusion. Most interesting, however, is the case in which individuals comply with norms that *go against* their privately held attitudes and opinions. For example, couples without religious convictions frequently get married in religious services, and male workers who hate neckties often wear them to work. In short, groups have an extraordinary range of rewards and punishments available to induce conformity to norms. In the next chapter, we will examine the process of conformity in detail.

Some Typical Norms Specifying a typical list of organizational norms is something like trying to describe the typical pattern of snowflakes. In an organization of any size, an incredibly complex pattern of norms might exist across formal groups, informal groups, and levels in the hierarchy. Nevertheless, there are some classes of norms that seem to crop up in most organizations to affect the behavior of members. They include the following:

- *Loyalty norms.* Groups and organizations frequently attempt to exact a strong degree of commitment and loyalty from their members. In the military, these norms are formalized with specific sanctions to be applied to traitors and deserters. In most other cases, loyalty norms tend to be informal. Managers frequently perceive that they must work late, come in on weekends, and accept transfers to other cities in order to prove their loyalty to the company and to their peers.[10] Despite official policy, police officers might refuse to "squeal" on fellow officers who commit brutality or accept favors.

- *Dress norms.* Social norms frequently dictate the kind of clothing worn to work. Again, formal norms tend to be invoked by military and quasi-military organizations, which support polished buttons and razor-edged creases. Of course, sometimes normative expectations from above confront informal counternorms from below. A certain pub that is popular with university students required its waiters to wear ties. They did so—usually with jeans and hunting shirts! Even when there are no dress codes, social norms are remarkably effective in dictating who should wear what on the job:

  > Managers of whatever sex were likely to present a tailored, conservative appearance. . . . (Nonmanagers), on the other hand, were likely to be dressed much less "professionally." "You can tell the professional women from the secretaries by their shoes," one person reported. "The professionals wear pumps; the secretaries wear four-inch wedgies."[11]

- *Reward allocation norms.* There are at least four norms that might dictate how rewards such as pay, promotions, and informal favors could be allocated in organizations:

  —Equity—reward according to inputs such as effort, performance, or seniority
  —Equality—reward everyone equally
  —Reciprocity—reward people the way they reward you
  —Social responsibility—reward those who truly need the reward[12]

Officially, of course, most organizations tend to stress allocation according to some combination of equity and equality norms—give employees what they deserve, but no favoritism. However, further normative forces may come into play in reward allocation. In the preceding chapter it was mentioned that managers often equalize pay increases awarded to subordinates under merit pay plans. In this case, equality subverts equity. If overtime is awarded according to seniority (equity) or randomly (equality), a work group might invoke a social responsibility norm to insist that a financially needy co-worker be given special consideration. Finally, the reciprocity norm is frequently invoked, especially among managers. Those who rise in

The top managers of Ben & Jerry's Ice Cream. Dress norms can vary enormously between organizations. (Steve Kagan/Gamma-Liaison)

rank might feel that they owe special favors to those who sponsored their progress.

- *Performance norms.* The performance of organizational members might be as much a function of social expectations as it is of inherent ability, personal motivation, or technology.[13] Work groups provide their members with potent cues about what is judged to be an appropriate level of performance, and new group members are alert for these cues: Is it OK to take a break now? Under what circumstances can I be absent from work without being punished? Of course, the official organizational norms that are sent to subordinates by managers usually favor high performance. However, work groups often establish their own informal performance norms, such as those that restrict productivity under a piecerate pay system (Chapter 7).[14]

In the early days of Triton Computers, obvious norms included dressing casually, working long hours, and helping others with their projects.

Roles

In addition to size and norms, roles constitute another characteristic of group structure. **Roles** are positions in a group that have attached to them a set of expected behaviors. Thus, in a sense, roles represent "packages" of norms that apply to particular group members. As implied in the previous section, many norms apply to all group members in order to be sure that they engage in *similar* behaviors (such as restricting productivity or dressing a certain way). However, the development of roles is indicative of the fact that group members might also be required to act *differently* from one another. For example, in a committee meeting, not every member is required to function as a secretary or a chairperson, and these become specific roles that are fulfilled by particular people.

In organizations, we find two basic kinds of roles. First, we can identify designated or assigned roles. These are roles that are formally prescribed by an organization as a means of dividing labor and responsibility. In general, assigned roles indicate "who does what" and "who can tell others what to do." In a manufacturing organization, labels that might be applied to formal roles include president, engineer, machinist, manager, and subordinate. In a university, such labels might include department chairperson, professor, and student. In addition to assigned roles, we invariably see the development of emergent roles. These are roles that develop naturally to meet the social-emotional needs of group members or to assist in formal job accomplishment. The class clown and the office gossip fulfill emergent social-emotional roles, while an "old pro" might emerge to assist new group members learn their jobs. Other emergent roles might be assumed by informal leaders or scapegoats who are the targets of group hostility.

Individuals might encounter difficulties in the assumption of organizational roles. In this regard, it is instructive to contrast real-life roles with those played by actors in films and plays. Peter Sellers excepted, actors are fortunate in that they usually act only one role at a time. The real world is a lot more complicated, because we must simultaneously fulfill the requirements of a number of roles. For example, most managerial role incumbents must also fulfill a subordinate role vis-à-vis their bosses. In addition, actors are fortunate to have a script and an attentive director. As we shall see, some organizational roles lack a clear script and careful direction. Finally, actors can reject roles that don't suit their personalities or career plans. This option might be less likely for many organizational roles. Now, let's consider these matters more systematically.

Role Ambiguity **Role ambiguity** exists when the goals of one's job or the methods of performing it are unclear. Ambiguity might be characterized by confusion about how performance is evaluated, how good performance can be achieved, or what the limits of one's authority and responsibility are.

Exhibit 8–3 shows a model of the process that is involved in assuming an organizational role. As you can see, certain organizational factors lead role senders (such as managers) to develop role expectations and "send" roles to focal people (such as subordinates). The focal person "receives" the role and then tries

EXHIBIT   A model of the role assumption process.

8–3

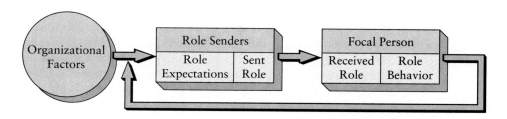

Source: Adapted from Katz, D., et al. (1966, 1978). *The social psychology of organizations.* New York: Wiley, p. 196. Copyright © 1966, 1978, by John Wiley & Sons, Inc. Reprinted by permission of John Wiley & Sons, Inc.

to engage in behavior to fulfill the role. This model reveals a variety of elements that can lead to ambiguity:

- *Organizational factors.* Some roles seem inherently ambiguous because of their function in the organization. For example, middle management roles might fail to provide the "big picture" that upper management roles do or do not require the attention to supervision necessary in lower management roles. Thus, two factors that can contribute to role clarity are absent. Similarly, staff specialists who have the role of advising managers or generating information might find their jobs unclear. The theoretical physicist charged by a communications firm to "generate new knowledge" might feel uncertain about the direction her work should take or the criteria that will be used to evaluate its worth.
- *The role sender.* Role senders might have unclear expectations of a focal person. A male sales manager who obtains his first female salesperson might vacillate about her exact role requirements—should he expect her to have dinner with male customers and "go out with the boys" after sales meetings? Even when the sender has specific role expectations, they might be ineffectively sent to the focal person. A weak orientation session, vague performance reviews, or inconsistent feedback and discipline may send ambiguous role messages to subordinates.
- *The focal person.* Even role expectations that are clearly developed and sent might not be fully digested by the focal person. This is especially true when he or she is new to the role. Ambiguity tends to decrease as length of time in the job role increases.[15]

   What are the practical consequences of role ambiguity? The most frequent outcomes appear to be job dissatisfaction, reduced organizational commitment, tension, anxiety, and intentions to quit.[16] In fact, you will recall that at Triton Computers, several employees found the ambiguity of the unstructured roles not to their liking and quit. It must be emphasized, however, that few workers would prefer a perfectly clear role stemming from repetitive job duties, close supervision, and a myriad of rules and regulations. Rather, it is probably *unnecessary* ambiguity stemming from the role sender that causes the most problems.

Role Conflict   Role conflict exists when an individual is faced with incompatible role expectations. Conflict can be distinguished from ambiguity in that role expectations might be crystal clear but incompatible in the sense that they are mutually exclusive, can't be fulfilled simultaneously, or don't suit the role occupant. Since expectations can be incompatible for various reasons, it is useful to distinguish among several forms of role conflict:

- **Intra-sender role conflict** occurs when a single role sender provides incompatible role expectations to the role occupant. For example, a manager might tell a subordinate to take it easy and not work so hard while delivering yet another batch of reports that requires immediate attention. This form of role conflict seems especially likely to also provoke ambiguity. For an example, see In Focus 8–1.
- If two or more role senders differ in their expectations for a role occupant, **inter-sender role conflict** can develop. Boundary role occupants who straddle the boundary between the organization and its clients or customers are especially likely to encounter this form of conflict. Salespeople, police officers, and teachers may face very different sets of demands from those inside and those outside of the organization. For example, a school principal might insist that teachers treat children equally, while a parent might insist on special treatment for his Sally. Inter-sender conflict can also stem exclusively from within the organization. The classic example here is the first-level supervisor, who serves as the interface between "management" and "the workers." From above, the supervisor might be pressured to get the work out and keep the troops in line. From below, he or she might be encouraged to behave in a considerate and friendly manner. Finally, inter-sender role conflict can stem exclusively from senders outside of the organization. A police chief might have to contend with community groups that desire law and order and those that assert that police officers exercise too much power.
- Especially if we include roles external to the organization, organizational members necessarily play several roles at one time. Often, the expectations inherent in these several roles are incompatible, and **inter-role conflict** results.[17] One person, for example, might fulfill the roles of a functional expert in marketing, head of the market research group, subordinate to the vice-president of marketing, and member of a product development task force. As a member of the task force, this individual might have to contribute to plans that go against the best interests of her research group. To complicate matters, she also fulfills a number of roles outside of the organization, including wife, mother, daughter, daughter-in-law, and so on. This is

obviously a busy person, and competing demands for time are a frequent symptom of inter-role conflict.

IN FOCUS 8–1

▼
. . . .

New Emphasis on Service Causes Role Ambiguity and Conflict at GTE

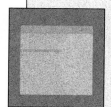

Workers at GTE Corp.'s GTE California unit are confused. After conducting a survey earlier this year, officials of the phone company were upset to find that most customer service representatives thought speed came before customers.

To change this impression, GTE California pumped $170,000 into weekend seminars for 850 employees who were paid overtime if they chose to attend. The events, held in tony hotels, featured a motivational speaker who preached that when you pick up the phone, "you own the problem."

To spice things up, actors parading as "The Sisters of Satisfaction" and "The Brothers of Boogie" sang about "Good Phonin' " to the tune of the rock oldie "Good Lovin.' "

John Bailey, a GTE manager for consumer operations who organized the seminars, says response was so favorable that he keeps the comment cards in his desk drawer, so he can look at them when he feels down.

But the message got muddied: While employees now believe that the customer comes first, they remain confused by GTE's continued emphasis on speed, which includes timing how long workers talk to each caller.

Nine-year customer service veteran Ramona Kies-Moore says she now tries to "own the problem" when a customer complains. For instance, if an installer is late, instead of writing up the problem for her manager to solve—as she is supposed to—Ms. Kies-Moore will sometimes take a few extra minutes to track down the installer herself. Unfortunately, she says, "that shows up bad on your talk time."

GTE is trying to change that. "We're trying to evolve and change attitudes," says Mary Velis, a GTE customer representative supervisor. "We have to learn to mix both of them together," she says of speed and quality. "It's very hard."

Source: Excerpted from Rigdon, J. E. (1990, December 5). More firms try to reward good service, but incentives may backfire in long run. *The Wall Street Journal*, B1, B6. Copyright © 1990 by Dow Jones & Company, Inc. Reprinted by permission.

- Even when role demands are clear and otherwise congruent, they might be incompatible with the personality or skills of the role occupant—thus, **person-role conflict** results.[18] As shown in Exhibit 8–3, the received role must be converted into adequate role behavior, and some individuals might simply be unwilling or unable to effect this conversion. It is reasonable to assume that much person-role conflict is precluded by self-selection. That is, people will normally try to avoid assuming roles with which they are personally incompatible. However, an employee might still end up in a role for which he or she is unsuited. At Triton Computers, you will recall that computer designer Wayne Griggs experienced person-role conflict when he was required to work as production manager.

As with role ambiguity, the most consistent consequences of role conflict are dissatisfaction, stress reactions, lowered organizational commitment, and turnover intentions.[19]

Status

One janitor to another:

> You should see the executive bathrooms on my end of the building!
> Amazing! Marble sinks, gold-plated spigots, thick carpeting, shoe
> shine machines, bottles of cologne. Wanna dry your hands? They got
> a choice of hot air, regular towels, or paper towels. That's class!
> Always nice and tidy, not like the locker room where *you* work.

Status is the rank, or social position, or prestige accorded to group members. Put another way, it represents the group's *evaluation* of a member. Just *what* is evaluated depends on the status system in question. However, when a status system works smoothly, the group will exhibit clear norms about who should be awarded more or less status.

The above example illustrates three curiosities about status. First, status, like beauty, is in the eye of the beholder. Second, we often obtain our own status from a connection (however removed) with those who have more.[20] Finally, we are extremely adept at detecting (or inventing) differences in status when they can benefit us. However, as we shall see, status is not one person's fantasy. Rather, it is another characteristic of *social* structure that depends upon some degree of agreement among group members about who has it and who doesn't.

Formal Status Systems All organizations have both formal and informal status systems. Since formal systems are most obvious to observers, let's begin there. The formal status system represents management's attempt to publicly identify those people who have more status than others. It is so obvious because this identification is implemented by the application of **status symbols** that are tangible indicators of status. Status symbols might include titles, particular working relationships, the pay package, the work schedule, and the physical working envi-

Source: Duncan/
©Punch/Rothco

*"Emily, I'm just phoning to say I've been promoted to assistant regional manager.
Please see to it in the future that my sandwiches are upgraded accordingly."*

ronment (see In Focus 8–2 on page 266). Just what are the criteria for achieving formal organizational status? One criterion is often seniority in one's work group. Employees who have been with the group longer might acquire the privilege of choosing steady daylight work or a more favorable office location. Even more important than seniority, however, is one's assigned role in the organization, one's job (see the cartoon). Because they perform different jobs, secretaries, laborers, supervisors, and executives acquire different statuses. Organizations often go to great pains to ensure that status symbols are appropriately tied to assigned roles, as this description of telephone allocation at Western Electric indicates:

> As the junior manager moves up through the ranks, he will usually first have a Touch-Tone desk set. He will then progressively move up to a colored Touch-Tone desk set, a Touch-Tone set with a "hands free" device, a Touch-Tone telephone with a set of programmed cards to insert that dial the desired number; an electronic preset dialing system requiring only the touch of one button to dial a specific number; and—for the president and executive vice-presidents—a Picturephone.[21]

Why do organizations go to all this trouble to differentiate status? For one thing, status and the symbols connected to it serve as powerful magnets to induce members to aspire to higher organizational positions (recall Maslow's need for esteem). Second, status differentiation reinforces the authority hierarchy in work

▼
....

Rug Ranking at Canadian Broadcasting Corporation and Air Canada

In just about every big company, allocating office space is a complicated game, played according to strict rules and regulations.

Insiders call the game rug ranking, and virtually all major corporations do it—whether they admit it or not.

Some bureaucracies, like our federal civil service, have abandoned all pretence of secrecy and actually print up copies of their codified guidelines. These regulations lay down the perks of power in the minutest detail. For example, executives above a certain level may have the right to a leather-covered water pitcher; those below get plastic. One of the almost universal rules is: the higher the floor, the more important the person. Another: Don't tamper with what an employee perceives as his acquired space.

The master players in the rug-ranking game are government bureaucracies and Crown [government-owned] corporations, which some say invented the rules. The Canadian Broadcasting Corporation, to cite one example, has its own "space committee," which decides who gets to sit where according to formal guidelines.

Corporation vice-presidents, according to the rules, are entitled to "no less than 600 sq. ft., where feasible; directors: 225 sq. ft., where feasible; departmental employees and support staff: 150 and 100 sq. ft. respectively."

Richard Chambers, director of public relations at the CBC, explained that the corporation "tries to give executives what they want, what they deserve, whatever. They may not always have walls around their desks, but they almost always have the exact square footage they're entitled to."

Air Canada used to play the game in earnest, but when it moved from offices in Place Ville Marie to its own headquarters building, it had to modify the rules a little.

Because of the unique cruciform floor plan at PVM, the airline had been able to assign eight corner office suites per floor. The new building, by contrast, provided only four. Needless to say, some officers suffered serious blows to their egos.

For all the preoccupation with the space provided to executives on their rise to the top, the fact remains that the largest office in any company is not necessarily that of the president or vice-presidents. More often than not, that distinction belongs to the receptionist.

Source: Abridged from Hustak, A. (1990, March 10). Rug ranking. *The Gazette* (Montreal), p. J4. Reprinted by permission of The Gazette.

groups and in the organization as a whole, since people *pay attention* to high-status individuals. At Triton Computers, Max Bart's suits and private office served as a symbol of his growing status to both Triton employees and outsiders.

Of course, there is a downside to such obsessive status differentiation. In particular, it works against creating a culture of teamwork and cooperation across ranks. For this reason, many corporations have begun to downplay status differences by doing away with unnecessary symbols. The high-tech culture of Silicon Valley has always been pretty egalitarian, but even old-line industries are getting on the bandwagon. For example, Union Carbide's Connecticut headquarters has equal-sized offices and no executive dining rooms or parking lots.

The differences in formal status that exist within organizations usually carry over to the evaluation of the status of occupations by the public at large. Thus, doctors have more prestige than nurses in the community, just as they do in the hospital. Exhibit 8–4 summarizes ratings of occupational prestige obtained from a number of cross-national surveys. In general, surveys of this nature show remarkable stability over time and good agreement across various societies. In addition, people who themselves differ in status tend to agree very closely in their ratings of the prestige of various occupations.[22] Thus, status judgments of the public at large are influenced by some of the same factors that indirectly lead to formal status differences in organizations—the skill, training, and education of the people being judged.

Informal Status Systems   In addition to formal status systems, we can detect informal status systems in organizations. Such systems are not well advertised, and they might lack the conspicuous symbols and systematic support that are usually accorded to the formal system. Nevertheless, they can operate just as effectively. Sometimes, job performance is a basis for the acquisition of informal status. The "power hitters" on a baseball team or the "cool heads" in a hospital emergency unit might be highly evaluated by co-workers for their ability to assist in task accomplishment. Some managers who perform well early in their careers are identified as "fast trackers" and given special job assignments that correspond to their elevated status. Just as frequently, though, informal status is linked to factors other than job performance. Blacks and women might be accorded low status in spite of good performance. Also, some jobs might be informally perceived as glamor jobs, elevating the status of their occupants. In an industrial supply firm these might be sales positions, and in a high technology firm they might be engineering positions. Of course, reality might follow fiction as employees are promoted into management positions from these glamor jobs and accorded *formal* status. Finally, even the most apparently irrelevant nonwork associations might contribute to informal status on the job. Consider this interaction among three machine operators:

> The "professor theme" was the cream of verbal interaction. It
> involved George's connection with higher learning. His daughter had
> married the son of a professor who instructed in one of the local col-

leges. The professor theme was not in the strictest sense a conversation piece. When the subject came up, George did all the talking. The two Jewish operators remained silent as they listened with deep

EXHIBIT

8–4

Standard prestige scores for various occupations.

78 College and university teachers; physicians
72 Architects; lawyers
70 Dentists
69 Chemists
67 Bank officers and financial managers
66 Psychologists; airplane pilots; chemical and mechanical engineers
63 Controllers and treasurers
62 Accountants
60 Clergymen; economists
57 Elementary school teachers
56 Stock and bond salesmen; painters and sculptors
55 Office managers; draftsmen
54 Librarians; registered nurses
52 Sales managers (non-retail); actors
51 Computer programmers
50 Radio and television announcers; airline stewardesses
49 Real estate agents and brokers
48 Bank tellers
45 Musicians and composers
44 Insurance agents, brokers, and underwriters
43 Automobile mechanics
40 Farmers; policemen and detectives
39 Foremen
38 Receptionists
37 Air traffic controllers
34 Funeral directors
33 Mail carriers; truck drivers
31 File clerks
23 Bartenders; waiters
22 Garage workers and gas station attendants
14 Newsboys
13 Garbage collectors

Note: Scores can range from 92 to −2. They are derived from studies of occupational prestige carried out in many countries around the world and applied to the 1970 U.S. Census Detailed Occupational Classifications. This is why some labels are sex-typed.

Source: From Donald J. Treiman, *Occupational prestige in comparative perspective,* pp. 306–315. Copyright © 1977 by Academic Press, Inc. Reprinted by permission of the author and the publisher.

respect, if not actual awe, to George's accounts. . . . I came to the conclusion that it was the professor connection . . . which provided the fount of George's superior status in the group.[23]

As we said earlier, status is in the eye of the beholder!

Consequences of Status What are the consequences of status differences in groups and organizations? One of the most obvious is the manner in which individuals who differ in status address each other.[24] Social units develop clear norms about such matters, and the violation of these norms can lead to considerable confusion and embarrassment. Mr. Jennings, the president of a large firm, may address his secretary as "Marie," but Ms. Garcia, the secretary, must address him as "Mr. Jennings," not "Bob." Of course, such norms depend upon the social setting. A doctor and nurse who are well acquainted might use first names when alone, but the nurse will most likely revert to the title "Doctor" when others are present.

Status affects communication in ways other than form of address. For one thing, most people wish to communicate with others at their own status level or higher, rather than with people who are below them.[25] The result is a tendency for communication to move up the status hierarchy. Thus, people at each level of a group's status hierarchy could be expected to direct more comments toward their peers and "betters" than would be directed downward. Why does this occur? Perhaps equals and people of higher status are perceived as attractive, and if they are not seen as attractive, they are perceived as powerful. In either case, we might try to enhance our *own* status by interacting with them. (Recall George and "the professor," and observe the popularity of the star on a Little League team.)

Status also affects the *amount* of communication engaged in by various group members and their influence in group affairs. As you might guess, higher-status members do more talking and have more influence.[26] Some of the most convincing evidence comes from studies of jury deliberations, in which jurors with higher social status (such as managers and professionals) participate more and have more effect on the verdict.[27] Thus, if the plant superintendent, the production manager, and a production supervisor make the rounds on an assembly line, we can offer a pretty good guess about who will do the most talking. The relationship of status to amount of communication and influence probably stems from several factors. First, since high-status members are *targets* of a lot of communication, they have a disproportionate opportunity to respond. Second, high-status group members might be perceived as more knowledgeable about the issue at hand (even if they aren't). Also, awareness of one's high status might promote self-confidence and assertiveness, leading one to contribute ideas more forcefully.

Finally, who should conform more readily to group norms, high-status members or low-status members? In the next chapter we will consider this important issue.

GROUP COHESIVENESS

You will recall from the story that began the chapter that the founders of Triton Computers worked in the early days as a closely knit team. That is a casual description of a characteristic known more formally as **group cohesiveness.** Cohesive groups are those that are especially attractive to their members. Because of this attractiveness, members are especially desirous of staying in the group, and tend to describe the group in favorable terms.[28]

The arch-stereotype of a cohesive group is the major league baseball team that begins September looking like a good bet to win its division and get into the World Series. On the field we see well-oiled, precision teamwork. In the clubhouse, all is sweetness and joviality, and interviewed players tell the world how fine it is to be playing with "a great bunch of guys."

Two initial points about cohesiveness are worth noting. First, cohesiveness is a relative, rather than absolute, property of groups. While some groups are more cohesive than others, there is no objective line between cohesive and noncohesive groups. Thus, we will use the adjective *cohesive* to refer to groups that are more attractive than average for their members. Second, cohesiveness is an informal, emergent group process. However, the manager who clearly understands why cohesiveness occurs might be able to affect the extent to which it develops in a work unit.

Factors Influencing Cohesiveness

What makes some groups more cohesive than others? There is probably no single factor that will make a particular group highly cohesive. Rather, a number of factors in combination contribute to cohesiveness.

Threat and Competition   Earlier, we pointed out that groups often form to accomplish social-emotional goals. Thus, any factor that increases the importance of these goals for the group should promote cohesiveness. External threat to the survival of the group has been shown to increase cohesiveness in a wide variety of situations.[29] As an example, consider the wrangling, uncoordinated corporate board of directors that quickly forms a united front in the face of a takeover bid. Honest competition with another group can also promote cohesiveness.[30] This is the case with the World Series contenders mentioned earlier.

Why do groups often become more cohesive in response to threat or competition? They probably feel a need to improve communication and coordination so that they can better cope with the situation at hand. The group is now perceived as more attractive because it is seen as capable of doing what has to be done to ward off threat or to win. There are, of course, limits to this. Under *extreme* threat or very *unbalanced* competition, increased cohesiveness will serve little purpose. For example, the partners in a firm faced with certain financial disaster would be unlikely to exhibit cohesiveness because it would do nothing to combat the severe threat.

Success It should come as no surprise that a group becomes more attractive to its members when it has successfully accomplished some important goal, such as defending itself against threat or winning a prize.[31] By the same token, cohesiveness should decrease after failure, although there may be "misery loves company" exceptions. The situation for competition is shown graphically in Exhibit 8–5. Fit-Rite Jeans owns two small clothing stores (A and B) in a large city. To boost sales, it holds a contest between the two stores, offering $150 worth of merchandise to each employee of the store that achieves the highest sales during the next business quarter. Before the competition begins, the staffs of the two stores are equally cohesive. As suggested above, as the competition begins, both groups become more cohesive. The members become more cooperative with each other, and in each store there is much talk about "we" versus "they." At the end of the quarter, store A wins the prize and becomes yet more cohesive. The group is especially attractive to its members because it has succeeded in the attainment of a desired goal. On the other hand, cohesiveness plummets in losing store B—the group has become less attractive to its members.

In general, the accomplishment of any goal that the group feels is important should facilitate cohesiveness—even if the goal is only having fun or establishing a friendly work atmosphere.

Similarity of Members Earlier, it was pointed out that similarity of attitudes tends to increase the attraction between individuals and thus promotes group formation. A logical extension of this would suggest that similarity of attitudes among group members would increase cohesiveness and that, furthermore, simi-

**EXHIBIT
8–5**

Competition, success, and cohesiveness.

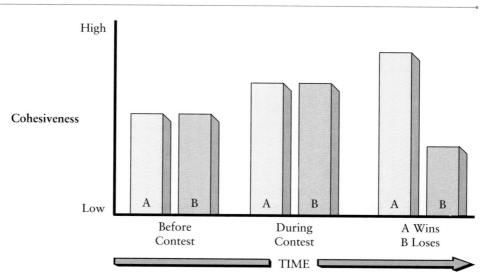

lar background characteristics such as race, age, and education might do the same. In fact, this appears to be true when the group's primary goal is that of creating a friendly climate. However, if the group is especially interested in accomplishing some particular task, its success in performing the task will usually outweigh member similarity in determining cohesiveness.[32] For example, one study found no relationship between cohesiveness and similarity of age or education for industrial work groups.[33] Similarly, another study found that the cohesiveness of groups composed of black and white southern soldiers was dependent upon successful task accomplishment rather than racial composition.[34]

Size   Other things being equal, bigger groups should have a more difficult time becoming and staying cohesive. In general, such groups should have a more difficult time agreeing on goals and more problems communicating and coordinating effort to achieve these goals. Earlier, it was pointed out that large groups frequently divide into subgroups. Clearly, such subgrouping is contrary to the cohesiveness of the larger group. There is, however, a potential exception to this rule. A larger group might exhibit high cohesiveness if its very size aids in goal accomplishment. For example, a large coalition of dissatisfied workers might threaten a wildcat strike if its demands are not met. In this case, size might promote cohesiveness because it enhances chances for success.

Toughness of Initiation   Despite its rigorous admissions policies, the Harvard Business School doesn't lack applicants. Similarly, exclusive yacht and golf clubs might have waiting lists for membership extending several years into the future. All of this suggests that groups that are tough to get into should be more attractive than those that are easy to join. Indeed, one study of university fraternities showed that those that had more rigorous "hazing" practices for potential members tended to be more cohesive.[35] This effect is well known in the military, where rigorous physical training and stressful "survival schools" precede entry into elite units such as the Special Forces or the Rangers. Of course, there might be an element of dissonance operating here. Having worked so hard to join a group, new members might be psychologically compelled to find the group attractive.

Consequences of Cohesiveness

From the previous section, it should be clear that managers (or group members) might be able to influence the level of cohesiveness of work groups by inducing competition or threat, varying group size or composition, or manipulating membership requirements. The question remains, however, as to whether *more* or *less* cohesiveness is a desirable group property. This, of course, depends on the consequences of group cohesiveness and who is doing the judging.

More Participation in Group Affairs   Because cohesive groups are attractive to their membership, members should be especially motivated to participate (in several senses of the word) in group affairs. For one thing, because members wish to remain in the group, voluntary turnover from cohesive groups should be low. For another, members like being with each other; therefore, absence should be lower than that exhibited by less cohesive groups. During the Fit-Rite sales contest, for example, we might expect casual absence in both stores to drop as the sales staff members become more reliant on each other to achieve their goal. In a third sense, participation should be reflected in a high degree of communication within the group as members strive to cooperate with and assist each other. In addition, this communication might well be of a more friendly and supportive nature, depending on the key goals of the group.[36]

More Conformity Because they are so attractive and coordinated, cohesive groups are well equipped to supply information, rewards, and punishment to individual members. These factors take on special significance when they are administered by those who hold a special interest for us. Thus, highly cohesive groups are in a superb position to induce conformity to group norms because "they have so much to offer."

Members of cohesive groups should be especially motivated to engage in activities that will *keep* the group cohesive. Chief among these activities is applying pressure to deviants to get them to comply with group norms. Cohesive groups react to deviants by increasing the amount of communication directed at these individuals.[37] Presumably, such communication contains information to help the deviant "see the light," as well as veiled threats about what might happen if he or she doesn't. Over time, if such communication is ineffective in inducing conformity, it tends to decrease. This is a signal that the group has isolated the deviant member to maintain cohesiveness among the majority.

More Success Above, it was pointed out that successful goal accomplishment contributes to group cohesiveness. In line with the old saying that nothing succeeds like success, it is also true that cohesiveness contributes to group success—in general, cohesive groups are good at achieving their goals. Thus, there is a reciprocal relationship between success and cohesiveness:

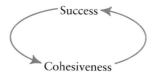

Why are cohesive groups effective at goal accomplishment? Probably because of the other consequences of cohesiveness noted above. A high degree of participation and communication, coupled with active conformity to group norms, should ensure a high degree of agreement about the goals to be pursued and the methods to be used to achieve these goals. Thus, coordinated effort pays dividends to the group.

Now for a very important question: Since cohesiveness contributes to goal accomplishment, should managers attempt to increase the cohesiveness of work groups by juggling the factors that influence cohesiveness? To answer this question, it must be emphasized that cohesive groups are especially effective at accomplishing *their own* goals. If these goals happen to correspond with those of the organization, increased cohesiveness should have substantial benefits for group performance. If not, organizational effectiveness might be threatened. For example, during the Vietnam War, cohesive units of U.S. soldiers occasionally united to defy a command to move into dangerous territory. In this case, the goals of the cohesive GIs (to remain safe and secure) did not correspond to those of the military brass (to pursue the enemy). Your own value system will tell you who was right and wrong here. However, from the army command's perspective, this was a case in which cohesiveness threatened organizational effectiveness.

Studies of industrial work groups have contributed to our understanding of the consequences of cohesiveness with regard to the productivity of individual group members. In particular, one large-scale study reached the following conclusions:

- In highly cohesive groups, the productivity of individual group members tends to be fairly similar to that of other members. In less cohesive groups there is more variation in productivity.
- Highly cohesive groups tend to be *more* or *less* productive than less cohesive groups.[38]

These two facts are shown graphically in Exhibit 8–6. The lower variability of productivity in more cohesive groups stems from the power of such groups to

EXHIBIT 8–6   **Hypothetical productivity curves for groups varying in cohesiveness.**

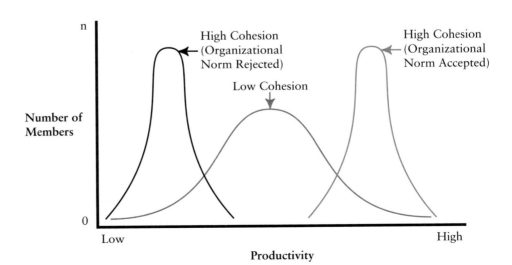

induce conformity. To the extent that work groups have productivity norms, more cohesive groups should be better able to enforce them. Furthermore, if cohesive groups accept organizational norms regarding productivity, they should be highly productive. If cohesive groups reject such norms, they are especially effective in limiting productivity.

The moral here should be clear: Cohesive groups tend to be successful in accomplishing what they wish to accomplish. In a good labor relations climate, group cohesiveness should contribute to high productivity. If the climate is marked by tension and disagreement, cohesive groups might effectively pursue goals that result in low productivity.

To return to the story at the beginning of the chapter, early adversity, common interests, and early success led to high cohesiveness among the founders of Triton Computers. This in turn stimulated the successful introduction of the personal computer. However, growth, turnover, and the addition of less committed members now threaten cohesiveness.

DESIGNING EFFECTIVE WORK GROUPS

The double-edged nature of group cohesiveness suggests that a delicate balance of factors dictates whether a work group is effective or ineffective. In turn, this raises the idea that organizations should pay considerable attention to how work groups are designed and managed. At first, the notion of designing a work group might seem strange. After all, don't work groups just "happen" in response to the demands of the organization's goals, technology, and so on? While these factors surely set some limits on how groups are organized and managed, organizations are finding that there is still plenty of scope for creativity in work group design.

A good model for thinking about the design of effective work groups is to consider a successful sports team, whether professional or amateur. In most cases, such teams are small groups made up of highly skilled individuals who are able to meld these skills into a cohesive effort. The task being performed is intrinsically motivating and provides very direct feedback. If there are status differences on the team, the basis for these differences is contribution to the team, not some extraneous factor. The team shows an obsessive concern with obtaining the right personnel, relying on tryouts or player drafts, and the team is "coached," not supervised. With this informal model in mind, let's examine the concept of group effectiveness more closely.

J. Richard Hackman of Harvard University (co-developer of the Job Characteristics Model, Chapter 7) has written extensively about work group effectiveness.[39] According to Hackman, a work group is effective when (1) its physical or intellectual output is acceptable to management and to the other parts of the organization that use this output, (2) group members' needs are satisfied rather than frustrated by the group, and (3) the group experience enables members to *continue* to work together.

What leads to group effectiveness? In colloquial language, we might say "sweat, smarts, and style." More formally, Hackman notes that group effectiveness will be boosted when high effort is directed toward the group's task, when great knowledge and skill are directed toward the task, and when the group adopts sensible strategies for accomplishing its goals. And just how does an organization achieve this? There is growing awareness in many organizations that the answer is **self-managed work groups.** Although the exact details vary tremendously, such groups generally provide their members with the opportunity to do challenging work under reduced supervision. Other labels that are often applied to such groups are autonomous, semiautonomous, self-regulated, superteams, and so on. The general idea, which is more important than the label, is that the groups tend to regulate much of their own members' behavior.

Critical to the success of self-managed work groups are the nature of the task, the composition of the group, and various support mechanisms.

Tasks for Self-Managed Groups

Experts agree that tasks assigned to self-managed work groups should be complex and challenging, requiring high interdependence among team members for accomplishment. In general, these tasks should have the qualities of enriched jobs, described in Chapter 7. Thus, the task will be seen as significant, it will be performed from beginning to end, it will involve a variety of skills, and so on. The point here is that self-managed teams have to have something useful to self-manage, and it is complex tasks that capitalize on the diverse knowledge and skills of a group. Taking a bunch of olive stuffers on a food-processing assembly line, putting them in distinctive jumpsuits, calling them the Olive Squad, and telling them to self-manage will be unlikely to yield dividends in terms of effort expended or brainpower employed. The basic task will still be boring!

Outside of the complexity requirement, the actual range of tasks for which self-managed teams have been used is great, spanning both blue- and white-collar jobs. In the white-collar domain, complex service and design jobs seem especially conducive to self-management. Organizations such as 3M, Aetna Life & Casualty, and Federal Express make extensive use of teams. At Federal Express, for example, self-managed back-office clerical teams are credited with improving billing accuracy and reducing lost packages for a savings of millions of dollars.[40] Similarly, companies such as United Parcel and Times Mirror have recently developed multiskilled sales teams to sell complex products or services. Mixing people from various functional areas (design, manufacturing) can do wonders for customer service.

In the blue-collar domain, Kodak, General Mills, GM's Saturn plant, and Chaparral Steel of Midlothian, Texas, make extensive use of self-managed work groups. In general, these groups are responsible for dividing labor among various subtasks as they see fit and making a variety of decisions about matters that impinge on the group. When a work site is formed from scratch and lacks an existing culture, the range of these activities can be very broad. Consider the self-managed groups formed in a new English confectionery plant:

> Production employees worked in groups of 8 to 12 people, all of whom were expected to carry out each of eight types of jobs involved in the production process. Group members were collectively responsible for allocating jobs among themselves, reaching production targets and meeting quality and hygiene standards, solving local production problems, recording production data for information systems, organizing breaks, ordering and collecting raw materials and delivering finished goods to stores, calling for engineering support, and training new recruits. They also participated in selecting new employees. Within each group, individuals had considerable control over the amount of variety they experienced by rotating their tasks, and each production group was responsible for one product line. Group members interacted informally throughout the working day but made the most important decisions—for example, regarding job allocation—at formal weekly group meetings where performance was also discussed.[41]

Self-managed work groups at Federal Express have saved millions of dollars by improving work procedures. (Karen Kasmauski/ Woodfin Camp & Associates)

Corning, Inc. opened a ceramic filter plant in Blacksburg, Virginia, that is organized along similar principles. Autonomous, flexible teams resulted in outstanding profitability.

If a theme runs through this discussion of tasks for self-managed groups, it is the breakdown of traditional, conventional, specialized *roles* in the group. Group members adopt roles that will make the group effective, not ones that are simply related to their own narrow specialty—marketers learn something about engineering, blue collar workers learn something about training, and so on.

At this point, why not pause and consider Ford's problem in You Be the Manager?

The Composition of Self-Managed Groups

How should self-managed groups be assembled to ensure effectiveness? "Stable, small, and smart" might be a fast answer.[42]

Stability Self-managed groups require considerable interaction among their members. This in turn requires understanding and trust. To achieve this, group membership must be fairly stable. Rotating members into and out of the group will cause it to fail to develop a true group identity.[43]

Size In keeping with the demands of the task, self-managed teams should be as small as is feasible. The goal here is to keep process losses and "social loafing" to a minimum. These negative factors can be a problem for all groups, but they can be especially difficult for self-managed groups. This is because reduced supervision means that there is no boss to coordinate the group's activities and ride herd over social loafers who don't do their share.

Expertise It goes without saying that group members should have a high level of expertise about the task at hand. Everybody doesn't have to know everything, but the group as a *whole* should be very knowledgeable about the task. Again, reduced supervision discourages "running to the boss" when problems are encountered, and the group must have the resources to successfully solve these problems. One set of skills that should probably be possessed to some degree by all members is *social skills*. Understanding how to talk things out, communicate effectively, and resolve conflict is especially important for self-managed groups.

Diversity Put simply, a work group should have members who are similar enough to work well together and diverse enough to bring a variety of perspectives and skills to the task at hand. A product planning group consisting exclusively of new male M.B.A.s might work well together but lack the different perspectives that are necessary for creativity.

One way of maintaining appropriate group composition might be to let the group choose its own members, as occurred at the confectionery plant noted above. In the GM Saturn startup, a panel of union and management members

YOU BE THE MANAGER

Manager

Designing Ford's Taurus

Before it even began designing the Ford Taurus/Mercury Sable, the management of Ford Motor Company knew it had to try something different. The usual North American way of designing cars was neither efficient nor effective. Traditionally, this design is carried out in a relay-like fashion. First, stylists determine what the car will look like and then pass their design on to engineering, which develops mechanical specifications and blueprints. In turn, manufacturing is then required to consider how to construct what has been designed. Somewhere on down the line, marketing and accounting get their say. This process leads to problems. One link in the chain might have a difficult time understanding what the previous link meant. Worse, one department might resist the ideas of another simply because they "weren't invented here." Frequently, concepts have to "go back to the drawing board" when they encounter downstream resistance.

The results of this approach were all too obvious to Ford management. The average design cycle for a North American car took over five years, compared to three years for Japanese cars. The delay meant greater development expenses, and the imperfect coordination left gaps in details that resulted in low quality for early production models.

Ford management felt that there had to be a better way. How about *you*?

1. How might the concepts of roles, status, and cohesiveness explain the problems with the traditional design sequence?

2. Was there a better way to design the new Taurus/Sable?

To learn what Ford did, see The Manager's Notebook at the end of the chapter.

Source: Waterman, R. H., Jr. (1987). *The renewal factor.* New York: Bantam Books; McElroy, J. (1985, April). Ford's new way to build cars. *Road & Track,* 156–158.

evaluated applications for all blue- and white-collar jobs, paying particular attention to social skills.[44]

The theme running through this discussion of group composition is that of
loading the dice in favor of *high cohesiveness* and the development of group
norms that stress group effectiveness.

Supporting Self-Managed Groups

A number of support factors can assist self-managed groups in becoming and
staying effective. One of these is adequate training in technical and social skills
when necessary. At Saturn, for example, new workers receive a full five days of
training, a figure unheard of in the traditional U.S. auto industry. Another involves some careful thinking about how the organization's reward system corresponds to a team concept. Ideally, perhaps, the group would be paid according to
its success as a *team,* and in some companies, groups are paid in accordance with
gain-sharing principles (Chapter 7). Another tactic is to pay group members according to the number of specific team skills that they have mastered (e.g., weld-

■

EXHIBIT   Factors influencing work group effectiveness.

8–7

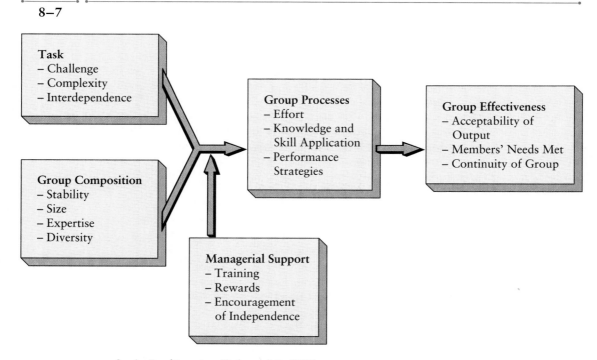

Source: Based in part on Hackman, J. R. (1987).

ing, machining, and assembly). This is sensible in that a formal status symbol, pay, is made contingent on behavior that should help the team accomplish its goals. A better distribution of skills gives the group more options about how to organize its work. On the other hand, some firms that have adopted self-managed groups have made an effort to do away with status symbols that have nothing to do with group effectiveness (such as reserved parking and dining areas).

Finally, self-managed teams will not receive the best support when managers feel threatened by self-management and see it as reducing their own power or promotion opportunities. A recent study found that the most effective managers in a self-management environment encouraged groups to observe, evaluate, and reinforce their own task behavior.[45] This suggests that coaching groups to be independent enhances their effectiveness.[46] Exhibit 8–7 summarizes the factors that influence work group effectiveness.

THE MANAGER'S NOTEBOOK

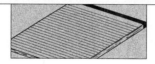

Designing Ford's Taurus

1. The tradition of relaying car designs through departments causes employees to isolate themselves in their narrow professional roles at the expense of the larger project ("I'm a stylist. What do I care about engineering?"). It can also stimulate group cohesiveness at the expense of the larger project ("We engineers have to stick together."). Finally, the professionals in one department might see themselves as having superior status to those in other departments ("We engineers are superior to those blue-sky stylists.").

2. At the outset of the project, Ford formed Team Taurus, a group that incorporated people from all the departments that ultimately influence the design of a car (even down to the legal department). This early involvement built mutual understanding and reduced confusion so that expensive last-minute design changes were unnecessary. The company estimates that Team Taurus saved $400 million in development funds. The resulting product was literally an award-winning design. General Motors used a similar team approach in the design of the Saturn.

SUMMARY

- A group consists of two or more people interacting interdependently to achieve a common goal. The formation and maintenance of groups depend upon opportunity for interaction, potential for goal accomplishment, and the personal characteristics of members.

- As groups get bigger, they provide less opportunity for member satisfaction. When tasks are additive (performance depends upon the addition of individual effort) or disjunctive (performance depends upon that of the best member), larger groups should perform better than smaller groups if process losses due to poor coordination and communication can be avoided. When tasks are conjunctive (performance is limited by the weakest member), performance decreases as the group gets bigger because the chance of adding a weak member increases.
- Norms are expectations that group members have about each other's behavior. They provide consistency to behavior and develop as a function of shared attitudes. In organizations, both formal and informal norms often develop to control loyalty, dress, reward allocation, and performance.
- Roles are positions in a group that have associated with them a set of expected behaviors. Role ambiguity refers to a lack of clarity of job goals or methods. Role conflict exists when an individual is faced with incompatible role expectations, and it can take four forms: intra-sender, inter-sender, inter-role, and person-role. Both ambiguity and conflict have been shown to provoke job dissatisfaction, tension, anxiety, and lowered commitment.
- Status is the rank or prestige accorded to group members by the group. Formal status systems are designed by the organization to reinforce the authority hierarchy and reward progression up the hierarchy. In practice, this involves allocating status symbols to individuals on the basis of seniority and formal organizational roles. Informal status systems also operate in organizations, though they might lack conspicuous status symbols. Higher-status members are usually addressed more formally, communicate more, and have more influence than lower status members.
- Cohesive groups are especially attractive to their members. Threat, competition, success, and small size contribute to cohesiveness, as does a tough initiation into the group. The consequences of cohesiveness include increased participation in group affairs, improved communication, and increased conformity. Cohesive groups are especially effective in accomplishing their own goals, which might or might not be those of the organization.
- Members of self-managed work groups do challenging work under reduced supervision. For greatest effectiveness, such groups should be stable, small, well trained, and moderately diverse in membership.

KEY CONCEPTS

Group	Norms	Inter-role conflict
Formal work groups	Roles	Person-role conflict
Informal groups	Role ambiguity	Status
Additive tasks	Role conflict	Status symbols
Disjunctive tasks	Intra-sender conflict	Group cohesiveness
Conjunctive tasks	Inter-sender conflict	Self-managed work groups

DISCUSSION QUESTIONS

1. Pick a group of which you are a member. Why did this group form, and why does it continue to persist as a group? Consider the issues of opportunity for interaction, potential for goal accomplishment, and the personal characteristics of members.

2. Give an example of an observation that you have made of group formation under stress. What functions did the formation of this group serve? Did it remain intact when and if the stress was removed? Does stress always lead to group formation? Consider the behavior that might occur on a rapidly sinking ship before answering.

3. Consider a large office in an insurance firm that consists of clerks, typists, and claims processors. Suppose that several informal friendship groups have formed on the basis of proximity and attitude similarity. Discuss the potential pros and cons of these groups for the organization. Does the existence of such informal groups make special demands upon office managers? Should organizations try to prevent the development of such groups?

4. Suppose that a group of United Nations representatives from various countries forms to draft a reso-

lution regarding world hunger. Does this appear to be an additive, disjunctive, or conjunctive task? What kinds of process losses would such a group be likely to suffer? Can you offer a prediction about the size of this group and its performance?

5. State several norms that exist in your classroom or in your work group. What functions do these norms serve? What are the shared attitudes that underlie these norms? How are the norms enforced?

6. Describe some work roles that seem inherently ambiguous because of organizational factors. Describe some factors that cause professors or supervisors to send ambiguous role messages to students or subordinates.

7. Mark Allen, a representative for an international engineering company, is a very religious person and an elder in his church. Mark's direct superior has instructed him to use "any legal means" to sell a large construction project to a South American government. The vice-president of international operations had informed Mark that he can offer a generous "kickback" to government officials to clinch the deal, although such practices are illegal. Discuss the three kinds of role conflict that Mark is experiencing.

8. Some organizations have made concerted efforts to do away with many of the status symbols associated with differences in organizational rank. All employees park in the same lot, eat in the same dining room, and have similar offices and privileges. Discuss the pros and cons of such a strategy. How might such a change affect organizational communications?

9. You are an executive in a consumer products corporation. The president assigns you to form a task force to develop new marketing strategies for the organization. You are permitted to choose its members. What things would you do to make this group as cohesive as possible?

10. Discuss the dangers of group cohesiveness for the group itself and for the organization of which the group is a part.

EXPERIENTIAL EXERCISE

Lost at Sea

The purpose of this exercise is to compare individual and group problem solving and to explore the group dynamics that occur in a problem-solving session. It can also be used in conjunction with Chapter 12.

The Scenario

You are adrift on a private yacht in the South Pacific. As a consequence of a fire of unknown origin, much of the yacht and its contents have been destroyed. The yacht is now slowly sinking. Your location is unclear because of the destruction of critical navigational equipment and because you and the crew were distracted by trying to bring the fire under control. Your best estimate is that you are approximately one thousand miles south-southwest of the nearest land.

Shown in Exhibit 1 is a list of fifteen items that are intact and undamaged after the fire. In addition to these articles, you have a serviceable rubber life raft with oars that is large enough to carry yourself, the crew, and all the items listed. The total contents of all survivors' pockets are a package of cigarettes, several books of matches, five one-dollar bills, and seventeen credit cards.

Instructions

The instructor will form groups of four to seven members. The general task is to rank the fifteen items in terms of their importance for survival.

EXHIBIT

1

Items	1 Individual Ranking	2 Group Ranking	3 Survival Experts' Ranking	4 Difference Between 1 and 3	5 Difference Between 2 and 3
Sextant					
Shaving mirror					
Five-gallon can of water					
Mosquito netting					
One case of U.S. Army C rations					
Maps of the Pacific Ocean					
Seat cushion (flotation device approved by the Coast Guard)					
Two-gallon can of oil-gas mixture					
Small transistor radio					
Shark repellent					
Twenty square feet of opaque plastic					
One quart of 160-proof Puerto Rican rum					
Fifteen feet of nylon rope					
Two boxes of chocolate bars					
Fishing kit					
TOTALS =					
				Individual Accuracy	Group Accuracy

Step 1: Working *individually,* each group member should rank order the fifteen items in terms of their survival value, giving a 1 to the most useful item, a 2 to the next most useful item, and so on. The least useful item will be ranked 15. List your answers in Column 1 of the grid. (10 minutes)

Step 2: The group will proceed to discuss the value of the fifteen items as a group and to develop a consensus ranking. In doing this, be open to the ideas of others and take advantage of different perspectives. Do *not* vote or average your answers. Try to reach consensus on the ranking by talking it out. Put your group's ranking in Column 2 of the grid. (30 minutes)

Step 3: Your instructor will provide you with the expert ranking of the items provided by officers of the U.S. Merchant Marines. Write the expert ranking in Column 3 of the grid.

Step 4: Take the absolute difference between your individual ranking (Column 1) and the experts' ranking (Column 3) for each item and write this difference in Column 4 of the grid. ("Absolute difference" means to ignore plus or minus signs.)

Step 5: Take the absolute difference between the group ranking (Column 2) and the experts' ranking (Column 3) for each item and write this difference in Column 5 of the grid.

Step 6: Calculate your individual accuracy score by totaling the numbers in Column 4 of the grid. The lower the score, the better.

Step 7: Calculate the group's accuracy score by totaling the numbers in Column 5 of the grid. The lower the score, the better.

Step 8: Calculate the *average* individual score for your group by adding up the individual accuracy scores (Step 6) and dividing by the number of members in your group.

Discussion

The instructor will summarize the results on the board for each group, including (a) average individual accuracy score, (b) group accuracy score, (c) gain or loss between the average individual score and the group score, and (d) the lowest individual score (i.e., the best score) in each group.

The following questions will help to guide the discussion:

_____ 1. As a group task, is the Lost at Sea exercise an additive, disjunctive, or conjunctive task?

_____ 2. What would be the impact of group size on performance in this task?

_____ 3. Did any norms develop in your group that guided how information was exchanged or how the decision was reached?

_____ 4. Did any special roles emerge in your group? These could include a leader, a secretary, an "expert," a critic, a humorist, and so on. How did these roles contribute to or hinder group performance?

_____ 5. Consider the factors that contribute to effective self-managed groups. How do they pertain to a group's performance in the Lost at Sea exercise?

Source: Adapted from Pfeiffer, J. W., & Jones, J. E. (1975). *The 1975 Annual Handbook for Group Facilitators,* San Diego, CA: University Associates, Inc. Used with permission.

The Kingston Company

The Kingston Company, located in Ontario, was a medium-sized manufacturing firm which made a line of machine parts and marketed them to plants in the southeastern section of the province. Harold Kingston, the president and majority shareholder in the company held a Master of Business Administration degree from an American university, and was a vigorous supporter of the usefulness and value of a graduate business education. As a result, he had on his staff a group of four young MBA's to whom he referred as "the think group" or "the troubleshooters."

The four members of the group ranged in age from the youngest at 23 to the oldest at 35, with the two intermediate members being 27. They were all from different universities, and had different academic backgrounds. Their areas of interest were Marketing, Organizational Behavior, Operations Research, and Finance. All had been hired simultaneously and placed together in the "think group" by Mr. Kingston because, as he put it, "With their diverse knowledge and intelligence they ought to be able to solve any of this company's problems."

For their first month on the job, the "Big Four," as they became known in the firm, familiarized themselves with the company's operations and employees. They spent a half-day every week in conference with Mr. Kingston and his executive committee, discussing the goals and objectives of the company, and going over the history of the major policy decisions made by the firm over the years. While the process of familiarization was a continuing one, the group decided after four weeks that it had uncovered some of the firm's problems and that it would begin to set out recommendations for the solution of these problems.

From the beginning, the members of the group had worked long hours and could usually be found in the

Source: Stuart-Kotze, R. (1980). *Introduction to organizational behavior: A situational approach*. Reston, VA: Reston. © 1980, pp. 320–323. Reprinted by permission of Prentice-Hall, Inc., Englewood Cliffs, NJ.

office, well after the plant had closed, discussing their findings and trading opinions and ideas. The approach to problem solving which they adopted was to attack each problem as a group and to pool their ideas. This seemed to give a number of different slants to the problems, and many times helped clear away the bias which inevitably crept into each member's analyses.

Mike Norton, the finance specialist, and the youngest member of the group, and Jim Thorne and Dave Knight, the operations research man and the behavior management man, respectively, spent a lot of time together outside the work environment. They seemed to have similar interests, playing tennis and golf together, and generally having a keen interest in sports. They managed to get tickets together to watch the local professional football games, and ice-hockey tickets, etc. The fourth and oldest member of the group, Cy Gittinger did not share these interests. The only "sports" he played were shuffleboard and croquet, and he didn't join the other three too often after work for a beer in a local bar, since he also abstained from alcohol.

The group, from the beginning, was purposely unstructured. All the members agreed to consider themselves equals. They occupied one large office, each having a desk in an opposite corner, with the middle of the room acting as a "common." Basic decisions were usually made with the four men pacing about in the open area, leaning against the walls and desks, and either squeezing or bouncing "worry balls" of a rubber-putty substance, used for cleaning typewriters, off the walls. The atmosphere was completely informal, and the rest of the firm kidded the members of the group about the inordinately large amount of typewriter cleaner used in the room when there were no typewriters to be seen.

While consensus was not required, the group found that they were able to agree on a course of action most of the time. When they were unable to do so, they presented their differing opinions to Mr. Kingston, in whose hands the final decision rested. They acted in a purely staff capacity, and unless requested to help a particular manager, and authorized to do so by Mr. Kingston, they confined their reports to the president and his executive committee. Reports were usually presented in written form, with all four members of the group present and contributing verbal support and summation.

The group realized that working in close contact would result in strained relations on occasion, and they agreed to attempt to express their feelings accurately and try to understand issues from the other members' point of view. Jokes about "happiness boys," "peddlers," and "formula babies" were bandied about, and each of the four made a conscious effort to see the biases introduced by his field of interest. Attempts at controlling the discussion and establishing a leadership position were handled by pointing out the behavior to the individual involved.

However, as the months passed, there seemed to be a growing uneasiness in the relationship between Norton, Thorne and Knight, and the fourth member, Gittinger. The three brought their feelings out one day when they were playing golf. At the nineteenth hole, over a drink, Thorne commented on the amount of time Gittinger spent talking to Mr. Kingston in his office. They all spent a great deal of time out of their office talking to managers and workers all through the plant, gathering data on various problems, but, Thorne remarked, Gittinger seemed to confine his activities to the upper levels of management far more than the others did. The other two had made the same observation, but felt that it was really hard to put a finger on anything "wrong" about consulting with the president continually. They agreed that their fact finding did not generally require as much time at higher levels as Gittinger was devoting, but when the point was brought up in subsequent discussion at the office, Cy explained that in order to get information from Mr. Kingston, he found an "indirect" approach, which entailed a certain amount of small talk, was most successful.

After the group had been functioning for ten months, Kingston called them in to a meeting with his executive committee and went through an appraisal of their performance. He was, he said, tremendously pleased that his "think group" had performed so well, and he felt vindicated in his belief in the potency of applying the skills learned in graduate business school. His executives added their words of praise. Then Mr. Kingston brought up a suggestion he said he and Cy Gittinger had been discussing for the past month and a half, to appoint one of the group members as a coordinator. The coordinator's job would be to form a liaison between Kingston and the executive committee on the one hand, and the group on the other, and also to guide the group, as a result of the closer ties of the coordinator with the management team, in establishing a set of priorities for different problem areas. When Kingston had finished describing the pro-

posal, which, it seemed, met with his and the committee's approval, Jim Thorne remarked that this procedure seemed to be unnecessary in the light of the previous smooth functioning of the group, and began to explain that such a change would upset the structure and goals of the group. He was interrupted by Mr. Kingston who said he had an important engagement. "We'll leave the working out of all the details to you men," he said. "We don't want to impose anything on you, and we have all agreed that you should be the ones to work out just how this new plan can be implemented." At this point, the meeting ended.

As the group walked back to their office, Gittinger was the only one who talked. He wondered aloud who would be the most suitable man for the coordinator's job, and repeated Kingston's words, citing the advantages that would accrue to the company with the creation of such a position. Since it was 4:45 P.M., they all cleared their desks and left the plant together, splitting up outside to go home.

At 6:00 P.M., Thorne called Norton to ask him what he thought about the developments of the afternoon. The latter expressed surprise, anger, and resentment that the decision had been made without the consultation of the group, and remarked that Knight, to whom he had just been talking, felt the same way. The trio made arrangements to meet for dinner at their downtown athletic club at 7:00 P.M. that evening to discuss the situation.

1. What are some of the norms that developed among the "Big Four" as they began their work at the Kingston Company?

2. Discuss the role dynamics and status differences within the think group as they evolved over time.

3. Compare the cohesiveness of the group after its formation with its cohesiveness at the end of the case. In both instances, what factors influenced its level of cohesiveness?

4. Analyze and evaluate the effectiveness of the think group, using the material on self-managed groups and the concepts summarized in Exhibit 8–7.

5. Why is the trio of younger men worried about Mr. Kingston's suggestion?

6. What are the pros and cons of Mr. Kingston's idea in terms of overall benefit to the company?

REFERENCES

1. For a detailed analysis of the motives for informal group formation, see Tichy, N. (1973). An analysis of clique formation and structure in organizations. *Administrative Science Quarterly, 18,* 194–208.

2. For a partial review, see Kahn, A., & McGaughey, T. A. (1977). Distance and liking: When moving close produces increased liking. *Sociometry, 40,* 138–144.

3. Byrne, D. (1969). Attitudes and attraction. In L. Berkowitz (Ed.), *Advances in experimental social psychology* (Vol. 4). New York: Academic Press.

4. Shaw, M. E. (1981). *Group dynamics: The psychology of small group behavior* (3rd ed.). New York: McGraw-Hill; Jones, E. E., & Gerard, H. B. (1967). *Foundations of social psychology.* New York: Wiley.

5. Hare, A. P. (1976). *A handbook of small group research.* New York: The Free Press; Shaw, 1981.

6. Hare, 1976; Shaw, 1981.

7. The following discussion relies upon Steiner, I. D. (1972). *Group process and productivity.* New York: Academic Press.

8. Steiner, 1972; Hill, G. W. (1982). Group versus individual performance: Are n + 1 heads better than one? *Psychological Bulletin, 91,* 517–539.

9. For an example of the social process by which this sharing may be negotiated in a new group, see Bettenhausen, K., & Murnighan, J. K. (1985). The emergence of norms in competitive decision-making groups. *Administrative Science Quarterly, 30,* 350–372.

10. For a good discussion of this, see Kanter, R. M. (1977). *Men and women of the corporation.* New York: Basic Books, pp. 63–67.

11. Kanter, 1977, p. 37.

12. Leventhal, G. S. (1976). The distribution of rewards and resources in groups and organizations. In L. Berkowitz & E. Walster (Eds.), *Advances in experimental social psychology* (Vol. 9). New York: Academic Press.

13. See Mitchell, T. R., Rothman, M., & Liden, R. C. (1985). Effects of normative information on task performance. *Journal of Applied Psychology, 70,* 48–55.

14. See Roy, D. (1952). Quota restriction and gold-bricking in a machine shop. *American Journal of Sociology, 57,* 426–442.

15. Jackson, S. E., & Schuler, R. S. (1985). A meta-analysis and conceptual critique of research on role ambiguity and role conflict in work settings. *Organizational Behavior and Human Decision Processes, 36,* 16–78. For a methodological critique of this domain, see King, L. A., & King, D. W. (1990). Role conflict and role ambiguity: A critical assessment of construct validity. *Psychological Bulletin, 107,* 48–64.

16. Jackson & Schuler, 1985.

17. Cooke, R. A., & Rousseau, D. M. (1984). Stress and strain from family roles and work-role expectations. *Journal of Applied Psychology, 69,* 252–260; Beutell, N. J., & Greenhaus, J. H. (1983). Integration of home and nonhome roles: Women's conflict and coping behavior. *Journal of Applied Psychology, 68,* 43–48.

18. See Latack, J. C. (1981). Person/role conflict: Holland's model extended to role-stress research, stress management, and career development. *Academy of Management Review, 6,* 89–103.

19. Jackson & Schuler, 1985.

20. Rafaeli, A. (1989). When cashiers meet customers: An analysis of the role of supermarket cashiers. *Academy of Management Journal, 32,* 245–273.

21. Robbins, S. P. (1978). *Personnel: The management of human resources.* Englewood Cliffs, NJ: Prentice-Hall, p. 294.

22. Treiman, D. J. (1977). *Occupational prestige in comparative perspective.* New York: Academic Press.

23. Roy, D. F. (1960). "Banana time": Job satisfaction and informal interaction. *Human Organization, 18,* 158–169, p. 164.

24. Ervin-Tripp, S. M. (1969). Sociolinguistics. In L. Berkowitz (Ed.), *Advances in experimental social psychology* (Vol. 4). New York: Academic Press.

25. Shaw, 1981.

26. Berger, J., Cohen, B. P., & Zelditch, M., Jr. (1972). Status characteristics and social interaction. *American Sociological Review, 37,* 241–255.

27. Strodbeck, F. L., James, R. M., & Hawkins, C. (1957). Social status in jury deliberations. *American Sociological Review, 22,* 713–719.

28. For other definitions and a discussion of their differences, see Mudrack, P. E. (1989). Defining group cohesiveness: A legacy of confusion? *Small Group Behavior, 20,* 37–49.

29. Stein, A. (1976). Conflict and cohesion: A review of the literature. *Journal of Conflict Resolution, 20,* 143–172.

30. Cartwright, D. (1968). The nature of group cohesiveness. In D. Cartwright & A. Zander (Eds.), *Group dynamics* (3rd ed.). New York: Harper & Row.

31. Lott, A., & Lott, B. (1965). Group cohesiveness as interpersonal attraction: A review of relationships with antecedent and consequent variables. *Psychological Bulletin, 64,* 259–309.

32. Anderson, A. B. (1975). Combined effects of interpersonal attraction and goal-path clarity on the cohesiveness of task-oriented groups. *Journal of Personality and Social Psychology, 31,* 68–75. Also see Cartwright, 1968.

33. Seashore, S. (1954). *Group cohesiveness in the industrial workgroup.* Ann Arbor, MI: Institute for Social Research.

34. Blanchard, F. A., Adelman, L., & Cook, S. W. (1975). Effect of group success and failure upon interpersonal attraction in cooperating interracial groups. *Journal of Personality and Social Psychology, 31,* 1020–1030.

35. Walker, M. (1968). Organizational type, rites of incorporation, and group solidarity: A study of fraternity hell week. *Dissertation Abstracts, 29*(2-A), 689–690. Also see Aronson, E., & Mills, J. (1959). The effects of severity of initiation on liking for a group. *Journal of Abnormal and Social Psychology, 59,* 177–181.

36. Cartwright, 1968; Shaw, 1981.

37. Schacter, S. (1951). Deviation, rejection, and communication. *Journal of Abnormal and Social Psychology, 46,* 190–207.

38. Seashore, 1954. Also see Stogdill, R. M. (1972). Group productivity, drive, and cohesiveness. *Organizational Behavior and Human Performance, 8,* 26–43. For a recent critique, see Mudrack, P. E. (1989). Group cohesiveness and productivity: A closer look. *Human Relations, 42,* 771–785.

39. Hackman, J. R. (1987). The design of work teams. In J. W. Lorsch (Ed.), *Handbook of organizational behavior.* Englewood Cliffs, NJ: Prentice-Hall.

40. Dumaine, B. (1990, May 7). Who needs a boss? *Fortune,* 52–60.

41. Wall, T. D., Kemp, N. J., Jackson, P. R., & Clegg, C. W. (1986). Outcomes of autonomous workgroups: A field experiment. *Academy of Management Journal, 29,* 280–304, p. 283.

42. Parts of this section rely on Hackman, 1987.

43. See Ashforth, B. E., & Mael, F. (1989). Social identity theory and the organization. *Academy of Management Review, 14,* 20–39.

44. Treece, J. (1990, April 9). Here comes GM's Saturn. *Business Week,* 56–62.

45. Manz, C. C., & Sims, H. P., Jr. (1987). Leading workers to lead themselves: The external leadership of self-managing work teams. *Administrative Science Quarterly, 32,* 106–128.

46. For reviews of research on self-managed groups, see Chapter 3 of Cummings, T. G., & Molloy, E. S. (1977). *Improving productivity and the quality of working life.* New York: Praeger; Goodman, P. S., Devadas, R., & Hughes, T. L. G. (1988). Groups and productivity: Analyzing the effectiveness of self-managing teams. In J. P. Campbell & R. J. Campbell (Eds.), *Productivity in organizations.* San Francisco: Jossey-Bass.

SOCIAL INFLUENCE, SOCIALIZATION, AND CULTURE

WALT DISNEY COMPANY

The Walt Disney Company empire includes Disney Studios, California's Disneyland, Florida's Disney World, and a lucrative licensing arrangement for products based on Disney characters. It is universally agreed that Disney has been successful, especially in its theme parks and associated resorts, by virtue of an unwavering dedication to excellent customer service. In fact, firms such as General Motors and DuPont have sent executives to Disney-sponsored seminars to understand how Disney has managed to provide guests with such a clean, pleasant, friendly environment for all of these years.

By all appearances, the task doesn't seem easy. The work force is mostly young and not especially well paid. They are particularly likely to be scheduled to work on busy holidays and vacation periods, just when they would like to spend time with friends and family. Much of the work itself is basically routine and boring (try uttering "Welcome Voyager" with conviction thousands of times a day to the hordes who visit Space Mountain!). Also, Disney has some of the most rigid grooming standards in the industry, forbidding beards, mustaches, and dangling jewelry. The company even provides samples of which basic black shoes are acceptable. The image here is cleancut and conservative.

If individuality is discouraged, all-American friendliness is encouraged. Elaborate group selection interviews stress attitudes and personality over academic credentials, and a film is shown to warn job candidates about expected standards of grooming and behavior. If they are accepted, new employees attend "Disney University" and take the courses Traditions I and II, which expose them to the lingo and lore of Disneyana. In the Disney vocabulary, they are hosts or cast members, not employees, and customers are guests. Their uniforms are referred to as costumes, and they are said to be on stage when they are in the public part of the park. Groups tests are given ("Name the seven dwarves in Snow White.") to foster teamwork. Cast members learn that their role in creating happiness includes picking up any stray trash that they see and being able to answer any conceivable question a guest asks. When everyone does this, employees serve as role models for each other. After the group training at Disney U., employees are assigned to experienced peers who train them in the techniques of their specific job assignment. This "paired training," along with the Traditions classes, is much more extensive than is typical in most service organizations. Thus, guests have little reason to expect poor performance from a new cast member, who has been well versed in Walt Disney's values regarding family entertainment.

Disney relies heavily on promotion from within, even in its management ranks. Its white-collar turnover is low by any standard, and its turnover rate is well below average for hourly service employees. Part of this might be due to a system of decidedly social rewards and perks that appeal to younger employees. These include company sports leagues, employee nights at the park, and company picnics and beach parties.

In the old days, the cry "Walt's in the park" would motivate cast members to do their very best. Today, Disney U. trainers often exhort students with "Walt's *always* in the park now." The spirit lives.[1]

Michael Eisner, CEO of the Walt Disney Company, with employees. (Sygma)

This description of a successful service organization raises a number of interesting questions. How does Disney attract and retain employees despite low pay, curtailed individuality, and fairly routine work? Do employees actually accept the ideals and values that they encounter in their training? What has maintained the Disney obsession with excellent service over the years? These are the kinds of questions that we will probe in this chapter.

First, we will examine the general issue of social influence in organizations, how members have an impact on each other's behavior and attitudes. Social norms hold an organization together, and conformity to such norms is a product of social influence. Thus, the next section discusses conformity. Following this, we consider the elaborate process of socialization, the learning of the organization's norms and roles. Socialization both contributes to and results from the organizational culture, the final area that we will explore.

SOCIAL INFLUENCE IN ORGANIZATIONS

In the previous chapter, it was pointed out that groups exert influence over the attitudes and behavior of their individual members. As a result of social influence, people often feel or act differently than they would as independent operators. What accounts for such influence? In short, in many social settings, and especially in groups, people are highly *dependent* upon others. This dependence sets the stage for influence to occur.

Information Dependence

We are frequently dependent upon others for information about the adequacy and appropriateness of our behavior, thoughts, and feelings. How satisfying is this job of mine? How nice is our boss? How much work should I take home to do over the weekend? Should we protest the bad design at the meeting? Objective, concrete answers to such questions might be hard to come by. Thus, we must often rely upon information provided by others. In turn, this **information dependence** gives others the opportunity to influence our thoughts, feelings, and actions via the signals they send to us.[2]

Individuals are often motivated to compare their own thoughts, feelings, and actions with those of others as a means of acquiring information about their adequacy.[3] In one well-known series of studies designed to explore this hypothesis, students volunteered to participate in an experiment concerning the effects of electric shock on physiological functioning. Some were led to believe that they would receive very painful shocks, a condition that was reinforced by the presence of a forbidding "shock generator." Others were led to expect very mild tingling shocks and were reassured that the experience would not be harmful. While the equipment was being readied, the volunteers were given the option of waiting with someone else or alone. Actually, no shocks were delivered, and when the subjects had made their choice, the experiment was over. In sum, 63 percent of those who expected nasty shocks chose to wait with others, while only 33 percent of those who expected mild shocks chose to do so.[4] Subsequent studies suggested that those in the high threat condition wished to wait with others to obtain *information* about how they should be feeling and behaving in a threatening situation.

Some people are more in need of information than others. In the shock studies, those who faced more frightening prospects were more motivated to seek information. In general, novel, threatening, or confusing settings should increase information dependence. At the Disney Company, young new employees with little work experience would be especially tuned in to information conveyed by the more experienced members, not to mention each other.

Some people are better *sources* of information than others. In the shock studies, the volunteers who were in the threatening condition did not wish to wait with just anyone. Rather, they revealed this tendency only when the potential company was about to undergo the same experience. As this illustrates, *peers* are often a preferred source of information. Thus, in deciding how satisfying your job is, you would be especially likely to rely on the impressions of your co-workers. In other cases, we might seek information from *experts* rather than peers. An expert is simply someone whom we perceive to be especially knowledgeable about the situation at hand. At Disney, the Traditions trainers are drawn from the ranks of experienced park workers. As such, they serve as an important source of expert information for the new recruits.

In summary, groups often influence members via the information that they provide about important issues. The effects of social information can be very strong, often exerting as much or more influence over others as objective reality.[5]

Effect Dependence

As if group members were not busy enough tuning in to information provided by the group, they must also be sensitive to the rewards and punishments the group has at its disposal. Thus, individuals are dependent upon the *effects* of their behavior as determined by the rewards and punishments provided by others. **Effect dependence** actually involves two complementary processes. First, the group frequently has a vested interest in how individual members think and act because such matters can affect the goal attainment of the group. Second, the member frequently desires the approval of the group. In combination, these circumstances promote effect dependence.

In organizational settings plenty of effects are available to keep individual members "under the influence." Superiors typically have a fair array of rewards and punishments available, including promotions, raises, and the assignment of more or less favorable tasks. At the informal level, the variety of such effects available for use by co-workers is staggering. Cooperative behavior might be rewarded with praise, friendship, and a helping hand on the job. Lack of cooperation might result in nagging, harassment, name calling, social isolation, and even physical punishment.

CONFORMITY: SOCIAL INFLUENCE IN ACTION

One of the most obvious consequences of information and effect dependence is the tendency for group members to conform to the norms that have been established by the group. In the last chapter we discussed the development and function of such norms, but we have postponed until now the discussion of why norms are supported. Put simply, much of the information and many of the effects upon which group members are dependent are oriented toward enforcing group norms.

Motives for Conformity

It might occur to you that **conformity** is a rather general term. After all, the fact that Roman Catholic priests conform to the norms of the Church hierarchy seems rather different from the case in which convicts conform to norms established by prison officials. Clearly, the motives for conformity differ in these two cases. What is needed, then, is some system to classify different motives for conformity.[6]

Compliance **Compliance** is the simplest, most direct motive for conformity to group norms. It occurs because a member wishes to acquire rewards from the group and avoid punishment. As such, it primarily involves effect dependence. Although the complying individual adjusts his or her behavior to the norm, he or she does not really subscribe to the beliefs, values, and attitudes that underlie the norm. Most convicts conform to formal prison norms out of compliance. Similarly, very young children behave themselves only because of external forces.

Identification Some individuals conform because they find other supporters of the norm attractive. In this case, the individual identifies with these supporters and sees himself or herself as similar to them. Although there are elements of effect dependence here, information dependence is especially important—if someone is basically similar to you, then you will be motivated to rely on them for information about how to think and act. **Identification** as a motive for conformity is often revealed by an imitation process in which established members serve as models for the behavior of others. For example, a newly promoted executive might attempt to dress and talk like her successful, admired boss. Similarly, as children get older, they might be motivated to behave themselves because such behavior corresponds to that of an admired parent with whom they are beginning to identify.

Internalization Some conformity to norms occurs because individuals have truly and wholly accepted the beliefs, values, and attitudes that underlie the norm. As such, **internalization** of the norm has happened, and conformity occurs because it is seen as *right,* not because it achieves rewards, avoids punishment, or pleases others. That is, conformity is due to internal, rather than external, forces. In general, we expect that most religious leaders conform to the norms of their religion for this reason. Similarly, the career army officer might come to support the strict discipline of the military because it seems right and proper, not simply because such discipline is supported by colleagues. In certain organizational settings, some of these motives for conformity are more likely than others. For example, it is highly unlikely that many Disneyland recruits fully internalize the material covered in Traditions I and II. Rather, they appear to *identify* with the company and its experienced members:

> Like employees everywhere, there is a limit to which such overt company propaganda can be effective. Students and trainers alike seem to agree on where the line is drawn, for there is much satirical banter, mischievous winkings, and playful exaggeration in the classroom. All are aware that the label "Disneyland" has both an unserious and artificial connotation and that a full embrace of the Disneyland role would be as deviant as its full rejection. It does seem, however, because of the corporate imagery, the recruiting and selection procedures, the goodwill trainees hold toward the organization at entry, the peer-based employment context, and the smooth fit with real student calendars, the job is considered by most to be a good one. The University of Disneyland, it appears, graduates students with a modest amount of pride and a considerable amount of fact and faith firmly ingrained as important things to know (and accept).[7]

Experiments in Conformity

The various motives for conformity can be illustrated by two well-known studies of the conformity process. In turn, we can use these studies to illustrate the conditions under which conformity is more or less likely to occur.

The Asch Study In a study by Solomon Asch, subjects were led to believe that they were participating in an experiment on visual perception.[8] They were seated last in a row of seven to nine other individuals and exposed to lines of the type shown in Exhibit 9–1. The object was to indicate which of the three comparison lines was equal in length to the standard line. Judgments were given successively, and the subject was the last to respond. On the first two trials, things went smoothly, and all of the people agreed as to which line matched the standard. On the third trial an amazing thing happened. The first person to respond gave a clearly inaccurate answer, and this response was also given by the others. Quickly, it was the subject's turn to respond. What would you do? As you might have guessed, the other people in the row were confederates of the experimenter, and this was a study in conformity rather than perception. Over a number of trials, the confederates communicated a "false norm" several times. Conformity to this false norm occurred about one third of the time by subjects that had remarkably varied degrees of independence.

In this study, why was there so much conformity to the false norm? Clearly, the perceptual task was very easy; control subjects who performed the task alone

EXHIBIT

9–1

Which comparison line matches the standard? The Asch conformity study task.

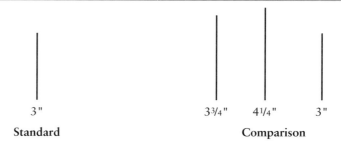

3"		3¾" 4¼" 3"
Standard		Comparison

Source: From Asch, S. A. (1956). Studies of independence and conformity: A minority of one against a unanimous majority. *Psychological Monographs: General and Applied,* Vol. 70, No. 9. Whole No. 416, p. 7. Copyright 1956 by the American Psychological Association. Adapted by permission of the author.

made few errors in judgment. When asked why they had yielded, most subjects said something to the effect that "I knew they were wrong, but I gave in anyway." The majority of the subjects did not believe that the false norm was correct, but they doubted both the majority's perceptions and their own capacities to judge and were torn in conflicting directions. Evidently, they were in a state of effect dependence, anticipating rejection or other punishment by the others if they disagreed.

The Sherif Study Research by Muzafer Sherif was also explained to the participants as an exercise in visual perception. What they were required to do was to estimate the amount of movement of a point of light in a darkened room. In fact, the light was absolutely stationary. However, in this situation, observers invariably report some movement. This phenomenon is called the autokinetic (self-movement) effect, and it is due to certain physiological processes. Because there is no frame of reference in a completely dark environment, individuals usually give widely differing estimates of the distance the light has "moved."

First, Sherif tested subjects individually to determine their estimates without social influence. Then, subjects were assembled into groups of two or three and asked to judge the movement over a series of trials. On each trial, they made simultaneous judgments. The results were clear-cut. Over the series of trials, the estimates of the movement of the group members tended to *converge.* Gradually, those who initially reported large movements decreased their estimates, and vice versa—in other words, a compromise was reached. Sherif argued that this convergence represented the development of a norm to which group members conformed.[9]

Notice that the situation here is very different from that in the Asch line study. This is clearly an ambiguous situation, and the subjects are in certain need of information. Thus, minimally, it would appear that identification occurred among group members. The case here is not so much that they found each other attractive as that they recognized each other as equally bemused. In such cases, we often rely upon others for information about how to think or act. In fact, it would appear that the compromise norm was frequently *internalized* as representing correct information. When subjects were tested alone after the group experience, they tended to respond with the group-established norm. Amazingly, this effect has been shown to persist a whole year after the group interaction.[10]

It is important to recognize that there are many decision tasks facing existing groups that have elements in common with the Asch and Sherif experimental situations. For example, imagine the negotiating committee of a trade union that is trying to decide whether to accept a company contract offer. Each member offers a successive opinion about the course of action to be taken. If the first three unionists all favor acceptance, will the fourth be willing to offer a contrary view? (Asch situation). Similarly, consider three partners who own a restaurant who are trying to decide whether they should expand their premises during an uncertain economic climate. Initially, one favors no expansion, one favors a large expansion, and one falls in the middle (Sherif situation). Will they compromise on a medium-sized expansion? To answer questions of this nature, we must explore the variables that influence degree of conformity.

Factors Influencing Conformity

What determines the extent to which a particular group member will be likely to conform to group norms? Put simply, factors that increase or decrease information and effect dependence should influence the extent of conformity of individual group members.

Publicity In the Asch setting, one obvious way to reduce the conformity of the naive subject to the false norm is to permit the subject to render opinions about line length in secret. Such a condition reduces effect dependence. For example, suppose an executive group has two equally strong informal norms—not cheating on expense accounts and not leaving the office before six o'clock. Other things being equal, an executive who disagrees with both norms would be more likely to comply with the leaving-time norm than the cheating norm because violation of the former would be more obvious. In some piecerate pay situations in which groups have developed norms to restrict productivity, workers will lie about their own output to prevent pressure from their co-workers.

Size of the Opposition Any tendency to "go along with the crowd" is enhanced when the "crowd" is bigger because a large opposition contains more sources of information and more sources of reward and punishment. In the Asch setting, subjects are less likely to conform to the false norm when confronting only one or two others than when there are seven or eight.[11] Research on jury size shows that small juries tend to render less consistent verdicts than large juries.[12] This might

Source: Drawing
by Handelsman; ©
1972 The New
Yorker Magazine,
Inc.

"Well, heck! If all you smart cookies agree, who am I to dissent?"

stem in part from the fact that dissenters in small juries feel freer to stand their ground. (For a related view on the judicial perspective, see the cartoon!)

Dissension Imagine that, in the Asch setting, the naive subject finds that he or she has a "partner in crime" somewhere earlier in the lineup, that is, someone who also rejects the false norm and gives correct responses. As you might guess, such a condition strongly reduces the subject's tendency to conform. Dissenters provide alternative sources of information to the group consensus and change potential reward and punishment patterns.

The Issue at Hand In the Asch routine, it is possible to increase the naive subject's tendency to conform to the false norm by making the stimulus lines more nearly equal in length. In general, difficult, ambiguous issues increase the tendency toward conformity to group norms. For example, suppose four sales managers are asked to nominate one of their subordinates for promotion to manager. The subordinates are usually on the road, and there has been little opportunity to observe their managerial abilities. If, for some reason, three of the managers favor a particular candidate, it should be difficult for the fourth to dissent, since the choice is difficult and ambiguous.

Other things being equal, issues that are directly relevant to a group's goal accomplishment are also likely to prompt high conformity. For example, suppose a college history department is interested in increasing its national reputation so that it can hire well-known scholars. In this case, we should see more conformity to a norm that insists on a high publication rate than to a norm that favors conservative tweed clothing.

Status The relationship between status in the group and conformity is complex but easy to understand. If nonconformity occurs, it should usually occur among two classes of people—high-status members or low-status members who have been actively rejected by the group (the latter have often been socially isolated or serve as scapegoats). High-status members have often *achieved* their high status because they have generally conformed to group norms. Thus, on an issue chosen at random, it is often safe to predict conformity from such a person. However, high-status members also receive **idiosyncrasy credits** from the group because of their history of conformity. This means that having paid their dues to the group, they are permitted to occasionally deviate without fear of censure.[13] On the other hand, low-status isolates and scapegoats have already rejected the group as a source of information and suffered the negative effects of doing so. Thus, they have little to gain by conforming in a particular case. Finally, low-status members who are striving to become fully integrated into the group (usually *new* members) should reveal a strong tendency to conform, since they are both effect and information dependent (Exhibit 9–2).

For an example of nonconformity in the form of "whistleblowing," see Ethical Focus 9–1 on page 300.

The Subtle Power of Compliance

In many of the examples given in the previous section, especially those dealing with increased effect dependence, it is obvious that the doubting group member is motivated to conform only in the *compliance* mode. That is, he or she really doesn't support the belief, value, and attitude structure underlying the norm but conforms simply to avoid trouble or obtain rewards. Of course, this happens all the time. Individuals without religious beliefs or values might agree to be married in a church service to please others. Similarly, a bank teller might verify that a small check being cashed by a familiar customer is covered by sufficient funds even though he feels that the whole process is a waste of time. These examples of

EXHIBIT 9–2

Status, idiosyncrasy credits, and conformity.

Status	Idiosyncrasy Credits?	Use Credits?	Conform?
High	Yes	Yes	No
		No	Yes
Low (Rejected Member)	No	Can't	No
Low (New Member)	No	Can't	Yes

compliance seem trivial enough, but as we shall now see, a little compliance can go a long way, in at least two senses.

First, consider the **foot-in-the-door phenomenon**, named for a well-known technique used by door-to-door salespeople. This concept refers to the tendency for compliance with a fairly minor request to prime persons to be receptive to

---

ETHICAL FOCUS 9–1

▼
....
Whistleblowing—Ethical Nonconformity

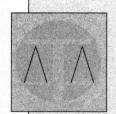

A. Earnest Fitzgerald, a former high-level manager in the U.S. Air Force and Lockheed CEO, revealed to Congress and the press that the Air Force and Lockheed systematically practiced a strategy of underbidding in order to gain Air Force contracts for Lockheed, which then billed the Air Force and received payments for cost overruns on the contracts. Fitzgerald was fired for his trouble, but eventually received his job back. The underbidding/cost overruns, on at least the C-5/A cargo plane, were stopped.

The events described here by Richard Nielsen are an example of whistleblowing—an act of nonconformity by an organizational member who calls attention to some serious wrongdoing.

Myron and Penina Glazer conducted an in-depth study of fifty-five whistleblowers in both the public and private sectors. Far from being perennial malcontents, virtually all of them were dedicated, long-service employees who were finally unable to reconcile unethical organizational practices with their strong sense of individual responsibility. Long service was no protection from retaliation. Many whistleblowers were fired, transferred, blackballed, demoted, or personally intimidated and harassed for their lack of conformity.

Of course, not all whistleblowers face retaliation. Janet Near and Marcia Miceli studied the severity of retaliation against whistleblowers who were U.S. federal employees. Retaliation was more likely when the whistleblowers lacked managerial support, when the wrongdoing was particularly serious, and when the person went outside the organization to blow the whistle. Interestingly, retaliation was not related to position in the organization.

Source: Nielsen, R. P. (1989). Changing unethical organizational behavior. *Academy of Management Executive*, 3, 123–130, p. 125; Glazer, M. P., & Glazer, P. M. (1986, August). Whistleblowing. *Psychology Today*, 36–43; Near, J. P., & Miceli, M. P. (1986). Retaliation against whistleblowers: Predictors and effects. *Journal of Applied Psychology*, 71, 137–145.

more demanding requests.[14] For instance, suppose an employee asks a co-worker to "punch out" for him one day so that he can leave work early. The co-worker reluctantly complies. The following week, the employee asks the co-worker to punch in for him in the morning for the next three days because his car is in the shop and he must take a late bus to work. According to the "foot" phenomenon, the co-worker should be more likely to comply with this more demanding request than he would be if he had not first complied with the less demanding request. Why does the "foot" phenomenon occur? Probably because the initial compliance slightly changes the complier's self-image vis-à-vis the other person ("I punched out for him. I'm a helpful person to him."). Confronted with a more demanding request, the complier then needs to maintain this self-image. Let the innocent complier beware!

Over time, the effects of compliance can be even more powerful and more subtle. Specifically, the compliant individual is necessarily *doing* something that is contrary to the way he or she *thinks* or *feels*. As pointed out in our discussion of attitudes in Chapter 5, such a situation is highly dissonant and arouses a certain tension in the individual. Now one way to reduce this dissonance is to cease conformity. However, this might require the person to adopt an isolate or scapegoat role, equally unpleasant prospects. The other method of reducing dissonance is to gradually accept the beliefs, values, and attitudes that support the norm in question. In practice, how might this occur?

Consider Joan, an idealistic graduate of a college social work program who acquires a job with a social services agency. Joan loves helping people but hates the bureaucratic red tape and reams of paperwork that are necessary to accomplish this goal. However, to acquire the approval of her boss and co-workers, and to avoid trouble, she follows the rules to the letter of the law. This is pure compliance. Over time, however, Joan begins to *identify* with her boss and more experienced co-workers because they are in the enviable position of controlling those very rewards and punishments that are so important to her. Obviously, if she is to *be* one of them, she must begin to think and feel like them. Finally, Joan is promoted to a supervisory position partly because she is so cooperative. Breaking in a new social worker, Joan is heard to say, "Our rules and forms are very important. You don't understand now, but you will." The metamorphosis is complete—Joan has *internalized* the beliefs and values that support the bureaucratic norms of her agency.

Although this story is slightly dramatized, the point that it makes is accurate—simple compliance can set the stage for more complete involvement with organizational norms and roles.

SOCIALIZATION: GETTING (SOME) CONFORMITY FROM MEMBERS

The story of Joan the social worker in the previous section describes how one individual was socialized into a particular organization. **Socialization** is the process by which people learn the norms and roles that are necessary to function in a group or organization. As we shall see, some of this process might occur before membership formally begins. Furthermore, socialization is an ongoing process by virtue of continuous interaction with others in the workplace. However, there is good reason to believe that socialization is most potent during certain periods of membership transition, such as when one is promoted or assigned to a new work group, and especially when one joins a new organization.[15]

Stages of Socialization

Since organizational socialization is an ongoing process, it is useful to divide this process into three stages.[16] One of these stages occurs before entry, another immediately follows entry, and the last occurs after one has been a member for some period of time. In a sense, the first two stages represent hurdles for achieving passage into the third stage (see Exhibit 9–3).

Anticipatory Socialization   A considerable amount of socialization might occur even before a person becomes a member of a particular organization. This process is called anticipatory socialization. Some anticipatory socialization includes a formal process of skill and attitude acquisition, such as that which might occur by attending university. Other anticipatory socialization might be informal, such as that acquired through a series of summer jobs or even by watching the portrayal of organizational life in television shows and movies. As we shall see shortly, organizations vary in the extent to which they encourage anticipatory socializa-

EXHIBIT 9–3

Stages of organizational socialization.

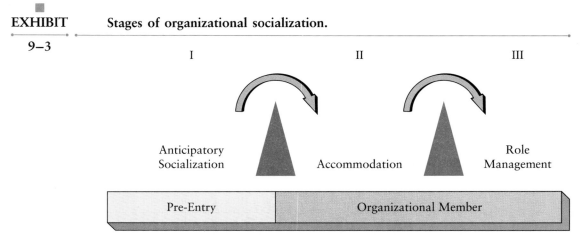

Source: Based on Feldman, D. C. (1976). A contingency theory of socialization. *Administrative Science Quarterly, 21*, 433–452 by permission of *Administrative Science Quarterly*. Copyright © 1976 by Administrative Science Quarterly.

tion in advance of entry. Also, we shall see that not all anticipatory socialization is accurate and useful for the new member.

Accommodation In the accommodation stage, the new recruit, armed with some expectations about organizational life, encounters the day-to-day reality of this life. Formal aspects of this stage might include orientation programs, training programs (such as that at Disney), and rotation through various parts of the organization. Informal aspects include getting to know and understand the style and personality of one's boss and co-workers. At this stage, the organization and its experienced members are looking for an acceptable degree of conformity to organizational norms and the gradual acquisition of appropriate role behavior. Recruits, on the other hand, are interested in having their personal needs and expectations fulfilled. If accommodation is reached, the recruit will have complied with critical organizational norms and should begin to identify with experienced organizational members.

Role Management Having survived the accommodation process and acquired basic role behaviors, the member's attention shifts to fine-tuning and actively managing his or her role in the organization. He or she might be expected to exercise some idiosyncrasy credits and modify the role to better serve the organization. This might require forming connections outside the immediate work group. And the organizational member must confront balancing the now-familiar organizational role with nonwork roles and family demands. Each of these experiences provides additional socialization to the role occupant, who might begin to internalize the norms and values that are prominent in the organization.

Now that we have seen a basic sketch of how socialization proceeds, let's look in greater detail at some of the key issues in the process.

The Naive New Member

People seldom join organizations without expectations about what membership will be like. In fact, it is just such expectations that lead them to choose one career or job over another. Management majors have some expectations about what they will be doing when they become management trainees in the Ajax Company. Similarly, even eighteen-year-old army recruits have notions about what military life will be like.

Research indicates that many expectations that are held by entering organizational members are inaccurate and often unrealistically high.[17] In one study of telephone operators, for example, expectations about the nature of the job were obtained before employment commenced, and perceptions of the actual job were obtained shortly after. The results indicated that many perceptions were less favorable than expectations. A similar result occurred for students entering a Master of Business Administration program.[18] Such changes, which are fairly common, give support to the notion that socialization has an important impact on new organizational members.[19]

Why do new members often have unrealistic expectations about the organizations they join? To some extent, occupational stereotypes such as those discussed in Chapter 4 could be responsible. Such stereotypes are often communicated by the media. For example, a person entering nurses' training might have gained some expectations about hospital life from watching *General Hospital*. Those of us who teach might also be guilty of communicating stereotypes. After four years of study, the new management trainee at Ajax might be dismayed to find that the emphasis is on *trainee* rather than *management!* Finally, unrealistic expectations may also stem from overzealous recruiters who paint rosy pictures in order to attract job candidates to the organization. Taken together, these factors demonstrate the need for socialization.

The Dilemmas of Socialization

Individuals enter organizations with a unique set of skills, interests, and attitudes. This fact of life poses interesting dilemmas for both the individual and the organization.

On one hand, new members wish to maintain their individual identity and self-respect by retaining their unique qualities and building upon them. On the other hand, they are also anxious to learn the ropes of the organization and use these unique qualities in a manner acceptable to peers and superiors. The organization and its experienced members also face a similar dilemma. On one hand, new members must to some extent be encouraged to support the norms and role requirements of the organization. Without this support, organizational goals will be impossible to achieve because the firm or institution simply won't be *organized*. On the other hand, complete and total allegiance to existing norms and role requirements will render the organization dinosaurlike, unable to adapt to a changing environment. In this case, creative and innovative behaviors on the part of individual members are stifled, and existing norms and roles take on a life of their own. In Chapter 1, you learned that two very basic conditions for organizational survival are reliable role behavior *and* creative, innovative activity.

These, then, are the dilemmas of socialization: How should individuals react to socialization practices? And how can organizations socialize members to an adequate extent without frustrating them or stifling their uniqueness?

From the individual's viewpoint, many people simply avoid joining organizations whose socialization practices are incompatible with their needs. Of course, this can be tricky business given the inaccurate perceptions of organizational practices held by many outsiders. Finding themselves at the mercy of socialization that doesn't meet their needs, individuals might effect a compromise or decide to seek employment elsewhere.

Organizations attempt to solve *their* socialization dilemmas by tailoring socialization practices to their particular needs. Intuitively, this seems reasonable. Somehow, the making of a priest seems different from the making of a stockbroker! Let's now turn to the different schemes that various organizations employ to meet their particular needs.

Methods of Socialization

For various jobs, organizations differ in terms of *who* does the socializing, *how* it is done, and *how much* is done. In turn, these differences affect the job behavior of those who are socialized.

Reliance on External Agents Organizations differ in the extent to which they make use of *other* organizations to help socialize their members. For example, hospitals do not develop experienced cardiologists from scratch. Rather, they depend on medical schools to socialize potential doctors in the basic role requirements of being a physician. Similarly, business firms rely upon university business schools to send them recruits who think and act in a businesslike manner. In this way, a fair degree of anticipatory socialization may exist before a person joins an organization. On the other hand, organizations such as police forces, the military, and religious institutions are less likely to rely upon external socializers. Police academies, boot camps, and seminaries are set up as extensions of these organizations to aid in socialization.

It appears that organizations that handle their own socialization are especially interested in maintaining the continuity and stability of job behaviors over a period of time. Conversely, those that rely on external agencies to perform anticipatory socialization are oriented toward maintaining the potential for creative, innovative behavior on the part of members—there is less "inbreeding." Of course, reliance on external agents might present problems. The engineer who is socialized in university courses to respect design elegance might find it difficult to accept cost restrictions when he or she is employed by an engineering firm. For this reason, organizations that rely heavily upon external socialization always supplement it with formal training and orientation or informal on-the-job training.

At Disney, hiring young employees and promoting from within suggest relatively little reliance on external agents. Perhaps the company is trying to avoid "bad habits" that could be picked up in less meticulous service organizations!

Collective Versus Individual A collective socialization strategy or an individual strategy may be employed.[20] In the collective case, a number of new or aspiring members are socialized as a group, going through the same experiences and facing the same challenges. Army boot camps, fraternity pledge classes, and training classes for salespeople and airline attendants are examples. Under an individual system, socialization is tailor-made for each new member. Simple on-the-job training and apprenticeship to develop skilled craftspeople constitute individual socialization.

Collective socialization is often used to promote organizational loyalty, esprit de corps, and uniformity of behavior among those being socialized. This last characteristic is often very important. No matter where they are in the world, soldiers know whom to salute and how to do it. Similarly, air passengers need not expect any surprises from cabin attendants, thanks to the attendants' collective socialization. Collective socialization is especially effective in inducing uniform behavior because there are so many models present who are undergoing the same experience. In addition, the individuals being socialized might pressure each other to toe the line and "do things right." Thus, in collective socialization, one's peers prove to be especially potent sources of information.

Under individual socialization, new members are more likely to take on the particular characteristics and style of their socializers. Thus, two newly hired real estate agents who receive on-the-job training from their bosses might soon think and act more like their bosses than like each other. As you can see, uniformity is less likely under individual socialization.

It must be mentioned that collective socialization is always followed up by individual socialization as the member joins his or her regular work unit. For example, rookie police officers are routinely partnered with more experienced officers. At this point, they will begin to develop some individuality in the style with which they perform their jobs. At Disney, collective socialization in Traditions I and II is followed up with the more individualized paired training.

Debasement and Hazing   Organizations frequently put new members through a series of experiences that are designed to humble them and strip away some of their initial self-confidence. These experiences are called **debasement** (or, informally, hazing). Often, debasement is seen as a way of testing the commitment of new members and correcting for faulty anticipatory socialization. Having been humbled and stripped of preconceptions, members are then seen as ready to learn the norms of the organization. Some debasement experiences are formal and planned (see Global Focus 9–2). An extreme example is the rough treatment and shaved heads experienced by Marine Corps recruits. A little less extreme are Disney's strict grooming standards. Even new college graduates are not immune to debasement:

> This may sound like brainwashing or boot camp, but it usually just takes the form of pouring on more work than the newcomer can possibly do. IBM and Morgan Guaranty socialize with training programs in which, to quote one participant, "You work every night until 2 A.M. on your own material, and then help others." Proctor & Gamble achieves the same result with what might be called upending experiences—requiring a recent college graduate to color in a map of sales territories, for example. The message is clear: while you may be accomplished in many respects, you are in kindergarten as far as what you know about this organization.[21]

Not all debasement experiences are formally designed. The immediate work group might take it upon itself to test the new member through informal hazing. For example, the newly hired engineer might be asked to explain the plans for an impossible or "nonsense" electrical circuit. Similarly, the rookie cop might be sent in alone to shake down a bar that is frequented by unfriendly bikers. Often, such experiences are designed to illustrate how group members must depend upon each other.

Debasement experiences most commonly occur in entry-level jobs, whether blue-collar or white-collar. A new executive vice-president would be unlikely to suffer debasement unless he or she was entering a hostile environment.

GLOBAL FOCUS 9–2

▼
. . . .
Debasement at Japan's Mister Donut

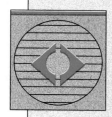

OSAKA, Japan—It can be argued that anyone who opens a Mister Donut franchise in Japan really wants to. On the first day of management training, the future entrepreneurs are sent by bus to a Kyoto residential district, where they go from house to house, knocking on doors and politely asking permission to scrub the family toilet. According to members of the company, it is an exercise intended to instill a sense of community service.

After that, all franchise owners and shop managers enroll in the company's "Donut University," a five-week training course covering everything from quality control to fire prevention. Meals, which are included, consist almost solely of doughnuts and coffee.

"Unless they can live with doughnuts for five weeks, we feel they cannot serve doughnuts with pride," says Keji Chiba, general manager and director of food industries for the Duskin Company, the privately owned concern that franchises Mister Donut in Japan.

"Every success story of an American business here in Japan has a Chiba," said Kenichi Ohmae, managing director of McKinsey & Company in Tokyo. "Everyone talks of the importance of the group, but I don't think a group can create a business. It's the result of one or two men using principles of Japanese management."

The spirit of thanksgiving is not dead in the Mister Donut operation today—and it also pinpoints the difference between Japan's Mister Donut and its American counterpart. Each year on Jan. 27, the day it was decided to introduce Mister Donut in Japan, every shop manager, sales person and baker in the Japanese operation is dispatched to clean a public washroom in the spirit of "self-reflection and gratitude," as a company leaflet describes it.

Source: Abridged from Trucco, T. (1982, December 26). Serving Mr. Donut and the community. *The New York Times*. Copyright © 1982 by The New York Times Company. Reprinted by permission.

Extent of Socialization   Under some circumstances, organizations are pretty much willing to make do with what they get in terms of recruits. That is, they attempt to build upon the characteristics that the person brings into the setting rather than attempting radical socialization. Many volunteer organizations such as charities and community groups are like this, since they have little power over recruits. Similarly, if a university physics department hires a prominent but eccentric physicist, socialization will probably consist of showing her the library and the computer center and hoping that she will win the Nobel Prize soon! At the other extreme, some organizations have as their goal the radical socialization of members, hoping to strip them of old beliefs, values, and attitudes and get them to internalize new ones. Whether they are successful or not, prisons, mental hospitals, and religious orders have this orientation toward inmates, patients, and novitiates. Of course, most organizations fall between these extremes, and try to exact a degree of conformity that is needed to regulate behavior while permitting necessary innovation.[22]

Realistic Job Previews

It was noted earlier that new organizational members often harbor unrealistically inflated expectations about what their jobs will be like. When the job is actually begun, it fails to live up to these expectations, "reality shock" is experienced, and job dissatisfaction results. As a consequence, costly turnover is most likely to occur among newer employees who are unable to survive the discrepancy between expectations and reality. For the organization, this sequence of events represents a failure of socialization.

Obviously, organizations cannot control all sources of unrealistic job expectations, such as those provided by television shows and glorified occupational stereotypes. However, they *can* control those generated during the recruiting process by providing job applicants with realistic job previews. **Realistic job previews** provide a balanced, realistic picture of the positive and negative aspects of the job to job applicants.[23] Thus, they provide "corrective action" to expectations at the anticipatory socialization stage. Exhibit 9–4 compares the realistic job preview process with the traditional preview process that often sets expectations too high by ignoring the negative aspects of the job.

How are realistic job previews designed and conducted? Generally, experienced employees and personnel officers are interviewed to obtain their views on the positive and negative aspects of the job. Then, these views are incorporated into booklets or videotape presentations for applicants.[24] For example, a video presentation might involve interviews with job incumbents discussing the pros and cons of their jobs. In its video, Disney stresses grooming standards. Realistic previews have been designed for jobs as diverse as telephone operator, life insurance salesperson, Marine Corps recruit, and supermarket worker. Exhibit 9–5, on page 310 shows the elements of a realistic preview for bank tellers that was conducted by using booklets.

Realistic job previews have been shown to be effective in reducing turnover. What is less clear is exactly why this reduction occurs. Reduced expectations and increased job satisfaction are part of the answer. Less clear is whether or not realistic previews cause those who are not cut out for the job to withdraw from the application process.[25] Although the turnover reductions from realistic previews are small, they can result in substantial financial savings for organizations.[26]

EXHIBIT 9–4

Traditional and realistic job previews compared.

Traditional Procedures	Realistic Procedures
Set Initial Job Expectations too High	Set Job Expectations Realistically
Job Is Typically Viewed as Attractive	Job May or May Not Be Attractive, Depending on Individual's Needs
High Rate of Job Offer Acceptance	Some Accept, Some Reject Job Offer
Work Experience Disconfirms Expectations	Work Experience Confirms Expectations
Dissatisfaction and Realization That Job Not Matched To Needs	Satisfaction; Needs Matched To Job
Low Job Survival, Dissatisfaction, Frequent Thoughts of Quitting	High Job Survival, Satisfaction, Infrequent Thoughts of Quitting

■
EXHIBIT

9–5

Elements covered in a realistic job preview for bank tellers.

Topic	Job Preview Coverage
Training	Training described Final exam at the end of training mentioned Failure rate during training reported
Work	Banking transactions described Accuracy important and it is checked daily Working under pressure, e.g., Mondays & Fridays Manager schedules work 1 week in advance Working on your feet Working may become routine and repetitive
Customers	Courtesy is always required Rude customers encountered
Career opportunities	Promotion criteria specified Average promotion rates for each job given How to move into branch management (college degree needed)
Compensation	Pay rates specified Employee benefits described How pay increases are determined
Summary of major points	Summary included—½ page long, titled "It's not for everyone"

Source: Adapted from Dean, R. A., & Wanous, J. P. (1984). Effects of realistic preview on hiring bank tellers. *Journal of Applied Psychology, 69,* 61–68. Copyright © 1984 by American Psychological Association. Reprinted by permission.

The Power of Socialization

Socialization can be a powerful process, even overcoming cultural boundaries in the case of multinational corporations:

> It was in Brussels, at the annual ITT (International Telephone and Telegraph) barbecue for managers from all over the world, that I first felt the full impact. . . . Belgian waiters were cooking steaks and sweet corn on the charcoal grills, while the polyglot managers queued up docilely with their plates. . . . It was not immediately easy to tell the Europeans from the Americans, except perhaps by the shoes and trousers, for the Europeans, too—whether Swedish, Greek, or even French—had a hail-fellow style and spoke fluent American, joshing and reminiscing about old times in Copenhagen and Rio. I soon had

a sense of being enveloped by the company, by its rites, customs, and arcane organogram, of being swept right away from Brussels, or Europe, or anywhere.[27]

ORGANIZATIONAL CULTURE

The last several pages have been concerned with socialization into an organization. To a large degree, the course of that socialization both depends on and shapes the culture of the organization. Let's examine culture, a concept that has rapidly gained the attention of both researchers and practicing managers.

What Is Organizational Culture?

At the outset, it can be said that organizational culture is not the easiest concept to define. Informally, culture might be thought of as an organization's style, atmosphere, or personality. This style, atmosphere, or personality is most obvious when we contrast what it must be like to work in various organizations such as IBM, Sears, the U.S. Marine Corps, or the New York Yankees. Even from their mention in the popular press, we can imagine that these organizations provide very different work environments. Thus, culture provides uniqueness and social identity to organizations.

More formally, **organizational culture** consists of the shared beliefs, values, and assumptions that exist in an organization.[28] In turn, these shared beliefs, values, and assumptions determine the norms that develop and the patterns of behavior that emerge from these norms. The term *shared* does not necessarily mean that members are in close agreement on these matters, although they might well be. Rather, it means that they have been uniformly exposed to them and have some minimum common understanding of them. Several other characteristics of culture can be noted:

- Culture represents a true "way of life" for organizational members, who often take its influence for granted. Frequently, an organization's culture becomes obvious only when it is contrasted with that of other organizations or when it undergoes changes.
- Because culture involves basic assumptions, values, and beliefs, it tends to be fairly stable over time. In addition, once a culture is well established, it can persist despite turnover among organizational personnel, providing social continuity.
- The content of a culture can involve matters that are internal to the organization or external. Internally, a culture might support innovation, risk taking, or secrecy of information. Externally, a culture might support "putting the customer first" or behaving unethically toward competitors.
- Culture can have a strong impact on both organizational performance and member satisfaction.

It is important to note that culture is truly a social variable, reflecting yet another aspect of the kind of social influence that we have been discussing in this chapter. Thus, culture is not simply an automatic consequence of an organization's technology, products, or size. For example, there is some tendency for organizations to become more bureaucratic as they get larger. However, the culture of a particular large organization might support an informal, nonbureaucratic atmosphere.

Can an organization have several cultures? The answer is yes. Often unique subcultures develop that reflect departmental differences or differences in occupation or training. A researcher who studied Silicon Valley computer companies found that technical and professional employees divided into "hardware types" and "software types." In turn, hardware types subdivided into engineers and technicians, and software types subdivided into software engineers and computer scientists. Each group was seen to have its own values, beliefs, and assumptions about how to design computer systems.[29] Effective organizations will develop an overarching culture that manages such divisions. For instance, a widely shared norm might exist that in effect says, "We fight like hell until a final design is chosen, and then we all pull together."

The "Strong Culture" Concept

Some cultures have more impact on the behavior of organizational members than others. In a **strong culture,** the beliefs, values, and assumptions that make up the culture are both intense and pervasive across the organization.[30] In other words, the beliefs, values, and assumptions are strongly supported by the majority of members, even cutting across any subcultures that might exist. Thus, the strong culture provides great consensus concerning "what the organization is about" or what it stands for. In weak cultures, on the other hand, beliefs, values, and assumptions are less strongly ingrained and/or less widely shared across the organization. Weak cultures are thus fragmented and have less impact on organizational members. All organizations can be said to have a culture, although it might be hard to detect the details of weak cultures.

To firm up your understanding of strong cultures, let's consider thumbnail sketches of three organizations that are generally agreed to have strong cultures:[31]

- *Procter & Gamble*. This Cincinnati-based consumer products giant markets everything from Crest toothpaste to Pampers. Known for fanatical attention to product quality and consumer tastes. Also known for rigorous employee selection practices and inducing healthy competition among its brand managers.
- *IBM*. Every employee at this computer giant knows and understands the company's complete devotion to customer service. This is backed by knowledge that extensive training and education are an ongoing way of life at IBM. Strong attention to details, right down to the clothing worn by company representatives.

- *3M.* This Minneapolis-based company produces tape, adhesives, abrasives, and building materials. Known for its extreme dedication to product innovation. Employees are rewarded for creativity and risk taking to this end, and failure is accepted as part of the game.

Three points are worth emphasizing about these examples of strong cultures. First, an organization need not be big to have a strong culture. If its members agree strongly about certain beliefs, values, and assumptions, a small business, school, or social service agency can have a strong culture. Second, strong cultures do not necessarily result in blind conformity. For example, the strong culture at 3M supports and rewards *non*conformity in the form of innovation and creativity. Finally, Procter & Gamble, IBM, and 3M are obviously successful organizations. Do strong cultures always result in organizational success?

Assets and Liabilities of Strong Cultures

Ever since the publication of the immensely popular book *In Search of Excellence,* observers have been interested in the possible advantages for organizational effectiveness that might result from having a strong culture.[32] In this book, Thomas Peters and Robert Waterman list what they claim are the best-run, most innovative American companies, firms such as Hewlett-Packard, Texas Instruments, Kodak, Revlon, DuPont, and the three discussed above. They then go on to cite the common characteristics that these firms share (Exhibit 9–6), many of which contribute to a strong culture. For instance, "stick to the knitting" (point 6 in Exhibit 9–6) means that successful firms have generally limited their business to areas with which they are familiar, allowing them to concentrate on core values (point 5), including staying close to the customer (point 2). Similarly, they argue that successful firms are loose (point 8) in granting employees autonomy (point 3) but tight when it comes to reinforcing core values.

**EXHIBIT
9–6**

Characteristics of excellent organizations according to Peters and Waterman.

1. A bias for action.
2. Close to the customer.
3. Autonomy and entrepreneurship.
4. Productivity through people.
5. Hands-on, value driven.
6. Stick to the knitting.
7. Simple form, lean staff.
8. Simultaneous loose-tight properties.

Source: Peters, T. J., & Waterman, R. H., Jr. (1982). *In search of excellence: Lessons from America's best-run companies.* Copyright © 1982 by Peters, T. J., & Waterman, R. H., Jr. Reprinted by permission of HarperCollins Publishers, Inc.

Both the companies chosen and the characteristics noted by Peters and Waterman have received some criticism. It is probably most sensible to treat their ideas as advocacy rather than scientific fact.[33] However, there is growing consensus that strong cultures contribute to organizational success *when the culture supports the mission, goals, and strategy of the organization.*[34] In this case, a strong common culture should ease communication and coordination and provide a means for dealing with conflict when it arises.

On the other side of the coin, strong cultures can prove to be a liability under certain circumstances. First, the mission, goals, or strategy of an organization may change, and the strong culture that supported past success might not suit the new order. Later, we will examine how deregulation in the telecommunications industry challenged the strong traditional culture of AT&T.

Second, strong cultures can mix as badly as oil and water when a merger or acquisition pushes two of them together under the same corporate banner. Both General Electric and Xerox, large organizations with strong cultures of their own, had interesting experiences when they acquired small high-technology Silicon Valley companies with unique cultures:

> So Versatec retained its first-come, first-served parking lot, its volleyball courts, its raucous Halloween party, its pension and health plans, its cookies and coffee on silver trays outside the chief executive's office, and the freewheeling, egalitarian attitudes that go along with these things. In the early days Xerox kept sending in its helpful minions. First came the security men, munificently offering to install the corporate badge system at Versatec headquarters. Zaphiropoulos fed them coffee and cookies and patiently explained that though doubtless his company would someday embrace badges gratefully, now was too soon. Later came the facilities department, offering to oversee the construction of Versatec's second building and refusing to take no for an answer. Zaphiropoulos bowed to necessity but served notice not to interfere again by ignoring the bill that later arrived.[35]

Finally, some strong cultures can threaten organizational effectiveness simply because the cultures are in some sense pathological.[36] Such cultures may be based on beliefs, values, and assumptions that support infighting, secrecy, and paranoia, pursuits that hardly leave time for doing business. Here's an example of an unsuccessful semiconductor firm whose culture exhibited considerable paranoia:

> The two founders took all kinds of precautions to prevent their ideas from being stolen. They fragmented jobs and processes so that only a few key people in the company really understood the products. They rarely subcontracted work. And they paid employees very high salaries to give them an incentive to stay with the firm. These three precautions combined to make Paratech's costs among the highest in the industry.[37]

Contributors to the Culture

How are cultures built and maintained? In this section we consider two key factors that contribute to the foundation and continuation of organizational cultures.

The Founder's Role   It is certainly possible for cultures to emerge over time without the guidance of a key individual. However, it is remarkable how many cultures, especially strong cultures, reflect the values of an organization's founder.[38] The imprint of Walt Disney on the Disney Company, Sam Walton on Wal-Mart, Ray Kroc on McDonald's, T. J. Watson on IBM, and Bill Gates on Microsoft is obvious. As we shall note shortly, such imprint is often kept alive through a series of stories about the founder that is passed on to successive generations of new employees. This provides continuing reinforcement for the firm's core values. In a similar vein, it is usually agreed that the organization's culture is strongly shaped by top management. The culture will usually begin to emulate what top management "pays attention to." Sometimes, the culture begun by the founder can cause conflict when top management wishes to see an organization change directions. At Apple Computer, Steven Jobs nurtured a culture based on new technology and new products—innovation was everything. When this strategy was perceived by top management to be damaging profits, a series of controls and changes was introduced by management that led to Jobs's resignation as chairman.[39]

Socialization   The precise nature of the socialization process is a key contributor to the culture that emerges in an organization, because socialization is the means by which the culture's beliefs, values, and assumptions are learned. Weak or fragmented cultures often feature haphazard selection and a nearly random series of job assignments that fail to present the new hire with a coherent set of experiences. On the other hand, Richard Pascale of Stanford University notes that organizations with strong cultures go to great pains to expose employees to a careful step-by-step socialization process (Exhibit 9–7).[40]

- *Step 1.* New employees are carefully selected to obtain those who will be able to adapt to the existing culture, and realistic job previews are provided to allow candidates to deselect themselves. As an example, Pascale cites Procter & Gamble's series of individual interviews, group interviews, and tests for brand management positions.
- *Step 2.* Debasement and hazing are used to provoke humility in new hires so that they are open to the norms of the organization.
- *Step 3.* Employees are trained "in the trenches" so that they begin to master one of the core areas of the organization. For example, even experienced M.B.A.s will be required to start on the bottom of the professional ladder to ensure that they understand how *this* organization works. At Lincoln

Electric, an extremely successful producer of industrial products, new M.B.A.s literally spend eight weeks on the welding line so that they truly come to understand and appreciate Lincoln's unique shopfloor culture.

- *Step 4.* The reward and promotion system is carefully used to reinforce

EXHIBIT

9–7

Socialization steps in strong cultures.

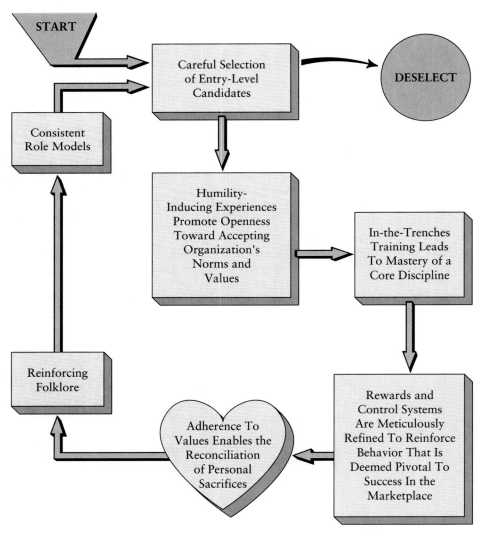

Source: Pascale, R. (1985, Winter). The paradox of "corporate culture": Reconciling ourselves to socialization. *California Management Review, 27*(2), 26–41. Copyright © by The Regents of the University of California. By permission of The Regents of the University of California and the author.

those employees who perform well in areas that support the goals of the organization.

- *Step 5.* Again and again, the culture's core beliefs, values, and assumptions are asserted to provide guidance for member behavior. This is done to emphasize that the personal sacrifices required by the socialization process have a true purpose.
- *Step 6.* Members are exposed to folklore about the organization, stories that reinforce the nature of the culture. We examine this in more detail below.
- *Step 7.* Role models who are consistent with the culture are identified as "fast-trackers" to serve as tangible examples to imitate.

Pascale is careful to note that it is the *consistency* among these steps and their mutually reinforcing properties that make for a strong culture. Given that they are socializing theme park employees rather than rocket scientists, it is remarkable how many of these tactics Disney uses. Selection is rigorous, and grooming standards serve as mild debasement. Everyone begins at the bottom of the hierarchy. Pay is low, but promotion is tied to performance. Folklore stresses core values ("Walt's in the park."). Better performers are chosen to serve as role models at Disney U. or in paired training.

Diagnosing a Culture

Earlier, it was noted that culture represents a "way of life" for organizational members. Even when the culture is strong, this way of life might be difficult for uninitiated outsiders to read and understand. One way to grasp a culture is to examine the symbols, rituals, and stories that characterize the organization's way of life. For insiders, these symbols, rituals, and stories are mechanisms that teach and reinforce the culture.

Symbols At IBM, the sayings "IBM means service" and "respect for the individual" are seen and heard again and again. Observers generally concede that these sayings have a powerful symbolic impact on employees because the organization tries to live by them.[41] On the other hand, consider the corrupt police force that has "Integrity and Honor" painted on the sides of all its squad cars. Here, the corrupt culture is reinforced by the irony of the motto. Former Porsche Managing Director Peter Schutz was asked why his company is involved in auto racing. After citing the publicity and product development benefits of racing, Schutz noted its symbolic cultural function:

> Probably the most important dimension, though, from my point of
> view, is the contribution that racing makes to our corporate culture.
> The racing activity is highly visible, and it has a couple of characteristics that I find extremely valuable in achieving the kind of quality we
> want. One of them is the concept that work has to be ready on time.
> You have to develop a critical path and plan all of your material
> flow. Whether you do this formally or informally, you have to get

your arms around the vital dimensions of the project. And, of course, it introduces the idea that you work until the job is done, not until it's quitting time. Our racing team would never think of going home just because it's evening. If there's a race the next day, the car has to be finished. And that gets transferred to other areas of the company. It becomes part of the fiber of the entire company.[42]

Some executives are particularly skilled at using symbols consciously to reinforce cultural values. CEO Carl Reichardt of Wells Fargo is known as a fanatic cost cutter. A story is told of him receiving managers requesting capital budget increases while sitting in a tatty chair. As managers made their cases, Reichardt picked at the chair's exposed stuffing, sending a strong symbolic message of fiscal austerity. This was in case they had missed the message conveyed by having to pay for their own coffee and their own office Christmas decorations![43]

Rituals   Observers have noted how rites, rituals, and ceremonies can convey the essence of a culture.[44] For example, at Tandem, a California computer company, Friday afternoon "popcorn parties" are a regular ritual. (For years, these parties were called "beer busts." I'll leave it up to you to decide whether this change of names is symbolic of a major cultural shift!) The parties reinforce a "work hard, play hard" atmosphere and reaffirm the idea that weekly conflicts can be forgotten. (See In Focus 9–3.) The Disney picnics, beach parties, and employee nights are indicative of a peer-oriented, youth-oriented culture. At Mary Kay Cosmetics, elaborate "seminars" with the flavor of a Hollywood premiere combined with a

Porsche uses its racing team to symbolically reinforce the key elements of its corporate culture. (Michael H. Dunn/The Stock Market)

▼
....

Fun—A Corporate Ritual at Ben & Jerry's Ice Cream and Odetics Robotics

More and more, fun is becoming part of the corporate culture in America. Nowhere is the practice of putting a grin on workers' faces held more sacred than at the Waterbury, Vt., headquarters of those dastardly mashers Ben (Cohen) and Jerry (Greenfield) of home-made ice-cream fame.

Ben & Jerry employees always had the fun—though highly caloric—benefits of taking home three pints of ice cream a day, sampling new flavors like jalapeno and grapefruit champagne or enjoying a sundae at their desk from the company ice-cream parlor.

During a busy period last summer, masseuses were provided during work hours to untie the stress knots. "People could go out, have a massage and relax for half an hour," said Peter Lind, head of research and development, who lauds Ben & Jerry for spreading joy on a constant basis.

Six months ago, because things were getting a little too serious, Ben & Jerry formed an employee Joy Committee. Even that name, however, was considered too serious, so now it's the Joy Gang, said company spokeswoman Maureen Martin.

The gang, headed by Lind, has arranged such employee events as Barry Manilow Appreciation Day, when the music of he who writes the songs that make the whole world happy spewed out of the company's Muzak system.

"It was held on Manilow's birthday, which someone found on a calendar," said Martin. "We had a contest and voted *At the Copa* his best song."

At Odetics, a high-tech robotics firm in Anaheim, Calif., a Fun Committee has been around for seven years, arranging employee events like "Fifties Day," which featured hula-hoop contests, feats of bubblegum blowing and telephone-booth stuffing competitions.

Odetics spokeswoman Judy Artunian said that you can't get much more of an interaction between all levels of employees than when a company janitor is stuffed in a phone booth with a senior vice president.

"Everyone is on a first-name basis because of these events," said Artunian, who noted that a high-tech mascot named Odex 1 is part of the fun. Employee encounters with Odex 1 are routine, as the six-legged multifunctional robot has the run of the company.

Source: Abridged from Gentile, D. (1989, July 31). Fun becomes part of corporate culture. *The Gazette* (Montreal), p. B-9. Originally appeared in *The New York Daily News*, 1989.

revival meeting are used to make the sales force feel good about themselves and the company. Pink Cadillacs and other extravagant sales awards reinforce the cultural imperative that any Mary Kay woman can be successful. Rituals need not be so exotic to send a cultural message. In some companies, the annual performance review is seen as an act of feedback and development. In others, it might be viewed as an exercise in punishment and debasement.

Stories As noted above, the folklore of organizations as expressed in stories about past organizational events is a common aspect of culture. These stories, told repeatedly to successive generations of new employees, are evidently meant to communicate "how things work," whether they are true, false, or a bit of both. Anyone who has spent much time in a particular organization is familiar with such stories, and they often appear to reflect the uniqueness of organizational cultures. However, research indicates that a few common themes underlie many organizational stories:

- Is the big boss human?
- Can the little person rise to the top?
- Will I get fired?
- Will the organization help me when I have to move?
- How will the boss react to mistakes?
- How will the organization deal with obstacles?[45]

Issues of equality, security, and control underlie the stories that pursue these themes. Also, such stories often have a "good" version, in which things turn out well, and a "bad" version, in which things go sour. For example, there is a story that Ray Kroc, McDonald's founder, cancelled a franchise after finding a single fly in the restaurant.[46] This is an example of a sour ending to a "how will the boss react to mistakes?" story. Whether the story is true or not, its retelling is indicative of one of the core values of the McDonald's culture—a fanatical dedication to clean premises. To see an application of cultural diagnosis, consult You Be the Manager.

AT&T—A Culture in Transition

To conclude our discussion of culture, let's examine an organization that has undergone a radical cultural transition in recent years.[47] On January 1, 1984, AT&T was required by a U.S. Justice Department Consent Decree to divest itself of its local telephone company operations. This was one of a long series of deregulation changes that forced the former monopoly to confront a new competitive marketplace. The "physical" consequences of the consent decree were impressive in themselves, as the work force was reduced considerably and millions of dollars in assets were sold. Equally important, however, was the change that was required in AT&T's culture.

Prior to the years leading up to the divestiture, AT&T had a strong corporate culture based on providing universal telephone service at a reasonable price. The

YOU BE THE MANAGER

Cultural Change at BankAmerica

A. P. Giannini, then a successful executive, founded the Bank of America to provide banking services for the Italian immigrants of San Francisco. The innovation and risk taking that are inherent in catering to people of little means were to exemplify the bank's culture for many years. Under A. P.'s leadership, the bank pioneered many service innovations that made banking more "customer friendly," including advertising, branch banking, and less forbidding open landscape banking premises. More stodgy competitors were forced to imitate Bank of America to remain competitive. At the same time, A. P. successfully backed several risky bond and loan ventures, including the building of the Golden Gate Bridge and the production of Disney's *Snow White and the Seven Dwarfs*.

By the 1980s, management had become concerned that the bank was no longer focused on the values set down by its founder, especially those involving customer service. Years of operating in an increasingly regulated environment had caused the pioneer to itself become stodgy and bureaucratic. It had lost strategic focus, lost market share, and been the object of a hostile takeover attempt. This was no way to face the increasing competition prompted by federal deregulation of financial services. Management was convinced that a change in BankAmerica culture was necessary. How would *you* go about this task?

1. Before making any radical changes, the bank wanted to accurately assess its current culture. How would you do this? What do you think you would find in terms of cultural beliefs and norms?

2. How can the culture of a large organization be changed? How do we begin?

To find out what BankAmerica did, see The Manager's Notebook at the end of the chapter.

Source: Adapted from Beck, R. N. (1987, February). Visions, values and strategies: Changing attitudes and culture. *Academy of Management Executive*, 33–39.

core values were oriented toward excellent service, and stories are told with pride about the dedication of Bell System staff to keeping the lines open. To support this mission, cultural emphasis was placed on loyalty, lifetime careers, and promotion from within. Since it was a monopoly, product development could proceed slowly, and aggressive sales tactics were not necessary.

With deregulation, AT&T was required to change its mission to include the development and sale of innovative communications products and services. A new culture that was supportive of this mission would have to be grounded on entrepreneurship, fast decision making, and creative risk taking. To accomplish this, the company gave increased power to the marketing function and took increased pains to tie rewards to individual performance. Sales personnel were placed on commission, and service personnel were given more autonomy in doing their jobs. The changes were supported by information campaigns in which top management regularly asserted the need for a new culture at AT&T.

Some AT&T employees enjoy the new "action" and the increased job autonomy offered by the cultural change. Others, however, have expressed anxiety and uncertainty regarding the changed way of life that the new culture requires. Some worry that the service ethic will be sacrificed for the sales ethic. As we noted earlier, strong cultures can be difficult to change. And as we have noted throughout the chapter, social influence has a strong impact on organizational members.

THE MANAGER'S NOTEBOOK

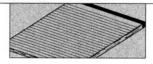

Cultural Change at BankAmerica

Coupled with a change in business strategy, BankAmerica's cultural change led to a considerable competitive turnaround. The cultural change is noteworthy in that it relied strongly on behavioral science research techniques (Chapter 2) and several rounds of employee surveys (Chapters 5, 11, and 17).

1. External consultants and in-house staff interviewed employees to assess their views of the current culture. These interviews revealed several specific beliefs and norms that contributed to the bank's current problems and showed a departure from the values espoused by founder A. P. Giannini. These included: Don't risk failure; take a short term view; don't be frank when evaluating products or programs; seniority is more important than performance; study a new idea to death; protect your own turf.

2. A new set of core values was developed that included putting the customer first and respecting, recognizing, and rewarding both customers and bank employees. Also, it was deemed important that top management aggressively share bank strategy with all employees. This talk of values and strategy began with the CEO and cascaded down the hierarchy via meetings, publications, and training programs. In-house management development courses were designed and tested by using surveys to measure *subordinate* reactions to their boss's new behavior. Finally, great pains were taken to truly tie pay to performance to reinforce innovation, cooperation, and sensible risk taking.

SUMMARY

- There are two basic forms of social dependence. Information dependence means that we rely upon others for information about how we should think, feel, and act. Effect dependence means that we rely on rewards and punishments provided by others. Both contribute to conformity to norms.
- There are several motives for conformity. One is compliance, in which conformity occurs mainly to achieve rewards and avoid punishment. It is mostly indicative of effect dependence. Another motive for conformity is identification with other group members. Here, the person sees himself or herself as similar to them and relies upon them for information. Finally, conformity may be motivated by the internalization of norms, and the person is no longer conforming simply because of social dependence.
- Conformity to norms is most likely when others will be aware of deviance, when the opposition is big and unanimous, and when the issue at hand is ambiguous or important to the group. High-status group members have generally achieved their status by conformity to group norms. However, they may deviate on a particular issue by exercising idiosyncrasy credits that they have built up by previous conformity. Low-status members who are new to the group are especially likely to exhibit conformity, while those who have been rejected by the group have nothing to gain by conformity.
- Conformity due to simple compliance can have strong long-term effects. The foot-in-the-door phenomenon suggests that complying with minor requests sets the stage for conformity to more demanding requests. In addition, the person who complies with norms simply to gain rewards or avoid punishment might feel dissonance, since the behavior does not correspond to private attitudes. One way to reduce this dissonance is to adopt the belief and value structure underlying the norm.
- Organizational members learn norm and role requirements through stages of socialization. Some organizations rely on other organizations to do a certain amount of anticipatory socialization, while others handle the process themselves. Some rely on collective socialization, in which new members learn the ropes as a group, while others socialize new members on an individual basis. Debasement and hazing may be used to test the stuff of new members. Also, realistic job previews can be used to cope with initial unrealistic expectations.
- Organizational culture consists of the shared beliefs, values, and assumptions that exist in an organization. Strong cultures can be an asset when they support the mission and strategy of the organization, but they can pose problems when change is necessary. The organization's founder and its socialization process can be strong contributors to the shape of the culture, which is often revealed by symbols, rituals, and stories.

KEY CONCEPTS

Information dependence	Internalization	Debasement
Effect dependence	Idiosyncrasy credits	Realistic job previews
Conformity	Foot-in-the-door phenomenon	Organizational culture
Compliance	Socialization	Strong culture
Identification		

DISCUSSION QUESTIONS

1. Compare and contrast information dependence with effect dependence. Under which conditions should people be especially information-dependent? Under which conditions should people be especially effect-dependent?

2. Describe an instance of conformity that you have observed in an organizational setting. Was this incident motivated by compliance, identification, or internalization? Were the results beneficial for the organization? Were they beneficial to the individual involved?

3. Imagine that a large organization is charged with

making illegal financial contributions to a political campaign. What are the situational factors that might prompt executives to conform to such organizational norms at the expense of societal norms that stand against such behavior?

4. Consider how you were socialized into the college or university where you are taking your organizational behavior course. Did you have some unrealistic expectations? Where did your expectations come from? What outside experiences prepared you for college or university? Are you experiencing collective or individual socialization? What is the extent of socialization required by most colleges and universities?

5. Contrast the socialization process used by the army with that employed by the typical business firm. Why do they differ?

6. What are the pros and cons of providing realistic job previews for a job that is objectively pretty bad?

7. Imagine that you are starting a new business in the retail trade. You are strongly oriented toward providing excellent customer service. What could you do to nurture a strong organizational culture that would support such a mission?

8. Discuss the advantages and disadvantages of developing a strong organizational culture.

EXPERIENTIAL EXERCISE

A Debate: AT&T's Project Miracles

More and more North American organizations are exposing their managers to intense outdoor experiences as a management development technique. The purpose of this exercise is for you to critically evaluate the pros and cons of one such program, AT&T's Project Miracles. Speaking generally, intense outdoor programs have been touted as a way to increase morale, motivation, trust, teamwork, and communication. They have also been described as methods to mold organizational culture. Let's debate the issue!

Option 1: Informal Debate

The instructor will divide the class into small learning groups that will informally debate the pros and cons of Project Miracles. Each group should be prepared to present its conclusions to the class.

Option 2: Formal Debate

The instructor will assign a pro-Miracles position to one small learning group and an anti-Miracles position to another. While the groups meet to plan their presentations, other learning groups will debate informally as above. Each of the formal groups should plan for a seven-minute opening statement, a three-minute rebuttal, and a three-minute closing. The class will vote on the winner.

 In debating, use your intuition and experience, but also try to use the theories and concepts that we have been studying. Here are some questions to guide your arguments:

_____ 1. Is it plausible that intense outdoor experiences increase job satisfaction? (Chapter 5)

_____ 2. Exactly how would outdoor experiences stimulate motivation? (Chapter 6)

_____ 3. Can outdoor experiences stimulate group effectiveness and teamwork? (Chapter 8)

_____ 4. Do outdoor experiences contribute to socialization and shape the culture? (This chapter)

—————— 5. Are people truly free to decline participation in outdoor exercises? Are such exercises ethical? (This chapter)

Project Miracles

"I was feeling victimized," said Jeff McCollum of the period in his career after American Telephone and Telegraph abruptly ended his stint as an acting vice president. "I was very bitter."

McCollum's experience is not unusual among long-time AT&T employees. In 1984, when the federal government forced the company to divest its local telephone companies, an enormous wave of restructuring and layoffs ensued. The consumer products division, where McCollum is currently the education director, went from 17,000 employees to 8,500 in two years, he said.

To deal with the sagging morale of employees who survived the divestiture, the company spent more than a year researching and developing a motivational training program, known as Project Miracles, that uses intense outdoor experiences. McCollum, one of the earliest participants, said that the program helped him to rethink his career goals and priorities, and get beyond his feeling that "being a vice president was the be-all and end-all of why I was at work." He said he is now quite happy in his current position. Small groups of employees participate in a week-long retreat at an outdoor camp, led by staff from one of several outside agencies that carry out the program for AT&T.

The actual course of the retreat varies somewhat from one agency to another. SportsMind, the Seattle-based firm that helped AT&T develop its program, tailors the length and activities of its programs to fit different clients. Typically, employees do 15 hours each day of aerobic exercise, teamwork experiences, and discussions of the role of individual integrity, honesty and choice in the work place.

AT&T and SportsMind officials, as well as many past participants, believe that the highlight of the program is the afternoon of physically and psychologically intense outdoor experiences.

The activities often are challenges to the participants' fear of heights. "Trust falls," where a participant stands on a five- to six-foot high platform and falls backward into the arms of fellow employees, are a frequent feature. Ropes courses, where participants teeter across ropes strung in trees 20 or even 40 feet off the ground, are also common. For safety, parachute harnesses are used in the ropes courses and other dangerous activities to ensure participants' safety.

According to Bentz, the outdoor work challenges participants to "do more than they thought they could, and after that they're exhilarated." People say to themselves, "maybe there are lots of areas where I'm saying 'I can't' when I can," he said.

Bentz attributes the popularity of SportsMind and similar programs to changes in the workplace. "Companies are looking for ways to increase the level of trust, honesty and openness in communication, and improve the ability of people to work together and solve problems under pressure," he said.

But both AT&T and SportsMind officials acknowledge the potential for employees to be pressured to undergo physical and psychological stress against their will.

Bentz said SportsMind addresses the coercion issue by making discussions of choice a major part of the programs. "At every point, we give people the opportunity to choose" to sit out of activities, he said. "If somebody's got a bad back or a bad knee, we ask them to choose to sit out." He acknowledged, however, that in teamwork building situations such as a group scramble over a high wall, "there's a lot of pressure" to participate. "Any kind of challenge involves some stress," he added.

AT&T employees often return from Project Miracles feeling refreshed and "dewy eyed," said Stinson of AT&T. But, he added, "if after 30 or 60 days, people are back in their normal frame of mind and normal way of doing business, then you've wasted your time."

McCollum, the former AT&T vice president, recalled the first time that he participated in Project Miracles.

"I was scared" of the tree-top and mountainside coursework, he said. But he found that acknowledging and verbalizing his fear made it "much more manageable" than pretending he wasn't afraid. "A very difficult thing for me across my adult life was to ask for support," he added. Project Miracles' emphasis on teamwork helped him address that issue personally, and has also spurred attitude change across his division, he said. "One of the organizational changes that we see is that we regard a request for support as a sign of strength," he said.

AT&T has put several thousand employees through Project Miracles since 1987. The cost per employee varies, depending on which agency carries out the program; SportsMind charges corporations about $1,500 for each participant.

When the first managers returned from a pilot run of the program, they offered overwhelming support for it on employee attitude surveys.

"Eighty percent related the personal value of the program to be extraordinary or very high," McCollum said. "And more than 90 percent recommended that we offer it to other managers as well as to non-management personnel in the organization."

In one department, research showed that measurable output as well as attitudes improved after employees participated in Project Miracles. Sales rates increased, levels of cooperation increased and backlogs fell, McCollum said.

That is the kind of news that corporate management likes to hear. AT&T will continue to evaluate the attitudes and performance of employees to determine whether the company should forge ahead or scale back its efforts, according to Stinson.

But virtually no data have been collected at AT&T or through independent research that would indicate whether specifically challenging employees physically and psychologically in outdoor coursework really pays off back at the office. How the outdoor programs measure up against more conventional motivational training, how long the effects last, and what factors help or hinder the retention of training are all questions thus far unanswered.

■

Source: Story abridged from Moses, S. (1990, January). Morale programs face effectiveness questions. *APA Monitor*, p. 20. Copyright 1990 by The American Psychological Association. Reprinted by permission.

CASE STUDY

United Chemical Company

The United Chemical Company is a large producer and distributor of commodity chemicals with five chemical production plants in the United States. The main plant in Baytown, Texas, includes not only production equipment but also the company's research and engineering center.

The process design group consists of eight male engineers and the supervisor, Max Kane. The group has worked together steadily for a number of years, and good relationships had developed among all members. When the work load began to increase, Max hired a new design engineer, Sue Davis, a recent masters degree graduate from one of the foremost engineering schools in the country. Sue was assigned to a project whose goal was expansion of one of the existing plant facility's capacity. Three other design engineers were assigned to the project along with Sue: Jack Keller (age thirty-eight, fifteen years with the company), Sam Sims (age forty, ten years with the company), and Lance Madison (age thirty-two, eight years with the company).

As a new employee, Sue was very enthusiastic about the opportunity to work at United. She liked her work because it was challenging and offered her a chance to apply much of the knowledge she had gained in her university studies. On the job, Sue kept fairly much to herself and her design work. Her relations with her fellow project members were friendly, but she did not go out of her way to have informal conversations during or after working hours.

Sue was a diligent employee who took her work quite seriously. On occasions when a difficult problem arose, she would stay after hours to come up with a solution. Because of her persistence, coupled with her more current education, Sue usually completed her portion of the various project stages a number of days before her

colleagues. This was somewhat irritating to her because on these occasions she went to Max to ask for additional work to keep her busy until her fellow workers caught up to her. Initially she had offered to help Jack, Sam, and Lance with their portions of the project, but each time she was turned down very tersely.

About five months after Sue had joined the design group, Jack asked to see Max about a problem the group was having. The conversation between Max and Jack was as follows:

MAX: Jack, I understand you wanted to discuss a problem with me.

JACK: Yes, Max. I didn't want to waste your time, but some of the other design engineers wanted me to discuss Sue with you. She is irritating everyone with her know-it-all, pompous attitude. She just is not the kind of person that we want to work with.

MAX: I can't understand that, Jack. She's an excellent worker whose design work is always well done and usually flawless. She's doing everything the company wants her to do.

JACK: The company never asked her to disturb the morale of the group or to tell us how to do our work. The animosity of the group can eventually result in lower-quality work for the whole unit.

MAX: I'll tell you what I'll do. Sue has a meeting with me next week to discuss her six-month performance. I'll keep your thoughts in mind, but I can't promise an improvement in what you and the others believe is a pompous attitude.

Source: Szilagyi, A. A., Jr., & Wallace, J. J., Jr. (1983). *Organizational behavior and performance* (3rd ed.). Copyright © 1983 by HarperCollins Publishers. Reprinted by permission.

JACK: Immediate improvement in her behavior is not the problem; it's her coaching others when she has no right to engage in publicly showing others what to do. You'd think she was lecturing an advance class in design with all her high-power, useless equations and formulas. She'd better back off soon, or some of us will quit or transfer.

During the next week, Max thought carefully about his meeting with Jack. He knew that Jack was the informal leader of the design engineers and generally spoke for the other group members. On Thursday of the following week, Max called Sue into his office for her midyear review. Certain excerpts of the conversation were as follows:

MAX: There is one other aspect of your performance I'd like to discuss with you. As I just said, your technical performance has been excellent; however, there are some questions about your relationships with the other workers.

SUE: I don't understand—what questions are you talking about?

MAX: Well, to be specific, certain members of the design group have complained about your apparent "know-it-all attitude" and the manner in which you try to tell them how to do their job. You're going to have to be patient with them and not publicly call them out about their performance. This is a good group of engineers, and their work over the years has been more than acceptable. I don't want any problems that will cause the group to produce less effectively.

SUE: Let me make a few comments. First of all, I have never publicly criticized their performance to them or to you. Initially, when I was finished ahead of them, I offered to help them with their work, but was bluntly told to mind my own business. I took the hint and concentrated on my part of the work.

MAX: Okay, I understand that.

SUE: What you don't understand is that after five months of working in this group, I have come to the conclusion that what is going on is a "rip-off" of the company. The other engineers are "goldbricking" and setting a work pace much less than they're capable of. They're more interested in the music from Sam's radio, the local football team, and the bar they're going to go to for TGIF. I'm sorry, but this is just not the way I was raised or trained. And finally, they've never looked on me as a qualified engineer, but as a woman who has broken their professional barrier.

MAX: The assessment and motivation of the engineers is a managerial job. Your job is to do your work as well as you can without interfering with the work of others. As for the male-female comment, this company hired you because of your qualifications, not your sex. Your future at United is quite promising if you do the engineering and leave the management to me.

Sue left the meeting very depressed. She knew that she was performing well and that the other design engineers were not working up to their capacity. This knowledge frustrated her more and more as the weeks passed.

1. Speculate about the culture of the design group. What would be some of its specific norms?

2. Account for Sue's failure to conform to the norms of the design group. As a new member, isn't she highly dependent on the group?

3. Account for Jack and the group's fairly strong reaction against Sue. Why don't they simply ignore her?

4. How do various aspects of socialization apply to the events in the case? Be sure to cover Sue's anticipatory socialization.

5. Would a formal realistic job preview have prevented Sue's problem?

6. What should Sue do now?

7. What should Max do now?

REFERENCES

1. This case is based on Burka, P. (1988, November 8). What they teach you at Disney U. *Fortune,* Special advertising section; Solomon, C. M. (1989, December). How does Disney do it? *Personnel,* 50–57; Van Maanen, J. V., & Kunda, G. (1989). "Real feelings": Emotional expression and organizational culture. *Research in Organizational Behavior, 11,* 43–103.

2. The terms "information dependence" and "effect dependence" are used by Jones, E. E., & Gerard, H. B. (1967). *Foundations of social psychology.* New York: Wiley.

3. Festinger, L. (1954). A theory of social comparison processes. *Human Relations, 7,* 117–140.

4. Schacter, S. (1959). *The psychology of affiliation.* Stanford, CA: Stanford University Press.

5. For a review of social influence effects on perceptions of task design, see Thomas, J., & Griffin, R. (1983). The social information processing model of task design: A review of the literature. *Academy of Management Review, 8,* 672–682.

6. Kelman, H. C. (1961). Processes of opinion change. *Public Opinion Quarterly, 25,* 57–78.

7. Van Maanen & Kunda, 1989, p. 65.

8. Asch, S. E. (1952). *Social psychology.* Englewood Cliffs, NJ: Prentice-Hall.

9. Sherif, M. (1935). A study of some social factors in perception. *Archives of Psychology, 27,* No. 187.

10. Rohrer, J., Baron, S., Hoffman, E., & Swander, D. (1954). The stability of autokinetic judgments. *Journal of Abnormal and Social Psychology, 49,* 595–597.

11. Asch, 1952; Gerard, H., Wilhelmy, R., & Connolley, E. (1968). Conformity and group size. *Journal of Personality and Social Psychology, 8,* 79–82.

12. Saks, M. J. (1977). *Jury verdicts.* Lexington, MA: Heath.

13. Hollander, E. P. (1958). Conformity, status, and idiosyncrasy credit. *Psychological Review, 65,* 117–127; Hollander, E. P. (1964). *Leaders, groups, and influence.* New York: Oxford University Press.

14. Freedman, J. L., & Fraser, S. C. (1966). Compliance without pressure: The foot-in-the-door technique. *Journal of Personality and Social Psychology, 4,* 195–202; Seligman, C., Bush, M., & Kirsch, K. (1976). Relationship between compliance in the foot-in-the-door paradigm and size of the first request. *Journal of Personality and Social Psychology, 33,* 517–520.

15. Van Maanen, J., & Schein, E. H. (1979). Toward a theory of organizational socialization. *Research in Organizational Behavior, 1,* 209–264.

16. Feldman, D. C. (1976). A contingency theory of socialization. *Administrative Science Quarterly, 21,* 433–452.

17. Wanous, J. P. (1980). *Organizational entry: Recruitment, selection, and socialization of newcomers.* Reading, MA: Addison-Wesley.

18. Wanous, J. P. (1976). Organizational entry: From naive expectations to realistic beliefs. *Journal of Applied Psychology, 61,* 22–29.

19. For other such studies, see Van Maanen, J., & Schein, E. H. (1977). Career development. In J. R. Hackman & J. L. Suttle (Eds.), *Improving life at work: Behavioral science approaches to organizational change.* Glenview, IL: Scott, Foresman.

20. Van Maanen & Schein, 1979.

21. Pascale, R. (1984, May 28). Fitting new employees into the company culture. *Fortune,* 28–43, p. 30.

22. This discussion draws upon Van Maanen & Schein, 1979, but differs in detail.

23. Wanous, 1980.

24. Wanous, 1980.

25. Premack, S. L., & Wanous, J. P. (1985). A meta-analysis of realistic job preview experiments. *Journal of Applied Psychology, 70,* 706–719.

26. Premack & Wanous, 1985; McEvoy, G. M., & Cascio, W. F. (1985). Strategies for reducing employee turnover: A meta-analysis. *Journal of Applied Psychology, 70,* 342–353.

27. Sampson, A. (1973). *The sovereign state of ITT.* Greenwich, CT: Fawcett, pp. 13–14.

28. For a more complete discussion of various definitions, theories, and concepts of culture, see Smircich, L. (1983). Concepts of culture and organizational analysis. *Administrative Science Quarterly, 28,* 339–358; Schein, E. H. (1985). *Organizational culture and leadership.* San Francisco: Jossey-Bass; Allaire, Y., & Firsirotu, M. E. (1984). Theories of organizational culture. *Organization Studies, 5,* 193–226; Wiener, Y. (1988). Forms of value systems: A focus on organizational effectiveness and cultural change and maintenance. *Academy of Management Review, 13,* 534–545.

29. Gregory, K. L. (1983). Native-view paradigms: Multiple cultures and culture conflicts in organizations. *Administrative Science Quarterly, 28,* 359–376.

30. Kilmann, R., Saxton, M. J., & Serpa, R. (1986, Winter). Issues in understanding and changing culture. *California Management Review*, 87–94; Deal, T. E., & Kennedy, A. A. (1982). *Corporate cultures: The rites and rituals of corporate life*. Reading, MA: Addison-Wesley. For a critique, see Saffold, G. S., III. (1988). Culture traits, strength, and organizational performance: Moving beyond "strong" culture. *Academy of Management Review, 13,* 546–558.

31. These sketches are drawn in part from Peters, T. J., & Waterman, R. H., Jr. (1982). *In search of excellence: Lessons from America's best-run companies*. New York: Harper & Row.

32. Peters & Waterman, 1982.

33. Hitt, M. A., & Ireland, R. D. (1987, May). Peters and Waterman revisited: The unended quest for excellence. *Academy of Management Executive,* 91–98.

34. Lorsch, J. W. (1986, Winter). Managing culture: The invisible barrier to strategic change. *California Management Review,* 95–109.

35. Magnet, M. (1984, November 12). Acquiring without smothering. *Fortune,* 22–30, p. 28.

36. Kets de Vries, M. F. R., & Miller, D. (1984). *The neurotic organization: Diagnosing and changing counterproductive styles of management*. San Francisco: Jossey-Bass.

37. Kets de Vries, M. F. R., & Miller, D. (1984, October). Unstable at the top. *Psychology Today,* 26–34, p. 32.

38. See Schein, 1985.

39. Uttal, B. (1985, August 5). Behind the fall of Steve Jobs. *Fortune,* 20–24.

40. Pascale, R. (1985, Winter). The paradox of "corporate culture": Reconciling ourselves to socialization. *California Management Review,* 26–41; Pascale, 1984; for some research support, see Caldwell, D. F., Chatman, J. A., & O'Reilly, C. A. (1990). Building organizational commitment: A multifirm study. *Journal of Occupational Psychology, 63,* 245–261.

41. Ornstein, S. (1986). Organizational symbols: A study of their meanings and influences on perceived organizational climate. *Organizational Behavior and Human Decision Processes, 38,* 207–229.

42. Gumpert, D. E. (1986, March–April). Porsche on nichemanship. *Harvard Business Review,* 98–106, p. 100.

43. Nulty, P. (1989, February 27). America's toughest bosses. *Fortune,* 40–54.

44. Trice, H. M., and Beyer, J. M. (1984). Studying organizational cultures through rites and ceremonials. *Academy of Management Review, 9,* 653–669.

45. Martin, J., Feldman, M. S., Hatch, M. J., & Sitkin, S. B. (1983). The uniqueness paradox in organizational stories. *Administrative Science Quarterly, 28,* 438–453.

46. Peters, T., & Austin, N. (1985). *A passion for excellence: The leadership difference*. New York: Random House.

47. The following draws on Tunstall, W. C. (1986, Winter). The breakup of the Bell system: A case study in culture transformation. *California Management Review,* 110–124; Main, J. (1984, December 24). Waking up at AT&T: There's life after culture shock. *Fortune,* 66–74.

CHAPTER

10

LEADERSHIP

ELECTROCO

Electroco is a small electronics design and manufacturing firm located south of San Francisco that is concerned with the application of sophisticated silicon technology to everyday devices such as police radar units, automotive ignition systems, and children's toys. Last April, as a result of resignations, Electroco acquired two new managers. Both were having their problems.

Bernie Reiman had enlisted in the army straight out of high school and remained there for seven years, rising to the rank of sergeant. Seeking a career change, he then enrolled in a local community college and earned an Associate degree in industrial supervision. Bernie was hired as a production supervisor at Electroco because the president was impressed by his combination of army experience and academic credentials.

The jobs that Bernie supervised were routine and boring, consisting of the assembly of various small electronic units. Most of the jobs could be learned in a few days. Despite this, the work force performed well and exhibited little turnover and absence. On the basis of his army experience, Bernie made a conscious effort to remain aloof from his subordinates and not involve himself personally with them. To impress the production manager, Bernie monitored productivity carefully and spent most of his time on the shop floor, observing his workers, making suggestions, and giving advice.

Evidently, something was wrong with these tactics. In the months following Bernie's hiring, productivity fell, several workers resigned, and absenteeism increased. Several workers were heard mumbling, "I wish he'd stay off my back and let me do my work."

At the other end of the Electroco complex a different kind of leadership problem had developed. Dr. Charles Hackett had been appointed as head of the research and development group, which consisted of sixteen engineers who were electronics specialists. This group experimented with sophisticated silicon electronics, and their findings were then passed to a design team for adaptation to practical problems. The jobs were challenging, although their goals were often vague. Hackett had been hired away from his position as chairman of the electrical engineering department at a California university. His Ph.D. in solid state electronics and his leadership experience as department chairman had convinced Electroco's president that he was the right man to head the R&D group.

Hackett had quickly decided that he could manage the R&D group the way he had run his university department. First, he got to know all of the engineers on a friendly personal basis and assured them that they could come to him if they had problems. He insisted that they were all professional equals. Then he retired to his office, where he spent most of his time reading scientific and technical journals. "After all," he thought, "these people have advanced degrees. They know what to do."

During the next several months, two of Hackett's engineers resigned. Frequent quarrels broke out about who was supposed to be doing what work. Worst of all, Hackett discovered that two engineers had been working independently on the same research problem for over a month. Neither engineer was aware of what the other had been doing.

Ironically, Bernie Reiman and Charles Hackett responded to their problems in the same way—both decided to involve their subordinates in decision making about their jobs. However, Bernie failed, while Charles acted successfully.

Considerable problems often occurred on the production line when a change of products was made. There was usually great confusion, and productivity often remained low for some time following the change. Since a change was coming up, Reiman told his subordinates to develop a plan for easing the transition. They worked hard and came up with a plan for phasing out the current product line while simultaneously starting up the new line. The plan was for several workers to gradually train others on the new assemblies. Bernie thought the idea was great, and he took it to his boss, the production manager. The production manager thought it was great too, except for one problem—the components for the new production run wouldn't be available until the last minute. The phase-in plan was impossible. When Bernie told his unit about this, morale sank even lower. The workers felt cheated.

Charles Hackett was more fortunate when he asked his subordinates for suggestions. The engineers proposed regular team meetings and a peer review system to work out and monitor research assignments. In addition, they requested that Charles meet with each engineer every two weeks to go over his or her progress and to provide clear feedback. Charles readily agreed, and within a month things were operating smoothly.

Meanwhile, Electroco's president was debating whether to fire Bernie Reiman. Also, he was wondering whether a consultant could use psychological tests to choose leaders with the proper personality.

■

This story poses several questions of practical importance. Why weren't Bernie and Charles able to translate their previously acquired leadership skills to their new jobs? Why didn't Bernie's directive approach work on the production job? Why didn't Charles' easy-going approach work on the R&D job? Why did the involvement of subordinates in decision making work for Charles but not for Bernie? Could personality tests have been used to choose good leaders in these situations? These are the kinds of questions that we will attempt to answer in this chapter.

First, we will define leadership and consider the possibility that special leadership traits can be identified. After this, we will explore how leaders emerge in groups. Next, we will examine the consequences of various leadership behaviors and examine two theories suggesting that effective leadership depends upon the nature of the work situation. Following this are discussions of participation, transformational leadership, and charisma. We will conclude by critically evaluating the importance of leadership in organizations.

WHAT IS LEADERSHIP?

We see the headlines all the time:

- *Senator Charges Leadership Crisis in Executive Branch*
- *Strong Leadership Boosts Leadbottom Mines Productivity*
- *Rookie Quarterback Demonstrates Leadership in Big Game*
- *Union Leadership Says No to Contract Offer*

Although the meaning of such headlines poses no mysteries for us as newspaper readers, we can gain some understanding of the essence of leadership by examining the common notion underlying each one. Basically, they say:

- The Senator feels that the President isn't exerting enough influence.
- Leadbottom Mines executives influenced their work force to work harder and produce more.
- The quarterback influenced other team members to perform well.
- Influential union members vetoed the contract offer.

In other words, **leadership** occurs when particular individuals exert influence upon others in an organizational context. Thus, while the Senator thinks that the President isn't doing enough leading, financial observers feel that Leadbottom executives are doing a good job of leading. Effective leadership involves exerting influence in a way that achieves the organization's goals by enhancing the productivity and satisfaction of the work force.

In theory, *any* organizational member can exert influence on other members, thus engaging in leadership. In practice, though, some members are in a better position to be leaders than others. Individuals with titles such as manager, executive, supervisor, and department head occupy formal or assigned leadership roles (Chapter 8). As part of these roles they are *expected* to influence others, and they are given specific authority to direct subordinates. At Electroco, Bernie Reiman (production supervisor) and Charles Hackett (head of R&D) occupied formal leadership roles. The presence of a formal leadership role is no guarantee that any leading will be done. Some managers and supervisors fail to exert any influence on others. These people will usually be judged ineffective leaders. Thus, leadership involves going beyond formal role requirements to influence others.

Individuals might also emerge to occupy informal leadership roles. Since informal leaders do not have formal authority, they must rely on being well liked or being perceived as highly skilled in order to exert influence. In this chapter we will concentrate on formal leadership, although we will consider informal leadership as well.

Leadership involves status differences as well as role differences, and leaders are almost always granted higher status than those who serve as followers. Thus, there is generally no shortage of candidates who aspire to leadership roles. But who is actually likely to become a leader?

THE (SOMEWHAT ELUSIVE) SEARCH FOR LEADERSHIP TRAITS

Throughout history, social observers have been fascinated by obvious examples of successful interpersonal influence, whether the consequences of this influence were good, bad, or mixed. Individuals such as Henry Ford, Martin Luther King, Jr., Ralph Nader, and Joan of Arc have been analyzed and reanalyzed to discover what made them leaders and what set them apart from less successful leaders. The implicit assumption here is that those who become leaders and do a good job of it possess a special set of traits that distinguish them from the masses of followers. While such a position has been advocated by philosophers and the popular media for centuries, trait theories of leadership did not receive serious scientific attention until the 1900s.

Research on Leadership Traits

During World War I the U.S. military recognized that it had a leadership problem. Never before had such a massive war effort been mounted, and able officers were in short supply. Thus, the search for leadership traits that might be useful in identifying potential officers began. Following the war, and continuing through World War II, this interest expanded to include searching for leadership traits in populations as diverse as school children and business executives. Some studies tried to differentiate traits of leaders and followers, while others were a search for traits that predicted leader effectiveness or separated lower-level leaders from higher-level leaders.[1]

Just what is a trait, anyway? **Traits** are personal characteristics of the individual, including physical characteristics, social background, intellectual ability, personality, task orientation, and social skills. Exhibit 10–1 lists just a few examples of the dozens of traits that have been investigated in the study of leadership.

You will recall that the president of Electroco wondered whether personality tests could be used to select better leaders. Similarly, the sergeant shown in the cartoon evidently embraces the trait theory of leadership. But are traits associated with the assumption or the successful performance of leadership?

A cautious assessment would indicate that the results of the trait approach have been disappointing. Hundreds of studies suggest that many traits are unassociated with leadership, while others are inconsistently or weakly related. However, a somewhat more liberal and selective view of this work suggests that several traits are frequently (though still weakly) associated with the assumption or performance of leadership duties.[2]

Intelligence	Energy
Education	Self-confidence
Social status	Dominance
Participativeness	Need for achievement

As you would expect, leaders (or more successful leaders) tend to be higher than average on these dimensions. Also, intelligence and dominance are especially associated with perceptions by others that one is a leader.[3] However, the *usefulness* of such findings is open to some question.

EXHIBIT

10–1

Examples of traits investigated in leadership studies.

Physical Characteristics	Social Background	Intellectual Ability
Energy	Education	Intelligence
Age	Social status	Judgment
Height	Mobility	Verbal fluency
Weight		Problem solving

Personality	Task Orientation	Social Skills
Dominance	Achievement need	Administrative ability
Aggressiveness	Responsibility need	Cooperativeness
Self-confidence	Initiative	Popularity
Originality		Interpersonal competence
Stress tolerance		Participativeness
Emotional balance		Tact

Source: From Stogdill, R. M. (1974). *Handbook of leadership.* Adapted with permission from The Free Press, a Division of Macmillan, Inc. Copyright © 1974 by The Free Press.

Source: Distributed
by King Features
Syndicate, Inc.

Problems with the Trait Approach

Even though some traits appear to be related to leadership, there are several reasons for the trait approach not being the best means of understanding and improving leadership.

In many cases, it is difficult to determine whether traits make the leader or the opportunity for leadership produces the traits. For example, do dominant individuals tend to become leaders, or do employees become more dominant *after* they successfully occupy leadership roles? This distinction is important. If the former is true, we might wish to seek out dominant people and appoint them to leadership roles. If the latter is true, this strategy will not work.

Even if we know that dominance, intelligence, or tallness is associated with effective leadership, we have few clues about what dominant or intelligent or tall people *do* to influence others successfully. As a result, we have no information about how to train and develop leaders and no way to diagnose failures of leadership.

The most crucial problem of the trait approach to leadership is its failure to take into account the *situation* in which leadership occurs. Intuitively, it seems reasonable that top executives and first-level supervisors might require different traits to be successful. Similarly, physical prowess might be useful in directing a logging crew but irrelevant to managing a team of scientists.

LESSONS FROM EMERGENT LEADERSHIP

The trait approach is mainly concerned with what leaders *bring* to a group setting. Discouragement with this approach gradually promoted an interest in what leaders *do* in group settings. Of particular concern were the behaviors in which certain group members engage that cause them to *become* leaders. As we shall see, this study of **emergent leadership** gives us some good clues about what formally assigned or appointed leaders must do to be effective.

Imagine that a grass-roots organization has assembled to support the election of a local politician to the state legislature. In response to a newspaper ad, thirty individuals show up, all of whom admire Jonathan Greed, the aspiring candidate. The self-appointed chairperson begins the meeting and asks for volunteers for various subcommittees. The publicity subcommittee sounds interesting, so you volunteer and find yourself with six other volunteers, none of whom knows each other. Your assigned goal is to develop an effective public relations campaign for Greed. From experience, you are aware that someone will emerge to become the leader of this group. Who will it be?

Without even seeing your group interact, we can make a pretty good guess as to who will become the leader. Quite simply, it will be the person who *talks* the most, as long as he or she is perceived as having relevant expertise.[4] Remember, leadership is a form of influence, and one important way to influence the group is by speaking a lot. What would the "big talker" talk about? Probably about planning strategy, getting organized, dividing labor, and so on—things to get the task at hand accomplished. Social psychologists often call such a leader a **task leader** because he or she is most concerned with accomplishing the task at hand.

Suppose I also ask the group members who they *liked* the most in the group. Usually, there will be a fair amount of agreement, and the nominated person might be called the **social-emotional leader.** Social-emotional influence is more subtle than task influence, and it involves reducing tension, patching up disagreements, settling arguments, and maintaining morale.

In many cases, the task and social-emotional leadership roles are performed by the same group member.[5] In some instances, though, two separate leaders emerge

The task leader is the member of the group who stimulates the others to accomplish the task at hand. Not surprisingly, this is usually the person who does the most talking. (The Photographers' Library/ Uniphoto)

to fill these roles. When this happens, these two leaders usually get along well with each other and respect each other's complementary skills.[6] In fact, for better or worse, in the typical North American family, the father often assumes the task role and the mother the social-emotional role.

Such emergence of two leadership roles has been noted again and again in a wide variety of groups. This suggests that task and social-emotional leadership are two important functions that must occur in groups. On one hand, the group must be structured and organized to accomplish its tasks. On the other hand, the group must stick together and function well as a social unit, or the best structure and organization will be useless. Thus, in general, leaders must be concerned with both the social-emotional and task functions. Furthermore, organizations almost never appoint *two* formal leaders to a work group. Thus, the formal appointed leader must often be concerned with juggling the demands of two distinct roles.

There is an important qualifier to the preceding paragraph. It should be obvious that task and social-emotional functions are both especially important in the case of newly developing groups. However, for mature, ongoing groups, one leadership role might be more important than the other. For example, if group members have learned to get along well with each other, the social-emotional role might decrease in importance. Also, the two leadership roles may be differentially important in different situations. Suppose a team of geologists is doing a routine series of mineral prospecting studies in a humid, bug-infested jungle. In this case, its leader might be most concerned with monitoring morale and reducing tensions provoked by the uncomfortable conditions. If the team is attacked by hostile natives, task leadership should become more important—a defense must be mounted and a plan for retreat developed.

THE BEHAVIOR OF ASSIGNED LEADERS

We turn now to the behavior of assigned or appointed leaders, as opposed to emergent leaders. What are the crucial behaviors engaged in by such leaders, and how do these behaviors influence subordinate performance and satisfaction? In other words, is there a particular *leadership style* that is more effective than other possible styles? In the case that began the chapter, Bernie Reiman and Charles Hackett exhibited different leadership styles. Are such differences important?

Consideration and Initiating Structure

The most involved, systematic study of leadership to date was begun at Ohio State University in the late 1940s. The Ohio State researchers began by having subordinates describe their superiors along a number of behavioral dimensions. Statistical analyses of these descriptions revealed that they boiled down to two basic kinds of behavior—consideration and initiating structure.

Consideration involves the extent to which the leader is approachable and shows personal concern for subordinates. The considerate leader is seen as friendly, egalitarian, and protective of group welfare. Obviously, consideration is related to the social-emotional function discovered in studies of emergent leadership. As you will recall, Charles Hackett adopted a considerate leadership style at Electroco.

Initiating structure involves the degree to which the leader concentrates on group goal attainment. The structuring leader stresses standard procedures, schedules the work to be done, and assigns subordinates to particular tasks. Clearly, initiating structure is related to the task function revealed in studies of emergent leadership. At Electroco, Bernie Reiman based his leadership style on initiating structure.

Theoretically, consideration and initiating structure are not incompatible. Presumably, a leader could be high, low, or average on one or both dimensions. Given our earlier discussion of emergent leadership functions, you might assume that a leader who is high on both dimensions would be the most effective. In the next section we shall consider this possibility.

The Consequences of Consideration and Structure

The association between leader consideration, leader initiating structure, and subordinate responses has been the subject of hundreds of research studies. At first glance, the results of these studies seem confusing and often contradictory.[7] Sometimes consideration seems to promote satisfaction or high performance, and sometimes it does not. Sometimes structure prompts satisfaction or performance, and sometimes it does not. However, when we consider the particular *situation* in which the leader finds himself or herself, a clearer picture emerges:

- When subordinates are under a high degree of pressure due to deadlines, unclear tasks, or external threat, initiating structure increases satisfaction and performance. (Soldiers stranded behind enemy lines should perform better under directive leadership.)
- When the task itself is intrinsically satisfying, the need for high consideration and high structure is generally reduced. (The teacher who really enjoys teaching should be able to function with less social-emotional support and less direction from the principal.)
- When the goals and methods of performing the job are very clear and certain, consideration should promote subordinate satisfaction, while structure should promote dissatisfaction. (The job of garbage collection is clear in goals and methods. Here, subordinates should appreciate social support but view excessive structure as redundant and unnecessary.)
- When subordinates lack knowledge as to how to perform a job, or the job itself has vague goals or methods, consideration becomes less important, while initiating structure takes on additional importance. (The new astronaut recruit should appreciate direction in learning a complex, unfamiliar job.)[8]

As you can see from the above propositions, the effects of consideration and initiating structure depend upon characteristics of the task, the subordinate, and the setting in which work is performed. Thus, the leader who is high in both consideration and structure will not always perform better than other types of leaders.[9] In some cases, one type of behavior or the other might be unhelpful or even damaging to subordinate performance or satisfaction.

You should now be able to understand why Bernie Reiman and Charles Hackett had leadership troubles at Electroco. Bernie attempted to use a high degree of initiating structure in supervising jobs that were routine and easily learned, and his subordinates resented this leadership style. Charles, on the other hand, relied on a considerate approach to supervise jobs that were complex and had unclear goals. His subordinates craved direction, but he was not providing it.

Leader Reward and Punishment Behaviors

Consideration and initiating structure are the leader behaviors that have received the greatest attention from behavioral scientists. However, assigned leaders can do other things besides initiate structure and be considerate. For example, a leader might set goals for subordinate performance, redesign jobs to better suit subordinate needs, or assign subordinates to particular tasks in which they are likely to be effective.[10] From previous chapters, it should be clear that these behaviors will prove effective when they are pursued in an intelligent and systematic way.

Two additional leader behaviors that have been the focus of research are leader reward behavior and leader punishment behavior. **Leader reward behavior** involves providing subordinates with compliments, tangible benefits, and deserved special treatment. When such rewards *are made contingent on performance,* subordinates perform at a high level and experience job satisfaction.[11] Under such leadership, subordinates have a clear picture of what is expected of them, and they understand that positive outcomes will occur if they achieve these expectations. Put another way, contingent rewards serve as positive reinforcers (Chapter 3) for desired subordinate responses.

Leader punishment behavior involves the use of reprimands or unfavorable task assignments and the active withholding of raises, promotions, and other rewards. Compared with reward behavior, the consequences of leader punishment are much less favorable.[12] At best, punishment seems to have little impact on satisfaction or productivity. At worst, when punishment is perceived as random and not contingent on subordinate behavior, subordinates react with great dissatisfaction. You will recall from Chapter 3 that punishment is extremely difficult to use effectively, and these results seem to prove the point.

Leaders vary considerably in their access to reward opportunities, and this in turn can affect their tendency to resort to punishment. At lower organizational levels, leaders often exert little control over promotion opportunities or salary decisions. Also, they might have so many subordinates that individualized rewards are difficult to administer. Finally, rigid technologies at lower organizational levels (such as assembly lines) might prohibit leaders from redesigning jobs or giving subordinates favorable task assignments. Limited by time, technology, or an absence of tangible rewards, supervisors might resort to searching for negative behavior and punishing it.[13] Organizations that want supervisors to be effective leaders must ensure that they have the tools to do so!

Leader Behavior: An Evaluation

The study of leader behavior represents an improvement over the trait approach, since it is concerned specifically with what leaders actually *do* in their leadership roles. However, the traditional exploration of leader behavior is not without its weaknesses.

In this section, we have been speaking as if certain leader behaviors *cause* subordinate satisfaction or performance. Doubtless, this is often true. However, the reverse is also possible. That is, subordinates who exhibit a particular level of satisfaction or performance might themselves cause the leader to act in certain ways.[14] For example, computer programmers who are especially productive might cause their supervisor to be considerate rather than the other way around. The point here, of course, is that leadership involves *interaction* between leaders and followers, and both parties have the capability to influence each other. Leadership styles that appear to be effective might sometimes be the results, rather than the causes, of subordinate behavior.

Another problem of the traditional behavioral approach to leadership has been its neglect of the situation in which leadership occurs. In this regard, the behavioral approach is guilty of the sins of the trait approach. However, as we observed in discussing consideration an initiating structure, it is possible to identify certain situations in which one combination of leader behaviors is more effective than another. We now turn to two theories of leadership that take the situation into account.

SITUATIONAL THEORIES OF LEADERSHIP

We have referred to the potential impact of the situation on leadership effectiveness several times. Specifically, *situation* refers to the *setting* in which influence attempts occur. This setting includes the nature of the subordinates being led, the nature of the task they are performing, and characteristics of the organization. The two leadership theories that follow consider situational variables that seem especially likely to influence leadership effectiveness.

Fiedler's Contingency Theory

Fred Fiedler of the University of Washington has spent over two decades developing and refining a situational theory of leadership called **Contingency Theory**.[15]

This name stems from the notion that the association between *leadership orientation* and *group effectiveness* is contingent upon (depends upon) the extent to which the *situation is favorable* for the exertion of influence. In other words, some situations are more favorable for leadership than others, and these situations require different orientations on the part of the leader. Let's examine some aspects of this theory.

Leadership Orientation Fiedler has measured leadership orientation by having leaders describe their **Least Preferred Co-Worker (LPC)**. This person may be a current or past co-worker. In either case, it is someone with whom the leader has had a difficult time getting the job done. To obtain an LPC score, the troublesome co-worker is described on eighteen scales of the following nature:

$$\text{PLEASANT}:\underline{\ }:\underline{\ }:\underline{\ }:\underline{\ }:\underline{\ }:\underline{\ }:\underline{\ }:\underline{\ }:\text{UNPLEASANT}$$
$$\phantom{\text{PLEASANT}:}8\ \ 7\ \ 6\ \ 5\ \ 4\ \ 3\ \ 2\ \ 1$$
$$\text{FRIENDLY}:\underline{\ }:\underline{\ }:\underline{\ }:\underline{\ }:\underline{\ }:\underline{\ }:\underline{\ }:\underline{\ }:\text{UNFRIENDLY}$$
$$\phantom{\text{FRIENDLY}:}8\ \ 7\ \ 6\ \ 5\ \ 4\ \ 3\ \ 2\ \ 1$$

The leader who describes the LPC relatively favorably (a high LPC score) can be considered *relationship* oriented. That is, despite the fact that LPC is or was difficult to work with, the leader can still find positive qualities in him or her. On the other hand, the leader who describes the LPC unfavorably (a low LPC score) can be considered *task* oriented. This person allows the low task competence of the LPC to color his or her views of the personal qualities of the LPC ("If he's no good at the job, then he's not good, period.").

Fiedler has argued that the LPC score reveals a personality trait that reflects the leader's motivational structure. High LPC leaders are motivated to maintain interpersonal relations, while low LPC leaders are motivated to accomplish the task. Despite the apparent similarity, the LPC score is *not* a measure of consideration or initiating structure. These are observed *behaviors,* while the LPC score is evidently an *attitude* of the leader toward work relationships.

Situational Favorableness Situational favorableness is the "contingency" part of Contingency Theory. That is, it specifies when a particular LPC orientation should contribute most to group effectiveness. According to Fiedler, a favorable leadership situation exists when the leader has a high degree of control and when the results of this control are very predictable. Factors that affect situational favorableness, in order of importance, are the following:

- *Leader-member relations.* When the relationship between the leader and the group members is good, the leader is in a favorable situation to exert influence. Loyal, supportive subordinates should trust the leader and follow his or her directives with little complaint. A poor relationship should damage the leader's influence and even lead to insubordination or sabotage.
- *Task structure.* When the task at hand is highly structured, the leader should be able to exert considerable influence on the group. Clear goals, clear procedures to achieve these goals, and straightforward performance

measures enable the leader to set performance standards and hold subordinates responsible ("Fill ten of these crates an hour."). When the task is unstructured ("Devise a plan to improve the quality of life in our city."), the leader might be in a poor position to evaluate subordinate work or to prove that her approach is superior to that of the group.

- *Position power.* Position power is formal authority to tell others what to do that is granted by the organization. The more position power held by the leader, the more favorable the leadership situation. In general, committee chairpersons and leaders in volunteer organizations have weak position power. Managers, supervisors, and military officers have strong position power.

In summary, the situation is most favorable for leadership when leader-member relations are good, the task is structured, and the leader has strong position power—for example, a well-liked army sergeant who is in charge of servicing jeeps in the base motor pool. The situation is least favorable when leader-member relations are poor, the task is unstructured, and the leader has weak position power—for instance, the disliked chairperson of a voluntary homeowner's association who is trying to get agreement on a list of community improvement projects.

The Contingency Model Under what conditions is one leadership orientation more effective than another? As shown in Exhibit 10–2, the various possible combinations of situational factors can be arranged into eight octants, which form a continuum of favorability. The model indicates that a task orientation (low LPC) is most effective when the leadership situation is very favorable (octants I, II, and III) *or* when it is very unfavorable (octant VIII). On the other hand,

EXHIBIT 10–2

Predictions of leader effectiveness from Fiedler's Contingency Theory of leadership.

Favorableness	High							Low
Leader-Member Relations	Good				Poor			
Task Structure	Structured		Unstructured		Structured		Unstructured	
Position Power	Strong	Weak	Strong	Weak	Strong	Weak	Strong	Weak
	I	II	III	IV	V	VI	VII	VIII
Most Effective Leader Orientation	Task				Relationship			Task

a relationship orientation (high LPC) is most effective in conditions of medium favorability (octants IV, V, VI, and VII). Why is this so? In essence, Fiedler argues that leaders can "get away" with a task orientation when the situation is favorable—subordinates are "ready" to be influenced. Conversely, when the situation is very unfavorable for leadership, task orientation is necessary to get anything accomplished. In conditions of medium favorability, the boss is faced with some combination of an unclear task or a poor relationship with subordinates. Here, a relationship orientation will help to make the best of a situation that is stress-provoking but not impossibly bad.

Evidence and Criticism   The conclusions about leadership effectiveness shown in Exhibit 10–2 are derived from many studies summarized by Fiedler.[16] However, the Contingency Theory has been subjected to as much debate as any theory in organizational behavior.[17] Critics have argued that Fiedler has applied questionable statistical techniques, and the results of laboratory studies have not always matched those found in natural settings. Also, Fiedler's explanation for the superior performance of high LPC leaders in the middle octants is not especially convincing, and the exact meaning of the LPC score is one of the great mysteries of organizational behavior. It does not seem to be correlated with other personality measures or predictive of specific leader behavior. It now appears that a major source of the many inconsistent findings regarding Contingency Theory is the small sample sizes used in many of the studies. Advances in correcting for this problem statistically have led recent reviewers to conclude that there is reasonable support for the theory.[18] However, Fiedler's prescription for task leadership in octant II (good relations, structured task, weak position power) seems contradicted by the evidence, suggesting that the theory needs some adjustment.

Despite the controversy, Fred Fiedler's contribution to our understanding of leadership should not be underestimated. The Contingency Theory was the first theory of leadership to take the role of the situation seriously. Let's now examine another such theory.

House's Path-Goal Theory

Robert House of the University of Toronto has proposed a situational theory of leadership called Path-Goal Theory.[19] Unlike Fiedler's Contingency Theory, which relies on the somewhat ambiguous LPC trait, **Path-Goal Theory** is concerned with the situations under which various leader *behaviors* are most effective.

The Theory   Why did House choose the name Path-Goal for his theory? According to House, the most important activities of leaders are those that clarify the paths to various goals of interest to subordinates. Such goals might include a promotion, a sense of accomplishment, or a pleasant work climate. In turn, the opportunity to achieve such goals should promote job satisfaction, leader acceptance, and high effort. Thus, *the effective leader forms a connection between subordinate goals and organizational goals.*

House argues that, to provide *job satisfaction* and *leader acceptance,* leader behavior must be perceived as immediately satisfying or as leading to future satisfaction. Leader behavior that is seen as unnecessary or unhelpful will be resented. House contends that, to promote subordinate *effort,* leaders must make rewards dependent on performance and ensure that subordinates have a clear picture of how these rewards can be achieved. To do this, the leader might have to provide support through direction, guidance, and coaching. For example, the bank teller who wishes to be promoted to supervisor should exhibit superior effort when his boss promises a recommendation contingent on good work and explains carefully how the teller can do better on his current job.

Leader Behavior Path-Goal Theory is concerned with four specific kinds of leader behavior. These include:

- *Directive behavior.* Directive leaders schedule work, maintain performance standards, and let subordinates know what is expected of them. This behavior is essentially identical to initiating structure.
- *Supportive behavior.* Supportive leaders are friendly, approachable, and concerned with pleasant interpersonal relationships. This behavior is essentially identical to consideration.
- *Participative behavior.* Participative leaders consult with subordinates about work-related matters and consider their opinions.
- *Achievement-oriented behavior.* Achievement-oriented leaders encourage subordinates to exert high effort and strive for a high level of goal accomplishment. They express confidence that these goals can be reached.

According to Path-Goal Theory, the effectiveness of each set of behaviors depends upon the situation which the leader encounters.

Situational Factors. Path-Goal Theory has concerned itself with two primary classes of situational factors—subordinate characteristics and environmental factors. Exhibit 10–3 illustrates the role of these situational factors in the theory. Put simply, the impact of leader behavior on subordinate satisfaction, effort, and acceptance of the leader depends upon the nature of the subordinates and the work environment. Let's consider these two situational factors in turn, along with some of the theory's predictions.

According to the theory, different types of subordinates need or prefer different forms of leadership. For example:

- Subordinates who are high need achievers (Chapter 6) should work well under achievement-oriented leadership.
- Subordinates who prefer being told what to do should respond best to a directive leadership style.

- When subordinates feel that they have rather low task abilities, they should appreciate directive leadership and coaching behavior. When they feel quite capable of performing the task, such behaviors will be viewed as unnecessary and irritating.

As you can observe from these examples, leaders might have to tailor their behavior to the needs, abilities, and personalities of individual employees.

Also according to the theory, the effectiveness of leadership behavior depends upon the particular work environment. For example:

- When tasks are clear and routine, directive leadership should be perceived as a redundant and unnecessary imposition. This should reduce satisfaction and acceptance of the leader. Similarly, participative leadership would not seem to be useful when tasks are clear, since there is little in which to participate. Obviously, such tasks are most common at lower organizational levels.
- When tasks are challenging but ambiguous, both directive and participative leadership should be appreciated by subordinates. Such styles should clarify the path to good performance and demonstrate that the leader is concerned with helping subordinates to do a good job. Obviously, such tasks are most common at higher organizational levels.
- Frustrating, dissatisfying jobs should increase subordinate appreciation of supportive behavior. To some degree, such support should compensate for a disliked job, although it should probably do little to increase effort.

As you can see from these examples of environmental factors, effective leadership should *take advantage of* the motivating and satisfying aspects of jobs while *offsetting or compensating for* those job aspects that demotivate or dissatisfy. You will recall that Bernie Reiman chose a directive leadership style, even though

EXHIBIT

10–3

The Path-Goal Theory of leadership.

Leader Behavior	Situational Factors	Subordinate Outcomes
Directive		Job Satisfaction
Supportive	Subordinate Characteristics	Acceptance of Leader
Achievement-Oriented	Environmental Factors	
Participative		Effort

Source: From *Journal of Contemporary Business, 3*,(4), p. 89. Reprinted by permission.

the assembly jobs that he supervised were routine and clear and his subordinates were very competent. Not surprisingly, they viewed this direction as unnecessary and responded with dissatisfaction. On the other hand, Charles Hackett tried to be supportive in supervising challenging, ambiguous research jobs. His subordinates needed direction in order to clarify the path to task accomplishment, but he did not realize this. This provoked dissatisfaction and lowered the performance of the Research and Development unit.

Evidence and Criticism In general, there is some research support for most of the situational propositions discussed above. In particular, there is substantial evidence that supportive or considerate leader behavior is most beneficial in supervising routine, frustrating, or dissatisfying jobs and that directive or structuring leader behavior is most effective on ambiguous, less structured jobs.[20] The theory appears to work better in predicting subordinate job satisfaction and acceptance of the leader than in predicting subordinate performance.[21] This might be due in part to the difficulty of *measuring* performance accurately. However, the theory itself might be at fault here. For example, while employees performing clear, routine jobs might be grateful for supportive leadership, directive leadership might be necessary to get any work done, since the task itself doesn't seem inherently motivating.

PARTICIPATIVE LEADERSHIP: INVOLVING SUBORDINATES IN DECISIONS

In the discussion of Path-Goal Theory, the issue of participative leadership was raised. Because this is such an important topic, it is appropriate to devote further attention to participation.

What Is Participation?

At a very general level, **participative leadership** means involving subordinates in making work-related decisions. The term *involving* is intentionally broad. Participation is not a fixed or absolute property, but a relative concept. This is illustrated in Exhibit 10–4. Here, we see that leaders can vary in the extent to which they involve subordinates in decision making. Minimally, participation involves obtaining subordinate opinions before making a decision oneself. Maximally, it allows subordinates to make their own decisions within agreed-upon limits. As the "area of freedom" on the part of subordinates increases, the leader is behaving in a more participative manner. There is, however, an upper limit to the area of subordinate freedom available under participation. Participative leadership should not be confused with the *abdication* of leadership, which is almost always ineffective.

Participation can involve individual subordinates or the entire group of subordinates that reports to the leader. For example, participation on an individual basis might work best when setting performance goals for particular subordinates, planning subordinate development, or dealing with problem employees. On the other hand, the leader might involve the entire work group in decision making when determining vacation schedules, arranging for telephone coverage during lunch hour, or deciding how to allocate scarce resources such as travel money or secretarial help. As these examples suggest, the choice of an individual or group participation strategy should be tailored to specifc situations.

Potential Advantages of Participative Leadership

Just why might participation be a useful leadership technique? What are its potential advantages?

Motivation Participation can increase the motivation of subordinates.[22] In some cases, participation permits them to contribute to the establishment of work goals and to decide how these goals can be accomplished. For example, suppose that, early in the spring quarter, a university department chairperson projects that she will have some budget money remaining at the end of the academic year. She informs her department members, and they decide to use the money to fund a trip

■
EXHIBIT   **Subordinate participation in decision making can vary.**
10–4

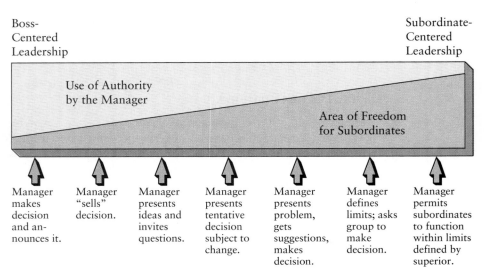

Source: Reprinted by permission of the Harvard Business Review. An exhibit from "How To Choose a Leadership Pattern" by Robert Tannenbaum and Warren H. Schmidt (March/April 1958). Copyright © 1958 by the President and Fellows of Harvard College; all rights reserved.

to a professional conference in New Orleans for the three professors who have the best student evaluations at the end of the quarter. Here, participation has clarified the path toward a valued goal, and the professors should be motivated to perform well in the classroom.

It might also occur to you that participation can increase intrinsic motivation by enriching subordinates' jobs. In Chapter 7 you learned that enriched jobs include high task variety and increased subordinate autonomy. Participation adds some variety to the job and promotes autonomy by increasing the "area of freedom" (Exhibit 10–4).

Quality An old saying argues that "two heads are better than one." While this is not always true, there do seem to be many cases in which "two heads" (participation) lead to higher-quality decisions than the leader could make alone.[23] In particular, this is most likely when subordinates have special *knowledge* to contribute to the decision. For example, when subordinates are in direct contact with clients while the leader is not, they should be the first to detect service problems. Salespeople for an office supply company will be the first to hear complaints about quality control problems. Similarly, desk clerks at city hall will be the first to find out that citizens are unable to understand the city's new building permit forms. A participative leadership style will increase the chances that such problems will be detected and corrected.

In many research and engineering departments, it is common for the professional subordinates to have technical knowledge that is superior to that of their boss. This occurs either because the boss is not a professional or because the boss's knowledge has become outdated. Under these conditions, participation in technical matters should enhance the quality of decisions.

Acceptance Even when participation does not promote motivation or increase the quality of decisions, it can increase the subordinates' acceptance of decisions. This is especially likely when issues of *fairness* are involved.[24] For example, consider the problems of scheduling vacations or scheduling telephone coverage during lunch hours. Here, the leader could probably make high-quality decisions without involving subordinates. However, the decisions might be totally unacceptable to the employees because they are perceived as unfair. Involving subordinates in decision making could result in solutions of equal quality that do not provoke dissatisfaction. Public commitment and ego involvement probably contribute to the acceptance of such decisions.

Potential Problems of Participative Leadership

You have no doubt caught on to the fact that every issue in organizational behavior has two sides. Consider the potential difficulties of participation.

Time and Energy Participation isn't a state of mind. It involves specific behaviors on the part of the leader (soliciting ideas, calling meetings), and these behaviors use time and energy. When a quick decision is needed, participation isn't an appropriate leadership strategy. The hospital emergency room isn't the place to implement participation on a continuous basis!

Jealousy When participation works well, it might provide the participators with benefits that provoke jealousy on the part of others who do not experience the enhanced status of this leadership style. For example, consider the department chairperson in a university who implemented participation to allocate the department's yearly budget. Department members made creative decisions that left a substantial balance for travel to conferences in exotic locations. Members of other departments that had not had the advantages of participation responded with envy and jealousy.

Loss of Power Some leaders feel that a participative style will reduce their power and influence. Sometimes, they respond by asking subordinates to make trivial decisions of the "what color shall we paint the lounge" type. Clearly, the consequences of such decisions (for motivation, quality, and acceptance) are near zero.

Lack of Receptivity or Knowledge Subordinates might not be receptive to participation. When the leader is distrusted, or when a poor labor climate exists, they might resent "having to do management's work." There is also evidence that certain personality characteristics might cause subordinates to reject participative leadership.[25] Even when receptive, subordinates might lack the knowledge to contribute effectively to decisions. Usually, this occurs because they are unaware of *external constraints* on their decisions. For example, consider the case of the toy factory with the following production process:

PARTS MADE → PARTS PAINTED → TOYS ASSEMBLED

In this factory, participation among the paint crew led them to establish elevated production levels that led to problems for the parts makers and toy assemblers. Management was forced to take control of production levels, and most of the painters quit.[26]

Our discussion of the advantages and problems of participation should clarify what happened to Bernie Reiman and Charles Hackett in the story that began the chapter. Bernie's subordinates came up with a sensible solution to the problem of introducing a new product line. Unfortunately, they lacked knowledge of the "big picture," which dictated that their solution was impossible to implement. On the other hand, Charles Hackett's R&D engineers had the expertise to identify their problems while avoiding external constraints. They used participation to come up with solutions that *took advantage of further participation* (team meetings, peer reviews, and frequent consultation with Hackett). These solutions clarified paths to valued goals for the engineers.

A Situational Model of Participation

How can leaders capitalize upon the potential advantages of participation while avoiding its pitfalls? Victor Vroom and Arthur Jago have presented a model that attempts to specify in a practical manner when participation should be used and to what extent it should be used (the model was originally developed by Vroom and Philip Yetton).[27]

Vroom and Jago begin with the recognition that there are various degrees of participation that can be exhibited by the leader. For issues involving the entire work group, the following range of behaviors is plausible (A stands for autocratic, C for consultative, and G for group):

AI. You solve the problem or make the decision yourself, using information available to you at the time.

AII. You obtain the necessary information from your subordinates, then decide the solution to the problem yourself. You may or may not tell your subordinates what the problem is in getting the information from them. The role played by your subordinates in making the decision is clearly one of providing the necessary information to you, rather than generating or evaluating alternative solutions.

CI. You share the problem with the relevant subordinates individually, getting their ideas and suggestions without bringing them together as a group. Then you make the decision, which may or may not reflect your subordinates' influence.

CII. You share the problem with your subordinates as a group, obtaining their collective ideas and suggestions. Then you make the decision, which may or may not reflect your subordinates' influence.

GII. You share the problem with your subordinates as a group. Together you generate and evaluate alternatives and attempt to reach agreement (consensus) on a solution. Your role is much like that of chairman. You do not try to influence the group to adopt "your" solution, and you are willing to accept and implement any solution which has the support of the entire group.[28]

Which of these strategies is most effective? According to Vroom and Jago, this depends on the situation or problem at hand. In general, the leader's goal should be to make high-quality decisions to which subordinates will be adequately committed without undue delay. To do this, he or she must consider the questions shown in Exhibit 10–5. The quality requirement (QR) for a problem might be low if it is very unlikely that a technically bad decision could be made or all feasible alternatives are equal in quality. Otherwise, it is probably high. The commitment requirement (CR) is likely to be high if subordinates are very concerned about which alternative is chosen or if they will have to actually implement the decision. The problem is structured (ST) when the leader understands the current situation, the desired situation, and how to get from one to the other.

EXHIBIT   **The Vroom and Jago decision tree for participative leadership.**

10–5

QR	Quality Requirement:	How important is the technical quality of this decision?
CR	Commitment Requirement:	How important is subordinate commitment to the decision?
LI	Leader's Information:	Do you have sufficient information to make a high-quality decision?
ST	Problem Structure:	Is the problem well structured?
CP	Commitment Probability:	If you were to make the decision by yourself, is it reasonably certain that your subordinate(s) would be commited to the decison?
GC	Goal Congruence:	Do subordinates share the organizational goals to be attained in solving the problem?
CO	Subordinate Conflict:	Is conflict among subordinates over preferred solutions likely?
SI	Subordinate Information:	Do subordinates have sufficient information to make a high-quality decision?

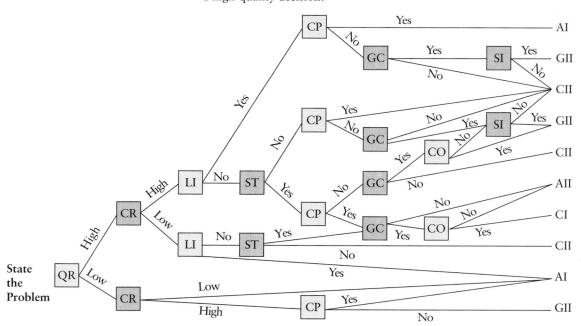

Source: Reprinted from Vroom, V. H., & Jago, A. G. (1988). *The new leadership: Managing participation in organizations.* Englewood Cliffs, NJ: Prentice-Hall. Copyright © 1987 by Vroom, V. H., & Jago, A. G.

Unfamiliarity, uncertainty, and novelty in any of these matters reduces problem structure. The other questions in Exhibit 10–5 are fairly self-explanatory. Notice, however, that all are oriented toward preserving either decision quality or commitment to the decision.

By tracing a problem through the decision tree, the leader encounters the prescribed degree of participation for that problem. In every case, the tree shows the fastest approach possible (i.e., the most autocratic) that still maintains decision quality and commitment. In many cases, if the leader is willing to sacrifice some speed, a more participative approach could be used to stimulate subordinate development (as long as quality or commitment is not threatened). In Focus 10–1 illustrates how the model is applied to a problem.

The original decision model developed by Vroom and Yetton, upon which the Vroom and Jago model is based, has substantial research support.[29] Successful managerial decisions are more likely than unsuccessful decisions to follow the model's prescriptions. The model has been used frequently in management development seminars.

Does Participation Work?

Now we come to the bottom line—does participative leadership result in beneficial outcomes? There is substantial evidence that employees who have the opportunity to participate in work-related decisions report more job satisfaction than those who do not. Thus, most workers seem to *prefer* a participative work environment. However, the positive effects of participation on productivity are open to some question. For participation to be translated into higher productivity, it would appear that certain facilitating conditions must exist. Specifically, participation should work best when subordinates feel favorable toward it, when they are intelligent and knowledgeable about the issue at hand, and when the task is complex enough to make participation useful.[30] In general, these conditions are incorporated into the Vroom and Jago model. Like any other leadership strategy, the usefulness of participation depends upon the constraints of the situation. In Chapter 12 we will consider group decision making, a topic that has additional relevance for participation.

TRANSFORMATIONAL LEADERSHIP AND CHARISMA

Thus far in the chapter we have been studying various aspects of what has been called transactional leadership. Transactional leadership is leadership that is based on a fairly straightforward exchange between the leader and the followers—subordinates perform well, and the leader rewards them; the leader uses a participatory style, and the subordinates come up with good ideas. Although it might be difficult to do well, such leadership is routine, in the sense that it is directed mainly toward bringing subordinate behavior in line with organizational goals. However, you might have some more dramatic examples of leadership in mind, examples in which leaders have had a more profound effect on followers by giving them a new vision that instilled true commitment to a project, a department, or an organization. Such leadership is called **transformational leadership** because the leader decisively changes the beliefs and attitudes of followers to correspond to this new vision.[31]

Popular examples of transformational leadership are easy to find—consider Disney CEO Michael Eisner's role in improving Disney's performance, Steven Jobs's vision in bringing the Apple Macintosh to fruition, Mary Ann Lawlor's turnaround of Drake Business Schools, or CEO Jack Welch's ongoing revision of

IN FOCUS 10–1

How the Vroom and Jago Model of Participation Works

Here is a case that illustrates how the Vroom and Jago model works. Read the case and trace the analysis through the decision tree. Vroom and Jago have used such cases to train leaders in decision-making skills.

You are the head of a research and development laboratory in the nuclear reactor division of a large corporation. Often it is not clear whether a particular piece of research is potentially of commercial interest or merely of "academic" interest to the researchers. In your judgment, one major area of research has advanced well beyond the level at which operating divisions pertinent to the area could possibly assimilate or make use of the data being generated.

Recently, two new areas with potentially high returns for commercial development have been proposed by one of the operating divisions. The team working in the area referred to in the previous paragraph is ideally qualified to research these new areas. Unfortunately, both the new areas are relatively devoid of scientific interest, while the project on which the team is currently engaged is of great scientific interest to all members.

At the moment, this is, or is close to being, your best research team. The team is very cohesive, has a high level of morale, and has been very productive. You are concerned not only that they would

General Electric's strategy (see In Focus 10–2). Each of these leaders went beyond a mere institutional figurehead role and even beyond a transactional leadership role to truly transform subordinates' thinking about the nature of their businesses. However, these prominent examples should not obscure the fact that transformational leadership can occur in less visible settings. For example, a new coach might revitalize a sorry peewee soccer team or an energetic new director might turn around a moribund community association using the same types of skills.

But what *are* the skills of these exceptional transformational leaders who encourage considerable effort and dedication on the part of followers? Professor Bernard Bass of the State University of New York at Binghamton has conducted

not want to switch their effort to these new areas, but also that forcing them to concentrate on these two new projects could adversely affect their morale, their good intragroup working relations, and their future productivity both as individuals and as a team.

You have to respond to the operating division within the next two weeks indicating what resources, if any, can be devoted to working on these projects. It would be possible for the team to work on more than one project but each project would need the combined skills of all the members of the team, so no fragmentation of the team is technically feasible. This fact, coupled with the fact that the team is very cohesive, means that a solution that satisfies any team member would very probably go a long way to satisfying everyone on the team.

Analysis

Quality Requirement	High Importance
Commitment Requirement	High Importance
Leader Information	Probably Yes
Problem Structure	Yes
Commitment Probability	No
Goal Congruence	Probably No
Subordinate Conflict	Probably No
Subordinate Information	No
Highest Overall Effectiveness:	CII

Source: Vroom, V. H., & Jago, A. G. (1988). *The new leadership: Managing participation in organizations.* Englewood Cliffs, NJ: Prentice-Hall, pp. 164–165. Reprinted by permission.

IN FOCUS 10–2

▼
....

General Electric's Jack Welch—A Transformational Leader

John F. (Jack) Welch, Jr., Chairman and CEO of General Electric since 1981, is widely recognized in business circles as a prime example of a transformational leader. What Welch has transformed is a once-stodgy giant that was destined to be unable to compete in global markets. A leaner, more aggressive, more globally active GE is the result. In conventional business terms, this was accomplished by divesting many operations, eliminating many jobs, and acquiring new business lines. As a result, GE is now a world-class performer in areas such as aircraft engines, circuit breakers, electric motors, lighting, and major appliances. Also, in the United States, it can boast ownership of broadcasting firm NBC.

How does one change a giant? In a *Harvard Business Review* interview, Welch said, "Good business leaders create a vision, articulate the vision, passionately own the vision, and relentlessly drive it to completion. Above all else though, good leaders are open. They go up, down, and around their organization to reach people. They don't stick to established channels. They're informal. They're straight with people."

Early on, Welch's vision involved convincing GE management that change was indeed necessary due to global competition, even though the firm was performing well. This led to strategic change that guided the series of divestitures and acquisitions. To implement this strategy, Welch attacked GE's entrenched bureaucracy. Management levels were removed, headquarters staff units were slashed, and self-protective "sign-offs" on product changes were reduced. This results in faster decisions and gives managers more responsibility for the consequences of those decisions.

Lately, Welch's vision has concentrated on boosting productivity in order to stimulate profits. Welch has long felt that GE stock is undervalued, and he is doing something about it by means of this productivity drive.

Source: Tichy, N., & Charan, R. (1989, September–October). Speed, simplicity, self-confidence: An interview with Jack Welch. *Harvard Business Review,* 112–120; Vogel, T. (1989, December 18). Big changes are galvanizing General Electric. *Business Week,* 100–102; Sherman, S. P. (1989, March 27). The mind of Jack Welch. *Fortune,* 38–50.

extensive research on transformational leaders.[32] Bass notes that transformational leaders are usually good at the transactional aspects of clarifying paths to goals, rewarding good performance, and so on. But he also notes three qualities that set transformational leaders apart from their transactional colleagues:

- Intellectual stimulation
- Individualized consideration
- Charisma

[Intellectual stimulation contributes in part to the "new vision" aspect of transformational leadership. People are stimulated to think about problems, issues, and strategies in new ways. Often, creativity and novelty are at work here.]For example, Steve Jobs was convinced that the Apple Macintosh had to be extremely user friendly. As you might imagine, many of the technical types who wanted to sign on to the Mac project needed to be convinced of the importance of this quality, and Jobs was just the person to do it, raising their consciousness about what it felt like to be a new computer user.

[Individualized consideration involves treating subordinates as distinct individuals, indicating concern for their personal development, and serving as a mentor when appropriate. The emphasis is a one-on-one attempt to meet the needs of the individual in question in the context of the overall goal or mission.]Bass implies that individualized consideration is particularly striking when it is exhibited by military leaders because the military culture generally stresses impersonality and "equal" treatment.

General Norman Schwarzkopf in the Persian Gulf region. One part of transformational leadership is giving subordinates individualized consideration. (David Turnley/Detroit Free Press/Black Star)

Charisma is the third, and by far the most important, aspect of transformational leadership. In fact, many authors simply talk about charismatic leadership, although a good case can be made that a person could have charisma without being a leader. Charisma is a term stemming from a Greek word meaning *favored* or *gifted*. Charismatic individuals have been portrayed throughout history as having personal qualities that give them the potential to have extraordinary influence over others. They tend to command strong loyalty and devotion, and this in turn inspires enthusiastic dedication and effort directed toward the leader's chosen mission. In terms of the concepts developed in Chapter 9, followers come to trust and *identify* with charismatic leaders and to *internalize* the values and goals held by them. Charisma provides the *emotional* aspect of transformational leadership.

It appears that the emergence of charisma is a complex function of traits, behaviors, and being in the right place at the right time.[33] Prominent traits include self-confidence, dominance, and a strong conviction in their own beliefs. Charismatics often act to create an impression of personal success and accomplishment. They hold high expectations for follower performance while at the same time expressing confidence in followers' capabilities. This enhances the self-esteem of the followers. The goals set by charismatic leaders often have a moral or ideological flavor to them. In addition, charismatic leaders often emerge to articulate the feelings of followers in times of stress or discord. If these feelings go against an existing power structure, the leader might be perceived as especially courageous.

One interesting view of the emergence of charisma portrays it as a stagelike process.[34] Although such stages probably do not occur in all instances of charisma, this portrayal does clarify the means by which charisma contributes to transformational leadership. In the first stage, the leader carefully evaluates the status quo for opportunities for change. Particular attention is devoted to assessing subordinate needs and organizational constraints. At the same time, the leader seeks out or even causes deficiencies in the status quo. For example, he or she might commission market research to show a strong demand for a product or service that the organization does not offer. In the second stage, the leader formulates a vision or mission that challenges the status quo but that somehow corresponds to the followers' needs and aspirations. For example, he or she might envision a product that will return the firm to its former eminence as a respected innovator in engineering. At this stage, impression management is important to articulate the vision to followers. Here is where rhetoric, self-confidence, and showing confidence in others come into play. The new mission's ability to change the unsatisfactory status quo is emphasized. In the final stage of charismatic emergence, the leader actually gets subordinates to achieve the new vision or mission, often by setting an example of self-sacrifice and flaunting unconventional expertise to build subordinate trust. For example, the leader might work extensive hours, make risky challenges to other organizational members who threaten the mission, and suggest unusual but workable technical solutions.

Charisma has been studied most intensively among political leaders and the leaders of social movements. Winston Churchill, Martin Luther King, and Gandhi appear to have been charismatic. Among U.S. Presidents, one study concludes that Jefferson, Jackson, Lincoln, Kennedy, and Reagan were charismatic, while Coolidge, Harding, and Buchanan were not.[35] Among business leaders, Mary Kay Ash and Lee Iacocca are often cited as charismatic (see In Focus 10–3).

In passing, it must also be mentioned that charisma has a dark side, a side that

IN FOCUS 10–3

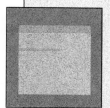

Does Lee Iacocca Have Charisma?

Can charisma be seen in the business world? Let's consider Lee Iacocca, dubbed by *Time* as "America's hottest new folk hero." When Iacocca took over the helm at Chrysler Corporation in 1979 the company's financial plight was so serious that many observers felt that it would not survive. Iacocca obtained federal loan guarantees against strong resistance and championed radical changes in marketing and management, and by 1984 Chrysler achieved a year of record-breaking profits.

But did charismatic leadership help Iacocca turn Chrysler around? Many observers think so. During the years of rebuilding, Iacocca exhibited resolute confidence in himself and in his employees. This confidence was played out publicly in a series of television commercials in which Iacocca starred ("If you can find a better car, buy it!"). The moral and ideological goal of defeating unfair foreign competition and preserving American manufacturing dominance was undisguised in his public speeches, hitting the right chord with the Chrysler work force and the public at large. Iacocca boldly and bluntly advocated import quotas against strong resistance from the federal administration. When the turnaround finally occurred, he gave tangible expression to his confidence in the workforce by awarding every one of Chrysler's 100,000 employees a $500 bonus.

During this period, Iacocca was being touted as a potential presidential candidate and receiving literally thousands of requests to make speeches. But it is the warm, enthusiastic reception that Iacocca received from groups of dealers and assembly line workers that reveals the likelihood of his charisma. Mobbed and cheered by well-wishers, it was clear that they shared with Iacocca the vision that had saved their jobs.

Source: Andersen, K. (1985, April 1). A spunky tycoon turned superstar. *Time*, 24–34. Reprinted by permission of Time, Inc.; Flax, S. (1985, January 7). Can Chrysler keep rolling along? *Fortune*, 34–39. Reprinted by permission of Fortune.

is revealed when charismatics abuse their strong influence over others for purely personal reasons.[36] The needs of followers are often exploited to pursue a reckless goal or mission. Adolf Hitler and the Reverend Jim Jones personify extreme examples of charismatic abuse. We will explore the abuse of power further in Chapter 13.

To summarize, transformational leaders provide intellectual stimulation and individualized consideration to followers. Most important, though, they exhibit charisma. The recent research evidence suggests that such leaders are perceived as especially effective by subordinates in stimulating both satisfaction and effort.[37] Before continuing, pause and consider the You Be the Manager feature about leadership development.

DOES LEADERSHIP MATTER?

Does leadership really *matter?* That is, does it have a strong influence on the effectiveness of organizations? This might seem like an incredible question after we have devoted so many pages to consideration, initiating structure, situational influence, participation, and transformation. However, as you have seen, the study of leadership, despite its great volume, has not produced perfect agreement about what constitutes effective leadership. Perhaps we are tilting at windmills. Maybe leadership just isn't important to organizations. Let's examine the pros and cons of this issue.

Mary Kay Ash of Mary Kay Cosmetics: a transformational charismatic leader. (Courtesy Mary Kay Cosmetics, Inc.)

M
anager

Leadership Development
at General Electric

To achieve CEO Jack Welch's vision of a more global, less hierarchical company (see In Focus 10–2), General Electric's management development staff realized that GE managers would require a new set of leadership skills. To implement these skills, the company relied on its Crotonville, New York, Management Development Institute. The institute proceeded to develop a complete curriculum that is oriented toward providing leadership development at various career transitions, such as when they join GE, become a manager, or become identified as a high potential executive.

Of particular concern was a course called the Business Management Course (BMC), a four-week program for upper-level middle managers who had been designated as having special potential for advancement. This group would play a critical role in "leading the charge" toward a revitalized GE. Traditionally, the BMC had been taught by using lectures, discussions, business games, and case studies of past business decisions. However, GE's management development experts were concerned that these approaches were too passive, not current enough in terms of GE's new reality, and not team-oriented enough. Also, they lacked an element of real risk to make the course an intense, high-impact experience, and they lacked a real global orientation. Besides, this was a lot of high-priced talent to be tied up for four weeks. Could the company get anything *from* the executives while exposing them to new global, team-oriented leadership skills?

How do *you* recommend revising the BMC?

1. Leadership development programs often face the problem of transfer of skills to the work environment. Why is this a particular problem with the traditional BMC approach?

2. What would you do to make the BMC experience relevant and timely for GE managers?

To find out what GE did, see The Manager's Notebook at the end of the chapter.

Source: Adapted from Noel, J. L., & Charan, R. (1988, Winter). Leadership development at GE's Crotonville. *Human Resource Management*, 433–447; Tichy, N. M. (1989, May). GE's Crotonville: A staging ground for corporate revolution. *Academy of Management Executive*, 99–106.

Pros and Cons

The notion that leadership is important rests mainly on the premise that special influence is necessary to get things done because organizations aren't and can't be designed perfectly and completely. You have probably experienced this phenomenon. The university financial office can't give you a refund until it is okayed by the registrar. The registrar can't okay the refund until it is approved by the professor. And the professor just went on sabbatical to Tasmania! *Here's* a case in which leadership is necessary! In other words, schools, hospitals, and business firms exhibit many loose ends or gaps that can be dealt with only by effective leadership. More specifically:

- Organizations do not have a rule or policy for every contingency. (The boss decides whether a particular absence is legitimate or illegitimate.)
- Organizational environments change, and someone must be responsive to this change. (If the economy takes a downturn, some members of the firm must convince others what the firm's response should be.)
- Organizational members differ in their needs and goals. (A sensitive manager might be able to motivate one employee with challenging work assignments and another with the promise of a raise in pay.)[38]

Conditions of this nature suggest that there is considerable *latitude* for leadership actions that can help or hinder the organization in achieving its goals.[39]

The notion that leadership isn't so important rests mainly on the premise that a number of factors conspire to constrain the influence that individuals in leadership roles might have. In other words, the potential for influence is inhibited, and the leader's latitude is more apparent than real. One author has argued that the following factors limit leader impact:[40]

- In most organizations, rigid selection and promotion policies dictate that those who achieve leadership positions have very similar leadership styles. (If all the managers in a government office behave similarly, they should have similar influence—one manager is easily replaceable by another who should be equally effective.)
- The leader's performance can be strongly affected by external factors beyond his or her control. (The best boss in the company might not be able to overcome subordinates' resentment of the dirty, boring work required by a particular technology.)

Obviously, the argument that leadership matters and the position that leadership doesn't matter both sound pretty rational. This suggests that both positions may be true under certain circumstances. Let's examine what these circumstances might be.

Leadership Neutralizers and Substitutes

Some interesting ideas have been proposed in response to the dilemma of whether leadership matters.[41] First, it has been argued that certain subordinate, task, and organizational characteristics can serve as **neutralizers of leadership.** When these factors are present in the work setting, the opportunities for leaders to exercise influence are reduced. In this case, then, leadership might not "matter" because the leader's influence attempts are stymied. When such factors are not present, the leader might have an important effect on subordinate satisfaction and performance. For example, consider the following situations:

> Martin is a petroleum engineer for a major oil company. He is a troubleshooter who deals with company problems around the world, and he is constantly "on the go." He sees his boss about every two months. Martin is very interested in his job, and he doesn't care about what performance rating or merit raise he receives.

> Shawn is a management trainee in a large insurance company. Her office is beside that of her boss, and she consults with him about ten times a day. Shawn hopes to obtain a good performance rating so that she can receive a lucrative promotion.

Obviously, Shawn's boss is in a better position to exercise influence than Martin's boss. The latter's leadership potential is to some extent neutralized by the fact that he seldom sees Martin and because Martin is unresponsive to the rewards he can provide.

Going a step further, some neutralizers of leadership can actually serve as **substitutes for leadership.** In other words, some subordinate, task, and organizational characteristics might operate to make leadership unnecessary or redundant. While simple neutralizers reduce the *effectiveness* of leadership attempts, substitutes reduce the *necessity* for leadership. For example, consider these situations:

> A group of ten welders and riveters is assembling a large natural gas pipeline. All of them are highly experienced, and they work well together as a friendly, cohesive unit. Their task is clear and unambiguous—assemble fifty yards of pipe each day.

> A group of computer experts has decided to start a new company to design and market software packages. Although they are all technical experts, they know nothing about financing their venture or marketing their proposed products. There is much disagreement about how to establish the new enterprise and how to choose which software to develop.

In which of these situations does leadership seem more necessary? For the pipe crew, the straightforwardness of the task at hand and the friendly, cooperative working relationships could well serve as substitutes for active, formal leadership. We would not be surprised to see the crew work well if the boss called in sick for several days. On the other hand, the proposed computer firm is begging for leadership. Its goals are unclear, and its founders are unlikely to reach an easy agreement. There are no substitutes for leadership here.

Exhibit 10–6 summarizes a number of potential neutralizers of leadership. In some cases, these neutralizers can also serve as substitutes. In the first example discussed above (Martin versus Shawn), indifference toward rewards and spatial distance were presented as simple neutralizers. These factors reduce the impact of leadership, but they do not reduce the need for leadership. In the second example, a clear task, experienced workers, and a cohesive work group served as substitutes for formal leadership for the pipe crew. The computer group did not have the advantages of these substitutes. Notice that some factors neutralize social-emotional influence, some neutralize task influence, and some neutralize both. For example, highly experienced, knowledgeable subordinates might need little task leadership, but they still require social-emotional support from the leader.

In summary, it would appear that leadership "matters" most when neutralizers and substitutes are not present in subordinates' skills and attitudes, task design, or the organizational design. When neutralizers and substitutes are present, the impact of formal leadership is reduced.[42]

EXHIBIT 10–6

Neutralizers of leadership.

Neutralizing Characteristics	Will Neutralize Considerate or Social-Emotional Leadership	Will Neutralize Initiating Structure or Task Leadership
Of Subordinate		
Ability, experience, knowledge		X
Professional orientation	X	X
Indifference toward rewards	X	X
Of Task		
Routine and clear		X
Provides its own feedback		X
Intrinsically satisfying	X	
Of Organization		
Inflexible rules and procedures		X
Cohesive work groups	X	X
Spatial distance between leader and subordinate	X	X

Source: From Kerr, S., & Jermier, J. M. (1978). Substitutes for leadership: Their meaning and measurement. *Organizational Behavior and Human Performance, 22,* p. 378. Copyright © 1978 by Academic Press. Reprinted by permission.

THE MANAGER'S NOTEBOOK

Leadership Development at General Electric

1. The problem with transfer of leadership skills back to the work environment is that the traditional Business Management Course was oriented toward the old GE rather than the new GE. Transformational and team-oriented skills were necessary in the more global and less hierarchical company.

2. The BMC was reorganized around a series of consulting projects that involve providing recommendations for solutions to real problems faced by GE business units. Two teams of five or six managers are assigned to each problem, and the teams work independently to develop alternative solutions. Extensive fieldwork is done, and a ninety-minute presentation to top executives of the unit caps the effort. This work has sometimes been conducted in Europe to provide an appreciation for the global aspect of GE's business. Team recommendations have often been implemented. The course begins with a series of intense outdoor experiences that are designed to instill team spirit.

SUMMARY

- Leadership occurs when an individual exerts influence upon others in an organizational context. Early studies of leadership were concerned with identifying physical, psychological, and intellectual traits that might predict leader effectiveness. While some traits appear weakly related to leadership capacity, there are no traits that guarantee leadership across various situations.

- Studies of emergent leadership have identified two important leadership functions—the task function and the social-emotional function. The former involves helping the group achieve its goals through planning and organizing, while the latter involves resolving disputes and maintaining a pleasant group environment. Explorations of the behavior of assigned leaders have concentrated on initiating structure and consideration, which are similar to task behavior and social-emotional behavior. The effectiveness of consideration and structure depends upon the nature of the task and the subordinates. Leader reward behavior is probably a more foolproof strategy than leader punishment behavior.

- Two situational theories of leadership were discussed. Fiedler's Contingency Theory suggests that different leadership orientations are necessary depending upon the favorableness of the situation for the leader. Favorableness depends upon the structure of the task, the position power of the leader, and the satisfactoriness of the relationship between the leader and the group. Fiedler argues that task-oriented leaders perform best in situations that are either very favorable or very unfavorable. Relationship-oriented leaders are said to perform best in situations of medium favorability. House's Path-Goal Theory suggests that leaders will be most effective when they are able to clarify the paths to various subordinate goals that are also of interest to the organization. According to House, the effectiveness of directive, supportive, participative, and achievement-oriented behavior depends upon the nature of the subordinates and the characteristics of the work environment.

- Participative leader behavior involves subordinates in work decisions. Participation can increase subordinate motivation and lead to higher-quality and more acceptable decisions. The Vroom and Jago model specifies how much participation should be used for various kinds of decisions. Participation works best when subordinates are desirous of participation, when they are intelligent and knowledgeable, and when the task is reasonably complex.

- Transformational leaders modify the beliefs and attitudes of followers to correspond to a new vision. They provide intellectual stimulation and individualized consideration. They also have charisma, the ability to command extraordinary loyalty, dedication, and effort from followers.
- Leadership is most important when few neutralizers or substitutes for leadership exist. Neutralizers are factors that make leadership attempts less effective, and substitutes are factors that can act in place of leader influence.

KEY CONCEPTS

Leadership	Initiating structure	Participative leadership
Traits	Leader reward behavior	Transformational leadership
Emergent leadership	Leader punishment behavior	Charisma
Task leader	Fiedler's Contingency Theory	Neutralizers of leadership
Social-emotional leader	Least Preferred Co-Worker (LPC)	Substitutes for leadership
Consideration	House's Path-Goal Theory	

DISCUSSION QUESTIONS

1. Name a physical, intellectual, or personality trait that might be associated with effective leadership and defend your position. Then discuss a situation in which this trait might *not* be associated with effective leadership.

2. Discuss a case of emergent leadership that you have observed. Why did the person in question emerge as a leader? Did he or she fulfill the task role, the social-emotional role, or both?

3. Contrast the relative merits of consideration and initiating structure in the following leadership situations: running the daily operations of a branch bank; commanding an army unit under enemy fire; supervising a group of college students who are performing a hot, dirty, boring summer job. Use House's Path-Goal Theory to support your arguments.

4. Fred Fiedler argues that leader LPC is difficult to change and that situations should be "engineered" to fit the leader's LPC orientation. Suppose that a relationship-oriented (high LPC) person finds herself assigned to a situation with poor leader-member relations, an unstructured task, and weak position power. What could she do to make the situation more favorable for her relationship-oriented leadership?

5. Describe a situation that would be ideal for having subordinates participate in a work-related decision.

Discuss the subordinates, the problem, and the setting. Describe a situation in which participative decision making would be an especially unwise leadership strategy. Why is this so?

6. Discuss the pros and cons of the following statement: Even when a manager can make an adequate decision on his or her own, the manager should attempt to involve subordinates in the decision.

7. Distinguish between neutralizers of leadership and substitutes for leadership. Give an example of each.

8. Julio is an extremely experienced salesperson of sophisticated electronic equipment. He has an M.Sc. in electrical engineering and is on the road eleven months a year. He really enjoys his job, and he is extremely interested in the high commissions the job offers. Discuss Julio's situation from the perspective of neutralizers of and substitutes for the leadership of his sales manager.

9. What are charismatic individuals skilled at doing that gives them extraordinary influence over others?

10. Describe a leadership situation in which a highly charismatic transformational leader would probably *not* be the right person for the job.

EXPERIENTIAL EXERCISE

Leadership Style

Below are three cases in which a leader confronts a problem that requires a decision to be made. After reading each case, use your intuition to decide which of Vroom and Jago's five decision strategies (AI, AII, CI, CII, GII) the leader should use. Then reread each case and trace its characteristics through the decision tree shown in Exhibit 10–5. Did your intuitive answers differ from those provided by the decision tree analysis? If so, what factors led to the difference?

Case I

You are general foreman in charge of a large gang laying an oil pipeline. It is now necessary to estimate your expected rate of progress in order to schedule material deliveries to the next field site.

You know the nature of the terrain you will be traveling and have the historical data needed to compute the mean and variance in the rate of speed over that type of terrain. Given these two variables it is a simple matter to calculate the earliest and latest times at which materials and support facilities will be needed at the next site. It is important that your estimate be reasonably accurate. Underestimates result in idle foremen and workers, and an overestimate results in tying up materials for a period of time before they are to be used.

Progress has been good and your five foremen and other members of the gang stand to receive substantial bonuses if the project is completed ahead of schedule.

Case II

You are on the division manager's staff and work on a wide variety of problems of both administrative and technical nature. You have been given the assignment of developing a universal method to be used in each of the five plants in the division for manually reading equipment registers, recording the readings, and transmitting the scorings to a centralized information system. All plants are located in a relatively small geographical region.

Until now there has been a high error rate in the reading and/or transmittal of the data. Some locations have considerably higher error rates than others, and the methods used to record and transmit the data vary between plants. It is probable, therefore, that part of the error variance is a function of specific local conditions rather than anything else, and this will complicate the establishment of any system common to all plants. You have the information on error rates but no information on the local practices that generate these errors or on the local conditions that necessitate the different practices.

Everyone would benefit from an improvement in the quality of the data, as it is used in a number of important decisions. Your contacts with the plants are through the quality-control supervisors who are responsible for collecting the data. They are a conscientious group committed to doing their jobs well, but they are highly sensitive to interference on the part of higher management in their own operations. Any solution that does not receive the active support of the various plant supervisors is unlikely to reduce the error rate significantly.

Case III

You are the head of a staff unit reporting to the vice-president of finance. He has asked you to provide a report on the firm's current portfolio including recommendations for changes in the selection criteria currently employed. Doubts have been raised about the efficiency of the existing system in the current market conditions, and there is considerable dissatisfaction with prevailing rates of return.

You plan to write the report, but at the moment you are quite perplexed about the approach to take. Your own specialty is the bond market, and it is clear to you that a detailed knowledge of the equity market, which you lack, would greatly enhance the value of the report. Fortunately, four members of your staff are specialists in different segments of the equity market. Together they possess a vast amount of knowledge about the intricacies of investment. However, they seldom agree on the best way to achieve anything when it comes to the stock market. While they are obviously conscientious as well as knowledgeable, they have major differences when it comes to investment philosophy and strategy.

You have six weeks before the report is due. You have already begun to familiarize yourself with the firm's current portfolio and have been provided by management with a specific set of constraints that any portfolio must satisfy. Your immediate problem is to come up with some alternatives to the firm's present practices and select the most promising for detailed analysis in your report.

Source of Cases: Vroom, V. H., & Yetton, P. W. (1973). *Leadership and decision-making*. Pittsburgh: University of Pittsburgh Press. © 1973 by University of Pittsburgh Press. Reprinted by permission.

Jean Hall's Dilemma

Jean Hall had worked for the Contronica Corporation for about five years. She was 29 years old, was single, and had acquired both her B.B.A. and M.B.A. from the University of Florida, where she majored in finance and management. Her performance at Contronica, first as an analyst in the Corporate Planning group, and then as a consultant in the Management Audit Department, was typically described by her supervisors and co-workers as "excellent" or "outstanding." She was recognized as having exceptional analytical ability, and the studies she completed for Contronica were regarded by at least one of the company's division managers as "models in their own right." Jean was affable and openly communicative in her relationships with people; she seemed to be generally well liked in return and had been considered "one of the team" in both departments in which she had worked.

Despite this, Jean had begun to experience some self-doubt and anxiety in the last few days. A month earlier she received a promotion as director of the Management Audit Department, a middle management position which reported to the Vice-President of Administration. Her predecessor, Roger Davis, had been transferred to cover an important line position left vacant by the sudden death of the incumbent.

The function of the Management Audit Department was to conduct reviews and studies of the systems and general operations of the various divisions throughout the company with the objective of recommending, and assisting in implementing, changes to improve the effectiveness or efficiency of these divisions. These studies were conducted on a pre-arranged rotational basis, or by invitation of the divisions. In effect, the department worked as in-house resource group and consulting arm of the company.

Jean's anxiety stemmed from the task which had been thrust upon her and her department, and from her uncertainty concerning the leadership approach she should use in getting the job accomplished. Only three weeks after assuming her new position, she received a hurried phone call from her superior, Bill Handelman, the Vice-President of Administration. Handelman had received feedback from the Marketing Division to the effect that the company was losing literally "hundreds of thousands" in dollar sales volume as a result of an apparent failure to meet delivery dates on orders for the company's new portable fax machine. Both the Marketing and Manufacturing personnel seemed to agree that the problem was in the production and inventory control system which had been installed by an external management consulting firm some three years earlier. The company's President had also learned of the problem and was "hopping mad." Jean was directed by Handelman to "get you and your department working on that problem . . . and fast. We need action and solutions . . . no delays . . . no blue-sky fooling around." While Handelman's own manner could largely be explained by the pressure he himself felt in the circumstances, nonetheless, it was not totally unrepresentative of the approach of the corporation's top executives to management problems. As one middle manager stated "they (top management) are very, very 'hard nosed.'"

From her own experience and from the preliminary investigations she conducted, Jean knew that the real underlying cause for the company's problem might not necessarily lie in the production and inventory control system. As far as she was concerned, the causes still had to be determined; there would likely be numerous obstacles for which there were probably no pre-packaged solutions. Jean personally did not know very much about the production and control system used in the company. Most of her own experience had been acquired working on problems related to procurement, distribution, sales forecasting, and the like. However, she had a good opinion of the people now working for her. She had an opportunity to get to know most of them as colleagues in the previous three years. In her view, they had both

Source: This case is an adaptation from "Montronics Corporation: The New Manager's Dilemma," by Professor Peter E. Pitsiladis, Concordia University, Montreal, 1991. All names and other selected data have been disguised. Used by permission.

the competence and breadth of technical knowledge to respond to the situation.

There were 17 people working for Jean, about half men and half women: four consultants, nine analysts, and four audit assistants with the duties of the latter including secretarial work. All of the consultants and analysts had university degrees, mostly in business, but some in engineering and science. Two of the four consultants were themselves M.B.A.'s. Jean knew that at least three of the analysts and one of the consultants had done some work in the Manufacturing Division on production control problems, so she could count on their knowledge and input.

On reflection, Jean was convinced that interpersonal relations among members of her department were generally quite good. There was some competition among some of them, and conflict was evident at times, but none of it was out of the ordinary. Jean perceived most of the members of the department to be responsible and reasonably cognizant of, and committed to, the goals of the department. There were a few natural or informal sub-group formations or cliques in the department, but the sharing of information and technical know-how was not blocked because of this. Jean felt that this openness could in part be explained by the procedures used in the department for assigning personnel to the study projects.

Traditionally, the Management Audit Department assigned two or three main teams to a study. One of the consultants usually served as the project leader. Teams would thus be formed around a study, and when the work was completed the members would be separately re-assigned to other projects. In this way, over a period of six months or a year, each member of the department would have had task interactions with most of the other members. Because of the rotating nature of the assignments, each consultant could expect to occasionally work under the team leadership of one of the other consultants. The leadership behavior of these consultants varied considerably: Two appeared to be task and job oriented; one of them appeared to stress participation and interpersonal relations; the fourth seemed to exhibit varying degrees of both orientations.

While Jean had not perceived any clear relationship between leadership behaviors and team performance, it was not, she was certain, because such relationships did not exist. In running the department as a whole, Jean's predecessor, Roger Davis, had clearly been of the "hard nose," directive tradition. This was illustrated in the manner with which he frequently established objectives and schedules for the study teams, occasionally omitting to even get input from the team members for the purpose. Yet he had not been particularly disliked by the department. It seemed to Jean that reaction to her predecessor's approach varied from resentment and frustration on the one hand to mild disinterest and acceptance on the other. As a measure of its performance, the department appeared to have won the acceptance of top management and in the previous two years had generated proposals that resulted in significant improvements and

dollar savings for the company. These savings were more than 12 times greater than the costs associated with running the department. To some of the top management group, Davis had been the corporate "golden boy."

As a co-worker, Jean had had good working relationships with other members of the department as previously indicated. As their "new" boss however, she was not certain about the extent to which she had their loyalty, confidence, and support. There were indications of at least some mild resentment on the part of three consultants over their having lost out in the competition for the directorship of the Management Audit Department. Jean's performance in the company however, had put her in a good position; at the time of her appointment to her new job she was given "full authority to hire, fire, and run the department as she saw fit, so long as she produced results."

Jean pondered this situation and was trying to determine what leadership approach would be most effective. She knew that she was very much "on trial" by top management and by her own subordinates. To the extent that she could produce results by solving the order delivery problem she and her department would look good in the eyes of the top executives. On the other hand, the initial perceptions of her managerial approach by the subordinates in the department would be very much influenced by her style with the project team members—and these initial perceptions, Jean knew, might very well affect the tenor of her relationships in the department in the future.

1. Describe the role conflict (Chapter 8) currently being faced by Jean Hall.

2. Use House's Path-Goal Theory to analyze the leadership situation confronting Jean. Which leadership style does the theory suggest?

3. Use Fiedler's Contingency Theory to analyze the leadership situation confronting Jean. Which leadership style does the theory suggest?

4. Run the portable fax problem through the Vroom and Jago decision tree (Exhibit 10–5). What level of participation is indicated?

5. Discuss the merits of transformational or charismatic leadership in this setting.

6. Are there any factors at Contronica that might neutralize Jean Hall's attempts at leadership? Are there any substitutes for leadership in this setting? Does "leadership matter" in the Management Audit Department?

7. What should Jean Hall do now?

REFERENCES

1. Bass, B. M. (1981). *Stogdill's handbook of leadership: A survey of research* (rev. ed.). New York: Free Press.

2. This list is derived from Bass, 1981, and House, R. J., & Baetz, M. L. (1979). Leadership: Some empirical generalizations and new research directions. *Research in Organizational Behavior, 1,* 341–423.

3. Lord, R. G., DeVader, C. L., & Alliger, G. M. (1986). A meta-analysis of the relationship between personality traits and leadership perceptions: An application of validity generalization procedures. *Journal of Applied Psychology, 71,* 402–410.

4. Bottger, P. C. (1984). Expertise and air time as bases of actual and perceived influence in problem-solving groups. *Journal of Applied Psychology, 69,* 214–221.

5. Lewis, G. H. (1972). Role differentiation. *American Sociological Review, 37,* 424–434.

6. Bales, R. F., & Slater, P. E. (1955). Role differentiation in small decision-making groups. In T. Parsons, et al. (Eds.), *Family, socialization, and interaction process.* Glencoe, IL: Free Press; Slater, P. E. (1955). Role differentiation in small groups. *American Sociological Review, 20,* 300–310.

7. For a pessimistic review, see Korman, A. K. (1966). "Consideration," "initiating structure," and organizational criteria—A review. *Personnel Psychology, 19,* 349–361. For an optimistic update, see Kerr, S., & Schriesheim, C. (1974). Consideration, initiating struture, and organizational criteria—An update of Korman's 1966 review. *Personnel Psychology, 27,* 555–568.

8. Kerr, S., Schriesheim, C. A., Murphy, C. J., & Stogdill, R. M. (1974). Toward a contingency theory of leadership based upon the consideration and initiating structure literature. *Organizational Behavior and Human Performance, 12,* 62–82.

9. For a review of the evidence, see Filley, A. C., House, R. J., & Kerr, S. (1976). *Managerial process and organizational behavior* (2nd ed.). Glenview, IL: Scott, Foresman. Also see Larson, L. L., Hunt, J.G., & Osborn, R.N. (1976). The great hi-hi leader behavior myth: A lesson from Occam's razor. *Academy of Management Journal, 19,* 628–641.

10. Oldham, G. R. (1976). The motivational strategies used by supervisors: Relationships to effectiveness indicators. *Organizational Behavior and Human Performance, 15,* 66–86.

11. Ashour, A. S., & Johns, G. (1983). Leader influence through operant principles: A theoretical and methodological framework. *Human Relations, 36,* 603–626; Podsakoff, P. M., & Schriesheim, C. A. (1984). Leader reward and punishment behavior: A review of the literature. In D. F. Ray (Ed.), *Southern Management Association Proceedings,* 12–14.

12. Ashour & Johns, 1983; Podsakoff & Schriesheim, 1984.

13. Ashour & Johns, 1983. Also see Podsakoff, P. M. (1982). Determinants of a supervisor's use of rewards and punishments: A literature review and suggestions for further research. *Organizational Behavior and Human Performance, 29,* 58–83.

14. For a review of evidence, see Kerr & Schriesheim, 1974.

15. Fiedler, F. E. (1967). *A theory of leadership effectiveness.* New York: McGraw-Hill; Fiedler, F. E., & Chemers, M. M. (1974). *Leadership and effective management.* Glenview, IL: Scott, Foresman; Fiedler, F. E. (1978). The contingency model and the dynamics of the leadership process. In L. Berkowitz (Ed.), *Advances in experimental social psychology* (Vol. 11). New York: Academic Press.

16. For a summary, see Fiedler, 1978.

17. See Ashour, A. S. (1973). The contingency model of leader effectiveness: An evaluation. *Organizational Behavior and Human Performance, 9,* 339–355; Graen, G. B., Alvares, D., Orris, J. B., & Martella, J. A. (1970). The contingency model of leadership effectiveness: Antecedent and evidential results. *Psychological Bulletin, 74,* 285–296.

18. Peters, L. H., Hartke, D. D., & Pohlmann, J. T. (1985). Fiedler's contingency theory of leadership: An application of the meta-analysis procedures of Schmidt and Hunter. *Psychological Bulletin, 97,* 274–285; Strube, M. J., & Garcia, J. E. (1981). A meta-analytic investigation of Fiedler's contingency model of leadership effectiveness. *Psychological Bulletin, 90,* 307–321.

19. The best descriptions of the theory can be found in House, R. J., & Dessler, G. (1974). The path-goal theory of leadership: Some post hoc and a priori tests. In J. G. Hunt & L. L. Larson (Eds.), *Contingency approaches to leadership.* Carbondale, IL: Southern Illinois University Press; House, R. J., & Mitchell, T. R. (1974, Autumn). Path-goal theory of leadership. *Journal of Contemporary Business,* 81–97; Filley, House, & Kerr, 1976.

20. House & Dessler, 1974; House & Mitchell, 1974; Filley, House, & Kerr, 1976.

21. See, for example, Greene, C. N. (1979). Questions of causation in the path-goal theory of leadership. *Academy of Management Journal, 22,* 22–41; Griffin, R. W. (1980). Relationships among indi-

vidual, task design, and leader behavior variables. *Academy of Management Journal, 23,* 665–683.

22. Mitchell, T. R. (1973). Motivation and participation: An integration. *Academy of Management Journal, 16,* 160–179.

23. Maier, N. R. F. (1973). *Psychology in industrial organizations* (4th ed.). Boston: Houghton Mifflin; Maier, N. R. F. (1970). *Problem solving and creativity in individuals and groups.* Belmont, CA: Brooks/Cole.

24. Maier, 1970, 1973.

25. House & Baetz, 1979.

26. Strauss, G. (1955). Group dynamics and intergroup relations. In W. F. Whyte, *Money and motivation.* New York: Harper & Row.

27. Vroom, V. H., & Jago, A. G. (1988). *The new leadership: Managing participation in organizations.* Englewood Cliffs, NJ: Prentice-Hall; Vroom, V. H., & Yetton, P. W. (1973). *Leadership and decision-making.* Pittsburgh: University of Pittsburgh Press.

28. Vroom & Yetton, 1973, p. 13.

29. See Vroom & Yago, 1988, for a review. See also Field, R. H. G., Wedley, W. C., & Hayward, M. W. J. (1989). Criteria used in selecting Vroom-Yetton decision styles. *Canadian Journal of Administrative Sciences, 6(2),* 18–24.

30. Reviews on participation reveal a complicated pattern of results. See Miller, K. I., & Monge, P. R. (1986). Participation, satisfaction, and productivity: A meta-analytic review. *Academy of Management Journal, 29,* 727–753; Wagner, J. A., III, & Gooding, R. Z. (1987). Shared influence and organizational behavior: A meta-analysis of situational variables expected to moderate participation-outcome relationships. *Academy of Management Journal, 30,* 524–541; Wagner, J. A., III, & Gooding, R. Z. (1987). Effects of societal trends on participation research. *Administrative Science Quarterly, 32,* 241–262.

31. The transformational/transactional distinction is credited to Burns, J. M. (1978). *Leadership.* New York: Harper & Row.

32. Bass, B. M. (1985). *Leadership and performance beyond expectations.* New York: Free Press; Bass, B. M. (1990, Winter). From transactional to transformational leadership: Learning to share the vision. *Organizational Dynamics,* 19–31.

33. House, R. J. (1977). A 1976 theory of charismatic leadership. In J. G. Hunt & L. L. Larson (Eds.), *Leadership: The cutting edge.* Carbondale, IL: Southern Illinois University Press.

34. Conger, J. A., & Kanungo, R. N. (1988). Behav-

ioral dimensions of charismatic leadership. In J. A. Conger & R. N. Kanungo (Eds.), *Charismatic leadership: The elusive factor in organizational effectiveness.* San Francisco: Jossey-Bass; Conger, J. A., & Kanungo, R. N. (1987). Toward a behavioral theory of charismatic leadership in organizational settings. *Academy of Management Review, 12,* 637–647.

35. House, R. J., Woycke, J., & Fodor, E. M. (1988). Charismatic and noncharismatic leaders: Differences in behavior and effectiveness. In J. A. Conger & R. N. Kanungo (Eds.), *Charismatic leadership: The elusive factor in organizational effectiveness.* San Francisco: Jossey-Bass.

36. Howell, J. M. (1988). Two faces of charisma: Socialized and personalized leadership in organizations. In J. A. Conger & R. N. Kanungo (Eds.), *Charismatic leadership: The elusive factor in organizational effectiveness.* San Francisco: Jossey-Bass.

37. Hater, J. J., & Bass, B. M. (1988). Superiors' evaluations and subordinates' perceptions of transformational and transactional leadership. *Journal of Applied Psychology, 73,* 695–702; Avolio, B. J., & Bass, B. M. (1988). Transformational leadership, charisma, and beyond. In J. G. Hunt, B. R. Baglia, H. P. Dachler, & C. A. Schriesheim (Eds.), *Emerging leadership vistas.* Lexington, MA: Lexington Books.

38. Adapted from Katz, D., & Kahn, R. L. (1978). *The social psychology of organizations* (2nd ed.). New York: Wiley.

39. For a review of the evidence that concludes that leadership matters, see House & Baetz, 1979. For further discussion of this issue, see Thomas, A. B. (1988). Does leadership make a difference in organizational performance? *Administrative Science Quarterly, 33,* 388–400.

40. Pfeffer, J. (1977). The ambiguity of leadership. *Academy of Management Review, 2,* 104–112. Pfeffer also cites evidence that leadership is less important than other organizational factors.

41. Kerr, S. (1977). Substitutes for leadership: Some implications for organizational design. *Organizational and Administrative Sciences, 8,* 135–146; Kerr, S., & Jermier, J. M. (1978). Substitutes for leadership: Their meaning and measurement. *Organizational Behavior and Human Performance, 22,* 375–403.

42. Sheridan, J. E., Vredenburgh, D. J., & Abelson, M. A. (1984). Contextual model of leadership influence in hospital units. *Academy of Management Journal, 27,* 57–78; Howell, J. P., & Dorfman, P. W. (1981). Substitutes for leadership: Test of a construct. *Academy of Management Journal, 24,* 714–728.

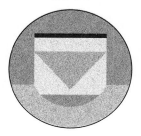

COMMUNICATION

TRI-CITY SOCIAL SERVICES AGENCY

Myra Greenfield sat at her desk and wondered why everything had gone so badly. A supervisor with Tri-City Social Services Agency, she had just had a performance review session with Otis Roberts, one of the social workers who reported to her. The meeting had begun well enough. Myra started by reviewing a number of positive points about Otis's performance. In doing this, she cited specific examples of his dedication to his clients and his skill in assisting them in improving their lives.

When Myra began to detail some of Otis's performance problems, things went sour fast. She could see him tense up and observed a scowl engulf his face. Most of his problems involved a blatant disregard of agency procedures and regulations in helping his clients. The most recent example involved his visiting a police station at midnight to help the jailed son of one of his clients. Visits of this nature were frowned upon by the agency, which had special channels established for such contacts. Myra had been told about the "midnight ride" by another supervisor, who had heard it from another social worker whose husband was a police officer. Although Myra had meant to discuss such incidents with Otis in the past, she had always put if off.

When Myra finished, Otis broke into an angry tirade.

"Look, Myra, I can't believe this! If you objected to some of my work tactics, why didn't you tell me before now? I've been doing these things for months and they've been helping my clients. It isn't fair to spring all this on me at performance review time. And how did you find out about my visit to the cop shop? Have you been spying on me? I went to the station directly because it just takes too long to get anything done through channels around here. That kid needed help fast! I knew it was wrong to go there, and I wanted to talk to you about it. But I just don't feel very welcome in your office, Myra. It's not what you say, it's how you *act*. Somehow, you just don't seem very interested in the problems of your social workers. And you sure don't seem to have much time for us."

■

This incident is interesting because it illustrates a communication breakdown caused by an earlier series of communication events. Otis went outside of approved channels of communication to help his clients. Myra found out about it through her own informal channels. Otis somehow felt that Myra wasn't interested in his work problems, even though she said she was. Both avoided communicating bad news to each other.

In this chapter we shall explore these and other aspects of communication in organizations. First, communication will be defined, a model of the communication process will be presented, and the importance of communication will be illustrated. Then two hypothetical extreme forms that organizational communication could take will be discussed. An exploration of the reality of organizational communication will explain why these extremes are not achieved. After this, superior-subordinate communication, the "grapevine," the verbal and nonverbal language of work, and cross-cultural communication will be investigated. Finally, several means of improving communication will be evaluated.

WHAT IS COMMUNICATION?

Communication is the process by which information is exchanged between a sender and a receiver. This seductively simple definition is broad enough to cover a wide variety of information exchanges. For example, the wall thermostat and the furnace in your house are constantly engaged in communication. The thermostat (sender) tells the furnace (receiver) how hot it should run. In turn, the furnace (sender) gives the thermostat (receiver) feedback about how hot it is running. This ongoing exchange of information contributes to your comfort.

The kind of communication we are concerned with in this chapter is *interpersonal* communication—the exchange of information between people. The most simple prototype for interpersonal communication is a one-on-one exchange between two individuals. Exhibit 11–1 presents a model of the interpersonal communication process and an example of a communication episode between a purchasing manager and her assistant. As you can see, the sender must encode his or her thoughts into some form that can be *transmitted* to the receiver. In this case, the manager has chosen to encode her thoughts in writing and transmit them via electronic mail. Alternatively, the manager could have encoded her thoughts in speech and transmitted them via a tape recording or face-to-face. The assistant, as a receiver, must *perceive* the message and accurately decode it to achieve accurate understanding. In this case, the assistant uses a parts catalog to decode the meaning of an "A-40." To provide *feedback*, the assistant might send the manager a copy of the order form for the flange bolts. Such feedback involves yet another communication episode that tells the original sender that her message has been received and understood.

This simple communication model is valuable because it points out the complexity of the communication process and demonstrates a number of points at which errors can occur. Such errors lead to a lack of correspondence between the sender's initial thoughts and the receiver's understanding of the intended message. A slip of the finger on the keyboard can lead to improper encoding. A poor electronic mail system can lead to ineffective transmission. An outdated parts catalog can result in inaccurate decoding.

EXHIBIT

11–1

A model of the communication process and an example.

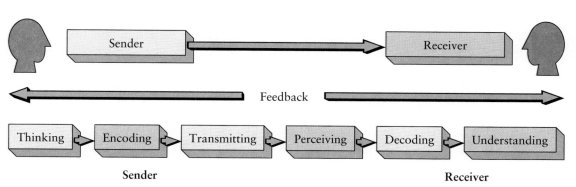

Thinking:
Purchasing manager says to herself, "I think we're getting short on A-40s."

Encoding:
Keyboards memo to assistant instructing him to order A-40s.

Transmitting:
Sends memo through electronic mail.

Perceiving:
Assistant reads memo.

Decoding:
Checks parts catalogue to find out what an A-40 is.

Understanding:
Realizes that he must place an order for flange bolts.

Source: From Glueck, W. F. (1980). *Management,* (2nd ed.). New York: Holt, Rinehart and Winston. Copyright © 1977 by Holt, Rinehart and Winston, Inc. Reprinted by permission of the publisher.

THE IMPORTANCE OF COMMUNICATION

The importance of communication for effective organizational functioning can be illustrated in two ways. First, we can consider the relationship between communication and the topics covered earlier in the book. Then, we can explore how much time organizational members spend communicating.

Think back to our discussion of the nature of organizations in Chapter 1. There, we defined organizations as social inventions for accomplishing goals through group effort. Obviously, organizational goals will not be accomplished if they are inadequately communicated to the individuals and groups that comprise the organization—members will work at cross-purposes. Going a step further, in Chapter 8 we defined groups as people interacting interdependently to achieve a common goal. The interaction referred to in this definition is a form of communication. Thus, at the most basic level, organizations wouldn't *be* organizations without communication among their members.

Less abstractly, it should be clear to you that *every* chapter in the book so far has been concerned implicitly with the exchange of information among organizational members. For example, the application of reinforcement and punishment (Chapter 3) is a form of communication because these stimuli contain important information. By the same token, our discussion of perceiving the motives of others in Chapter 4 described how we try to decode the social cues that they provide. In addition, our discussions of attitude change (Chapter 5), motivation (Chapter 6), and socialization (Chapter 9) revealed that these processes are often accomplished through interpersonal communication. Thus, communication is necessary for organizational effectiveness.

The importance of communication is also revealed by analyses of how organizational members spend their time at work. Careful studies of production workers indicate that they participate in between sixteen and forty-six communication episodes per hour.[1] Even the low figure of sixteen episodes works out to one episode every four minutes. As we move up the organization's hierarchy, it is evident that more and more time is spent communicating. For first-level supervisors of production jobs, various studies show that 20 to 50 percent of the boss's time at work is spent in verbal communication. When communication through paperwork is added, these figures increase to between 29 and 64 percent.[2] Moving our scrutiny to the levels of middle and upper management, we find that from 66 to 89 percent of managers' time is spent in verbal (face-to-face and telephone) communication.[3] Since these figures exclude other forms of communication (such as reading and writing letters, memos, and reports), it is obvious that the content of many managerial jobs is composed almost exclusively of communication tasks.

In summary, communication is important because it defines the nature of organizations, because it is a part of so many important organizational processes, and because it requires so much time.

THE EXTREMES OF ORGANIZATIONAL COMMUNICATION

To understand some of the basic issues involved in communication in organizations, let's consider two hypothetical extreme forms that such communication could take. As we shall see, the reality of organizational communication falls somewhere between these extremes. To do this, we will examine Blake Plastics, a hypothetical designer and producer of high-impact plastic products. A partial organizational chart for Blake is shown in Exhibit 11–2. Imagine that Blake has seventy members in total.

All-Channel Communication

At one extreme, each employee at Blake could in theory communicate with any of sixty-nine other members, for a staggering total of 2,415 potential communica-

EXHIBIT 11–2   **Partial organizational chart for Blake Plastics.**

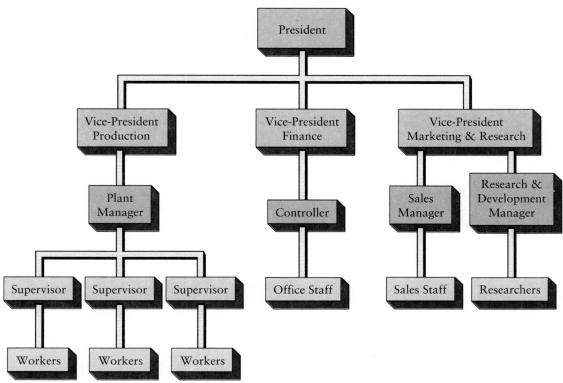

tion channels! (The relevant formula here is $N(N-1)/2$, where N equals the number of organizational members.) In fact, of course, this **all-channel communication** doesn't happen. For one thing, organizations are *designed* in part to discourage the completely free flow of information. This is one thing that separates an organization from a random collection of individuals. For example, if a salesperson receives evidence from a client that a particular product has flaws, the salesperson would not be encouraged to enter the plant and complain directly to the mold operator who had produced the product. Rather, there are "proper channels" that should be observed. Second, many organizational members may be *disinterested* in communicating with other members and even be unaware of their existence. For instance, a production worker might not know what a controller is, or who the controller is, even though the controller signs his paycheck! In summary, considerably fewer than Blake's 2,415 potential communication channels would actually be used.

Strict Chain of Command

Now let's consider the other extreme. The lines on Blake's organizational chart represent lines of authority and reporting relationships. For example, a vice-president has authority over the plant manager, who has authority over the production supervisors, and so on. Conversely, production workers report to their supervisors, who report to the plant manager, and so on. In theory, organizational communication could stick to this strict **chain of command.** Under this system, three necessary forms of communication can be accomplished.

- **Downward communication.** This is communication that flows from the top of the organization toward the bottom. For example, the vice-president of production might instruct the plant manager to gear up for manufacturing a new product. In turn, the plant manager would provide specifics to supervisors, who would instruct the production workers accordingly.
- **Upward communication.** This form of communication flows from the bottom of the organization toward the top. For instance, a research engineer might conceive a new plastic formula with unique properties. She might then pass this on to the research and development manager, who would then inform the relevant vice-president.
- **Horizontal communication.** This is communication that occurs between departments or functional units, usually as a means of coordinating effort. Within a strict chain of command, such communication would flow up to and then down from a *common superior*. For example, suppose a salesperson gets an idea for a new product from a customer. To get this idea to the research staff, it would have to be transmitted up to and down from the vice-president of marketing and research, the common superiors for these departments.

Clearly, a lot of organizational communication does follow the formal lines of authority shown on organizational charts. This is especially true with regard to the examples of upward and downward communication given above—directives and instructions usually pass downward through the chain of command, and ideas and suggestions pass upward. However, the reality of organizational communication suggests that the formal chain of command provides an underestimate of all the channels of communication that actually exist in organizations. Thus, the communication channels in any organization fall somewhere between the theoretical maximum of all-channel communication and the severely limited number prescribed by strict chain of command.

THE REALITY OF ORGANIZATIONAL COMMUNICATION

There are two major reasons why a formal chain of command is an underestimation of the number of communication channels within organizations.

Informal Communication

The chain of command obviously fails to consider *informal* communication between members. In previous chapters we discussed in some detail how informal interaction helps people accomplish their jobs more effectively. Within a particular work group, it helps employees coordinate their work efforts. Thus, two researchers in Blake's research and development unit might make an informal agreement to review each other's calculations and written reports before they are submitted to the boss. Similarly, the research and development manager might meet the plant manager on the golf course and ask whether any problems have been encountered in introducing a new product line. Of course, not all informal communication benefits the organization. An informal grapevine might spread unsavory, inaccurate rumors across the organization. We will discuss this process shortly.

The Chain of Command Is Often Ineffective

The formal chain of command also underestimates the number of communication channels that exist in organizations because managers recognize that sticking strictly to the chain is often ineffective. **Effective communication** occurs when the right people receive the right information in a timely manner (see Global Focus 11–1 on page 380). If any of these three conditions is violated, a particular communication episode is ineffective. In the story that began the chapter, Otis Roberts felt that communicating with the police through formal channels would be ineffective because it would not be timely.

Getting the right information to the right people is often inhibited by filtering. **Filtering** is the tendency for a message to be watered down or stopped altogether at some point during transmission, and it is something of a double-edged sword.

GLOBAL FOCUS 11–1

▼
....
At Benetton, Effective Communication Speeds Sales

Even the world's fastest factory won't offer much competitive advantage if everything it produces gets snagged in the distribution chain, a lesson Benetton the Italian sportswear company, has knit in its heart. Located in Ponzano, Italy, Benetton makes and distributes 50 million pieces of clothing worldwide each year, mostly sweaters, slacks, and dresses.

Benetton found that the fastest way to run a distribution system is to create an electronic loop linking sales agent, factory, and warehouse. If, say, a saleswoman in one of Benetton's Los Angeles shops finds that she is starting to run out of a best-selling red sweater in early October, she calls one of Benetton's 80 sales agents, who enters the order in his personal computer, which sends it to a mainframe in Italy. Because the red sweater was originally created on a computer-aided design system, the mainframe has all its measurements on hand in digital code, which can be transmitted to a knitting machine. The machine makes the sweaters, which factory workers put in a box with a bar code label containing the address of the Los Angeles store, and the box goes into the warehouse. That's right—one warehouse serves Benetton's 5,000 stores in 60 countries around the world. It cost $30 million, but this distribution center, run by only eight people, moves 230,000 pieces of clothing a day.

Once the red sweaters are sitting snugly in one of 300,000 slots in the warehouse, a computer sends a robot flying. By reading the bar codes, the robot finds the right box and any other boxes being shipped to the Los Angeles store, picks them up, and loads them onto a truck. Including manufacturing time, Benetton can get the order to Los Angeles in four weeks. If the company already has red sweaters in stock, it takes one week. That's quite a performance in the notoriously slow garment industry, where hardly anyone else will even bother with reorders. And if Benetton suddenly realizes that it didn't make any, say, black cardigans and purple blouses this year and they're hot, it can manufacture and ship a "flash collection" of black cardigans and purple blouses in huge quantities in a few weeks.

Source: Exerpted from Dumaine, B. (1989, February 13). How managers can succeed through speed. *Fortune*, 54–59, p. 13. Reprinted by permission of Fortune.

On one hand, employees are *supposed* to filter information. For example, production workers are not expected to inform their bosses of every trivial event that occurs on the job. Similarly, vice-presidents are not expected to communicate every detail of the management of the company clear to the shop floor. On the other side of the coin, overzealous filtering will preclude the right people from getting the right information, and the organization will suffer accordingly. Upward filtering often occurs because subordinates are afraid that their boss will use the information against them. Downward filtering is often due to time pressures or simple lack of attention to detail, but more sinister motives may be at work. As the old saying goes, "information is power," and some managers filter downward communications to maintain an edge on their subordinates. For example, a manager who feels that an up-and-coming subordinate could be promoted over her might filter crucial information to make the subordinate look bad at a staff meeting. The performance review at Tri-City Social Services indicated that both Myra and Otis had been filtering information.

Obviously, the potential for filtering increases with the number of links in the communication chain. For this reason, many organizations establish channels in addition to those revealed in the formal chain of command. For instance, many managers establish an **open door policy** in which any organizational member below them can communicate directly without going through the chain. Such a policy should decrease the upward filtering of sensitive information if subordinates trust the system. To prevent downward filtering, many organizations attempt to communicate directly with potential receivers, bypassing the chain of command. For example, the president of Blake Plastics might use the public address system to accurately inform employees about intended layoffs. Research has shown that certain types of information are more likely to be filtered than are others, thus indicating the selective need for alternative channels of communication. For example, information that is concerned directly with production might pass down through the hierarchy relatively intact, while that concerned with nonproduction matters (such as a change in the parking regulations) might be subjected to considerable filtering.[4]

The need for effective horizontal communication between departments probably provides the best example of why communication channels are established outside the formal chain of command. Returning to Blake Plastics, suppose the plant manager has an idea for cutting costs by modifying the construction of a particular product. Such an idea should be evaluated by the research and development manager and passed on to the research staff for detailed tests. Following the strict chain of command, this message would pass through the following sequence: Plant Manager → Vice-President Production → President → Vice-President Marketing and Research → Research and Development Manager. Obviously, this form of transmission is very inefficient. The large number of links in the chain increases the probability of filtering, and even if the message remains unfiltered, transmission time could be prohibitive. For this reason, many organizations form semiformal "bridges" or "gangplanks" between horizontal functions that need coordination.[5] At Blake, the plant manager would probably be encouraged to consult directly with the research and development manager.

In summary, informal communication and the recognition of filtering and time constraints guarantee that organizations will develop channels of communication beyond the strict chain of command. However, these channels will seldom approximate the total number available. Now, let's examine several aspects of organizational communication in detail.

SUPERIOR-SUBORDINATE COMMUNICATION

Superior-subordinate communication consists of the one-to-one exchange of information between a boss and a subordinate. As such, it represents a key element in upward and downward communication in organizations. Ideally, such exchange should enable the boss to instruct the subordinate in proper task performance, clarify reward contingencies, and provide social-emotional support. In addition, it should permit the subordinate to ask questions about his or her work role and make suggestions that might further the goals of the company or institution. As the story that began the chapter illustrated, such ideals may be difficult to achieve.

A survey of 32,000 employees in the United States and Canada asked them to rank their preferred and current sources of organizational information. As shown in Exhibit 11–3, the immediate supervisor was the actual source *and* the preferred source of most information.[6] In addition, perceptions that supervisors are good communicators tend to be correlated positively with organizational performance.[7] Thus, any organization would wish to establish good superior-subordinate communication.

How Good Is It?

The extent to which superiors and subordinates agree about work-related matters and are sensitive to each other's point of view is one index of good communication. Although the parties might "agree to disagree" about certain matters, extreme and persistent perceptual differences are problematic. Research has indicated that superiors and subordinates often differ in their perceptions of the following matters:

- How subordinates should and do allocate time
- How long it takes to learn a job
- The importance subordinates attach to pay
- The amount of authority the subordinate has
- The subordinate's skills and abilities
- The subordinate's performance and obstacles to good performance
- The superior's leadership style[8]

Perceptual differences of this nature suggest a lack of openness in communication, which might contribute to much role conflict and ambiguity, especially on the part of subordinates. In addition, there is substantial evidence that a lack of openness in communication reduces subordinate job satisfaction.[9]

Inhibiting Factors

What are the factors that contribute to communication problems between superiors and subordinates?

Conflicting Role Demands In the previous chapter we noted that the leadership role requires superiors to attend to both task and social-emotional functions. That is, the boss must simultaneously direct and control the subordinate's work *and* be attentive to the emotional needs and desires of the subordinate. Many superiors have difficulties balancing these two role demands. For example, imagine the following memo from a sales manager to one of the company's younger sales representatives:

> I would like to congratulate you on being named Sales Rep of the Month for March. You can be very proud of this achievement. I now

■
EXHIBIT

11–3

Preferred and current sources of information about organizational issues.

Preferred Ranking	Sources of Information	Current Ranking
1	My immediate supervisor	1
2	Small group meetings	4
3	Top executives	11
4	Employee handbook/other brochures	3
5	Local employee publication	8
6	Orientation program	12
7	Organization-wide employee publication	6
8	Annual state-of-the-business report	7
9	Bulletin boards	5
10	Upward communication program	14
11	The union	9
12	Mass meetings	10
13	Audiovisual programs	15
14	Mass media	13
15	The grapevine	2

Source: Foltz, R. G. (1985). Communication in contemporary organizations. In Reuss, C. & Silvis, D. (Eds.), *Inside organizational communication* (2nd ed.). New York: Longman, p. 10. Copyright © 1985 by Longman Publishing Group. Reprinted with permission of Longman Publishing Group.

look forward to your increased contribution to our sales efforts, and I
hope you can begin to bring some new accounts into the company.
After all, new accounts are the key to our success.

In congratulating the young sales rep and in suggesting that he increase his performance in the future, the manager tries to take care of social-emotional business
and task business in one memo. Unfortunately, the sales rep might be greatly
offended by this communication episode, feeling that it slights his achievement
and implies that he has not been pulling his weight in the company. In this case,
two separate communiques, one dealing with congratulations and the other with
the performance directive, would probably be more effective. Given misunder-
standings of this nature, it is not surprising that superiors and subordinates often
differ in their descriptions of the superior's leadership style.[10]

The Mum Effect Another factor inhibiting effective superior-subordinate communication is the **mum effect**. This distinctive term refers to the tendency to avoid
communicating unfavorable news to others.[11] Evidently, people would rather
"keep mum" than convey bad news that might provoke negative reactions on the
part of the receiver. For example, physicians are often reluctant to inform patients
or their families of the existence of terminal illness. At Tri-City Social Services,
Otis Roberts kept mum about his unorthodox work procedures, while Myra
Greenfield kept mum about her objections to them.

As the example involving the physician illustrates, the sender need not be *responsible* for the bad news in order for the mum effect to occur. For instance, a
structural engineer might be reluctant to tell her boss that cracks have been discovered in the foundation of a building, even though a subcontractor was responsible for the faulty work. It should be obvious, though, that the mum effect is
probably even more likely when the sender *is* responsible for the bad news. For
example, the nurse who mistakenly administers an incorrect drug dosage might
be very reluctant to inform the head nurse of her error. Research has shown that
subordinates with strong aspirations for upward mobility are especially likely to
encounter communication difficulties with their bosses.[12] This might be due in
part to the mum effect—employees who desire to impress their bosses to achieve
a promotion have strong motives to withhold bad news.[13]

As the story that began the chapter illustrates, the mum effect does not apply
only to subordinates. The boss might be reluctant to transmit bad news downward. In my research in one organization, I found that subordinates who had
good performance ratings were more likely to be informed of those ratings than
subordinates who had bad ratings. Managers evidently avoided communicating
bad news for which they were partly responsible, since they themselves had done
the performance ratings. Given this state of affairs, it is not surprising that managers and their subordinates often differ in their perceptions of subordinate performance.[14]

Status Effects A third factor that might inhibit superior-subordinate communication is the tendency for superiors to *devalue* communication with their subordi-

nates. In Chapter 8 it was pointed out that the status of group members affects communication patterns—people reveal a clear desire to communicate with people of a similar or higher status, rather than those of a lower status. From this, it follows that necessary communications with people of lower status, such as one's subordinates, might be viewed negatively. In an interesting study designed to test this proposal, managers were asked to record every communication episode that they engaged in during a week at work.[15] In addition to specifying the method of communication and identifying the other party, they were asked to report their attitude toward each episode on scales of the following nature:

Valuable							Worthless
Dissatisfying							Satisfying
Boring							Interesting
Precise							Vague

The results indicated a clear tendency for the managers to react more favorably to episodes with higher-status organizational members than to those involving their subordinates. It is reasonable to expect that subordinates catch on to such negative reactions and begin to withhold information, a situation that contributes to poor communication.

Time A final factor that might lead to poor superior-subordinate communication is the simple constraint of time. This is especially true at lower organizational levels. You will recall that we concluded that first-level supervisors spend between 20 and 50 percent of their working time in verbal communication. Furthermore, these studies reveal that most of this time is spent communicating with subordinates. Now, on the face of it, this seems pretty generous—subordinates may receive up to 50 percent of the boss's time on the job. However, there is a catch here. It must be remembered that many first-level supervisors have more than twenty subordinates reporting to them. Thus, simple division indicates that *each* subordinate might receive less than 1 percent of the boss's total time on the job each day. Indeed, three studies have indicated that superior-subordinate communication on production jobs averages only *four minutes* a day![16] Thus, it is entirely possible that Otis Roberts was correct when he said that Myra Greenfield didn't seem to have much time for her subordinates.

Before continuing, pause and consider the impact of telecommuting on informal communication and superior-subordinate communication. See the You Be the Manager feature.

THE GRAPEVINE

Just inside the gate of a steel mill there was a large sign that read "X days without a major accident." The sign was revised each day to impress upon the work force the importance of safe working practices. A zero posted on the sign caught one's

YOU BE THE MANAGER

Telecommuting at Pacific Bell

The large telecommunications company Pacific Bell is based in California. In recent years, the company has gradually become increasingly interested in the concept of telecommuting. By telecommuting, employees are able to work at home but stay in touch with their offices via the computer network, voice mail, and electronic messages.

The possibilities of telecommuting were first called to Pacific Bell's attention during the Los Angeles Olympics, when it was adopted as a temporary measure to avoid the horrendous automotive gridlock that was expected when games visitors were added to the city's already clogged freeways. Shortly thereafter, Pacific Bell implemented a pilot project to examine telecommuting, using 100 volunteer managers. On hearing about the project, 400 other managers developed informal arrangements with their bosses to begin telecommuting. Necessity was added to popularity when a large earthquake struck the San Francisco area in fall of 1989. With the Bay Bridge damaged, leading to impossibly long commutes, the value of telecommuting in times of emergency was obvious.

During this period, Pacific Bell realized that it had to get a clear fix on the consequences of telecommuting. Thus, it conducted a survey of managers' opinions. Also, it realized that it had to develop a company policy concerning telecommuting.

Considering its implications for organization communication, what are *your* views about telecommuting?

1. What are the pros and cons of telecommuting?
2. What are some policies you would put in place concerning telecommuting?

To find out what Pacific Bell's survey showed and some details of its telecommuting policy, see The Manager's Notebook at the end of the chapter.

Source: Adapted from Bailey, D. S., & Foley, J. (1990, August). Pacific Bell works long distance. *HR Magazine*, 50–52.

attention immediately, since this meant that a serious accident or fatality had just occurred. Seeing a zero upon entering the mill, workers seldom took more than five minutes to find someone who knew the details. While the victim's name might be unknown, the location and nature of the accident were always accurate, even though the mill was very large and the accident had often occurred on the previous shift. How did this information get around so quickly? It travelled through the "grapevine." In the story that began the chapter, Myra found out about Otis's "midnight ride" to the police station through the grapevine.

Characteristics of the Grapevine

The **grapevine** is the informal communication network that exists in any organization. As such, the grapevine often cuts across formal lines of communication that are recognized by management. Observation suggests several distinguishing features of grapevine systems:

- We generally think of the grapevine as communicating information by word of mouth. However, written notes and fax massages may contribute to the transmission of information. For example, a fax operator in the New York office might tell the Zurich office that the chairman's wife just had a baby.
- Organizations often have several grapevine systems, some of which may be loosely coordinated. For instance, a secretary who is part of the "office grapevine" might communicate information to a mail carrier, who passes it on to the "warehouse grapevine."
- The grapevine may transmit information relevant to the performance of the organization as well as personal gossip. Many times, it is difficult to distinguish between the two: "You won't *believe* who just got fired!"

How accurate is the grapevine? One expert concludes that at least 75 percent of the noncontroversial organizationally-related information carried by the grapevine is correct.[17] Personal information and emotionally charged information are most likely to be distorted.

Grapevine information does not run through organizations in a neat chain in which person A tells only person B who tells only person C, etc. Neither does it sweep across the organization like a tidal wave, with each sender telling six or seven others, who each in turn transmit the information to six or seven *other* members. Rather, only a proportion of those who receive grapevine news pass it on, with the net effect that more "know" than "tell."[18]

Who Participates in the Grapevine?

Just who is likely to tell? That is, who is likely to be a transmitter of grapevine information? Personality characteristics may play a role. For instance, extroverts might be more likely to pass on information than introverts. Similarly, those who lack self-esteem might pass on information that gives them a personal advantage.

The nature of the information might also influence who chooses to pass it on. In a hospital, the news that a doctor has obtained a substantial cancer research grant might follow a very different path from news involving his affair with a nurse!

Finally, it is obvious that the *physical* location of organizational members is related to their opportunity to both receive and transmit news via the "vine." Occupants of work stations that receive a lot of traffic are good candidates to be grapevine transmitters. A warm control room in a cold plant or an air-conditioned computer room in a sweltering factory might provide their occupants with a steady stream of potential receivers for juicy information. On the other side of the coin, jobs that require movement throughout the organization also give their holders much opportunity to serve as grapevine transmitters. Mail carriers and maintenance personnel are good examples. Or, consider the daily arrival of the man who picked up the production of an isolated group of factory workers:

> The arrival . . . was always a noisy one, like the arrival of a daily passenger train in an isolated small town. Interaction attained a quick peak of intensity to crowd into a few minutes all communications necessary and otherwise. . . . News items would be dropped, some of serious import, such as reports of accomplished or impending layoffs in the various plants of the company, or of gains or losses in orders for company products. Most of the news items, however, involved bits of information on plant employees told in a light vein.[19]

Pros and Cons of the Grapevine

Is the grapevine desirable from the organization's point of view or not? As the above quotation illustrates, it can keep employees informed about important organizational matters such as job security. In some organizations, management is so notoriously lax at this that the grapevine is a regular substitute for formal communication. (As shown in Exhibit 11–3, the grapevine is perceived as the second most common but least preferred source of information!) The grapevine can also provide a test of employee reactions to proposed changes without making formal commitments. Managers have been known to "leak" ideas (such as a change to a four-day workweek) to the grapevine in order to probe their potential acceptance. Finally, participation in the grapevine can add a little interest and diversion to the work setting. In this context, it is simply part of the informal grouping system discussed in Chapter 8.

The grapevine can become a real problem for the organization when it becomes a constant pipeline for rumors. A **rumor** is an unverified belief that is in general circulation.[20] The key word here is *unverified*—although it is possible for a rumor to be true, it is not likely to *remain* true as it runs through the grapevine (see the cartoon.) Because the information cannot be verified as accurate, rumors are susceptible to severe distortion as they are passed from person to person.

Source: Drawing by Ziegler, © 1972 The New Yorker Magazine, Inc.

The distortion of rumors can take two forms. Some rumors seem to get longer and more complex as each sender adds his or her "two cents' worth." Other rumors are simplified through retelling, enhancing ease of communication. When this occurs, unfamiliar, difficult-to-remember details will usually be omitted, while interesting, dynamic details will be embellished. For example, a rumor that begins as:

> Paul Jones was laid off because of the installation of that new automated casting machine. They think he'll be back on another job soon.

may end up as:

> Word is that automation will cost a lot of jobs around here. Some guys are already gone.

Rumors seem to spread fastest and farthest when the information is especially ambiguous, when the content of the rumor is important to those involved, and when the recipient is emotionally aroused.[21] Thus, the rumor about Paul Jones would probably circulate most widely among production workers rather than office personnel, and it would probably be more potent if the economic climate of the community was bad.

Increasingly difficult global competition, staff reductions, and restructuring have placed a recent premium on rumor control. At the same time, the tendency to be mum about giving bad news should be avoided. DuPont is a firm that has received good marks for communicating with employees early and accurately about impending staff reductions. Similarly, Equitable Life acted quickly and effectively to quash rumors that it was going bankrupt.

THE VERBAL LANGUAGE OF WORK

A friend of mine just moved into a new neighborhood. In casual conversation with a neighbor, he mentioned that he was "writing a book on OB." She replied with some enthusiasm, "Oh, that's great. My husband's in obstetrics too!" My friend, of course, is a management professor who was writing an organizational behavior book. The neighbor's husband was a physician who specialized in delivering babies.

Every student knows what it means to do a little "cramming" in the "caf" before an exam. Although this phrase might sound vaguely obscene to the uninitiated listener, it reveals how circumstances shape our language and how we often take this shaping for granted. In many jobs, occupations, and organizations we see the development of a specialized language or **jargon** that associates use to communicate with each other. Thus, OB means organizational behavior to management professors and obstetrics to physicians.

Dr. Rosabeth Moss Kanter, in studying a large corporation, discovered its attempt to foster COMVOC, or "common vocabulary," among its managers.[22] Here, the goal was to facilitate communication among employees who were often geographically separated, unknown to each other, and "meeting" impersonally through telex or memo. COMVOC provided a common basis for interaction among virtual strangers. In addition, managers developed their own informal supplements to COMVOC. Upward mobility, an especially important topic in the corporation, was reflected in multiple labels for the same concept:

Fast trackers	One performers
High fliers	Boy (girl) wonders
Superstars	Water walkers

While jargon is an efficient means of communicating with peers and provides a touch of status to those who have mastered it, it can also serve as a *barrier* to communicating with others. For example, local jargon might serve as a barrier to clear communication between departments such as sales and engineering. New organizational members often find the use of jargon especially intimidating and confusing. For instance, consider the fledgling computer scientist who found himself assigned to a project group to develop a new computer:

> A *canard* was anything false, usually a wrongheaded notion entertained by some other group or company; things could be done in ways that created *no muss, no fuss*, that were *quick and dirty*, that were *clean*. *Fundamentals* were the source of all right thinking, and

weighty sentences often began with the adverb *fundamentally*, while *realistically* prefaced many flights of fancy. There was talk of *wars, shootouts, hired guns* and people who *shot from the hip*. The *win* was the object of all this sport and the *big win* was something that could be achieved by *maximizing* the smaller one.[23]

A second serious problem with the use of jargon is the communication barrier that it presents to those *outside* of the organization or profession. Consider the language of the corporate takeover, with its greenmail, poison pills, and white knights! Kanter, the researcher who studied COMVOC in a large corporation, found that wives of male executives could generate a total of 103 unfamiliar terms and phrases used by their husbands in relation to work![24] Such a situation might contribute to a poor understanding of what the spouse does at work and how work can make such heavy demands on family life.

THE NONVERBAL LANGUAGE OF WORK

Have you ever come away from a conversation having heard one thing yet believing the opposite of what was said? Professors frequently hear students say that they understand a concept but somehow know that they don't. Students often hear professors say, "Come up to my office any time," but somehow know that they don't mean it. In the case that began the chapter, Otis Roberts reported that he didn't feel welcome in his boss's office despite what she said. How can we account for these messages that we receive in spite of the words we hear? The answer is often nonverbal communication.

Nonverbal communication refers to the transmission of messages by some medium other than speech or writing. As indicated above, nonverbal messages can be very powerful in that they often convey "the real stuff" while words serve as a smoke screen. Raised eyebrows, an emphatic shrug, or an abrupt departure can communicate a lot of information with great economy. The minutes of dramatic meetings (or even verbatim transcripts) can make for extremely boring reading because they are stripped of nonverbal cues. These examples involve the transmission of information by so-called body language. Below we consider body language and the manipulation of objects as major forms of nonverbal communication.

Body Language

Body language is nonverbal communication that occurs by means of the sender's bodily motions and facial expressions or the sender's physical location in relation to the receiver.[25] Although a variety of information can be communicated via body language, two important messages involve the extent to which the sender likes and is interested in the receiver and the sender's views concerning the relative status of the sender and the receiver.

In general, senders communicate liking and interest in the receiver when they:

- Position themselves physically close to the receiver
- Touch the receiver during the interaction
- Maintain eye contact with the receiver
- Lean forward during the interaction
- Direct the torso toward the receiver[26]

As you can see, each of these behaviors demonstrates that the sender has genuine consideration for the receiver's point of view.

Senders who feel themselves to be of higher status than the receiver act more *relaxed* than those who perceive themselves to be of lower status. Relaxation is demonstrated by:

- The casual, asymmetrical placement of arms and legs
- A reclining, nonerect seating position
- A lack of fidgeting and nervous activity[27]

In other words, the greater the difference in relaxation between two parties, the more they communicate a status differential to each other.

As indicated earlier, when a contradiction exists between verbal behavior and body language, we tend to rely more heavily upon the information transmitted via body language. For example, the boss who claims to be interested in a subordinate's problem while positioning herself across the room, failing to maintain eye contact, and orienting her body away from the subordinate will doubtless signal a true lack of interest.

One area in which body language has been shown to have an impact is on the outcome of employment interview decisions. Employment interviewers are usually faced with applicants who are motivated to make a good verbal impression. Thus, in accord with the idea that "the body doesn't lie," interviewers might consciously or unconsciously turn their attention to nonverbal cues on the assumption that they are less likely to be censored than verbal cues. Research has shown that nonverbal behaviors such as smiling, gesturing, and maintaining eye contact have a favorable impact on interviewers when they are not overdone.[28] However, it is unlikely that such body language can overcome bad credentials or poor verbal performance.[29] Rather, increased body language might give the edge to applicants who are otherwise equally well qualified. Remember, in an employment interview, it's not just what you say, but also what you do!

Props, Artifacts, and Costumes

In addition to the use of body language, nonverbal communication can also occur through the use of various *objects* such as props, artifacts, and costumes. Consider the spontaneous use of a handy prop to make a nonverbal point:

> I have observed a plant superintendent in a concrete-block plant who absentmindedly picked up a small piece of broken brick while talking

to the foreman. As soon as he had left, the foreman ordered a half-hour of overtime for the entire crew to clean up the plant. Nothing had been actually said about it.[30]

Most of us are probably less creative than the superintendent and thus tend to do our communicating with less transient objects. For example, consider the manner in which people decorate and arrange their offices. Does this tell visitors anything about the occupant? Does it communicate any useful information? One observer thinks so:

> The more a person does influence his own surroundings, however, through decoration, personal artifacts, rearrangement, bringing in his own furniture, and the like, the more data he provides about who he is. A visitor can then get information fairly quickly about similarities and differences between himself and the occupant of the place. This can help in establishing a new relationship, since it provides more data about what realistic expectations the visitor may have of the occupant, and it may stimulate the visitor to disclose more information about himself than he would if they were in some anonymous place, starting from zero information.[31]

If personalization of one's office does communicate something about the personality of the occupant, another observer suggests that, in the company she studied, secretaries were more open than their bosses:

> Secretaries added a personal touch to Industrial Supply Corporation workplaces. Professional and managerial offices tended to be austere: generally uniform in size and coloring, and unadorned except for a few family snapshots or discrete artworks. . . . But secretaries' desks were surrounded by splashes of color, displays of special events, signs of individuality and taste of the residents: postcards from friends' or bosses' travels pasted on walls, newspaper cartoons, large posters with funny captions, huge computer printouts that formed the names of the secretaries in gothic letters.[32]

Does careful research confirm these observations of the decor and arrangement of offices transmitting nonverbal information? The answer is yes. One typical study found that students would feel more welcome and comfortable in professors' offices when the office was (1) tidy, (2) decorated with posters and plants, and (3) the desk was against the wall instead of between the student and the professor.[33] A neat office evidently signaled that the prof was well organized and had time to talk to them. Perhaps personal decoration signaled, "I'm human." When the desk was against the wall, a tangible barrier between the parties was removed. Other research has shown that persons who arrange their desks and visitors' chairs in an open and inviting manner are more outgoing and internally controlled.[34] Thus, it appears that visitor responses to variations in office decor might have some validity.

Frequently, the first few minutes of plays and movies have no dialogue. Despite this lack of verbal communication, we often learn much about the actors by means of the costumes they wear. In the right setting, proper costumes send clear messages—"I'm a stuffy English butler;" "I'm a damsel in distress;" "I'm a tough gangster." It stands to reason that the costumes worn by people in organizational settings also send nonverbal communications.

Does clothing communicate? "Wardrobe engineer" John T. Molloy is convinced that the clothing worn by organizational members sends clear signals about their competence, seriousness, and promotability. That is, receivers unconsciously attach certain stereotyped meanings to various clothing and then treat the wearer accordingly. For example, Molloy insists that a black raincoat is the kiss of death for an aspiring male executive. He claims that black raincoats signal "lower middle class," while beige raincoats lead to "executive" treatment both inside and outside of the firm. For the same reason, Molloy strongly vetoes sweaters for women executives. Molloy stresses that proper clothing will not make up for a lack of ambition, intelligence, and savvy. Rather, he argues that the wrong clothing will prevent these qualities from being detected. To this end, he prescribes detailed "business uniforms," the men's built around a conservative suit and the women's around a skirted suit and blouse.[35] The popularity of such thinking is revealed by a rise in the number of image consultants who help aspiring executives to "dress for success."

Research is beginning to reveal that clothing does indeed communicate.[36] Even at the ages of ten to twelve, children associate various brand names of jeans with different personality characteristics of the wearer! Such effects persist in adulthood, in which research simulations have shown that more masculinely dressed and groomed women are more likely to be selected for executive jobs. However, one study shows that there might be a point at which women's dress becomes "too masculine" and thus damages their prospects.[37] Observers note that women's clothing styles have been of special research interest because there is less clear consensus about just how female executives should dress.

If clothing does indeed communicate, it might do so in part because of the impact it has on the wearer's own self-image. Proper clothing might enhance self-esteem and self-confidence to a noticeable degree. One study contrived to have some student job applicants appear for an interview in street clothes, while others had time to dress in more appropriate formal interview gear. Those who wore more formal clothes felt that they had made a better impression on the interviewer. They also asked for a starting salary that was $4,000 higher than the job seekers who wore street clothes![38]

CROSS-CULTURAL COMMUNICATION

Consider a commonplace exchange in the world of international business:

A Japanese businessman wants to tell his Norwegian client that he is uninterested in a particular sale. To be polite, the Japanese says, "That will be very difficult." The Norwegian interprets the statement to mean that there are still unresolved problems, not that the deal is off. He responds by asking how his company can help solve the problems. The Japanese, believing he has sent the message that there will be no sale, is mystified by the response.[39]

Obviously, ineffective communication has occurred between our international businesspeople, since the Norwegian has not received the right information about the (non)sale. From the Norwegian's point of view, the Japanese has not encoded his message in a clear manner. The Japanese, on the other hand, might criticize the weak decoding skills of his Scandinavian client. Thus, we see that problems in communication across cultures go right to the heart of the communication model that we studied at the beginning of the chapter.

In Chapter 5 we learned that various societies differ in their underlying value systems. In turn, these differences lead to divergent attitudes about a whole host of matters ranging from what it means to be on time for a meeting to how to say "no" to a business deal (as illustrated above). In Chapter 5 we also noted that a surprising number of managers do not work out well in international assignments. It is reasonable to attribute many of these failures to problems in cross-cultural communication. Let's examine some important dimensions of such communication.

Language

Communication is generally better between individuals or groups that share similar cultural values. This is all the more so when they share a common language. Thus, despite acknowledged differences in terminology ("lift" versus "elevator," "petrol" versus "gasoline"), language should not prove to be a communication barrier for the American executive who is posted to a British subsidiary. Despite this generality, the role of language in communication involves some subtle ironies. For example, a common language can sometimes cause visitors to misunderstand or be surprised by legitimate cultural differences because they get lulled into complacency. Boarding a Qantas Airlines flight in Australia, I was attempting to pick up a magazine from a rack in the 747 when I was admonished by a male steward with the sharp words "First class, mate." I grinned sheepishly and headed back to my tourist class seat without the magazine. Wise to the ways of Australia, I was not offended by this display of brash informality. However, a less familiar North American, assuming that "They speak English, they're just like us," might have been less forgiving, attributing the steward's behavior to a rude personality rather than national style. By the same token, the steward would be surprised to learn that someone might be offended by his words.

As the Qantas example indicates, speaking the same language is no guarantee of perfect communication. In fact, the Norwegian and Japanese businesspeople described above might have negotiated in a common language, such as English.

Even then, the Norwegian didn't get the message. Speaking generally, however, learning a second language should facilitate cross-cultural communication. This is especially true when the second-language facility provides extra insight into the "communication style" of the other culture. Thus, the Norwegian would profit from understanding that the Japanese have sixteen subtle ways to say no, even if he couldn't understand the language perfectly.[40] Even though Americans are notoriously adverse to second-language learning, many executives seem to be getting the message in the face of the increasing globalization of business. (See Global Focus 11–2.) Although the language of international business is surely gravitating

---

GLOBAL FOCUS 11–2

▼
....
Second Language Helps Global Communication

Faced with ongoing globalization of their businesses, an increasing number of U.S. executives are learning a second language. **Du Pont** chief Executive Edgar S. Woolard Jr. just completed a crash course in Japanese. Other Du Pont managers are cramming second languages as well. So, too, are their counterparts at **Eastman Kodak, Citicorp, General Electric**'s Medical Systems division, and other corporations.

Says Phyllis Piano, a manager in the human resources department at GE Medical Systems: "Language does not make a person think globally, but it's a start." In 1985 only 13% of GE Medical Systems' business was overseas. That has grown to almost 50%, partly as a result of a 1987 deal where GE traded its consumer electronics business for cash and the medical equipment operation of French electronics giant **Thomson SA.**

Most big companies sign up with 111-year-old **Berlitz International** to teach executives to speak another language. Says Berlitz marketing director Patricia Sze: "There's been a steady upswing in corporate clients over the past four years." Enrollment in the company's corporate-oriented total emersion and other classes increased more than 50% between 1985 and 1988. Among the most popular languages for Americans attending Berlitz classes: French and German, though Japanese is picking up fast.

English classes account for 64% of Berlitz's business, internationally. No wonder. Many international companies have declared English as their official language, among them **Philips,** the Dutch electronics firm.

Source: Teitelbaum, R. S. (1989, December 4). Language: One way to think globally. *Fortune*, 11, 14. Reprinted by permission of Fortune.

toward English, learning the second language should provide better insight into the nuances of a business partner's culture.

Nonverbal Communication Across Cultures

From our earlier discussion of nonverbal communication, you might be tempted to assume that it would hold up better than verbal communication across cultures. While there are some similarities across cultures in nonverbal communication, there are also many differences. Here are a few examples:

- *Facial expressions.* People are very good at decoding basic, simple emotions in facial expressions, even across cultures. Americans, Japanese, and members of primitive New Guinea tribes can accurately detect anger, surprise, fear, and sadness in the same set of facial photographs.[41] Thus, paying particular attention to the face in cross-cultural encounters will often yield communication dividends. However, this doesn't always work because some cultures (such as that of Japan) frown upon the display of negative facial expressions, no doubt prompting the "inscrutable" label.
- *Gestures.* Except for literal mimicry ("I need food," "Sign here"), gestures do not translate well across cultures. This is because they involve symbolism that isn't shared. Most amusing are those cases in which the same gesture has different meanings across cultures:

  > In the United States a raised thumb is used as a signal of approval or approbation, the 'thumbs up' signal, but in Greece it is employed as an insult, often being associated with the expression 'katsa pano' or 'sit on this'. Another example is the ring sign, performed by bringing the tips of the thumb and finger together so that they form a circle. For most English-speaking people it means O.K. and is in fact known as the 'O.K. gesture'. But in some sections of France the ring means zero or worthless. In English-speaking countries disagreement is signalled by shaking the head, but in Greece and southern Italy the head-toss is employed to signify 'no'.[42]

- *Gaze.* There are considerable cross-cultural differences in the extent to which it is considered suitable to look others directly in the eye. Latin Americans and Arabs favor an extended gaze, while Europeans do not.
- *Touch.* In some cultures, people tend to stand close to one another when meeting and often touch each other as an adjunct to conversation. This is common in Arab, Latin American, and South European countries. On the other hand, North Europeans and North Americans prefer to "keep their distance."[43]

In an interesting experiment on nonverbal cross-cultural communication, English people were trained in social skills that were appropriate to the Arab world. These included standing or sitting close to others and looking into their eyes, coupled with extensive touching, smiling, and handshaking. Arabs were then introduced to a trained subject and to a control subject who had only been exposed to general information about the Middle East. When asked whom they liked better, the Arabs preferred the people who had been trained in their own nonverbal communication style.[44] We can well imagine a business meeting between English and Saudi bankers, both true to their cultures. The Saudis, gazing and touching, finish the meeting wondering why the English are so inattentive and aloof. The English, avoiding eye contact and shrinking from touch, wonder why the Saudis are so aggressive and threatening!

Etiquette and Politeness

Cultures differ considerably in how etiquette and politeness are expressed.[45] Very often, this involves saying things that one doesn't literally mean. The problem is that the exact form that this takes varies across cultures, and careful decoding is necessary to avoid confusion and embarrassment. Literal decoding will almost always lead to trouble. Consider the North American manager who says to a subordinate, "Would you like to calculate those figures for me?" This is really a mild order, not an opportunity to say no to the boss's "invitation." However, put yourself in the place of a foreign subordinate who has learned that Americans generally speak directly and expect directness in return. Should she say no to the boss? In some cultures, politeness is expressed with modesty that seems excessive to North Americans. Consider, for example, the Chinese visitor's response to a Canadian who told him that his wife was very attractive. The Chinese modestly responded, "No, no, my wife is ugly." Needless to say, what was said wasn't what was meant.

In social situations the Japanese are particularly interested in maintaining feelings of interdependence and harmony. To do this, they use a large number of set phrases or "lubricant expressions" that are designed to express sympathy and understanding, soften rejection, say no indirectly, or facilitate apology. To Europeans and North Americans who do not understand the purpose of these ritual expressions, they seem at best to be small talk and at worst to be insincere:

> Learning to use lubricant expressions may be as difficult and painful as it is important, particularly in cases where Japanese norms and values are in conflict with those commonly held by Americans. For instance, an American executive who attributes his success in the American business world to his being articulate, assertive, and decisive is likely to feel strong resistance to using softening lubricant expressions such as, "Well, I'm not really sure about this but . . . " or "It's difficult to say exactly but . . . " in English *or* in Japanese. The area of apologizing also often raises vehement negative reactions from Americans: "I'm not going to say 'I'm sorry' if I didn't do anything wrong"; "They're the ones who are at fault, so why should I apologize?"; "It seems almost dishonest to say we're sorry when we

aren't." Japanese, however, are more concerned with smoothing relationships and maintaining harmony than with "objective" determination of who is at fault. Thus, there are a number of rhetorical lubricant expressions of apology that are used regardless of whether one is "truly sorry" or "really at fault."[46]

Social Conventions

Over and above the issue of politeness and etiquette, there are a number of social conventions that vary across cultures and can lead to communication problems.[47] We have already alluded to the issue of directness. Especially in business dealings, North Americans tend to favor "getting down to brass tacks" and being specific about the issue at hand. Thus, the uninitiated businessperson might be quite surprised at the rather long period of informal chat that will begin business meetings in the Arab world or the indirectness and vagueness of many Japanese negotiators.

What is considered a proper degree of loudness for speech varies across cultures, and people from "quieter" societies (such as the United Kingdom) might unfairly view those from "louder" societies (such as the Middle East) as pushy or intimidating. What is considered proper punctuality also varies greatly around the world. In North America and Japan, punctuality at meetings and social engagements is expected and esteemed. In the Arab world and Latin America, being late for a meeting is not viewed negatively. In fact, one study found that being on time for an appointment connoted success in the United States and being *late* connoted success in Brazil.[48] Notice how an American businessperson might decode a Brazilian's lateness as disrespect, while the Brazilian was just trying to make a proper impression.

Finally, nepotism, favoring one's relatives in spite of their qualifications, is generally frowned upon in more individualistic societies such as North America and North Europe. However, in more collective cultures, such as those found in Africa and Latin America, people are expected to help their relatives. Hence, an American manager might view his Nigerian colleague's hiring his own son as irresponsible. The Nigerian might see it as irresponsible *not* to hire his own flesh and blood.

IMPROVING ORGANIZATIONAL COMMUNICATION

Thus far, we have discussed a variety of barriers to effective communication in organizations. In this section we shall discuss some relatively straightforward techniques that have been proposed to improve communication. More complex techniques will be considered in Chapter 13 (with regard to conflict reduction) and Chapter 17 (with regard to organizational development).

Choosing the Correct Medium

To communicate effectively, it is important to choose the correct medium to properly convey your intended message. Of particular importance is choosing a medium that can transmit information of appropriate richness. **Information richness** is the potential information-carrying capacity of a communication medium.[49] As shown in Exhibit 11–4, various media can be rank-ordered in terms of their information richness. A face-to-face transmission of information is very high in richness because the sender is personally present, audio and visual channels are used, body language and verbal language are occurring, and feedback to the sender is immediate and ongoing. A telephone conversation is also fairly rich, but it is limited to the audio channel, and it doesn't permit the observation of body language. At the other extreme, communicating via numeric computer output lacks richness because it is impersonal and uses only numeric language. Feedback to such communication might also be very slow.

At first thought, always using a rich medium might seem attractive. However, reflection indicates that this is not a good idea. Rich information media can be expensive and time consuming to use, and the messages that they convey can be difficult to send to a large number of receivers. Also, very rich media can inhibit some aspects of communication. For example, research shows that strangers working in face-to-face groups tend to use more inhibited speech than those

---

EXHIBIT

11–4

Communication media and information richness.

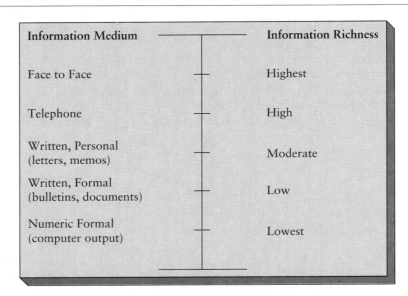

Information Medium		Information Richness
Face to Face		Highest
Telephone		High
Written, Personal (letters, memos)		Moderate
Written, Formal (bulletins, documents)		Low
Numeric Formal (computer output)		Lowest

Source: Daft, R. L., & Lengel, R. H. (1984). Information richness: A new approach to managerial behavior and organization design. *Research in Organizational Behavior, 6*, 191–233, p. 196. Reprinted by permission of JAI Press, Inc.

interacting via computer screens.[50] Also, participation tends to be more equal across group members when they interact via computer, a medium that is richer than a letter (because of fast feedback) but not as rich as the telephone (because of the lack of audio cues). Evidently, people (especially quiet types) are less likely to censor themselves when they are protected by the distance afforded by the computer.

A good rule to follow is that less routine messages require richer communication media.[51] Memos and written reports are fine for recurrent, noncontroversial, impersonal communication. New news, intended changes, controversial messages, and emotional issues generally call for richer (i.e., face-to-face or video) media. For example, faced with low product quality, senior management at luxury car maker Jaguar wanted to get the attention of middle management and then effectively implement change:

> They had middle managers listen to taped interviews with customers rather than read survey results. Each manager heard the intensity of customers' feelings abut dirty waiting rooms, incompetent mechanics, indifferent dealers, and "service that stinks." Hearing the customers' own words energized managers to do something about it. Jaguar senior managers then used face-to-face communications (speeches, task forces, one-on-one meetings) to implement the new strategic objective of high quality products.[52]

Middle managers at Jaguar listened to tapes of customer complaints. The depth of customer dissatisfaction required a rich communication medium. (Impact Photos/ Tony Stone Worldwide)

Exit Interviews

Exit interviews are interviews conducted with resigning or dismissed employees to gain useful information about problems affecting those who remain employed. As such, they represent an attempt to improve upward communication. The interviews are traditionally conducted by a management representative, the person's immediate superior, or someone from the personnel department.

In theory, exit interviews should provide some frank information about the work situation that employees who remain might be afraid to report for fear of reprisal. In fact, they don't appear to accomplish this goal. Several studies have demonstrated that reasons for resignation given in traditional exit interviews do not correspond to those given in follow-ups by researchers.[53] Since those provided to researchers tend to be more negative, it can be concluded that resigning employees hide their true feelings so as not to "burn their bridges" with management. Clearly, traditional exit interviews provide a poor source of upward communication.

Employee Surveys and Survey Feedback

In contrast to exit interviews, surveys of the attitudes and opinions of current employees can provide a useful means of upward communication. Since surveys are usually conducted with questionnaires that provide for anonymous responses, employees should feel free to voice their genuine views. A good **employee survey** contains questions that reliably tap employee concerns and also provide information that is useful for practical purposes. Survey specialists must summarize (encode) results in a manner that is easily decoded by management. Surveys are especially useful when they are administered periodically. In this case, managers can detect changes in employee feelings that might deserve attention. For example, a radical decrease in satisfaction with pay might be a precursor of labor troubles and signal needed revision of the compensation package.

When survey results are fed back to employees, along with management responses and any plans for changes, downward communication should be enhanced. Survey feedback shows workers that their comments have been heard and considered by management. Plans for changes in response to survey concerns indicate a commitment to two-way communication.[54]

Suggestion Systems, Query Systems, and Hotlines

Suggestion systems are designed to enhance upward communication by soliciting ideas for improved work operations from nonmanagerial employees. They represent a formal attempt to encourage useful ideas and prevent their filtering through the chain of command. The simplest example of a suggestion system involves the use of a suggestion box into which employees put written ideas for improvements (usually anonymously). This simple system is usually not very effective, since there is no tangible incentive for making a submission and no clear mechanism to show that a submission has been considered.

Much better are programs that *reward* employees for suggestions that are actually adopted and provide feedback as to how each suggestion was evaluated. For simple suggestions a flat fee is usually paid (perhaps $100). For complex suggestions of a technical nature that might result in substantial savings to the firm, a percentage of the anticipated savings is often awarded (perhaps several thousand dollars). An example of such a suggestion might be how to perform machinery maintenance without costly long-term shutdowns. When strong publicity is given to the adopted suggestions (such as explaining them in the organization's employee newsletter), downward communication is also enhanced, since employees receive information about the kind of innovations desired.

Related to suggestion systems are *query systems* that provide a formal means of answering questions that employees may have about the organization. These systems foster two-way communication and are most effective when questions and answers are widely disseminated. Many organizations have a column of questions and answers in their employee newsletters, the content ranging from questions about benefits to the firm's stock performance. Many libraries have adopted a similar system to answer queries from users about library services. One provides "Library Dialogue" forms that are routed to the library official most qualified to respond. Most completed forms and responses are then posted in a prominent location in the library so that others may learn from the dialogue.

Many organizations have adopted *telephone hotlines* to further communication. Some are actually query systems in that employees can call in for answers to their questions. For example, AT&T developed a "Let's Talk" program to answer employee questions about the impact of its antitrust divestiture, and C&P Telephone Companies has an interactive system to handle queries about equal employment opportunity and affirmative action. More common are hotlines that use a news format to present company information. News may be presented live at prearranged times or recorded for 24-hour availability. Such hotlines prove especially valuable at times of crisis such as storms, strikes, and so on.[55]

Supervisor Training

Is good communication a mysterious inherited art, or can bosses be trained to communicate more effectively with subordinates? The evidence suggests that proper training can improve the communication skills of supervisors. Notice the specific use of the word *skills* here. Vague lectures about the importance of good communication simply don't tell supervisors *how* to communicate better. However, isolating specific communication skills and giving the boss an opportunity to practice these skills should have positive effects. The supervisor who has confidence in how to handle delicate matters should be better able to handle the balance between social-emotional and task demands.

Effective training programs usually present videotaped models correctly handling a typical communication problem. Supervisors then role-play the problem and are reinforced by the trainers when they exhibit effective skills. At General Electric, for example, typical communication problems addressed with this kind of training have included discussing undesirable work habits, reviewing work performance, discussing salary changes, and dealing with subordinate-initiated discussions.[56]

It might seem that training of this nature is essentially focused on downward communication. However, there is much evidence that the disclosure of one's attitudes and feelings promotes reciprocity on the part of the receiver. Thus, the boss who can communicate effectively downward can expect increased upward communication in return.[57]

THE MANAGER'S NOTEBOOK

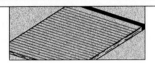

Telecommuting at Pacific Bell

1. Over 3,000 managers responded to Pacific Bell's survey about telecommuting. Expected advantages of the practice included increased job satisfaction and productivity and decreased stress. Many felt that productivity would be enhanced because of fewer interruptions (i.e., less unscheduled informal communication). Stress reduction was linked to the opportunity to avoid grinding commutes in urban areas. Negative aspects of telecommuting, although not strongly endorsed, centered on its potential damage to informal communication. These included decreased visibility when promotions were considered, problems in handling rush projects, and workload spillover for nontelecommuters.

2. Pacific Bell's telecommuting policy is designed to clarify the telecommuter's role so that superior-subordinate communication problems about the practice do not develop. Both parties sign an agreement, and either can terminate the telecommuting arrangement at any time. Telecommuting is generally done only on a part-time basis and for jobs in which productivity can be measured objectively. Telecommuters are required to be accessible during standard business hours and have a dedicated work space in their homes.

SUMMARY

- Communication is the process by which information is exchanged between a sender and a receiver. Organizational members (especially managers) spend a considerable portion of their time communicating. Effective communication involves getting the right information to the right people in a timely manner.
- In theory, any organizational member could communicate with any other in a totally random fashion. At the other extreme, communication could follow the strict chain of command. Both of these hypothetical extremes are unrealistic. All-channel communication is discouraged by the organization, while the chain of command fails to account for informal communication and may be extremely ineffective. This ineffectiveness stems from filtering and the long time it can take for information to pass through the chain.
- Superior-subordinate communication is frequently ineffective. The superior might have difficulty balancing task and social-emotional demands, and both superiors and subordinates might be

reluctant to inform each other of bad news (the mum effect). Also, superiors might devalue communicating with subordinates or simply not have enough time to spend interacting with them.

- The grapevine is the organization's informal communication network. Only a portion of people who receive grapevine information pass it on. Key physical locations or jobs that require movement around the organization encourage certain members to pass on information. The grapevine can be useful to the organization, and it often transmits information accurately. However, it becomes problematic when rumors (unverified beliefs) circulate.

- Verbal language that is tailored to the needs of a particular occupation or organization is known as jargon. While jargon aids communication between experienced associates, it can often prove confusing for new organizational members and people outside the organization. Nonverbal communication involves the transmission of messages by a medium other than speech or writing. One major form is body language, which involves body movement or the placement of the body in relation to the receiver. Much body language is subtle and automatic, communicating factors such as liking, interest, and status differences. Other forms of nonverbal communication involve office decoration, office arrangement, and the clothing worn at work.

- Communication across cultures can be difficult owing to obvious language differences but also to less obvious differences in nonverbal style, social conventions, and matters of etiquette.

- Richer communication media are necessary for less routine messages. Traditional exit interviews do little to enhance communication, while employee surveys and survey feedback, suggestion and query systems, and supervisor training may be useful in improving communication.

KEY CONCEPTS

Communication	Filtering	Nonverbal communication
All-channel communication	Open door policy	Body language
Chain of command	Mum effect	Information richness
Downward communication	Grapevine	Exit interviews
Upward communication	Rumor	Employee surveys
Horizontal communication	Jargon	Suggestion systems
Effective communication		

DISCUSSION QUESTIONS

1. Using Exhibit 11–1 as a guide, describe a communication episode that you have observed in an organization. Who were the sender and receiver? Was the episode effective? Why or why not?

2. Debate: Since more and more global business is being conducted in English, North Americans will not have cross-cultural communication problems in the future.

3. Why does the proportion of working time devoted to communication increase as we move up the hierarchy of the organization?

4. Describe or invent a situation in which communicating strictly by the chain of command would be very ineffective.

5. "It is very difficult to establish good superior-subordinate communication." What evidence would support this position?

6. Discuss the pros and cons of the existence of the grapevine in organizations. Suppose an organization wanted to "kill" the grapevine. How easy do you think this would be?

7. Interview someone who performs a job with which you are unfamiliar. Make a list of the unusual language or jargon used on this job and define the terminology. Why was this jargon developed?

8. Discuss a case in which you heard one message communicated verbally and "saw" another transmitted nonverbally. What was the content of each message? Which one did you believe?

9. Under what conditions might body language or clothing have a strong communicative effect? When might the effect be weaker?

■

EXPERIENTIAL EXERCISE

Cross-Cultural Confusion

The purpose of this exercise is to find out whether you can diagnose the reasons for the apparent work-related "cross-cultural confusion" illustrated in the three incidents below. In thinking through your diagnosis, you will be required to consider the relative impact of differences in cultural values versus other factors that might have caused the problem.

Working alone, read each incident and rank-order the potential explanations given for the problem in terms of their likelihood. Give a rank of 1 to the most likely, 2 to the next most likely, and so on. Also, jot down a brief rationale for your ranking that considers the cultural difference and other factors. Why or why not is a particular explanation correct? Following this, one of two procedures can be used:

_____ 1. The instructor can discuss the rankings with the class as a whole.
_____ 2. The class can break into small learning groups, discuss each incident, and develop a group ranking for each incident. Following this, the instructor can compare the group rankings and discuss them with the class as a whole.

Your instructor will give you the expert opinion about the explanations for the events given the cultures involved and the situational factors mentioned in the incidents. Of course, individuals are unique. The correctness of these explanations is based on a "typical" cultural response in the absence of other information.

Incident 1: Who's in Charge?

The president of Janice Tani's firm asked her, as chief executive of the marketing division, and her staff (three male MBAs) to set up and close an important contract with a Japanese firm. He thought his choice especially good as Janice (a Japanese American from California) knew the industry well and could also speak Japanese.

As she and her staff were being introduced, Janice noticed a quizzical look on Mr. Yamamoto's face and heard him repeat "chief executive" to his assistant in an unsure manner. After Janice had presented the merits of the strategy in Japanese, referring to notes provided by her staff, she asked Mr. Yamamoto what he thought. He responded by saying that he needed to discuss some things further with the head of her department. Janice explained that was why she was there. Smiling, Mr. Yamamoto replied that she had done an especially good job of explaining, but that he wanted to talk things over with the person in charge. Beginning to be frustrated, Janice stated that she had authority for her company. Mr. Yamamoto glanced at his assistant, still smiling, and he arranged to meet with Janice at another time.

Why did Mr. Yamamoto keep asking Janice about the executive in charge?

_____ 1. He did not really believe that she was actually telling the truth about who she was.
_____ 2. He had never heard the term "executive" before and did not understand the meaning of "chief executive."
_____ 3. He had never personally dealt with a woman in Janice's position, and her language ability caused him to think of her in another capacity.
_____ 4. He really did not like her presentation and did not want to deal with her firm.
_____ 5. He was attracted to her and wanted to meet with her alone.

Incident 2: Shaping Up the Office

Ronald, an ambitious young executive, had been sent to take over the Sales branch of his American company in São Paulo, Brazil. He spent a few weeks learning routines with the departing manager and was somewhat disturbed by the informality and lack of discipline that seemed to characterize the office. People seemed to indulge in excessive socializing, conversations seemed to deal more with personal than business matters and no one seemed to keep to their set schedules. Once he had formally taken over, he resolved to do something about this general slackness and called the staff together for a general meeting. He told them bluntly that work rates and schedules would have to be adhered to and hoped that a more businesslike atmosphere would prevail. Over the next few months he concentrated on improving office efficiency, offering higher bonuses and incentives to those who worked well and private warnings to those who didn't. By the end of the first quarter he felt he had considerably improved the situation and was therefore somewhat surprised to find sales figures had significantly dropped since his takeover.

What reason would you give to Ronald for this drop in sales?

_____ 1. He has probably lowered the office morale.

_____ 2. The salesmen probably resent his management style and are deliberately trying to make him look bad.

_____ 3. The salesmen would probably have responded better to a more participative approach to the problems.

_____ 4. Key Brazilian workers lost face through Ronald's actions.

Incident 3: Transmitting Information on Transmission Systems

"Adjustment to Japan has been much easier than I thought," Ted Owens told his wife about a year after their move from the United States. Ted had been sent by an automobile company in Detroit to see if he could establish production facilities for transmission systems that would be built in Japan and imported to the United States. Having been told that negotiations take a long time in Japan, he was not disappointed that it had taken a year for a major meeting to be set up with the key Japanese counterparts. But the Japanese had studied the proposal and were ready to discuss it this morning, and Ted was excited as he left for work. At the meeting people discussed matters that were already in the written proposal that had been circulated beforehand. Suddenly it occurred to Ted that there was an aspect of quality control inspection that he had left out of the proposal. He knew that the Japanese should know of this concern since it was important to the long-range success of the project. Ted asked the senior person at the meeting if he could speak, apologized for not having already introduced the quality control concern he was about to raise, and then went into his addition to the proposal. His presentation was met with silence, and the meeting was later adjourned without a decision having been made on the whole manufacture-importation program. Since Ted thought that a decision would be made that day, he was puzzled.

What was the reason for Ted's difficulty?

_____ 1. Ted had brought up quality control, an issue about which the Japanese are very proud. The Japanese thought that Ted was questioning their commitment to quality control.

_____ 2. Ted had brought up an issue on which there had not been prior discussion among the people somehow involved in that specific issue.

_____ 3. Ted had asked the senior person about speaking; in actuality, there was a younger person present who was in charge and Ted should have deferred to this person.

_____ 4. Expecting a decision in a year is still unrealistic. Ted should be more patient.

■

Source: Incidents from Brislin, R. W., Cushner, K., Cherrie, C., & Yong, M. (1986). *Intercultural interactions: A practical guide.* Pp. 157–158, 164–165, 172. Copyright © 1986 by Sage Communications, Inc. Reprinted by permission of Sage Communications, Inc.

The Nomizu Sake Company

The Nomizu Sake Company was founded in 1982 as a joint-venture between Nomizu International, a Japanese liquor importing firm based in southern California, and Woodland Farms Inc., an American rice-milling company with headquarters in northern California. The company was established in the San Francisco Bay Area, at an antiquated dairy factory which was renovated to suit the technological needs of sake production.

In its formative stage, the company brought over a team of Japanese sake makers from a small, agricultural village in northern Japan known for its sake making expertise. This team was led by a sake master, Mr. Toshiyuki Kawate, a good-natured, rotund, middle-aged man, characterized by his serene, Buddha-like disposition, steadfast traditional values, and sizable physical strength (he held a fifth-level black-belt standing in Judo). The Japanese team was originally housed in trailers on the factory premises and shared common kitchen and lavatory facilities. The younger sake makers took turns at being the group cook and shared housekeeping responsibilities. They worked long hours to set up the sake production area and develop a resilient yeast culture which would successfully serve as a catalyst for the rice fermentation process in the United States. A typical day for the Japanese team began with a thirty minute morning exercise routine which was led by Kawate, the sake master. Their day ended with a formal ceremonious work song which praised one another for their group effort and achievement for the day.

Nomizu Sake Company's management team was made up of Mr. Steven James, Sr., Chairman of the Board and President of Woodland Farms, Inc., his son, Steven James, Jr., Executive Vice-President, and Mr. Kenichi Nagano, Vice-President of Distribution and President of Nomizu International. James, Jr. was the only one of the triumvirate with an office at the company

site. Mr. Nagano was stationed at Nomizu International headquarters in Los Angeles and Steven James, Sr. at Woodland Farms, Inc. in Woodland. Steven James, Jr., a blonde-haired, blue-eyed, native San Franciscan, was typically American in his individualistic, entrepreneurial, straight-forward way of doing business. Outwardly cosmopolitan, he was in fact quite provincial in his attitudes toward the Japanese.

As the company grew, an American marketing, public relations and financial staff were brought in at company headquarters, as well as a Japanese/American salesforce. When full production commenced in the Fall of 1983, Mr. Kawate was promoted to Production Manager and additional production line workers were hired from the immediate vicinity of the factory to meet increased production demands. These workers came from a variety of backgrounds including students, expatriate housewives, student drop-outs, blue-collar workers, blacks, whites, Hispanics and Asian-Americans.

From the onset of the venture, management exhibited an awareness of certain problems that an international joining of this sort would produce. This awareness was limited, however, to the obvious communication difficulties that would arise from having monolingual Japanese nationals and Americans working under the same roof. Management made initial efforts to rectify this language problem by hiring Wendy Suzuki in 1982, at the company's inception, as the chief language instructor for the Japanese faction. A Japanese American born and raised in Japan, she gave private English lessons to the sake master six hours a week, after working hours, focusing on technical and basic survival skills. In addition, she conducted group English lessons for the junior sake makers.

It did not take much time to elapse before further problems of a more complex intercultural nature began to emerge in the company. As soon as full production began and production support was increased by hiring from the heterogeneous population of the San Francisco Bay Area, Kawate's monocultural methods of production management met with sizable resistance from the new

Source: Case prepared by Mary Yoko Brannen. From Morgan, G. (1989). *Creative organization theory: A resource book*. Newbury Park, CA: Sage, 1989. Reprinted by permission of the author.

workforce. A split in the workforce between the Japanese nationals and the multicultural Americans became pronounced. The newly hired Americans who had no cultural or artistic investment in sake making saw their job as a basic nine to five commitment of wage labor. They were characterized by their sense of individual identity, equal sense of status, informal style and direct assertiveness. In comparison, the Japanese nationals were characterized by a sense of group identity, respect for hierarchical status, formal style and indirect expression. Consequently, the American portion of the workforce, though initially intrigued by the novelty of Kawate's management techniques, soon grew tired of having to work past five o'clock p.m. to meet daily production quotas, as did their Japanese counterparts.

Consequently, Kawate called a meeting with James, Jr., to discuss the problems he was facing in the production area. James, Jr. called Wendy in to interpret for this session, and, after a brief discussion, he explained to Kawate that in America employees could not be expected to work overtime without some kind of monetary compensation. He went on to explain that since the Japanese workers were being paid on a salaried basis, overtime without compensation was not an unreasonable demand. If Kawate insisted that the other American workers, who were being paid on an hourly basis, should work overtime, then they would have to receive time and a half compensation. He further elaborated that because the Japanese workers would not have to receive extra compensation for overtime, and since they readily agreed to put in extra work, it was much more cost effective for the company to allow the Japanese to work overtime until production quotas were met and let the Americans go home at five o'clock as they wished.

As soon as the Japanese nationals saw that the seemingly aberrant behavior of their American co-workers was accepted by the management rather than reprimanded, they began to feel resentment and jealousy. Two of the younger Japanese workers followed the lead of their American co-workers and began punching out at five o'clock sharp. Group morale began to decline not only among the production workers as a whole, but also among the Japanese subunit as well.

By this time James, Jr., who had already increased Wendy's responsibilities to include becoming his private language tutor in an act of good faith toward the Japanese faction of the company, found it necessary to increase her responsibilities further. As more and more complex intercultural problems of the nature described above began to emerge and productivity and morale began to decline, she was called upon more frequently to interpret for James, Jr. and Kawate. These sessions which started out as short, thirty minute formalities, soon grew into frantic, five to six hour sessions of heated discussion, characterized by a high level of frustration on the part of everyone, where Wendy would continually try to find common cultural ground on which to center the issues at hand. James, Jr. was frustrated by what he called Kawate's "Japanese farmboy" mentality; Kawate was frustrated because he just could

not understand why what he thought were "givens" in effective management practice were being questioned; and Wendy was frustrated because the sessions were too long and strenuous for effective simultaneous interpretation and because she could not stay impartial throughout the whole process; sometimes she took the American side, sometimes the Japanese, and many times she felt too embarrassed and compromised to translate the vulgarities and accusations that were expressed.

In 1984 a tasting room was opened to encourage the public to try sake, and a director of the tasting room was hired, Ms. Carolyn Yuen, a young Chinese woman from Taiwan who was a recent college graduate with a degree in Public Relations. Wendy was called upon at this time to provide advice and educational background for the tasting room staff so that they would be better prepared to answer the various questions that their customers might have regarding Japan and sake. In addition she put together a verbal accompaniment to a slide show to be shown at tastings on the sake making process.

Occasionally, to supplement her income and for job diversity, Wendy would help serve sake and speak with customers in the tasting room. On one such occasion, she witnessed a slide show and much to her surprise and embarrassment, she saw that the tasting room staff had added a slide of Mr. Kawate's portrait to which the verbal accompaniment went something like this: "Mr. Kawate, the sake master at Nomizu Sake Company, nobly left his hometown of Niigata, Japan to come to the United States on a mission to share his art of sake making. His mission was not without sacrifice because by leaving Japan, Mr. Kawate has blacklisted himself from the profession of sake masters in Japan, never again to be able to return and resume his position in Japan." Immediately upon hearing this Wendy spoke with the director of the tasting room, Carolyn Yuen, and asked her how this addition had come about. She said she did not know who originated it, but it was a gallant story and the customers were always interested in it. Wendy's response was that it was outrageous, unkind and insensitive to fabricate a story which was not only untrue, but also quite seriously an attack on Kawate's moral character. She added that perhaps this was all done in innocence, but that the cultural implications of Kawate's losing face among his colleagues in Japan were very serious and that this practice should be stopped immediately before Kawate would catch wind of it. Despite Wendy's admonition, the tasting room staff continued to use the same story.

Finally, in a culture session with Kawate he told Wendy that he was aware that his portrait was being used in the slide show and asked her to translate the accompanying storyline. He understood most of it but was baffled by the meaning of the word "blacklist." Knowing that she too could share in Kawate's loss of face by owning up to her role in the situation—in Japan the whole organization loses face when an employee makes an error—she apologized for not having been effective in putting an end to the story and then proceeded to translate it for him. Kawate's reaction was very grave, as she had anticipated it would be. He immediately took her by the arm and led her into James, Jr.'s office, entered without knocking, and had her repeat to James, Jr. what she had translated. He then demanded an explanation from James, Jr. James, Jr. assured Kawate that he had not known about this and that he would take care of it right away. He would have the tasting room staff discontinue the story and make Kawate a formal apology. After Kawate had left James, Jr. demanded an explanation from Wendy as to why she had not come to see him before this had gotten back to Kawate. He punctuated his anger with accusatory phrases such as "How could you have let something as inconsequential as this get so out of hand?" and "Where are your loyalties placed anyway?" The next day Wendy was told at a formal meeting of the tasting room staff that her services there were no longer needed. From that time on she was called upon less frequently to interpret and work as cultural liaison for James, Jr. Within a period of about three months she ceased to hear from the company.

1. How effective is communication at the Nomizu Sake Company? Cite specific examples in which ineffective communication occurred.

2. Is there evidence of the mum effect in the case?

3. Discuss how different cultural values between Japan and the United States shape the events in the case.

4. Discuss some of the more subtle problems caused by a lack of a common language between James, Jr. and Mr. Kawate.

5. Evaluate Wendy Suzuki's effectiveness. Is there anything that she should have done differently?

6. Evaluate James, Jr.'s effectiveness. What could he have done to improve communication at Nomizu?

REFERENCES

1. Meissner, M. (1976). The language of work. In R. Dubin (Ed.), *Handbook of work, organization, and society*. Chicago: Rand McNally.

2. Meissner, 1976.

3. Mintzberg, H. (1973). *The nature of managerial work*. New York: Harper & Row.

4. Davis, K. (1968). Success of chain-of-command oral communication in a manufacturing management group. *Academy of Management Journal, 11*, 379–387.

5. Fayol, H. (1916/1949). *General and industrial management* (trans. by C. Storrs). New York: Pitman.

6. Foltz, R. G. (1985). Communication in contemporary organizations. In C. Reuss & D. Silvis (Eds.), *Inside organizational communication* (2nd ed.). New York: Longman.

7. Snyder, R. A., & Morris, J. H. (1984). Organizational communication and performance. *Journal of Applied Psychology, 69*, 461–465.

8. From an unpublished review by the author. Some studies are cited in Jablin, F. M. (1979). Superior-subordinate communication: The state of the art. *Psychological Bulletin, 86*, 1201–1222. See also Dansereau, F., & Markham, S. E. (1987). Superior-subordinate communication: Multiple levels of analysis. In F. Jablin, L. Putnam, K. H. Roberts, & L. W. Porter (Eds.), *Handbook of organizational communication*. Newbury Park, CA: Sage.

9. Jablin, 1979.

10. Mitchell, T. R. (1970). The construct validity of three dimensions of leadership research. *Journal of Social Psychology, 80*, 89–94; Jago, A. G., & Vroom, V. H. (1975). Perceptions of leadership style: Superior and subordinate descriptions of decision-making behavior. *Organizational and Administrative Sciences, 6*, 103–120.

11. Tesser, A., & Rosen, S. (1975). The reluctance to transmit bad news. In L. Berkowitz (Ed.), *Advances in experimental social psychology* (Vol. 8). New York: Academic Press.

12. Read, W. (1962). Upward communication in industrial hierarchies. *Human Relations, 15*, 3–16; For related studies, see Jablin, 1979.

13. Evidence that subordinates tend to suppress communicating negative news to the boss can be found in O'Reilly, C. A., & Roberts, K. H. (1974). Information filtration in organizations: Three experiments. *Organizational Behavior and Human Performance, 11*, 253–265.

14. Thornton, G. C., III. (1980). Psychometric properties of self-appraisals of job performance. *Personnel Psychology, 33*, 263–271; Ashford, S. J. (1989). Self-assessments in organizations: A literature review and integrated model. *Research in Organizational Behavior, 11*, 133–174.

15. Lawler, E. E., III, Porter, L. W., & Tennenbaum, A. (1968). Managers' attitudes

toward interaction episodes. *Journal of Applied Psychology, 52,* 432–439. For a similar study with similar results, see Whitely, W. (1984). An exploratory study of managers' reactions to properties of verbal communication. *Personnel Psychology, 37,* 41–59.

16. Reviewed by Meissner, 1976.

17. Davis, K. (1977). *Human behavior at work* (5th ed.). New York: McGraw-Hill.

18. Davis, K. (1953). Management communication and the grapevine. *Harvard Business Review,* 31(5), 43–49; Sutton, H., & Porter, L. W. (1968). A study of the grapevine in a governmental organization. *Personnel Psychology, 21,* 223–230.

19. Roy, D. F. (1960). "Banana time": Job satisfaction and informal interaction. *Human Organization, 18,* 158–168, p. 162.

20. Rosnow, R. L. (1980). Psychology of rumor reconsidered. *Psychological Bulletin, 87,* 578–591.

21. However, as Rosnow, 1980, points out, the evidence for these conditions is sparse. Specifically, rumors might become important because they are rumors, rather than the other way around.

22. Kanter, R. M. (1977). *Men and women of the corporation.* New York: Basic Books.

23. Kidder, T. (1981). *The soul of a new machine.* Boston: Little, Brown, p. 46.

24. Kanter, 1977.

25. For reviews, see Heslin, R., & Patterson, M. L. (1982). *Nonverbal behavior and social psychology.* New York: Plenum; Harper, R. G., Wiens, A. N., & Matarazzo, J. D. (1978). *Nonverbal communication: The state of the art.* New York: Wiley.

26. Mehrabian, A. (1972). *Nonverbal communication.* Chicago: Aldine-Atherton.

27. Mehrabian, 1972.

28. Edinger, J. A., & Patterson, M. L. (1983). Nonverbal involvement and social control. *Psychological Bulletin, 93,* 30–56.

29. Rasmussen, K. G., Jr. (1984). Nonverbal behavior, verbal behavior, resume credentials, and selection interview outcomes. *Journal of Applied Psychology, 69,* 551–556.

30. Meissner, 1976, p. 244.

31. Steele, F. I. (1973). *Physical settings and organizational development.* Reading, MA: Addison-Wesley.

32. Kanter, 1977, p. 69.

33. Campbell, D. E. (1979). Interior office design and visitor response. *Journal of Applied Psychology, 64,* 648–653. For a replication, see Morrow, P. C., & McElroy, J. C. (1981). Interior office design and visitor response: A constructive replication. *Journal of Applied Psychology, 66,* 646–650.

34. McElroy, J. C., Morrow, P. C., & Ackerman, R. J. (1983). Personality and interior office design: Exploring the accuracy of visitor attributions. *Journal of Applied Psychology, 68,* 541–544.

35. Molloy, J. T. (1975). *Dress for success.* New York: Warner; Molloy, J. T. (1977). *The woman's dress for success book.* Chicago: Follett.

36. Solomon, M. R. (1986, April). Dress for effect. *Psychology Today,* 20–28; Solomon, M. R. (Ed.). (1985). *The psychology of fashion.* New York: Lexington.

37. Forsythe, S., Drake, M. F., & Cox, C. E. (1985). Influence of applicant's dress on interviewer's selection decisions. *Journal of Applied Psychology, 70,* 374–378.

38. Solomon, 1986.

39. Adler, N. J. (1986). *International dimensions of organizational behavior.* Boston: Kent, p. 53.

40. Ramsey, S., & Birk, J. (1983). Preparation of North Americans for interaction with Japanese: Considerations of language and communication style. In D. Landis & R. W. Brislin (Eds.), *Handbook of intercultural training* (Vol. III). New York: Pergamon.

41. Ekman, P. (Ed.). (1982). *Emotion in the human face* (2nd ed.). Cambridge: Cambridge University Press.

42. Furnham, A., & Bocher, S. (1986). *Culture shock: Psychological reactions to unfamiliar environments.* London: Methuen, pp. 207–208.

43. Examples on gaze and touch draw on Furnham & Bocher, 1986; Argyle, M. (1982). Inter-cultural communication. In S. Bochner (Ed.), *Cultures in contact: Studies in cross-cultural interaction.* Oxford: Pergamon.

44. Collett, P. (1971). Training Englishmen in the non-verbal behaviour of Arabs: An experiment on intercultural communication. *International Journal of Psychology, 6,* 209–215.

45. Furnham & Bochner, 1986; Argyle, 1982.

46. Ramsey & Birk, 1983, p. 235.

47. Furnham & Bochner, 1986; Argyle, 1982.

48. Levine, R., West, L. J., & Reis, H. T. (1980). Perceptions of time and punctuality in the United States and Brazil. *Journal of Personality and Social Psychology, 38,* 541–550.

49. Daft, R. L., & Lengel, R. H. (1984). Information richness: A new approach to managerial behavior and organizational design. *Research in Organizational Behavior, 6,* 191–233.

50. Siegel, J., Dubrovsky, V., Kiesler, S., & McGuire, T. W. (1986). Group processing in computer medi-

ated communication. *Organizational Behavior and Human Decision Processes, 37,* 157–187.

51. Lengel, R. H., & Daft, R. L. (1988, August). The selection of communication media as an executive skill. *Academy of Management Executive,* 225–232.

52. Lengel & Daft, 1988, p. 230.

53. Lefkowitz, J., & Katz, M. L. (1969). Validity of exit interviews. *Personnel Psychology, 22,* 445–456; Hinrichs, J. R. (1975). Measurement of reasons for resignation of professionals: Questionnaire versus company and consultant exit interviews. *Journal of Applied Psychology, 60,* 530–532.

54. For a good description of how to develop and use organizational surveys, see Dunham, R. B., & Smith, F. J. (1979). *Organizational surveys.* Glenview, IL: Scott, Foresman.

55. Taft, W. F. (1985). Bulletin boards, exhibits, hotlines. In C. Reuss & D. Silvis (Eds.), *Inside organizational communication* (2nd ed.). New York: Longman.

56. Burnaska, R. (1976). The effects of behavior modeling training upon managers' behaviors and employees' perceptions. *Personnel Psychology, 29,* 329–335.

57. Capella, J. N. (1981). Mutual influence in expressive behavior: Adult-adult and infant-adult dyadic interaction. *Psychological Bulletin, 89,* 101–132.

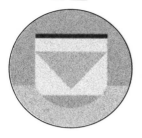

CHAPTER 12

DECISION MAKING

Barbara Lane's bedside phone rang at 3:21 A.M. She answered groggily, and it took several moments for the news to sink in. Matt Klein was dead, killed in a car accident on his way home from a party. Barbara was chairperson of the board of directors of Glamor International, an East Coast chain of retail clothing stores. Matt Klein had been Glamor's successful president for eight years.

Guiding her Mercedes through the morning rush hour, Barbara reflected that it would be a problem to find a good replacement for Matt. He had been a real "hands-on" executive, doing much of the important fashion buying personally. He spoke French fluently and was well acquainted with the customs and business practices of the Far East. Thus, his frequent buying trips to France, Hong Kong, and Taiwan had always been very successful. To Barbara, the issue was clear: Find a replacement just like Matt.

When she arrived at the office, Barbara called the members of the board and advised them of her intended course of action. She would call several headhunting agencies with experience in the fashion trade and have them screen applicants. Also, she would consult with several executives she knew in the industry.

Within two weeks, twelve candidates for the job had been identified. Barbara had their résumés and dossiers copied and sent by courier to the board members. A meeting was called for the next day to decide who would be interviewed by the board. Although many members found the lengthy file too much to digest in one evening, none mentioned this.

Barbara opened the meeting with a short, pointed speech. "Ladies and gentlemen, the obvious problem we face here is finding a new president who is as similar as possible to our able former president, Matt Klein. We must present a united front in this matter. We have worked together well in the past, and I know I can count on your total support. Now, let me tell you who I think the best candidate is. . . ."

There had been no objections to her suggestion. A week later, the board interviewed Roger Nesmith, an executive with a large New York department store.
Nesmith had been a head fashion buyer for the store and had experience in France
and the Far East. After the interview, Barbara spoke.

"I suggest we go with this man. He has experience in France and the Far East, and
our competitors aren't waiting around for us to make a decision."

One board member protested that several other candidates should be interviewed,
but he was quickly chastised by two other members for being too cautious. A vote
was taken, and Roger Nesmith assumed the presidency of Glamor International.

A year later, Glamor was in trouble. Sales were down, and it was clear that
Nesmith had poor judgment about which fashions would prove popular.

After a meeting to discuss the sales problem, several of the board members remi-
nisced about Nesmith's selection. One said, "I knew all along that he wasn't the best
candidate, but I thought everyone else felt differently." Another said "Don't blame
yourself. Those headhunting agencies are worthless."

Why did the board make a faulty decision? Did they have enough information?
Did they have too much information? Was finding a replacement just like Matt
Klein the real problem? Why wasn't there more discussion during the meetings?
Why didn't they interview more candidates? These are the kinds of questions that
we will attempt to answer in this chapter.

First, decision making will be defined, and a model of a rational decision-
making process will be presented. As we work through this model, we shall be
especially concerned with the practical limitations of rationality. Then, the types
of problems that require organizational decisions will be discussed. After this, the
use of groups to make decisions will be investigated. Then, we will look at the
ethics of decision making. Finally, some techniques to improve decision making
will be evaluated.

WHAT IS DECISION MAKING?

Consider the following questions that might arise in a variety of organizational
settings:

- How much inventory should our store carry?
- Where should the proposed community mental health center go?
- Should I remain on this job or accept another?
- How many classes of Philosophy 200 should our department offer next
  semester?
- Should our bank grant this loan?
- Should our diplomats attend the summit conference?

Common sense tells us that questions such as these have something to do with decision making. Specifically, they suggest that someone is going to have to do some decision making to provide answers!

Decision making is the process of developing a commitment to some course of action.[1] Three things are noteworthy about this definition. First, decision making involves making a *choice* among several action alternatives—the store can carry more or less inventory, and the mental health center can be located on the north or south end of town. Second, decision making is a *process* that involves more than simply the final choice among alternatives—if the worker mentioned above decides to accept the offer of a new job, we want to know *how* this decision was reached. Finally, the "commitment" mentioned in the definition usually involves some commitment of *resources* such as time, money, or personnel—if the store carries a large inventory, it will tie up cash; if the chairperson of Philosophy offers too many introductory classes, he might have no one available to teach a graduate seminar. As a consequence, incorrect decisions can be very costly to the organization.

In addition to conceiving of decision making as the commitment of resources, we can also describe it as a process of problem solving.[2] A **problem** exists when a gap is perceived between some existing state and some desired state. For example, the chairperson of the Philosophy department might observe that there is a projected increase in university enrollment for the upcoming year and that his course schedule is not completed (existing state). In addition, he might wish to adequately service the new students with Philosophy 200 classes and at the same time satisfy his Dean with a timely, sensible schedule (desired state). In this case, the decision-making process involves the perception of the existing state, the conception of the desired state, and the steps that the chairperson takes to move from one state to the other. At Glamor International, the board had a problem—how to fill an empty position (existing state) with a good candidate (desired state).

It should be clear that decision making is at the heart of the correct application of many of the topics that we have discussed thus far in the book. Choosing a correct motivational strategy for subordinates or deciding on the proper degree of participation to utilize depends upon a careful process of decision making.

THE COMPLEAT DECISION MAKER— A RATIONAL DECISION-MAKING MODEL

Exhibit 12–1 presents a model of the decision process that might be used by a rational decision maker. When a problem is identified, a search for information is begun. This information clarifies the nature of the problem and suggests alternative solutions. These are carefully evaluated, and the best is chosen for implementation. The implemented solution is then monitored over time to ensure its immediate and continued effectiveness. If difficulties occur at any point in the process, repetition or recycling may be effected.

It might occur to you that we have not yet determined exactly what is meant by a "rational" decision maker. Before we discuss the specific steps of the model in detail, let's contrast two forms of rationality.

Perfect Versus Bounded Rationality

The prototype for **perfect rationality** is the familiar Economic Person (formerly Economic Man), whom we meet in the first chapter of most introductory textbooks in economics. Economic Person is the perfect cool, calculating decision maker. More specifically, he or she:

- Can gather information about problems and solutions without cost and is thus completely informed

EXHIBIT

12–1

The rational decision-making process.

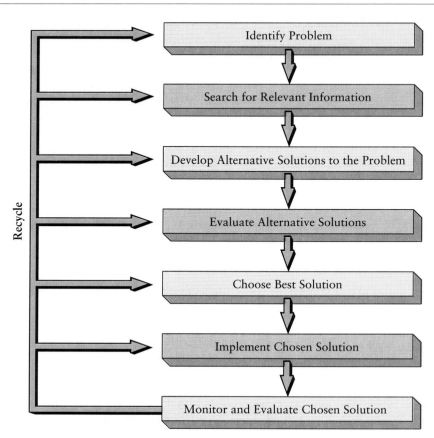

- Is perfectly logical—if solution A is preferred over solution B, and B is preferred over C, then A is necessarily preferrable to C
- Has only one criterion for decision making—economic gain

While Economic Person is useful for theoretical purposes, the perfectly rational characteristics embodied in Economic Person do not exist in real decision makers. This point has been recognized by Nobel Prize winner Herbert Simon. Simon suggests that administrators exhibit **bounded rationality** rather than perfect rationality.[3] That is, while they try to act rationally, they are limited in their capacity to acquire and process information. In addition, time constraints and political considerations (such as the need to please others in the organization) act as bounds to rationality.

Now let's examine the steps in the decision-making process, with two goals in mind: you can use these steps as a way to solve problems; and by contrasting how these steps are handled with perfect rationality and bounded rationality, you will see how bad decisions are made.

Problem Identification

You will recall that a problem exists when a gap occurs between existing and desired conditions. Such gaps might be signaled by dissatisfied customers or vigilant superiors or subordinates. Similarly, the press might contain articles about legislation or ads for competing products that signal difficulties for the organization. The perfectly rational decision maker, infinitely sensitive and completely informed, should be a great problem identifier. Bounded rationality, however, can lead to difficulties in problem identification:

- *Perceptual defense.* In Chapter 4 we pointed out that the perceptual system may act to defend the perceiver against unpleasant perceptions. As a consequence, problems in one's own work domain might go undetected. For example, a marketing manager might fail to identify a sales problem even though she is sensitive to problems outside her area of responsibility (e.g., production).
- *Problem defined in terms of solution.* This form of jumping to conclusions effectively short-circuits the rational decision-making process. In the story that began the chapter, Barbara Lane defined Glamor's problem in terms of a solution—find a replacement "just like Matt." This might have led her to look for similarities and overlook differences. When Coca-Cola changed its time-honored formula to produce a "new" Coke, it appears that its market share problem was prematurely defined in terms of a particular solution—we need to change our existing product.
- *Problem diagnosed in terms of symptoms.* "What we have here is a morale problem." While this might be true, a concentration on surface symptoms will provide the decision maker with few clues about an adequate solution. The *real* problem here involves the *cause* of the morale problem. Low

morale due to poor pay suggests different solutions than does low morale due to boring work.[4]

Information Search

As you can see in Exhibit 12–1, once a problem is identified, a search for information is instigated. This information search may clarify the nature or extent of the problem and begin to suggest alternative solutions. Again, our perfectly rational Economic Person is in good shape at this second stage of the decision-making process. He or she has free and instantaneous access to all information necessary to clarify the problem and develop alternative solutions. Bounded rationality, however, presents a different picture. Information search might be slow and costly. For example, the executive who has a vague suspicion that a morale problem exists might have to decide whether to order a costly and time-consuming attitude survey. If this survey indicates dissatisfaction with pay, he might then have to decide whether to authorize another costly and time-consuming survey of the pay rates provided by competitors (decisions, decisions, decisions!). At Glamor International, Barbara Lane screened many résumés but seemed to limit her interest to candidates with experience in France and the Far East.

Of course, surveys, company records, and input from others are not the only sources of information available to the decision maker. Decision makers frequently rely on their own *memory* to provide information—"Have I ever encountered a problem like this before? How did we solve it?" Here, the bounds of rationality again intrude. Specifically, we are most likely to recall events that happened *frequently* in the past, or *unusual* or *exotic* events.[5] While such events might prove irrelevant in the context of the current problem, we nonetheless rely on our past experience. The manager who remembers that "every time we went to an outside supplier for parts, we got burned" might be ignoring the uniqueness of her current problem.

While the bounds of rationality often force us to make decisions with incomplete or imperfect information, *too much* information can also damage the quality of decisions. Consider the example of former General Electric CEO Reginald Jones:

> Translated and amplified by his subordinates, Jones's thirst for data led to ridiculous excess. Dennis Dammerman, 43, now GE's chief financial officer, says that he had to stop computers in one GE business from spitting out seven daily reports. Just one made a stack of paper 12 feet high, containing product-by-product sales information— accurate to the penny—on hundreds of thousands of items. The bureaucracy routinely emasculated top executives by overwhelming them with useless information and enslaved middle managers with the need to gather it. Old-timers say that as mastery of the facts became impossible, illusion sufficed. Briefing books had grown to such dense impenetrability that managers simply skipped reading them. Instead,

they relied on staffers to feed them tough questions—"gotchas" in
GE lingo—with which to intimidate subordinates at meetings.[6]

And you think your course assignments are heavy! This **information overload** is
the reception of more information than is necessary to make effective decisions.

As you might guess, information overload can lead to errors, omissions, delays, and cut corners.[7] In addition, decision makers facing overload often attempt
to use all of the information at hand, then get confused and permit low-quality
information or irrelevant information to influence their decisions.[8] Perhaps you
have experienced this when writing a term paper—trying to incorporate too
many references and too many viewpoints into a short paper can lead to a confusing, low-quality end product. More isn't necessarily better.

However, decision makers seem to *think* that more is better. In one study, even
though information overload resulted in lower-quality decisions, overloaded decision makers were more *satisfied* than those who did not experience overload.[9]
Why is this so? For one thing, even if decisions do not improve with additional
information, *confidence* in the decisions may increase ("I did the best I could").
Second, decision makers may fear being "kept in the dark" and associate the
possession of information with power. One research review draws the following
conclusions about information gathering and use:[10]

- Much information that is gathered has little decision relevance.
- Much information that is used to justify a decision is collected and inter-
  preted *after* the decision has been made.
- Much requested information is not used in making the decision for which it
  was requested.
- Regardless of the information available, more information is requested.
- Complaints occur that not enough information is available to make a deci-
  sion even though available information is ignored.

In conclusion, although good information improves decisions, organizational
members often obtain more information than is necessary for adequate decisions.

Alternative Development, Evaluation, and Choice

Perfectly informed or not, the decision maker can now list alternative solutions to
the problem, examine the solutions, and choose the best one. For the perfectly
rational, totally informed, ideal decision maker, this is easy. He or she:

- Can conceive of all alternatives
- Knows the ultimate value of each alternative
- Knows the probability that each alternative will work

In this case, the decision maker can exhibit **maximization**—that is, he or she
can choose the alternative with the greatest expected value. Consider a simple
example.

	Ultimate Value	Probability	Expected Value
Alternative 1	$100,000 Profit	.4	$40,000 Profit
Alternative 2	$ 60,000 Profit	.8	$48,000 Profit

Here, the expected value of each alternative is calculated by multiplying its ultimate value by its probability. In this case, the perfectly rational decision maker would choose to implement the second alternative.

Unfortunately, things do not go so smoothly for the decision maker working under bounded rationality. Not all alternative solutions are known, and the decision maker might be ignorant of the ultimate values and probabilities of success of those that are known:

> A colleague and I were talking after having accepted our first jobs. Contemplating the misery of moving, we discussed whether to send our libraries to either our respective university offices, or to our new homes (wherever those might be). We noted that there was no way to intelligently make this choice, for the information necessary to make it would not even exist until several months after the decision was finalized. That is, *we could not know* what our offices or homes would be like until we had moved and arranged these matters, but we needed to make the choice months before the event could occur.[11]

Obviously, the new professors lacked adequate information to make a wise decision. However, there is strong evidence that humans are poor intuitive statisticians even when they have adequate experience with some event. People are particularly bad at revising probability estimates as they acquire information.[12] For example, an employment interviewer might screen hundreds of applicants without learning that source of referral (saw ad in newspaper, heard about job from friend, etc.) is associated with different probabilities of good job performance.

Finally, the perfectly rational decision maker can evaluate alternative solutions against a single criterion—economic gain. The decision maker who is bounded by reality might have to factor in other criteria as well, such as the political acceptability of the solution to other organizational members—will the boss like it? Since these additional criteria have their own values and probabilities, the decision-making task increases in complexity.

The bottom line here is that the decision maker working under bounded rationality frequently "satisfices" rather than maximizes.[13] **Satisficing** means that the decision maker establishes an adequate level of acceptability for a solution and then screens solutions until one that exceeds this level is found. When this occurs, evaluation of alternatives ceases, and the solution is chosen for implementation. For instance, the personnel manager who feels that absenteeism has become too high might choose a somewhat arbitrary acceptable level (e.g., the rate one year earlier), then accept the first solution that seems likely to achieve this level. Few organizations seek to *maximize* attendance.

Solution Implementation

When a decision is made to choose a particular solution to a problem, the solution must be implemented. The perfectly rational decision maker will have factored any possible implementation problems into his or her choice of solutions. Of course, the bounded decision maker will attempt to do the same when estimating probabilities of success. However, in organizations, decision makers are often dependent upon others to implement their decisions, and it might be difficult to anticipate their ability or motivation to do so. The French architect Roger Taillibert conceived a brilliant technical and aesthetic solution for the design of Montreal's Olympic Stadium. Unfortunately, the design was so complex that Quebec construction workers encountered tremendous problems in getting the stadium built on time. These unanticipated implementation problems contributed to extreme cost overruns.

Solution Evaluation

When the time comes to evaluate the implemented solution, the decision maker is effectively examining the possibility that a new problem has occurred: Does the (new) existing state match the desired state? Has the decision been effective? For all the reasons stated previously, the perfectly rational decision maker should be able to evaluate the effectiveness of the decision with calm, objective detachment. Again, however, the bounded decision maker might encounter problems at this stage of the process.

Justification   There is substantial evidence that people tend to be overconfident about the adequacy of their decisions.[14] This suggests that substantial dissonance can be aroused when a decision turns out to be faulty. One way to prevent such dissonance is to avoid careful tests of the adequacy of the decision. As a result, many organizations are notoriously lax when it comes to evaluating the effectiveness of expensive training programs or advertising campaigns. If the bad news cannot be avoided, the erring decision maker might devote his or her energy to trying to justify the faulty decision.[15]

The justification of faulty decisions is best seen in the irrational treatment of sunk costs. **Sunk costs** are permanent losses of resources incurred as the result of a decision.[16] The key word here is "permanent." Since these resources have been lost (sunk) due to a past decision, they should not enter into future decisions. Despite this, people often "throw good resources after bad," acting as if sunk costs can be recouped. This process is termed **escalation of commitment** to a course of action, in which the escalation involves devoting more and more resources to actions implied by the decision.[17] For example, suppose an executive authorizes the purchase of several microcomputers to improve office productivity. The machines turn out to be very unreliable, and they are frequently out of commission for repair. Perfect rationality suggests admitting to a mistake here. However, the executive might authorize an order for more machines from the same manufacturer to "prove" that he was right all along, hoping to recoup sunk costs with improved productivity from an even greater number of machines.

Dissonance reduction is not the only reason that escalation of commitment to a faulty decision may occur. In addition, a social norm that favors *consistent* behavior by administrators might be at work.[18] Changing one's mind and reversing previous decisions might be perceived as a sign of weakness, a fate to be avoided at all costs.

Escalation of commitment is sometimes observed even when the current decision maker is not responsible for previous sunk costs. For example, politicians might continue an expensive unnecessary public works project even though it was begun by a previous political administration. Here, dissonance reduction and the appearance of consistency are irrelevant, and some other causes of escalation are suggested. For one thing, decision makers might be motivated not to appear wasteful.[19] ("Even though the airport construction is way over budget and flight traffic doesn't justify a new airport, let's finish the thing. Otherwise, the taxpayers will think we've squandered their money.") Also, escalation of commitment might be due to the way in which decision makers frame the problem once some resources have been sunk. Rather than seeing the savings involved in reversing the decision, the problem might be framed as a decision between a sure loss of x dollars (which have been sunk) and an uncertain loss of $x + y$ dollars (maybe the additional investment will succeed). Research shows that when problems are framed this way, people tend to avoid the certain loss and go with the riskier choice, which in this case involves escalation.[20] (For another perspective on risk, see In Focus 12–1.)

One interesting example of escalation of commitment and an inability to write off sunk costs involved the epic western film *Heaven's Gate*. Writer-director Mi-

The film *Heaven's Gate* was a financial disaster because its backers escalated their commitment and could not bring themselves to write off sunk costs. (Yoram Kahana/Shooting Star)

chael Cimino initially proposed to United Artists that the film would cost $7.5 million. By the time production began, this figure had increased to $10 million. Production was behind schedule from the very first week, and Cimino was spending $200,000 a day. At this rate, the projected cost of the film would be close to $50 million, and the film would have had to do better than almost any movie ever made to break even! United Artists finally capped production costs at over three times the initial estimate and ordered Cimino to construct a commercial product from the thousands of feet of film he had shot. *Heaven's Gate* turned out to be one of the biggest box office flops in movie history.[21]

IN FOCUS 12–1

How Risky Are Executives?

Researchers Kenneth MacCrimmon and Donald Wehrung conducted a major study of the risk-taking propensity of 509 U.S. and Canadian senior business executives. They defined risk as exposure to a chance of a loss under conditions of decision uncertainty. A number of different techniques were used to study reactions to risk. Self-reported attitudes toward risk were measured, and the executives were asked to choose investment gambles and real money wagers that differed in risk. In addition, they made decisions about standardized business problems that varied in risk, such as how to respond to a patent violation lawsuit and a threatened labor strike. Also, the executives were asked to report their personal insurance holdings, debt, gambling activities, investment strategies, and any hazardous sports or hobbies they pursued. The research findings indicated that:

- The executives perceived themselves as being riskier than they actually were.
- The executives were more risk-averse when dealing with their own money than with their firms' money.
- There is no such thing as a "risky personality." People who take great risks in one domain may be very risk-averse in another domain.
- Comparatively, bankers, older managers, and those who had been with the same firm for a long time were risk-averse. Higher-level executives and those from smaller firms took more risks.
- The most successful executives took the most risks.

Source: Reprinted by permission of The Free Press, a division of Macmillan Publishing Company, Inc. from pp 268–274 in MacCrimmon, K. R., & Wehrung, D. A. (1986). *Taking risks: The management of uncertainty.* Copyright © 1986 by MacCrimmon, K. R. & Wehrung, D. A.

Hindsight   The careful evaluation of decisions is also inhibited by faulty hindsight. Hindsight refers to the tendency to review the decision-making process that we used in order to find out what we did right (in the case of success) or wrong (in the case of failure). While hindsight can prove useful, it is also open to some serious errors.

The classic example of hindsight involves the armchair quarterback who "knew" that a chancy intercepted pass in the first quarter was unnecessary because the team won the game anyway! The armchair critic is exhibiting the **knew-it-all-along effect.** This is the tendency to assume after the fact that we knew all along what the outcome of a decision would be. In effect, our faulty memory adjusts the probabilities that we estimated before making the decision to correspond to what actually happened.[22] This can prove quite dangerous. The money manager who consciously makes a very risky investment that turns out to be successful might revise her memory to assume that the decision was a sure thing. The next time, the now-confident investor might not be so lucky!

Another form of faulty hindsight is the tendency to take personal responsibility for successful decision outcomes while denying responsibility for unsuccessful outcomes.[23] Thus, when things work out well, it is because *we* made a careful, logical decision. When things go poorly, some unexpected *external* factor messed up our sensible decision! For example, students are very willing to take responsibility for good grades, while bad grades are attributed to poor teaching or a heavy course load. Similarly, the marketing manager who approves an advertising campaign resulting in increased sales will assume that she planned the campaign properly. A downturn in sales might be attributed to the poor economy or the unanticipated actions of a competitor. Sometimes this tendency reflects conscious excuse-making. Usually, however, it probably reflects an unconscious search for additional information when poor decision outcomes occur.

When the board members of Glamor International realized that they had chosen the wrong person as president, they exhibited hindsight. They knew all along that headhunting agencies couldn't be trusted.

Rational Decision Making—A Summary

The rational decision-making model shown in Exhibit 12–1 provides a good guide for how many decisions *should* be made but only a partially accurate view of how they *are* made. Research shows that for complex, unfamiliar decisions, such as choosing an occupation, the rational model provides a pretty good picture of how people actually make decisions.[24] Also, organizational decision makers often follow the rational model when they agree about the goals they are pursuing.[25] On the other hand, there is plenty of case study evidence of the rational model being short-circuited in organizational decisions, in part because of the biases discussed above.[26] Also, true experts in a field appear to short-circuit the rational model, using their knowledge base stored in memory to skip steps logically.[27] At every stage of the rational decision-making process, the bounds on rationality present difficulties. Exhibit 12–2 summarizes the operation of perfect and bounded rationality at each stage of the decision process.

TYPES OF PROBLEMS

It probably doesn't surprise you that people try to behave rationally and analytically when making a decision such as choosing a career. This is obviously a tough decision with important consequences. For many, in fact, it is literally a once-in-a-lifetime decision and not something that one gets a lot of practice at. In contrast, it has probably occurred to you that many decisions appear to be made almost automatically, as if they made themselves. In many of these cases, it might even be difficult to believe that a true "decision" has been made—the dentist

EXHIBIT

12–2

Perfectly rational decision making contrasted with bounded rationality.

Stage	Perfect Rationality	Bounded Rationality
Problem identification	Easy, accurate perception of gaps that constitute problems	Perceptual defense; jump to solutions; attention to symptoms rather than problems
Information Search	Free; fast; right amount obtained	Slow; costly; reliance on flawed memory; obtain too little or too much
Development of Alternative Solutions	Can conceive of all	Not all known
Evaluation of Alternative Solutions	Ultimate value of each known; probability of each known; only criterion is economic gain	Potential ignorance of or miscalculation of values and probabilities; criteria include political factors
Solution Choice	Maximizes	Satisfices
Solution Implementation	Considered in evaluation of alternatives	May be difficult owing to reliance on others
Solution Evaluation	Objective, according to previous steps	May involve justification, escalation to recover sunk costs, faulty hindsight

reaches quickly and confidently for a particular drill; the clerk routes the invoice to shipping without a thought.

This discussion suggests that the elaborate rational decision-making model presented earlier applies more to some problems than to others. Let's contrast two kinds of problems encountered in organizations.

Well-Structured Problems

For **well-structured problems,** the existing state is clear, the desired state is clear, and how to get from one state to the other is fairly obvious.[28] Intuitively, these problems are simple, and their solutions arouse little controversy. This is because such problems are repetitive and familiar. Here are some examples:

- Assistant bank manager—Which of these ten automobile loan applications should I approve?
- Typist—Should this go on a letterhead or memo paper?
- Merchant—Is it time to reorder garden hoses?
- Welfare officer—How much assistance should this client receive?
- Truck driver—How much weight should I carry?

Because decision making takes time and is prone to error, organizations (and individuals), attempt to program the decision making for well-structured problems. A **program** is simply a standardized way of solving a problem. As such, programs short-circuit the rational decision-making process by enabling the decision maker to go directly from problem identification to solution.

Programs usually go under labels such as *rules, routines, standard operating procedures, rules of thumb,* and so on. Sometimes, they come from experience and exist only "in the head." For example, the merchant might have a rule of thumb that says to order more hoses when inventory drops below fifty in the summer or ten in the winter. Other programs are more formal. You are probably aware that routine loan applications are "scored" by banks according to a fixed formula that takes into account income, debt, previous credit, and so on. Similarly, the welfare officer will score applicants for assistance according to family size, other sources of income, etc. Some programs exist in the form of straightforward rules—"Truck drivers will always carry between 85 and 95 percent of legal weight."

Many of the problems encountered in organizations are well-structured, and programmed decision making provides a useful means of solving these problems. However, programs are only as good as the hopefully rational decision-making process that led to the adoption of the program in the first place. In computer terminology, "garbage in" will result in "garbage out." Another difficulty with decision programs is their tendency to persist even when problem conditions change. Decision makers thus continue to use programs even when they become ineffective.

These difficulties of programmed decision making are seen in the ineffective hiring procedures that some firms use. To solve the recurrent problem of choosing employees for lower-level jobs, almost all companies use application forms. These forms are part of a decision program. However, some firms have persisted in asking for information that violates equal employment and human rights legislation enacted in the past two decades. Costly lawsuits have resulted. Furthermore, there is no evidence that this information is a valid predictor of performance in any event (garbage in–garbage out).

Ill-Structured Problems

The extreme example of an **ill-structured problem** is one in which the existing and desired states are unclear, and the method of getting to the desired state (even if clarified) is unknown. For example, a vice-president of marketing might have a vague feeling that the sales of a particular product are too low. However, she might lack precise information about the product's market share (existing state) and the market share of its most successful competitor (ideal state). In addition, she might be unaware of exactly how to increase the sales of this particular product.

Ill-structured problems are generally unique. That is, they are unusual and have not been encountered before. In addition, they tend to be complex, and they involve a high degree of uncertainty. As a result, they frequently arouse controversy and conflict among the people who are interested in the decision. Although the choice of a new president at Glamor was an ill-structured problem, controversy was suppressed. Other examples of ill-structured problems are the following:

- Should we vaccinate the population against a new flu strain when the vaccination might have some bad side effects?
- Should a risky attempt to rescue political hostages be implemented?
- In which part of the country should we build a new plant?
- A new surgery procedure could save this patient, but not much is known about the technique. Should I try it?

It should be obvious that ill-structured problems such as these cannot be solved with programmed decisions. Rather, the decision makers must resort to **nonprogrammed decision making.** This simply means that they are likely to try to implement the full rational decision-making model shown in Exhibit 12–1. Clearly, though, ill-structured problems test the bounds of rationality very severely. They involve much uncertainty, and they might stimulate strong political considerations.

As illustrated in Exhibit 12–3, there is a tendency for more ill-structured problems to be encountered as one moves up the hierarchy of an organization. Consequently, more nonprogrammed decision making is necessary at higher levels. This isn't especially surprising. People in the upper ranks are paid more and given more status partially because they are expected to be able to make tough decisions. At lower organizational levels, we find more well-structured problems and greater reliance on programmed decision making. Of course, there are exceptions

■
EXHIBIT

12–3

Problem types and decision strategies at different organizational levels.

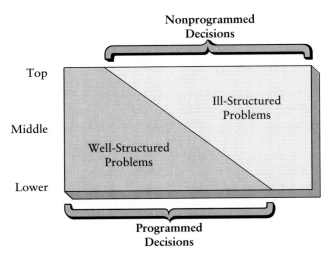

Source: From Donnelly, J. H., Jr., et. al. (1978). *Fundamentals of management* (3rd ed.). © 1978 by Business Publications, Inc. Reprinted by permission of Richard D. Irwin, Inc.

to this general rule. The president of a small firm might scan sales data and order needed adjustments in production according to a routine rule of thumb. Conversely, a janitor might discover a broken water pipe and act in a nonprogrammed manner to solve the problem.

Because ill-structured problems involve complexity, uncertainty, and potential controversy, organizations often rely upon groups rather than individuals to provide solutions. Let's examine group decision making.

GROUP DECISION MAKING

Many, many organizational decisions are made by groups rather than individuals. If you reconsider the examples of ill-structured problems noted in the previous section, you will see how unlikely it would be for them to be solved by a lone decision maker. Presidents are usually chosen by boards of directors. The surgeon who is considering an unproven operating technique will voluntarily consult with colleagues, and his or her hospital probably has a formal review committee for such procedures.

In this section we shall consider the advantages and problems of group decision making.

Why Use Groups?

There are a number of reasons for groups being employed to make organizational decisions.

Decision Quality It is often argued that groups can make higher-quality decisions than individuals. There are three assumptions to this argument:

- Groups are *more vigilant* than individuals—more people are scanning the environment.
- Groups can *generate more ideas* than individuals.
- Groups can *evaluate ideas better* than individuals.

A reexamination of the decision process shown in Exhibit 12–1 indicates why these should be valuable characteristics.

At the problem identification and information search stages, vigilance is especially advantageous. A problem that is missed by some group members might be identified by others. For example, a member of the board of directors might notice a short article in an obscure business publication that has great relevance for the firm. In searching for information to clarify the problem suggested in the article, other members of the board might possess unique information that proves useful.

When it comes to developing alternative solutions, more people should literally have more ideas, if only because someone remembers something that others have forgotten. In addition, members with different backgrounds and experiences may bring different perspectives to the problem. This is why undergraduate students, graduate students, faculty, and administrators are often included on university task forces to improve the library or develop a course evaluation system. Finally, in listening to each other's ideas, group members can combine information to develop unique solutions that no single member could conceive.

When it comes to evaluating solutions and choosing the best one, groups have the advantage of checks and balances. That is, an extreme position or incorrect notion held by one member should be offset by the pooled judgments of the rest of the group.

In summary, these characteristics suggest that groups *should* make higher-quality decisions than individuals. Shortly, we will find out whether they actually do so.

Decision Acceptance As pointed out in our discussion of participative leadership in Chapter 10, groups are often used to make decisions on the premise that a decision made in this way will be more acceptable to those involved. Again, there are several assumptions underlying this premise:

- People wish to be involved in decisions that will affect them.
- People will better understand a decision in which they participated.
- People will be more committed to a decision in which they invested personal time and energy.

The acceptability of group decisions is especially useful in dealing with a problem described earlier—getting the decision implemented. If decision makers truly understand the decision and feel committed to it, they should be willing to follow through and see that it is carried out.

Diffusion of Responsibility High quality and acceptance are sensible reasons for using groups to make decisions. As you may recall from Chapter 10, a somewhat less admirable reason to employ groups is to **diffuse responsibility** across the members in case the decision turns out poorly. In this case, each member of the group will share part of the burden of the negative consequences, and no one person will be singled out for punishment. Of course, when this happens, individual group members often "abandon ship" and exhibit biased hindsight—"I knew all along that the bid was too high to be accepted, but they made me go along with them."

Do Groups Actually Make Higher-Quality Decisions Than Individuals?

The discussion in the first part of the previous section suggested that groups *should* make higher-quality decisions than individuals. But *do* they? Is the frequent use of groups to make decisions warranted by evidence? The answer is yes. One review concludes that *"groups usually produce more and better solutions to problems than do individuals working alone."*[29] Another concludes that group performance is superior to that of the average individual in the group.[30]

As you might suspect, this conclusion may be qualified by the exact nature of the problem and the composition of the group. More specifically, groups should perform better than individuals when:

- The group members differ in relevant skills and abilities, as long as they don't differ so much that conflict occurs.
- Some division of labor can occur.
- Memory for facts is an important issue.
- Individual judgments can be combined by weighting them to reflect the expertise of the various members.[31]

To consolidate your understanding of these conditions, consider a situation that should favor group decision making: A small construction company wishes to bid on a contract to build an apartment complex. The president, the controller, a construction boss, and an engineer work together to formulate the bid. Since they have diverse backgrounds and skills, they divide the task initially. The president reviews recent bids on similar projects in the community; the controller gets estimates on materials costs; the engineer and boss review the blueprints. During this process, each racks his brain to recall lessons learned from making previous bids. Finally, they put their information together, and each member voices an opinion about what the bid should be. The president decides to average these opinions to arrive at the actual bid, since each person is equally expert in his own area.

Disadvantages of Group Decision Making

Although groups have the ability to develop high-quality, acceptable decisions, there are a number of potential disadvantages to group decision making.

Time Groups seldom work quickly or efficiently when compared to individuals. This is because of the process losses (Chapter 8) involved in discussion, debate, and coordination. The time problem increases with group size. When the speed of arriving at a solution to a problem is a prime factor, the use of groups should be avoided.

Escalation of Demands Participation in group decisions can be a rewarding experience. In a sense, such participation may constitute a form of job enrichment. Thus, the opportunity to incorporate one's own values into an acceptable decision may escalate demands for participation in other decisions that are not suitable for a group approach.

Conflict Many times, participants in group decisions have their own personal axes to grind or their own resources to protect. When this occurs, decision quality may take a back seat to political wrangling and infighting. In the example about the construction company presented earlier, the construction boss might see it being to his advantage to overestimate the size of the crew required to build the apartments. On the other hand, the controller might make it his personal crusade to pare labor costs. A simple compromise between these two extreme points of view might not result in the highest-quality decision.

Groupthink In retrospect, have you ever been involved in a group decision that you knew was a "loser" but that you felt unable to protest? Perhaps you thought you were the only one who had doubts about the chosen course of action. Perhaps you tried to speak up, but others criticized you for not being on the team. Maybe you found yourself searching for information to confirm that the decision was correct and ignoring evidence that the decision was bad. What was happening? Were you suffering from some strange form of possession? Mind control?

In Chapter 9 we discussed the process of conformity in social settings. As you might expect, conformity can have a strong influence on the decisions that groups make. The most extreme influence is seen when **groupthink** occurs. This happens when group pressures lead to reduced mental efficiency, poor testing of reality, and lax moral judgments.[32] In effect, unanimous acceptance of decisions is stressed over quality of decisions.

Psychologist Irving Janis, who developed the groupthink concept, felt that high group cohesiveness was at its root. It now appears that other factors might be equally important or more important. These include concern for approval from the group and the isolation of the group from other sources of information. However, the promotion of a particular decision by the group leader appears to be the strongest cause.[33] In any event, Janis provides a detailed list of groupthink symptoms:

- *Illusion of invulnerability*. Members are overconfident and willing to assume great risks. They ignore obvious danger signals.
- *Rationalization*. Problems and counterarguments that can't be ignored are "rationalized away."
- *Illusion of morality*. The decisions adopted by the group are not only perceived as sensible, they are also perceived as *morally* correct.
- *Stereotypes of outsiders*. The group constructs unfavorable stereotypes of those outside the group who are the targets of their decisions.
- *Pressure for conformity*. Members pressure each other to fall into line and conform with the group's views.
- *Self-censorship*. Members convince themselves to avoid voicing opinions contrary to the group.
- *Illusion of unanimity*. Members perceive that unanimous support exists for the chosen course of action.
- *Mindguards*. Some group members may adopt the role of "protecting" the group from information that goes against its decisions.[34]

Obviously, victims of groupthink are operating in an atmosphere of unreality that should lead to low-quality decisions. As an example, Janis cites the disastrous Cuban Bay of Pigs invasion that was planned by President Kennedy and his advisors during the early 1960s. All of the above symptoms of groupthink were present during the planning sessions: State Department doubts about the invasion were ignored and rationalized; the Cuban army was stereotyped as ineffective; various advisors subsequently reported having censored their own doubts. Janis also describes similar examples from the Vietnam era.

In the business world, the design and marketing of the ill-fated Edsel automobile have been attributed to groupthink. Similarly, individuals as diverse as Wall Street investors and corporate price fixers have been described as succumbing to its pressures.[35] In the story that began the chapter, groupthink was exhibited. Controversy was stifled as the board members quickly agreed to the choice of a new Glamor president.

Shortly, we shall consider some techniques for improving decision making in organizations. You will notice that some of these techniques should help prevent groupthink.

How Do Groups Handle Risk?

Almost by definition, problems that are suitable for group decision making involve some degree of risk and uncertainty. This raises a very important question: Do groups make decisions that are more or less risky than those of individuals?

Or will the degree of risk assumed by the group simply equal the average risk preferred by its individual members? The answer here is obviously important. Consider the following scenarios:

> An accident has just occurred at a nuclear power plant. Several corrections exist, ranging from expensive and safe to low-cost but risky. On the way to an emergency meeting, each nuclear engineer formulates an opinion about what should be done. But what will the group decide?

> A company has been sued for $10 million in a product liability case. A conservative strategy indicates settling out of court. A riskier strategy suggests going to court and fighting the case. Each top executive has a private opinion about the matter. But what will they decide when they meet together?

Conventional wisdom provides few clear predictions about what the groups of engineers and executives will decide to do. On one hand, it is sometimes argued that groups will make riskier decisions than individuals because there is security in numbers. That is, diffusion of responsibility for a bad decision encourages the group to take greater chances. On the other hand, it is often argued that groups are cautious, with the members checking and balancing each other so much that a conservative outcome is sure to occur. Just contrast the committee-laden civil service with the swashbuckling style of independent operators such as Ted Turner and Donald Trump!

Given this contradiction of common sense, the history of research into group decision making and risk is both interesting and instructive. In 1961, a student at the Massachusetts Institute of Technology reported in a Master's thesis that he had discovered clear evidence of a **risky shift** in decision making.[36] Participants in the research were asked to review hypothetical cases involving risk, such as those involving career choices or investment decisions. As individuals, they recommended a course of action. Then they were formed into groups, and the groups discussed each case and came to a joint decision. In general, the groups tended to advise riskier courses of action than the average risk initially advocated by their members. This is the risky shift. As studies were conducted to explore the reasons for its causes, things got more complicated. For some groups and some decisions, **conservative shifts** were observed. In other words, groups came to decisions that were *less* risky than those of the individual members before interaction.

It is now clear that both risky and conservative shifts are possible, and they occur in a wide variety of real settings, including investment and purchasing decisions. But what determines which kind of shift occurs? A key factor appears to be the initial positions of the group members before they discuss the problem. This is illustrated in Exhibit 12–4. As you can see, when group members are somewhat conservative before interaction (the x's), they tend to exhibit a conservative shift when they discuss the problem. When group members are somewhat risky initially (the ●'s), they exhibit a risky shift after discussion. In other words, *group discussion seems to polarize or exaggerate the initial position of the group.*[37] Returning to the nuclear accident, if the engineers initially prefer a somewhat conservative solution, they should adopt an even more conservative strategy during the meeting.

Why do risky and conservative shifts occur when groups make decisions? Evidence seems to indicate three main factors:

- Group discussion generates ideas and arguments that individual members haven't considered before. This information naturally favors the members' initial tendency toward risk or toward conservatism. Since discussion provides "more" and "better" reasons for the initial tendency, the tendency ends up being exaggerated.
- Group members try to present themselves as basically similar to other members but "even better." Thus, they try to one-up others in discussion by adopting a slightly more extreme version of the group's initial stance.
- When the group's initial position is somewhat risky, diffusion of responsibility may contribute to a risky shift. The consequences of a bad decision can be distributed over the group.[38]

In summary, administrators should be aware of the tendency for group interaction to polarize initial risk levels. If this polarization results from the sensible exchange of information, it might actually improve the group's decision. However, if it results from one-upmanship or diffusion of responsibility, it might lead to low-quality decisions.

■

EXHIBIT   The dynamics of risky and conservative shifts for two groups.

12–4

Position of Group Members Before Discussion:

Most   Medium   Most
Conservative   Risk   Risky
Alternative   Alternative

Position of Group Members After Discussion:

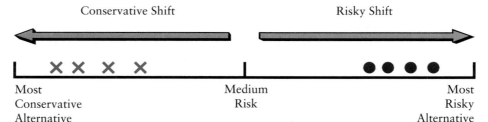

Conservative Shift   Risky Shift

Most   Medium   Most
Conservative   Risk   Risky
Alternative   Alternative

ETHICS IN DECISION MAKING

In 1982 and 1986, the Johnson & Johnson subsidiary that was responsible for Tylenol quickly and decisively withdrew the product from the market after poison-laced examples of it were discovered. During the same era, the retail broker E. F. Hutton was busy implementing a check-overdraft scheme that is said to have defrauded hundreds of small banks out of millions of dollars. How can we account for the radical difference in ethics reflected in the decisions that underpinned these actions?

For our purposes, **ethics** can be defined as systematic thinking about the moral consequences of decisions. Moral consequences can be framed in terms of the potential for harm to any stakeholders in the decision, ranging from the decision makers themselves to "innocent bystanders" who might be affected by the decision.[39] Ethics is a major branch of philosophy, and no attempt will be made to describe the various schools of ethical thought. Instead, we will focus on the kinds of ethical issues that organizational decision makers face and some of the factors that stimulate unethical decisions.

Over the years, a number of surveys have been conducted to determine managers' views about the ethics of decision making in business.[40] Some striking similarities across studies provide an interesting picture of the popular psychology of business ethics. First, far from being shy about the subject, a large majority agree that unethical practices occur in business. Furthermore, a substantial proportion (between 40 and 90 percent, according to the particular study) report that they have been pressured to compromise their own ethical standards when making organizational decisions. Finally, in line with the concept of self-serving attributions, managers invariably tend to see themselves as having higher ethical standards than their peers and sometimes their superiors. The unpleasant picture being painted here is one in which managers are often tempted to behave unethically, and sometimes succumb, but feel that they still do better than others on moral grounds.

In case you think that students are purer than organizational decision makers, think again. Research is fairly consistent in showing that business students have looser ethical standards than practicing managers, at least when responding to written descriptions of ethical issues.[41]

The Nature of Ethical Dilemmas

What are the kinds of ethical dilemmas that most frequently face organizational decision makers? Exhibit 12–5, on page 436, shows the results of a Conference Board survey of 300 companies around the world. As you can see, conflicts of interest, questionable gift giving, and sexual harassment top the list of ethical concerns (while executive salaries are seen to present fewer problems!). Especially noteworthy is the fact that 77 percent of firms report problems in dealing with foreign business practices that are contrary to their own ethical norms.

Of course, ethical issues often tend to be peculiar to the specific domain in which we're usually making decisions. As an example, let's consider the ethical dilemmas that are faced by the various subspecialties of marketing.[42] Among market researchers, accurately identifying to subjects the true sponsor of the re-

EXHIBIT

12–5

A survey of ethical issues.

The Conference Board asked executives at 300 companies worldwide whether the following constituted ethical issues for business. The percentage of affirmative responses is listed next to the issue.

Issue	Percent
Employee conflicts of interest	91
Inappropriate gifts to corporate personnel	91
Sexual harassment	91
Unauthorized payments	85
Affirmative action	84
Employee privacy	84
Environmental issues	82
Employee health screening	79
Conflicts between company's ethics and foreign business practices	77
Security of company records	76
Workplace safety	76
Advertising content	74
Product safety standards	74
Corporate contributions	68
Shareholder interests	68
Corporate due process	65
Whistleblowing	63
Employment at will	62
Disinvestment	59
Government contract issues	59
Financial and cash management procedures	55
Plant/facility closures and downsizing	55
Political action committees	55
Social issues raised by religious organizations	47
Comparable worth	43
Product pricing	42
Executive salaries	37

Source: From *Corporate Ethics*, a Conference Board research report (New York: The Conference Board). Reprinted by permission.

search has been an ongoing topic of debate. Among purchasing managers, where to draw the line in accepting favors (e.g., sports tickets) from vendors poses ethical problems. Among product managers, issues of planned obsolescence, unnecessary packaging, and differential pricing (e.g., charging more in the inner city) raise ethical concerns. When it comes to salespeople, how far to go in enticing customers and how to be fair in expense account use have been prominent ethical themes. Finally, in advertising, the range of ethical issues can (and does) fill books. Consider, for example, the decision to use sexual allure to sell a product.

In contrast to these occupationally specific ethical dilemmas, what are the *common themes* that run through ethical issues faced by managers? An in-depth interview study of an occupationally diverse group of managers discovered seven themes that defined their moral standards for decision making.[43] Here are those themes and some typical examples of associated ethical behavior:

- *Honest communication.* Evaluate subordinates candidly; advertise and label honestly; don't slant proposals to senior management.
- *Fair treatment.* Pay equitably; respect the sealed bid process; don't give preference to suppliers with political connections; don't use lower-level people as scapegoats.
- *Special consideration.* The "fair treatment" standard can be modified for special cases, such as helping out a long-time employee, giving preference to hiring the disabled, or giving business to a loyal but troubled supplier.
- *Fair competition.* Avoid bribes and kickbacks to obtain business; don't fix prices with competitors.
- *Responsibility to organization.* Act for the good of the organization as a whole, not for self-interest; avoid waste and inefficiency.
- *Corporate social responsibility.* Don't pollute; think about the community impact of plant closures; show concern for employee health and safety.
- *Respect for law.* Avoid taxes, don't evade them; don't bribe government inspectors; follow the letter and spirit of labor laws.

It is useful to recognize that many ethical dilemmas faced by decision makers are actually forms of role conflict (Chapter 8). For example, consider the ethical theme of corporate social responsibility. Here, an executive's role of custodian of the environment (don't pollute) might be at odds with his or her role as a community employer (don't close the plant that pollutes).

Causes of Unethical Decisions

What are the causes of unethical decisions? The answer to this question is important so that in your role as a decision maker you can anticipate the circumstances in which special vigilance might be warranted. Knowing the causes of unethical behavior can aid in its prevention. Because the topic is sensitive, you should appreciate that this is not the easiest area to research. The major evidence comes from surveys of executive opinion, case studies of prominent ethical failures, business game simulations, and responses to written scenarios involving ethical dilemmas (such as the exercise at the end of this chapter).

Gain Although the point might seem mundane, it is critical to recognize the role of temptation in unethical decision making. The anticipation of healthy reinforcement for following an unethical course of action, especially if no punishment is expected, should promote unethical decisions.[44] Consider, for example, Dennis Levine, the Drexel Burnham Lambert investment banker who was convicted of insider trading in Wall Street's biggest scandal:

> It was just so easy. In seven years I built $39,750 into $11.5 million, and all it took was a 20-second phone call to my offshore bank a couple of times a month—maybe 200 calls total. My account was growing at 125% a year, compounded. Believe me, I felt a rush when I would check the price of one of my stocks on the office Quotron and learn I'd just made several hundred thousand dollars. I was confident that the elaborate veils of secrecy I had created—plus overseas bank-privacy laws—would protect me.[45]

Dennis Levine committed unethical behavior for the promise of enormous gain. (Rick Maiman/ Sygma)

Competition It has long been recognized that stiff competition for scarce resources can stimulate unethical decisions. This has been observed in both business game simulations and industry studies of illegal acts, in which trade offenses such as price fixing and monopoly violations have been shown to increase with industry decline.[46] For example, observers cite a crowded and mature market as one factor prompting price fixing violations in the folding-carton packaging industry.[47] One exception to the "competition stresses ethics" thesis should be noted. In cases in which essentially *no* competition exists, there is also a strong temptation to make unethical decisions. This is because the opportunity to make large gains is not offset by market checks and balances. Prominent examples have occurred in the defense industry, in which monopoly contracts to produce military hardware have been accompanied by some remarkable examples of overcharging the taxpayers.

Personality Are there certain types of personalities that are prone to unethical decisions? Perhaps. Business game simulations have shown that people with strong economic value orientations (Chapter 5) are more likely to behave unethically than those with weaker economic values.[48] Also, there are marked individual differences in the degree of sophistication that people use in thinking about moral issues.[49] Other things being equal, it is sensible to expect that people who are more self-conscious about moral matters will be more likely to avoid unethical decisions. Finally, people with a high need for power (Chapter 6) might be prone to make unethical decisions when this power is used to further self-interests rather than for the good of the organization as a whole. In the next chapter, the ethics of power and politics will be considered further.

In closing this section, let's recall that we have a tendency to exaggerate the role of dispositional factors, such as personality, in explaining the behavior of others (Chapter 4). Thus, when we see unethical behavior, we should look at situational factors, such as competition and the organization's culture, as well as the personality of the actor.

Culture A recent study found that there were considerable differences in ethical values across the organizations studied.[50] These differences involved factors such as consideration for employees, respect for the law, respect for organizational rules and so on. In addition, there were differences across groups within these organizations. This suggests that aspects of an organization's culture (and its subcultures) can influence the ethics of decision making. This corresponds to the repeated finding in executive surveys that peer and superior conduct are viewed as strongly influencing ethical behavior, for good or for bad. The presence of role models helps to shape the culture (Chapter 9). If these models are actually rewarded for unethical behavior rather than punished, the development of an unethical culture is likely.

Observers of the folding-carton price-fixing scandal mentioned above note how top managers frequently seemed out of touch with the difficulty of selling boxes in a mature, crowded market. They put in place goal setting and reward

Source: *Harvard Business Review,* March–April 1989, p. 112, The New Yorker Magazine, Inc.

"Be careful what you say in front of Nevelstrom; he's some kind of ethics nut."

systems (e.g., commission forming 60 percent of income) that almost guaranteed unethical decisions, systems that are much more appropriate for products on a growth cycle.[51]

Finally, a consideration of culture suggests the conditions under which corporate codes of ethics might actually have an impact on decision making. If such codes are specific, are tied to the actual business being done, and correspond to the reward system, they should bolster an ethical climate. If vague codes that do not correspond to other cultural elements exist, the negative symbolism might actually damage the ethical climate.

Employing Ethical Guidelines

A few simple guidelines, regularly used, should help in the ethical screening of decisions. The point isn't to paralyze your decision making (see the cartoon) but to get you to think seriously about the moral implications of your decisions *before* they are made.[52]

- Identify the stakeholders that will be affected by any decision.
- Identify the costs and benefits of various decision alternatives to these stakeholders.

- Consider the relevant moral *expectations* that surround a particular decision. These might stem from professional norms, laws, organizational ethics codes, and principles such as honest communication and fair treatment.
- Be familiar with the common ethical dilemmas that are faced by decision makers in your organizational role or profession.
- Discuss ethical matters with decision stakeholders and others. Don't think ethics without talking about ethics.

The limited evidence so far suggests that formal education in ethics does have a positive impact on ethical attitudes.[53] For an example of one program, see Ethical Focus 12–2 on page 442.

Before continuing, consider the You Be the Manager feature on page 444. Did the events described there constitute an ethical dilemma?

IMPROVING DECISION MAKING IN ORGANIZATIONS

It stands to reason that organizational decision making can be improved if decision makers can be encouraged to think ethically and to approximate more closely the rational decision-making models shown in Exhibit 12–1. This should help to preclude the various biases and errors that we have alluded to throughout the chapter. Each of the following techniques has this goal.

Training Discussion Leaders

When group decision making is utilized, an appointed leader often convenes the group and guides the discussion. The actions of this leader can "make or break" the decision. On one hand, if the leader behaves autocratically, trying to "sell" a preconceived decision, the advantages of using a group are obliterated, and decision acceptance can suffer. If the leader fails to exert *any* influence, however, the group might develop a low-quality solution that does not meet the needs of the organization. One expert has argued that discussion leaders should be trained to develop the following skills:

- State the problem in a nondefensive, objective manner. Do not suggest solutions or preferences.
- Supply essential facts and clarify any constraints on solutions (e.g., "We can't spend more than $5000").
- Draw out all group members. Prevent domination by one person and protect members from being attacked or severely criticized.
- Wait out pauses. Don't make suggestions or ask leading questions.
- Ask stimulating questions that move the discussion forward.
- Summarize and clarify at several points to mark progress.[54]

Notice that these skills are not vague attitudes, but specific behaviors. Thus, they are subject to training and practice. There is good evidence that this training can be accomplished through role-playing and that it can increase the quality and acceptance of group decisions.[55]

ETHICAL FOCUS 12–2

▼
....
Arthur Andersen Starts Ethics Program

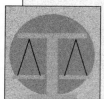

Can business ethics be taught? Arthur Andersen & Co. thinks so. About a year ago, the Chicago-based Big Eight accounting firm called together ethics experts from business and academia to develop a program promoting education in undergraduate and graduate-level business schools.

The result of their brainstorming: PACE, a series of free case studies schools can incorporate into existing ethics programs. Professors can get acquainted with the cases during free seminars at the firm's Center for Professional Education in St. Charles, Ill. Arthur Andersen has earmarked $5 million to fund the program for at least five years, and also plans to sell it to companies for employee training sessions.

Covering finance, marketing, economics, management, and accounting, the case studies highlight ethical issues that an entry-level employee might face, such as accepting gifts and tips, truthfulness in advertising, plant closures, and sexual harassment. The materials don't offer a "right" or "wrong" solution or espouse a particular ethical or religious school of thought. "Our goal," says Don Baker, head of Arthur Andersen's university relations program, "is for the students to be walking out of the class period arguing with each other."

Why is Arthur Andersen going to the trouble and expense of designing and disseminating an ethics program? For starters, the firm hires some 4,000 graduates from U.S. universities each year. Their ability to handle ethical dilemmas greatly affects their employer and their industry. "Business has been on the defensive for some time now with respect to accusations of unethical behavior," notes Charles Brown, former chairman of AT&T and an adjunct member of Andersen's Advisory Council on Ethics. "Ask yourself: When was the last time you watched a TV sitcom in which a businessperson was the hero?"

Source: Fusco, M. A. C. (1989, Spring/Summer). Ethics game plan: Taking the offensive. *Business Week Careers*, p. 51.

Stimulating and Managing Controversy

Full-blown conflict among organizational members is hardly conducive to good decision making. Information is certain to be withheld, and personal or group goals will take precedence over developing a decision that solves organizational problems. On the other hand, a complete lack of controversy can be equally damaging, since alternative points of view that may be very relevant to the issue at hand will never surface. Such a lack of controversy is partially responsible for the groupthink effect, and it also contributes to many cases of escalation of commitment to flawed courses of action. For example, it is now clear that stifled controversy played a part in the disastrous launch of the space shuttle Challenger (In Focus 12–3, page 445).

Research shows that controversy can be stimulated in decision-making groups by incorporating members with diverse ideas and backgrounds, forming subgroups to "tear the problem apart," and establishing norms that favor the open sharing of information.[56] However, these tactics must be managed carefully to ensure that open conflict does not result. The discussion skills covered in the previous section can help here.

One interesting method of controversy stimulation is the appointment of a **devil's advocate** to challenge existing plans and strategies. The advocate's role is to challenge the weaknesses of the plan or strategy and state why it should not be adopted. For example, a bank might be considering offering an interest-paying checking account plan. Details to be decided include interest rate, required minimum balance, and so on. A committee might be assigned to develop a position

Business professors learn how to teach ethics at Arthur Andersen. See Ethical Focus 12-2. (Courtesy of Arthur Andersen & Co., S.C.)

paper. Before a decision is made, someone would be assigned to read the paper and "tear it apart," noting potential weaknesses. Thus, a decision is made in full recognition of the pros and cons of the plan.

YOU BE THE MANAGER

Manager

Fuji, Kodak, and the University of Rochester

The University of Rochester, located in Rochester, New York, is particularly well regarded in the fields of science, engineering, and technology. Despite this, or because of it, the university's graduate business school had a problem. The business school had accepted one Tsuneo Sakai for fall admission. The problem was that Mr. Sakai worked for the Japanese film and photographic products firm Fuji.

The university has always enjoyed a close and cooperative relationship with Kodak, which is based in Rochester. Kodak provides significant funding to the university and provides it with access to some of its databases. Kodak strategy and technology are frequently the object of classroom discussions.

For some time, Kodak and Fuji had been locked in strong competition. Fuji beat out Kodak to become the official film of the Los Angeles Olympic games. Kodak responded by introducing its new disposable camera the day before Fuji's was introduced.

When Kodak heard about the admission of Mr. Sakai to Rochester, it requested that the offer be rescinded. It was concerned that he might learn the firm's proprietary information during classroom discussions.

As Dean of the Rochester business school, what would *you* do?

1. What are the merits of trying to program a decision of this nature?
2. What are some ethical considerations raised by this case?

To find out what Rochester did, see The Manager's Notebook at the end of the chapter.

Source: Adapted from Picht, R. (1987, September 2). Kodak forces school to reject Fuji employee. *The Globe and Mail*, p. B10. (Associated Press).

▼
....

Space Shuttle Decision Making Flawed

On January 28, 1986, a clear, bright day, the space shuttle *Challenger* exploded little more than a minute after lift-off from the Kennedy Space Center in Florida. All seven of its crew were killed. Not surprisingly, early news coverage focused on the possible technical reasons for the disaster. In quick order, with the help of video replays of the explosion, attention was directed toward the giant solid rocket boosters that served to propel the shuttle off the launch pad. Speculation, later confirmed, suggested that the synthetic O-ring seals that separated the booster segments had failed, causing the uncontrolled explosion. It had been unusually cold on the launch pad that morning, and the seals did not respond well to low temperatures.

Even before these technical flaws were confirmed, attention began to shift to the behavioral aspects of the launch. Who actually approved the launch? And weren't there any warnings about the problematic seals? The answers to these and other questions were provided several months later by a presidential committee of inquiry into the *Challenger* disaster that was chaired by former Secretary of State William Rogers. The commission concluded that "there was a serious flaw in the decision-making process" used by NASA.

An especially conspicuous aspect of the decision-making process was the suppression of controversial information that might have contributed to a delay of the fatal launch and even a rethink of shuttle design. It is now clear that engineers at Morton Thiokol, the producer of the boosters, had expressed fears about the integrity of the O-rings to their management for some time, but this information was evidently not passed on to NASA. NASA itself had detected O-ring erosion in previous flights but did not order a suspension of launches, and top NASA management claimed that it had never heard of the seal problem. The night before the launch, cold weather was expected, and a telephone conference was held to discuss its probable effects. Morton Thiokol engineers strongly opposed the launch. However, Thiokol managers, pressured by NASA flight managers at the Marshall Space Flight Center in Alabama, finally agreed to sign off on the launch. Since Thiokol "agreed" to the flight, top NASA management was never informed of the controversy.

Observers noted that the safety consciousness of the earlier space program had been replaced by schedule consciousness as NASA attempted to demonstrate the commercial capabilities of the shuttle. Reports surfaced that astronauts who dissented from this line were pressured by NASA to keep their thoughts to themselves.

Source: Magnuson, E. (1986, March 10). "A serious deficiency." *Time*, 42–44; Marbach, W. D. (1986, February 10). What went wrong? *Newsweek*, 32–34; various articles, *New York Times*, June 10, 1986.

Evidence indicates that the controversy promoted by the devil's advocate improves decision quality.[57] However, to be effective, the advocate must present his or her views in an objective, unemotional manner.

Brainstorming

Brainstorming is the "brain child" of a Madison Avenue advertising executive.[58] Its major purpose is to increase the number of creative solution alternatives to problems. Thus, **brainstorming** focuses on the *generation* of ideas rather than the *evaluation* of ideas. If a large number of ideas can be generated, the chance of obtaining a truly creative solution is increased.

Brainstorming was originally conceived as a group technique. It was assumed that in generating ideas, group members could feed off each other's suggestions and be stimulated to offer more creative solutions. To ensure this, the group is encouraged to operate in a free-wheeling, off-the-wall manner. No ideas should be considered too extreme or unusual to be voiced. In addition, no criticism of ideas should be offered, since this can inhibit useful lines of thinking. For instance, an advertising agency might convene a group to generate names for a new

A flawed decision making process contributed to the Challenger disaster. See In Focus 12-3. (NASA)

Source: Drawing
by Drucker; ©
1977 The New
Yorker Magazine,
Inc.

"On second thought, let's <u>not</u> take another crack at it."

toothpaste or soft drink (as in our cartoon). Similarly, a government agency might convene a group to generate possible solutions for welfare fraud.

Traditional brainstorming has not fulfilled its creative promise. Research has shown conclusively that individuals working alone tend to generate more ideas than when in groups. In other words, four people working independently (and encouraged to be creative and nonevaluative) will usually generate more ideas than the same people working as a team. Why is this? Likely explanations include inhibition, domination of the group by an ineffective member, or the sheer physical limitations of people trying to talk simultaneously. Research on "electronic" brainstorming confirms this. When people can enter their ideas at will into computer terminals, group brainstorming works as well as individual brainstorming.[59] Here, people are more anonymous, and they don't have to wait until others finish "talking."

Nominal Group Technique

The fact that nominal (in name only) brainstorming groups generate more ideas than interacting brainstorming groups gave rise to the **nominal group technique**

(NGT) of decision making. Unlike brainstorming, NGT is concerned with both the generation of ideas and the evaluation of these ideas:

> Imagine a meeting room in which seven to ten individuals are sitting around a table in full view of each other; however, at the beginning of the meeting they do not speak to each other. Instead, each individual is writing ideas on a pad of paper in front of him or her. At the end of five to ten minutes, a structured sharing of ideas takes place. Each individual, in round-robin fashion, presents one idea from his or her private list. A recorder writes that idea on a flip chart in full view of other members. There is still no discussion at this point of the meeting—only the recording of privately narrated ideas. Round-robin listing continues until all members indicate they have no further ideas to share.
>
> Discussion follows during the next phase of the meeting; however, it is structured so that each idea receives attention before independent voting. This is accomplished by asking for clarification, or stating support or nonsupport of each idea listed on the flip chart. Independent voting then takes place. Each member privately, in writing, selects priorities by rank-ordering (or rating). The group decision is the mathematically pooled outcome of the individual votes.[60]

As you can observe, NGT carefully separates the generation of ideas from their evaluation. Ideas are generated nominally (without interaction) to prevent inhibition and conformity. Evaluation permits interaction and discussion, but it occurs in a fairly structured manner to be sure that each idea gets adequate attention.

NGT has been used in a variety of organizational settings, including business and the health care field. Its chief disadvantage would seem to be the time and resources required to assemble the group for face-to-face interaction. The Delphi technique was developed in part to overcome this problem.

The Delphi Technique

The **Delphi technique** of decision making was developed at the Rand Corporation to forecast changes in technology. Its name derives from the future-telling of the famous Greek Delphic Oracle.[61] Unlike NGT, the Delphi process relies solely upon a nominal group—participants do not engage in face-to-face interaction. Thus, it is possible to poll a large number of experts without assembling them in the same place at the same time. It should be emphasized that these experts do not actually make a final decision; rather, they provide information for organizational decision makers.

The heart of Delphi is a series of questionnaires mailed to respondents. Minimally, two waves of questionnaires would be used, but more are not unusual. The first questionnaire is usually general in nature and permits free responses to the problem. For example, suppose the vice-president of personnel of a large multibranch corporation wishes to evaluate and improve the firm's Management by Objectives program. A random sample of managers who have worked with MBO might be identified and sent an initial questionnaire asking them to list the strengths and weaknesses of the program. The personnel staff would collate the responses and develop a second questionnaire that might share these responses and ask for suggested improvements. A final questionnaire might then be sent asking respondents to rate or rank each improvement. The staff would then merge the ratings or rankings mathematically and present them to the vice-president for consideration.

A chief disadvantage of Delphi is the rather lengthy time frame involved in the questionnaire phases (Exhibit 12–6). In addition, its effectiveness depends upon

■
EXHIBIT

12–6

The plan for a typical Delphi exercise.

Activities	Estimated Minimum Time for Accomplishment
1) Develop the Delphi question	$\frac{1}{2}$ day
2) Select and contact respondents	2 days
3) Select sample size	$\frac{1}{2}$ day
4) Develop Questionnaire #1 and test	1 day
a. Type and send out	1 day
b. Response time	5 days
c. Reminder time	3 days
5) Analysis of Questionnaire #1	$\frac{1}{2}$ day
6) Develop Questionnaire #2 and test	2 days
a. Type and send out	1 day
b. Response time	5 days
c. Reminder time	3 days
7) Analysis of Questionnaire #2	1 day
8) Develop Questionnaire #3 and test	2 days
a. Type and send out	1 day
b. Response time	5 days
c. Reminder time	3 days
9) Analysis of Questionnaire #3	1 day
10) Prepare a final report	4 days
a. Type report and send out	1 day
b. Prepare respondents' report	1 day
c. Type report and send out	1 day
Total estimated minimum time	$44\frac{1}{2}$ days

Source: Delbecq, A. L., Van de Ven, A. H., & Gustafson, D. *Group techniques for program planning.* Reprinted by permission of A. L. Delbecq.

the writing skills of the respondents and their interest in the problem, since they must work on their own rather than as part of an actual group. Despite these problems, Delphi is an efficient method of pooling a large number of expert judgments while avoiding the problems of conformity and domination that can occur in interacting groups.

The University of Michigan Transportation Research Institute uses a Delphi survey to poll auto executives about future trends in automobile design and marketing. The industry can then use this informed opinion as part of its decision-making process.[62]

THE MANAGER'S NOTEBOOK

Fuji, Kodak, and the University of Rochester

Kodak was successful in convincing Rochester to rescind Fuji employee Tsuneo Sakai's acceptance at the business school. Mr. Sakai enrolled at the Massachusetts Institute of Technology.

1. There is considerable merit to developing rules or policies to program such decisions. These rules or policies make clear in advance to applicants what constitute the exact criteria for acceptance or rejection. They also clarify the university's position to interested outsiders, such as Kodak and Fuji, and thus prevent the intentional or unintentional exertion of pressure on admissions personnel. Formulating such rules and policies requires decision makers to think through the implications of their decisions.

2. Examining the stakeholders in the decision, Kodak could lose trade secrets to Fuji with the admission of Mr. Sakai. Also, Rochester could lose some support from Kodak. On the other hand, what about the rights of the individual? Should Mr. Sakai be denied an education at Rochester simply because of his place of employment? If Rochester is morally obligated to ignore religion and ethnic background in making admissions, should it be able to consider whom one works for? Was Mr. Sakai a victim of marketing wars rather than a potential industrial spy? What would *you* have done?

SUMMARY

- Decision making is the process of developing a commitment to some course of action. Alternatively, it is a problem-solving process. A problem exists when a gap is perceived between some existing state and some desired state.
- Rational decision making involves (1) problem identification, (2) information search, (3) development of alternative solutions, (4) evaluation of alternatives, (5) choice of best alternative, (6) implementation, and (7) ongoing evaluation of the implemented alternative. The imaginary perfectly rational decision maker has free and easy access to all relevant information, can

process it accurately, and has a single ultimate goal—economic maximization. Real decision makers must suffer with bounded rationality. They do not have free and easy access to information, and the human mind has limited information processing capacity. In addition, time constraints and political considerations can outweigh anticipated economic gain. As a result, bounded decision makers usually satisfice (choose a solution that is "good enough") rather than maximize. Perceptual defense, faulty hindsight, attempts to recover sunk costs, and information overload may damage the quality of decisions.

- Some problems are well structured. This means that existing and desired states are clear, as is the means of getting from one state to the other. Well-structured problems are often solved with programs, which simply standardize solutions. Programmed decision making is effective as long as the program is developed rationally and as long as conditions do not change.
- Ill-structured problems involve some combination of an unclear existing state, an unclear desired state, or unclear methods of getting from one state to the other. They tend to be unique and nonrecurrent, and they require nonprogrammed decision making, in which the rational model comes into play.
- It is often assumed that groups can make higher-quality decisions than individuals because of their vigilance and their potential capacity to generate and evaluate more ideas. Also, group members might accept more readily a decision in which they have been involved. Given the proper problem, groups will frequently make higher-quality decisions than individuals. However, using groups takes a lot of time, can lead to demands for greater participation, and might provoke conflict. In addition, groups might fall prey to groupthink, in which social pressures to conform to a particular decision outweigh rationality. Groups might also make decisions that are more risky or conservative than those of individuals.
- Ethics involves systematic thinking about the moral consequences of decisions. Personality, extreme competition, the organizational culture, and opportunity for gain can all stimulate unethical decisions.
- Attempts to improve decision making have involved training discussion leaders, stimulating controversy, brainstorming, the nominal group technique, and the Delphi technique.

KEY CONCEPTS

Decision making	Escalation of commitment	Risky shift
Problem	Knew-it-all-along effect	Conservative shift
Perfect rationality	Well-structured problems	Ethics
Bounded rationality	Program	Devil's advocate
Information overload	Ill-structured problems	Brainstorming
Maximization	Nonprogrammed decision making	Nominal group technique
Satisficing	Diffusion of responsibility	Delphi technique
Sunk costs	Groupthink	

DISCUSSION QUESTIONS

1. The director of an urban hospital feels that there is a turnover problem among the hospital's nurses. About 25 percent of the staff resigns each year, leading to high replacement costs and disruption of services. Use the decision model shown in Exhibit 12–1 to explore how the director might proceed to solve this problem. Discuss probable bounds to the rationality of the director's decision.

2. Debate the following: Business schools spend too much time teaching students to be maximizers. What they should do is teach students how to be more effective satisficers.

3. Describe a decision-making episode (in school, work, or personal life) in which you experienced information overload. How did you respond to this overload? Did it affect the quality of your decision?

4. Many universities must register thousands of students for courses each semester. Is this a well-structured problem or an ill-structured problem? Does it require programmed decisions or nonprogrammed decisions? Elaborate.

5. An auditing team fails to detect a case of embezzlement that has gone on for several months at a

bank. How might the team members use hindsight to justify their faulty decisions?

6. A very cohesive planning group for a major oil company is about to develop a long-range strategic plan. The head of the unit is aware of the groupthink problem and wishes to prevent it. What steps should she take?

7. Discuss the implications of diffusion of responsibility, risky shift, and conservative shift for the members of a parole board.

8. Discuss how the concepts of groupthink and escalation of commitment might be related to some cases of unethical decision making (and its coverup) in business.

9. What are the similarities and differences of the nominal group technique and the Delphi technique? What are the comparative advantages and disadvantages?

10. Discuss the reasons why decision makers might continue to commit resources to a failing course of action.

■

EXPERIENTIAL EXERCISE

Ethical Decision Making

The purpose of this exercise is to get you to consider some of the ethical aspects of decision making. Imagine that you are a marketing executive. Given below are several decision dilemmas, each of which might have an ethical dimension to it. Working alone, consider each dilemma in turn. For each dilemma, decide and record whether you would agree with the suggested course of action (yes) or disagree with the suggested course of action (no).

Students will then form into small learning groups and discuss each decision dilemma. After each dilemma is discussed, the group should calculate the *percentage* of its members that *agree* with each proposed course of action (some people might have changed their minds after discussion). The instructor will record the percentage of each group favoring each alternative on the board and discuss the results. DO NOT READ THE DEBRIEFING UNTIL TOLD TO DO SO BY THE INSTRUCTOR!

Dilemmas

_____ 1. One of your dealers in an important territory has had family troubles recently and is not producing the sales he used to. He was one of the company's top producers in the past. It is not clear how long it will take before his family trouble straightens out. In the meantime, many sales are being lost. There is a legal way to terminate the dealer's franchise and replace him. What would you do?

_____ 2. You have a chance to win a big account that will mean a lot to you and your company. The purchasing agent hinted that he would be influenced by a "gift." Your assistant recommends sending a fine color television set to his home. What would you do?

_____ 3. You have heard that a competitor has a new product feature that will make a big difference in sales. He will have a hospitality suite at the annual trade show and unveil this feature at a party thrown for his dealers. You can easily send a snooper to this meeting to learn what the new feature is. What would you do?

_____ 4. You are eager to win a big contract, and during sales negotiations you learn that the buyer is looking for a better job. You have no intention of hiring him, but if you hinted that you might, he would probably give you the order. What would you do?

_____ 5. You are a marketing vice president working for a beer company, and you have learned that a particularly lucrative state is planning to raise the minimum legal drinking age from 18 to 21. You have been asked to join other breweries in lobbying against this bill and to make contributions. What would you do?

_____ 6. You want to interview a sample of customers about their reactions to a competitive product. It has been suggested that you invent an innocuous name like the Marketing Research Institute and interview people. What would you do?

_____ 7. You produce an antidandruff shampoo that is effective with one application. Your assistant says that the product would turn over faster if the instructions on the label recommended two applications. What would you do?

Debriefing

George M. Zinkham, Michael Bisesi, and Mary Jane Saxton gave this ethics quiz to M.B.A. students at a major southwestern university over a number of semesters between fall 1981 and spring 1987. Below are the percentages of the students who agreed with the suggestion posed in each dilemma, including the highest semester, the lowest semester, and the average over twelve semesters:

	High %	Low %	Twelve-semester average
1. Terminate franchise?	65	0	18
2. Bribe agent?	35	16	27
3. Send snooper?	88	48	63
4. Hint at job?	25	4	12
5. Join lobby?	70	53	60
6. Invent name?	78	30	48
7. Recommend double dose?	72	32	49

Were there any trends in these responses over time? The researchers found that there was an increasing trend over time to bribe an agent (2), send a snooper (3), and invent a name of a research institute (6). However, recent responses were more resistant to joining an alcohol lobby (5).

■

Source: Dilemmas from Kotter, P. (1980). *Marketing management: Analysis, Planning and Control*, (4th ed.). © 1980, pp. 706–707. Reprinted by permission of Prentice-Hall, Inc., Englewood Cliffs, NJ. Research results from Zinkham, G. M., Bisesi, M., & Saxton, M. M. (1989). MBAs' changing attitudes toward marketing dilemmas: 1981–1987. *Journal of Business Ethics, 8,* 963–974. Reprinted by permission of Kluwer Academic Publishers.

CASE STUDY

Odessy
Communications

Odessy Communication Systems is a company specializing in the distribution of computer software programs. The company was established six years ago by Colin Bright and Jessica Thom, two friends who had studied together in the University. In its first year, Odessy had grown to a staff of eight. Six of the original members were still with the company; and two new members, Stacey Ratton and Brad Broad, had joined a year before.

The management philosophy shared by all members of Odessy was that frequent group discussions, participatory decision making, and an open and supportive climate would allow Odessy to grow and prosper. To promote the philosophy, the following policies were created in the initial stages of Odessy's development:

- Weekly meetings would allow consideration of problems, airing of grievances, and discussion of new ideas.
- Consensus would be reached on all major decisions.
- To create an open climate, activities such as sports, social gatherings, and membership in a software club would be encouraged. Also, a comfortable, informal dining area would be created; and offices would be bright and comfortable, easily accessible by everyone.

Six months ago, Odessy introduced a new line of software called "Dear John," a collection of prewritten letters in various styles and for a variety of occasions. The user simply had to fill out a series of questions on the requirements for the letter; and the software, drawing from its collection, would automatically compose a letter.

At first, the software had received good publicity and had produced good profits; in the last several months, however, Odessy had received many complaints from

Source: Case prepared by Jenepher Lennox. From Ferguson, S. D., & Ferguson, S. (Eds.). (1988). *Organizational communication* (2nd ed.). Copyright © 1988 by Transaction. Reprinted by permission.

dissatisfied users. Apparently, the software was creating letters that did not meet the needs of its users.

A discussion session was called, to be attended by all staff members. Two members, Jim and Sheila, entered the meeting together.

Jim: I don't know what could be wrong with "Dear John." It's the most exciting new software on the market since we designed "Filer" two years ago.

Sheila: I know. We spent so much time conceptualizing and designing it.

Jim: I'm sure that the trouble is with the retailers. Their attempts to demonstrate and sell the products are a farce. Even without real sales experience, I know that any of us could do a better job of selling.

The rest of the staff was seated; so all turned their attention to Colin, who began to outline the problem.

Colin: I guess you've all heard that "Dear John" is generating some complaints and receiving some pretty bad publicity. I've brought the complaints report and the press clipping file so that we can all take a look to see what the problem is.

Amanda: Well, I've read the complaints report, and I can pretty well summarize it for all of you. People don't feel that the letters written by "Dear John" are meeting their needs. The tone and working don't match the occasion.

Tony: The press clippings mainly say the same thing. The critics say that the letters that come out of "Dear John" are too much the same from one to the next. They claim that anyone receiving a "Dear John" feels like it's the same letter that everyone else got. (Everyone laughs)

Jessica: OK, so it sounds like a problem of poor PR. The customers just aren't being shown how individual each letter is. They need to be convinced that "Dear John" is a necessary and valuable tool in their work.

(Nodding heads, several voices of agreement)

Brad: Isn't it possible that "Dear John" is just lacking in originality? If it's the tone and working that people don't like, how will better publicity change that?

(Several members voice their disagreement)

Jim: We all know it's a super product. We did numerous tests; we did consumer surveys; and we're the only company marketing anything like "Dear John."

Amanda: You agreed that it was great, Brad, when we were doing the original tests. Product promotion has a huge effect on how the product is perceived by consumers; so if "Dear John" is not getting the right kind of marketing, we can't blame the software for the lack of positive response.

Jessica: Right. Now, we have to decide how to market "Dear John" so that consumers will appreciate it as the useful product it is. Any suggestions?

Jim: What if we invest in some quality advertising on television and in the newspaper? If we hire a good ad agency, we'll get the message across.

(Nodding heads, murmurs of agreements)

Brad: Before we embark on an ad campaign, don't you think that we should decide whether the product should be modified, or even withdrawn? I mean, we can't ignore the fact that there are more than superficial problems with it.

Amanda: Are you kidding? After the months we've all spent working on "Dear John," designing it, testing it, perfecting it, and finally putting it on the market? We can't just forget all that work and abandon the whole project!

Jim: Yeah, we know it's good. If we put out a couple of thousand dollars to really promote the product, show people its good qualities, then we won't have to worry about a few letters of complaint. Besides there are always a few people who don't like a product, no matter how good it is. You know, those natural complainer types.

Brad: No way, you can't ignore the facts and try to camouflage the product under a glossy ad campaign. You have to look at the problems in "Dear John" and correct them.

Colin: You know, Brad, every time we get started on some good ideas, you break in with your negative attitude. If you can't suggest anything constructive, then don't waste time arguing and criticizing.

Nodding in agreement, the other group members began discussing the ad campaign. The group reached consensus on the final plans, although Brad avoided participating in the planning sessions. After the meeting, Jim and Sheila left together.

Jim: Well, I can't wait to see the results of the ad campaign. The public can't help but be persuaded to buy the product after being exposed to this campaign.

Sheila: Yes, it does look good. I was thinking though about what Brad was saying, that there may be problems with the product itself. We didn't really examine that question. I wonder if some of those consumer complaints may be valid. I didn't want to mention my doubts, though, because everyone else seemed to feel so strongly about "Dear John." I didn't want to seem pessimistic.

Jim: No, it's a good thing you didn't say anything. There was no need. It would have put people on edge and maybe hurt some feelings. Oh, are you meeting us for a baseball game at lunch tomorrow?

Sheila: You bet I will!

They parted, waving, contented with their accomplishments and another successful day at Odessy Communication Systems.

■

1. Is the problem about which the group is meeting ill-structured or well-structured? How does the *group* perceive the problem in terms of structure?

2. Use the rational decision-making model shown in Exhibit 12–1 to describe and evaluate the decision-making process described in the case.

3. Apply the concepts of sunk costs and escalation of commitment to the events in the case.

4. Discuss the group dynamics illustrated in the case. Did groupthink occur? Give specific evidence to support your answer.

5. What are the ethical issues raised in the case?

6. Using the material in the chapter, what could have been done to improve the group's decision-making process?

■

REFERENCES

1. Mintzberg, H. (1979). *The structuring of organizations*. Englewood Cliffs, NJ: Prentice-Hall.

2. MacCrimmon, K. R., & Taylor, R. N. (1976). Decision making and problem solving. In M. D. Dunnette (Ed.), *Handbook of industrial and organizational psychology*. Chicago: Rand McNally.

3. Simon, H. A. (1957). *Administrative behavior* (2nd ed.). New York: Free Press.

4. The latter two difficulties are discussed by Huber, G. P. (1980). *Managerial decision making.* Glenview, IL: Scott, Foresman. For further discussion of problem identification, see Kiesler, S., & Sproull, L. (1982). Managerial response to changing environments: Perspectives on problem sensing from social cognition. *Administrative Science Quarterly, 27,* 548–570; Cowan, D. A. (1986). Developing a process model of problem recognition. *Academy of Management Review, 11,* 763–776.

5. Tversky, A., & Kahneman, D. (1973). Availability: A heuristic for judging frequency and probability. *Cognitive Psychology, 5,* 207–232. Also see Taylor, S. E., and Fiske, S. T. (1978). Salience, attention, and attribution: Top of the head phenomena. In L. Berkowitz (Ed.), *Advances in experimental social psychology* (Vol. 11). New York: Academic Press.

6. Sherman, S. P. (1989, March 26). The mind of Jack Welch. *Fortune,* 38–50, p. 42.

7. Miller, J. G. (1960). Information input, overload, and psychopathology. *American Journal of Psychiatry, 116,* 695–704.

8. Manis, M., Fichman, M., & Platt, M. (1978). Cognitive integration and referential communication: Effects of information quality and quantity in message decoding. *Organizational Behavior and Human Performance, 22,* 417–430; Troutman, C. M., & Shanteau, J. (1977). Inferences based on nondiagnostic information. *Organizational Behavior and Human Performance, 19,* 43–55.

9. O'Reilly, C. A., III. (1980). Individuals and information overload in organizations: Is more necessarily better? *Academy of Management Journal, 23,* 684–696.

10. Feldman, M. S., & March, J. G. (1981). Information in organizations as signal and symbol. *Administrative Science Quarterly, 26,* 171–186.

11. Bonoma, T. V. (1977). Business decision making: Marketing implications. In M. F. Kaplan & S. Schwartz (Eds.), *Human judgment and decision processes in applied settings.* New York: Academic Press.

12. MacCrimmon & Taylor, 1976.

13. Simon, H. A. (1957). *Models of man.* New York: Wiley; Cyert, R. M., & March, J. G. (1963). *A behavioral theory of the firm.* Englewood Cliffs, NJ: Prentice-Hall.

14. Slovic, P., Fischhoff, B., & Lichtenstein, S. (1977). Behavioral decision theory. *Annual Review of Psychology, 28,* 1–39.

15. Staw, B. M. (1980). Rationality and justification in organizational life. *Research in Organizational Behavior, 2,* 45–80.

16. For a detailed treatment and other perspectives, see Northcraft, G. B., & Wolf, G. (1984). Dollars, sense, and sunk costs: A life cycle model of resource allocation decisions. *Academy of Management Review, 9,* 225–234.

17. Staw, B. M. (1981). The escalation of commitment to a course of action. *Academy of Management Review, 6,* 577–587. For alternative views, see Bowen, M. G. (1987). The escalation phenomenon revisited: Decision dilemmas or decision errors? *Academy of Management Review, 12,* 52–66.

18. Staw, 1981. For the limitations on this view, see Knight, P. A. (1984). Heroism versus competence: Competing explanations for the effects of experimenting and consistent management. *Organizational Behavior and Human Performance, 33,* 307–322.

19. Arkes, H. R., & Blumer, C. (1985). The psychology of sunk cost. *Organizational Behavior and Human Decision Processes, 35,* 124–140.

20. Whyte, G. (1986). Escalating commitment to a course of action: A reinterpretation. *Academy of Management Review, 11,* 311–321.

21. Bach, S. (1985). *Final cut: Dreams and disaster in the making of Heaven's Gate.* New York: Morrow.

22. Hawkins, S. A., & Hastie, R. (1990). Hindsight: Biased judgments of past events after outcomes are known. *Psychological Bulletin, 107,* 311–327.

23. Greenwald, A. G. (1980). The totalitarian ego: Fabrication and revision of personal history. *American Psychologist, 35,* 603–618.

24. Mitchell, T. R., & Beach, L. R. Expectancy theory, decision theory, and occupational preference and choice. In Kaplan & Schwartz, 1977.

25. Pinfield, L. T. (1986). A field evaluation of perspectives on organizational decision making. *Administrative Science Quarterly, 31,* 365–388.

26. Nutt, P. C. (1984). Types of organizational decision processes. *Administrative Science Quarterly, 29,* 414–450.

27. Lord, R. G., & Maher, K. J. (1990). Alternative information-processing models and their implications for theory, research, and practice. *Academy of Management Review, 15,* 9–28.

28. MacCrimmon & Taylor, 1976.

29. Shaw, M. E. (1981). *Group dynamics* (3rd ed.). New York: McGraw-Hill, p. 78.

30. Hill, G. W. (1982). Group versus individual performance: Are n + 1 heads better than one? *Psychological Bulletin, 91,* 517–539.

31. Shaw, 1981; Davis, J. H. (1969). *Group performance.* Reading, MA: Addison-Wesley; Libby, R., Trotman, K. T., & Zimmer, I. (1987). Member variation, recognition of expertise, and group performance. *Journal of Applied Psychology, 72,* 81–87.

32. Janis, I. L. (1972). *Victims of groupthink*. Boston: Houghton Mifflin.

33. McCauley, C. (1989). The nature of social influence in groupthink: Compliance and internalization. *Journal of Personality and Social Psychology, 57*, 250–260. For another view of causes, see Whyte, G. F. (1989). Groupthink reconsidered. *Academy of Management Review, 14*, 40–56.

34. Janis, 1972.

35. Huseman, R. C., & Driver, R. W. (1979). Groupthink: Implications for small-group decision making in business. In R. Huseman & A. B. Carroll (Eds.), *Readings in organizational behavior: Dimensions of management actions*. Boston: Allyn and Bacon.

36. Stoner, J. A. F. (1961). *A comparison of individual and group decisions involving risk*. Unpublished Master's thesis. School of Industrial Management, Massachusetts Institute of Technology.

37. Lamm, H., & Myers, D. G. (1978). Group-induced polarization of attitudes and behavior. In L. Berkowitz (Ed.), *Advances in experimental social psychology* (Vol. 11). New York: Academic Press.

38. Lamm & Myers, 1978.

39. This draws loosely on Glenn, J. R., Jr. (1986). *Ethics in decision making*. New York: Wiley.

40. For reviews, see Tsalikis, J., & Fritzsche, D. J. (1989). Business ethics: A literature review with a focus on marketing ethics. *Journal of Business Ethics, 8*, 695–743; Trevino, L. K. (1986). Ethical decision making in organizations: A person-situation interactionist model. *Academy of Management Review, 11*, 601–617.

41. Tsalikis & Fritzsche, 1989.

42. Tsalikis & Fritzsche, 1989.

43. Bird, F., & Waters, J. A. (1987). The nature of managerial moral standards. *Journal of Business Ethics, 6*, 1–13.

44. Trevino, L. K., Sutton, C. D., & Woodman, R. W. (1985). *Effects of reinforcement contingencies and cognitive moral development on ethical decision-making behavior: An experiment*. Paper presented at the annual meeting of the Academy of Management, San Diego; Hegarty, W. H., & Sims, H. P., Jr. (1978). Some determinants of unethical behavior: An experiment. *Journal of Applied Psychology, 63*, 451–457.

45. Levine, D. B. (1990, May 21). The inside story of an inside trader. *Fortune*, 80–89, p. 82.

46. Staw, B. M., & Szwajkowski, E. W. (1975). The scarcity-munificence component of organizational environments and the commission of illegal acts. *Administrative Science Quarterly, 20*, 345–354.

47. Sonnenfeld, J., & Lawrence, P. R. (1989). Why do companies succumb to price fixing? In K. R. Andrew (Ed.), *Ethics in practice: Managing the moral corporation*. Boston: Harvard Business School Press.

48. Hegarty & Sims, 1978; Hegarty, W. H., & Sims, H. P., Jr. (1979). Organizational philosophy, policies, and objectives related to unethical decision behavior: A laboratory experiment. *Journal of Applied Psychology, 64*, 331–338.

49. Colby, A., & Kohlberg, L. (1987). *The measurement of moral judgment. Volume 1: Theoretical foundations and research validation*. Cambridge: Cambridge University Press; also see Trevino, 1986.

50. Victor, B., & Cullen, J. B. (1988). The organizational bases of ethical work climates. *Administrative Science Quarterly, 33*, 101–125.

51. Sonnenfeld & Lawrence, 1989. See also Hosmer, L. T. (1987). The institutionalization of unethical behavior. *Journal of Business Ethics, 6*, 439–447.

52. This draws on Waters, J. A., & Bird, F. (1988). *A note on what a well-educated manager should be able to do with respect to moral issues in management*. Unpublished manuscript.

53. Weber, J. (1990). Measuring the impact of teaching ethics to future managers: A review, assessment, and recommendations. *Journal of Business Ethics, 9*, 183–190.

54. Maier, N. R. F. (1973). *Psychology in industrial organizations* (4th ed.). Boston: Houghton Mifflin.

55. Maier, N. R. F. (1970). *Problem solving and creativity in individuals and groups*. Belmont, CA: Brooks/Cole.

56. Tjosvold, D. (1985). Implications of controversy research for management. *Journal of Management, 11*(3), 21–37.

57. Schwenk, C. R. (1984). Devil's advocacy in managerial decision-making. *Journal of Management Studies, 21*, 153–168. For a recent study, see Schweiger, D. M., Sandberg, W. R., & Ragan, J. W. (1986). Group approaches for improving strategic decision making: A comparative analysis of dialectical inquiry, devil's advocacy, and consensus. *Academy of Management Journal, 29*, 51–71.

58. Osborn, A. F. (1957). *Applied imagination*. New York: Scribners.

59. Gallupe, R. B., Bastianutti, L. M., & Cooper, W. H. (1991). Unblocking brainstorms. *Journal of Applied Psychology, 76*, 137–142.

60. Delbecq, A. L., Van de Ven, A. H., & Gustafson, D. H. (1975). *Group techniques for program planning*. Glenview, IL: Scott, Foresman, p. 8.

61. Delbecq et al., 1975.

62. 1992 cars: Not too far out. (1984, March 26). *Autoweek*, p. 4.

POWER, POLITICS, AND CONFLICT

MARY CUNNINGHAM

Mary Cunningham entered the Harvard Business School. Two years later, at age twenty-seven, she graduated and proceeded to exhibit one of the fastest starts to a business career ever seen in North America. Faced with a variety of job offers, she accepted a position as executive assistant to William Agee, chairman of Bendix Corporation. In this job, she wrote his speeches and prepared testimony for him to offer in hearings in Washington. A year later, Ms. Cunningham was promoted to vice-president for corporate and public affairs and headed up a task force to review the firm's North American automotive supplies activities. Three months after this, she was again promoted, this time to vice-president for strategic planning. Two months later, Cunningham resigned from Bendix. Her resignation followed an extraordinary meeting of 600 employees in which Agee denied that her rapid advancement was due to personal involvement with him.

What accounted for the rise and fall of Mary Cunningham? As for the rise, there is no doubt that she was extremely bright and highly motivated to obtain power. In addition, Agee took a strong interest in her career development, admiring her expertise. They were clearly kindred spirits. At best, critics attributed her rise to unwarranted favoritism on the part of Agee. At worst, they hinted at an affair.

Several factors probably accounted for the ill will toward Cunningham. For one thing, some executives did not share Agee's view about Cunningham's expertise, especially in the automotive parts field. Some felt that her task force report yielded little new information. In addition, some managers were angered that Cunningham had not consulted them in the preparation of the report, and some senior executives were upset that she had been promoted over them. Finally, Cunningham had become closely identified with Agee's plan to move Bendix away from automobile parts and into high technology. Although most executives agreed that this change was necessary, some might have feared the rapid redistribution of power that was occurring.

Mary Cunningham survived a vote of confidence from the board of directors but resigned because the controversy had reduced her effectiveness within the company. Shortly thereafter, she took a planning position at Seagrams. Sometime later, Agee himself was forced out of Bendix. Eventually, Cunningham and Agee married and set up a consulting firm.[1]

This true story illustrates the main themes of this chapter—power, politics, and conflict. First, power will be defined, and the bases of individual power will be discussed. Then we shall examine how organizational members get power and who seeks power. After this we shall explore how organizational subunits, such as particular departments, obtain power. Organizational politics will be defined, and the relationship of politics to power will be explored. The final topic of the chapter is conflict. The causes and results of conflict will be examined, and the pros and cons of conflict will be considered. Finally, some methods of managing conflict will be disccussed.

SEE NO EVIL, HEAR NO EVIL, SPEAK NO EVIL—A PROLOGUE

"But no matter how we're going to word it, to the manager of Corporate Services our recommendation is going to say that he has done

Mary Cunningham-Agee. Her career tells us a lot about organizational politics and conflict. (David R. Frazier Photolibrary)

a lousy job. And naturally he is resisting. He is resisting because he thinks he's got some power. Not he himself but someone higher up; he's got contacts. And we think we've got some power; and we've got people who can bring influence to bear upon this question. It isn't a matter of who is right; it's who's got the power. And a lot of times the support is not because our facts are 100 per cent correct, but because some guy likes what we're doing. Or he likes the individuals. Or he thinks, politically speaking, he should back us. And right now, politically speaking, it's going to be favorable for some big guy to back us because of the slump in the economy—see?"[2]

We see! We see! And somehow we *know* that many organizational decisions do not depend upon who is "100 per cent correct." Rather, as the speaker insists, decisions often depend upon power dynamics and political considerations. And, as he implies, this often promotes organizational conflict.

Until fairly recently, power, politics, and conflict were not considered polite topics for coverage in organizational behavior textbooks. At best, they were seen as irrational, and at worst, as evil. Now, though, theorists and researchers have begun to recognize what managers have known all along—that power, politics, and conflict are *natural* expressions of life in organizations. They often develop as a rational response to a complex set of needs and goals, and their expression may be beneficial rather than evil.

WHAT IS POWER?

Power is the capacity to influence others who are in a state of dependence. Several points about this definition deserve elaboration. First, notice that power is the *capacity* to influence the behavior of others. Power is not always exercised.[3] For example, most professors hold a great degree of potential power over students in terms of grades, assignment load, and the ability to embarrass students in class. Under normal circumstances, only a small amount of this power is actually used.

Second, the fact that the target of power is dependent upon the powerholder does not imply that a poor relationship exists between the two. For instance, your best friend has power to influence your behavior and attitudes because you are dependent upon him or her for friendly reactions and social support. Presumably, you can exert reciprocal influence for similar reasons.

Third, power can flow in any direction in an organization. Often, members at higher organizational levels have more power than those at lower levels. However, in specific cases, reversals can occur. For example, the janitor who finds the president in a compromising position with a secretary might find himself in a powerful position if the president wishes to maintain his reputation in the organization!

Finally, power is a broad concept that applies to both individuals and groups. On one hand, an individual production manager might exert considerable influence over the supervisors who report to him. On the other, the marketing department at XYZ Foods might be the most powerful department in the company, able to get its way more often than other departments. But from where do the production manager and the marketing department obtain their power? This issue is explored in the following sections. First, we will consider individual bases of power and how they are obtained. Then we will examine how organizational subunits (such as the marketing department) obtain power.

THE BASES OF INDIVIDUAL POWER

If you wanted to marshal some power to influence others in your organization, where would you get it? Put simply, power can be found in the *position* that you occupy in the organization or the *resources* that you are able to command. The first base of power to be discussed, legitimate power, is dependent upon one's position or job. The other bases (reward, coercive, referent, and expert power) involve the control of important resources. If other organizational members do not respect your position or value the resources that you command, they will not be dependent on you, and you will lack power to influence them.[4]

Legitimate Power

Legitimate power derives from a person's position or job in the organization. It constitutes the organization's judgment about who is formally permitted to influence whom, and it is often called authority. As we move up the organization's hierarchy, we find that members possess more and more legitimate power. In theory, organizational equals (e.g., all vice-presidents) have equal legitimate power. Of course, some people are more likely than others to *invoke* their legitimate power—"Look, *I'm* the boss around here."

Organizations differ greatly in the extent to which they emphasize and reinforce legitimate power. At one extreme is the U.S. Army, which has many levels of command, differentiating uniforms, and rituals (e.g., salutes), all designed to emphasize legitimate power. On the other hand, the academic hierarchy of universities tends to downplay differences in the legitimate power of lecturers, professors, chairpeople, and deans.

When legitimate power works, it does so because people have been socialized to accept its influence. Experiences with parents, teachers, and law enforcement officials cause members to enter organizations with a degree of readiness to submit to (and exercise) legitimate power. In fact, studies consistently show that employees cite legitimate power as a major reason for following their boss's directives, even across various cultures.[5]

Reward Power

Reward power exists when the powerholder can exert influence by providing positive outcomes and preventing negative outcomes. In general, it corresponds to the concept of positive reinforcement discussed in Chapter 3. Reward power is often used to back up legitimate power. That is, managers and supervisors are given the chance to recommend raises, do performance evaluations, and assign preferred tasks to subordinates. Of course, *any* organizational member can attempt to exert influence over others with praise, compliments, and flattery, which also constitute rewards.

Coercive Power

Coercive power is available when the powerholder can exert influence by the use of punishment and threat. Like reward power, it is often used as a support for legitimate power. Supervisors and managers might be permitted to dock pay, assign unfavorable tasks, or block promotions. Despite a strong civil service system, even U.S. government agencies provide their executives with plenty of coercive power:

> Some agencies have a Siberia—an unpleasant or professionally unproductive duty station, to which rebellious employees may be reassigned. Faced with Siberia, an employee may, of course, resign, but even if he accepts exile, he is effectively removed from the position in which he caused difficulty.
>
> "You'd be surprised how many resignations we had when people discovered they had been reassigned to Anchorage," said one former Federal Aeronautics Administration official.[6]

Of course, coercive power is not perfectly correlated with legitimate power. Lower-level organizational members can also apply their share of coercion. For example, work-to-rule campaigns, designed to slow productivity by adhering religiously to organizational procedures, may be employed. Cohesive work groups are especially skillful at enforcing such campaigns.

In Chapter 3 it was pointed out that the use of punishment to control behavior is very problematic because of emotional side effects. Thus, it is not surprising that the use of coercive power by managers is generally ineffective.[7]

Referent Power

Referent power exists when the powerholder is *well liked* by others. It is not surprising that we are readily influenced by people we like. We are prone to consider their points of view, ignore their failures, and seek their approval. In fact, it is often highly dissonant to hold a point of view that is discrepant from that held by someone we like.[8]

Referent power is especially potent for two reasons. First, it stems from *identification* with the powerholder. Thus, it seems to represent a truer or deeper base of power than reward or coercion, which may stimulate mere compliance to achieve rewards or avoid punishment. Second, *anyone* in the organization may be well liked, irrespective of their other bases of power. Thus, referent power is available to everyone from the janitor to the president.

Friendly interpersonal relations often permit influence to be extended across the organization, outside of the usual channels of legitimate authority, reward, and coercion. For example, a production manager who becomes friendly with the design engineer through participation in a task force might later use this contact to ask for a favor in solving a production problem.

Expert Power

A person has **expert power** when he or she has special expertise that is valued by the organization. In any circumstance, we tend to be influenced by experts or by those who are known to perform their jobs well. However, the more crucial and unusual this expertise, the greater the expert power available. Thus, expert power corresponds to difficulty of replacement. Consider the business school that has one highly published professor who is an internationally known scholar and past presidential cabinet member. Such a person would obviously be difficult to replace and should have much greater expert power than an unpublished lecturer.

One of the most fascinating aspects of expert power occurs when it is accrued by lower-level organizational members. Many secretaries have acquired expert power through long experience in dealing with clients, keeping records, or sparring with the bureaucracy. Frequently, they have been around longer than those they serve. In this case, it is not unusual for bosses to create special titles and develop new job classifications to reward their expertise and prevent their resignation.

Expert power is especially likely to exist for lower-level members in scientific and technical areas. Consider the solid-state physicist who has just completed her Ph.D. dissertation on a topic of particular interest to her new employer. Although new to the firm, she might have considerable expert power. Put simply, she *knows* more than her boss, whose scientific knowledge in this area is now outdated. At the Bendix Corporation, some executives granted Mary Cunningham expert power while others did not. William Agee marvelled at her expertise, but some others felt that she had little understanding of the automotive supplies area.

Studies show that expert power is a valuable asset for managers. Of all the bases of power, expertise is most consistently associated with subordinate effectiveness.[9]

HOW DO INDIVIDUALS OBTAIN POWER?

Now that we have discussed the individual bases of power, we can turn to the issue of how people *get* power. That is, how do organizational members obtain promotions to positions of legitimate power, demonstrate their expertise, and get others to like them? And how do they acquire the ability to provide others with rewards and punishment? Rosabeth Moss Kanter, an organizational sociologist, has provided some succinct answers—Do the right things, and cultivate the right people.[10]

✳ Doing the Right Things

We would hope that most organizational members do the "right thing" most of the time. However, according to Kanter, some activities are "righter" than others for obtaining power. She argues that activities lead to power when they are extraordinary, highly visible, and especially relevant to the solution of organizational problems.

Extraordinary Activities Excellent performance of a routine job might not be enough to obtain power. This is especially true in the management and professional ranks, in which one is generally expected to demonstrate a high level of competence. What is needed to obtain power, according to Kanter, is excellent performance in *unusual* or *nonroutine* activities. In the large company that she studied, these activities included occupying new positions, managing substantial changes, and taking great risks. For example, consider the business school professor who establishes and directs a new M.B.A. program. This is a risky major change that involves the occupancy of a new position. If successful, the professor should acquire substantial power in the school.

Visible Activities Extraordinary activities will fail to generate power if no one knows about them. This is a special problem in large, geographically dispersed organizations. The manager who successfully "turns around" the Peoria plant might go unrecognized by executives in New York. People who have an interest in power are especially good at identifying visible activities and publicizing them. The successful marketing executive whose philosophy is profiled in *Fortune* will reap the benefits of power. Similarly, the innovative surgeon whose techniques are reported in the *New England Journal of Medicine* will enhance her influence in the hospital.

Relevant Activities Extraordinary, visible work may fail to generate power if no one cares. If the work is not seen as relevant to the solution of important organizational problems, it will not add to one's influence. The English professor who wins two Pulitzer prizes will probably not accrue much power if his small college is financially strapped and hurting for students. The same might apply to an innovative personnel manager in a company that is fighting for survival. Neither is seen as contributing to the solution of pressing organizational problems. As we shall see shortly, being in the right place at the right time is crucial to the acquisition of power. In another college or company, these extraordinary, visible activities might generate considerable influence.

At Bendix, Mary Cunningham's activities were perceived by some as extraordinary, visible, and relevant. Running the special task force was an important, visible job because the company was rethinking its heavy involvement in the automotive field.

Cultivating the Right People

An old saying advises "It's not what you know, it's *who* you know." In reference to power in organizations, there is probably more than a grain of truth to the latter part of this statement. Developing informal relationships with the right people (especially when coupled with doing the right things) can prove a useful means of acquiring power. Dr. Kanter suggests that the right people can include organizational subordinates, peers, and superiors. To these we might add certain crucial outsiders.

Outsiders Establishing good relationships with key people outside of one's organization can lead to increased power within the organization. Sometimes this power is merely a reflection of the status of the outsider, but all the same it may add to one's internal influence. The assistant director of a hospital who is friendly with the president of the American Medical Association might find herself holding power by association. Cultivating outsiders may also contribute to more tangible sources of power. Organizational members who are on the boards of directors of other companies might acquire critical information about business conditions that they can use in their own firms. The purchasing agent who develops good relations with suppliers might be able to "work wonders" when shortages exist, thus adding to his power base. The tendency for business leaders to cultivate relationships with members of Congress is no accident!

Subordinates At first blush, it might seem unlikely that power can be enhanced by cultivating relationships with subordinates. However, as Kanter notes, influence can be accrued by being closely identified with certain up-and-coming subordinates—"I taught her everything she knows." In academics, some professors are better known for the brilliant Ph.D. students they have supervised than for their own published work. Of course, there is also the possibility that an outstanding subordinate will one day become one's boss! Having cultivated the relationship earlier, one might then be rewarded with special influence.

Cultivating subordinate interests can also provide power when a manager can demonstrate that he or she is backed by a cohesive team. The research director who can oppose a policy change by honestly insisting that "My people won't stand for this" knows that there is strength in numbers.

Peers Cultivating good relationships with peers is mainly a means of ensuring that nothing gets in the way of one's *future* acquisition of power. As one moves up through the ranks, favors can be asked of former associates, and fears of being "stabbed in the back" for a past misdeed are precluded. Organizations often reward good "team players" with promotions on the assumption that they have demonstrated good interpersonal skills. For instance, the military sometimes uses peer ratings as an input in promotion decisions.

Superiors Liaisons with key superiors probably represent the best way of obtaining power through cultivating others. Such superiors are often called mentors or sponsors because of the special interest they show in a promising subordinate. Mentors can provide power in several ways. Obviously, it is useful to be identified as a protégé of someone higher in the organization. More concretely, mentors can provide special information and useful introductions to other "right people."

It is often argued that mentors are especially important for women junior executives because of the general lack of female role models at higher organizational ranks. It is absolutely clear that Mary Cunningham acquired power at Bendix because William Agee served as her mentor. Her story also points out a common problem with the mentor-protégé relationship—some organizational members might attack the protégé as an indirect means of damaging his or her mentor. We will discuss mentorship in more detail in Chapter 18.

WHO WANTS POWER?

Who wants power? At first glance, the answer would seem to be *everybody*. After all, it is both convenient and rewarding to be able to exert influence over others. Power whisks celebrities to the front of movie lines, gets rock stars the best restaurant tables, and enables executives to shape organizations in their own image. Actually, there are considerable individual differences in the extent to which individuals pursue and enjoy power. On television talk shows, we occasionally see celebrities recount considerable embarrassment over the unwarranted power that public recognition brings.

Earlier it was indicated that power is often considered a manifestation of evil. This is due in no small part to the image of power seekers that has historically been portrayed by some psychologists and political scientists. Several aspects of this image are strikingly similar:

- Power seekers are neurotics who are covering up feelings of inferiority.
- Power seekers are striving to compensate for childhood deprivation.
- Power seekers are substituting power for lack of affection.[11]

There can be little doubt that these characteristics do apply to some power seekers. Underlying this negative image of power seeking is the idea that some power seekers feel weak and resort primarily to coercive power to cover up, compensate for, or substitute for this weakness.[12] Power is sought for its own sake and is used irresponsibly to hurt others. Adolf Hitler comes to mind as an extreme example.

But can power be used responsibly to influence others? Psychologist David McClelland says yes. In Chapter 6 we discussed McClelland's research on need for power (*n* Pow). You will recall that *n* Pow is defined as the need to have strong influence over others. This need is a reliable personality characteristic—some people have more *n* Pow than others.[13] Also, just as many women have high *n* Pow as men.[14] In "pure" form, people who are high in *n* Pow conform to the negative stereotype depicted above—they are rude, sexually exploitive, and abusive of alcohol and show a great concern with status symbols. However, when *n* Pow is used in a responsible and controlled manner, these negative properties are not observed. Specifically, McClelland argues that the most effective managers:

- Have high *n* Pow
- Use their power to achieve organizational goals
- Adopt a participative or "coaching" leadership style
- Are relatively unconcerned with how much others like them

McClelland calls such managers *institutional managers* because they use their power for the good of the institution rather than for self-aggrandizement. They refrain from coercive leadership but don't play favorites, since they aren't worried about being well liked. His research reveals that institutional managers are more effective than *personal power managers,* who use their power for personal gain, and *affiliative managers,* who are more concerned with being liked than with exercising power. Exhibit 13-1 on page 468 shows that institutional managers are generally superior in giving subordinates a sense of responsibility, clarifying organizational priorities, and instilling team spirit.[15] We can conclude that the need for power can be a useful asset as long as it is not a neurotic expression of perceived weakness.

Finally, what happens when people want power but can't get it because they are locked in a low-level job or faced with excessive rules and regulations? People react to such powerlessness by trying to gain control, but if they can't succeed, they feel helpless and become alienated from their work.[16]

CONTROLLING STRATEGIC CONTINGENCIES—HOW SUBUNITS OBTAIN POWER

Thus far we have been concerned with the bases of *individual* power and how individual organizational members obtain influence. In this section we shift our concern to **subunit power.** Most straightforwardly, the term *subunit* applies to organizational departments. In a business firm these departments might include production, marketing, finance, research, and personnel. In a university they might include personnel, registration, records, maintenance, and the various academic departments (e.g., history, chemistry, and management). In some cases, subunits could also refer to particular jobs, such as those held by intensive-care nurses, mechanics, or mail carriers.

EXHIBIT
13–1

Responses of subordinates of managers with different motive profiles.

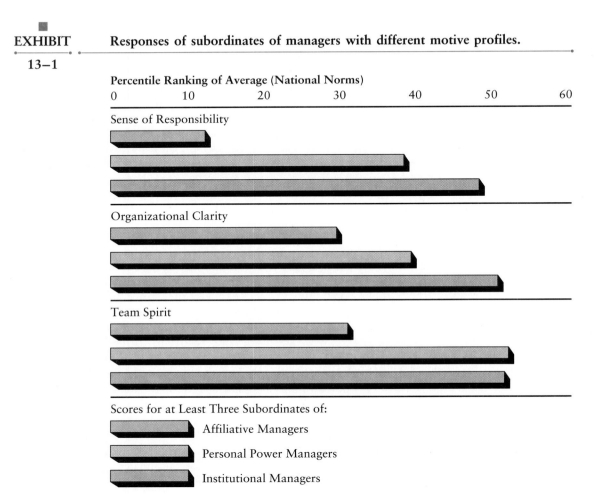

Percentile Ranking of Average (National Norms)

| 0 | 10 | 20 | 30 | 40 | 50 | 60 |

Sense of Responsibility

Organizational Clarity

Team Spirit

Scores for at Least Three Subordinates of:

Affiliative Managers

Personal Power Managers

Institutional Managers

How do organizational subunits acquire power? That is, how do they achieve influence that enables them to grow in size, get a bigger share of the budget, obtain better facilities, and have greater impact on decisions? In short, they control **strategic contingencies.** This means that the work performed by *other* subunits is contingent upon the activities and performance of a key subunit. Again, we see the critical role of *dependence* in power relationships. If some subunits are dependent upon others for smooth operations (or their very existence), they are susceptible to influence. We turn now to the conditions under which subunits can control strategic contingencies.

Scarcity

Differences in subunit power are likely to be magnified when resources become scarce.[17] When there is plenty of budget money or office space or support staff for all subunits, they will seldom waste their energies jockeying for power. If cutbacks occur, however, differences in power will become apparent. For example, well-funded quality of worklife programs or organizational development efforts might disappear when economic setbacks occur because the subunits that control them are not essential to the firm's existence.

Subunits tend to acquire power when they are able to *secure* scarce resources that are important to the organization as a whole. One study of a large state university found that the power of academic departments was associated with their ability to obtain funds through consulting contracts and research grants. This mastery over economic resources was more crucial to their power than was the number of undergraduates taught by the department.[18]

Uncertainty

Organizations detest the unknown. Unanticipated events wreak havoc with financial commitments, long-range plans, and tomorrow's operations. The basic sources of uncertainty exist mainly in the organization's environment—government policies might change, sources of supply and demand might dry up, or the economy might take an unanticipated turn. It stands to reason that the subunits that are most capable of coping with uncertainty will tend to acquire power.[19] In a sense, these subunits are able to protect the others from serious problems. By the same token, uncertainty promotes confusion, which permits *changes* in power priorities as the organizational environment changes:

> The most power goes to those people in those functions that provide greater control over what the organization finds currently problematic: sales and marketing people when markets are competitive; production experts when materials are scarce and demand is high; personnel or labor relations specialists when labor is scarce; lawyers, lobbyists, and external relations specialists when government regulations impinge; finance and accounting types when business is bad and money tight. There is a turning to those elements of the system that seem to have the power to create more certainty in the face of dependency, to generate a more advantageous position for the organization.[20]

A dramatic example of a shift in subunit power has occurred for the personnel or human resource departments of large corporations during the past twenty years. For many years, the personnel function in most organizations had relatively little power. However, beginning in the 1970s, increased government intervention into personnel policies began. This was especially true in the area of employment discrimination, in which legislation provoked considerable uncertainty. In coming to the rescue, personnel departments acquired a long-awaited measure of power. Currently, the uncertainty provoked by downsizing, new technology, and mergers and acquisitions has continued the trend.

Centrality

Other things being equal, subunits whose activities are most central to the work flow of the organization should acquire more power than those whose activities are more peripheral.[21] A subunit's activities can be central in at least three senses. First, they may influence the work of most other subunits. The finance or accounting department is a good example here—its authority to approve expenses and make payments affects every other department in the firm.

Centrality also exists when a subunit has an especially crucial impact on the quantity or quality of the organization's key product or service. This is one reason for the traditional low power of personnel departments—their activities are fairly remote from the primary goals of the organization. Similarly, a production department should have more power than a research and development department that only "fine-tunes" existing products.

Finally, a subunit's activities are more central when their impact is more immediate. As an example, consider a large city government that includes a fire department, a police department, and a public works department. The impact of a lapse in fire or police services will be felt more immediately than a lapse in street repairs. This gives the former departments more potential for power acquisition.

One prominent trend in large North American organizations has been the reduction in power of corporate headquarters staff units (see In Focus 13-1). An example would be a marketing research department that is set up to do studies for several divisional product lines. Many organizations have found that, because of their centrality (literal and figurative) in the decision process, such units slow decision making and damage communication between top management and the field. This is out of step with the increasing global pace of business. One reaction has been to slash corporate staff and push more of their responsibilities down into the divisions.

Substitutability

A subunit will have relatively little power if its activities can be performed by others inside or outside of the organization. If the subunit's staff is nonsubstitutable, however, it can acquire substantial power.[22] One crucial factor here is the labor market for the specialty performed by the subunit. A change in the labor market can result in a change in the subunit's influence:

> In the 1950s, when there were relatively few engineers to service an expanding American economy, engineers had great prestige and power. They could force employers to provide them with large salaries and benefits, by threatening to withhold their services. By the

IN FOCUS 13–1

▼
....

Headquarters Staff Loses Power at GE, Owens-Illinois, and Heinz

Fortune magazine has noted the decline in the power of headquarters staff units in recent years. This has occurred as many CEOs have attempted to delegate more authority to lower-level managers in operating units to nurture their leadership opportunities:

Staff are second-guessers by nature. Says Harvard's [John] Kotter: "Staff make it very, very difficult to nurture leadership. The emerging leader will run into 16 staff guys, these checkers. They eat leaders."

More CEOs are coming to understand this. Reginald Jones ran General Electric using a strong staff system that his successor, Jack Welch, has dismantled. Five years ago at Owens-Illinois, says CEO Robert Lanigan, "There was a lot of time spent in exercising the power of this office through the corporate staff." Staff has been dramatically reduced, and line managers' salaries pegged higher than those of staffers. The result, according to Lanigan: "The staff are there as consultants, as advisers to me and to other line people."

At Heinz, Chairman Anthony J.F. O'Reilly has cut the staff out of the loop completely. "There is no interface between staff and the presidents of the affiliates," says O'Reilly. "No ambassadors, no courtiers, no *fonctionnaires*. It's me and the president of an affiliate, one on one." Out of a worldwide work force of 50,000, only 150 are on the corporate staff.

The staff-like units that remain are located deeper in the Heinz organization, and their relationship to operating units has changed. Mary Ann McCollough runs one such unit. As general manager of marketing services for Heinz USA, she provides consumer research, promotion and advertising support, and test-kitchen services principally to the four divisions of Heinz USA, including Weight Watchers. She has no direct reporting relationship with her clients. And "clients" is the word: McCullough bills the line businesses for her unit's services. Market dynamics, not a hierarchy, determine what her unit does. Its day-to-day work is more likely to be critiqued—pro or con—by the units she serves than by the VP to whom she reports.

Source: Stewart, T. A. (1989, November 6). New ways to exercise power. *Fortune*, 52–64, pp. 54, 55.

early 1970s, however, many persons had become engineers and consequently the bargaining power of engineers with employers was practically nil.[23]

In the 1990s there is again a shortage of engineers (and scientists), with a consequent increase in their bargaining power. Precisely in line with the strategic contingencies idea, observers note how this shortage has provided real opportunities for properly trained women and members of minorities to move into positions of power from which they were excluded when there were plenty of white male engineers and scientists to go around.[24]

If the labor market is constant, subunits whose staffs are highly trained in technical areas tend to be less substitutable than those which involve minimal technical expertise. For example, consider the large telephone company that makes extensive use of a computerized management information system. The department in charge of this system might acquire considerable power because its computer analysts perform specialized work that can't be done by others in the company. On the other hand, if telephone operators go on strike, management personnel can substitute for them by handling the phones.

Finally, if work can be contracted out, the power of the subunit that usually performs these activities is reduced. Typical examples include temporary office help, off-premises data entry, and contracted maintenance and laboratory services. The subunits that control these activities often lack power because the threat of "going outside" can be used to counter their influence attempts.

Scientists and engineers, like the biomedical researcher pictured here, are again in great demand in American business. This can give them power within their organizations. (Barry Bomzer/ Tony Stone Worldwide)

Some Final Considerations

The strategic contingencies theory presents a very rational view of subunit power—power gravitates to where it is needed to solve pressing organizational problems. In the previous chapter, however, we covered in some detail how many organizational decisions are made on less-than-rational terms, and the acquisition of power by subunits is no exception. For example, we have all heard of empire building, the process by which departments expand in size or responsibility beyond what is necessary in terms of strict effectiveness. Similarly, a study in the semiconductor industry showed that the founder's functional background (e.g., engineering, science) influenced which department had the most power in newly founded companies.[25] Another study showed that when top management saw a department's values as being similar to its own, that department tended to have power over and above its ability to cope with strategic contingencies.[26]

When a subunit acquires power, however it gets it, it will often attempt to hold onto that power. This goal is aided considerably by the fact that it *has* power at its disposal to influence other departments and their key members. Thus, power can get institutionalized in a department even though organizational priorities appear to have changed. This is often accomplished by playing organizational politics, a topic to which we now turn.

ORGANIZATIONAL POLITICS— USING AND ABUSING POWER

In previous pages, we have avoided using the terms *politics* or *political* in describing the acquisition and use of power. This is because not all uses of power constitute politics.

The Basics of Organizational Politics

Organizational politics is the pursuit of self-interest within an organization, whether or not this self-interest corresponds to organizational goals.[27] Frequently, politics involves using means of influence that are not sanctioned by the organization and/or pursuing ends or goals that are not sanctioned by the organization.[28]

Several preliminary points should be made about organizational politics. First, political activity is self-conscious and intentional. This separates politics from ignorance, stupidity, or lack of experience with approved means and ends. Second, implicit in all but the mildest examples of politics is the idea of resistance, the idea that political influence would be countered if detected by those with different agendas. Third, we can conceive of politics as either individual activity or subunit activity. Either a person or a whole department could act politically. Finally, it is possible for political activity to have beneficial outcomes for the organization, even though these outcomes are achieved by questionable tactics.

We can explore organizational politics using the means/ends matrix shown in Exhibit 13-2. It is the association between influence means and influence ends that determines whether activities are political and whether these activities benefit the organization.

I. *Sanctioned means/sanctioned ends.* Here, power is used routinely to pursue agreed-upon goals. Familiar, accepted means of influence are employed to achieve sanctioned outcomes. For example, a manager agrees to recommend a raise for a subordinate if she increases her net sales 30 percent in the next six months. There is nothing political about this.

II. *Sanctioned means/nonsanctioned ends.* In this case, acceptable means of influence are abused to pursue goals that are not approved by the organization. For instance, a head nurse agrees to assign a subordinate nurse to a more favorable job if the nurse agrees not to report the superior for stealing medical supplies. While job assignment is often a sanctioned means of influence, covering up theft is not a sanctioned end. This is dysfunctional political behavior.

III. *Nonsanctioned means/sanctioned ends.* Here, ends that are useful for the organization are pursued through questionable means. For example, a commercial artist is vying with a co-worker to have his proposal accepted for an advertising campaign. Feeling that his proposal is truly better, the artist takes the account executive to dinner, flatters him, and subtly discredits the co-worker's proposal. Currying favor and discrediting others are seldom approved methods of influence. However, if the proposal is really superior, the consequences might be beneficial for the firm. This is obviously a gray area of politics. At Bendix, some observers felt that Mary Cunningham acted politically in not consulting key managers about

---

EXHIBIT

13–2

The dimensions of organizational politics.

Influence Means	Influence Ends	
	Organizationally Sanctioned	Not Sanctioned by Organization
Organizationally Sanctioned	Non-Political Job Behavior I	II Organizationally Dysfunctional Political Behavior
Not Sanctioned by Organization	Political Behavior III Potentially Functional to the Organization	IV Organizationally Dysfunctional Political Behavior

Source: From Mayes, B. T., & Allen, R. T. (1977, October) Conceptual notes—Toward a definition of organizational politics, *The Academy of Management Review,* Vol. 2, No. 4, p. 675. Reprinted by permission.

her task force report. Still, it appears that she had the firm's interests at heart.

IV. *Nonsanctioned means/nonsanctioned ends.* This quadrant may exemplify the most flagrant abuse of power, since disapproved tactics are used to pursue disapproved outcomes. For example, to increase his personal power, the head of an already overstaffed legal department wishes to increase its size. He intends to hire several of his friends in the process. To do this, he falsifies workload documents and promises special service to the accounting department in exchange for the support of its manager.

We have all seen cases in which politics have been played out publicly in order to "teach someone a lesson." More frequently, though, politicians are motivated to conceal their activities with a "cover story" or "smoke screen" designed to make them appear legitimate.[29] Such a tactic will increase the odds of success and avoid punishment from superiors. A common strategy is to cover nonsanctioned means and ends with a cloak of rationality:

> The head of a research unit requests permission to review another research group's proposal in case she can add information to improve the project. Her covert intent is to maintain her current power which will be endangered if the other research group carries out the project. Using her informational power base, her covert means are to introduce irrelevant information and pose further questions. If she sufficiently confuses the issues, she can discredit the research group and prevent the project from being carried out. She covers these covert intents and means with the overt ones of improving the project and reviewing its content.[30]

Do political activities occur under particular conditions or in particular locations in organizations? Some tentative conclusions include the following:

- Managers report that most political maneuvering occurs among middle and upper management levels rather than at lower levels.
- Some subunits are more prone to politicking than others. Clear goals and routine tasks (e.g., production) might provoke less political activity than vague goals and complex tasks (e.g., research and development).
- Some issues are more likely than others to stimulate political activity. Budget allocation, reorganization, and personnel changes are likely to be the subjects of politicking. Setting performance standards and purchasing equipment are not.
- In general, scarce resources, uncertainty, and important issues provoke political behavior.[31]

Machiavellianism—The Harder Side of Politics

Have you ever known people in an organization or another social setting who had the following characteristics?

- Act very much in their own self-interest, even at the expense of others
- Cool and calculating, especially when others get emotional
- High self-esteem and self-confidence
- Form alliances with powerful people to achieve their goals

These are some of the characteristics of individuals who are high on a personality dimension known as Machiavellianism. **Machiavellianism** is a set of cynical beliefs about human nature, morality, and the permissibility of using various tactics to achieve one's ends. The term derives from the sixteenth-century writings of the Italian civil servant Niccolo Machiavelli, who was concerned with how people achieve social influence and the ability to manipulate others. Psychologists have suggested that the degree of an individual's endorsement of the beliefs expressed by Machiavelli is representative of a stable psychological trait.

Compared with "low Machs," "high Machs" are more likely to advocate the use of lying and deceit to achieve desired goals and to argue that morality can be compromised to fit the situation in question. In addition, high Machs assume that many people are excessively gullible and do not know what is best for themselves. Thus, in interpersonal situations, the high Mach acts in an exceedingly practical manner, assuming that the ends justify the means. Not surprisingly, high Machs tend to be convincing liars and good at "psyching out" competitors by creating diversions. Furthermore, they are quite willing to form coalitions with others to outmaneuver or defeat people who get in their way.[32] In summary, high Machs are likely to be enthusiastic organizational politicians.[33]

This discussion of the Machiavellian personality trait probably raises two questions on your part. First, you might wonder, do high Machs feel *guilty* about the social tactics that they utilize? The answer would appear to be no. Since they are cool and calculating, rather than emotional, high Machs seem to be able to insulate themselves from the negative social consequences of their tactics. Second, you might wonder how *successful* high Machs are at manipulating others and why such manipulation would be tolerated by others. After all, the characteristics detailed above are hardly likely to win a popularity contest, and you might assume that targets of a high Mach's tactics would vigorously resist manipulation by such a person. Again, the high Mach's rationality seems to provide an answer to this question. Put simply, it appears that high Machs are able to accurately identify situations in which their favored tactics will work. Such situations have the following characteristics:

- The high Mach can deal face-to-face with those to be influenced.
- The interaction occurs under fairly emotional circumstances.
- The situation is fairly unstructured, with few guidelines for appropriate forms of interaction.[34]

In combination, these characteristics reveal a situation in which the high Mach can use his or her tactics because others are distracted by emotion. High Machs, by remaining calm and rational, can create a social structure that facilitates their personal goals at the expense of others. Thus, it would appear that high Machs are especially skilled at getting their way when power vacuums or novel situations confront a group, department, or organization. For example, imagine a small family-run manufacturing company whose president dies suddenly, and no special plans for succession have been made. In this power vacuum, a high Mach vice-president would have an excellent chance of manipulating the choice of a new president. The situation is novel, emotion-provoking, and unstructured, since no guidelines for succession exist. In addition, the decision-making body would be small enough for face-to-face influence and coalition formation.

Networking—The Softer Side of Politics

Only a small proportion of the population has the personality profile characteristic of the hardball Machiavellian politician. Despite this, political influence is often necessary to enable organizational members to achieve their goals, especially if these goals involve some degree of change or innovation. Thus, a more common and more subtle form of political behavior involves networking. **Networking** can be defined as establishing good relations with key organizational members and/or outsiders in order to accomplish one's goals. If these goals are beneficial to the organization, we can describe networking as functional political behavior. In essence, networking involves developing informal social contacts that can be used to enlist the cooperation of others when their support is necessary. Upper-level managers often establish very large political networks both inside and outside of the organization (see Exhibit 13-3). Lower-level organiza-

People with Machiavellian tendencies succeed in organizational politics by remaining calm in the face of conflict. (Melanie Carr Uniphoto)

EXHIBIT 13–3 A typical general manager's network.

Financial sources, bankers, stockholders, and so on	Customers, suppliers, and competition	The government, the press, and the public
Varies a bit depending on the type of mangement job. Will have a close working relationship with some of these people and know dozens of them.	Often is aquainted with hundreds of these people, some very well. Not unusual to see a close relationship with 50 people.	Varies a bit, but not unusual to know many of these people and to be close to some of them.

External

Internal

General Manager

Bosses and/or board of directors	Peers and their bosses and subordinates	Immediate subordinates	Subordinates of subordinates
Usually has a good working relationship wth 10 to 20 people. Often has a very close relationship with some of them.	Varies depending on the manager's job. Sometimes there are no peers. At other extreme may know and have a good working relationship with dozens of people in this category.	Usually has a good working relationship with 5 to 15 people. Often has a very close relationship with some of them and has them molded into a team of people that work well together.	Knows quite a few of these people (from 5 to 500), recognizes still more, and has a close relationship with a few. Often has created an environment in which these people have a fairly clear sense of direction and work well together.

Source: Reprinted by permission of the *Harvard Business Review*. An exhibit from "What Effective General Managers Really Do," by John P. Kotter (November/December 1982). Copyright © 1982 by the President and Fellows of Harvard College; all rights reserved.

tional members might have a more restricted network, but the principle remains the same.

Some networking is a function of one's location in the organization's work flow and formal communication channels.[35] A key location provides the opportunity to interact with and establish influence over others. However, individuals can also pursue networking more aggressively. One study of general managers found that they used face-to-face encounters and informal small talk to bolster their political networks. They also did favors for others and stressed the obligations of others to them. Personnel were hired, fired, and transferred to bolster a workable network, and the managers forged connections *among* network members to create a climate conducive to goal accomplishment.[36]

Is Playing Politics Ethical?

Is political activity ethical? We have noted that organizational politics is conscious, intentional behavior. Thus, much of our extensive discussion of ethics and decision making in the previous chapter applies here. It is particularly important to be clear about who the relevant *stakeholders* are when we decide to act politically. Because politics by definition involves *self*-interest, it is easy to gloss over others' legitimate interests when the game is being played.

Perhaps the most easily identified stakeholders are political opponents, if they exist for the particular political episode in question. For instance, we discussed above several examples of individuals or groups contending for resources or control. Political opponents may invoke very different ethical criteria to justify their actions, and these criteria might be difficult to reconcile. For example, at Bendix, political opponents of Cunningham and Agee questioned their conduct in anonymous letters to the board. The targets doubtless saw this as a cowardly invasion of privacy. The perpetrators doubtless saw themselves as protecting another stakeholder, the organization as a whole.

The larger organization's role as a stakeholder in political activity can itself be ethically complicated. One study found that managers who established a strong political network were most likely to obtain frequent promotions. However, in terms of setting performance standards and developing subordinate satisfaction and commitment, less political managers performed better, using their communication and human resource management skills. In the researchers' words, the political managers were more "successful" but less "effective."[37] However, it would be difficult to question the ethics of the political managers for shortchanging the organization when they were tangibly rewarded for acting politically!

This example raises a third category of stakeholders whose interests might be considered in the political arena—subordinates or co-workers who are affected by political activity. A common instance involves making unreasonable demands on subordinates to curry favor with superiors, as this R&D group leader explains:

> "There is no way we can meet all our objectives. Objectives are only added to the list, never taken off. On each project, [_____] wants

us to explore every possibility that higher management has suggested, no matter how illogical. Anything they want, he assures them we can do; and if we don't deliver, it's our fault. The situation has become so impossible, people don't care anymore."[38]

To conclude, politics, like power, is a natural occurrence in all organizations. Whether or not politics is functional for the organization depends upon the ends that are pursued and the influence means that are used.

CONFLICT BETWEEN INDIVIDUALS OR SUBUNITS

It is nearly impossible to discuss power and politics without considering conflict. For one thing, political maneuvering and the exercise of power are two of the many causes of conflict in organizations. Furthermore, power plays and politics often result as individuals or groups attempt to cope with conflict. In this chapter we are concerned with interpersonal conflict—conflict between people or groups.

What Is Interpersonal Conflict?

Interpersonal conflict is a process of antagonism that occurs when one person or organizational subunit frustrates the goal attainment of another. Notice that conflict can exist between individuals or between groups. The curator of a museum might be in conflict with the director over the purchase of a particular work of art. Likewise, the entire curatorial staff might be in conflict with the financial staff over cutbacks in acquisition funds.

Conflict involves the joint occurrence of antagonism and blocked goals. Antagonism may involve both attitudes and behaviors. As for attitudes, the conflicting parties might develop a dislike for each other, see each other as unreasonable, and develop negative stereotypes of their opposites. ("Those scientists should get out of the laboratory once in a while.") Antagonistic behaviors might include name calling, sabotage, or even physical aggression. Frustrated goals often indicate that mutual assistance between the conflicting parties is low. Rather than aiding each other in goal attainment, each party views its loss as the other's gain. Thus, conflict is characterized by high antagonism and low mutual assistance.

Conflict, Collaboration, and Competition

It is useful to contrast conflict with two other processes of interaction—collaboration and competition (Exhibit 13-4). **Collaboration** exists when mutual assistance is high and antagonism is low. For instance, carpenters and electricians on a construction site might consult frequently to be sure that their work is sequenced in an optimal manner. Such collaboration should help both groups

EXHIBIT
13–4

Relationships among conflict, competition, and collaboration.

	Conflict	Competition	Collaboration
Mutual Assistance	Low	Low	High
Antagonism	High	Low	Low

accomplish their work and prevent antagonism. As we shall see, organizations often attempt to stimulate collaboration to prevent or reduce conflict.

Competition exists when both mutual assistance and antagonism are low. Here, each party sees its loss as the other's gain, but this does not result in destructive attitudes or behavior. Sport probably provides the purest example of a competitive relationship. Although each tennis set or football game can have only one winner, and the opponents certainly don't attempt to help each other, hostility is the exception rather than the rule. Likewise, sales reps might compete for a quarterly sales prize without antagonism. Experience indicates that competitive relationships are delicate. When either party decides not to "play by the rules," antagonism develops, and competition deteriorates into conflict.[39] We have all seen "bad blood" develop between sports teams.

Since conflict is a process, we might expect to see it progress through a series of stages. We will consider the conflict process once some causes of conflict have been identified.

CAUSES OF ORGANIZATIONAL CONFLICT

It is possible to isolate a number of factors that contribute to organizational conflict. You should keep in mind that some of these factors may occur in combination.[40]

Interdependence

When individuals or subunits are mutually dependent upon each other to accomplish *their own* goals, the potential for conflict exists. For example, the sales staff is dependent upon the production department for the timely delivery of high-quality products. This is the only way sales can maintain the good will of its customers. On the other hand, production depends upon the sales staff to provide routine orders with adequate lead times. Custom-tailored emergency orders will wreak havoc with production schedules and make the production department look bad. In contrast, the sales staff and the office maintenance staff are not highly interdependent. Salespeople are on the road a lot and should not make great demands on maintenance. Conversely, a dirty office probably won't lose a sale!

Interdependence can set the stage for conflict for two reasons. First, it necessitates interaction between the parties so that they can coordinate their interests. Conflict will not develop if the parties can "go it alone." Second, as indicated at the beginning of the chapter, interdependence implies that each party has some *power* over the other. It is relatively easy for one side or the other to abuse its power and create antagonism.

It must be emphasized that interdependence does not *always* lead to conflict. In fact, it often provides a good basis for collaboration through mutual assistance. Whether or not interdependence prompts conflict depends upon the presence of other conditions, which we will now consider.

Differences in Power, Status, and Culture

Conflict can erupt when parties differ significantly in power, status, or culture.

Power If dependence is not mutual, but one way, the potential for conflict increases. If party A needs the collaboration of party B to accomplish its goals, but B does not need A's assistance, antagonism may develop. B has power over A, and A has nothing with which to bargain. A good example is the quality control system in many factories. Production workers might be highly dependent upon inspectors to approve their work, but this dependence is not reciprocated. The inspectors might have a separate boss, their own office, and their own circle of friends (other inspectors). In this case, production workers might begin to treat inspectors with hostility, one of the symptoms of conflict.

Status Status differences provide little impetus for conflict when people of lower status are dependent upon those of higher status. This is the way organizations are supposed to work, and most members are socialized to expect it. However, because of the design of the work, there are occasions when employees with technically lower status find themselves giving orders to, or controlling the tasks of, higher-status people. The restaurant business provides a good example. In many restaurants, lower-status waiters and waitresses give orders and initiate queries to higher-status cooks or chefs. The latter might come to resent this reversal of usual lines of influence.[41] The advent of the "electronic office" led to similar kinds of conflict. As secretaries mastered the complexities of electronic word processing, they found themselves having to educate executives about the capabilities and limitations of such systems. Some executives are defensive about this reversal of roles.

At Bendix, it is reasonable to expect that some older male executives resented taking orders from twenty-nine-year-old Mary Cunningham.

Culture In Chapter 9 we discussed the concept of organizational culture, defining it as consisting of shared beliefs, values, and assumptions within an organization. When two or more very different cultures develop in an organization, the clash in beliefs, values, and assumptions can result in overt conflict. For example, hospital administrators who develop a strong culture centered on efficiency and cost-effectiveness might find themselves in conflict with physicians who share a strong culture based on providing excellent patient care at any cost. A telling case of cultural conflict occurred when Apple Computer expanded and hired professionals away from several companies with their own strong cultures:

> The newcomers brought their own strands and strains. During the first couple of years Apple recruited heavily from Hewlett-Packard, National Semiconductor, and Intel, and the habits and differences in style among these companies were reflected in Cupertino. There was a general friction between the rough and tough ways of the semiconductor men (there were few women) and the people who made computers, calculators, and instruments at Hewlett-Packard. . . . Some of the Hewlett-Packard men began to see themselves as civilizing influences and were horrified at the uncouth rough-and-tumble practices of the brutes from the semiconductor industry. . . . Many of the men from National Semiconductor and other stern backgrounds harbored a similar contempt for the Hewlett-Packard recruits. They came to look on them as prissy fusspots. They didn't question their professionalism; they just seemed to feel that they were too professional.[42]

Ambiguity

Ambiguous goals, jurisdictions, or performance criteria can lead to conflict. Under such ambiguity the formal and informal rules that govern interaction break down. In addition, it might be difficult to accurately assign praise for good outcomes or blame for bad outcomes when it is hard to see who was responsible for what. For example, if sales drop following the introduction of a "new and improved" product, the design group might blame the marketing department for a poor advertising campaign. In response, the marketers might claim that the "improved" product is actually inferior to the old product. Obviously, it might be difficult to marshal evidence to prove who is correct.

Ambiguous jurisdictions are often revealed when new programs are introduced. This is a common occurrence in universities. For instance, the division of continuing education might initiate series of management development seminars that compete with those offered by the business school. Likewise, the political science department might wish to establish a master's degree in applied politics that is similar to a degree offered by the school of public administration. In both cases, charges of "poaching" are almost certain to occur.

Ambiguous performance criteria are a frequent cause of conflict between superiors and subordinates. The basic scientist who is charged by a chemical company to "discover new knowledge" might react negatively when her boss informs her that her work is inadequate. This rather open-ended assignment is susceptible to a variety of interpretations.

At Bendix Corporation, ambiguity occurred as the company shifted into the high-technology field and changed its organizational structure. This promoted conflict, some of which affected William Agee and Mary Cunningham.

Scarcity

Earlier, it was pointed out that differences in power are magnified when resources become scarce. This does not occur without a battle, however, and conflict often surfaces in the process of power jockeying. Limited budget money, secretarial support, or computer time can contribute to conflict. Consider the company that installs a new computer that is to be used for administrative and research purposes. At first, there is plenty of computer time and space for both uses. However, as both factions make more and more use of the computer, access becomes a problem. Conflict may erupt at this point.

Scarcity has a way of turning latent or disguised conflict into overt conflict. Two scientists who don't get along very well may be able to put up a peaceful front until a reduction in laboratory space provokes each to protect his domain. In conclusion, interdependence, ambiguity, scarcity, and differences in power, status, and culture can contribute to conflict.

THE CONFLICT PROCESS

Earlier, it was pointed out that conflict is a process. This means that a number of events occur when one or more of the causes of conflict noted above takes effect. We will assume here that the conflict in question occurs between groups, such as organizational departments. However, much of this is also relevant to conflict between individuals. Specifically, when conflict begins, we often see the following events transpire:

- "Winning" the conflict becomes more important than developing a good solution to the problem at hand.
- The parties begin to conceal information from each other or to pass distorted information.
- Each group becomes more cohesive. Deviants who speak of conciliation are punished, and strict conformity is expected.
- Contact with the opposite party is discouraged except under formalized, restricted conditions.
- While the opposite party is negatively stereotyped, the image of one's own position is boosted.
- On each side, more aggressive people who are skilled at engaging in conflict may emerge as leaders.[43]

You can certainly see the difficulty here. What begins as a problem of interdependence, ambiguity, or scarcity quickly escalates to the point that the conflict process *itself* becomes an additional problem. The elements of this process then work against the achievement of a peaceful solution. The conflict continues to cycle "on its own steam."

IS ALL CONFLICT BAD?

In everyday life, there has traditionally been an emphasis on the negative, dysfunctional aspects of conflict. This is not difficult to understand. Discord between parents and children, severe labor strife, and international disputes are unpleasant experiences. To some degree, this emphasis on the negative aspects of conflict is also characteristic of thinking in the area of organizational behavior. Recently, though, there has been growing awareness of the potential *benefits* of organizational conflict.

Further reflection on the conflict process presented above demonstrates why it is often dysfunctional for both the organization and its members. From the organization's standpoint, conflict can waste an excessive amount of time and energy, diverting people from their jobs. In fact, parties might collaborate briefly to conceal their conflict from organizational agents so that they can continue to fight without censure! In general, the excessive self-interest that characterizes conflict seems to work against the very reason organizations are formed. From the individual's perspective, severe conflict can lead to stress. Pressures for conformity and the spectre of "losing" may take a personal toll.

The argument that conflict can be functional rests mainly on the idea that it promotes necessary organizational change. One advocate of this position puts it this way:

CONFLICT → CHANGE → ADAPTATION → SURVIVAL[44]

In other words, for organizations to survive, they must adapt to their environments. This requires changes in strategy that may be stimulated through conflict. For example, consider the museum that relies heavily upon government funding and consistently mounts exhibits that are appreciated only by "true connoisseurs" of art. Under a severe funding cutback, the museum can survive only if it begins to mount more popular exhibits. Such a change might occur only after much conflict within the board of directors.

Just how does conflict promote change? For one thing, it might bring into consideration new ideas that would not be offered without conflict. In trying to "one up" the opponent, one of the parties might develop a unique idea that the other can't fail to appreciate. In a related way, conflict might promote change because each party begins to monitor the other's performance more carefully. This search for weaknesses means that it is more difficult to hide errors and problems from the rest of the organization. Such errors and problems (e.g., a failure to make deliveries on time) might be a signal that changes are necessary. Finally, conflict may promote useful change by signaling that a redistribution of power is necessary. Consider the personnel department that must battle with managers to get antidiscrimination programs implemented. This conflict might be a clue that some change is due in power priorities.[45]

The conclusion that we can draw is that some conflict is functional and some is dysfunctional. This indicates that conflict in organizations must be properly *managed*.

CONFLICT MANAGEMENT STRATEGIES

The previous section suggests that there are circumstances under which conflict should be resolved and others under which conflict should be stimulated. Let's examine these two basic conflict management strategies in turn.

Conflict Resolution

A large number of strategies for interpersonal **conflict resolution** have been suggested.[46] Although each might be effective in certain situations, several have little to recommend them because they fail to get at the *source* of the conflict. For example, a manager might issue a directive for warring parties to cease conflict or make a slightly more sophisticated attempt to smooth over conflict by emphasizing common interests. In each case, the source of the conflict remains, and the parties might simply respond by concealing or disguising their conflict behaviors.

Other resolution strategies have the potential to be effective but might be very difficult to implement. For example, the conflicting parties can attempt to withdraw from each other, effectively avoiding further hostile behavior. Unfortunately, this option is seldom available because interdependence and required interaction caused the conflict in the first place! Also, if a conflict is prompted by the demand for scarce resources, the manager can attempt to expand these resources. Again, however, this reasonable idea might be impossible to implement.

Several other resolution strategies seem to have the potential to affect the sources of conflict while not involving severe problems of implementation. These include compromise, problem solving, and the introduction of superordinate goals.

Compromise Compromise is a form of "horse trading" in which each party gives up something with the expectation that it will receive something in exchange. In effect, its goal is to establish *rules of exchange* to resolve conflict. Thus, compromise can be an effective means of resolving conflict stimulated by scarce resources. On the other hand, it should not be useful for resolving conflicts that stem from power asymmetry because the weaker party has little to offer the stronger party. Effective compromises are obviously highly dependent on the bargaining skills and good will of the bargainers.[47]

Compromise might be used to resolve the traditional conflict that can develop between sales and production. The sales manager and the production superintendent might be asked to develop a set of guidelines for salespeople to use in making promises to customers. These guidelines include provisions for volume of merchandise, delivery lead times, and custom-tailored orders.

Problem Solving **Problem solving** is an attempt to move from conflict to collaboration. It differs from compromise in that the parties are encouraged to *integrate* their needs so that both are fully satisfied. There is no assumption that something must be lost in the process. Rather, it is assumed that the solution to the conflict problem will leave each party in better condition. Problem solving probably works best when the conflict is not intense and when each party has information that is useful to the other. In addition, one expert suggests that several beliefs are helpful in stimulating problem solving:

- A mutually acceptable decision is desirable.
- Differences of opinion are valuable.
- People are essentially equals despite differences in knowledge, attitudes, and status.
- Others can be trusted.
- The other party has the ability to continue the conflict but has chosen to attempt collaboration.[48]

Obviously, an effective problem-solving effort can take time and practice to develop. However, its success should be self-reinforcing. Research evidence suggests that cooperation through problem solving frequently enhances productivity and achievement.[49]

Superordinate Goals **Superordinate goals** are attractive outcomes that can be achieved only by collaboration.[50] Neither party to a conflict can attain the goal on its own. In a sense, superordinate goals require a problem-solving orientation. However, their introduction may be especially useful when conflict is so extreme that the parties use normal problem-solving meetings only as an excuse to attack each other.

An excellent example of the imposition of a superordinate goal occurred in the Chrysler Corporation in 1980. With the prospect of bankruptcy and massive unemployment looming large, the United Auto Workers and Chrysler management collaborated on developing a scheme for keeping the company afloat. On a different scale, a feud between police detectives and uniformed officers might be put aside to pool information to solve a series of murders.

You will observe that a superordinate goal does not really change the underlying cause of the conflict. However, research suggests that the conflict may remain resolved even after the goal is achieved. In addition, the failure to achieve a superordinate goal does not seem to make the existing conflict worse.[51]

Before we examine conflict stimulation, have a look at conflict management at Honda in You Be the Manager.

M anager

Conflict Management at Honda

Japan's Honda Motor Company is widely regarded as one of the world's most successful organizations. Born out of the devastation of post–World War II Japan, the company has continued to perfect the culture set down by founder Soichiro Honda. That culture stresses technical excellence, the relentless pursuit of quality, and a trusting relationship among employees. Perhaps because of the stereotype that the Japanese value harmony so highly, it is not widely appreciated that Honda has many characteristics that could stimulate intense conflict. For example, to provoke innovation and constant questioning about its products, Honda has structurally separated its various functions (engineering, R&D, manufacturing, and sales) much more than is usually the case in the vehicle industry. This is traditionally a certain recipe for turf wars and poor cooperation. To complicate this extreme decentralization, management has constantly pressed for great increases in productivity and reductions in the cycle time for new product development. On top of this, the company is known for providing great opportunities for youthful managers and engineers, a practice that goes against the strong age-related status hierarchy of most industrial firms, especially in Japan.

Honda's plants at Marysville, Ohio, and Alliston, Ontario, are managed according to Honda corporate principles rather than conventional North American style. Much emphasis is placed on corporate values, team meetings, and employee flexibility to fill in on various jobs. Despite careful selection procedures, people are sometimes hired who do not adapt to the Honda culture. Firings have occurred at both sites. However, both sites have remained firmly nonunionized.

How do you account for Honda's success in managing conflict?

1. Speculate about how Honda might manage the turf wars among its functional units.

2. Speculate as to why firings in the North American plants have not led to unionization.

To see how Honda manages conflict, see The Manager's Notebook.

Source: Pascale, R. T. (1990). *Managing on the edge.* New York: Simon & Schuster; McCallum, T. (1990, Summer). Democracy at work. *Inside Guide,* 40–44; Shook, R. L. (1988). *Honda: An American success story.* New York: Prentice Hall Press.

Conflict Stimulation

Earlier, it was pointed out that conflict might be necessary to cause needed changes in the organization. This suggests that there are times when administrators will wish to *stimulate* conflict rather than reduce it. The implicit assumption here is that the strategy of **conflict stimulation** will result in changes that benefit the organization.

How does the manager know when some conflict might be a good thing? One signal is the existence of a "friendly rut," in which peaceful relationships take precedence over organizational goals. Another signal is seen when parties that should be interacting closely have chosen to withdraw from each other to avoid overt conflict. A third signal occurs when conflict is suppressed or downplayed by denying differences, ignoring controversy, and exaggerating points of agreement.[52]

The idea of intentionally stimulating conflict has received little research attention. However, logic suggests that the causes of conflict discussed earlier could be manipulated by managers to achieve change.[53] A few examples follow:

- *Scarcity*. The president and the controller of a manufacturing company felt that the budgets allocated to various departments were not a good reflection of changing priorities. They introduced a zero-base budget that required all departments to justify their needs regardless of past allocations. Since the departments were required to compete for a scarce resource, considerable conflict developed. It was agreed that this conflict helped to promote needed changes in funding emphasis.
- *Status differences*. The dean of a business school appointed a low-status assistant professor as director of a lethargic M.B.A. program. The "old guard" professors who staffed the program resented having to answer to the new director. To assert their superiority, they suggested a series of changes that revitalized the program.
- *Ambiguity*. The director of a medical research laboratory was very unhappy with the lack of coordination among the lab's research projects. The position of assistant director was opening up because of a retirement, and the director gave contradictory, ambiguous signals about who might be promoted to the job. This led to conflict, which magnified the lack of coordination so much that the researchers held meetings to resolve the problem.

THE MANAGER'S NOTEBOOK

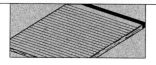

Conflict Management at Honda

Very generally, the Honda Motor Company's culture tends to stress good communication and speaking one's mind. Also, core values, such as enhancing product quality, provide a superordinate goal around which disputes can be resolved. However, some more specific conflict management tactics are seen at Honda.

1. Honda uses face-to-face sessions called *waigaya* ("chattering" or "hubbub") both to legitimate the value of conflict for learning purposes and to resolve conflict. In these sessions, traditional concessions to rank and status are put aside, and participants are encouraged to say what is truly on their minds. Anything goes, except direct criticism of one's colleagues or boss. *Waigaga* are used at all corporate levels, from the shopfloor to the executive suite. Frank discussion and a variety of viewpoints, coupled with a strong overarching culture, turn conflict into improved decisions.
2. When the North American Honda plants decide to terminate an employee, he or she can choose to appear before a review panel of other employees. If the review panel decides that the dismissal was unwarranted, the employee is reinstated. The existence of the review panel mechanism reminds supervisors to avoid capricious discipline and signals management trust in employee judgment.

SUMMARY

- Power is the capacity to influence other people who are in a state of dependence. Individuals have power by virtue of their position in the organization (legitimate power) or by virtue of the resources that they command (reward, coercion, friendship, or expertise).
- Organizational members can obtain power by doing the right things and cultivating the right people. Activities that lead to power acquisition need to be extraordinary, visible, and relevant to the needs of the organization. People to be cultivated include outsiders, subordinates, peers, and superiors. Managers with high need for power are effective when they use this power to achieve organizational goals.
- Organizational subunits obtain power by controlling strategic contingencies. This means that they are able to affect events that are critical to *other* subunits. Thus, departments that can obtain resources for the organization will acquire power. Similarly, subunits gain power when they are able to reduce uncertainty for the organization, when their function is central to the work flow, and when their tasks can't be performed by other subunits or outside contractors.
- Organizational politics occurs when influence means that are not sanctioned by the organization are used or when nonsanctioned ends are pursued. The pursuit of nonsanctioned ends is always dysfunctional, but the organization may benefit when nonsanctioned means are used to achieve approved goals. Machiavellian tactics represent an extreme form of politics, while networking represents a subtle form. Ethical questions about politics generally revolve around its impact on various stakeholders.
- Interpersonal conflict is a process of antagonism that occurs when one person or subunit frustrates the goal attainment of another. Causes of conflict include high interdependence, ambiguous jurisdictions, scarce resources, and differences in power, status, and culture.
- Conflict management includes both resolution and stimulation. One resolution tactic is compromise, in which each party agrees to make a sacrifice in exchange for some benefit. Another is problem solving, in which both parties work to effect a solution that meets their needs with no sacrifice. Also, superordinate goals that are attractive but not obtainable without collaboration may be introduced. Conflict stimulation generally involves manipulating the factors that are known to cause conflict. This might involve making resources less available or increasing ambiguity.

KEY CONCEPTS

Power	Coercive power	Subunit power
Legitimate power	Referent power	Strategic contingencies
Reward power	Expert power	Organizational politics

Machiavellianism   Competition   Problem solving
Networking   Conflict resolution   Superordinate goals
Interpersonal conflict   Compromise   Conflict stimulation
Collaboration

DISCUSSION QUESTIONS

1. Contrast the bases of power available to an army sergeant with those available to the president of a voluntary community association. How would these differences in power bases affect their influence tactics?

2. Are the bases of individual power easily substitutable for each other? Are they equally effective? For example, can coercive power substitute for expert power?

3. Present a profile of someone who acquires power in an organization. What activities does he or she pursue? What relationships does he or she cultivate?

4. Imagine that you are on a committee at work or in a group working on a project at school that includes a "high Mach" member. What could you do to neutralize the high Mach's attempts to manipulate the group?

5. Discuss the conditions under which the following subunits of an organization might gain or lose power: Legal department; research and development unit; public relations department. Use the

concepts of scarcity, uncertainty, centrality, and substitutability in your answers.

6. Differentiate between power and politics. Give an exmple of the use of power that is not political.

7. It has been said that "Politics is a way of life in organizations." Do you agree? Is political activity necessary for organizations to function?

8. Suppose two accounting majors are hired right out of college by an accounting firm. Being in a new and unfamiliar environment, they quickly develop a collaborative relationship, helping each other with work assignments and so on. What factors could turn this collaboration into competition? What factors could turn the competition into open conflict?

9. The manager of a fast food restaurant observes that conflict among the staff is damaging service. How might he or she implement a superordinate goal to reduce this conflict?

10. Describe a situation that you have observed in which conflict stimulation had a beneficial outcome. How was the conflict stimulated? Why was the conflict ultimately beneficial?

EXPERIENTIAL EXERCISE

Rate Your Boss

Below is a list of statements that may be used in describing behaviors that supervisors in work organizations can direct toward their subordinates. First carefully read each descriptive statement, thinking in terms of your supervisor (present or past). Then decide the extent to which you agree that your supervisor could do this to you. Mark the number that most closely represents how you feel. Use the following numbers for your answers:

    5 = Strongly agree

    4 = Agree

    3 = Neither agree nor disagree

    2 = Disagree

    1 = Strongly disagree

My supervisor can . . .

_____ 1. increase my pay level.
_____ 2. make me feel valued.
_____ 3. give me undesirable job assignments.
_____ 4. make me feel like he/she approves of me.
_____ 5. make me feel that I have commitments to meet.
_____ 6. make me feel personally accepted.
_____ 7. make me feel important.
_____ 8. give me good technical suggestions.
_____ 9. make my work difficult for me.
_____ 10. share with me his/her considerable experience and/or training.
_____ 11. make things unpleasant here.
_____ 12. make being at work distasteful.
_____ 13. influence my getting a pay raise.
_____ 14. make me feel like I should satisfy my job requirements.
_____ 15. provide me with sound job-related advice.
_____ 16. provide me with special benefits.
_____ 17. influence my getting a promotion.
_____ 18. give me the feeling I have responsibilities to fulfill.
_____ 19. provide me with needed technical knowledge.
_____ 20. make me recognize that I have tasks to accomplish.

Scoring and Interpretation

This questionnaire measures the extent to which you see your boss as possessing the various bases of individual power discussed at the beginning of the chapter. To score your questionnaire, simply add up the responses that you gave to the four questions that correspond to each power base:

Power base	Items
Legitimate	5, 14, 18, 20
Reward	1, 13, 16, 17
Coercive	3, 9, 11, 12
Referent	2, 4, 6, 7
Expert	8, 10, 15, 19

For each power base, the score should fall between 4 and 20. The higher the score, the higher the person is on that power base. The researchers who developed the scale, Timothy Hinkin and Chester Schriesheim, found that expert and referent power contributed positively to satisfaction with supervision. Coercive power contributed negatively.

■

Source: Hinkin, T. R., & Schriesheim, C. A. (1989). Development and application of new scales to measure the French and Raven (1959) bases of social power. *Journal of Applied Psychology, 74*, 561–567. Copyright © 1989 by the American Psychological Association. Reprinted by permission.

CASE STUDY

Information Access, Inc.

Information Access, Inc., specialized in the sale of econometric forecasts and consulting services to businesses around the United States. The firm prepared separate forecasts for a number of sectors of the nation's economy. Since IAI's primary output was specialized information, expertise was a central part of the overall product. Then shifting status and power structures within the firm began to cause major problems for management.

IAI's hierarchy, not surprisingly, was designed around the specialized forecasts. Each forecast had a product manager, who was typically an MBA and who was responsible for the depth and accuracy of the forecasts and of the insights the forecasts offered to customers. Expertise was the hallmark of these consultants, and their centrality to the primary product and close contact with customers made their position a very high status one. In fact, it was an open secret that some product managers had higher status than the president of the firm. On the other hand, the majority of positions within IAI were involved with computer operations, and the "databankers" who filled these positions had little or no customer contact.

IAI dealt with customers at two levels. Typically, managers from client firms negotiated for IAI's consulting services and signed a contract for both services and data to be supplied by IAI. The secretary or assistant to the client firm's manager then accessed the data directly from IAI's computer through a telephone link. For this reason, IAI had to deal with questions raised by the managers' subordinates about difficulties in accessing the information as well as with specialized questions raised by the managers themselves about how to interpret the data.

When IAI was first established, project managers, serving as consultants, dealt with *all* the questions—with

technical problems in accessing the data, with administrative problems in billings, and with problems in interpretation of data. But as the firm grew and faced more substantive competition, it was felt that an 800 number would be more efficient in responding to customer questions about technical and administrative problems. The original plan was for the number to be used in a reactive manner only. In other words, the phone line would only handle incoming calls from customers. A number of college graduates (mostly BAs) were hired to handle these calls. Since they staffed the phone banks, they were soon nicknamed "bankies." For most, it was their first job out of college.

The real reason for establishing the 800 number was, of course, to free up the consultants, and the bankies were instructed to respond directly to any issue that did not warrant the attention of a consultant. Soon after the number was put into service, however, there were some unplanned changes in procedure.

Susan Faraday was the first manager of the 800 number. She had been with IAI for six years and had been promoted quickly through several positions. Then in the course of reorganization, her job was eliminated. She applied for the job as manager of the 800 number, but was turned down because it was felt that she had too much seniority for the position; the low status envisioned for the job fit neither her salary nor her grade level. However, when no other suitable candidates for the job were found, she was given the position.

The 800 number was an immediate success with customers. Activities went smoothly under Faraday's direction, and everyone at IAI was pleased with the outcome. As soon as the dust settled, however, Faraday moved to increase the status of her position. Her first action was to propose that her group undertake some informal market research. After all, she argued, her subordinates spoke to clients across the United States. Over a two- or three-month period, her group had contact with the majority of the firm's clients and was in an excellent position to "ensure that clients were happy with their consultants."

Source: Sayles, L. R. (1989). *Leadership: Managing in real organizations* (2nd ed.) pp. 129–131. Copyright © 1989 by McGraw-Hill Publishing Company. Reprinted by permission.

The consultants reacted with some annoyance. It bothered them to think that some lowly bankie who handled a customer's minor questions would be "checking up" on their performance. The bankies would not be speaking with the decision makers who were responsible for the purchases in the first place, the consultants argued, but with people who would be able to provide only indirect evidence of their performance. A poor relationship between a client manager and his or her staff could easily affect the subordinate's perception of the consultant's work. In addition, the bankies would have no way to assess the status of the relationship of consultant and client at any given point in time. If the client firm was negotiating a new contract or was temporarily dissatisfied, any comments elicited might not be indicative of the normal status of the client-consultant relationship.

The consultants felt that the best way to evaluate the effectiveness of their work was by the amount of money that they brought in from clients. Regardless of what information the bankies collected, if the clients continued to purchase services then they must be reasonably satisfied. Faraday responded that under that philosophy, the only way that IAI would become aware of problems would be for clients to stop paying or to allow their contracts to lapse. By that time, the client-consultant problem would be too serious to resolve easily.

Though the consultants did not like the state of affairs, the bankies began to solicit information regarding customer satisfaction. Along with the change, of course, came a large boost in the status and power of Faraday's job. For a time, things progressed without a major incident. Then Faraday decided that her group should be more "proactive" in their client contact. The market research effort was no longer to be limited just to clients who called into the 800 number, but would extend to all IAI clients. Faraday assigned her bankies lists of firms to contact and query in regard to their relationships with IAI consultants. In addition, she began tabulating "client satisfaction sheets." The sheets effectively assigned "grades" to consultants based on the clients' perceptions of their work. Needles to say, the consultants hit the roof. To make matters worse, Faraday began to set up meetings at client sites to "straighten out the problems" created by consultants. Over the consultants' strong objections, Faraday was able to consolidate her position and accrue increasing status to her department at the expense of the once-powerful product managers.

1. Account for the apparent power and status of the project management consultants before the advent of the 800 number. Consider both their likely actions as individuals and the strategic contingencies controlled by the consulting function.

2. Account for the increasing power and status of the 800 number group under Susan Faraday. Consider both her actions as an individual and the strategic contingencies controlled by the 800 number group.

3. Analyze in detail the causes for conflict between the consultants and the "bankies."

4. Did Susan Faraday act politically in extending the influence of the 800 number group? Did she act ethically? Justify your answers.

5. As a top executive at Information Access, what steps would you take to manage the conflict between the consultants and the 800 number group?

REFERENCES

1. This case is based on Bernstein, P. B. (1980, November 3). Upheaval at Bendix. *Fortune*, 48–56; Sheehy, G. (1980, October 30). Gossip undoes top corporate woman. *The Gazette* (Montreal), p. 45.

2. Cohen, P. (1973). *The gospel according to the Harvard Business School*. New York: Penguin, p. 302.

3. Provan, K. G. (1980). Recognizing, measuring, and interpreting the potential/enacted power distinction in organizational research. *Academy of Management Review, 5*, 549–559.

4. These descriptions of bases of power were developed by French, J. R. P., Jr., & Raven, B. (1959). In D. Cartwright (Ed.), *Studies in social power*. Ann Arbor, MI: Institute for Social Research.

5. Rahim, M. A. (1989). Relationships of leader power to compliance and satisfaction with supervision: Evidence from a national sample of managers. *Journal of Management, 15*, 545–556; Tannenbaum, A. S. (1974). *Hierarchy in organizations*. San Francisco: Jossey-Bass.

6. Vaughn, R. (1975). *The spoiled system*. New York: Charterhouse, p. 19.

7. Podsakoff, P. M., & Schriesheim, C. A. (1985). Field studies of French and Raven's bases of power: Critique, reanalysis, and suggestions for future research. *Psychological Bulletin, 97*, 387–411.

8. Heider, F. (1958). *The psychology of interpersonal relations*. New York: Wiley.

9. Podsakoff & Schriesheim, 1985.

10. The following is based upon Kanter, R. M. (1977). *Men and women of the corporation*. New York: Basic Books.

11. Kipnis, D. (1976). *The powerholders*. Chicago: University of Chicago Press.

12. Some observers, such as Kipnis (1976), feel that all power seekers are motivated by some form of perceived weakness. I disagree.

13. McClelland, D. C. (1975). *Power: The inner experience*. New York: Irvington.

14. Winter, D. G. (1988). The power motive in women—and men. *Journal of Personality and Social Psychology, 54*, 510–519.

15. McClelland, D. C., & Burnham, D. H. (1976, March–April). Power is the great motivator. *Harvard Business Review*, 100–110.

16. Ashforth, B. E. (1989). The experience of powerlessness in organizations. *Organizational Behavior and Human Decision Processes, 43*, 207–242.

17. Salancik, G. R., & Pfeffer, J. (1977, Winter). Who gets power—and how they hold on to it: A strategic contingency model of power. *Organizational Dynamics*, 3–21.

18. Salancik, G. R., & Pfeffer, J. (1974). The bases and use of power in organizational decision making: The case of a university. *Administrative Science Quarterly, 19*, 453–473. Also see Pfeffer, J., & Moore, W. L. (1980). Power in university budgeting: A replication and extension. *Administrative Science Quarterly, 25*, 637–653. For conditions under which the power thesis breaks down, see Schick, A. G., Birch, J. B., & Tripp, R. E. (1986). Authority and power in university decision making: The case of a university personnel budget. *Canadian Journal of Administrative Sciences, 3*, 41–64.

19. Hickson, D. J., Hinings, C. R., Lee, C. A., Schneck, R. E., & Pennings, J. M. (1971). A strategic contingency theory of intraorganizational power. *Administrative Science Quarterly, 16*, 216–229; for support of this theory, see Hinings, C. R., Hickson, D. J., Pennings, J. M., & Schneck, R. E. (1974). Structural conditions of intraorganizational power. *Administrative Science Quarterly, 19*, 22–44; Saunders, C. S., & Scamell, R. (1982). Intraorganizational distributions of power: Replication research. *Academy of Management Journal, 25*, 192–200; Hambrick, D. C. (1981). Environment, strategy, and power within top management teams. *Administrative Science Quarterly, 26*, 253–276.

20. Kanter, 1977, pp. 170–171.

21. Hickson et al., 1971; Hinings et al., 1974.

22. Hickson et al., 1971; Hinings et al., 1974; Saunders & Scamell, 1982.

23. Kipnis, 1976, p. 159.

24. Nulty, P. (1989, July 31). The hot demand for new scientists. *Fortune*, 155–163.

25. Boeker, W. (1989). The development and institutionalization of subunit power in organizations. *Administrative Science Quarterly, 34*, 388–410.

26. Enz, C. A. (1988). The role of value congruity in intraorganizational power. *Administrative Science Quarterly, 33*, 284–304.

27. Nord, W. R., & Tucker, S. (1987). *Implementing routine and radical innovations*. Lexington, MA: Lexington Books.

28. Mayes, B. T. & Allen, R. W. (1977). Toward a definition of organizational politics. *Academy of Management Review, 2*, 672–678.

29. Porter, L. W., Allen, R. W., & Angle, H. L. (1981). The politics of upward influence in organizations. *Research in Organizational Behavior, 3*, 109–149.

30. Schein, V. E., (1977). Individual power and political behaviors in organizations: An inadequately explored reality. *Academy of Management Review, 2*, 64–72, p. 67.

31. Porter et al., 1981; Madison, D. L., Allen, R. W., Porter, L. W., Renwick, P. A., & Mayes, B. T. (1980). Organizational politics: An exploration of managers' perceptions. *Human Relations, 33*, 79–100.

32. Geis, F., & Christie, R. (1970). Overview of experimental research. In R. Christie & F. Geis (Eds.), *Studies in Machiavellianism*. New York: Academic Press.

33. See Ralston, D. A. (1985). Employee ingratiation: The role of management. *Academy of Management Review, 10*, 477–487.

34. Geis & Christie, 1970.

35. Brass, D. J. (1984). Being in the right place: A structural analysis of individual influence in an organization. *Administrative Science Quarterly, 29*, 518–539.

36. Kotter, J. P. (1982). *The general managers*. New York: Free Press.

37. Luthans, F., Hodgetts, R. M., & Rosenkrantz, S. A. (1988). *Real managers*. Cambridge, MA: Ballinger.

38. Kelly, C. M. (1987, Summer). The interrelationship of ethics and power in today's organizations. *Organizational Dynamics*, 4–18, p. 14.

39. For a discussion of the relationship between rules and conflict, see Thomas K. (1976). Conflict and conflict management. In M. D. Dunnette (Ed.), *Handbook of industrial and organizational psy-*

chology. Chicago: Rand McNally. Also see Katz, D., & Kahn, R. L. (1978). *The social psychology of organizations* (2nd ed.). New York: Wiley.

40. This section relies heavily on Walton, R. E., & Dutton J. M. (1969). The management of interdepartmental conflict: A model and review. *Administrative Science Quarterly, 14,* 73–84.

41. See Whyte, W. F. (1948). *Human relations in the restaurant industry.* New York: McGraw-Hill.

42. Moritz, M. (1984). *The little kingdom: The private story of Apple Computer.* New York: Morrow, pp. 246–247.

43. See Wilder, D. A. (1986). Social categorization: Implications for creation and reduction of intergroup bias. *Advances in Experimental Social Psychology, 19,* 291–349; Sherif, M. (1966). *In common predicament: Social psychology of intergroup conflict and cooperation.* Boston: Houghton Mifflin; Blake, R. R., Shepard, H. A., & Mouton, J. S. (1964). *Managing intergroup conflict in industry.* Houston: Gulf.

44. Robbins, S. P. (1974). *Managing organizational conflict: A nontraditional approach.* Englewood Cliffs, NJ: Prentice-Hall, p. 20.

45. For other advantages of conflict, see Thomas, 1976.

46. See Robbins, 1974; Filley, A. C. (1975). *Interpersonal conflict resolution.* Glenview, IL: Scott, Foresman.

47. For a review of bargaining tactics, see Lewicki, R. J., & Litterer, J. A. (1985). *Negotiation.* Homewood, IL: Irwin.

48. Filley, 1975.

49. Johnson, D. W., Maruyama, G., Johnson, R., Nelson, D., & Skon, L. (1981). Effects of cooperative, competitive, and individualistic goal structures on achievement: A meta-analysis. *Psychological Bulletin, 89,* 47–62. See also Tjosvold, D. (1986). *Working together to get things done.* Lexington, MA: D. C. Heath.

50. Sherif, 1966.

51. Hunger, J. D., & Stern, L. W. (1976). An assessment of the functionality of the superordinate goal in reducing conflict. *Academy of Management Journal, 19,* 591–605.

52. Brown, L. D. (1983). *Managing conflict at organizational interfaces.* Reading, MA: Addison-Wesley.

53. Robbins, 1974; also see Brown, 1983.

CHAPTER
14

STRESS

ALAN WINDSOR

At the age of twenty-eight, Alan Windsor graduated from a prestigious Eastern university with a Master of Business Administration degree. As one of the best students majoring in marketing, Alan received a number of job offers from the nation's top advertising agencies, and after much deliberation he chose a position in New York City. For a period of two years, Alan directed a number of marketing research studies and contributed many successful ideas to various account executives' advertising plans. Because of his excellent performance, Alan was offered a position as an account executive. Although he enjoyed the technical aspects of market research, he realized that the account executive job was the "fast track" through the organization, and he accepted it. More than anything, Alan wanted to succeed in the new position. The following months proved both painful and educational for Alan. Put simply, he was an exceedingly *shy* individual who found it difficult to establish new interpersonal relationships. When Alan had first started with the organization, his co-workers and superiors had noticed this quality, but it seemed to wear off as he became acquainted with the staff. However, the account executive job required him to entertain potential clients and sell them on his ideas, and this proved very difficult. Most problematic were the crucial presentations of a completed advertising campaign proposal to "strangers" from a client organization. In these meetings, Alan stuttered badly and was generally unconvincing. Although the proposals were considered technically excellent by Ann Howe, Alan's superior, she was convinced that his inability to establish rapport with clients was responsible for his failure to land several important accounts. This situation was very threatening for Alan, who became more and more hostile toward his support personnel, often blaming them for the failure of his proposals. Alan eventually resigned to accept a marketing research position with a major producer of food products. During the job interview, he had been happy to learn that the new position would require a fairly narrow and stable range of interactions solely within the company.

Alan Windsor accepted a new assignment that was incompatible with his personality and experienced considerable stress as a result. In this chapter we will explore the phenomenon of stress in organizations. First, a model of a stress episode will be presented and dissected in some detail. Particular attention will be paid to the causes of stress at various points in organizations and to the consequences that stress can have for the individual and the organization. Finally, some strategies for reducing or coping with stress will be considered.

STRESS IN ORGANIZATIONS—A PROLOGUE

It is easy to imagine situations that must surely prove stressful for organizational members. Hockey players battling for the Stanley Cup, the White House staff during the Iraq invasion of Kuwait, and personnel working in power plants during nuclear accidents have obviously been exposed to elevated levels of tension. However, these dramatic cases should not obscure the fact that stress is part of the everyday routine of organizations. We often experience stress-provoking situations outside of organizations, and it would be naive to assume that things are different behind organizational walls. In fact, many individuals are employed by organizations primarily for their ability to respond effectively to stressful conditions. Police officers, firefighters, and hospital emergency room personnel all occupy positions that are thought of as stressful. Even apparently routine jobs can provide stress when the routine becomes unbearable or when a minor change in the routine is implemented. Some teachers experience stress when they are required to teach the same course year after year, while others experience stress when they are asked to teach a new course.

A MODEL OF ORGANIZATIONAL STRESS

The story that began the chapter provides an example of a typical stress episode that can serve as a prototype for our subsequent discussion. We can divide this episode into three key stages:

1. Alan Windsor assumed a new position in the advertising agency that was incompatible with his personality (*stressor*).
2. Alan was unable to achieve his goal of performing well as an account executive and experienced considerable anxiety (*stress*).
3. Alan blamed his support staff for his problem but set out to find a job that was compatible with his personality (*stress reactions*).

A model of a stress episode is shown in Exhibit 14–1.

Stressors

Stressors are environmental events or conditions that have the potential to induce stress. As we shall see shortly, organizational stressors might include the nature of a person's job, the organizational setting in which the job is performed, and the people encountered at work. In Alan Windsor's case, the job itself proved to be the key stressor. The requirement for him to interact with clients was the beginning of his problem. There are probably some conditions that would prove stressful for just about everyone. These include things like extreme heat, extreme cold, isolation, or the presence of hostile others. More interesting is the fact that the individual personality often determines the extent to which a potential stressor becomes a real stressor and actually induces stress. Thus, Alan's shyness led him to *interpret* his new position as stress-provoking. Evidently, the same job requirements did not serve as stressors for other account executives with different personality makeups.

Stress

Stress is a psychological reaction to the demands inherent in a stressor that has the potential to make a person feel tense or anxious because the person does not feel capable of coping with these demands.[1] Alan Windsor wanted to be successful in fulfilling the demands of his new job, but he felt incapable of doing so.

It should be understood that stress is not intrinsically bad. All individuals require a certain level of stimulation from their environment, and moderate levels of stress can serve this function. In fact, one would wonder about the perceptual accuracy of a person who *never* experienced frustration or conflict. On the other hand, stress does become a problem when it leads to especially high levels of anxiety and tension. People reveal individual differences in their ability to *tolerate*

EXHIBIT
14–1

Model of a stress episode.

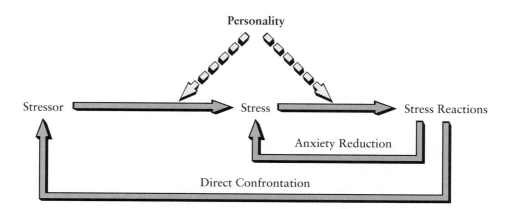

stress. Despite his shyness, Alan Windsor had a high need for achievement, and this need evidently led to great anxiety in response to his frustration. An equally frustrated individual with a lower need for achievement might have been much less anxious.

Stress Reactions

Stress reactions are the behavioral, psychological, and physiological consequences of stress. Some of these reactions are essentially passive responses over which the individual has little direct control, such as elevated blood pressure or the development of stomach ulcers. Other reactions are active attempts to *cope* with some previous aspect of the stress episode. Exhibit 14–1 indicates that stress reactions that involve coping attempts might be directed toward dealing directly with the stressor or simply reducing the anxiety generated by stress. In general, the former strategy has more potential for effectiveness than the latter because the chances of the stress episode being *terminated* are increased.[2] The executive under extreme pressure to complete a difficult report by Friday will do well to work on the report. This activity confronts the stressor directly, and it should terminate the stress episode. On the other hand, "throwing a drunk" might temporarily reduce anxiety, but it would not end the stress episode—the report is still due by Friday. Again, notice that personality characteristics often intervene between the experience of stress and the enactment of stress reactions. For example, individuals who usually feel that self-initiative, personal actions, and free will determine their behavior tend to confront stressors directly. Those who habitually feel that fate, luck, and chance determine what happens to them are more prone to simple anxiety-reduction strategies.[3]

Alan Windsor used a mixed coping strategy for dealing with the stress episode that he encountered. Blaming his support staff probably temporarily reduced his anxiety and made him feel a little better. Seeking out and accepting a new job directly confronted the stressor (the account executive job requirements) and terminated the stress cycle. Later we will discuss a number of stress reactions that are typical of organizational stress episodes.

Often, reactions that are useful for the individual in dealing with a stress episode may be very costly to the organization. The individual who is conveniently absent from work on the day of a difficult inventory check might prevent personal stress but leave the organization short-handed (provoking stress in others). This simple example shows that organizations should be interested in the stress that individual employees experience. Stress is *motivational,* and the organization will not always benefit from the reactions that stress motivates.

Personality and Stress

In the previous sections we have noted in a general sense how personality can intervene to influence the extent to which stressors lead to actual stress. We have also seen how personality can affect which stress reactions are exhibited in response to stress. A question remains, however, as to whether there is any particular type of personality that is especially likely to experience stress and to exhibit negative reactions to it. In recent years, physicians, psychologists, and management scholars have developed an interest in one such personality type, that defined by the Type A behavior pattern.

Interest in the Type A behavior pattern began when physicians noticed that many sufferers of coronary heart disease, especially those who developed the disease relatively young, tended to exhibit a distinctive pattern of behaviors and emotions.[4] This pattern of behaviors and emotions contributed to heart disease even when cigarette smoking, cholesterol level, and elevated blood pressure were accounted for. Individuals who exhibit the **Type A behavior pattern** tend to be aggressive and ambitious. Their hostility is easily aroused, and they feel a great sense of time urgency. They are impatient, competitive, and preoccupied with their work. The Type A individual is often contrasted with the Type B, who does not exhibit these extreme characteristics. Close to half of the urban population seems prone to the Type A behavior pattern. Although more men than women are Type A, the negative effects of the Type A personality are equivalent for men and women.[5] Research suggests that the Type A pattern might have its beginnings in childhood[6].

Is stress a key factor in the Type A equation? In other words, is the elevated heart disease seen in Type A individuals a physiological reaction to stress? The answer seems to be yes. Compared to Type B individuals, Type A people report heavier workloads, longer work hours, and more conflicting work demands.[7] Whether or not these reports are accurate, we will see later that such factors turn out to be potent stressors. Thus, either Type A people encounter more stressful situations than Type Bs, or they perceive themselves as doing so. In turn, Type A individuals are likely to exhibit adverse physiological reactions in response to stress. These include elevated blood pressure, elevated heart rate, and modified blood chemistry. Frustrating, difficult, or competitive events are especially likely to prompt these adverse reactions. In addition, Type A people perform better than Type Bs in situations that call for persistence, endurance, or speed. They can ignore fatigue and distraction to accomplish their goals. Type A individuals seem to have a strong need to control their work environment. This is doubtless a full-time task that stimulates their feelings of time urgency and leads them to overextend themselves physically.[8]

As research has accumulated, it has become increasingly clear that the major component of Type A behavior that contributes to adverse physiological reactions is hostility and repressed anger. This may also be accompanied by exaggerated cynicism and distrust of others. When these factors are prominent in a particular Type A individual's personality, stress is most likely to take its toll.[9]

The Type A behavior pattern has some interesting ramifications. For one thing, Type A people do not generally *report* more tension, anxiety, or job dissatisfaction than Type Bs, even though they do report more of the stressors noted earlier.[10] Thus, Type A people might be unaware of the impact that work stress has on them. To complicate matters, many work organizations reward the very behaviors that Type A people favor—achievement orientation, long work hours, and extreme work involvement. Thus, it is not surprising that Type A individuals as a group tend to reach higher organizational levels and achieve higher occupational success than Type Bs. The message here is that organizations might be unintentionally threatening the health and well-being of their best performers.

STRESSORS IN ORGANIZATIONAL LIFE

In this section we will examine potential stressors in detail. Some stressors can affect almost everyone in any organization, while others seem especially likely to affect people who perform particular roles in organizations. We will examine first some role-specific stressors and then some more general stressors.

Executive and Managerial Stressors

Executives and managers make key organizational decisions and direct the work of others. In these capacities, they seem to experience special forms of stress.

Role Overload **Role overload** occurs when too many tasks must be performed in too short a time period. Research indicates that role overload is an especially common stressor for managers.[11] In Chapter 2, Henry Mintzberg's observational study of managers was discussed. Mintzberg summarizes his findings in the following way:

> My own study of chief executives found no break in the pace of activity during office hours. The mail (average of 36 pieces per day), telephone calls (average of 5 per day), and meetings (average of 8) accounted for almost every minute from the moment these men entered their offices in the morning until they departed in the evenings. A true break seldom occurred. Coffee was taken during meetings, and lunchtime was almost always devoted to formal or informal meetings. When free time appeared, ever present subordinates quickly usurped it.
>
> Thus the work of managing an organization may be described as taxing. The quantity of work to be done, or that the manager chooses to do, during the day is substantial and the pace is unrelenting. After hours, the chief executive (and probably many other managers as well) appears to be able to escape neither from an environment that recognizes the power and status of his position nor from his own mind, which has been well trained to search continually for new information.[12]

Mintzberg argues that the open-ended nature of the managerial job is responsible for this heavy and protracted workload. Management is an ongoing *process,* and there are few signposts to signify that a task is complete and that rest and relaxation are permitted. Even when managers truly enjoy confronting their heavy workload, they are often frustrated by their inability to contemplate or perfect some strategy. "When can I get some time to *think* around here?" is a frequently heard complaint. In addition, the heavy workload might frustrate the executive's attempt to develop other skills and interests. Many a project such as a partially restored vintage automobile or a partly built summer cottage languish while organizational fires are fought. Especially when coupled with frequent moves or excessive travel demands, a heavy workload often provokes conflict between the manager's role as an organizational member and his or her role as a spouse or parent. Such role conflicts can be especially stressful because they involve incompatible demands made by parties who are both important to the executive, and the rewards for complying with one party involve negative consequences from the other party. Thus, role overload may provoke stress while at the same time preventing the executive from enjoying the pleasures of life that can reduce stress. Some executives even ignore threats to their health in combatting role overload:

> Ray Brant, vice-president for human relations at National Semiconductor, contracted a rare blood disease that had to be treated with intravenous medication twenty-four hours a day. The disease required hospitalization, but Brant talked his way out of that because of his heavy workload. The semiconductor executive carried his intravenous

Working mothers can suffer stress from role overload. (Jeffry W. Myers/Uniphoto)

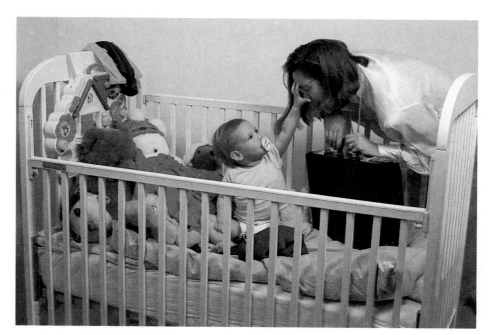

bottle and pump with him to business meetings and arranged his car so the medication pumped as he drove. "If I backed off work for six weeks, I'd be too far offstream when I came back," he said.[13]

See Global Focus 14–1 for another perspective on role overload.

Heavy Responsibility Not only is the workload of the executive heavy, but it can have extremely important consequences for the organization and its members. The president of a company might have the final say on the implementation of a million-dollar marketing plan. Similarly, a vice-president of labor relations might be in charge of a negotiation strategy that could result in either labor peace or a protracted and bitter strike. These "make-or-break" responsibilities can confront executives with severe cases of conflict, since each of several strategies will have pros and cons and a decision must be made with incomplete information. To complicate matters, the personal consequences of an incorrect decision can be staggering. For example, the courts have fined or even jailed executives who have engaged in illegal activities on behalf of their organizations. Clearly, the anticipation of imprisonment for an incorrect business decision falls into the stressor category! Finally, it should be noted that executives are responsible for people, as well as things, and this influence over the future of others has the potential to induce stress. The executive who must terminate the operation of an unprofitable plant, putting many out of work, or the manager who must fire a subordinate, putting one out of work, might experience guilt and tension.[14]

Professional Stressors

Professionals are individuals who have acquired highly specialized training in a particular area of expertise. They typically subscribe to a particular set of beliefs, values, and attitudes regarding their work and are members of a professional organization that sets standards for training and disciplining its members. Scientists, engineers, accountants, psychologists, doctors, lawyers, and teachers are among those individuals who are often considered professionals. Like managers, professionals are sometimes exposed to a particular set of stressors.

Profession Versus Organization One stressor that professionals often confront is contradictory demands from the employing organization and their profession. These contradictory demands lead to a form of role conflict in which one's role as a professional is at odds with one's role as an employee. In general, when professionals are employed by organizations that specialize in the professional service, such conflicts are rare. Accountants who work in public accounting firms and lawyers who work in law firms find themselves in an organizational environment that supports their professional values. However, when the professional is employed by an organization that does not offer the professional's service as its main product, role conflict can develop. For example, the accountant who is the controller of a manufacturing firm might experience stress when asked by the president to institute some questionable bookkeeping practices. Similarly, the scientist who values "knowledge for its own sake" might encounter stress when required by an electronics firm to terminate an interesting basic research project for a more

---

GLOBAL FOCUS 14–1

▼
....
Role Overload, Japanese Style

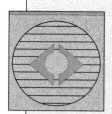

Despite their country's status as the world's biggest creditor nation, Japanese workers continue to put in the greatest amount of work time of any major industrialized country: on average, they spend as much as 500 more hours a year on the job than do their counterparts in West Germany and France, 200 more than those in the U.S. and Britain. Only 1 out of 3 workers enjoys a five-day workweek. Employees by and large use just half their paid vacation time, generally 15 days a year. "They worry that if they take time off, there will be too much work when they return, or it will cause trouble to their co-workers," says Osamu Naito of the leisure-development section at the Ministry of International Trade and Industry (MITI).

Sensitive to foreign criticism that Japanese work too hard and spend too little, the government has set a goal to reduce work time—from the current average of 261 work days per year to 223 days by 1992. This month, under a new law passed by the Diet, public offices began closing two Saturdays a month. Previously, government offices were open half-days on Saturdays, and civil servants were required to work every other Saturday. But "as long as the office is open, there are meetings and such, and it's difficult to take time off," says a government official.

MITI has also begun to rate corporations on their so-called comfort margin, taking into account such ingredients as work hours, holidays and pay scales. So far, 25 companies have won high marks, including Jujo Paper, Mitsubishi Electric and the Japanese subsidiary of Mobil Oil. Not all firms wanted the distinction: about half asked to remain anonymous, arguing that the comfort margin was nothing to be proud of.

This year MITI has proposed a "conjugal day" for workers. Translation: husbands are being urged to take their wives out for a night on the town, a rare event for middle-aged and older couples. In fact, MITI may be pushing the limits of the possible. When the ministry suggested that the conjugal day could eventually become a national holiday, some part-time workers protested that another mandatory day off would infringe upon their right to work.

Source: Abridged from Maklhara, K. (1989, January 30). Coming to grips with *Karoshi. Time*, p. 50. Copyright © 1989 by The Time Inc. Magazine Company. Reprinted by permission.

practical investigation of some specific problem. In both cases, the organization and the profession can be characterized as competing for the *loyalty* of the professional. For instance, one study of scientists and managers in an aerospace company found that only 15 percent of the scientists identified with their organization more than their profession. In contrast, 68 percent of the managers studied identified most strongly with the organization.[15]

Lack of Authority   Even though professionals in a nonprofessional-oriented organization have the power of special knowledge in their area of expertise, they frequently lack formal authority to implement decisions and influence organizational policy. This happens because professionals are usually found in staff jobs in which they generate information on which managers take action. As such, they serve in essentially advisory roles. Speaking of scientists, one writer has said:

> Since the scientist enters the organization at the lower end of the hierarchy, he finds his immediate group subordinated to several decision-making and coordinating echelons. When the upper echelons generate policies that disrupt his work or change its direction, he often reacts with irritation and frustration.[16]

The irritation and frustration to which this writer refers also stem from the fact that professionals must consistently "sell" their ideas to those organizational members who have the authority to implement them. For example, industrial psychologists who work as personnel specialists for large organizations must frequently find a department or divisional manager who is willing to sponsor their ideas for a new motivational scheme or performance evaluation plan. This puts the specialist in the potentially stressful position of having to convince the busy manager to devote substantial time and resources to a plan of action that might have an unclear or delayed payoff. If lack of authority were not problematic enough in inducing stress, it can be compounded by the fact that professionals are frequently supervised by nonprofessional personnel. The psychologists referred to above might report to a Director of Human Resources who is not a psychologist. Similarly, the lawyers who work in the claims department of an insurance firm might report to a manager who is not a lawyer. This condition can lead to poor communication and a lack of support for professionals even *within* their own organizational units.

Operative-Level Stressors

Operatives are individuals who occupy nonprofessional and nonmanagerial positions in organizations. In a manufacturing organization, operatives perform the work on the shopfloor and range from skilled craftspeople to unskilled laborers. As is the case with other organizational roles, the occupants of operative positions are sometimes exposed to a special set of stressors.

Poor Physical Working Conditions   Operative-level employees are more likely than managers and professionals to be exposed to physically unpleasant and even dangerous working conditions. Although social sensibility and the actions of unions have improved working conditions over the years, many employees must still face excessive heat, cold, noise, pollution, and the chance of accidents. A spot welder in an automobile assembly plant had this to say about his job:

> I don't know if you've heard of plant pollution. It's really terrible. Especially where I work, you have the sparks and smoke. . . . If you don't turn the fans down, the smoke'll come right up. . . . I usually go outside to get a breath of fresh air. The further you are from the front door the worse it is. You can cut the heat with a knife, especially when it gets up in the nineties. You get them carbon monoxide fumes, it's just hell.[17]

Speaking about the stress involved in maintaining safe working conditions, a crane operator reported:

> It's not so much the physical, it's the mental. When you're working on a tunnel and you're down in a hole two hundred feet, you use hand signals. You can't see these. You have to have something else that's your eyes. There has been men dropped and such because some fellow gave the wrong signal. . . . The average crane operator lives to be fifty-five years old. They don't live the best sort of life. There's a lot of tension. We've had an awful lot of people have had heart attacks.[18]

Poor Job Design   We have all heard stories about individuals with Master's degrees who drive taxicabs for a living. In fact, the educational level of the North American work force has risen consistently over the years. This rise in educational level has been accompanied by greater expectations of interesting work and a greater desire for influence over work-related decisions.[19] These changes have been paralleled by an increase in the proportion of white-collar jobs, especially in the public sector and service industries. However, many of these jobs, as well as traditional lower-level blue-collar jobs, do not offer challenge and opportunity commensurate with the education and skills of their incumbents.[20] While bad job design can provoke stress at any organizational level (executive role overload is an example), lower-level blue- and white-collar jobs are particular culprits. It might seem paradoxical that jobs that are too simple or not challenging enough can act as stressors. However, monotony and boredom can prove extremely frustrating to individuals who see themselves as capable of handling more complex tasks.

Jobs that make high demands on workers while giving them little control over workplace decisions seem especially prone to produce stress and negative stress reactions.[21] High demands might include a hectic work pace, excessive workload, limited time to accomplish tasks, or responsibility for extreme economic loss. Lack of control involves limited decision latitude and authority. Jobs that often involve high demand and little control include telephone operators, nurse's aides, assembly line workers, and garment stitchers. As shown in Exhibit 14–2, these jobs fall into a zone of increased risk for heart disease (the area to the right of the dashed curve). Stress might be partially responsible for this elevated risk.

■
EXHIBIT   **Heart disease risk among males.**

14–2

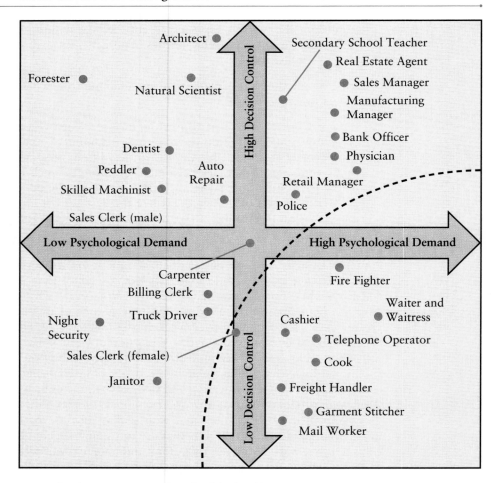

Note: High-risk occupations are to the right of the dotted line.

Source: Nelson, B. (1983, April 1). Bosses face less risk than bossed. *The New York Times*, Section E, p. 16. Copyright © 1983 by The New York Times Company. Reprinted by permission.

Boundary Role Stressors

Boundary roles are positions in which organizational members are required to interact with members of other organizations or with the public. As such, boundary roles exist at the executive, professional, and operative levels of organizations. For example, a vice-president of public relations is responsible for representing his or her company to the public, while the vice-president of labor relations is responsible for interacting with a variety of union organizations. In the professional domain, a medical doctor who works for a pharmaceutical company might be required to represent the company before a congressional committee. At the operative level, receptionists, salespeople, and installers often interact with the public or representatives of other organizations.

There is evidence suggesting that occupants of boundary role positions are especially likely to experience stress as they straddle the imaginary boundary between the organization and its environment.[22] This is yet another form of role conflict in which one's role as an organizational member might be incompatible with the demands made by the public or other organizations. A classic case of boundary role stress involves salespeople, especially those who sell to other organizations such as wholesalers and retailers. In extreme cases, these buyers desire fast delivery of a large quantity of custom-tailored products. The salesperson might be tempted to "offer the moon" but is at the same time aware that such an order could place a severe strain on his or her organization's production facilities. Thus, the salesperson is faced with the dilemma of doing his or her primary job (selling) while protecting another function (production) from unreasonable demands that could result in a broken delivery contract.

A particular form of stress experienced by some boundary role occupants is burnout. **Burnout** is defined as a combination "of emotional exhaustion, depersonalization, and reduced personal accomplishment that can occur among individuals who work with people in some capacity."[23] Frequently, these other people are organizational clients who require very special attention or who are experiencing severe problems. Thus, teachers, nurses, paramedics, social workers, and police are especially likely candidates for burnout.

Burnout appears to follow a stagelike process that begins with emotional exhaustion (see Exhibit 14–3). The person feels fatigued in the morning, drained by the work, and frustrated by the day's events. One way to deal with this extreme exhaustion is to distance oneself from one's clients, the "cause" of the exhaustion. In an extreme form, this might involve treating them like objects and lacking concern for what happens to them. The clients might also be seen as blaming the employee for their problems. Finally, the burned-out individual develops feelings of low personal accomplishment—"I can't deal with these people, I'm not helping them, I don't understand them." In fact, because of the exhaustion and depersonalization, there might be more than a grain of truth to those feelings. Although the exact details of this progression are open to some question, these three sets of symptoms appear to paint a reliable picture of burnout.[24]

■
EXHIBIT

14–3

The stages of burnout and their symptoms.

Emotional Exhaustion $\longrightarrow$	Depersonalization $\longrightarrow$	Low Personal Accomplishment
Feel drained by work	Have become calloused by job	Cannot deal with problems effectively
Feel fatigued in the morning	Treat people like objects	Am not having a positive influence on others
Feel burned out	Don't care what happens to people	Cannot understand others' problems or empathize with them
Frustrated	Feel others blame you for their problems	
Don't want to work with people		No longer feel exhilarated by job

Source: Jackson, S. E. (1984). Organizational practices for preventing burnout. In A. S. Sethi & R. S. Schuler (Eds.), *Handbook of stress coping strategies*. Copyright © 1984 by HarperCollins Publishers, Inc. Reprinted by permission of the publisher. p. 92.

Burnout seems to be most common among people who entered their jobs with especially high ideals. Their expectations of being able to "change the world" are badly frustrated when they encounter the reality shock of troubled clients (who are often perceived as unappreciative) and the inability of the organization to help them. Teachers get fed up with being disciplinarians, nurses get upset when patients die, and police officers get depressed when they must constantly deal with the "losers" of society.[25]

What are the consequences of burnout? Some individuals bravely pursue a new occupation, often experiencing guilt about not having been able to cope in the old one. Others stay in the same occupation but seek a new job. For instance, the burned-out nurse might go into nursing education to avoid contact with sick patients. In a related vein, some people pursue administrative careers in their profession, attempting to "climb above" the source of their difficulties. These people often set cynical examples for idealistic subordinates. Finally, some people stay in their jobs and become part of the legion of "deadwood," collecting their paychecks but doing little to contribute to the mission of the organization. Many "good bureaucrats" seem to choose this route.[26]

Some General Stressors

To conclude our discussion of stressors that are encountered in organizational life, we will consider some stressors that are probably experienced equally by occupants of executive, professional, operative, and boundary roles.

Job Insecurity Secure employment is an important goal for almost everyone, and stress may be encountered when secure employment is threatened. At the operative level, unionization has provided a degree of employment security for many, but the vagaries of the economy and the threat of automation hang heavy over many workers. Among professionals, a curious paradox exists. In many cases, the very specialization that enables them to obtain satisfactory jobs becomes a millstone whenever social or economic forces change. For example, aerospace scientists and engineers have long been prey to the boom and bust nature of their industry. When layoffs occur, these people are often perceived as overqualified or too specialized to easily obtain jobs in related industries. Another source of insecurity for many professionals is the ease with which one's knowledge of a particular field can become obsolete. Especially in highly technical fields such as science, the undergraduate's knowledge of today might be the Ph.D.'s knowledge of yesterday. Finally, the executive suite does not escape job insecurity. Recent pressures for corporate performance have made cost cutting a top priority for many companies. One of the surest ways to cut costs in the short run is to reduce executive positions and thus reduce the total management payroll. Many top corporations have greatly thinned their executive ranks in recent years (see In Focus 14–2).

Role Ambiguity We have already noted how role conflict, having to deal with incompatible role expectations, can provoke stress. There is also substantial evidence that role ambiguity can provoke stress.[27] From Chapter 8, you will recall that role ambiguity exists when the goals of one's job or the methods of performing the job are unclear. Such a lack of direction can prove stressful, especially for people who are low in their tolerance for such ambiguity. Almost by definition, many managerial and executive jobs seem prone to ambiguity. For example, the president of a manufacturing firm might be instructed by the board of directors to increase profits and cut costs. While this goal seems clear enough, the means by which it can be achieved might be unclear. This ambiguity can be devastating, especially when the organization is doing poorly and no strategy seems to improve things. In general, jobs that are lower in the organization seem clearer in method and may have less intrinsic role ambiguity. However, even at lower levels, ambiguity can exist when supervision is weak or inconsistent in its demands and direction. Severe stress can be encountered when one is told to do one thing one minute and something contradictory the next. Often, both the task and the boss can contribute to role ambiguity. A former copywriter in an advertising agency described a typical assignment this way:

> I would go to the boss and he'd tell me what he wanted. I'd go back to my room and try to write it, and get mad and break pencils and pound on the wall. Then finish it and take it in to him, and change it and change it, and then I'd go back and write it over again and take it in to him and he'd change it again, and I'd take it back. This

IN FOCUS 14–2

▼
....
Westinghouse Downsizing Provokes Stress

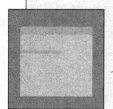

Researchers have found a higher than expected prevalence of depression among white-collar workers at Westinghouse Electric Corp., and evidence that such a condition reduces their productivity.

Information for the study was gathered in 1987, shortly after the company announced a restructuring and layoffs, developments that would be expected to increase stress among employees. Because dozens of U.S. companies have retrenched in recent years, the results are likely to reflect conditions beyond Westinghouse. "This is about the American workplace in the last half of the 1980s," says Carroll Curtis, medical director at Westinghouse. "They've been difficult times for people. We wanted to know what's happening in our workplace" in order to address the problem.

In a study of 1,870 employees, researchers found that 23% of men and 36% of women reported having a major episode of depression, often lasting 10 weeks or longer, at least once in their lives; 9% of men and 17% of women said they'd had such episodes in the year before the study, in the midst of the restructuring.

"Those rates are much higher than would have been predicted by general population studies," says Evelyn J. Bromet, a professor of psychiatry at the State University of New York, Stony Brook, and one of the investigators on the study. Rates in previous studies ranged from 5% to 21% in a lifetime, she says, though comparisons are difficult because studies vary widely in approach.

The Westinghouse study also found that 14% of employees who had suffered from depression said they had missed deadlines on projects; 6% said supervisors questioned their work performance; and 8% had unfavorable performance reviews. They also reported difficulty concentrating and relating to colleagues. Just 25% of men and one-third of women had sought professional advice or treatment for depression, the researchers say.

Among other things, data from the study will be used to strengthen the company's employee assistance program and to develop ways to help employees struggling with caring for elderly parents, troublesome children and other sources of stress at home, Dr. Curtis says. "It's kind of a landmark study," he says. "If we have problems, we need to know about them. [Otherwise,] we're flying by the seat of our pants."

Source: Winslow, R. (1989, December 13). Workplace turmoil is reflected in depression among employees. *The Wall Street Journal*, p. B1. Copyright © 1989 by Dow Jones & Company, Inc. Reprinted by permission.

would happen thirty or forty times and then we'd move to another man. He'd put his feet on the desk and change it again.[28]

Interpersonal Incompatibility   So-called "personality clashes" are unpleasant enough outside of organizations to provoke a considerable degree of stress. When such unpleasantries occur within an organization, they would seem to have the potential to induce even more stress. For one thing, outside of the organization, one can often simply cease interaction with the disliked person. This option is frequently unavailable when people are working together. Second, the stress stemming from incompatibility can have substantial spillover in an organization. That is, not only is the incompatibility stress-provoking in and of itself, but it can create further stress by interfering with perceived or actual job performance. A personality clash with the boss might lead the boss to give the subordinate a poor performance rating, only exacerbating the subordinate's stress. In addition, the subordinate might spend so much time complaining about the boss or trying to "mend fences" that his or her actual performance suffers. Clearly, interpersonal problems with peers, superiors, and subordinates can extend from the shopfloor to the executive suite.

Exhibit 14–4 summarizes the sources of stress at various points in the organization. Before continuing, consider the stressful situation described in You Be the Manager.

Fear of layoffs can be a major source of stress in the airline industry, because of frequent mergers, restructurings and bankruptcies. See also In Focus 14-2. (Dany Krist/ Uniphoto)

REACTIONS TO ORGANIZATIONAL STRESS

In this section we shall examine the reactions that individuals who experience organizational stress might exhibit. These reactions can be divided into behavioral, psychological, and physiological responses.

Behavioral Reactions to Stress

Behavioral reactions to stress involve overt activities that the stressed individual uses in an attempt to cope with the stress. They include problem solving, withdrawal, and the use of addictive substances.

Problem Solving We would hope that problem solving is the most typical response to organizational stress. In general, **problem solving** is directed toward terminating the stressor or reducing its potency, not toward simply making the person feel better in the short run. Problem solving is reality oriented, and while it is not always effective in combatting the stressor, it reveals flexibility and realistic use of feedback. Thus, if an attempted solution to a stress problem is not effective, the person feels capable of trying another approach. Most examples of a problem-solving response to stress are undramatic because problem solving is generally the routine, sensible, obvious approach that an objective observer might suggest.

■
EXHIBIT   **Sources of stress at various points in the organization.**

14–4

Executives and Managers
• Heavy, Continuing Workload
• Heavy Responsibility

Boundary Roles
• Role Conflict

All Employees
• Job Insecurity
• Role Ambiguity
• Interpersonal Incompatibility

Professionals
• Profession vs. Organization
• Lack of Authority

Operative Employees
• Poor Physical Conditions
• Poor Job Design

YOU BE THE MANAGER

Manager

For Sale: Gulfstream Aerospace

In the "good old days," organizations sold off unwanted divisions or subsidiaries secretly—investment bankers would find a buyer, and a sale would be made without a word to employees. However, the 1980s saw the advent of a new tactic in which organizations began to declare publicly that they wished to sell a division or subsidiary. This tactic was used in various cases to prompt a bidding war, boost stock prices, or convince creditors that a cash flow problem would soon end. Lost in the frenzy were the feelings of the employees of the soon-to-be-divested firm, who often had to endure months of stressful confusion and uncertainty about the future.

The management of Gulfstream Aerospace of Savannah, Georgia, knew all too well the stresses of such a situation. Gulfstream, a manufacturer and servicer of aircraft, had experienced a "public auction" in 1985. Rumors of layoffs flew, and productivity and morale plummeted. When it was announced that Chrysler Corporation was the buyer, rumors surfaced that the operation would be moved to Detroit. Many talented personnel resigned without waiting to see what the new owners would be like.

In late 1989, Chrysler decided to divest itself of Gulfstream. Gulfstream management, having regained employee confidence after the 1985 sale, knew that it had to do something to avoid the stress and rumors this time around. The company simply couldn't afford the turnover and loss of morale that had accompanied the previous sale.

What would *you* do to manage this stressful situation?

1. What are the key stressors that are present in an acquisition situation such as that experienced by Gulfstream?
2. What would you do to prevent or alleviate the stress that the Gulfstream employees face?

To find out what Gulfstream did, see The Manager's Notebook.

Source: Adapted from Deutsch, C. H. (1990, March 4). Letting employees in on the news. *The New York Times*, p. F37. Copyright © 1990 by The New York Times Company, Inc. Reprinted by permission.

Some examples of problem-solving reactions to stress include the following:

- *Delegation.* A busy executive reduces her stress-provoking workload by delegating some of her many tasks to a capable subordinate.
- *Time management.* A manager who finds the day too short writes a daily schedule, forces his subordinates to make formal appointments to see him, and instructs his secretary to screen phone calls more selectively.
- *Talking it out.* A professional engineer who is experiencing stress because of poor communication with her nonengineer superior resolves to sit down with the boss and hammer out an agreement concerning the priorities on a project.
- *Asking for help.* A salesperson who is anxious about his company's ability to fill a difficult order asks the production manager to provide a realistic estimate of the probable delivery date.
- *Searching for alternatives.* A machine operator who finds his monotonous job stress-provoking applies for a transfer to a more interesting position for which the pay is identical.

The presence of stress or stressors is sometimes implicated in reduced job performance.[29] Notice that these problem-solving responses will often reduce stress *and* stimulate performance, benefitting both the individual and the organization.

Withdrawal Withdrawal from the stressor is one of the most basic reactions to stress. In organizations, this withdrawal takes the form of absence and turnover. Compared with problem-solving reactions to stress, absenteeism fails to attack the stressor directly. Rather, the absent individual is simply attempting some short-term reduction of the anxiety prompted by the stressor. When the person returns to the job, the stress is still there. From this point of view, absence is a dysfunctional reaction to stress for both the individual and the organization. The same can be said about turnover when a person resigns from a stressful job on the spur of the moment merely to escape stress. However, a good case can be made for a well-planned resignation in which the intent is to assume another job that should be less stressful. This is actually a problem-solving reaction that should benefit both the individual and the organization in the long run. We are as yet unsure just how much absence and turnover represent specific withdrawal from stress. However, there is some evidence that stress-prone operative jobs are likely to prompt absence.[30] In addition, several potential stressors discussed earlier (role ambiguity and underutilization of potential) are associated with absence.[31] Turnover and turnover intentions have often been linked with stress and its causes.[32]

Use of Addictive Substances Smoking, drinking, and drug use represent the least satisfactory behavioral responses to stress for both the individual and the organization. These activities fail to terminate stress episodes, and they leave employees less physically and mentally prepared to perform their jobs. We have all heard of hard-drinking newspaper reporters and advertising executives, and it is tempting to infer that the stress of their boundary role positions is responsible for their drinking. Unfortunately, like these, most reports of the relationship between stress and the use of addictive substances are anecdotal. However, there are indications that cigarette use and alcohol abuse are associated with the presence of work-related stress.[33]

Psychological Reactions to Stress

Psychological reactions to stress primarily involve emotions and thought processes, rather than overt behavior, although these reactions are frequently revealed in the individual's speech and actions. The most common psychological reaction to stress is the use of defense mechanisms. **Defense mechanisms** are psychological attempts to reduce the anxiety associated with stress. Notice that, by definition, defense mechanisms concentrate on *anxiety reduction,* rather than actually confronting or dealing with the stressor. The use of defense mechanisms is usually automatic and unconscious; the individual is unaware of his or her defensiveness. However, in some cases the person might be aware of such defensiveness or intentionally implement a defense. Some common defense mechanisms include the following:

- **Rationalization** involves attributing socially acceptable reasons or motives to one's actions so that they will appear reasonable and sensible, at least to oneself. For example, a male nurse who becomes very angry and abusive when learning that he will not be promoted to supervisor might justify his anger by claiming that the head nurse discriminates against men.
- **Projection** involves attributing one's own undesirable ideas and motives to others so that they seem less negative. For example, a sales executive who is undergoing conflict about offering a bribe to an official of a foreign government might reason that the *official* is corrupt.
- **Displacement** involves directing feelings of anger at a "safe" target rather than expressing them where they may be punished. For example, a construction worker who is severely criticized by the boss for sloppy workmanship might go home and kick the family dog.
- **Reaction formation** involves expressing oneself in a manner that is directly opposite to the way one truly feels, rather than risking negative reactions to one's true position. For example, a low-status member of a committee might vote with the majority on a crucial issue rather than stating his true position and opening himself to attack.
- **Compensation** involves applying one's skills in a particular area to make up for failure in another area. For example, a professor who is unable to get her research published might resolve to become a superb teacher.
- **Repression** involves preventing threatening ideas from becoming conscious, so that the stressor need not be confronted. For example, the assembly line worker who finds his routine but demanding job stressful might honestly forget to set his alarm clock and consequently wake up too late to go to work.

You will recall that Alan Windsor responded defensively to the stress generated by his failure as an account executive when he blamed his support staff for his problems. This involved a combination of rationalization and projection. By projecting his own inadequacies onto his staff, he was trying to rationalize his inability to land accounts.

Is the use of defense mechanisms a good or bad reaction to stress? Used occasionally to temporarily reduce anxiety, they appear to be a useful reaction. For example, the construction worker who displaces aggression onto the family dog rather than attacking the frustrating boss might calm down, return to work the next day, and "talk it out" with the boss. (Note that this is a problem-solving reaction. We hope he would also make up with the dog!) Thus, the occasional use of defense mechanisms as short-term anxiety reducers probably benefits both the individual and the organization. In fact, people with "weak defenses" might be incapacitated by anxiety and resort to dysfunctional withdrawal or addiction.

When the use of defense mechanisms becomes a chronic reaction to stress, however, the picture changes radically. The problem stems from the very character of defense mechanisms—they simply don't change the objective character of the stressor, and the basic conflict or frustration remains in operation. After some short-term relief from anxiety, the basic problem remains unresolved. In fact, the stress might *increase* with the knowledge that the defense has been essentially ineffective. In addition, as the above examples illustrate, all defense mechanisms involve a certain degree of detachment from the *reality* of the stress episode. As defense is piled upon defense, it might be more and more difficult for individuals to accurately assess the true reason for their anxiety. In this case, they become less and less likely to engage in sensible problem-solving responses to the stressor.

Physiological Reactions to Stress

Can work-related stress kill you? This is clearly an important question for organizations, and it is even more important for individuals who experience excessive stress at work. Most studies of physiological reactions to stress have concentrated on the cardiovascular system, specifically on the various risk factors that might prompt heart attacks. For example, there is evidence that work stress is associated with electrocardiogram irregularities and elevated levels of blood pressure, cholesterol, and pulse.[34] However, most of the studies have been correlational in nature, comparing the incidence of these risk factors across occupations that were *assumed* to differ in the presence of stressors. In Chapter 2 you learned that correlation does not imply causation, and it is possible that individuals who are already high coronary risks *choose* to go into certain occupations. In this case, certain occupations would indeed appear to promote adverse physiological reactions, mainly because they attracted high-risk candidates.

Although dentists probably cause *you* stress, you might be surprised to learn that *they* also suffer from a fairly high rate of physiological problems that might be associated with stress. One study found that the difficulties of building a dental practice, the image of the dentist as an inflictor of pain, and a lack of appreciation from patients were related to various cardiovascular risks among dentists.[35]

REDUCING OR COPING WITH STRESS

This chapter would be incomplete without a discussion of the strategies that might be used to reduce or cope with stress. Some observers divide such strategies into organizational strategies—things that organizations can do to deal with stress—and strategies that might be used by individual employees. However, this distinction is somewhat artificial. If organizations can prepare employees for stress, individual employees might also be able to seek out information about anticipated stress. If companies can institute fitness programs, individual employees can also pursue a personal fitness regimen.

Prepare for Stress

One approach to preparing employees for anticipated stress might be to institute *realistic job previews,* which attempt to clearly specify the nature of the work to be encountered before the person is hired (Chapter 9). In their zeal to hire people, many recruiters tend to gloss over negative aspects of a job, including its potential to induce stress. A realistic preview should permit applicants who feel incapable of coping with stress to decline a job offer or to go into a job adequately forewarned. Although such previews have been shown to facilitate job satisfaction and reduce turnover, their effects on stress have not been closely examined. However, they might prove especially valuable in alerting idealistic candidates for burnout-prone jobs to the demands that could be posed by difficult clients. Realistic job previews could also be used to inform candidates for promotion or internal transfer about possible stressors in the new job.

In a similar vein, many multinational firms have instituted seminars to help employees and their families prepare for the stress that might be encountered in moving to another country and experiencing culture shock. Such programs warn transferees about the difficulties that might be confronted and provide them with an arsenal of stress-preventing suggestions. Similar plans have also been implemented by the armed forces. For example, the U.S. Air Force introduces military families who are about to be transferred to a foreign base to a local "sponsor family" that is currently stationed at that base. This enables the departing family to obtain first-hand information about the kinds of problems that might be encountered in the foreign environment and provides an established connection for them once they arrive there.

Job Redesign and Staffing

As indicated earlier, many jobs seem to have the potential for stress designed into them. For this reason, organizations might implement plans to redesign jobs to reduce their stressful characteristics. In theory, jobs anywhere in the organization could be redesigned to this end. Thus, an overloaded executive might be given an assistant to reduce the number of tasks he or she must perform. In practice, most formal job redesign efforts have involved enriching operative-level jobs to make them more stimulating and challenging. As noted in Chapter 7, this is usually accomplished by giving employees more control over the pace of their work and permitting them to use more of their skills and abilities. Although enrichment often increases job satisfaction and reduces withdrawal, there have been almost no studies of the impact of enrichment on stress reduction or physiological indicators of stress. One exception is a study in the production and packing department of a candy producer that showed distinct improvements in employee mental health after job enrichment.[36] Such tests are important because it is conceivable that job enrichment could provoke stress rather than reduce it. In general, job redesign is an important method of dealing with stress because it attempts to *remove* stressors rather than simply helping employees to *cope with* stressors.

When jobs cannot be redesigned, various staffing practices can serve to combat stress, especially when their use as such is approved by the organizational culture. Job posting refers to publicizing job openings within the organization and encouraging current employees to apply for the openings. A promotion-from-within policy refers to the notion that all jobs except those at the entry level will be staffed (if possible) by promoting people who are already employed by the organization. Effectively managed, these schemes might serve as stress reducers by allowing employees to gravitate to jobs that are compatible with their personalities and stress-tolerance characteristics. For example, job posting might allow a worker to request a lateral transfer (to a job at the same level) that is perceived as less stressful. Similarly, a promotion-from-within policy might permit an employee to escape the stress experienced in a routine, monotonous job. However, the promotion-from-within policy must be administered carefully to ensure that individuals do not feel *forced* to accept higher-level jobs that might involve more responsibility and thus prove more stressful.

Social Support

Everyday experience suggests to us that the support of others can help us deal with stress. We have all seen children who are facing a tense experience run to an adult for support and comfort, and we have all seen on television the victims of natural disasters finding solace in others. Although the dynamics of job stress might be more subtle, there is every reason to believe that social support should work the same way for people who experience job stress.

Speaking generally, social support simply refers to having close ties with other people. In turn, these close ties could affect stress by bolstering self-esteem, providing useful information, offering comfort and humor, or even providing material resources (such as a loan). Research evidence shows that the benefits of social support are double-barreled. First, people with stronger social networks exhibit better psychological and physical well-being. Second, when stressful events are encountered, people with good social networks are likely to cope more positively. Thus, the social network acts as a buffer against stress.[37]

Off the job, social support might be found in a spouse, family, or friends. On the job, social support might be available from one's superior or co-workers. Logic and some research evidence suggest that the buffering aspects of social support are most potent when they are directly connected to the source of stress. This means that co-workers and superiors might be the best sources of support for dealing with *work*-related stress. In particular, most managers could be better trained to recognize subordinate stress symptoms, clarify role requirements, and so on. Unfortunately, some organizational cultures, especially those that are very competitive, do not encourage members to seek support in a direct fashion. In this event, relationships that are developed in professional associations can sometimes serve as an informed source of social support.

Sabbaticals

In a sense, *sabbaticals* represent "time off for good behavior" in the organizational environment. They have been popularized by colleges and universities, in which professors are relieved of their usual duties for several months to engage in research, writing, or travel. Presumably, sabbaticals permit self-development and rejuvenation by removing the individual from the stresses of the regular job. Sabbaticals have occasionally been used by business firms, usually at the executive level. Prominent users include Time Inc., Intel, and Apple Computer. Xerox and IBM permit paid sabbaticals for community service projects. Other firms occasionally implement exchange programs with governments or universities to permit their executives to utilize their talents in different, less stressful settings. Sabbaticals would seem especially useful for combatting stress in burnout-prone jobs.

Stress Management Programs

In recent years, some organizations have begun to experiment with programs designed to help employees "manage" work-related stress. Such programs are also available from independent off-work sources. Some of these programs are designed to help physically and mentally healthy workers prevent problems due to stress. Others are therapeutic in nature, aimed at individuals who are already experiencing stress problems. Although the exact content of the programs varies, most involve one or more of the following techniques:[38]

- Meditation
- Training in muscle-relaxation exercises
- Biofeedback training to control physiological processes
- Skills training in time management
- Training to think more positively and realistically about sources of job stress

Although each of these techniques has been shown to be useful in reducing anxiety and tension in other contexts, they have only recently been applied in the work setting. Tentative evidence suggests that these applications are useful in reducing physiological arousal, sleep disturbances, and self-reported tension and anxiety.[39]

Some authors, including some who have designed successful stress management programs, have raised questions about their ethical implications.[40] Many of these programs take job or role requirements as given and then train workers to cope with the resulting stress. This approach does not try to permanently remove sources of stress, as job redesign might do. Is this strategy ethical? To some degree the answer to this question depends on the situation. If one is dealing with a large number of Type A individuals, who are evidently especially sensitive to stressors, a stress management program seems sensible and ethical because the source of much stress is within the employee. On the other hand, if clear and obvious stressors to which almost anyone would object are present (such as extreme overload or horrible working conditions), stress management programs look a lot less ethical.

Fitness Programs

It is often argued that physical exercise can reduce stress and counteract some of the adverse physiological effects of stress. The basic mechanics involve muscle

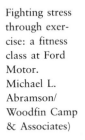

Fighting stress through exercise: a fitness class at Ford Motor. Michael L. Abramson/ Woodfin Camp & Associates)

relaxation, modified blood chemistry, and simple distraction from the daily grind. To this end, some organizations have established fitness programs for their members. These range from simple arrangements with local health clubs or YMCAs to complete in-house facilities with resident trainers.

> Companies like Xerox, Rockwell International, Weyerhaeuser, and Pepsi-Cola are spending tens of thousands of dollars for gyms equipped with treadmills, exercycles, and jogging tracks—and full-time staff. One of the more impressive operations is Kimberly-Clark, where $2.5 million have been invested in a 7,000 square foot health testing facility and a 32,000 square foot physical fitness facility staffed by fifteen full-time health care personnel.[41]

Physical fitness training is a strategy that has received some research attention. Studies have shown that fitness training is associated with improved mood, a better self-concept, reduced absenteeism, and reports of better performance.[42] Some of these improvements probably involve stress reduction.

THE MANAGER'S NOTEBOOK

For Sale: Gulfstream Aerospace

Within twenty-four hours of the announcement that Gulfstream was up for sale, its own founder and CEO, Allen Paulson, made public a plan to buy the company. Having seen the stress of the 1985 acquisition, Paulson was determined to reduce employee uncertainty. Still, other bids for the company were to be solicited by Chrysler.

1. A chief stressor in such acquisitions is job insecurity. The acquiring firm might have its own staff specialists or management team to put in place. Similarly, cost cutting measures might dictate blue-collar layoffs. Also, anticipated role ambiguity or conflict can surface if the acquiring firm is thought to have a very different culture or style of operations (for example, it could be a foreign company).

2. To reduce or prevent stress for Gulfstream employees, management communicated with them continuously about the sale. Each manager held meetings once a week and responded to *all* rumors in a straightforward fashion. The employees were particularly concerned about a rumored purchase by Mitsubishi. Management quickly announced that the Japanese firm was interested in another Chrysler subsidiary, not Gulfstream. Because of the careful and honest information campaign, there was no personnel turnover during the acquisition period.

SUMMARY

- Stressors are environmental conditions that have the potential to induce stress. Stress is a psychological reaction that can prompt tension or anxiety because an individual feels incapable of coping with the demands made by a stressor.
- Personality characteristics can cause some individuals to perceive more stressors than others, experience more stress, and react more negatively to this stress. In particular, people with the Type A behavior pattern are prone to such reactions. Type A individuals are aggressive, ambitious, and often hostile. They are preoccupied with their work and feel a great sense of time urgency. Hostility is the key factor in physiological risk.
- At the managerial or executive level, common stressors include role overload and high responsibility. Among professionals, conflict between professional demands and organizational demands, as well as lack of authority, may provoke stress. At the operative level, poor physical working conditions and underutilization of potential due to poor job design are common stressors. Boundary role occupants often experience stress in the form of conflict between demands from inside the employing organization and demands from outside. Burnout may occur when interaction with clients produces emotional exhaustion, depersonalization, and low accomplishment. Job insecurity, role ambiguity, and interpersonal incompatibility have the potential to induce stress in all organizational members.
- Behavioral reactions to stress include problem solving, withdrawal, and the use of addictive substances. Problem solving is the most effective reaction because it confronts the stressor directly and thus has the potential to terminate the stress episode. The most common psychological reaction to stress is the use of defense mechanisms to temporarily reduce anxiety. The most studied physiological reactions to stress are cardiovascular risk factors.
- Strategies that might be used to reduce organizational stress include preparation for anticipated stress, job redesign, careful staffing, social support, sabbaticals, stress management programs, and exercise programs.

KEY CONCEPTS

Stressors	Boundary roles	Projection
Stress	Burnout	Displacement
Stress reactions	Problem solving	Reaction formation
Type A behavior pattern	Defense mechanisms	Compensation
Role overload	Rationalization	Repression

DISCUSSION QUESTIONS

1. Two social workers just out of college join the same county welfare agency. Both find their case loads very heavy and their roles very ambiguous. One exhibits negative stress reactions, including absence and elevated alcohol use. The other seems to cope very well. Use the stress episode model to explain why this might occur.

2. Imagine that a person who greatly dislikes bureaucracy assumes her first job as an investigator in a very bureaucratic government tax office. Describe the stressors that might be encountered in this situation. Give an example of a problem-solving reaction to this stress. Give an example of a defensive reaction to it.

3. The jobs in the previous two questions are boundary role jobs. Explain this, and describe why boundary roles often prove stressful.

4. Give an example of a role conflict that might provoke anxiety. Describe a problem-solving reaction to this anxiety.

5. Compare and contrast the stressors that might be experienced by an assembly line worker and the president of a company.

6. Discuss the advantages and disadvantages of hiring employees with Type A personality characteristics.

7. Discuss the following three propositions: a) Organizations have a moral obligation to their employees

to make the organizational environment as stress-free as possible. b) Stress reduction in organizations makes good business sense. c) Not only would a stress-free organization be impossible to achieve, but such an environment would not be entirely desirable for either the individual or the organization.

EXPERIENTIAL EXERCISE

Coping with Stress

To what extent does each of the following fit as a description of you? (Circle one number in each line across:)

	Very true	Quite true	Some-what true	Not very true	Not at all true
1. I "roll with the punches" when problems come up.	1	2	3	4	5
2. I spend almost all of my time thinking about my work.	5	4	3	2	1
3. I treat other people as individuals and care about their feelings and opinions.	1	2	3	4	5
4. I recognize and accept my own limitations and assets.	1	2	3	4	5
5. There are quite a few people I could describe as "good friends."	1	2	3	4	5
6. I enjoy using my skills and abilities both on and off the job.	1	2	3	4	5
7. I get bored easily.	5	4	3	2	1
8. I enjoy meeting and talking with people who have different ways of thinking about the world.	1	2	3	4	5
9. Often in my job I "bite off more than I can chew."	5	4	3	2	1
10. I'm usually very active on weekends with projects or recreation.	1	2	3	4	5

	Very true	Quite true	Some- what true	Not very true	Not at all true
11. I prefer working with people who are very much like myself.	5	4	3	2	1
12. I work primarily because I have to survive, and not necessarily because I enjoy what I do.	5	4	3	2	1
13. I believe I have a realistic picture of my personal strengths and weakness.	1	2	3	4	5
14. Often I get into arguments with people who don't think my way.	5	4	3	2	1
15. Often I have trouble getting much done on my job.	5	4	3	2	1
16. I'm interested in a lot of different topics.	1	2	3	4	5
17. I get upset when things don't go my way.	5	4	3	2	1
18. Often I'm not sure how I stand on a controversial topic.	5	4	3	2	1
19. I'm usually able to find a way around anything which blocks me from an important goal.	1	2	3	4	5
20. I often disagree with my boss or others at work.	5	4	3	2	1

Scoring and Interpretation

Dr. Alan A. McLean, who developed this checklist, feels that people who cope with stress effectively have five characteristics. First, they know themselves well and accept their own strengths and weaknesses. Second, they have a variety of interests off the job, and they are not total "workaholics." Third, they exhibit a variety of reactions to stress, rather than always getting a headache or always becoming depressed. Fourth, they are accepting of others who have values or styles different from their own. Finally, good copers are active and productive both on and off the job.

Add together the numbers you circled for the four questions contained in each of the five coping scales.

Coping scale	Add together your responses to these questions	Your score (write in)
Knows self	4, 9, 13, 18	_____
Many interests	2, 5, 7, 16	_____
Variety of reactions	1, 11, 17, 19	_____
Accepts other's values	3, 8, 14, 20	_____
Active and productive	6, 10, 12, 15	_____

Then, add the five scores together for your overall total score: _____
Scores on each of the five areas can vary between 5 and 20. Scores of 12 or above perhaps suggest that it might be useful to direct more attention to the area.

The overall total score can range between 20 and 100. Scores of 60 or more may suggest some general difficulty in coping on the dimensions covered.

Source: McLean, A. A. (1979). *Work stress*. Reading, MA: Addison-Wesley, pp. 126–127. Copyright © 1976 by Management Decision Systems, Inc. Reprinted by permission.

Helen Malley (A)

Valerie Hyatt, the new manager of Federation Bank's Mid-Town Mall branch, started to work through the pile of paper that she had found waiting for her on her arrival at the branch a week ago. The previous manager, who had recently left the bank to work for a trust company, had left a number of things which required fairly urgent attention. One of the items was a performance appraisal form for Helen Malley. To her dismay, Valerie Hyatt saw that the form had been completed about two months previously, but it had not been discussed with Helen Malley.

As she read through it, it became clear that her first impressions of Helen Malley were being confirmed by her predecessor's appraisal. The performance was rated as "low competent," and it stated that Mrs. Malley was deficient in a number of areas of her work. In the last week, as she surveyed the operation, Valerie Hyatt had noticed how slowly Helen Malley, a liability clerk, appeared to work and how uncertain she was in her actions. Just the previous day she had asked Malley a rather simple question about where a particular account should be placed, and Malley had appeared not to know. A recent inspection report by the bank's internal auditors had shown a number of problems emanating from Malley's area. Malley appeared to be the source of many of the problems.

Helen Malley

Before she sent for Malley to discuss the performance appraisal, Valerie Hyatt decided to review Malley's file. This, in itself, was a major task since the material in the file was extensive. Helen Malley had been with the bank for 16 years and had worked in a number of clerical positions, starting off as a junior teller and rotating through several jobs including customer service clerk,

Source: Prepared by Jeffrey Gandz. Copyright 1983, The University of Western Ontario. Reprinted by permission.

liability clerk, deposits clerk, and back to teller. She had been in the position of liability clerk at the mall branch for 18 months.

Aged 59, Malley was separated from her husband and had three children, one of whom—a teenage son—still lived with her. She lived just a few hundred yards from the branch.

In her early years with the bank, Malley had always been considered a competent employee. All her performance appraisals, conducted at annual intervals, had indicated competent, although not outstanding performance. There was one exception to this. Four years ago she had a series of disagreements with her administration manager at a former branch, culminating in her request for a transfer from that branch. The reasons for the conflict were not explained in the file, nor was there any documentation other than her request for transfer for "personal reasons."

Two years ago Malley had a total of 23 days of absence, most of these in one or two day episodes. This was noted on her subsequent performance appraisal but did not, apparently, justify giving her a "low competent" appraisal. In the summer following the appraisal Malley complained of severe back pains. She said that she had been hurt the week previously when the steel gate of a vault swung closed behind her and hit her back as she was bending down to open a drawer. No one in the branch had noticed this accident and she had not complained to anybody about it at the time. During the past year Malley again had a total of 23 days of absence, 15 of which she attributed to treatment for this back condition. Her physician had certified that she required that time off work.

As far as Valerie Hyatt could tell from the records in the file, a pattern of sporadic absence had continued through the following winter. Starting in March of this year, Malley was off work for a total of six weeks for what was described in the file as a "nervous disorder." There was a good deal of correspondence in the file indicating that the bank's medical director had been in touch with her physician and had agreed to continue short-term disability benefits until she returned to work. Following her return to work there was some evidence of a deterioration in work performance. Malley appeared much slower at her job, hesitant and nervous, and this had been noted on her performance appraisal by the previous manager. This manager had left the bank in September before discussing the appraisal with her, and this is the situation which Valerie Hyatt had inherited.

The Performance Appraisal Interview

Having reviewed the file she decided that it was appropriate to conduct a performance appraisal interview with Malley. In Hyatt's mind there was absolutely nothing to be gained from glossing over the inadequate performance. Therefore, she confronted Malley with the performance appraisal that the previous manager had written up.

Malley burst into tears when advised that the evaluation was negative. She claimed, apparently with considerable sincerity, that she had never received an inadequate performance appraisal in all her years with the bank. This was the first negative feedback that she had apparently ever received. When Hyatt reviewed each dimension of performance with her, Malley's comments were always the same. She stated that she had never been adequately trained in any of the functions of the liability clerk. Furthermore, she stated that her absenteeism in the previous two years had been due to the fact that her back gave her a great deal of difficulty when she had to stand or move around, and that she was often in pain. While it wasn't sufficient for her to stay at home in bed, she said it was adversely affecting her performance.

One aspect of the performance appraisal that Hyatt brought to Malley's attention was her apparent brusqueness and curtness with customers and with fellow staff. Malley explained that she was in pain a lot of the time and really didn't feel that she was able to work.

Malley also said that for years she had felt incompetent when having to deal with customers. She had never felt that she had been adequately trained for her jobs. Most times, when she had been assigned to a new task, she was just "thrown into the deep end and expected to swim." She said that this treatment had made her very nervous, and she never felt that she really knew what she was doing.

Malley refused to sign the performance appraisal review that Hyatt had conducted with her. Hyatt stated that the review would be sent to head office anyway. She indicated clearly to Malley that she had six weeks to significantly improve her performance in a number of dimensions, otherwise her employment would be terminated. In response, Malley said that she really didn't think that she would ever be able to do the job of liability clerk. Throughout this interview, Malley was crying and it was clear that she would not be able to work any more that day.

Subsequent Developments

The following morning Miss Hyatt received a telephone call. Malley's family physician, Dr. Reginald, told her that Malley has experienced an extreme stress reaction and had come close to a nervous breakdown in his office the previous afternoon after her conversation with Hyatt. He advised Hyatt that Malley would be off work for a number of weeks and that he would write to the bank's medical director explaining the circumstances. Hyatt also received a letter signed by Malley which she thought had been drafted by a lawyer. This letter refused the "charges" of poor performance made in the appraisal and reiterated Malley's exemplary record.

Throughout the fall Malley remained off work. Every few weeks her physician would contact the bank's medical department indicating that she was still unfit to return to work. Meanwhile, at the Mid-Town Mall branch, she had been replaced by another employee who took over the liability clerk's job, and the operation was running much more smoothly. As she got to know the people in the branch well, it was clear to Hyatt that they were all relieved that Malley was no longer there. She hadn't been doing her share of work in the branch for some months, and the staff really felt some animosity toward her because of this. Several customers mentioned in passing that they were quite pleased that she was no longer there and felt much more at ease discussing their loss details with her replacement. On the other hand, a number of customers commented that they missed Malley and preferred discussing their problems with an older person.

In early December Hyatt heard directly from Malley that she was feeling much better and expected to return to work early in the new year. Hyatt did not look forward to this, since she was convinced, from her discussions with Malley, that she just couldn't perform the job at a competent level. But she didn't really know what she could do under the circumstances nor how she should treat Malley when she returned to work.

1. Is Helen Malley experiencing work-related stress? First, answer the question intuitively and give your reasoning. Then apply the stress model shown in Exhibit 14–1 to Helen's situation, noting signs of stressors, stress, and stress reactions. Be sure to consider the role demands faced by Helen.

2. Does Helen Malley exhibit a Type A behavior pattern? Is she suffering from burnout?

3. Evaluate Valerie Hyatt's performance as a manager in the episode recounted in the case.

4. What should Helen Malley do now? What should Valerie Hyatt do now?

REFERENCES

1. McGrath, J. E. (1970). A conceptual formulation for research on stress. In J. E. McGrath (Ed.), *Social and psychological factors in stress*. New York: Holt, Rinehart, Winston.

2. Roth, S., & Cohen, L. J. (1986). Approach, avoidance, and coping with stress. *American Psychologist, 41*, 813–819.

3. Anderson, C. R. (1977). Locus of control, coping behaviors and performance in a stress setting: A longitudinal study. *Journal of Applied Psychology, 62*, 446–451.

4. Friedman, M., & Rosenman, R. (1974). *Type A Behavior and your heart*. New York: Knopf.

5. Chesney, M. A., & Rosenman, R. (1980). Type A behavior in the work setting. In C. L. Cooper and R. Payne (Eds.), *Current concerns in occupational stress*. Chichester, England: Wiley.

6. Steinberg, L. (1985). Early temperamental antecedents of adult Type-A behaviors. *Developmental Psychology, 21*, 1171–1180.

7. Chesney & Rosenman, 1980.

8. Matthews, K. A. (1982). Psychological perspectives on the Type A behavior pattern. *Psychological Bulletin, 91*, 293–323. For a representative study, see Ivancevich, J. M., Matteson, M. T., & Preston, C. (1982). Occupational stress, Type A behavior, and physical well-being. *Academy of Management Journal, 25*, 373–391.

9. Booth-Kewley, S., & Friedman, H. S. (1987). Psychological predictors of heart disease: A quantitative review. *Psychological Bulletin, 101*, 343–362; Williams, R. (1989). *The trusting heart: Great news about Type A behavior*. New York: Random House.

10. Chesney & Rosenman, 1980.

11. Parasuraman, S., & Alutto, J. A. (1981). An examination of the organizational antecedents of stressors at work. *Academy of Management Journal, 24*, 48–67.

12. Mintzberg, H. (1973). *The nature of managerial work*. New York: Harper & Row, p. 30.

13. Rogers, E. M., & Larsen, J. K. (1984). *Silicon valley fever: Growth of a high-technology culture*. New York: Basic Books, p. 138.

14. An excellent review of managerial stressors can be found in Marshall, J., & Cooper, C. L. (1979). *Executives under pressure*. New York: Praeger.

15. La Porte, T. R. (1965). Conditions of strain and accommodation in industrial research organizations. *Administrative Science Quarterly, 10*, 21–38.

16. La Porte, 1965, p. 24.

17. Terkel, S. (1972). *Working*. New York: Avon, pp. 227–228.

18. Terkel, 1972, pp. 50–51.

19. Lawler, E. E., III. (1985). Education, managerial style, and organizational effectiveness. *Personnel Psychology, 38*, 1–26.

20. For a more optimistic view, see Kirkland, R. I., Jr., (1985, June 10). Are service jobs good jobs?, *Fortune*, 38–43.

21. Karasek, R. A., Jr. (1979). Job demands, job decision latitude, and mental strain: Implications for job redesign. *Administrative Science Quarterly, 24*, 285–308. Also see Martin, R., & Wall, T. D. (1989). Attentional demand and cost as stressors in shopfloor jobs. *Academy of Management Journal, 32*, 69–86.

22. Miles, R. H. Organizational boundary roles. In Cooper & Payne, 1980.

23. Maslach, C., & Jackson, S. E. (1984). Burnout in organizational settings. In S. Oskamp (Ed.), *Applied social psychology annual* (Vol. 5). Beverly Hills, CA: Sage, p. 134.

24. Lee, R. T., & Ashforth, B. E. (In press). A longitudinal study of burnout among supervisors and managers: Comparisons of the Leiter and Maslach (1988) and Golembiewski et al. (1986) models. *Organizational Behavior and Human Decision Processes*.

25. For a study of burnout among police personnel, see Burke, R. J., & Deszca, E. (1986). Correlates of psychological burnout phases among police officers. *Human Relations, 39*, 487–501.

26. See Pines, A. M., & Aronson, E. (1981). *Burnout: From tedium to personal growth*. New York: The Free Press.

27. Jackson, S. E., & Schuler, R. S. (1985). Meta-analysis and conceptual critique of research on role ambiguity and conflict in work settings. *Organizational Behavior and Human Decision Processes, 36*, 16–78. For a critique of some of this research, see Fineman, S., & Payne, R. (1981). Role stress—A methodological trap? *Journal of Occupational Behaviour, 2*, 51–64.

28. Terkel, 1972, pp. 115–116.

29. Jamal, M. (1984). Job stress and job performance controversy: An empirical assessment. *Organizational Behavior and Human Performance, 33*, 1–21; Motowidlo, S. J., Packard, J. S., & Manning, M. R. (1986). Occupational stress: Its causes and consequences for job performance. *Journal of Applied Psychology, 71*, 618–629.

30. Katz, D., & Kahn, R. L. (1978). *The social psy-

chology of organizations (2nd ed.). New York: Wiley.

31. Gupta, N., & Beehr, T. A. (1979). Job stress and employee behavior. *Organizational Behavior and Human Performance, 23,* 373–387.

32. See Kemery, E. R., Bedian, A. G., Mossholder, K. W., & Touliatos, J. (1985). Outcomes of role stress: A multisample constructive replication. *Academy of Management Journal, 28,* 363–375; Parasuraman, S., & Alutto, J. A. (1984). Sources and outcomes of stress in organizational settings: Toward the development of a structural model. *Academy of Management Journal, 27,* 330–350.

33. Beehr, T. A., & Newman, J. E. (1978). Job stress, employee health, and organizational effectiveness: A facet analysis, model, and literature review. *Personnel Psychology, 32,* 665–699.

34. Beehr & Newman, 1978. For a later review and a strong critique of this work, see Fried, Y., Rowland, K. M., & Ferris, G. R. (1984). The physiological measurement of work stress: A critique. *Personnel Psychology, 37,* 583–615. See also Fried, Y. (1989). The future of physiological assessments in work situations. In C. L. Cooper & R. Payne (Eds.), *Causes, coping, and consequences of stress at work.* Chichester, England: Wiley & Sons.

35. Cooper, C. L., Mallinger, M., & Kahn, R. (1978). Identifying sources of occupational stress among dentists. *Journal of Occupational Psychology, 61,* 163–174. See also Cooper, C. L., Watts, J., Baglioni, A. J., & Kelly, M. (1988). Occupational stress amongst general practice dentists. *Journal of Occupational Psychology, 61,* 163–174.

36. Wall, T. D., & Clegg, C. W. (1981). A longitudinal field study of group work redesign. *Journal of Occupational Behaviour, 2,* 31–49.

37. Cohen, S., & Wills, T. A. (1985). Stress, social support, and the buffering hypothesis. *Psychological Bulletin, 98,* 310–357.

38. Ivancevich, J. M., Matteson, M. T., Freedman, S. M., & Phillips, J. S. (1990). Worksite stress management interventions. *American Psychologist, 45,* 252–261; Murphy, L. R. (1984). Occupational stress management: A review and appraisal. *Journal of Occupational Psychology, 57,* 1–15.

39. Ivancevich et al., 1990; Murphy, 1984.

40. Johnston, D. C., Mayes, B. T., Sime, W. E., & Tharp, G. D. (1982). Managing occupational stress: A field experiment. *Journal of Applied Psychology, 67,* 533–542.

41. Ivancevich, J. M., & Matteson, M. T. (1980). *Stress at work: A managerial perspective.* Glenview, IL: Scott, Foresman, p. 215.

42. Gebhardt, D. L., & Crump, C. E. (1990). Employee fitness and wellness programs in the workplace. *American Psychologist, 45,* 262–272; Folkins, C. H., & Sime, W. E. (1981). Physical fitness training and mental health. *American Psychologist, 36,* 373–389; Falkenberg, L. E. (1987). Employee fitness programs: Their impact on the employee and the organization. *Academy of Management Review, 12,* 511–522.

PART FOUR

THE TOTAL ORGANIZATION

ORGANIZATIONAL STRUCTURE

STEEL VERSUS SOLAR

Bill Donovan reflected on his first eight months at Solar Components Corporation with a sense of satisfaction. "Now I understand this company," he thought. "Now I understand my role here." As Donovan's thoughts imply, things had not always been this way. In fact, his first four months as sales manager at Solar had been the most perplexing and challenging in his business career.

After graduating from high school, Donovan had obtained an engineering degree. However, he found the profession boring, and while working for one firm, he began to pursue an M.B.A. degree part-time, hoping to move into management. He had especially enjoyed his marketing courses, and this led to a fairly radical career change. Upon graduating, Donovan quit the engineering firm and took a job as a sales representative for Ohio Valley Steel. Starting in the field had been a wise move. In two years, Donovan was promoted to sales manager for finished steel products. Two years after this, he became general sales manager, with the managers for finished products and bulk steel reporting to him. Donovan occupied this position until he quit to become sales manager at Solar Components. Solar developed, designed, and constructed custom solar heating and cooling devices for residential and commercial buildings.

Bill Donovan's recent experience at Solar had led him to think a lot about his five years at Ohio Valley. In retrospect, selling steel had been a pretty routine business. Ohio Valley's product line had remained the same for years, and selling consisted mainly of calling on existing customers and keeping one's eyes open for new prospects who could use what Ohio produced. Sales contracts were standard and routine, and Donovan had encountered only a couple unusual cases in his whole career there. "After all," Donovan thought, "steel is steel. The winner in that business delivers on time and keeps quality high."

Ohio Valley Steel had been a formal, tightly controlled organization. Each position Donovan held had a detailed job description and a carefully written procedures manual. In addition, it had a long chain of command. Sales representatives reported to sales managers, who reported to the general sales manager. In turn, he reported to the marketing director, who then reported to the vice-president of marketing. Employees were encouraged to stick to the chain. This could be both comforting and frustrating. On one hand, there was always someone up the line to answer a question or deal with a problem. On the other, decisions could take *forever* to be made. In general, all important decisions were made at the top of the company. Donovan gradually came to understand the reason for this: Long production runs were most economical and easy to control in terms of quality. Only at the senior management level could sales orders be integrated into efficient production runs.

Even during his job interview, he was aware that things would be different at Solar Components. When he asked to see written job descriptions for the sales manager and sales reps, he was told there were none. Verbally, however, he learned that the jobs involved considerable latitude. He also realized that the chain of command at Solar was shorter than that at Ohio—just sales rep to sales manager to vice-president of marketing.

When he assumed his new job, it didn't take Donovan long to see the consequences of these differences. Unlike Ohio Valley's reps, the Solar sales reps had a high degree of technical training. Most were science graduates, and they worked closely with potential customers to develop custom solar systems that were suited to their individual needs. The solar technology was changing rapidly, and most salespeople consulted directly with the design department once a contact had been made. This procedure made Donovan nervous, so he asked to review all contacts before the reps went to design. However, he quickly realized that this didn't make any sense. Despite his engineering background, he simply didn't understand enough about solar systems to be helpful at this stage. Thus, he reinstituted the looser system of communication between sales and design.

Donovan also found out that the short chain of command discouraged pushing decisions "upstairs." When a sales rep came to him complaining about surface cracks in some solar panels that had just been delivered, he contacted his vice-president for advice. "I don't understand that stuff," he was told. "You and the rep get together with Michaels in production and Robbins in design and work it out. Whatever you decide is okay by me." Gradually, Donovan learned that such informal teamwork was common at Solar. Slowly, he settled into the job and learned to enjoy the system. Still, he wondered how two successful companies could be organized so differently.

This story reflects the common observation that different organizations are organized or structured differently. But why is this so? And how do these differences affect organizational members and the overall effectiveness of the organization? These are the kinds of questions that we shall attempt to answer in this chapter and the next.

First, organizational structure will be defined, and the methods by which labor is divided and departments are formed will be discussed. Then we will consider some methods by which labor is coordinated. Traditional structural characteristics and the relationship between size and structure will be considered. Finally, we will review some early prescriptions concerning structure and some signals of structural problems.

A PROLOGUE: THE ROLE OF ORGANIZATIONAL STRUCTURE

In previous chapters we were concerned primarily with the bits and pieces that make up organizations. First, we analyzed organizational behavior from the standpoint of the individual member—how his or her learning, perception, attitudes, and motivation affect behavior. Then we shifted our analysis to groups and to some of the processes that occur in organizations, including communication, leadership, and decision making. In this chapter we adopt yet another level of analysis by looking at the organization as a whole. Our primary interest is the causes and consequences of organizational structure.

Shortly, we will discuss organizational structure in detail. For now, it is enough to know that it broadly refers to how the organization's individuals and groups are *put together* or *organized* to accomplish work. This is an important issue. It is entirely possible to conceive of a firm or institution that has well-motivated individual members and properly led groups and still fails to fulfill its potential because of the way their efforts are divided and coordinated.

We are not used to thinking about the structure of organizations and how it affects us. Frequently, we confuse the effects of structure with motivation, leadership, or communication. For example, consider the Master's-level engineering student who must withdraw from a course that is cancelled because its enrollment is too small. She is able to withdraw from the course at the graduate office, but she is told that she must go to the accounts office to obtain a tuition refund. At the accounts office, she learns that she must have a note from the department that cancelled the course. Returning with a note from the electrical engineering department, she finds that she must also obtain a copy of her registration from the registrar's office before a refund can be granted. Ready to scream, she proceeds to give the poor accounts clerk a lecture on leadership, motivation, and communication. In fact, each of the subunits described in this example might be doing its own job perfectly well. It is the way the university is *structured* that is causing the student problems.

In Chapter 1 we defined organizations as social inventions for accomplishing goals through group effort. We also separated organizational goals into official goals (such as making a profit or curing the sick) and operative goals (such as keeping workers satisfied) that can assist in the achievement of official goals. In this chapter and the next, we shall see that organizational structure intervenes between goals and organizational accomplishments and thus influences organizational effectiveness.

WHAT IS ORGANIZATIONAL STRUCTURE?

Organizational structure is not the easiest concept to define precisely because the concept covers so much territory. However, we can get a little more precise than our previous allusion to structure as being how an organization is "put together" or "organized."

Let's begin this way: To achieve its goals, an organization has to do two very basic things—*divide* labor among its members and then *coordinate* what has been divided. The university mentioned above divided its labor—some members taught electrical engineering, some ran the graduate program, some took care of accounts, and some handled registration. It is simply unlikely that anyone could do *all* of these things well. Furthermore, within each of these subunits, labor would be further divided. For example, the registrar's office would include a director, secretaries, clerks, and so on. With all this division, some coordination is obviously necessary. Although the student didn't feel that the coordination was adequate, a good organizational detective would spot evidence of its existence— everyone knew whom she should see to solve her refund problem.

We can conclude that **organizational structure** is the manner in which an organization divides its labor into specific tasks and achieves coordination among these tasks.[1]

THE DIVISION AND COORDINATION OF LABOR

Labor must be divided because individuals have physical and intellectual limitations. *Everyone* can't do *everything;* even if this were possible, tremendous confusion and inefficiency would result. There are two basic dimensions to the division of labor, a vertical dimension and a horizontal dimension. Once labor is divided, it must be coordinated to achieve organizational effectiveness.

Vertical Division of Labor

The vertical division of labor is concerned primarily with apportioning authority for planning and decision making—who gets to tell whom what to do? As shown in Exhibit 15–1, in a manufacturing firm the vertical division of labor is usually signified by titles such as president, manager, and supervisor. In a university it might be denoted by titles such as president, dean, and chairperson. Organizations differ greatly in the extent to which labor is divided vertically. For example, the U.S. Army has nine levels of command ranging from four-star generals to sergeants. Similarly, Bell Canada has seven levels ranging from president to first-level supervisors. On the other hand, an automobile dealership might have only three levels, and a university would usually fall between these extremes. Separate departments, units, or functions *within* an organization will also often vary in the extent to which they vertically divide labor. A production unit might have several levels of management, ranging from supervisor to general manager. A research unit in the same company might have only two levels of management. A couple of key themes or issues underlie the vertical division of labor.

Autonomy and Control Holding other factors constant, the domain of decision making and authority is reduced as the number of levels in the hierarchy increases. Put another way, managers have less authority over fewer matters. This was illustrated in the story that began the chapter. Ohio Valley Steel had quite a few levels in its marketing hierarchy, and Bill Donovan found his authority to make decisions restricted. Solar Components, with fewer levels, pushed such authority lower and even involved the sales representatives in decisions.

Communication A second theme underlying the vertical division of labor is communication or coordination between levels. As labor is progressively divided vertically, timely communication and coordination can become harder to achieve. Recall that decisions took "forever" at Ohio Valley Steel. Also recall our discussion in Chapter 11 of information filtering as a barrier to communication. As the number of levels in the hierarchy increases, filtering is more likely to occur.

These two themes illustrate that labor must be divided vertically enough to ensure proper control but not so much as to make vertical communication and coordination impossible. The proper degree of such division will vary across organizations and across their functional units.

EXHIBIT

15–1

The dimensions of division of labor in a manufacturing firm.

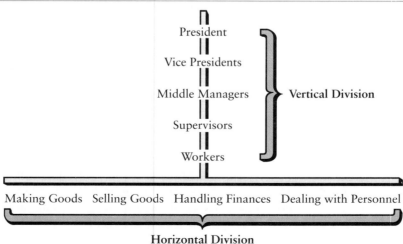

Horizontal Division of Labor

The horizontal division of labor involves grouping the basic tasks that must be performed into jobs and then into departments so that the organization can achieve its goals. The firm schematized in Exhibit 15–1 must produce and sell goods, keep its finances straight, and keep its employees happy. A hospital must admit patients, subject them to lab tests, fix what ails them, and keep them comfortable, all the while staying within its budget. Just as organizations differ in the extent to which they divide labor vertically, they also differ in the extent of horizontal division of labor. In a small business, the owner might be a "jack of all trades," making estimates, delivering the product or service, and keeping the books. As the organization grows, horizontal division of labor is likely, with different groups of employees assigned to perform each of these tasks. Thus, the horizontal division of labor suggests some specialization on the part of the work force. Up to a point, this increased specialization can promote efficiency. A couple of key themes or issues underlie the horizontal division of labor.

Job Design The horizontal division of labor is closely tied to our earlier consideration of job design (Chapter 7). An example will clarify this. Suppose that an organization offers a product or service that consists of A work, B work, and C work (e.g., fabrication, inspection, and packaging). There are at least three basic ways in which it might structure these tasks:

- Form an ABC Department in which all workers do ABC work
- Form an ABC Department in which workers specialize in A work, B work, or C work
- Form a separate A Department, B Department, and C Department

There is nothing inherently superior about any of these three designs. Notice, however, that each has implications for the jobs involved and how these jobs are coordinated. The first design provides for enriched jobs in which each worker can coordinate his or her own A work, B work, and C work. However, this design might require highly trained workers, and it might be impossible if A work, B work, and C work are complex specialties that require (for example) engineering, accounting, and legal skills. The second design involves increased horizontal division of labor in which employees specialize in tasks and in which the coordination of A work, B work, and C work becomes more critical. However, much of this coordination could be handled by properly designing the job of the head of the department. Finally, the third design offers the greatest horizontal division of labor in that A work, B work, and C work are actually performed in separate departments. This design provides for great control and accountability for the separate tasks, but it also suggests that someone above the department heads will have to get involved in coordination. There are several lessons here. First, the horizontal division of labor strongly affects job design. Second, it has profound implications for the degree of coordination necessary. Finally, it also has implications for the vertical division of labor and where control over work processes should logically reside.

Differentiation   A second theme occasioned by the horizontal division of labor is related to the first. As organizations engage in increased horizontal division of labor, they usually become more and more differentiated. **Differentiation** is the tendency for managers in separate functions or departments to differ in terms of goals, time spans, and interpersonal styles.[2] In tending to their own domains and problems, these managers might develop distinctly different psychological orientations toward the organization and its products or services. A classic case of differentiation is that which often occurs between marketing managers and those in research and development. The goals of the marketing managers might be external to the organization and oriented toward servicing the marketplace. Those of R&D managers might be oriented more toward excellence in design and state-of-the-art use of materials. While marketing managers want products to sell *now,* R&D managers might feel that "good designs take time." Finally, marketing managers might believe that dispute resolution with R&D is best accomplished by interpersonal tactics learned when they were on the sales force ("Let's discuss this over lunch"). R&D managers might feel that "the design data speaks for itself" when a conflict occurs. The essential problem here is that the marketing department and the R&D department *need* each other to do their jobs properly![3]

Differentiation is a natural and necessary consequence of the horizontal division of labor, but it again points to the need for coordination, a topic that we will consider in more detail below. For now, let's examine more closely how organizations can allocate work to departments.

Departmentation

As suggested above, once basic tasks have been combined into jobs, a question still remains as to how to group these jobs so that they can be managed effectively. The assignment of jobs to departments is called departmentation, and it represents one of the core aspects of the horizontal division of labor. It should be recognized that "department" is a generic term; some organizations use an alternative term such as unit, group, or division. There are several methods of departmentation, each of which has its strengths and weaknesses.

Functional Departmentation   This form of organization is basic and familiar. Under **functional departmentation,** workers with closely related skills and responsibilities (functions) are located in the same department (see Exhibit 15–2). Thus, those with skills in sales and advertising are assigned to the marketing department, those with skills in accounting and credit are assigned to the finance department, and so on. Under this kind of design, employees are grouped according to the kind of resources they contribute to achieving the overall goals of the organization.[4]

What are the advantages of functional departmentation? The most-cited advantage is that of efficiency. When all of the engineers are located in an engineering department, rather than scattered throughout the organization, it is easier to

EXHIBIT

15–2

Functional departmentation.

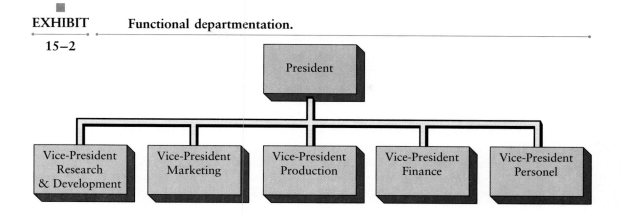

President

Vice-President Research & Development

Vice-President Marketing

Vice-President Production

Vice-President Finance

Vice-President Personel

be sure that they are neither overloaded nor underloaded with work. Also, support factors such as reference books, computer terminals, and laboratory space can be allocated more efficiently with less duplication. Some other advantages of functional departmentation include the following:

- Communication within departments should be enhanced, since everyone "speaks the same language."
- Career ladders and training opportunities within the function are enhanced.
- It should be easier to measure and evaluate the performance of functional specialists when they are all located in the same department.

What are the disadvantages of functional departmentation? Most of them stem from the specialization within departments that occurs in the functional arrangement. As a result, a high degree of differentiation can occur between functional departments. At best, this can lead to poor coordination and slow response to organizational problems. At worst, it can lead to open conflict between departments in which the needs of clients and customers are ignored. Departmental empires might be built at the expense of pursuing organizational goals.

There is consensus that functional departmentation works best in small to medium-sized firms that offer relatively few product lines or services. It can also be an effective means of organizing the smaller divisions of large corporations. When scale gets bigger and the output of the organization gets more complex, most firms gravitate toward product departmentation or its variations.

Product Departmentation Under **product departmentation**, departments are formed on the basis of a particular product, product line, or service. Each of these departments can operate fairly autonomously because it has its own set of functional specialists dedicated to the output of that department. For example, a computer firm might have a hardware division and a software division, each with its own staff of production people, marketers, and research and development personnel (see Exhibit 15–3).

What are the advantages of product departmentation? One key advantage is better coordination among the functional specialists who work on a particular product line. Since their attentions are focused on one product and they have fewer functional peers, fewer barriers to communication should develop. Other advantages include flexibility, since product lines can be added or deleted without great implications for the rest of the organization. Also, product-focused departments can be evaluated as profit centers, since they have independent control over costs and revenues. This is not feasible for most functional departments (e.g., the research and development department doesn't have revenues). Finally, product departmentation often serves the customer or client better, since the client can see more easily who produced the product (the software group, not Ajax Computers).

EXHIBIT   **Product departmentation.**

15–3

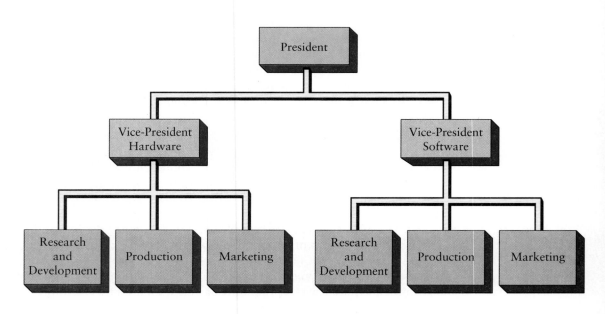

**EXHIBIT
15–4**

Geographic departmentation.

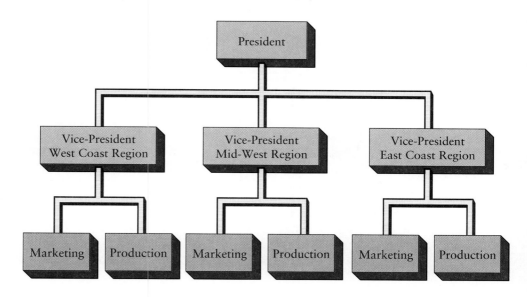

Are there any disadvantages to product departmentation? Professional development might suffer without a critical mass of professionals working in the same place at the same time. Also, economies of scale might be threatened and inefficiency might occur if relatively autonomous product-oriented departments are not coordinated. R&D personnel in an industrial products division and a consumer products division might work on a similar problem for months without being aware of each other's efforts. Worse, product-oriented departments might actually work at cross-purposes.

Other Forms of Departmentation Several other forms of departmentation can be observed.[5] Two of these are simply variations on product departmentation. One is called geographic departmentation. Under **geographic departmentation,** relatively self-contained units deliver the organization's products or services in specific geographic territories (Exhibit 15–4). This form of departmentation shortens communication channels, allows the organization to cater to regional tastes, and gives some appearance of local control to clients and customers. National retailers, insurance companies, and oil companies generally exhibit geographic departmentation.

Another form of departmentation that is closely related to product departmentation is called customer departmentation. Under **customer departmentation,** relatively self-contained units deliver the organization's products or services to specific customer groups (Exhibit 15–5). The obvious goal is to provide better service to each customer group by specialization. For example, many banks have

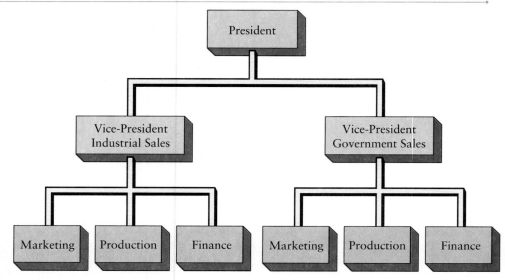

commercial lending divisions that are separate from the consumer loan operations. Universities might have separate graduate and undergraduate divisions. An
engineering firm might have separate divisions to cater to civilian and military
customers. In general, the advantages and disadvantages of geographic and customer departmentation parallel those for product departmentation.

Finally, it should be recognized that few organizations represent "pure" examples of functional, product, geographic, or customer departmentation. It is not
unusual to see **hybrid departmentation,** which involves some combination of
these structures. For example, a manufacturing firm might retain personnel, finance, and legal services in a functional form at headquarters but use product
departmentation to organize separate production and sales staffs for each product. Similarly, a large retail firm might departmentize buying functionally (all
buyers working out of the same headquarters department) even though it otherwise relies on geographic departmentation. The hybrids attempt to capitalize on
the strengths of various structures while avoiding the weaknesses of others.

In Focus 15–1 describes IBM's major restructuring.

Basic Methods of Coordinating Divided Labor

When the tasks that will help the organization achieve its goals have been divided
among individuals and departments, they must be coordinated so that goal accomplishment is actually realized. We can identify five basic methods of **coordination,** which is a process of facilitating timing, communication, and feedback.[6]

Direct Supervision This is a very traditional form of coordination. Working through the chain of command, designated supervisors or managers coordinate the work of their subordinates. For instance, a production supervisor coordinates the work of his or her subordinates. In turn, the production superintendent coordinates the activities of all the supervisors. This method of coordination is closely associated with our discussion of leadership in Chapter 10.

IN FOCUS 15–1

IBM Changes Structure

Computer giant IBM radically reorganized early in 1988. Until then, all major decisions (and many minor ones) about design, manufacturing, and marketing were made at corporate headquarters in Armonk, New York. There, eighteen senior executives, with the advice of a slew of staff advisors, charted IBM's course through the increasingly turbulent world of information technology. When this technology revolved around one main product category—mainframe computers—IBM's structure provided an impressive degree of coordination that made it a world leader. However, industry observers generally agree that this single-minded attention to mainframes distracted IBM from important developments in information technology. These included the popularity of personal computers and workstations, the need to build and service computer networks, and the demand for customized applications software. IBM competitors, including Apple, Digital, Sun, and Compaq, were able to exploit various of these developments at IBM's expense.

IBM's new structure has seven autonomous business units, which are essentially based on product lines. These include mainframes, personal computers, minicomputers, microchips, communications equipment, software, and programming. An eighth unit was set up to do the marketing for all the product units. A tough, respected senior vice-president was installed to serve as an integrator between the units. Thousands of employees were moved from headquarters staff units into these business units. The goal was to move IBM closer to its customers and speed decision making. Also, to better service the global marketplace, four worldwide geographic regions were established.

Source: Dreyfuss, J. (1989, August 14). Reinventing IBM. *Fortune*, 30–39; Staff (1988, February 15). Big changes at big blue. *Business Week*, 92–98; Sanger, D. E. (1988, January 3). The moment of truth for big blue. *The New York Times*, p. 1.

Standardization of Work Processes Some jobs are so routine that the technology itself provides a means of coordination. Little direct supervision is necessary for these jobs to be coordinated. The automobile assembly line provides a good example. When a car comes by, worker X bolts on the left A-frame assembly, and worker Y bolts on the right assembly. These workers do not have to interact, and they require minimal supervision. Work processes can also be standardized by rules and regulations. The procedures manual that Bill Donovan found at Ohio Valley Steel is an example.

Standardization of Outputs Even when direct supervision is minimal and work processes are not standardized, coordination can be achieved through the standardization of work outputs. Concern shifts from how the work is done to ensuring that the work meets certain physical or economic standards. For instance, workers in a machine shop might be required to construct complex valves that require a mixture of drilling, lathe work, and finishing. The physical specifications of the valves will dictate how this work is to be coordinated. Standardization of outputs is often used to coordinate the work of separate product or geographic divisions. Frequently, top management assigns each division a profit target. These standards ensure that each division "pulls its weight" in contributing to overall profit goals. Thus, budgets are a form of standardizing outputs.

Standardization of Skills Even when work processes and output cannot be standardized, and direct supervision is unfeasible, coordination can be achieved through standardization of skills. This is seen very commonly in the case of technicians and professionals. For example, a large surgery team can often coordinate its work with minimal verbal communication because of its high degree of interlocked training—surgeons, anesthesiologists, and nurses all know what to expect from each other because of their standard training.

Mutual Adjustment Mutual adjustment relies upon informal communication to coordinate tasks. Paradoxically, it is useful for coordinating the most simple and the most complicated divisions of labor. For example, imagine a small florist shop that consists of the owner-operator, a shop assistant, and a delivery person. It is very likely that these individuals will coordinate their work through informal processes, mutually adjusting to each other's needs. At the other extreme, consider the team that was responsible for designing the heat-shield tiles for the U.S. space shuttle craft. This complicated task reached to the very edge of current technology, requiring the collaboration of physicists, chemists, computer specialists, and aeronautical engineers. Here we see a unique task and a radical mix of specialists with different backgrounds and training. Again, mutual adjustment would be necessary to coordinate their efforts because standardization would be impossible. (Also, the more complex coordination mechanisms discussed below would be used.) At Solar Components, Bill Donovan found that mutual adjustment was necessary to coordinate the efforts of sales, production, and design. The customized nature of the product dictated that this approach be used.

   Now that we have reviewed the five methods of coordinating divided labor, a few comments are in order. First, as shown in Exhibit 15–6, the methods can be crudely ordered in terms of the degree of *discretion* they permit individual workers in terms of task performance; applied strictly, direct supervision permits little

EXHIBIT

15–6

Methods of coordination as a continuum of worker discretion.

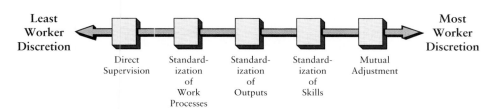

Source: From Mintzberg, H. (1979). *The structuring of organizations: A synthesis of the research*. Englewood Cliffs, NJ: Prentice-Hall, p. 198. © 1979. Reprinted by permission of Prentice-Hall, Inc., Englewood Cliffs, NJ.

discretion. Standardization of processes and outputs permits successively more discretion. (However, these forms of standardization can be "beaten" by clever workers.) Finally, standardization of skills and mutual adjustment put even more control into the hands of those who are actually doing the work.

Notice that just as division of labor affects the design of jobs, so does the method of coordination employed. As we move from the left side to the right side of the continuum of coordination, there is greater potential for jobs to be designed in an enriched manner. By the same token, an improper coordination strategy can destroy the intrinsic motivation of a job. Traditionally, much work performed by professionals (e.g., scientists and engineers) is coordinated by their own skill standardization. If the manager of a research lab decides to coordinate work with a high degree of direct supervision, the motivating potential of the scientists' jobs might be damaged. *She* is doing work that *they* should be doing.

It can also be observed that the use of the various methods of coordination tends to vary across different parts of the organization. These differences in coordination stem from the way labor has been divided. For example, upper management relies heavily upon mutual adjustment for coordination. Where tasks are more routine, such as in the lower part of the production subunit, we tend to see coordination via direct supervision or standardization of work processes or outputs.[7] Advisory subunits staffed by professionals, such as the legal department or the marketing research group, often rely upon a combination of skill standardization and mutual adjustment.

Finally, methods of coordination may change as task demands change. Under peacetime conditions or routine wartime conditions, the army relies heavily on direct supervision through a strict chain of command. However, this method of coordination can prove ineffective for fighting units under heavy fire. Here, we might see a sergeant with a radio instructing a captain where to direct artillery fire. This reversal of the chain of command is indicative of mutual adjustment.

Other Methods of Coordination

The forms of coordination discussed above are very basic in that almost every organization uses them. After all, when do we see an organization that *doesn't* exhibit some supervision, some standardization, and some talking things out? Sometimes, however, coordination problems are such that more customized, elaborate mechanisms are necessary to achieve coordination. This is especially true when we are speaking of lateral coordination across highly differentiated departments. Recall that the managers of such departments might vary greatly in goals, time spans, and interpersonal orientation. Figuratively, at least, they often "speak different languages." The process of obtaining coordination across differentiated departments usually goes by the special name of **integration**.[8] Good integration achieves coordination without reducing the differences that enable each department to do its own job well.[9] For example, in a high-technology firm, we don't *want* production and engineering to be so cozy that innovative tension is lost.[10]

In ascending order of elaboration, three methods of achieving integration include the use of liaison roles, task forces, and full-time integrators.[11]

Liaison Roles A **liaison role** is occupied by a person in one department who is assigned, as part of his or her job, to achieve coordination with another department. In other words, one person serves as a part-time link between two departments. Sometimes the second department might reciprocate by nominating its own liaison person. For example, in a university library, reference librarians might be required to serve as liaison people for certain academic departments or schools. In turn, an academic department might assign a faculty member to "touch base" with its liaison in the library. Sometimes, liaison people might actually be located physically in the corresponding department. For instance, a member of the engineering department might be assigned to an office in the plant to assist with production matters.

Task Forces When coordination problems arise that involve several departments simultaneously, liaison roles are not very effective. **Task forces** are temporary groups set up to solve coordination problems across several departments. Representatives from each department are included on a full-time or part-time basis, but when adequate integration is achieved, the task force is disbanded. The introduction of a new product or service might stimulate the establishment of a task force because of the degree of confusion and uncertainty. It might enable design, engineering, production, and sales to get their respective roles and time frames hammered out without referring the problem up into the hierarchy, where detailed knowledge might be lacking.

Integrators **Integrators** are organizational members who are permanently installed between two departments that are in clear need of coordination. In a sense, they are full-time problem solvers. Integrators are especially useful for dealing with conflict between (1) highly interdependent departments (2) which have very diverse goals and orientations (3) in a very ambiguous environment. Such a situation occurs in many high-technology companies.[12] For example, a solid-state electronics firm might introduce new products almost every month. This is a real strain on the production department, which might need the assistance of the design scientists to implement a production run. The scientists, on the other hand, rely on production to implement last-minute changes due to the rapidly changing technology. This situation badly requires coordination.

Integrators usually report directly to the executive to whom the heads of the two departments report. Ideally, they are rewarded according to the success of both units. A special kind of person is required for this job, since he or she has great responsibility but no direct authority in either department. The integrator must be unbiased, "speak the language" of both departments, and rely heavily on expert power.[13] An engineer with excellent interpersonal skills might be an effective integrator for the electronics firm.

TRADITIONAL STRUCTURAL CHARACTERISTICS

Every organization is unique in the exact way in which its labor is divided and coordinated. Few business firms, hospitals, or schools have perfectly identical structures. What is needed, then, is some efficient way to summarize the effects of the vertical and horizontal division of labor and its coordination on the structure of the organization. Over the years, management scholars and practicing managers have agreed upon a number of characteristics that summarize the structure of organizations.[14]

Span of Control

The **span of control** is the number of subordinates supervised by a superior. There is one essential fact about span of control: The larger the span, the less *potential* there is for coordination by direct supervision. As the span increases, the attention that can be devoted to each subordinate decreases. When work tasks are routine, coordination of labor through standardization of work processes or output often substitutes for direct supervision. Thus, at lower levels in production units, it is not unusual to see spans of control ranging to over twenty. In the managerial ranks, tasks are less routine, and adequate time might be necessary for informal mutual adjustment. As a result, spans at the upper levels tend to be smaller. Another factor might also be at work here. At lower organizational levels, workers with only one or a few specialties report to a supervisor. For instance, an office supervisor might supervise only clerks. As we climb the hierarchy, workers with radically different specialties might report to the boss. For example, the president might have to deal with vice-presidents of personnel, finance, production, and marketing. Again, the complexity of this task might dictate smaller spans.[15]

Flat Versus Tall

Holding size constant, a **flat organization** has relatively few levels in its hierarchy of authority, while a **tall organization** has relatively many levels. Thus, flatness versus tallness is an index of the vertical division of labor. Again, holding size constant, it should be obvious that flatness and tallness are associated with the average span of control. This is shown in Exhibit 15–7. Both schematized organizations have thirty-one members. However, the taller one has five hierarchical levels and an average span of two, while the flatter one has three levels and an average span of five. It is usually thought that flatter structures tend to push decision-making powers downward in the organization because a given number of decisions are apportioned among fewer levels. We saw this earlier in the comparison of Ohio Valley Steel and Solar Components. Also, flatter structures generally enhance vertical communication and coordination.

Radical differences in organizational height can exist even within industries. For example, at Ford and GM, the number of levels between the chief executive

EXHIBIT

15–7

The relationship between span of control and organizational flatness and tallness.

Tall Organization: 31 Members; 5 Levels; Average Span of Control Is 2

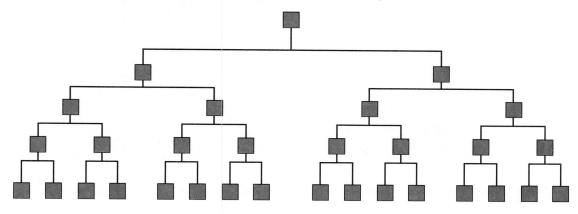

Flat Organization: 31 Members; 3 Levels; Average Span of Control Is 5

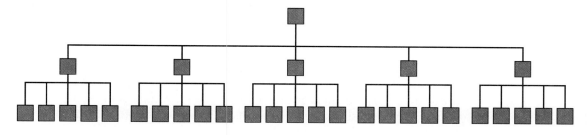

and plant workers varies between 17 and 22. At Toyota, only seven levels intervene.[16] Some analysts have argued that this reduced height is in part responsible for the ability of the Japanese manufacturer to get products to market more quickly.

Formalization

Formalization refers to the extent to which work roles are highly defined by the organization. A very formalized organization tolerates little variability in the way

The Toyota
MR2. A flat
organizational
structure helps
Toyota get new
products to
market quickly.
(Courtesy
Toyota, USA,
Inc.)

members perform their tasks. Some formalization stems from the nature of the job itself; the work requirements of the assembly line provide a good example of this. More interesting, however, is formalization that stems from rules, regulations, and procedures that the firm or institution chooses to implement. Detailed written job descriptions, thick procedures manuals, and the requirement to "put everything in writing" are evidence of such formalization. Many government organizations use this method of formalization. So does the fast food chain McDonald's:

> Rules and regulations are the gospel at McDonald's. The company's operating bible has 385 pages describing the most minute activities in each outlet. The manual prescribes that certain equipment—cigarette, candy, and pinball machines—is not permitted in the stores. It also prescribes strict standards for personal grooming. Men must keep their hair short and their shoes black and highly polished. Women are expected to wear hair nets and to use only very light makeup. The store manager is even provided with a maintenance reminder for each day of the year, such as "Lubricate and adjust potato-peeler belt."[17]

Centralization

Centralization refers to the extent to which decision-making power is localized in a particular part of the organization. In the most centralized organization, the power for all key decisions would rest in a single individual, such as the president. In a more decentralized organization, decision-making power would be dispersed

McDonald's in Moscow— formalization helps McDonald's maintain quality standards around the world. (F. Hibon/ Sygma)

down through the hierarchy and across departments. One observer suggests that limitations to individual brainpower often prompt decentralization:

> How can the Baghdad salesperson explain the nature of his clients to the Birmingham manager? Sometimes the information can be transmitted to one center, but a lack of cognitive capacity (brainpower) precludes it from being comprehended there. How can the president of the conglomerate corporation possibly learn about, say, 100 different product lines? Even if a report could be written on each, he would lack the time to study them all.[18]

Of course, the information-processing capacity of executives is not the only factor that dictates degree of centralization. Some organizations consciously pursue a more participative climate that can be achieved through decentralization. In others, top management might wish to maintain greater control and opt for stronger centralization. The successful North Carolina–based supermarket chain Food Lion has seen the merits of centralization for the fairly routine task of retailing food:

> Management controls a host of key operating details from headquarters, a sleek, two-story (soon to be four) brick and glass building located to the west of town by a distribution center the size of 15

football fields. Lights, heating, and refrigeration systems in all the stores, from Delaware to Florida, are turned on and off by a computer at headquarters. Virtually all major decisions—buying, pricing, merchandising—are made by the central brain trust. Explains [CEO Tom] Smith: "When we want to push a particular product, we can say, 'It goes here on the shelf or it goes here on display.' That way we've got somebody very experienced deciding the best place to put it, rather than having 500 people with their own ideas."[19]

Recalling the story that began the chapter, it should be obvious that Ohio Valley Steel was fairly tall, formalized, and centralized. Solar Components was flatter, less formal, and decentralized.

Complexity

Complexity refers to the extent to which organizations divide labor vertically, horizontally, and geographically.[20] A fairly simple organization will have few management levels (vertical division) and not many separate job titles (horizontal division). In addition, jobs will be grouped into a small number of departments, and work will be performed in only one physical location (geographic division). At the other extreme, a very complex organization will be tall, will have a large number of job titles and departments, and might be spread around the world. The essential characteristic of complexity is *variety*—as the organization becomes more complex, it has more kinds of people performing more kinds of tasks in more places, whether these places are departments or geographic territories.

Now that we have reviewed the traditional dimensions of structure, why not apply your knowledge by considering the You Be the Manager case (next page)?

ORGANIZATIONAL SIZE AND STRUCTURAL CHARACTERISTICS

It is perhaps trivial to note that the giant General Motors Corporation is structured differently from a small video rental shop. But exactly how does organizational size (measured by number of employees) affect the structure of organizations?

In general, there is much evidence that large organizations are more complex than small organizations.[21] For example, a small organization is unlikely to have its own legal department or market research group, and these tasks will probably be contracted out. Economies of scale enable large organizations to perform these functions themselves but with a consequent increase in the number of departments and job titles. In turn, this horizontal specialization often stimulates the need for additional complexity in the form of appointing integrators, creating planning departments, and so on. As horizontal specialization increases, manage-

YOU BE THE MANAGER

M̲anager

Reorganization at Hewlett-Packard

Hewlett-Packard is one of the most respected high-technology firms in the United States. From modest beginnings in 1939 (production literally began in a garage), the Palo Alto, California–based firm now employs over 80,000 people in the design and manufacture of test and measurement instruments, scientific calculators, computers, printers, and computer-aided engineering systems. For many years, H-P's success was predicated on a carefully calculated combination of business strategy and organizational culture. The strategy was to find market niches and fill them with the very best technology available. The emphasis was on first-class engineering. In turn, the culture was highly entrepreneurial and participatory. The structural result was a series of small, autonomous business units that designed, built, and sold their own products. These units were superb vehicles for management development, and they sometimes competed with each other for business.

The autonomous units were highly successful in serving the many specialized niche markets that constituted H-P's instrument business. However, as the firm became more and more involved in computer applications, the liabilities of the structure started to emerge. For example, customers frequently found that H-P hardware or software was not compatible because it was designed by separate divisions. Similarly, complex computer applications, such as the development of computer-aided engineering systems, were plagued with delays. Up to ten competing divisions that supplied components to the project were unable to coordinate their efforts.

H-P management knew that something had to be done to resolve these problems. What would *you* do?

1. Describe the departmentation and basic structure of H-P. Despite the problems, what are some of the merits of this design for H-P?
2. What structural changes would you make at H-P?

To find out what H-P did, see The Manager's Notebook.

Source: Pascale, R. T. (1990). *Managing at the edge.* New York: Simon and Schuster; Uttal, B. (1985, April 29). Mettle-test time for John Young. *Fortune*, 242–248; Uttal, B. (1984, October 29). Delays and defections at Hewlett-Packard. *Fortune*, p. 62; Harper, J. (1982, December 6). Can John Young redesign Hewlett-Packard? *Business Week*, 72–78.

ment levels must be added (making the organization taller) so that spans of control do not get out of hand.[22] To repeat, size is associated with increased complexity.

Complexity means coordination problems in spite of integrators, planning departments, and the like. This is where other structural characteristics come into play. In general, bigger organizations are less centralized than smaller organization.[23] In a small company, the president might be involved in all but the least critical decisions to be made. In a large company, the president would be overloaded with such decisions, and they could not be made in a timely manner. In addition, since the large organization will also be taller, top management is often too far removed from the action to make many operating decisions. How is control retained with decentralization? The answer is formalization—large organizations tend to be more formal than small organizations. Rules, regulations, and standard procedures help to ensure that decentralized decisions fall within accepted bounds. This comparison of a small, independent bank with a larger, more complex bank with several branches illustrates the point nicely:

> Interestingly, the larger bank may be much more decentralized than the small bank. In the small bank, the president may give final approval on all loans simply because time is available to do so. In large banks with many branches no one person can examine all the loan applications, so the decisions are decentralized to officers within the branches. However, this delegation of responsibility is accompanied by *standard procedures* for evaluating loan applications. Decision rules are carefully worked out in advance and communicated downward through policy updates, newsletters, and other formal documents. In this way the large organization can control its lower levels.[24]

Two further points about the relationship between size and structure should be emphasized. First, you will recall that product departmentation is often preferable to functional departmentation as the organization increases in size. Logically, then, organizations with product departmentation should exhibit more complexity and more decentralization than those with functional departmentation. A careful comparison of Exhibits 15–2 and 15–3 will confirm this logic. In the firm with the product structure, research, production, and marketing are duplicated, increasing complexity. In addition, since each product line is essentially self-contained, decisions can be made at a lower organizational level.

Finally, it should be recognized that size is only one determinant of organizational structure. Even at a given size, organizations might require different structures to be maximally effective. In the next chapter we will examine other determinants of structure.

Exhibit 15–8 (next page) summarizes the relationship between size and structural variables.

The relationship between size and structure.

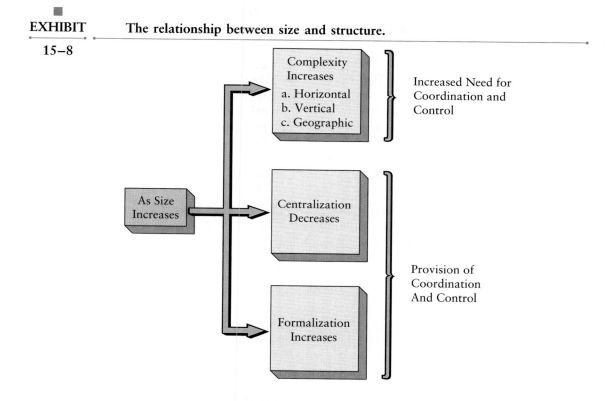

EMPLOYEE REACTIONS TO STRUCTURAL CHARACTERISTICS

What are the implications of structural characteristics for the job satisfaction of employees? The research literature provides us with some clues.[25]

There is no simple association between tallness or flatness and job satisfaction. Managers in organizations with fewer than 5000 employees seem to exhibit more job satisfaction when they operate under flatter structures. Those in organizations with over 5000 employees seem happier with taller structures.[26] We have noted that larger organizations tend to be taller. This suggests that exceptions to the general rule (i.e., small, tall organizations and large, flat organizations) prompt dissatisfaction. In the former, managers might have few opportunities for decision making. In the latter, coordination might be so poor that role ambiguity results.

Formalization often prompts job dissatisfaction, except for individuals who have very strong needs for the security that rules provide.[27] Formalization is a particular problem for boundary role occupants who must deal directly with outsiders.[28] Salespeople, welfare officers, and courthouse desk clerks often find themselves held to rules and red tape that damage their relationships with clients and customers and thus provoke considerable disillusionment.

There is no simple, straightforward relationship between job satisfaction and degree of organizational centralization. This might be because different degrees of centralization are appropriate for different subunits and across various kinds of organizations.

There has been very little study of individual reactions to varying spans of control. However, one study of sales representatives found that role ambiguity increased as more reps reported to the same manager.[29] This suggests that spans that are too large might contribute to communication and coordination problems. On the other hand, very small spans might reduce employee autonomy and provoke dissatisfaction, especially among well-trained and experienced personnel.

One important mechanism by which structural characteristics influence job satisfaction is job design.[30] We saw earlier that job design is affected by the way in which labor is divided and coordinated. For example, extreme division of labor might reduce the task variety of individual jobs and prompt dissatisfaction. Similarly, coordination of this divided labor by high formalization might reduce autonomy, again stimulating dissatisfaction.

EARLY PRESCRIPTIONS CONCERNING STRUCTURE

For many years, experts who were interested in organizational effectiveness concerned themselves with prescribing the "correct" way to structure an organization to achieve its goals. There were two basic phases to this prescription, which might be called the classical view and the human relations view. The following sketch of these viewpoints is necessarily brief and thus does some injustice to the subtle thinking underlying them. Nevertheless, the basic caricatures are accurate.

The Classical View and Bureaucracy

Most of the major advocates of the classical viewpoint were experienced managers or consultants who took the time to set down their thoughts on organizing in writing. For the most part, this activity occurred in the early 1900s. Frederick Taylor, the father of Scientific Management (Chapter 7), can be considered a contributor to the classical school, although he was mainly concerned with job design and the structure of work on the shopfloor.[31] You will recall that Taylor advocated extreme division of labor and specialization, even extending to the specialization of supervisors in roles such as trainer, disciplinarian, and so on. Also, he advocated careful standardization and regulation of work activities, rest pauses, and so on.

Other classical writers acquired their experience in military settings, mining operations, and factories that produced everything from cars to candy. Prominent names include Henri Fayol, James D. Mooney, and Lyndall Urwick.[32] Although exceptions existed, they tended to advocate a very high degree of specialization of labor and a very high degree of coordination. For example, they favored functional division of labor because this led to a high degree of specialization within departments. To coordinate these specialists, high formalization, a fairly tall structure, and an adequate degree of centralization were advocated. For the same reason, fairly small spans of control were suggested, except for lower-level jobs, in which machine pacing might substitute for close supervision.

The practicing managers had an academic ally in Max Weber, the distinguished German social theorist. Weber made the term *bureaucracy* famous by advocating it as a means of rationally managing complex organizations. During Weber's lifetime (1864–1920), managers were certainly in need of advice. In this time of industrial growth and development, most management was by intuition, and nepotism and favoritism were rampant. According to Weber, a **bureaucracy** has the following qualities:

- A strict chain of command in which each member reports to only a single superior
- Selection and promotion on the basis of impersonal technical skills rather than nepotism or favoritism
- Detailed rules, regulations, and procedures ensuring that the job gets done regardless of who the specific worker is
- Strict specialization to match duties with technical competence
- The centralization of power at the top of the organization[33]

It is important to understand that Weber saw bureaucracy as an "ideal type" or theoretical model that would standardize behavior in organizations and provide workers with security and a sense of purpose. Jobs would be performed *as intended* rather than according to the whims of the specific role occupant; in exchange for this conformity, workers would have a fair chance of being promoted and rising in the power structure. This sense of security was backed up by rules, regulations, and a clear-cut chain of command that further clarified required behavior.

We can summarize the prescriptions of the classical theorists by saying that they advocated mechanistic structures.[34] As summarized in Exhibit 15–9, **mechanistic structures** tend toward tallness, narrow spans, specialization, high centralization, and high formalization. Other structural and personnel aspects are designed to complement these basic structural prescriptions. By analogy, the organization is to be structured as a mechanical device, each part serving its separate function, each part closely coordinated with the others.

The Human Relations View and a Critique of Bureaucracy

The human relations movement is generally conceded to have begun with the famous Hawthorne studies of the 1920s and 1930s.[35] These studies, conducted at the Hawthorne plant of Western Electric near Chicago, began in the strict tradi-

■

EXHIBIT

15–9

Mechanistic and organic structures.

Organizational Characteristics	Types of Organization Structure	
Index	Organic	Mechanistic
Span of control	Wide	Narrow
Number of levels of authority	Few	Many
Ratio of administrative to production personnel	High	Low
Range of time span over which an employee can commit resources	Long	Short
Degree of centralization in decision making	Low	High
Proportion of persons in one unit having opportunity to interact with persons in other units	High	Low
Quantity of formal rules	Low	High
Specificity of job goals	Low	High
Specificity of required activities	Low	High
Content of communications	Advice and information	Instructions and decisions
Range of compensation	Narrow	Wide
Range of skill levels	Narrow	Wide
Knowledge-based authority	High	Low
Position-based authority	Low	High

Source: From Seiler, J. A. (1967). *Systems analysis in organizational behavior.* Homewood, IL: Irwin, p. 168. ©
Richard D. Irwin, Inc. 1967. This exhibit is an adaptation of one prepared by Paul R. Lawrence and Jay W.
Lorsch in an unpublished "Working Paper on Scientific Transfer and Organizational Structure," 1963. The
latter, in turn, draws heavily on criteria suggested by W. Evans. "Indices of the Hierarchical Structure of Industrial Organizations," *Management Science*, Vol. IX (1963), pp. 468–77, Burns and Stalker, *op. cit.*, and Woodward, *op. cit.*, as well as those suggested by R. H. Hall, "Intraorganizational Structure Variables," *Administrative Science Quarterly*, Vol. IX (1962), pp. 295–308.

tion of industrial engineering. They were concerned with the impact of fatigue,
rest pauses, and lighting on productivity. However, during the course of the studies, the researchers began to notice the impact that psychological and social processes had on productivity and work adjustment. This impact suggested that there
were dysfunctional aspects to the mechanistic organization of work. One obvious
sign was resistance to management through strong informal group mechanisms
such as norms that limited productivity. Gradually, this cause was taken up by a
number of other theorists and researchers (mostly academics), who proceeded to
take a hard look at the potential problems of mechanistic organizations. Their
views are usually described as a critique of bureaucracy, and some specific criti-
cisms include the following:

- Strict specialization and strong formalization are incompatible with human needs for growth and achievement.[36] This can lead to employee alienation from the organization and its clients or customers.
- Strong centralization and reliance upon formal authority often fail to take advantage of the creative ideas and knowledge possessed by lower-level members.[37] As a result, the organization will fail to learn from its mistakes, and innovation and adaptation will be threatened. Resistance to change will occur as a matter of course.
- Formalization through strict, impersonal rules leads members to adopt the *minimum* acceptable level of performance that the rules specify.[38] If a rule states that at least eight claims a day must be processed, eight claims will become the norm, even though higher performance levels are possible.
- Strong specialization combined with formalization causes employees to lose sight of the overall goals of the organization.[39] Forms, procedures, and required signatures become ends in themselves, divorced from the true needs of customers, clients, and other departments in the organization. This is the "red-tape mentality" that is sometimes observed in bureaucracies.

Obviously, not all mechanistic organizations exhibit these dysfunctions. However, they were observed commonly enough that human relations advocates and others began to call for the adoption of more organic organizational structures. As noted in Exhibit 15–9, **organic structures** rely upon less formalization, centralization, and specialization. Flexibility and informal communication are emphasized over rigidity and the strict chain of command.

The labels *mechanistic* and *organic* simply represent theoretical extremes, and organizational structures can obviously fall between these two extremes. Still, the question remains, is one structure superior to the other? A clue to the answer to this question can be found in the case that began the chapter. Ohio Valley Steel exhibited a more mechanistic structure, while Solar Components exhibited a more organic structure. However, both organizations were successful. In general (as long as the problems noted above are avoided), mechanistic structures are called for when the organizational environment is fairly stable and the technology is fairly routine (as at Ohio Valley Steel). Organic structures tend to work better when the environment is less stable and the technology is less routine (as in science-dependent, hi-tech Solar Components and W. L. Gore, discussed in In Focus 15–2).

In the next chapter we will examine in detail the impact of environment and technology on organizational structure. For now, it is enough to recognize that there is no "one best way" to organize.

A FOOTNOTE: SYMPTOMS OF STRUCTURAL PROBLEMS

At the beginning of the chapter, I observed that it is sometimes difficult to appreciate the impact of organizational structure on the behavior that occurs in organi-

IN FOCUS 15–2

▼
. . . .

W. L. Gore and Associates—An Organic Organization

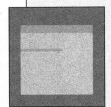

Joe Tanner doesn't have a boss. He has no title, other than one he shares with 5,000 co-workers, and he works only on projects that excite him. It may sound like a job created in a schoolyard or in heaven, but it's the way things operate at one of the most successful companies in the United States. Joe Tanner works for W. L. Gore and Associates, Inc. The Delaware-based company is best known for its waterproof breathable fabrics called Gore-Tex, but that's only a small part of its business. From a similar raw material, Gore also makes wires and cables for computers, medical grafts that can replace human tissue and filters which reduce air pollution. In total, this privately-owned company recorded workwide sales of more than U.S. $500 million during the past year. And it's all achieved by a system of non-management.

Gore is structured around what it calls a lattice system. Unlike a hierarchical chain of command, the lattice has no bosses, no orders and no titles—everyone is called an associate. And employees build their own project teams from which leaders emerge with the approval of their associates. If this seems like chaos, there is an underlying genius to it. In exchange for freedom and flexibility, Gore asks its associates to make commitments to projects and products. What they commit to and how they get it done is largely up to them, as long as they produce. "It's a system of freedom and self-commitment," says Tanner, 44, who works in the marketing department of Gore's fabrics division. "If you have an idea, you can run with it. You don't have to ask a boss if you can do it." However, an associate must sell the idea to enough associates to form a team that can develop and market the product. Senior associates, called sponsors, provide guidance and support but the decision-making is essentially left in the hands of those doing the work.

Obviously, the Gore philosophy is not suited to everyone. "We try to look for people who are quite flexible; people who don't require structure and who don't need to be told what to do," says corporate communications associate Carol Mongan. "It's probably the antithesis of the military, where orders are given. We've had people come here from the military and succeed but others found it didn't work out."

If there is a negative to the lattice system, it's a tendency to get excited about too many projects. "There is an awful lot of peer pressure," says Mongan. "You feel good about the team and you want to take on more responsibility. It's easy to overcommit."

Source: Abridged from Corbett, B. (1989, September). A system of non-management. *Canadian*, 14–20.

zations. Now that you have been through the basics of structure, your appreciation of this impact should be much improved. Let's conclude the chapter by considering some symptoms of structural problems in organizations.

- *Bad job design.* As was noted at several points, there is a reciprocal relationship between job design and organizational structure. Frequently, improper structural arrangements turn good jobs on paper into poor jobs in practice. A tall structure and narrow span of control in a research and development unit can reduce autonomy and turn exciting jobs into drudgery. An extremely large span of control can overload the most dedicated supervisor.

- *The right hand doesn't know what the left is doing.* If repeated examples of duplication of effort occur, or if parts of the organization work at cross-purposes, structure is suspect. One author gives the example of one division of a large organization laying off workers while another division was busy recruiting from the same labor pool![40] The general problem here is one of coordination and integration.

- *Persistent conflict between departments.* Managers are often inclined to attribute such conflicts to personality clashes between key personnel in the warring departments. Just as often, a failure of integration is the problem. One clue here is if the conflict persists even when personnel changes occur.

- *Slow response times.* Ideally, labor is divided and coordinated to do business quickly. Delayed responses might be due to improper structure. Centralization might speed responses when a few decisions about a few products are required (dictating functional departmentation). Decentralization might speed responses when many decisions about many products are required (dictating product departmentation).

- *Decisions made with incomplete information.* In Chapter 12 we noted that managers generally acquire more than enough information to make decisions. After the fact, if we find that decisions have been made with incomplete information, and the information existed somewhere in the organization, structure could be at fault. It is clear that structural deficiencies were in part responsible for keeping top NASA administrators unaware of the mechanical problems that contributed to the 1986 explosion of the space shuttle *Challenger*.[41] This information was known to NASA personnel, but it did not move up the hierarchy properly.

- *A proliferation of committees.* Committees exist in all organizations, and they often serve as one of the more routine kinds of integrating mechanisms. However, when committee is piled upon committee, or when task forces are being formed with great regularity, it is often a sign that the basic structure of the organization is being "patched up" because it doesn't work well.[42] A structural review might be in order if too many people are spending too much time in committee meetings.

THE MANAGER'S NOTEBOOK

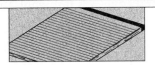

Reorganization at Hewlett-Packard

1. Hewlett-Packard was organized essentially by product departmentation—each of its small divisions was self-contained in terms of design, manufacturing, and sales. It was obviously complex and highly decentralized. This design made it easy to add divisions and keep tabs on division profits. It led to good coordination *within* divisions and gave the niche customer good service.

2. H-P management tried to increase the centralization of the firm. Much of this centralization was oriented toward an integrated marketing effort that would service multiple customer needs and ensure that H-P's various products were compatible with each other. In turn, the company began to revise its very strong product departmentation to a structure that was organized around several broad customer groups. This reorganization met with resistance from the product divisions and prompted turnover (rare for H-P). In response, organizational expert Richard Pascale contends that H-P management watered down the customer group concept to the point that the product divisions regained autonomy. He cites integration problems that remain because of this structure.

SUMMARY

- Organizational structure is the manner in which an organization divides its labor into specific tasks and achieves coordination among these tasks. Labor is divided vertically and horizontally. Vertical division of labor concerns the apportioning of authority. Horizontal division of labor involves designing jobs and grouping them into departments. While functional departmentation involves locating employees with similar skills in the same department, other forms of departmentation locate employees in accordance with product, geography, or customer requirements.

- Basic methods of coordinating divided labor include direct supervision, standardization of work processes, standardization of outputs, standardization of skills, and mutual adjustment. Workers are permitted more discretion as coordination moves from direct supervision through mutual adjustment. More elaborate methods of coordination are aimed specifically at achieving integration across departments. These include liaison roles, task forces, and integrators.

- Traditional structural characteristics include span of control, flatness versus tallness, formalization, centralization, and complexity. Larger organizations tend to be more complex, more formal, and less centralized than smaller organizations. Various structural characteristics influence the job satisfaction of the work force.

- The classical organizational theorists tended to favor mechanistic organizational structures (small spans, tall, formalized, and fairly centralized). The human relations theorists, having noted the flaws of bureaucracy, tended to favor organic structures (larger spans, flat, less formalized, and less centralized). However, there is no one best way to organize, and both mechanistic and organic structures have their places.

- Symptoms of structural problems include poor job design, extreme duplication of effort, conflict between departments, slow responses, too many committees, and decisions made with incomplete information.

KEY CONCEPTS

Organizational structure	Coordination	Tall organization
Differentiation	Integration	Formalization
Functional departmentation	Liaison role	Centralization
Product departmentation	Task force	Complexity
Geographic departmentation	Integrators	Bureaucracy
Customer departmentation	Span of control	Mechanistic structures
Hybrid departmentation	Flat organization	Organic structures

DISCUSSION QUESTIONS

1. Discuss the division of labor in a college classroom. What methods are used to coordinate this divided labor? Do differences exist between very small and very large classes?

2. Is the departmentation in a small college essentially functional or product-oriented? Defend your answer. (*Hint:* In what department will the historians find themselves? In what department will the grounds-keepers find themselves?)

3. Which basic method(s) of coordination is (are) most likely to be found in a pure research laboratory? On a football team? In a supermarket?

4. Most of the advocates of the classical approach to organizational structure were practicing managers or management consultants working in the early part of this century. Most of the advocates of the human relations approach were academics. How might these different backgrounds have affected their views about organizational structure?

5. Discuss the logic behind the following statement: "We don't want to remove the differentiation that exists between sales and production. What we want to do is achieve integration."

6. As Spinelli Construction Company grew in size, its founder and president, Joe Spinelli, found that he was overloaded with decisions. What two basic structural changes should Spinelli make to rectify this situation without losing control of the company?

7. Describe a situation in which a narrow span of control might be appropriate and contrast it with a situation in which a broad span might be appropriate.

8. Review some of the problems that bureaucratic or mechanistic structures might promote.

EXPERIENTIAL EXERCISE

Watermark Cards

In this activity, class members form miniature organizations, to see whether one or another type of structure works best.

_____ Step 1   Form groups of six to eight; the groups should be of equal size.

_____ Step 2   Half of the groups read the instructions headed "Watermark Cards: Eastern Region" while the other half read the instructions labeled "Watermark Cards: Western Region."

_____ Step 3   The instructor randomly selects one person in each group to be Regional Executive. Regional Executives are charged with carrying out the organizing guidelines given in their instructions. Allow about five minutes for this.

_____ Step 4   There will be at least three ten-minute production periods. The instructor acts as the CEO of Watermark Cards, at its national headquarters, and provides work requirements to Regional Executives as well as keeping track of time.

_____ Step 5   The first ten-minute work round begins. The CEO should make sure that everyone hears the two-minute signal that the round is about to end. When the round is over, the CEO briefly confers with the Regional Executives, meeting first with all Western Region Executives and then, separately with all Eastern Region Executives.

_____ Step 6   Begin the second work round, repeating the instructions in Step 5.

_____ Step 7   Begin the third work round, repeating the instructions in Step 5.

_____ Step 8   Announce that the activity is over. Each organization is to record on flip chart or newsprint its production record for each round.

_____ Step 9   Everyone moves around the room for a few minutes, to look over the various production records.

_____ Step 10   The entire group reassembles to review the exercise and discuss the results. Some relevant questions include:

- Was one or the other region consistently more productive? If so, why?
- Did the Western and Eastern Regional organizations face different problems? In what ways?
- Which organization—Eastern Region or Western Region—usually had more satisfied employees? Why?

Job Definitions and Task Activities

The raw materials used by the firm are blank sheets of 8 1/2″ × 11″ paper, and blue- or black-ink pens. *Materials preparation* consists of cutting the raw material (the 8 1/2″ × 11″ paper) precisely in half, and lightly folding each half to form a standard size greeting card blank.

Creative verse writers prepare the verses that the calligraphers copy onto the card blanks. Verses are always two line, and rhyme. Every verse is different; no duplications are permissible.

Calligraphers transcribe the verses onto the inside right hand pages of the card blanks. On the outside card blank cover, they print the occasion definition in block letters ("HAPPY BIRTH-DAY" for a general purpose birthday card, for instance). Inside lettering may be done in print or script, but must be of highest quality, that is neat and unsmeared, centered, and straight. Cards with defective calligraphy will be rejected.

The final prep task consists of checking the rhyme for rhythm and to make sure it matches the occasion definition, checking the calligraphy for neatness, etc., writing "REJECT" on the cover of cards that do not meet the standards and setting them aside, and folding and sorting by occasion those cards accepted. (If an unacceptable card is not rejected but is identified later by headquarters inspectors, a penalty will be assessed to the region by headquarters.)

Quarterly Plan

The CEO informs Regional Executives of the product mix for each quarter. The first quarter, for example, contains one major occasion—Valentine's Day—and a substantial proportion of cards produced during this quarter will be valentines. The second and subsequent quarters' production plans will be based on information provided by the CEO after the close of the preceding quarter.

Watermark Cards: Western Region

Watermark Cards, Inc., is one of the world's largest producers of greeting cards of all kinds. U.S. operations are divided into several regions, with each region operating relatively autonomously. Regional Executives are fully responsible for setting up their own organizations, and are accountable to headquarters only with regard to the quarterly plan, specifying the types of cards to be produced in the coming quarter (that is, so many percent will be Father's Day cards in the second quarter, so many percent will be Christmas cards in the fourth quarter, and so on).

The Regional Executive has set up the organization as product teams. That is each team is responsible for producing one or two types of card, from the preparation of materials, development of verses, and calligraphy to the sorting and folding of products in preparation for shipping.

If organization size is six, there will be two teams of two and a Teams Manager, in addition to the Regional Executive.

If organization size is seven there will be three teams of two *or* two teams of three (the Regional Executive is to decide) and the Regional Executive.

If the organization size is eight, there will be three teams of two *or* two teams of three, a Teams Manager, and the Regional Executive (the Regional Executive determines team size).

Watermark Cards: Eastern Region

Watermark Cards, Inc., is one of the world's largest producers of greeting cards of all kinds. U.S. operations are divided into several regions, with each region operating relatively autonomously. Regional Executives are fully responsible for setting up their own organizations, and are accountable to headquarters only with regard to the quarterly plan, specifying the types of cards to be produced in the coming quarter (that is, so many percent will be Father's Day cards in the second quarter, so many percent will be Christmas cards in the fourth quarter, and so on).

The Regional Executive has set up the organization in terms of functional departments. There is a materials preparation department, a creative verse department that makes up the verses that go on the cards, a calligraphy department that writes verses onto blank cards, and a final prep/shipping department.

If the organization size is six, two persons will be in the calligraphy department, one in the creative verse department, and one will handle both the materials preparation department and will also receive the products from the calligraphy department for final prep/shipping. One person will be Operations Manager and the remaining person is, of course, the Regional Executive.

If the organization size is seven, two persons will be in the calligraphy department, one in the creative verse department, one in the materials prep department, and one in the final prep/shipping department. One person will be Operations Manager and report to the Regional Executive.

If the organization size is eight, two persons will be in the calligraphy department, two in the creative verse department, one in materials prep, and one final prep/shipping. One person will be Operations Manager and report to the Regional Executive.

■

Source: Sashkin, M., & Morris, W. C. (1987). *Experiencing management.* © 1987 by Addison-Wesley Publishing Company, Inc. Reprinted with permission of the publisher.

National Business Machines

National Business Machines branch office number 120 is a marketing and service organization consisting of nearly 200 employees. The data-processing division is divided into four sections: two marketing units and two systems engineering units. This arrangement is depicted below.

The two marketing units sell new hardware. Each

■
EXHIBIT

1

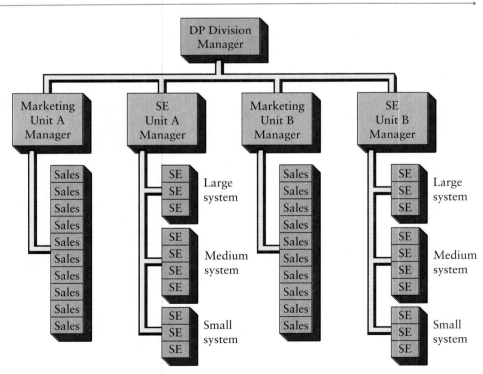

Source: Ford, R. C., Armandi, B. R., & Heaton, C. P. (1988). *Organization theory: An integrative approach.* Copyright © 1988 by Harper & Row, Publishers, Inc. Reprinted by permission of HarperCollins Inc.

marketing unit has ten salespersons. The two systems engineering (SE) units provide technical assistance to the marketing units. They help in selecting hardware, systems design, computer programming, operator training, installed systems review, computer application development, and many other functions associated with selling and installing computer systems. Each SE unit has ten systems engineers.

The SE units are independent of each other. One unit supports marketing unit A, and the other unit supports marketing unit B.

Systems engineering includes three types of skills and knowledge: those associated with small, medium, and large computer systems. Small systems are usually purchased by the brand-new data-processing user getting first exposure to the world of automation. Systems engineers in this area must of course be skilled systems analysts and programmers, but they must also be educators and psychologists. New data-processing users know only as much about the machines as the marketing representatives have told them. They are often unsure about whether they can deal with the machines. The small-system SE's must expand their knowledge and help them build confidence.

The medium-system SE works with a larger, higher-priced machine that has probably been installed for a few years. Users have their own data-processing staffs. Instead of being concerned with programming and operator training, the medium-system SE spends time looking for more advanced applications, such as installing terminals in different user departments.

The large-system SE deals with sophisticated data-processing installations. Large-system users are data-processing professionals with high standards, internal education programs and staffs of 50 or more.

The small-system SE may be working on five or six accounts per day, while the large-system SE may spend a week at one location.

In NBM branch office number 120, both SE units have systems engineers of all three types. This organizational structure has several advantages, but it also causes several problems.

The first problem occurs because the three data-processing system types—small, medium, and large—represent three quite different technologies. The effective SE manager must be well-versed in the latest trends of three separate disciplines. Both SE managers do a good job, but communications problems sometimes arise because they do not have experience in working on data-processing systems of all three kinds.

For example, both current SE managers have backgrounds in medium and large systems. The common misconception is that they should thoroughly understand small computer installations because small systems must be easier to install than large systems. However, in addition to designing the system and writing the programs, the small-system SE performs tasks that the SE's working on medium and large systems never perform. The small-system SE has to explain why the new user must spell

the customer's name in exactly the same way every time, or why a diskette created on one type of personal computer cannot be compatible with another. Mistakes in these details can cause unbelievable delays in an installation and can be very difficult to locate.

Another problem is the division's sales quota. Since NBM makes more money when installing large machines, the manager naturally meets the quota faster by installing large machines. Of course, everyone realizes the advantages of selling small machines to many customers in the expectation that they will later graduate to medium and large machines. However, the short-run emphasis always seems to be on the large systems.

This situation causes a morale problem among the small-system SE's. They see the large-system people getting the bonuses and the recognition at branch office meetings. The small-system SE's also think that their compensation is not proportionate to the compensation of the large-system SE's. Actually, most large-system SE's have worked longer for NBM and have developed more skills, so their average compensation is justifiably higher. However, the small-system SE's tend to overlook this fact.

Having two SE managers each control three SE classifications may be inherently inefficient. For instance, imagine this situation. Manager A needs a small-system SE and does not have one available. Manager B has an available SE with the proper talents. Manager A asks to borrow the SE. If manager B allows the borrowing, the borrowed SE may be needed by manager B but unavailable the very next day. On the other hand, NBM is a service organization, so manager B probably allows manager A to borrow the SE.

Consider the borrowed SE. Once assigned to the project, the SE will probably have to stay with it until it is finished, even if an SE from unit A becomes available. Once the borrowed SE gets to know the people and situation at the new installation and begins to design systems and develop programs, manager B will be reluctant to make a change. So the borrowed SE will be working for a manager who does not appraise performance or make salary recommendations. The borrowed SE may work 60 to 80 hours a week on a crash project, and manager B may never hear about it.

■

1. Noting that the case involves only the data-processing division of one branch of National Business Machines, speculate about the structure of the firm as a whole. Use concepts such as complexity, centralization, and formalization. What form of departmentation does the firm as a whole likely rely upon?

2. What form of departmentation is seen in NBM branch 120? Discuss the advantages and disadvantages of this form of departmentation with reference to the issues mentioned in the case.

3. Use the concepts of differentiation and integration to analyze the events in branch 120.

4. Suggest at least one structural alternative to that currently seen in branch 120. Explain how this alternative will deal with the problems cited in the case. Does the alternative design have any potential problems?

■

REFERENCES

1. Mintzberg, H. (1979). *The structuring of organizations*. Englewood Cliffs, NJ: Prentice-Hall.

2. Lawrence, P. R., & Lorsch, J. W. (1969). *Organization and environment: Managing differentiation and integration*. Homewood, IL: Irwin.

3. For an extended treatment of the role of interdependence between departments, see McCann, J., & Galbraith, J. R. (1981). Interdepartmental relations. In P. C. Nystrom & W. H. Starbuck (Eds.), *Handbook of organizational design* (Vol. 2). Oxford, England: Oxford University Press.

4. For a comparison of functional and product departmentation, see McCann & Galbraith, 1981; Walker, A. H., & Lorsch, J. W. (1968, November-December). Organizational choice: Product vs. function. *Harvard Business Review*, 129–138.

5. Contemporary treatment of these forms of departmentation can be found in Daft, R. L. (1989). *Organization theory and design* (3rd ed.). St. Paul, MN: West; Robey, D. (1991). *Designing organizations* (3rd ed.). Homewood, IL: Irwin.

6. Mintzberg, 1979.

7. See Hall, R. H. (1962). Intraorganizational structural variation: Application of the bureaucratic model. *Administrative Science Quarterly, 7*, 295–308.

8. Lawrence & Lorsch, 1969.

9. Galbraith, J. R. (1977). *Organization design*. Reading, MA: Addison-Wesley.

10. See Birnbaum, P. H. (1981). Integration and specialization in academic research. *Academy of Management Journal, 24*, 487–503.

11. This discussion relies on Galbraith, 1977.

12. Lawrence & Lorsch, 1969.

13. Galbraith, 1977.

14. These definitions of structural variables are common. However, there is considerable disagreement about how some variables should be measured. See Walton, E. J. (1981). The comparison of measures of organizational structure. *Academy of Management Review, 6*, 155–160.

15. Research on these hypotheses is sparse and not always in agreement. See Dewar, R. D., & Simet, D. P. (1981). A level specific prediction of spans of control examining effects of size, technology, and specialization. *Academy of Management Journal, 24*, 5–24; Van Fleet, D. D. (1983). Span of management research and issues. *Academy of Management Journal, 26*, 546–552.

16. Treece, J. B. (1990, April 9). Here comes GM's Saturn. *Business Week*, 56–62.

17. Daft, 1989, p. 179.

18. Mintzberg, 1979, p. 182.

19. Sheeline, W. E. (1988, August 15). Making them rich down home. *Fortune*, 50–55, p. 52.

20. Daft, 1989.

21. Much of this research was stimulated by Blau, P. M. (1970). A theory of differentiation in organizations. *American Sociological Review, 35*, 201–218. For a review and test, see Cullen, J. B., Anderson, K. S., & Baker, D. D. (1986). Blau's theory of structural differentiation revisited: A theory of structural change or scale? *Academy of Management Journal, 29*, 203–229.

22. Dewar, R., & Hage, J. (1978). Size, technology, complexity, and structural differentiation: Toward a theoretical synthesis. *Administrative Science Quarterly, 23*, 111–136; Marsh, R. M., & Mannari, H. (1981). Technology and size as determinants of the organizational structure of Japanese factories. *Administrative Science Quarterly, 26*, 33–57.

23. Mansfield, R. (1973). Bureaucracy and centralization: An examination of organizational structure. *Administrative Science Quarterly, 18*, 77–88; Hage, J., & Aiken, M. (1967). Relationship of centralization to other structural properties. *Administrative Science Quarterly, 12*, 79–91.

24. Robey, 1991, p. 103.

25. For comprehensive reviews, see Berger, C. J., & Cummings, L. L. (1979). Organizational structure, attitudes, and behavior. *Research in Organizational Behavior, 1*, 169–208; Porter, L. W., & Lawler,

E. E., III. (1965). Properties of organizational structure in relation to job attitudes and job behavior. *Psychological Bulletin, 81,* 23–51.

26. Porter & Lawler, 1965.

27. Crozier, M. (1964). *The bureaucratic phenomenon.* Chicago: University of Chicago Press.

28. Merton, R. K. (1957). *Social theory and social structure* (rev. ed.). New York: Free Press.

29. Chonko, L. B. (1982). The relationship of span of control to sales representatives' experienced role conflict and role ambiguity. *Academy of Management Journal, 25,* 452–456.

30. Oldham, G. R., & Hackman, J. R. (1981). Relationships between organizational structure and employee reactions: Comparing alternative frameworks. *Administrative Science Quarterly, 26,* 66–83.

31. Taylor, F. W. (1967). *The principles of scientific management.* New York: Norton.

32. For a summary of their work and relevant references, see Wren, D. A. (1979). *The evolution of management thought* (2nd ed.). New York: Wiley.

33. Weber, M. (1974). *The theory of social and economic organization* (A. M. Henderson & T. Parsons, Transl.). New York: Free Press.

34. The terms *mechanistic* and *organic* (to follow) were first used by Burns, T., & Stalker, G. M.

(1961). *The management of innovation.* London: Tavistock Publications. For a recent study, see Courtright, J. A., Fairhurst, G. T., & Rogers, L. E. (1989). Interaction patterns in organic and mechanistic systems. *Academy of Management Journal, 32,* 773–802.

35. Roethlisberger, F. J., & Dickson, W. J. (1939). *Management and the worker.* Cambridge, MA: Harvard University Press.

36. Argyris, C. (1957). *Personality and organization.* New York: Harper.

37. Likert, R. (1961). *New patterns of management.* New York: McGraw-Hill.

38. Gouldner, A. W. (1954). *Patterns of industrial bureaucracy.* New York: Free Press.

39. Selznick, P. (1949). *TVA and the grass roots: A study in the sociology of formal organizations.* Berkeley: University of California Press.

40. Child, J. (1984). *Organization: A guide to problems and practice.* London: Harper & Row.

41. Presidential Commission. (1986). *The report on the space shuttle Challenger accident.* Washington, DC: U.S. Government Printing Office.

42. Pugh, D. (1979, Winter). Effective coordination in organizations. *Advanced Management Journal,* 28–35.

ENVIRONMENT, STRATEGY, AND TECHNOLOGY

It was an amazing sight. Several prominent state governors appeared on the *Donahue* show to argue publicly the case for their states' obtaining the new General Motors Saturn plant. Shortly thereafter, the suspense ended when GM announced that Spring Hill, Tennessee, would be the beneficiary of its giant investment. The governors were obviously interested in the job opportunities and other economic spin-offs that would accrue if their states were chosen as the location for the Saturn plant. But what prompted GM to invest over $3 billion in a completely new division, its first since Pontiac?

Saturn is a totally new corporation, a wholly owned GM subsidiary that delivered its first cars in fall 1990. It is an autonomous division with its own sales and service operations. Why did GM decide to separate Saturn so decisively from the existing corporate structure, rather than just add yet another product line to its Chevrolet, Oldsmobile, Pontiac, Buick, and Cadillac lines? General Motors insiders and auto industry analysts cite two primary reasons. First, GM badly needed to find ways to cut costs to compete in the small car market, in which estimates suggested that Japanese manufacturers enjoyed a $2000 advantage per car. Second, top GM executives hope to use the Saturn venture as a testing ground for innovations that can be applied throughout the rest of the organization, especially ones that can get new models to the market more quickly. To accomplish both of these goals, the freedom of a completely "fresh start" and the protection offered by autonomy seemed to be essential.

Saturn is targeted at the same market as the Honda Civic, but at a decided price advantage. With the exception of the use of plastic for all vertical body parts, the cars themselves do not represent a radical technical departure for GM. Rather, it is the way in which the cars are designed, built, and marketed that is innovative. Even at the early design stages, representatives from engineering, manufacturing, and marketing worked together to ensure early coordination of efforts. This stands in sharp contrast to usual industry practice. Assembly is done by extensively trained self-managed work teams who maintain their own equipment, order supplies, set work schedules, and even select new members. To control quality and reduce transport costs, much subassembly is done by suppliers that are located close to the plant or even within the plant itself, thus fostering a close cooperative arrangement. Parts that do come in from the outside are delivered precisely when they are needed directly to the location where they are used in assembly. In the marketing domain, dealers are given more exclusive territories than is typical of North American auto manufacturers. As long as they meet stiff requirements in several key areas, they are given substantial autonomy to tailor their operations to local needs. Also, Saturn dealers helped to choose the company's advertising agency.

These changes in design procedure, manufacturing, and marketing are supported by a number of departures from conventional structure, management style, and labor relations practices. The Saturn corporation has a flatter management structure than the traditional GM divisions. A computerized "paperless" operation of electronic mail and a single, highly integrated database speed decisions and counter bureaucracy. Finally, GM agreed to a truly ground-breaking labor contract with the United Auto Workers. There are no time clocks, and workers are on salaries, although these salaries average only 80 percent of industry hourly wages. In addition, restrictive work rules were eliminated to support the team assembly concept. In exchange for these concessions, GM devotes 20 percent of the industry hourly wage to performance incentives and a profit-sharing plan for Saturn workers. In addition, 80 percent of the work force is

An assembly team at the Saturn plant in Spring Hill, Tennessee. These self-managed teams are one innovative feature of the Saturn project. (Courtesy of Saturn Corporation)

granted what amounts to lifetime employment security. Union representatives sit on all planning and organizing committees.

The Saturn project is not as radical as it was planned to be. The company rejected initial ideas for more extensive use of computers and robotics in assembly on the basis of recent experiences in some other GM plants. Instead, even more emphasis was placed on developing a motivated work force. Also Saturn's initial marketing scheme called for showrooms in malls, dealers without inventories, computerized ordering, and so on. Some of these plans were downscaled in part because of stringent state regulations about the permitted configuration of car dealerships.

General Motors lost substantial market share just during the conception and startup of Saturn. Time will tell whether Saturn has provided a new blueprint for success.[1]

■

The Saturn story illustrates some of the major questions that we will consider in this chapter. How does the external environment influence organizations? How can a strategy be developed to cope with this environment? And how can technology and other factors be used to implement strategy? In the previous chapter we concluded that there is no one best way to design an organization. In this chapter we will see that the proper organizational structure is contingent on environmental, strategic, and technological factors.

THE EXTERNAL ENVIRONMENT OF ORGANIZATIONS

In previous chapters we have been concerned primarily with the internal environments of organizations—those events and conditions inside the organization—that affect the attitudes and behaviors of members. In this section we turn our interest to the impact of the **external environment**—those events and conditions *surrounding* the organization that influence its activities.

There is ample evidence in everyday life that the external environment has tremendous influence on organizations. The OPEC oil embargo of 1973 and subsequent oil price increases shook Detroit automobile manufacturers to their foundations. Faced with gasoline shortages, increasing gasoline prices, and rising interest rates, consumers postponed automobile purchases or shifted to more economical foreign vehicles. As a consequence, American workers were laid off, plants were closed, and dealerships failed, while the manufacturers scrambled to develop more fuel-efficient smaller cars. The emphasis of advertising strategies changed from styling and comfort to economy and value. Significant portions of the manufacturers' environment (Middle East oil suppliers, American consumers, and Japanese competitors) prompted this radical regrouping.

Environmental conditions change, and by the mid-1980s an international oil surplus pushed gasoline prices down. Consumers responded with increased interest in size, styling, and performance. Auto industry analysts noted that some manufacturers responded to this shift faster than others. Chrysler, trimmed of bureaucracy by its near demise several years earlier, responded quickly and scored a number of marketing coups. General Motors responded less quickly. Along with a massive reorganization of its traditional divisions, the Saturn project is an attempt to enable the company to respond more quickly to environmental trends.

Saturn's launch coincided with yet another dramatic rise in oil prices due to Iraq's invasion of Kuwait. It also coincided with a period of intensified lobbying for more environmentally friendly cars. Although oil prices soon fell, environmental pressure remained high.

Organizations as Open Systems

Organizations can be described as open systems. **Open systems** are systems that take inputs from the external environment, transform some of these inputs, and send them back into the external environment as outputs (Exhibit 16–1).[2] Inputs include capital, energy, materials, information, technology, and people; outputs include various products and services. Some inputs are transformed (e.g., raw materials), while other inputs (e.g., skilled craftspeople) assist in the transformation process. Transformation processes may be physical (e.g., manufacturing or surgery), intellectual (e.g., teaching or programming), or even emotional (e.g., psychotherapy). For example, an insurance company imports actuarial experts, information about accidents and mortality, and capital in the form of insurance premiums. Through the application of financial knowledge, it transforms the capital into insurance coverage and investments in areas such as real estate. Universities import seasoned scholars and aspiring students from the environment.

EXHIBIT

16–1

The organization as an open system.

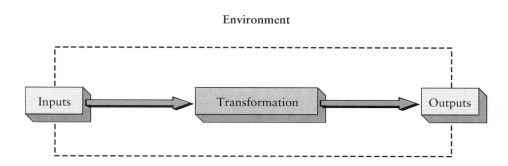

Through the teaching process, educated individuals are returned to the community as outputs.

The value of the open systems concept is that it sensitizes us to the need for organizations to cope with the demands of the environment on both the input side and the output side. As we will see, some of this coping involves adaptation to environmental demands. On the other hand, some coping may be oriented toward changing the environment.

First, let's examine the external environment in greater detail.

Components of the External Environment

The external environment of any given organization is obviously a "big" concept. Technically, it involves any person, group, event, or condition outside the direct domain of the organization. For this reason it is useful to divide the environment into a manageable number of components.[3]

The General Economy Organizations that survive by selling products or services often suffer from an economic downturn and profit by an upturn. When a downturn occurs, competition for remaining customers increases, and needed capital improvements might have to be postponed. Of course, some organizations thrive under a poor economy, including welfare offices and law firms that deal heavily in bankruptcies. In addition, if a poor economy is accompanied by high unemployment, some organizations might find it opportune to upgrade the quality of their staffs, since they will have an ample selection of candidates.

A clear example of the impact of the general economy can be seen in what happened to many savings and loan companies during the mid-1980s. Faced with double-digit inflation, they were forced to pay double-digit interest rates for capital while receiving only single-digit interest from the mature mortgages they held. Many companies failed because of this critical inability to manage inputs.

Customers All organizations have potential customers for their products and services. Piano makers have musicians, and consumer activist associations have disgruntled consumers. The customers of universities include not only students, but also the firms that employ their graduates and seek their research assistance. Organizations must be sensitive to changes in customer demands. For example, the small liberal arts college that resists developing a business school might be faced with declining enrollment.

Coca-Cola's past decision to introduce a "new," sweeter Coke in place of the traditional soft drink encountered tremendous customer resistance and forced the company finally to market two products in place of one—the new product and the relabeled Coke Classic. Most industry observers were not inpressed with this disregard of potential customer dissatisfaction. Successful firms are generally highly sensitive to customer reactions. Procter & Gamble deleted the 103-year-old man-in-the-moon logo from its packaging after it was unable to squelch rumors that the logo had satanic connotations.

Suppliers Organizations are dependent on the environment for supplies that include labor, raw materials, equipment, and component parts. Shortages can cause severe difficulties. For instance, the lack of a local technical school might prove troublesome for an electronics firm that requires skilled labor. Similarly, a strike by a company that supplies component parts might cause the purchaser to shut down its assembly line.

Jaguar, the British luxury car manufacturer, was almost forced out of the North American market because of its reputation for poor quality. Finally, Jaguar engineers traced many of the car's reliability problems to electrical accessories supplied by the Joseph Lucas company. (Lucas, a prominent supplier of lighting equipment, has often been dubbed by unfriendly observers as the Prince of Darkness!) Jaguar threatened and worked with Lucas to improve reliability, and the firm now does extremely well in North America.[4]

Competitors Environmental competitors vie for resources that include both customers and suppliers.[5] Thus, hospitals compete for patients, and consulting firms compete for clients. Similarly, utility companies compete for coal, and professional baseball teams compete for free agent ballplayers. Successful organizations devote considerable energy to monitoring the activities of competitors.

The economics of the photographic film business provide an example of the importance of the competitor component. One percent of the global market share translates into $40 million in revenues. When upstart Fuji outbid Kodak for designation as the official film of the Los Angeles Olympics, Kodak got the message, despite its strong dominance of the film market. Reorganization and a series of new products have helped Kodak maintain its dominance.[6]

Social/Political Factors Organizations cannot ignore the social and political events that occur around them. Changes in public attitudes toward racial integration, the proper age for retirement, or the proper role of big business will soon affect them. Frequently, these attitudes find expression in law through the political process. Thus, organizations must cope with a series of legal regulations that prescribe fair employment practices, proper competitive activities, product safety, and clients' rights.

One example of the impact of social trends on organizations is the increasing public interest in environmentalism. Many firms have been fairly proactive in their responses. For example, Pacific Gas & Electric works closely with environmental groups and has a dedicated environmentalist on its board. And McDonald's has become a visible proponent of recycling and an active educator of the public on environmental issues.[7]

An example of the conversion of a social trend into political and governmental action is seen in the deregulation of the U.S. and Canadian airline industries. Part of a general trend that has reduced federal regulation of business, this action spurred a long series of market entries, fare wars, route wars, mergers, acquisitions, and bankruptcies. Many a harried airline executive felt the target of the ancient Chinese curse "May you live in interesting times"!

Technology The environment contains a variety of technologies that are useful for achieving organizational goals. As we shall see, technology refers to ways of doing things, not simply to some form of machinery. The ability to adopt the proper technology should enhance the organization's effectiveness. For a business firm this might involve the choice of a proper computer system or production technique. For a mental health clinic it might involve implementing a particular form of psychotherapy that is effective for the kinds of clients serviced.

An example of the impact of technology on organizational life can be seen in the advent of computer-aided design (CAD). With CAD, designers, engineers, and draftspeople can produce quick, accurate drawings via computer. Databases can be stored, and simulations can be run that produce visual records of the reaction of objects to stress, vibration, and design changes. Some firms have found that

McDonald's responds to the social and political environment and widespread concern about ecology by refusing to use beef raised on land that was cleared by destroying tropical rainforests. (Courtesy McDonald's)

CAD reduces design lead times and increases productivity. Others have found that CAD systems have led to labor relations problems. Some traditional draftspeople have felt that their job security is threatened by CAD. Also, pay and status differences between those who learn CAD and those who do not can be difficult to resolve. In general, CAD seems destined to break down the traditional role differences between designers, engineers, and drawing technicians.

Now that we have outlined the basic components of organizational environments, a few more detailed comments are in order. First, this brief list does not provide a perfect picture of the large number of actual interest groups that can exist in an organization's environment. **Interest groups** are parties or organizations other than direct competitors who have some vested interest in how an organization is managed. For example, Exhibit 16–2 shows the interest groups that surround a small private college. As you can see, our list of six environmental components actually involves quite an array of individuals and agencies with which the college must contend. To complicate matters, some of these individuals and agencies might make competing or conflicting demands on the college. For instance, booster clubs might press the college to allocate more funds to field a

EXHIBIT

16–2

Interest groups in the external environment of a small private college.

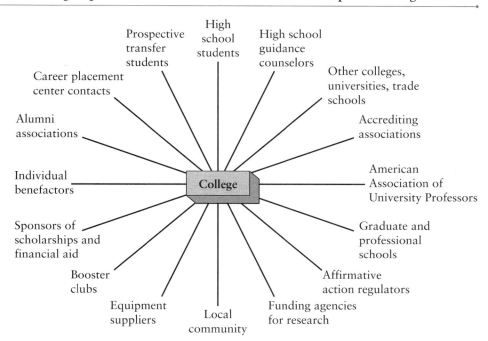

Source: From Brown, W. B., & Moberg, D. J. (1980). *Organization theory and management.* p. 45. Copyright © 1980, by John Wiley & Sons, Inc. Reprinted by permission of John Wiley & Sons, Inc.

winning football team, while scholarship sponsors might insist that the college match their donations for academic purposes.

Such competition for attention from different segments of the environment is not unusual. Iron City beer was boycotted by Pittsburgh area blacks who wanted the Pittsburgh Brewing Company to hire more blacks. When an agreement was reached and the black boycott ended, a counter-boycott was begun by some disgruntled whites![8] Similarly, while anti-drug organizations have sometimes supported the screening of employees for drug use, the American Civil Liberties Union has taken a keen interest in the violation of privacy that such tests can involve. Obviously, different interest groups evaluate organizational effectiveness according to different criteria.[9]

A second point to consider about the basic components of an organization's environment is that different parts of the organization will often be concerned with different components. For instance, we can expect a marketing department to be tuned in to customer demands and a legal department to be interested in regulations stemming from the social/political component. As indicated in the previous chapter, coordination of this natural division of interests is a crucial concern for all organizations. Also, as environmental demands change, it is important that power shifts occur to allow the appropriate functional units to cope with these demands.

Finally, events in various components of the environment provide both constraints and opportunities for organizations. Although environments with many constraints (e.g., high interest rates, strong competition, and so on) appear pretty hostile, an opportunity in one environmental sector might offset a constraint in another. For example, the firm that is faced with a dwindling customer base might find its salvation by exploiting new technologies that give it an edge in costs or new product development.

The Environment of Saturn

Let's return to the story that began the chapter and analyze some of the environmental components that shaped General Motors' plans regarding the Saturn project. A strong impetus for the Saturn venture was the $2000 cost advantage per small car that Japanese competitors held. However, cost reductions mean little unless the quality of the Saturn automobile is comparable to that of Japanese makes. To enhance quality, GM has exercised particular control over parts suppliers, inducing them to locate within or near the plant to facilitate communication with Saturn engineering and manufacturing personnel.

During the recessionary early 1980s, the general economy faltered, and unions lost considerable bargaining power. Union membership fell, and GM capitalized upon changing social attitudes toward unions to forge an innovative contract with the United Auto Workers. However, the legality of the contract was challenged by an interest group, the National Right to Work Legal Defense Foundation. This group, which provides legal aid to workers who do not wish to join unions, argued that it was improper for GM to specify the United Auto Workers as a bargaining agent in advance of any workers having been hired.[10] The challenge failed.

Several technological advances were exploited at Saturn, although not as many as were envisioned at the start of the project. Still, the plastic body parts are innovative, as is a sophisticated paperless database operation.

Finally, GM gambled that it could exploit a segment of customers that would not normally consider a domestic car—dedicated import buyers. It didn't wish to develop a new car only to divert sales from existing GM product lines.

Clearly, Saturn is a product of environmental constraints and opportunities. But exactly how do such constraints and opportunities affect the organization? To answer this question, we turn to the concepts of environmental uncertainty and resource dependence.

Environmental Uncertainty

One of the themes implied in our earlier discussion of environmental components is the fact that environments have considerable potential for causing confusion among managers. Customers may come and go, suppliers may turn from good to bad, and competitors may make surprising decisions. The resulting uncertainty can be both challenging and frustrating. **Environmental uncertainty** exists when an environment is vague, difficult to diagnose, and unpredictable. We all know that some environments are less certain than others. Your hometown provides you with a fairly certain environment. There, you are familiar with the transportation system, the language, and necessary social conventions. Thrust into the midst of a foreign culture, such as that found in India, you encounter a much less certain environment. How to greet a stranger, order a meal, and get around town become significant issues. There is nothing intrinsically bad about this uncertainty. It simply requires you to marshal a particular set of skills in order to be an effective visitor.

Like individuals, organizations can find themselves in more or less certain environments. But just exactly what makes an organizational environment uncertain? Put simply, uncertainty depends upon the environment's *complexity* (simple versus complex) and its *rate of change* (static versus dynamic).[11]

- *Simple environment.* A simple environment involves relatively few factors, and these factors are fairly similar to each other. For example, consider the pottery manufacturer that obtains its raw materials from two small firms and sells its entire output to three small pottery outlets.
- *Complex environment.* A complex environment contains a large number of dissimilar factors that affect the organization. For example, the college shown in Exhibit 16–2 has a more complex environment than the pottery manufacturer. In turn, the Saturn organization has a more complex environment than the college.
- *Static environment.* The components of this environment remain fairly stable over time. The small-town radio station that plays the same music format,

relies on the same advertisers, and works under the same FCC regulations year after year has a stable environment. (Of course, no environment is *completely* static; we are speaking in relative terms here.)

- *Dynamic environment.* The components of a highly dynamic environment are in a constant state of change. This change is unpredictable and irregular, not cyclical. For example, consider the firm that designs and manufactures microchips for electronics applications. New scientific and technological advances occur rapidly and unpredictably in this field. In addition, customer demands are highly dynamic as firms devise new uses for microchips. A similar dynamic environment faces Saturn, in part owing to the vagaries of the energy situation and in part owing to the fact that marketing automobiles has become an international business rather than a national business. For example, fluctuations in the relative value of international currencies can radically alter the cost of competing imported cars quite independently of anything Saturn management does.

As shown in Exhibit 16–3, rate of change and complexity can be arranged in a matrix (next page). A simple/static environment (cell 1) should provoke the least uncertainty, while a dynamic/complex environment (cell 4) should provoke the most. Some research suggests that change has more influence than complexity on uncertainty.[12] Thus, we might expect a static/complex environment (cell 2) to be somewhat more certain than a dynamic/simple environment (cell 3).

Earlier, it was stated that different portions of the organization are often interested in different components of the environment. To go a step further, it stands to reason that some aspects of the environment are less certain than others. Thus, some subunits might be faced with more uncertainty than others. For example, the research and development department of a microchip company would seem to face a more uncertain environment than the personnel department.

Increasing uncertainty has several predictable effects on organizations and their decision makers.[13] For one thing, as uncertainty increases, cause-and-effect relationships become less clear. If we are certain that a key competitor will not match our increased advertising budget, we may be confident that our escalated ad campaign will increase our market share. Uncertainty about the competitor's response reduces confidence in this causal inference. Second, environmental uncertainty tends to make priorities harder to agree upon, and it often stimulates a fair degree of political jockeying within the organization. To continue the example, if the consequences of increased advertising are unclear, other functional units might see the increased budget allocation as being "up for grabs." Finally, as environmental uncertainty increases, more information must be processed by the organization to make adequate decisions. Environmental scanning, planning, and formal management information systems will become more prominent. This illustrates that organizations will act to cope with or reduce uncertainty because uncertainty increases the difficulty of decision making and thus threatens organizational effectiveness. Shortly, we will examine in greater detail means of manag-

EXHIBIT

16–3

Environmental uncertainty as a function of complexity and rate of change.

		Complexity	
		Simple	Complex
Rate of Change	Static	**CELL 1** *Low Perceived Uncertainty* 1. Small number of factors and components in the environment 2. Factors and components are somewhat similar to one another 3. Factors and components remain basically the same and are not changing	**CELL 2** *Moderately Low Perceived Uncertainty* 1. Large number of factors and components in the environment 2. Factors and components are not similar to one another 3. Factors and components remain basically the same
	Dynamic	**CELL 3** *Moderately High Perceived Uncertainty* 1. Small number of factors and components in the environment 2. Factors and components are somewhat similar to one another 3. Factors and components of the environment are in continual process of change	**CELL 4** *High Perceived Uncertainty* 1. Large number of factors and components in the environment 2. Factors and components are not similar to one another 3. Factors and components of environment are in a continual process of change

Source: Duncan, R. B. (1972). Characteristics of organizational environments and perceived environmental uncertainty. Copyright © 1972 by the Administrative Science Quarterly, *17,* 313–327, p. 320. Reprinted by permission.

ing uncertainty. First we explore another aspect of the impact of the environment on organizations.

Resource Dependence

Earlier, it was noted that organizations are open systems that receive inputs from the external environment and transfer outputs into this environment. Many inputs from various components of the environment are valuable resources that are necessary for organizational survival. These include things such as capital, raw materials, and human resources. By the same token, other components of the environment (such as customers) represent valuable resources on the output end of the equation. All of this suggests that organizations are in a state of **resource dependence** with regard to their environments.[14] Carefully managing and coping with this resource dependence is a key to survival and success.

Several points about resource dependence deserve our attention. First, although all organizations are dependent upon their environments for resources, some organizations are more dependent than others. This is because some environments are more *munificent* than others (that is, they have a larger amount of readily accessible resources). Speaking very generally, the computer industry is currently located in a munificent environment. Capital is readily available, human resources are being trained in relevant fields, and new uses for computers are continually being developed. On the other hand, many organizations in traditional "smokestack" industries encounter a much less munificent environment. Investors are wary, customers are disappearing, and skilled human resources are attracted to situations with better career prospects. A classic case of a highly resource-dependent organization is a newly formed small business. Cautious bank managers, credit-wary suppliers, and a dearth of customers all teach the aspiring owner the meaning of dependence.

Second, it should be noted that a given organization might encounter ready resources in one sector of its environment and limited resources in another. For example, the U.S. military has generally had free and easy access to the latest in technological advances. On the other hand, the advent of the all-volunteer service has presented the military with constant problems in attracting and retaining highly qualified human resources.

Third, resource dependence can be fairly independent of environmental uncertainty, and dealing with one issue will not necessarily have an effect on the other.[15] For example, although the computer industry generally faces a munificent environment, this environment is uncertain, especially with regard to rate of change. On the other hand, many mature small businesses exist in a fairly certain environment but remain highly resource-dependent.

Finally, competitors, regulatory agencies, and various interest groups can have a considerable stake in how an organization obtains and transforms its resources.[16] In effect, the organization might be indirectly resource-dependent upon these bodies and thus susceptible to a fair degree of social control. For example, since Saturn is an independent corporation, it could have begun operations without unionization (the Nissan plant located in Tennessee is not unionized). However, other GM plants are organized by the United Auto Workers. To preclude labor difficulties and ensure the presence of committed human resources, GM agreed to United Auto Workers representation from the outset of the project.

The concept of resource dependence does not mean that organizations are totally at the mercy of their environments. Rather, it means that they must develop strategies for managing both resource dependence and environmental uncertainty.

STRATEGIC RESPONSES TO UNCERTAINTY AND RESOURCE DEPENDENCE

Organizations devote considerable effort to developing and implementing strategies to cope with environmental uncertainty and resource dependence. **Strategy** can be defined as the process by which top executives seek to cope with the constraints and opportunities posed by the organization's environment. Some views of the strategic process portray it as very conscious, planned, and rational. Other views portray the process as more intuitive, emerging from a stream of decisions made over time. The actual process of strategy formulation usually incorporates both approaches.

Exhibit 16–4 outlines the nature of the relationship between environment and strategy. At the top, the objective organizational environment is portrayed in terms of uncertainty and available resources, as discussed above. However, much of the impact that the environment has on organizations is indirect rather than direct, filtered through the perceptual system of managers and other organizational members.[17] By means of the perceptual process discussed in Chapter 4, personality characteristics and experience may color managers' perceptions of the environment. For example, the environment might seem much more complex and unstable for a manager who is new to his job than for one who has years of experience. Similarly, the optimistic manager might perceive more resources than the pessimistic manager.[18] It is the perceived environment that comprises the basis for strategy formulation.

Strategy formulation itself involves determining the mission, goals, and objectives of the organization. At the most basic level, for a business firm, this would even involve consideration of just what business the organization should pursue. Then, the organization's orientation toward the perceived environment must be determined. This might range from being defensive and protective of current interests (such as holding market share) to prospecting vigorously for new interests to exploit (such as developing totally new products).[19] There is no single correct strategy along this continuum. Rather, the chosen strategy must correspond to the constraints and opportunities of the environment. Finally, the strategy must be implemented by selecting appropriate managers for the task and employing appropriate techniques as shown in Exhibit 16–4. Correct choices here should have a decided impact on organizational effectiveness. For an example of an organization that has had some trouble choosing and implementing strategy, see In Focus 16–1.

One organization that pursued an interesting strategy in response to environmental constraints and opportunities and then modified that strategy was People Express airlines. Born in the heady days of airline deregulation, People began by offering "no-frills" service at discount prices rather than competing directly with established carriers for business customers. This strategy was successful for awhile, but as the established carriers responded with their own cut-rate fares, and the no-frills market became saturated, People changed its strategy also to cater to business travelers.[20] This change in strategy came too late, as People was shortly thereafter taken over by another airline. In its early days, People was small and had to pursue a strong cost-management strategy to reap profits from its low fares. To accomplish this, People had a remarkably organic structure, and it was not unusual to find pilots or flight attendants filling in as aircraft schedulers. As the airline got bigger, the structure became more formalized and mechanistic.[21]

EXHIBIT

16–4

Environment, strategy, and organizational effectiveness.

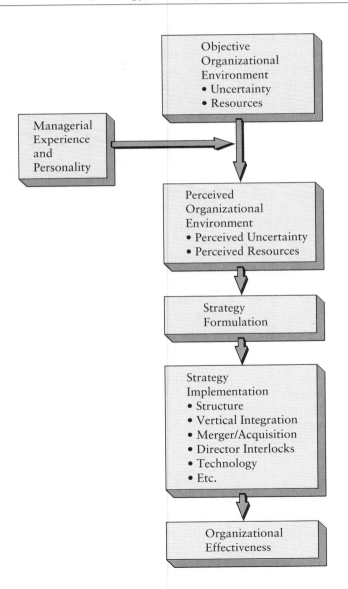

This is an example of using structure to implement strategy, a topic to which we now turn.

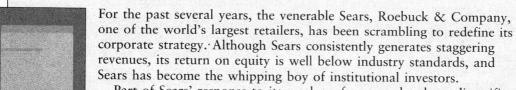

IN FOCUS 16–1

▼
....
Sears Changes Strategy

For the past several years, the venerable Sears, Roebuck & Company, one of the world's largest retailers, has been scrambling to redefine its corporate strategy. Although Sears consistently generates staggering revenues, its return on equity is well below industry standards, and Sears has become the whipping boy of institutional investors.

Part of Sears' response to its weak performance has been diversification into financial services, including the acquisition of the Dean Witter brokerage and Coldwell Banker real estate. To date, these acquisitions have not had a strong positive impact on the firm's financial picture, and opinions remain mixed as to what the future holds.

Merchandising is still the source of the bulk of Sears' revenues, and merchandising is the area in which the company has the most problems. Over the century, Sears built a giant bureaucracy to push its products throughout the country, and remnants of that bureaucracy seem permanently etched into the corporate culture. Costs, especially distribution costs, are well above those at arch-rival retailers K Mart and Wal-Mart. Furthermore, during the 1980s the Sears image became less clear to consumers. On one hand, it wasn't a deep discounter like K Mart or Wal-Mart. On the other hand, its emphasis on house brands and unexciting displays put it at a disadvantage against specialty stores such as The Limited (clothing) and Circuit City (appliances).

In 1989, Sears announced a new merchandising strategy, one that involved fancier displays, more brand names, and a more boutiquelike atmosphere. Equally important, it announced a new "everyday low price" policy that was meant to replace frequent promotions and sales. Within a year, it was clear that the new strategy had not worked well. Sales had not increased much, consumers did not perceive great changes at Sears, and several states were threatening suits, claiming that Sears' advertising was deceptive. Recently, Sears has reverted to value-for-money advertising while continuing to expand its brand name offerings.

Source: Fitzgerald, K. (1990, January 8). Sears' plan on the ropes. *Advertising Age*, p. 1; Saporito, B. (1989, December 18). Retailing's winners & losers. *Fortune*, 69–78; Oneal, M. (1988, October 17). Shaking Sears right down to its work boots. *Business Week*, 84–87.

Organizational Structure as a Strategic Response

How should organizations be structured to cope with environmental uncertainty? Paul Lawrence and Jay Lorsch of Harvard University have studied this problem.[22]

Lawrence and Lorsch chose for their research more and less successful organizations in three industries—plastics, packaged food products, and paper containers. These industries were chosen intentionally because it was assumed that they faced environments that differed in perceived uncertainty. This was subsequently confirmed by questionnaires and interviews. The environment of the plastics firms was perceived as very uncertain because of rapidly changing scientific knowledge, technology, and customer demands. Decisions had to be made even though feedback about their accuracy often involved considerable delay. At the opposite extreme, the container firms faced an environment that was perceived as much more certain. No major changes in technology had occurred in twenty years, and the name of the game was simply to produce high-quality standardized containers and get them to the customer quickly. The consequences of decisions could be learned in a short period of time. The perceived uncertainty faced by the producers of packaged foods fell between that experienced by the plastics producers and that faced by container firms.

Going a step further, Lawrence and Lorsch also examined the sectors of the environment that were faced by three departments in each company: sales (market environment), production (technical environment), and research (scientific environment). Their findings are shown in Exhibit 16–5. The crucial factor here

EXHIBIT 16–5   Relative perceived uncertainty of environmental sectors in the Lawrence and Lorsch study.

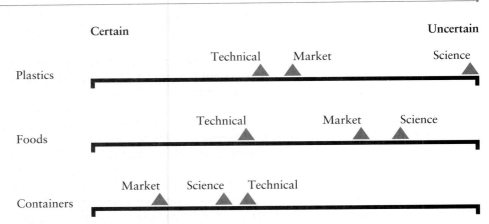

Source: Modified with permission from Paul R. Lawrence and Jay W. Lorsch, *Organization and Environment: Managing Differentiation and Integration.* Boston: Division of Research, Harvard Business School, 1967, p. 91. (Republished as a Harvard Business School Classic. Boston: Harvard Business School Press, 1986). Modified with permission.

is the *range* of uncertainty across the subenvironments faced by the various departments. In the container companies, producing, selling, and research (mostly quality control) were all fairly certain activities. In contrast, the range of uncertainty encountered by the plastics firms was quite broad. Research worked in a scientific environment that was extremely uncertain. On the other hand, production faced a technical environment that was a good bit more routine.

When Lawrence and Lorsch examined the attitudes of organizational managers, the impact of perceived environmental uncertainty became apparent. First of all, because the departments of the plastics firms had to cope with sectors of the environment that differed in certainty, the plastics firms tended to be highly differentiated (Chapter 15). Thus, their managers tended to differ rather greatly in terms of goals, interpersonal relationships, and time spans. For example, production managers were interested in immediate, short-term problems, while managers in the research department were concerned with longer-range scientific development. Conversely, the container firms were not highly differentiated because the environmental sectors with which they dealt were more similar in perceived certainty. The food packaging firms were more differentiated than the container firms but less differentiated than the plastic companies.

Because they faced a fairly certain environment and because they were fairly undifferentiated, the container firms had adopted mechanistic structures. The most successful was organized along strict functional lines and was highly centralized. Coordination was achieved through direct supervision and formalized written schedules. All in all, this container firm conformed closely to the classical prescriptions for structure. At the other extreme, the most successful plastics companies had adopted organic structures. This was the most sensible way to deal with an uncertain environment and high differentiation. Decision-making power was decentralized to locate it where the appropriate knowledge existed. Coordination was achieved through informal mutual adjustment, ad hoc teams that cut across departments, and special integrators who coordinated between departments (Chapter 15). In addition, the departments themselves were structured somewhat differently, research being the most organic and production the least organic.

The Lawrence and Lorsch study is important because it demonstrates a close connection between environment, structure, and effectiveness. However, follow-up research has not been entirely supportive of their findings, and several contradictory studies exist.[23] Part of the problem might rest in the difficulty of measuring uncertainty and in reconciling perceptions of the environment with objective environmental characteristics. How the "real" environment interacts with perceptions of the environment to affect strategy and structure remains to be determined.

Despite these spotty research findings, organizations very commonly tailor structure to strategy in coping with the environment. Consider Union Pacific Railroad, which was, like many American railroads, losing more and more market share to truckers. Why? It showed poor responsiveness to customers' needs. This included late pickups, late deliveries, dirty rail cars, and a host of other sins.

Mike Walsh, UP's new chief officer spearheaded a new strategy based on customer service and quality. To do this, he implemented a revised flatter structure that was designed to put more decision-making authority down where the customer is located:

> Nine layers of management stood between Walsh and the superintendents, the field officers responsible for the operations of trains in the territories. A super had to get permission from the bureaucracy in Omaha to spend more than a hundred bucks, and nobody outside the executive wing wanted to make a move without getting at least three signatures.
>
> Walsh eliminated six of the layers and reduced management ranks in the operating department by 800, or 50%. The superintendents now report to a single assistant vice president in Omaha, who reports to a single executive vice president, who reports to the chief. To get managers in the habit of acting quickly and innovatively, and without prodding from above, he has given superintendents power and a budget to manage; each has authority to spend as much as $25,000. This year a group of managers asked Walsh to approve a plan to forestall a shortage of grain cars. He said, "Look, you guys are at a pretty high level in the organization. If you can't make the decision, who can? I'd rather have to rein you in than kick you in the pants to get you going."[24]

Of course, UP still moved freight, a task that requires a lot of coordination. To provide these superintendents with adequate information, a new computer-controlled dispatching system was put in place.

Union Pacific's decentralization and reduction of bureaucracy correspond to a current trend that has been prompted in part by a more dynamic and/or more complex (e.g., global) business environment and accompanying revisions in strategic thinking. Part of the GM Saturn organization's strategy is to reduce the development time for new models. This helps to counteract uncertainty in the marketplace. To implement the strategy, the company opted for a flatter, more organic, less bureaucratic structure for Saturn.

The argument presented so far suggests that strategy always determines structure, rather than the other way around. This is a reasonable conclusion when considering an organization undergoing great change (such as Union Pacific) or the formation of a new organization (such as Saturn). However, for ongoing organizations, structure sometimes dictates strategy formulation. For instance, highly complex decentralized structures might dictate strategies that are the product of political bargaining between functional units. More centralized simple structures might produce strategies that appear more rational and less political (although not necessarily superior in effectiveness).[25]

Before continuing, please consult the You Be the Manager feature for an application to customer service of the material that we have been studying.

YOU BE THE MANAGER

M anager

Customer Service at United Services Automobile Agency

Consider the problem that faced United Services Automobile Agency (USAA):

> USAA was founded in 1922 to sell auto insurance to military offi-
> cers. The business was small and simple, and the customers had
> similar needs—few insurance companies were anxious to insure
> young officers. By the early 1980's, USAA expanded operations, first
> within property and casualty lines and then into other financial ser-
> vices. While keeping their niche focus, USAA opened a bank, an
> investment office, a real estate office, and even a merchandising arm
> that sold watches, cameras, and jewelry. These businesses were
> grown rapidly to meet the needs of an ever more affluent and aging
> customer base. As these customers grew older and retired from the
> military, they became more interested in investment and life style
> than in auto insurance. To facilitate growth of each business,
> product managers were given autonomy and the resources to
> proceed. Each required system's efforts to support their initiatives.
> Many found the central information systems group, long accustomed
> to marching to the drummer of the Property and Casualty division,
> was not always responsive to their needs. Some units elected to
> bring in consultants to build independent systems. Others built their
> own applications.

USAA had always prided itself on offering personalized service to its
customers, but it found that its fragmented information systems were
leading to service problems. You be the manager.

1. Speculate about the kind of customer service problems that USAA's
   fragmented information systems caused.
2. What is the proper structural response to regain USAA's strategic
   edge in service?

To find out what USAA did, see The Manager's Notebook.

Source: Ives, B., & Mason, R. O. (1990, November). Can information technology revitalize your customer service? *Academy of Management Executive*, 52–69, p. 55.

Other Forms of Strategic Response

Variations on organizational structure are not the only strategic response that organizations can make. Structural variations are often accompanied by other responses that are oriented toward coping with environmental uncertainty or resource dependence. Some forms of strategy implementation appear extremely routine, yet they might have a strong effect on the performance of the organization. For example, economic forecasting might be used to predict the demand for goods and services. In turn, formal planning might be employed to synchronize the organization's actions with the forecasts. All of this is done to reduce uncertainty and to predict trends in resource availability. Simple negotiating and contracting are also forms of implementing strategy. The innovative agreement between GM and the United Auto Workers regarding Saturn is one such example. General Motors' strategy here involved guaranteeing itself a ready supply of flexible labor at somewhat less than the going wage rate at its other plants. Some more elaborate forms of strategic response are worth a more detailed look.

Vertical Integration   Many managers live in fear of disruption on the input or output end of their organizations. A lack of raw materials to process or a snag in marketing products or services can threaten the very existence of the organization. One basic way to buffer the organization against such uncertainty over resource control is to use an inventory policy of stockpiling both inputs and outputs. For example, an automaker might stockpile chromium in anticipation of shortages due to political disruption in South Africa. At the same time, it might have thirty days' supply of new cars in its distribution system at all times. Both inventories serve as environmental "shock absorbers." A natural extension of this logic is **vertical integration,** the strategy of formally taking control of sources of supply and distribution.[26] Major oil companies, for instance, are highly vertically integrated, handling their own exploration, drilling, transport, refining, retail sales, and credit.[27] Again, environmental shock absorption is the goal, and it is no mystery that the activities of OPEC bolstered vertical integration on the supply end of this chain!

Mergers and Acquisitions   In recent years, we've seen the headlines again and again: General Electric acquires RCA; Nabisco is taken over by R. J. Reynolds, which itself is taken over; Philip Morris takes over Kraft. Such mergers of two firms or the acquisition of one firm by another are increasingly common strategic responses. Some mergers and acquisitions are stimulated by simple economies of scale. For example, a motel chain with one hundred motels might have the same advertising costs as one with fifty motels. Other mergers and acquisitions are pursued for purposes of vertical integration. For instance, a paper manufacturer might purchase a timber company. When mergers and acquisitions occur within the *same* industry, there is evidence that they are being effected partly to reduce the uncertainty prompted by competition. When they occur across *different* industries (a diversification strategy), the goal is often to reduce resource dependence on a particular segment of the environment. A portfolio is created so that if resources become threatened in one part of the environment, the organization can still prosper.[28] This was one motive for Philip Morris to take over food companies such as Kraft. Anti-smoking sentiments and legislation have provided much uncertainty for the firm's core business.

Strategic Alliances We've all heard about bad blood following a merger or acquisition, especially after a hostile takeover. This failure of cultures to integrate smoothly (Chapter 9) is only one reason that mergers that look good from a financial point of view often end up as operational disasters. Is there any way to have the benefits of matrimony without the attendant risks? Increasingly, the answer seems to be **strategic alliances,** actively cooperative relationships between legally separate organizations. The organizations in question retain their own cultures, but true cooperation replaces distrust, competition, or conflict for the project at hand. Properly designed, such alliances reduce risk and uncertainty for all parties, and resource *inter*dependence is recognized.

Organizations can engage in strategic alliances with competitors, suppliers, customers, and unions.[29] Among competitors, one common alliance is a research and development consortium in which companies band together to support basic research that is relevant for their products. For example, several Canadian producers of audio speakers have formed a consortium under the National Research Council to perfect the technology for "smart speakers" that adjust automatically to room configuration. Another common alliance between competitors is the joint venture, in which organizations combine complementary advantages for economic gain or new experience. The Toyota–General Motors joint venture in a California auto plant gave Toyota manufacturing access to the United States and gave GM experience with Japanese management techniques. This experience heavily influenced GM's subsequent decisions about how to structure and manage Saturn.

Strategic alliances with suppliers and customers have a similar theme of reducing friction and building trust and cooperation. At Union Pacific, for example, customers can place orders and track the progress of their own shipments by accessing UP's own mainframe. In manufacturing, it used to be standard procedure to have a number of suppliers that were chosen on the basis of low cost. If one supplier's quality or delivery was poor, it was dropped, and the slack was made up by another. Now it is becoming common for manufacturers to work closely with a small set of stable suppliers to ensure ongoing excellence in quality, delivery, and service. Hewlett-Packard, Ford, and General Motors are notably progressive in this.[30]

Finally, strategic alliances can occur between companies and unions. The innovative Saturn labor contract is just such an example.

Interlocking Directorates If we added up all the positions on boards of directors in the country and then added up all the people who serve as directors, the second number would be considerably smaller than the first. This is because of **interlocking directorates,** the condition that is said to exist when one person serves as a director on two or more boards. Such interlocking is prohibited by law when the firms are direct competitors, but as you can imagine, a fine line may exist as to the definition of a direct competitor. It has long been recognized that interlocking directorates provide a subtle but effective means of coping with environmental uncertainty and resource dependence. The director's expertise and experience with one organization can provide valuable information for another. Sometimes the value of the interlock is more direct. This is especially true when it is a "vertical interlock" in which one firm provides inputs to or receives outputs from the other (for instance, a director might serve on the board of a steel company and an auto producer):

> In addition to reducing uncertainty concerning inputs or outputs, a vertical interlock may also create a more efficient method of dealing with the environment. The outside director might be able not only to obtain the critical input, but also to procure favorable treatment such as a better price, better payment terms, or better delivery schedules. In addition, the search costs or the complexity involved in dealing with the environment may be reduced.[31]

Interlocks can also serve as a means of influencing public opinion about the wealth, status, or social conscience of a particular organization. Highly placed university officials, clergy, and union leaders are effectively board members in their own organizations, and they may be sought as board members by business firms to convey an impression of social responsibility to the wider public.[32] Resources are easier to obtain from a friendly environment than from a hostile environment!

The preceding are just a few examples of the kinds of strategic responses that organizations can implement to cope with the environment. Now, let's examine in greater detail another such response—technological choice.

THE TECHNOLOGIES OF ORGANIZATIONS

The term *technology* brings to mind physical devices such as turret lathes, handsaws, computers, and electron microscopes. However, as was pointed out earlier, this is an overly narrow view of the concept. To broaden this view, we might define **technology** as the activities, equipment, and knowledge that are necessary to turn organizational inputs into desired outputs. In a hospital, relevant inputs might include sick patients and naive interns, while desired outputs include well people and experienced doctors. In a steel mill, crucial inputs include scrap metal and energy, while desired outputs consist of finished steel. What technologies should the hospital and the steel mill use to facilitate this transformation? More important for our purposes, do different technologies require different organizational structures to be effective?

You will observe that the concepts of technology and environment are closely related.[33] The inputs that are transformed by the technology come from various segments of the organization's environment. In turn, the outputs that the technology creates are returned to the environment. In addition, the activities, equipment, and knowledge that constitute the technology itself seldom spring to life within the organization. Rather, they are imported from the technological segment of the environment to meet the organization's needs.

It should be emphasized that organizations choose their technologies.[34] In general, this choice will be predicated on a desired strategy. For example, the directors of a university mental health center might decide that they wish to deal only with students suffering from transitory anxiety or mild neuroses. Given these inputs, certain short-term psychotherapies would constitute a sensible technology. More disturbed students would be referred to clinics that have different strategies and different technologies.

Finally, it should be noted that different parts of the organization rely on different technologies, just as they respond to different aspects of the environment as a whole. For example, the personnel department uses a different technology than the finance department. However, research has often skirted this problem by concentrating on the "core" technology used by the key operating function (e.g., the production department in manufacturing firms).

Basic Dimensions of Technology

Organizational technology has been defined, conceptualized, and measured in literally dozens of different ways.[35] Some analysts have concentrated on degree of automation; others have focused on the degree of discretion granted to workers. Here we will consider other classifications of technologies developed by Charles Perrow and James D. Thompson. These classification schemes are advantageous because they can be applied both to manufacturing firms and to service organizations such as banks and schools.

Perrow's Routineness   According to Perrow, the key factor that differentiates various technologies is the routineness of the transformation task that confronts the department or organization.[36] **Technological routineness** is a function of two factors:

- *Exceptions.* Is the organization taking in standardized inputs and turning out standardized outputs (few exceptions)? Or is the organization encountering varied inputs or turning out varied outputs (many exceptions)? The technology becomes less routine as exceptions increase.
- *Problems.* When exceptions occur, are the problems easy to analyze or difficult to analyze? That is, can programmed decision making occur, or must workers resort to nonprogrammed decision making? The technology becomes less routine as problems become more difficult to analyze.

As shown in Exhibit 16–6, the exceptions and problems dimensions can be arranged to produce a matrix of technologies:

- *Craft technologies* typically deal with fairly standard inputs and outputs. Cabinetmakers use wood to make cabinets, and public schools attempt to educate "typical" students. However, when exceptions are encountered (a special order or a slow learner), analysis of the correct action might be difficult.

- *Routine technologies* such as assembly line operations and technical schools also deal with standardized inputs and outputs. However, when exceptions do occur (a new product line or a new subject to be taught), the correct response is fairly obvious.

- *Nonroutine technologies* must deal frequently with exceptional inputs or outputs, and the analysis of these exceptions is often difficult. By definition, research units are set up to deal with difficult, exceptional problems. Similarly, psychiatric hospitals encounter patients with a wide variety of disturbances. Deciding on a proper course of therapy can be problematic.

- *Engineering technologies* encounter many exceptions of input or required output, but these exceptions can be dealt with by using standardized responses. For example, individuals with a wide variety of physical conditions visit health spas, and each has a particular goal (e.g., weight loss, muscle development). Despite this variety, the recommendation of a training regimen for each individual is a fairly easy decision.

From most routine to least routine, Perrow's four technological classifications can be ordered in the following manner: routine, engineering, craft, nonroutine. Shortly, we will consider which structures are appropriate for these technologies. First, let's examine Thompson's technological classification.

EXHIBIT 16–6   **Perrow's matrix of technologies.**

		Exceptions	
		Few	Many
Problems	Difficult Analysis	**Craft Technology** Cabinet Making Public School	**Nonroutine Technology** Research Unit Psychiatric Hospital
	Easy Analysis	**Routine Technology** Assembly Line Vocational Training	**Engineering Technology** Heavy Machinery Construction Health Spa

Source: From Perrow, C. (1967, April). Framework for the comparative analysis of organizations, *ASR*, Vol. 32, No. 2, Figures 1 and 2, pp. 196, 198. Copyright © 1967 by the American Sociological Association. Reprinted by permission.

Thompson's Interdependence   In contrast to Perrow, James D. Thompson was interested in the way in which work activities are sequenced or "put together" during the transformation process.[37] A key factor here is **technological interdependence,** the extent to which organizational subunits depend on each other for resources, raw materials, or information. In order of increasing interdependence, Thompson proposed three classifications of technology (Exhibit 16–7):

- *Mediating technologies* operate under **pooled interdependence.** This means that each unit is to some extent dependent upon the pooled resources generated by the other units but is otherwise fairly independent of those units. Thompson gives rather abstract examples, such as banks, which mediate between depositors and borrowers, and post offices, which mediate between the senders and receivers of letters. However, the same argument can be applied more clearly to the branches of banks or post offices. The health of a bank as a whole might depend on the existence of several branches, but

■
EXHIBIT   **Thompson's technology classification.**

16–7

Mediating Technology (Pooled Interdependence):

Long-Linked Technology (Sequential Interdependence):

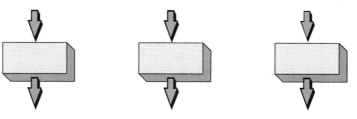

Intensive Technology (Reciprocal Interdependence):

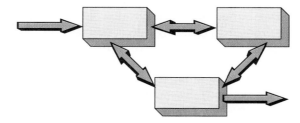

these branches operate almost independently of each other. Each has its own borrowers and depositors. Similarly, post office branches are dependent upon other branches to forward and receive mail, but this is the limit of their required interaction. A taxi company is another good example of pooled interdependence.

- *Long-linked technologies* operate under **sequential interdependence.** This means that each unit in the technology is dependent on the activity of the unit that preceded it in a sequence. The transformed product of each unit becomes a resource or raw material for the next unit. Mass production assembly lines are the classic example of long-linked technology. However, many "paper-processing" technologies, such as the claims department of an insurance company, are also sequentially interdependent (claims must be verified before they are adjusted and must be adjusted before they are settled).

- *Intensive technologies* operate under **reciprocal interdependence.** This means that considerable interplay and feedback must occur between the units performing the task in order to accomplish it properly. This is necessary because each task is unique, and the intensive technology is thus a customized technology. One example might be the technology employed by a multidisciplinary research team. Thompson cites a general hospital as a prime example of intensive technology.

> At any moment an emergency admission may require some combination of dietary, x-ray, laboratory, and housekeeping or hotel services, together with the various medical specialties, pharmaceutical services, occupational therapies, social work services, and spiritual or religious services. Which of these is needed, and when, can be determined only from evidence about the state of the patient.[38]

As technologies become increasingly interdependent, problems of coordination, communication, and decision making increase. To perform effectively, each technology requires a structure that is tailored to facilitate these tasks.

Structuring to Cope with Technology

How does technology affect organizational structure? According to Perrow, routine technologies should function best under mechanistic structures, while non-routine technologies call for more organic structures. In the former case, few exceptions to the normal course of events and easily analyzable problems suggest high formalization and centralization. In the latter case, many exceptions and difficult problems suggest that decision-making power should be located "where the action is." The craft and engineering technologies fall between these prescriptions. Perrow encountered difficulties in actually measuring routineness according to the dimensions of exceptions and ease of analysis.[39] However, simplified measures have generally supported his notion that more routine technologies adopt more mechanistic structures.[40]

According to Thompson, increasing technological interdependence must be accompanied by increased coordination or integration mechanisms. There is research evidence to support this proposition.[41] Furthermore, the *methods* used to achieve coordination should be reflected in structural differences across the technologies. Mediating technologies, operating only under pooled interdependence, should be able to achieve coordination via standardization of rules, regulations, and procedures. This formalization is indicative of a mechanistic structure (consider banks and the post office). Long-linked technologies must also be structured mechanistically, but the increased demands for coordination prompted by sequential interdependence must be met by planning, scheduling, and meetings. Finally, intensive technologies require intensive coordination, and this is best achieved by mutual adjustment and an organic structure that permits the free and ready flow of information among units.[42]

Without a doubt, the most famous study of the relationship between technology and structure was performed by Joan Woodward. Woodward examined the technology, structure, and organizational effectiveness of one hundred firms in South Essex, England.[43] This study is especially interesting because it began as an attempt to test the classical argument that mechanistic structures will prove most effective in all cases. In brief, this test failed—there was no simple, consistent relationship between organizational structure and effectiveness, and many of the successful firms exhibited organic structures. Woodward then analyzed and classified the technologies of the eighty firms in her sample that had clear-cut, stable production processes. She used these classifications:

- *Unit* (production of single units or small batches)
  - Custom-tailored units
  - Prototype production
  - Fabrication of large equipment in stages (e.g., locomotives)
  - Small batches to order
- *Mass* (production of large batches or mass production)
  - Large batches on assembly lines
  - Mass production (e.g., bakeries)
- *Process* (input transformed as an ongoing process)
  - Chemicals processed in batches
  - Continuous-flow production (e.g., gasoline, propane)

From top to bottom, this scale of technology seems to reflect both increasing smoothness of production and increasing impersonalization of task requirements.[44] Less and less personal intervention is necessary as machines control more and more of the work. Woodward's mass technology incorporates aspects of Perrow's routine technology and Thompson's long-linked technology. Her unit technology seems to cover Perrow's craft and engineering technologies and some aspects of Thompson's intensive technology. It is difficult to isolate Woodward's process technology in the Perrow or Thompson classifications.

Now for the key questions. Did organizational structures tend to vary with technology? If so, was this variance related to organizational effectiveness? The answer in both cases is yes. Each of the three technologies tended to have distinctive structures, and the most successful firms had structures that closely approximated the average of their technological groups. For instance, Woodward found that as the production process became smoother, more continuous, and more impersonal, the management of the system took on increasing importance. That is, moving from unit to mass to process, there were more managers relative to workers, more hierarchical levels, and lower labor costs. This is not difficult to understand. Unit production involves custom-tailored craftsmanship in which the workers can essentially manage their own work activity. However, it is very labor intensive. On the other hand, sophisticated continuous-process systems (such as those used to refine gasoline) take a great amount of management skill and technical attention to start up. Once rolling, a handful of workers can monitor and maintain the system.

Successful firms with unit and process technologies relied upon organic structures, while successful firms that engaged in mass production relied upon mechanistic structures. For example, the latter firms had more specialization of labor, more controls, and greater formalization (a reliance on written rather than verbal communication). At first glance, it might strike you as unusual that the firms at the extremes of the technology scale (unit and process) both tended to rely on organic structures. However, close consideration of the actual tasks performed under each technology resolves this apparent contradiction. Unit production generally involves custom-building complete units to customer specifications. As such, it relies upon skilled labor, teamwork, and coordination by mutual adjustment and standardized skills. The work itself is not machine-paced and is far from mechanistic. At the other extreme, process production is almost totally automated. The workers are essentially skilled technicians who monitor and maintain the system, and they again tend to work in teams. While the machinery itself operates according to a rigid schedule, workers can monitor and maintain it at their own pace. Informal relationships with supervisors replace close control.

Woodward's research is a landmark in demonstrating the general proposition that structure must be tailored to the technology that the organization adopts to achieve its strategic goals. Her findings have been replicated and extended by others.[45] However, there have been disconfirming studies, and a constant debate has gone on about the relative importance of organizational size versus technology in determining structure.[46]

The design of the Saturn organization shows evidence of an attempt to match structure to technology. In Woodward's terms, the core technology at Saturn is obviously mass production. However, some of its unique features, such as building automatic and manual transmissions on the same line to exactly match a car order, mean that the technology is somewhat less routine (in Perrow's terms) than the conventional monolithic assembly line. To take advantage of this, the shopfloor organization, with its work teams and reduced supervision, is more organic than is typical for the North American auto industry. This, then, is also reflected in the managerial and professional ranks, in which the technology for designing cars was modified. Instead of passing designs from department to department (Thompson's sequential interdependence), early involvement of all critical departments was obtained (Thompson's reciprocal interdependence). Again, this points to a more organic structure backed up by sophisticated electronic aids to facilitate coordination and communication. In fact, let's now turn our attention to advanced information technology.

IMPLICATIONS OF ADVANCED INFORMATION TECHNOLOGY

In concluding the chapter, let's consider some of the implications that ongoing advances in information technology are having for organizational behavior. Speaking broadly, **advanced information technology** refers to the generation, aggregation, storage, modification, and speedy transmission of information made possible by the advent of computers and related devices. Information technology is equally applicable in the factory or the office. In the factory, it controls such advances as robots, computer-numerically-controlled machine tools, and automated inventory management. In the office, it includes everything from word processing to electronic mail to automated filing to expert systems. Between the office and the factory, it includes computer-aided design and engineering.

The Two Faces of Advanced Technology

It is important to recognize that there has been much inaccurate hoopla about advanced information technology. This began even before the first mainframe computers were perfected, and it continues today. To exaggerate only slightly, doomsayers have painted a dark picture of job loss and deskilling, with technology running wild and stifling the human spirit. Opponents of this view (often vendors of hardware and software) have painted a rosy picture of improved productivity, superior decision making, and upgraded, happy employees. It probably doesn't surprise you that research fails to support either of these extremes as a general state of affairs. In the early days of mainframe batch data processing, deskilling, job pacing, and loss of routine clerical jobs did occur. However, as we shall see, the consequences of current advanced information technology are much less deterministic.

This discussion of extremes alerts us to a more realistic issue that might be called the "two faces" of technology.[47] This means that a given form of advanced information technology can have exactly *opposite* effects depending upon how it is employed. For example, the same system that is designed to monitor and control employees (say, by counting keystrokes) can be used to provide feedback and reduce supervision. Also, the same technology that can deskill jobs can be used to build skills *into* jobs. How can these opposite effects occur? They are possible because information technology is so *flexible*. In fact, we are discussing information technology separately from the core technologies discussed earlier because it is so flexible that it can be applied in conjunction with any of them.

The flexibility of information technology means that it is not deterministic of a particular organization structure or job design. Rather, it gives organizations *choices* about how to organize work. The company that wishes to decentralize can use information technology to provide lower-level employees with data to make decisions. The company that wishes to centralize can use the other face of the same technology to gather information from below to retain control. Such choices are a function of organizational culture and management values rather than inherent in the hardware. They should match the strategy being pursued, as our discussion of advanced manufacturing will show.

For purposes of discussion, we will distinguish between advanced manufacturing technology and advanced office technology. However, as we shall see, this distinction is artificial, since advanced technology has the capability to link the office more closely to the factory or to clients, customers, and suppliers in the outside environment.

Advanced Manufacturing Technology

Three major trends underlie advanced manufacturing technology.[48] The first is an obvious capitalization on computer intelligence and memory. The second is flexibility, in that the technology is configured to accomplish a changing variety of tasks. This is usually the product of an organizational strategy that favors adaptiveness, small batch production, and fast response. In turn, this strategy follows from attempting to find and exploit short-term "niches" in the marketplace rather than hoping to produce large volumes of the same product year after year. Consider this textile firm:

> Milliken has reduced its average production run from 20,000 to 4,000 yards and can dye lots as small as 1,000 yards. Apparel makers, textile and fiber firms, and retailers have recently joined to launch the so-called Quick Response program, designed to improve the flow of information among the various groups and speed order times. The program's goal is to cut the 66-week cycle from fiber to retail in the U.S. to 21 weeks.[49]

As a third trend, advanced manufacturing technologies are increasingly being designed to be integrated with *other* advanced technologies used by the organization. For example, the computer-aided design system that is used to design and modify a product can also be used to design, operate, and modify its production process via computer-aided manufacturing programs (the result being a so-called CAD/CAM system). Ultimately, using most of the technologies mentioned here, computer-integrated manufacturing systems (CIM) that integrate and automate all aspects of design, manufacturing, assembly, and inspection can be put in place. In turn, computerized information systems can link these tasks to supply and sales networks. Exhibit 16–8 compares highly flexible manufacturing systems with traditional mass production.[50]

■
EXHIBIT
16–8

Flexible manufacturing compared with traditional mass production.

Organizational Characteristic	Flexible Manufacturing	Mass Production
Strategy	• Adapt to environment	• Buffer against environment
	• Produce small batches	• Produce large batches
	• Small inventory, fast turnover	• Large inventory, slow turnover
	• Respond fast	• Respond predictably
Product	• Many variations, variable life cycles	• Few variations, long life cycles
Marketing	• Exploit niche markets	• Cater to mass market
Structure	• Organic, integrated	• Mechanistic, differentiated
Suppliers	• Few, chosen for reliability and responsiveness	• Many, chosen on basis of cost
Jobs	• Flexible jobs; teamwork	• Rigid, specialized jobs; little teamwork

What are the general implications of advanced manufacturing technology for organizational behavior? Such technology tends to automate the more routine information-processing and decision-making tasks. Depending on job design, what might remain for operators are the more complex tasks of a nonroutine nature, those dealing with system problems and exceptions. In addition, task interdependence tends to increase under advanced technologies. For example, design, manufacturing, and marketing might become more reciprocally than sequentially interdependent in a flexible manufacturing system. Finally, let's remember that such advanced technologies are adopted in part to cope with a less certain environment. Thus, many advanced technological systems result in nonroutine, highly interdependent tasks that are embedded in an uncertain environment.[51]

Organizational Structure What are the implications of this shift in technology? As shown in Exhibit 16–8, one effect is a movement toward flatter, more organic structures.[52] This corresponds to Woodward's finding that unit technologies require more organic designs than mass technologies, and the adoption of more flexible, short-term production batches is an example of unit technology. The expectation of flatter structures stems from the fact that more highly automated systems will handle information processing and diagnoses that were formerly performed by middle managers. Implications of advanced technology for centralization are interesting. On one hand, matters such as ordering raw materials and scheduling production should become more highly centralized. This is both re-

Designing the Airbus 320 at a CAD terminal, which is one of the most important new manufacturing technologies. (Brunode Hogues/Tony Stone Worldwide)

quired by the flexibility of the system and permitted by its enhanced information-processing capability. On the other hand, when problems or exceptions occur or when new designs are conceived, decentralization might be called for to locate decision making in the hands of lower-level specialists. However, the whole thrust of advanced technology dictates greater integration among specialties such as design, engineering, production, and marketing. This might require a retreat from the rigid functional structures (Chapter 15) that are common in manufacturing firms. Minimally, it suggests the increased use of integrators, task forces, planning committees, and other mechanisms that stimulate coordination.

Job Design   Advanced manufacturing technology can be expected to affect the design of jobs, and this is where the issue of choice alluded to earlier clearly comes into play. There is clear evidence that such technology can reduce worker control over shopfloor jobs and water down existing skills.[53] An example is having skilled machinists operate lathes that have been programmed by a remote technician. However, other choices are possible, including teaching the machinists to program the lathe or at least to edit existing programs for local conditions. The latter approaches are more likely to gain cooperation and commitment to the new technology. Following this logic, since advanced technology tends to automate routine tasks, operative workers must usually acquire advanced skills (e.g., computer skills). Also, since advanced technology tends to be flexible as well as expensive to operate, workers themselves must be flexible and fast to respond to problems. Extreme division of labor can be counterproductive in advanced technology. For example, operators simply might not be able to wait for someone else to perform routine maintenance and thus might have to have the flexibility to do this themselves. Similarly, traditional distinctions between roles (electrical maintenance versus mechanical maintenance or drafting versus design) begin to blur when the needs for coordination imposed by advanced technology are recognized.

All of this points to the design of jobs for advanced manufacturing technology according to the principles of job enrichment discussed in Chapter 7. In turn, this suggests that proper training is critical and that pay levels should be revised to fit the additional skills and responsibilities prompted by the technology. Many observers have recommended that self-managed teams (Chapter 8) be made responsible for setting up, running, and maintaining the system.[54] In fact, GM has adopted this scheme for the Saturn plant. Such teams permit cross-transfer of skills and provide the cross-task integration that is necessary to keep things working smoothly. The team concept is also applicable to other forms of advanced technology. For example, one company organized its CAD/CAM users into teams composed of two designers, a draftsperson, and a toolmaker.[55]

Advanced Office Technology

As noted above, the label advanced office technology can be applied sensibly to everything from word processing for secretaries to exotic expert systems for executives. Advanced office technology illustrates the coming together of some combination of three previously separate technologies—computers, office machines, and telecommunications (for example, a word processor combines a computer and a typewriter). The most common basic functions of the technology are the following:[56]

- Text processing
- Communication (e.g., electronic mail, fax)
- Information storage and retrieval
- Analysis and manipulation of information
- Administrative support (e.g., electronic calendars)

As with advanced manufacturing technology, we can point to some environmental and strategic concerns that have stimulated the adoption of advanced office technology, although these concerns are more general. One is obviously the potential for *labor saving.* Consider, for example, word processing (revisions are easy), video conferencing (a trip to the Coast is unnecessary), or spreadsheet analysis (many "What if?" scenarios can be probed by one manager). Another major concern stimulating the adoption of advanced technology is *responsiveness,* both within the organization and also to customers and suppliers. Speed and personalization of response are common goals (see In Focus 16–2, page 607). Finally, *improved decision making* is a goal of various decision support systems, expert systems, and the like.

The implications of advanced office technology are far reaching. What follows is an illustrative sample, again focusing on organization structure and job design.

Organizational Structure   At least as it pertains to management jobs, the link between office technology and organizational structure has been dominated by two related issues—the impact of information technology on tallness/flatness and centralization. Regarding tallness and flatness, there has been consistent speculation that advanced technology will enable a reduction in the number of supervisory and middle management personnel.[57] Fewer supervisors should be needed because electronic monitoring and feedback will replace routine supervision, and existing supervisors will be able to handle larger spans of control. With fewer supervisors, fewer middle managers will be required. Also, some advanced technology, such as decision support and expert systems, can make up for analyses performed by middle managers. For its size (over 40,000 employees), Federal Express is a flat organization, having only five levels. This is due in part to advanced electronic communication systems.

Actual research evidence on all this is rather scanty and mainly targeted at the middle management issue. Although some staff reductions have been reported, it is difficult to know how much of this is a direct result of office technology as opposed to flatness being imposed to make organizations more responsive to the external environment. Some research points to increased demands on middle management jobs as larger spans require them to be in charge of more diverse areas and as their performance is more monitorable by top management due to the technology.[58]

The impact of advanced office technology on centralization of decision making is most likely variable, precisely as it should be. Again, the key is the extreme flexibility of information technology. The same systems that allow senior managers to meddle in lower-level operations might enable junior staffers to assemble data and make decisions. Notice, though, that advanced technology does imply a freer, more democratic flow of information and general communication. This suggests that advanced technology enables a wider range of people and levels to be involved in organizational decision making.[59] Exactly how this capacity gets played out in decision-making practice is most likely a function of strategy and prevailing culture.

Finally, it should be noted that advanced information technologies actually raise questions about the physical limits of the organization and the office. Both "telecommuting" from home and the "portable office" (In Focus 16–3) illustrate this. Although these advances boost productivity, they can also result in less integration with the larger organization.

Job Design   The impact of advanced office technology on job design and related quality of working life differs considerably with job status. Among clerical and secretarial employees, when jobs have not been lost altogether, there is the potential for deskilling and reduced motivating potential.[60] A good case in point oc-

IN FOCUS 16–2

▼
....

The Portable Office Improves Customer Service

When a sales force has instant access to current pricing, inventory status, customer history, competitive activity, and a method for transmitting orders within minutes of receipt, it can dominate a market. Not only can it meet customer needs faster, it can anticipate them. In turn, the home office gets information on sales activity in "real time"—as it happens—and is better able to respond to market developments and competitive challenges. Remarks Kevin Mankin, director of product development, Zenith Data Systems, "Today more than ever, portable computers are being used by businesses to maximize their competitive advantage. Portable PCs allow valuable company information to be accessed from even the most remote locations. This allows information to be retrieved from the field, sent to the corporate office for interpretation, and immediately dispatched to everyone who needs it." Firms which rely on the effectiveness of a field sales force are beginning to realize such synergies make the computerization of these employees not just a possibility, but a necessity. Says David Takagi, senior vice president, office automation group, Panasonic, "Small, notebook-size computers that can be custom programmed for specific tasks are going to transform the periphery of countless companies. As you simplify the collection and dissemination of data in the field, costs go down and overall responsiveness and productivity increases."

A large insurance company equipped its agents with portable computers and portable printers to calculate and print out custom policies while on sales calls. Closing rates improved dramatically. Says Geoffrey J. Smith, manager, marketing and sales, personal printer products, Eastman Kodak, "Any situation involving on-site sales is greatly enhanced by the ability to generate a specific written proposal immediately. Prospects who can sign on the dotted line when their attention and interest are highest has resulted in increased closing rates of 40 percent or more." Since the system also cut the time spent on administrative work, agents found they were making more calls (productivity) and selling more policies (profitability).

Source: Excerpted from Finn, F. X. The portable office. Special advertising section, *Fortune*, February 26, 1990. Copyright © 1990 by The Time Inc. Magazine Company. Reprinted by permission.

curred in many organizations when word processing was introduced. Because the equipment was then expensive, secretarial support was often shifted into word processing pools to make efficient use of the hardware.[61] This frequently resulted in task specialization and a reduction in task identity. However, most observers agree that such technology can actually upgrade skills if it is used to optimal capacity and the work is not highly fragmented.[62] Yet again, the issue of flexibility and choice is seen.

Turning to quality of working life, word processing and related video display work have been known to provoke eyestrain, muscular strain, and stress symptoms. However, proper work station design and work pacing can cope with these problems. Computer monitoring (such as counting keystrokes or timing the length of phone calls by service workers) has also been linked to stress reactions. However, there are studies that show that such monitoring may be viewed favorably by employees when it is used for job feedback rather than as a basis for punishment.[63]

On the whole, professionals and managers seem to have taken to advanced office technology remarkably well. Routine aspects of such jobs (such as doing tedious calculations) have often been replaced by more cerebral pursuits. One exception may be some semiprofessional jobs, such as drafting, in which deskilling can occur without thoughtful job redesign.

Most of the foregoing is admittedly speculative, since research has really just begun on the organizational behavior implications of advanced information technology. However, there are many examples of organizations that have had poor success in introducing advanced technology because they ignored the human dimension. This raises the issue of implementing change in organizations, a concern of the next chapter.

THE MANAGER'S NOTEBOOK

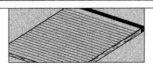

Customer Service at United Services Automobile Agency

1. The fragmented information systems resulted in multiple mailings to customers for each of USAA's product lines, each with a different telephone number to call. When calls were received, operators were unaware of the customers' association with other USAA businesses. Also, each of these businesses required a separate change of address form.

2. At first consideration, the decentralized information systems might appear to promote personalized service. However, they didn't because customer service personnel in USAA's various businesses were unaware of the "whole" customer and his or her related needs. USAA centralized its information systems around an all-inclusive customer file and used a single phone number to route customer calls to the appropriate service personnel.

SUMMARY

- Organizations are open systems that take inputs from the external environment, transform some of these inputs, and send them back into the environment as outputs. The external environment includes all of the events and conditions surrounding the organization that influence this process. Major components of the environment include the economy, customers, suppliers, competitors, social/political factors, and existing technologies.
- One key aspect of the external environment is its uncertainty. More uncertain environments are vague, difficult to diagnose, and unpredictable. Uncertainty is a function of complexity and rate of change. The most uncertain environments are complex and dynamic—they involve a large number of dissimilar components that are changing unpredictably. More certain environments are simple and stable—they involve a few similar components that exhibit little change. As environmental uncertainty increases, cause-effect relationships get harder to diagnose, and agreeing on priorities becomes more difficult because more information must be processed.
- Another key aspect of the external environment is the amount of resources it contains. Some environments are richer or more munificent than others, and all organizations are dependent upon their environments for resources.
- Strategy is the process by which executives seek to cope with the constraints and opportunities posed by the organization's environment, including uncertainty and scarce resources. One critical strategic response involves tailoring the organization's structure to suit the environment. In general, as demonstrated by the Lawrence and Lorsch study, mechanistic structures are most suitable for more certain environments, and organic structures are better suited to uncertain environments. Other strategic responses include vertical integration, mergers and acquisitions, strategic alliances, interlocking directorates, and technological choice.
- Technology includes the activities, equipment, and knowledge necessary to turn organizational inputs into desired outputs. One key aspect of technology is the extent of its routineness. A routine technology involves few exceptions to usual inputs or outputs and readily analyzable problems. A nonroutine technology involves many exceptions that are difficult to analyze. Another key aspect of technology is the degree of interdependence that exists between organizational units. This may range from simple pooling of resources to sequential activities to complex reciprocal interdependence.
- The most famous study of the relationship between technology and structure was performed by Joan Woodward. She determined that unit and process technologies performed best under organic structures, while mass production functioned best under a mechanistic structure. In general, less routine technologies and more interdependent technologies call for more organic structures.
- Advanced information technology generates, aggregates, stores, modifies, and speedily transmits information. In the factory, it permits flexible manufacturing that calls for organic structures, enriched jobs, and increased teamwork. In the office and the organization as a whole, the flexibility of advanced information technology means that its effects are highly dependent upon management values and culture.

KEY CONCEPTS

External environment	Vertical integration	Pooled interdependence
Open system	Strategic alliances	Sequential interdependence
Interest groups	Interlocking directorates	Reciprocal interdependence
Environmental uncertainty	Technology	Advanced information technology
Resource dependence	Technological routineness	
Strategy	Technological interdependence	

DISCUSSION QUESTIONS

1. Construct a diagram of the various interest groups in the external environment of CBS Television. Discuss how some of these interest groups may make competing or contradictory demands on CBS.

2. Describe a real or a hypothetical organization with a very uncertain environment. Do the same for an organization with a fairly certain environment. Be sure to cover both the complexity and rate of change dimensions.

3. Give an example of vertical integration. Use the concept of resource dependence to explain why an organization might choose a strategic response of vertical integration.

4. Discuss how interlocking directorates might reduce environmental uncertainty and help manage resource dependence.

5. Explain why organizations operating in more uncertain environments require more organic structures.

6. Locate the technology of a branch bank situated in a shopping center in Perrow's technology matrix (Exhibit 16–6). Defend your answer.

7. Distinguish among pooled interdependence, sequential interdependence, and reciprocal interdependence in terms of the key problem each poses for organizational effectiveness.

8. Give an example of unit technology, mass technology, and process technology. For which type of technology are the prescriptions of the classical organizational theorists best suited?

9. Imagine that a company is converting from conventional mass technology to a highly flexible, computerized, integrated production system. List structural and behavioral problems that might have to be anticipated in making this conversion.

10. Discuss this statement: The effects of advanced information technology on job design and organizational structure are highly predictable.

EXPERIENTIAL EXERCISE

Diagnosing an Organization

The purpose of this exercise is to choose an organization and to diagnose it in terms of the concepts covered in the chapter. Doing such a diagnosis should enable you to see better how the degree of "fit" among organizational structure, environment, strategy, and technology influences the effectiveness of the organization. The discussion throughout the chapter of the General Motors Saturn organization provides a general model for the nature of the exercise.

This exercise is suitable for an individual or group project completed outside of class or a class discussion guided by the instructor. In the case of the group project completed outside of class, a local organization might be chosen and contacted for information. Alternatively, library resources might be consulted to diagnose a prominent national or international organization. Your instructor might suggest one or more organizations for diagnosis.

_____ 1. Discuss in detail the external environment of the chosen organization.
   a) How has the general economy affected this organization recently? Is the organization especially sensitive to swings in the economy?
   b) Who are the organization's key customers? What demands do they make on the organization?
   c) Who are the organization's key suppliers? What impact do they have on the organization?

          d) Who are the organization's important competitors? What threats or opportunities do they pose for the organization?

          e) What general social and political factors (e.g., the law, social trends, environmental concerns) affect the organization in critical ways?

_____ 2. Drawing on your answers to question 1, discuss both the degree of environmental uncertainty and the nature of resource dependence faced by the organization. Be sure to locate the firm or institution in the appropriate cell of Exhibit 16–3 and defend your answer.

_____ 3. What broad strategies (excluding structure) has the organization chosen to cope with its environment?

_____ 4. Describe in as much detail as possible the structure of the organization and explain how this structure represents a strategic response to the demands of the environment. Is this the proper structure for the environment and broad strategies that you described in response to the earlier questions?
          a) How big is the organization?
          b) What form of departmentation is used?
          c) How big are spans of control?
          d) How tall is the organization?
          e) How much formalization is apparent?
          f) To what extent is the organization centralized?
          g) How complex is the organization?
          h) Where does the organization fall on a continuum from mechanistic to organic?

_____ 5. Describe the organization's core technology in terms of routiness (Exhibit 16–6) and interdependence (Exhibit 16–7). Is its structure appropriate for its technology?

_____ 6. What impact has advanced information technology had on the organization?

■

C & C Grocery Stores, Inc.

The first C & C grocery store was started in 1947 by Doug Cummins and his brother Bob. Both were veterans who wanted to run their own business, so they used their savings to start the small grocery store in Charlotte, North Carolina. The store was immediately successful. The location was good, and Doug Cummins had a winning personality. Store employees adopted Doug's informal style and "serve the customer" attitude. C & C's increasing circle of customers enjoyed an abundance of good meats and produce.

As business grew, Doug used the store's profits to open two additional stores in the Charlotte area. Over a period of twenty years the C & C chain expanded up the East coast and through the southeastern United States. Growth was at a moderate rate, because Doug did not want to overextend the chain's resources or take chances. Giving customers good service and value were more important than rapid growth. During the 1970s new stores were opened in the South and reached as far west as Texas.

By 1984, C & C had over 200 stores. A standard physical layout was used for new stores. Company head-quarters moved from Charlotte to Atlanta in 1975. The organization chart for C & C is shown in Exhibit 1. The central offices in Atlanta handled personnel, merchandising, financial, purchasing, real estate, and legal affairs for the entire chain. For management of individual stores, the organization was divided by regions. The southern, southeastern, and northeastern regions each had about seventy stores. Each region was divided into five districts of ten to fifteen stores each. A district director was responsible for supervision and coordination of activities for the ten to fifteen district stores.

Each district was divided into four lines of authority based upon functional specialty. Three of these lines reached into the stores. The produce department manager within each store reported directly to the produce specialist for the division, and the same was true for the meat department manager, who reported directly to the district meat specialist. The meat and produce managers were responsible for all activities associated with the acquisition and sale of perishable products. The store manager's responsibility included the grocery line, front-end departments, and store operations. The store manager was responsible for appearance of personnel, cleanliness, adequate check-out service, and price accuracy. A grocery manager reported to the store manager and maintained inventories and restocked shelves for grocery items. The district merchandising office was responsible for promotional campaigns, advertising circulars, district advertising, and for attracting customers into the stores. The grocery merchandisers were expected to coordinate their activities with each store in the district.

During the recession in 1980–81, business for the C & C chain dropped off in all regions and did not increase with improved economic times in 1983–84. This caused concern among senior executives. They also were aware that other supermarket chains were adopting a trend toward one-stop shopping, which meant the emergence of super stores that included a pharmacy, dry goods, and groceries—almost like a department store. Executives wondered whether C & C should move in this direction and how such changes could be assimilated into the current store organization. However, the most pressing problem was how to improve business with the grocery stores they now had. A consulting team from a major university was hired to investigate store structure and operations.

The consultants visited several stores in each region, talking to about fifty managers and employees. The

Source: Case prepared by Richard L. Daft. From Daft, R. L., & Steers, R. M. (1986). *Organizations: A micro/macro approach.* Glenview, IL: Scott, Foresman.

612

EXHIBIT

1

Organization structure for C & C Grocery Stores, Inc.

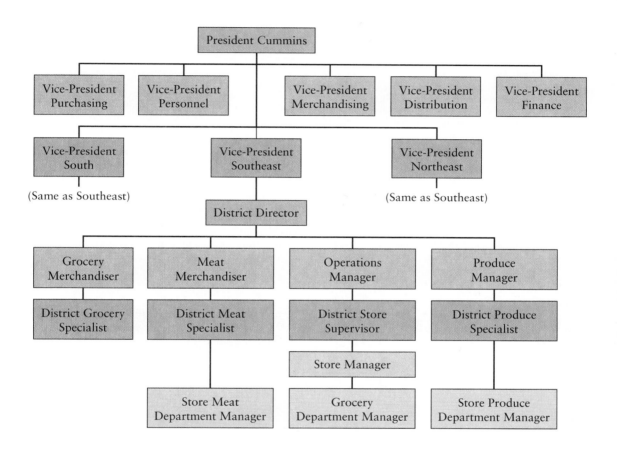

consultants wrote a report that pinpointed four problem areas to be addressed by store executives.

1. The chain is slow to adapt to change. Store layout and structure were the same as had been designed fifteen years ago. Each store did things the same way even though some stores were in low-income areas and other stores in suburban areas. A new grocery management system for ordering and stocking had been developed, but after two years was only partially implemented in the stores.

2. Roles of the district store supervisor and the store manager were causing dissatisfaction. The store managers wanted to learn general management skills for

potential promotion into district or regional management positions. However, their jobs restricted them to operational activities and they learned little about merchandising, meat, and produce. Moreover, district store supervisors used store visits to inspect for cleanliness and adherence to operating standards rather than to train the store manager and help coordinate operations with perishable departments. Close supervision on the operational details had become the focus of operations management rather than development, training, and coordination.

3. Cooperation within stores was low and morale was poor. The informal, friendly atmosphere originally created by Doug Cummins was gone. One example of

this problem occurred when the grocery merchandiser and store manager in a Louisiana store decided to promote Coke and Diet Coke as a loss leader. Thousands of cartons of Coke were brought in for the sale, but the stockroom was not prepared and did not have room. The store manager wanted to use floor area in the meat and produce sections to display Coke cartons, but those managers refused. The produce department manager said that Diet Coke did not help his sales and it was okay with him if there was no promotion at all.

4. Long-term growth and development of the store chain would probably require reevaluation of long-term strategy. The percent of market share going to traditional grocery stores was declining nationwide due to competition from large super stores and convenience stores. In the future, C & C might need to introduce non-food items into the stores for one-stop shopping, and add specialty sections within stores. Some stores could be limited to grocery items, but store location and marketing techniques should take advantage of the grocery emphasis.

To solve the first three problems, the consultants recommended reorganizing the district and the store structure as illustrated in Exhibit 2. Under this reorgani-

zation, the meat, grocery, and produce department managers would all report to the store manager. The store manager would have complete store control and would be responsible for coordination of all store activities. The district supervisor's role would be changed from supervision to training and development. The district supervisor would head a team that included himself and several meat, produce, and merchandise specialists who would visit area stores as a team to provide advice and help for the store managers and other employees. The team would act in a liaison capacity between district specialists and the stores.

The consultants were enthusiastic about the proposed structure. By removing one level of district operational supervision, store managers would have more freedom and responsibility. The district liaison team would establish a cooperative team approach to management that could be adopted within stores. The focus of store responsibility on a single manager would encourage coordination within stores, adaptation to local conditions, and provide a focus of responsibility for store-wide administrative changes.

The consultants also believe that the proposed structure could be expanded to accommodate non-grocery lines if enlarged stores were to be developed in the future. Within each store, a new department manager

EXHIBIT 2   Proposed reorganization of C & C Grocery Stores, Inc.

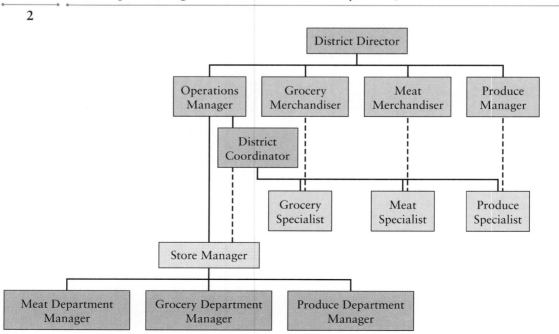

could be added for pharmacy, dry goods, or other major departments. The district team could be expanded to include specialists in these departments who would act as liaison for stores in the district.

■

1. Discuss the environmental components that are currently affecting C & C Grocery Stores.

2. Apply the concepts of environmental uncertainty, resource dependence, and strategy to the C & C case.

3. In Thompson's terms, what technology does a grocery store chain use to deliver service to customers? That is, do the stores exhibit pooled interdependence (mediating technology), sequential interdependence (long-linked technology), or reciprocal interdependence (intensive technology)? What are the implications of this technology for organizational design and coordination mechanisms?

4. Using concepts from Chapter 15, compare and contrast the current organizational structure with that proposed by the consultants.

5. Evaluate the proposed structure in terms of C & C's environment, strategy, and technology. How will various personnel respond to the new structure?

■

REFERENCES

1. This case is based on several sources: Treece, J. B. (1990, April 9). Here comes GM's Saturn. *Business Week,* 56–62; Staff. (1988, December 19). No deliveries at package pickup. *Autoweek,* p. 13; Taylor, A., III. (1988, August 1). Back to the future at Saturn. *Fortune,* 63–69; Fisher, A. B. (1985, November 11). Behind the hype at GM's Saturn. *Fortune,* 34–49.

2. Katz, D., & Kahn, R. L. (1978). *The social psychology of organizations* (2nd ed.). New York: Wiley.

3. This list relies upon Duncan, R. (1972). Characteristics of organization environments and perceived environmental uncertainty. *Administrative Science Quarterly, 17,* 313–327.

4. Coates, L. (1986, July 5). High-flying Jags no longer such a pain to take care of. *The Gazette* (Montreal), p. F–1.

5. See Khandwalla, P. (1981). Properties of competing organizations. In P. C. Nystrom & W. H. Starbuck (Eds.), *Handbook of organization design* (Vol. 1). Oxford: Oxford University Press.

6. Saporito, B. (1989, May 22). Companies that compete best. *Fortune,* 36–44.

7. Kirkpatrick, D. (1990, February 12). Environmentalism: The new crusade. *Fortune,* 44–55.

8. Pfeffer, J., & Salancik, G. R. (1978). *The external control of organizations: A resource dependence perspective.* New York: Harper & Row.

9. Connolly, T., Conlon, E. J., & Deutsch, S. J. (1980). Organizational effectiveness: A multiple-constituency approach. *Academy of Management Review, 5,* 211–217.

10. Fisher, 1985.

11. Duncan, 1972; Just how to measure uncertainty has provoked controversy. See Milliken, F. J. (1987). Three types of perceived uncertainty about the environment: State, effect, and response uncertainty. *Academy of Management Review, 12,* 133–143; Downey, H. K., & Ireland, R. D. (1979). Quantitative versus qualitative: Environmental assessment in organizational studies. *Administrative Science Quarterly, 24,* 630–637. For advances in quantitative measurement, see Snyder, N. H., & Glueck, W. F. (1982). Can environmental volatility be measured objectively? *Academy of Management Journal, 25,* 185–192; Dess, G. G., & Beard, D. W. (1984). Dimensions of organizational task environments. *Administrative Science Quarterly, 29,* 52–73.

12. Duncan, 1972; Tung, R. L. (1979). Dimensions of organizational environments: An exploratory study of their impact on organization structure. *Academy of Management Journal, 22,* 672–693. For contrary evidence, see Downey, H., Hellriegel, D., & Slocum, J. (1975). Environmental uncertainty: The construct and its application. *Administrative Science Quarterly, 20,* 613–629.

13. See also Leblebici, H., & Salancik, G. R. (1981). Effects of environmental uncertainty on information and decision processes in banks. *Administrative Science Quarterly, 26,* 578–596.

14. Pfeffer & Salancik, 1978; Yasai-Ardekani, M. (1989). Effects of environmental scarcity and munificence on the relationship of context to organizational structure. *Academy of Management Journal, 32,* 131–156.

15. Dess & Beard, 1984.

16. Pfeffer & Salancik, 1978.

17. See Yasai-Ardekani, M. (1986). Structural adaptations to environments. *Academy of Management Review, 11,* 9–21; Milliken, F. J. (1990). Perceiving and interpreting environmental change: An examination of college administrators' interpretation of changing demographics. *Academy of Management Journal, 33,* 42–63.

18. For an analog, see Miller, D., Dröge, C., & Toulouse, J. M. (1988). Strategic process and content as mediators between organizational context and structure. *Academy of Management Journal, 31,* 544–569.

19. Miles, R. C., & Snow, C. C. (1978). *Organizational strategy, structure, and process.* New York: McGraw-Hill.

20. Salpukas, A. (1986, May 3). People Express goes for first class. *The Gazette* (Montreal), p. I–14.

21. Labich, K. (1985, November 25). How long can quilting-bee management work? *Fortune,* p. 132.

22. Lawrence, P. R., & Lorsch, J. W. (1967). *Organization and environment: Managing differentiation and integration.* Homewood, IL: Irwin. For a follow-up study, see Lorsch, J. W., & Morse, J. J. (1974). *Organizations and their members: A contingency approach.* New York: Harper & Row.

23. For a review, see Miner, J. B. (1982). *Theories of organizational structure and process.* Chicago: Dryden.

24. Kupfer, A. (1989, December 18). An outsider fires up a railroad. *Fortune,* 133–146, p. 138.

25. Frederickson, J. W. (1986). The strategic decision process and organizational structure. *Academy of Management Review, 11,* 280–297.

26. Romme, A. G. L. (1990). Vertical integration as organizational strategy formation. *Organization Studies, 11,* 239–260.

27. Robey, D. (1986). *Designing organizations* (2nd ed.). Homewood, IL: Irwin.

28. Pfeffer & Salancik, 1978; Hill, C. W. L., & Hoskisson, R. E. (1987). Strategy and structure in the multiproduct firm. *Academy of Management Review, 12,* 331–341; Lubatkin, M., & O'Neill, H. M. (1987). Merger strategies and capital market risk. *Academy of Management Journal, 30,* 665–684.

29. Kanter, R. M. (1989, August). Becoming PALS: Pooling, allying, and linking across companies. *Academy of Management Executive,* 183–193.

30. Burtt, D. N. (1989, July–August). Managing suppliers up to speed. *Harvard Business Review,* 127–135.

31. Schoorman, F. D., Bazerman, M. H., & Atkin, R. S. (1981). Interlocking directorates: A strategy for reducing environmental uncertainty. *Academy of Management Review, 6,* 243–251, p. 244. For a

recent study, see Mizruchi, M. S., & Stearns, L. B. (1988). A longitudinal study of the formation of interlocking directorates. *Administrative Science Quarterly, 33,* 194–210.

32. Schoorman et al., 1981.

33. Rousseau, D. M. (1979). Assessment of technology in organizations: Closed versus open systems approaches. *Academy of Management Review, 4,* 531–542.

34. Child, J. (1972). Organizational structure, environment and performance: The role of strategic choice. *Sociology, 6,* 2–22.

35. Rousseau, 1979; Gillsepie, D. F., & Mileti, D. S. (1977). Technology and the study of organizations: An overview and appraisal. *Academy of Management Review, 2,* 7–16.

36. Perrow, C. A. (1967). A framework for the comparative analysis of organizations. *American Sociological Review, 32,* 194–208.

37. Thompson, J. D. (1967). *Organizations in action.* New York: McGraw-Hill.

38. Thompson, 1967, p. 17.

39. Perrow, C. A. (1970). *Organizational analysis: A sociological view.* Belmont, CA: Wadsworth. For an update on measurement, see Withey, M., Daft, R. L., & Cooper, W. H. (1983). Measures of Perrow's work unit technology: An empirical assessment and a new scale. *Academy of Management Journal, 26,* 45–63.

40. Tehrani, M., Montanari, J. R., & Carson, K. P. (1990). Technology as determinant of organization structure: A meta-analytic review. *Academy of Management Best Papers Proceedings,* 180–184; Gerwin, D. (1981). Relationships between structure and technology. In P. C. Nystrom & W. H. Starbuck (Eds.), *Handbook of organization design* (Vol. 2). Oxford: Oxford University Press.

41. Cheng, J. L. C. (1983). Interdependence and coordination in organizations: A role-system analysis. *Academy of Management Journal, 26,* 156–162.

42. Van de Ven, A. H., Delbecq, A. L., & Koenig, R., Jr. (1976). Determinants of coordination modes within organizations. *American Sociological Review, 41,* 322–338.

43. Woodward, J. (1965). *Industrial organization: Theory and practice.* London: Oxford University Press.

44. Mintzberg, H. (1979). *The structuring of organizations.* Englewood Cliffs, NJ: Prentice-Hall.

45. Marsh, R. M., & Mannari, H. (1981). Technology and size as determinants of the organizational structure of Japanese factories. *Administrative Science Quarterly, 26,* 33–57; Keller, R. T., Slocum, J. W., Jr., & Susman, G. J. (1974). Uncertainty and type of management in continuous process

organizations. *Academy of Management Journal, 17,* 56–68; Zwerman, W. L. (1970). *New perspectives on organizational theory.* Westport, CT: Greenwood.

46. Gerwin, 1981; Singh, J. V. (1986). Technology, size, and organizational structure: A reexamination of the Okayma study data. *Academy of Management Journal, 29,* 800–812.

47. Walton, R. E. (1989). *Up and running: Integrating information technology and the organization.* Boston: Harvard Business School Press.

48. Child, J. (1987). Organizational design for advanced manufacturing technology. In T. D. Wall, C. W. Clegg & N. J. Kemp (Eds.), *The human side of advanced manufacturing technology.* Sussex, England: Wiley.

49. From the Massachusetts Institute of Technology report *Made in America,* as excerpted in *Fortune,* May 22, 1989, p. 94.

50. This table draws in part on Nemetz, P. L., & Fry, L. W. (1988). Flexible manufacturing organizations: Implications for strategy formulation and organization design. *Academy of Management Review, 13,* 627–638; Main, J. (1990, May 21). Manufacturing the right way. *Fortune,* 54–64; Jelinek, M., & Goldhar, J. D. (1986). Maximizing strategic opportunities in implementing advanced manufacturing systems. In D. D. Davis (Ed.), *Managing technological innovation.* San Francisco: Jossey-Bass.

51. Cummings, T. G., & Blumberg, M. (1987). Advanced manufacturing technology and work design. In Wall et al.

52. Nemetz & Fry, 1988; Child, 1987. The following draws upon Child.

53. Wall, T. D., Corbett, J. M., Clegg, C. W., Jackson, P. R., & Martin, R. (1990). Advanced manufacturing technology and work design: Towards a theoretical framework. *Journal of Organizational Behavior, 11,* 201–219; Shaiken, H., Herzenberg, S., & Kuhn S. (1986). The work process under more flexible production. *Industrial Relations, 25,* 167–183.

54. Cummings & Blumberg, 1987; Blumberg, M., & Gerwin, D. (1984). Coping with advanced manufacturing technology. *Journal of Occupational Behaviour, 5,* 113–130.

55. From an unpublished paper by C. A. Voss, cited in Child, 1987.

56. Long, R. J. (1987). *New office information technology: Human and managerial implications.* London: Croom Helm.

57. Long, 1987.

58. Dopson, S., & Stewart, R. (1990). What *is* happening to middle management? *British Journal of Management, 1,* 3–16.

59. Huber, G. P. (1990). A theory of the effects of advanced information technologies on organizational design, intelligence, and decision making. *Academy of Management Review, 15,* 47–71.

60. Long, 1987; Hughes, K. D. (1989). Office automation: A review of the literature. *Relations Industrielles, 44,* 654–679.

61. Long, 1987.

62. Medcof, J. W. (1989). The effect and extent of use of information technology and job of the user upon task characteristics. *Human Relations, 42,* 23–41.

63. Long, 1987.

CHAPTER

17

ORGANIZATIONAL CHANGE, DEVELOPMENT, AND INNOVATION

FABER COLLEGE

Faber College was in trouble. Like many small, private colleges in the late 1980s, it was going broke. Located in the idyllic countryside of New Hampshire, Faber had been founded in 1912 by the wealthy philanthropist G. Roberts Faber. Its primary mission had always been to provide a high-quality undergraduate education in the liberal arts. However, in 1958, Faber had developed a Department of Economics and Business with funding from a local industrialist. With five faculty members, this department was the smallest in the college, and it had traditionally been regarded as the least prestigious and least powerful. However, this didn't inhibit its newfound popularity with students—the department's classes had been overflowing for the last three years. "Which is more than I can say for the other departments," thought Jean Marlow.

Dr. Jean Marlow had been president of Faber College for eighteen years. When she had been a professor of philosophy, and early in her term as president, Faber had been fairly prosperous. Students had been eager to obtain the personalized education offered by Faber at a cost not much greater than that of large, anonymous state universities. However, with few economies of scale and an expansive, old-fashioned campus to maintain, Faber's tuition and room and board expenses had climbed radically in recent years, outstripping those of the state schools. In addition, in the 1980s, students began to shift their interests to more practical, career-oriented courses, and Faber offered few of these. The net result was a sharp decline in enrollments and their accompanying fees. In fact, outside of the Department of Economics and Business, class enrollments had fallen to seminarlike levels. According to the Director of Finance, the writing was on the wall: Faber would be unable to meet its operating expenses within the next two years.

After long consultation with the board of regents, Jean Marlow called a general meeting of all Faber academic and support staff. She outlined Faber's dire economic situation, then made these points:

- Radical cuts would be made in support staff, strictly on a seniority basis.
- All academic departments except Economics and Business would have to reduce staff, beginning with untenured professors. Economics and Business would be expanded and marketed more aggressively to potential students.
- In some departments, tenured professors would be dismissed. She said that the guidelines set down by the American Association of University Professors would be followed, and she invited input from the Faber Faculty Association.
- All salaries would be frozen indefinitely.

The following weeks at Faber were filled with confusion, uncertainty, and conflict. Several excellent faculty members missed classes because of "personal business," which actually consisted of job-hunting trips out of town. Three tenured faculty members who were threatened with dismissal filed lawsuits against Faber. A meeting of the Faculty Association broke up in hostility because opinions were so highly polarized. Learning that several popular untenured professors were to be dismissed, Faber students held a protest march on Jean Marlow's office. Members of the Department of Economics and Business avoided walks across campus, having become the target of open hostility from other faculty members. The chairperson of Economics and Business wondered how he could recruit new faculty members with indefinitely frozen salaries and an atmosphere of tension surrounding the college.

At the height of the crisis, Paul Fellows, a junior faculty member in Economics and Business, learned an interesting fact while on a consulting assignment. A consortium of several small high-technology firms from around Boston was looking for a permanent retreat that it could use for periodic management development and technical refresher programs. Fellows had a brainstorm that Faber could approach the consortium with the following offer: The consortium would pay to renovate and upgrade an unused Faber dormitory, to be called the Faber Executive Center. In return, the consortium would be guaranteed so many days of use a year free of charge. The other days of the year, Faber would be free to rent the Executive Center to other groups for a profit and to develop its own management development programs. In all cases, Faber would provide catering on a for-profit basis. The proceeds from the Executive Center would be used to defray Faber's operating expenses. The Economics and Business chair was very enthusiastic about Fellows' idea and proceeded to sell it to Jean Marlow, who in turn sought approval from the board of regents.

Two years later, the Executive Center had turned out to be fairly successful. Its idyllic location was a change of pace for management development sessions but close enough to be easily accessible to Boston. The modest profits (with a clever tax treatment devised by Fellows) have helped Faber to remain solvent. As a spin-off, student enrollment has increased slightly as parents who visit the Executive Center on business have been exposed to the benefits of Faber.

As this story illustrates, organizations must often come to grips with the need for change. It also shows that the prospect of change can be an unpleasant experience. Why did the Faber administration ignore the trends that led to its problem? Why did various parties react so negatively to Jean Marlow's plans? Could she have proceeded in a more satisfactory manner? Could a consultant help Faber cope with change? What accounted for Paul Fellows' innovative idea? These are the kinds of questions that we will address in this chapter.

First, the concept of organizational change will be discussed, including the *whys* and *whats* of change. Then, the process by which change occurs will be considered, and problems involved in managing change will be examined. Following this, organizational development will be defined, and several development strategies will be explored. Finally, innovation, a special class of organizational change, will be explored.

THE CONCEPT OF ORGANIZATIONAL CHANGE

Common experience indicates that organizations are far from static. Our favorite small restaurant experiences success and expands. We return for a visit to our alma mater and observe a variety of new programs and new buildings. The local Oldsmobile dealer also begins to sell Toyotas. As consumers, we are aware that such changes may have a profound impact on our satisfaction with the product or service offered. By extension, we can also imagine that these changes have a strong impact on the people who work at the restaurant, university, or car dealership. In and of themselves, such changes are neither good nor bad. Rather, it is the way in which the changes are *implemented* and *managed* that is crucial to both customers and members. This is the focus of the present chapter.

In previous chapters we explored a number of specific techniques to improve organizational effectiveness, including job redesign, goal setting, and participative leadership. When such programs are introduced, they surely represent a change from the status quo. But what prompts such changes? And what ensures that they will be effective?

Why Organizations Must Change

All organizations face two basic sources of pressure to change—external sources and internal sources. Although this distinction is somewhat arbitrary, it provides a convenient basis for discussing forces for change.

In Chapter 16 it was pointed out that organizations are open systems that take inputs from the environment, transform some of these inputs, and send them back into the environment as outputs.[1] Most organizations work hard to stabilize their inputs and outputs. For example, a manufacturing firm might use a variety of suppliers to avoid a shortage or raw materials and attempt to turn out quality products to ensure demand. However, there are limits on the extent to which such control over the environment can occur. In this case, environmental changes must be matched by organizational changes if the organization is to remain effective. For example, consider the successful producer of slide rules in 1960. In less than a decade, the slide rule market virtually disappeared with the advent of reasonably priced electronic calculators. If the firm was unable to anticipate this by developing a new product and a market, it surely ceased to exist.

Probably the best recent example of the impact of the external environment in stimulating organizational change can be seen in the increased competitiveness of business. Brought on in part by a more global economy, North American businesses have had to become, as the cliche goes, leaner and meaner. Companies such as IBM and GM laid off thousands of employees in the late 1980s. Many firms did away with layers of middle managers, developing flatter structures so as to be more responsive to competitive demands. Mergers, acquisitions, and joint ventures with foreign firms have become commonplace, as have less adversarial relationships with unions and suppliers.

The story that began the chapter also illustrates the impact of the external environment on organizational change. Faber College was forced to change because its outputs (liberal arts graduates) were in less demand. Therefore, it attracted fewer crucial inputs (students and their fees).

Change can also be provoked by forces in the internal environment of the organization. Low productivity, conflict, strikes, sabotage, and high absenteeism and turnover are some of the factors that signal to management that change is necessary. Very often, internal forces for change occur in response to organizational changes that are designed to deal with the external environment. Thus, many mergers and acquisitions that were designed to bolster the competitiveness of an organization have been followed by cultural conflict between the merged parties. This conflict often stimulates further changes that were not anticipated at the time of the merger. At Faber College, severe internal disruptions occurred when Jean Marlow announced her solution to the enrollment problem. These internal forces suggested that additional changes would be necessary at Faber.

Two final points about the forces for change should be emphasized. First, the internal and external environments of various organizations will be more or less dynamic (a point made in Chapter 16 with regard to the external environment). In responding to this, organizations will therefore differ in the amount of change they should exhibit (Exhibit 17–1). As shown, organizations in a dynamic environment must generally exhibit more change to be effective than those operating in a more stable environment. Second, change in and of itself is not a good thing, and organizations can exhibit too much change as well as too little (Exhibit 17–1). The company that is in constant flux fails to establish the regular patterns of behavior that are necessary for effectiveness.

What Organizations Can Change

In theory, organizations can change just about any aspect of their operations they wish. Since change is a broad concept, it is useful to identify several specific domains in which modifications can occur. Of course, the choice of *what* to change depends upon a correct analysis of the internal and external forces that signal that change is necessary:[2]

- *Goals and strategies.* Organizations frequently change their goals and the strategies used to reach these goals. Expansion, the introduction of new products, and the pursuit of new markets represent such changes. At Faber College, the administration decided to expand the Economics and Business department to better tap the student market. Also, it developed the Executive Center to tap the management development market.
- *Technology.* Technological changes can vary from minor to major. The introduction of on-line computer access for bank tellers is a fairly minor change. Moving from a rigid assembly line to flexible manufacturing is a major change.
- *Job design.* Individual groups of jobs can be redesigned to offer more or less variety, autonomy, identity, significance, and feedback, as discussed in Chapter 7.
- *Structure.* Organizations can be modified from a functional to a product form or vice versa. Formalization and centralization can be manipulated, as can tallness and spans of control. Structural changes also include modifications in rules, policies, and procedures.
- *People.* The membership of an organization can be changed in two senses. First, the actual *content* of the membership can be changed through a process of hiring and firing. This is often done to introduce "new blood."

EXHIBIT

17–1

Relationships among environmental change, organizational change, and organizational effectiveness.

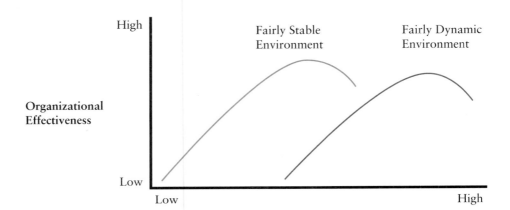

Second, the existing membership can be changed in terms of skills and attitudes by various training and development methods.

Two important points should be made abut the various areas in which change can be introduced. First, a change in one area very often calls for changes in others. Failure to recognize this systemic nature of change can lead to severe problems. For example, consider the functionally organized East Coast chemical firm that decides to expand its operations to the West Coast. To be effective, this goal and strategy change might require some major structural changes, including a more geographic form and decentralization of decision-making power.

Second, changes in goals, strategies, technology, structure, and job design almost always require that serious attention be given to people changes. As much as possible, necessary skills and favorable attitudes should be fostered *before* these changes are introduced. For example, although providing bank employees with a revised computer system is a fairly minor technological change, it might provoke anxiety on the part of those whose jobs are affected. Adequate technical training and clear, open communication about the change can do much to alleviate this anxiety. At Faber College, the administration decided on a change in goals and strategies without giving enough attention to people changes. This aroused anxiety, anger, and conflict.

The Change Process

By definition, change involves a sequence of organizational events or a psychological process that occurs over time. The distinguished psychologist Kurt Lewin has suggested that this sequence or process involves three basic stages—unfreezing, changing, and refreezing.[3]

Unfreezing Unfreezing occurs when recognition exists that some current state of affairs is inadequate. This might involve the realization that the present structure, task design, or technology is ineffective or that member skills or attitudes are inappropriate. *Crises* are especially likely to stimulate unfreezing. A dramatic drop in sales, a big lawsuit, and an unexpected strike are examples of such crises. At Faber College, the enrollment crisis unfroze the administration. In the past, an economic crisis unfroze the United Auto Workers' traditional attitudes toward union-company relations, and wage cutbacks were accepted to keep plants open. Of course, unfreezing can also occur without crisis. Regular attitude surveys and accounting data are often used to anticipate problems and initiate change before crises are reached.

Change Change occurs when some program or plan is implemented to move the organization and/or its members to a more adequate state. The terms *program* and *plan* are used rather loosely here, since some change efforts reveal inadequate planning. Change efforts can range from minor to major. A simple skills training program and a revised hiring procedure constitute fairly minor changes in which few organizational members are involved. Conversely, major changes that involve many members might include extensive job enrichment, radical restructuring, or serious attempts at extending participation in decision making.

Refreezing   When changes occur, the newly developed behaviors, attitudes, or structures must be subjected to **refreezing** to become an enduring part of the organizational system. At this point, the effectiveness of the change can be examined, and the desirability of extending the change further can be considered.

ISSUES IN THE CHANGE PROCESS

The simple sketch of the change process presented in the preceding section ignores several important issues that must be confronted during the process. These issues represent problems that must be overcome if the process is to be effective. Exhibit 17–2 illustrates the relationship between the stages of change and these problems.

Diagnosis

Accurate organizational diagnosis serves two important functions. First, **diagnosis** can provide information that contributes to unfreezing by showing that a problem exists. Second, once unfreezing occurs, further diagnosis can clarify the problem and suggest just what changes should be implemented. It is one thing to feel that "hospital morale has fallen drastically" but quite another to be sure that this is true and to decide what to do about it. These are critical decision points in the change process, and our discussion of decision making in Chapter 12 suggests the potential for many errors. This is especially true if unfreezing has been stimulated by a crisis. For instance, at Faber College the diagnosis of economic problems was correct, but the initial strategy that was used to correct them was hotly disputed.

Diagnosis can take a variety of forms and be performed by a variety of individuals. Relatively routine problems might be handled through existing channels. For example, suppose the director of a hospital laboratory has reason to believe

EXHIBIT

17–2

The change process and change problems.

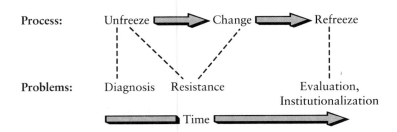

that many of his lab technicians do not possess adequate technical skills. In conjunction with the hospital personnel manager, the director might arrange for a formal test of these skills. A training program could be devised to correct inadequacies, and a more stringent selection program could be established to hire better personnel. At Faber College, a routine mechanism (the Board of Regents) was used to diagnose a very nonroutine problem.

For more complex, nonroutine problems, there is considerable merit in seeking out the diagnostic skills of a change agent. **Change agents** are experts in the application of behavioral science knowledge to organizational diagnosis and change. Some large firms have in-house change agents who are available for consultation. In other cases, outside consultants might be brought in. In any event, the change agent brings an independent, objective perspective to the diagnosis while working with the people who are about to undergo change.

Diagnostic information can be obtained through a combination of observations, interviews, questionnaires, and the scrutiny of records. As the next section will show, there is usually considerable merit in using questionnaires and interviews to involve the intended targets of change in the diagnostic process. The next section will also show why the change agent must be perceived as *trustworthy* by his or her clients.

The importance of careful diagnosis cannot be overemphasized. Properly done, diagnosis clarifies the problem, suggests *what* should be changed, and suggests the proper *strategy* for implementing change without resistance.[4]

Resistance

As the saying goes, people are creatures of habit, and change is frequently resisted by those at whom it is targeted. More precisely, both unfreezing and change may be resisted. At the unfreezing stage, defense mechanisms (Chapter 14) might be activated to deny or rationalize the signals that change is needed. Even if there is agreement that change is necessary, any specific plan for change might be resisted. This has been commonplace in recent years in U.S. national politics. Although Congress has recognized the need to enhance federal revenues or reduce spending to reduce the budget deficit, many specific plans to do one or both have encountered strong resistance. The faculty, staff, and students were doubtless aware of Faber College's financial troubles. Despite this, specific plans for change were opposed.

Resistance to change occurs when people either overtly or covertly fail to support the change effort. Why does such failure of support occur? Several common reasons include the following:[5]

- *Politics and self-interest.* People might feel that they personally will lose status or power with the advent of the change.
- *Low individual tolerance for change.* Predispositions in personality might make some people uncomfortable with changes in established routines.
- *Misunderstanding.* The reason for the change or the exact course that the change will take might be misunderstood.

- *Lack of trust.* People might clearly understand the arguments being made for change but not trust the motives of those proposing the change.
- *Different assessments of the situation.* The targets of change might sincerely feel that the situation does not warrant the proposed change and that the advocates of change have misread the situation.
- *A resistant organizational culture.* Some organizational cultures have especially stressed and rewarded stability and tradition. Advocates of change in such cultures are viewed as misguided deviants or aberrant outsiders. (When deregulation forced massive changes at AT&T, the resistant traditionalists were labeled "bellheads" by the new guard!)[6]

A common thread underlying all of these reasons for resistance is the implicit calculation that the costs of change will outweigh the benefits. But how can the scale be tipped to counter resistance? In large part, this depends on the exact reason for resistance.[7]

Low tolerance for change is mainly an individual matter, and it can often be overcome with supportive, patient supervision.

If politics and self-interest are at the root of resistance, it might be possible to co-opt the reluctant by giving them a special, desirable role in the change process or by negotiating special incentives for change. For example, consider office computing. Many heads of information services resisted the proliferation of personal computers, feeling that this change would reduce their power as departments moved away from dependence on the mainframe. Some organizations countered this resistance by giving information services control over the purchase, maintenance, and networking of personal computers, providing an incentive for change.

If misunderstanding, lack of trust, or different assessments are provoking resistance, good communication can pay off. Contemporary organizations are learning that obsessive secrecy about strategy and competition can have more internal costs than external benefits. It is particularly critical that *lower-level managers* understand the diagnosis underlying intended change and the details of the change so that they can convey this information to employees accurately. Springing "secret" changes on employees, especially when these changes involve matters such as work force reduction, is sure to provoke resistance. We saw this in the Faber College example.

Resistance to change can often be reduced by involving the people who are the targets of change in the change process (a point that was essentially ignored by the Faber College administration).[8] This is especially appropriate when there is adequate time for participation, when true commitment ("ownership") to the change is critical, and when the people who will be affected by the change have unique knowledge to offer. Some of the most striking examples of using participation to overcome potential resistance have involved changes in pay systems. This is ironic because the design of pay systems has traditionally been considered by management as inappropriate for participation. In one study, workers who exhibited high absenteeism helped to design a cash bonus plan to reward good attendance. When implemented, the plan led to significant reductions in absence, a goal that would traditionally provoke resistance.[9]

Finally, transformational leaders (Chapter 10) are particularly adept at overcoming resistance to change. One way they accomplish this is by "striking while the iron is hot," that is, by being especially sensitive to when followers are *ready* for change. For example, when Lee Iacocca became president of Chrysler, the situation was so bad that employees knew that change would have to occur. The other way is to unfreeze current thinking by installing practices that constantly examine and question the status quo. One research study of CEOs who were transformational leaders noted the following unfreezing practices:[10]

- An atmosphere is established in which dissent is not only tolerated but encouraged. Proposals and ideas are given tough objective reviews, and disagreement is not viewed as disloyalty.
- The environment is scanned for objective information about the organization's true performance. This might involve putting lots of outsiders on the board of directors or sending technical types out to meet customers.
- Organizational members are sent to other organizations and even other countries to see how things are done elsewhere.
- The organization compares itself along a wide range of criteria *against the competition,* rather than simply comparing its performance against last year's. This avoids complacency.

Transformational leaders are skilled at using the new ideas that stem from these practices to create a revised vision for followers about what the organization can do or be. Often, a radically reshaped culture is the result. In the process, as suggested in Chapter 10, they are good at inspiring trust and encouraging followers to subordinate their individual self-interests for the good of the organization. This is their particular strength in overcoming resistance.

Evaluation and Institutionalization

It seems only reasonable to evaluate effected changes to determine whether they accomplished what they were supposed to and whether that accomplishment is now considered adequate. Obviously, objective goals such as return on investment or market share might be easiest and most likely to be evaluated. Thus, Faber College knew that its new Management Center was at least moderately successful in terms of its impact on its balance sheet. Of course, organizational politics can intrude to cloud even the most objective evaluation.

Organizations are notorious for doing a weak job of evaluating "soft" change programs that involve skills, attitudes, and values. However, it is possible to do a thorough evaluation by considering a range of variables:

- Reactions—Did participants like the change program?
- Learning—What was acquired in the program?
- Behavior—What changes in job behavior occurred?
- Outcomes—What changes in productivity, absence, etc., occurred?[11]

To some extent, reactions measure resistance, learning reflects change, and behavior reflects successful refreezing. Outcomes indicate whether refreezing is useful for the organization. Unfortunately, many evaluations of change efforts never go beyond the measurement of reactions. Again, part of the reason for this may be political. The members of the organization who propose the change effort fear reprisal if failure occurs.

If the outcome of change is evaluated favorably, the organization will wish to institutionalize that change. This means that the change becomes a permanent part of the organizational system, a social fact that persists over time despite possible turnover by the members who originally experienced the change.[12]

Logic suggests that it should be fairly easy to institutionalize a change that has been deemed successful. However, we noted that many change efforts go un-evaluated or are only weakly evaluated, and without hard proof of success it is very easy for institutionalization to be rejected by disaffected parties. This is a special problem for extensive, broad-based change programs that call for a large amount of commitment from a variety of parties (e.g., extensive participation, job enrichment, or work restructuring). It is one thing to institutionalize a simple training program but quite another to do the same for complex interventions that can be judged from a variety of perspectives.

Studies of more complex change efforts indicate that a number of factors can inhibit institutionalization. For example, promised extrinsic rewards (such as pay bonuses) might not be developed to accompany changes. Similarly, initial changes might provide intrinsic rewards that create higher expectations that cannot be fulfilled. Institutionalization might also be damaged if new hires are not carefully socialized to understand the unique environment of the changed organization. As turnover occurs naturally, the change effort might backslide. In a similar vein, key management supporters of the change effort might resign or be transferred. Finally, environmental pressures such as decreased sales or profits can cause management to regress to more familiar behaviors and abandon change efforts.[13]

It stands to reason that many of the problems of evaluation and institutionalization can be overcome by careful planning and goal setting during the diagnostic stage. In fact, *planning* is a key issue in any change effort. Let's now examine organizational development, a means of effecting planned change.

ORGANIZATIONAL DEVELOPMENT: PLANNED CHANGE, ETC., ETC.

The heading of this section is meant to convey some of the difficulty that one encounters in trying to precisely define organizational development (OD). There is a message to be gained from this difficulty. OD is a continuously changing art and science that uses a wide variety of specific techniques and strategies to change organizations. As such, its character is difficult to summarize in a sentence. While all OD seeks to change organizations, not all change efforts can be classed as OD. With this preamble, I present a definition that seems to synthesize current thinking.[14]

Organizational development (OD) is a planned, ongoing effort to change organizations to be more effective and more human. It uses the knowledge of behavioral science to foster a culture of organizational self-examination and readiness for change. A strong emphasis is placed on interpersonal and group processes.

The fact that OD is *planned* distinguishes it from the haphazard, accidental, or routine changes that occur in all organizations. OD efforts tend to be *ongoing* in at least two senses. First, many OD programs extend over a long period of time, involving several distinct phases of activities. Second, if OD becomes institutionalized, continual reexamination and readiness for further change become permanent parts of the culture. In trying to make organizations more *effective* and more *human,* OD gives recognition to the critical link between personal processes such as leadership, decision making, and communication and organizational outcomes such as productivity and efficiency. The fact that OD uses *behavioral science knowledge* distinguishes it from other change strategies that rely solely upon principles of accounting, finance, or engineering. However, an OD intervention may also incorporate these principles. OD seeks to modify *cultural norms and roles* so that the organization remains self-conscious and prepared for adaptation. Finally, a focus on *interpersonal* and *group* processes recognizes that all organizational change affects members and is implemented with their cooperation.

To summarize the above, we can say that OD recognizes that systematic attitude change must accompany changes in behavior, whether these behavior changes are required by revisions in tasks, work procedures, organizational structure, or business strategies.

A few words should be said about the values and assumptions of change agents who practice OD. Traditionally, these values and assumptions have been decidedly humanistic and democratic. Thus, self-actualization, trust, cooperation, and the open expression of feelings among all organizational members have been viewed as desirable.[15] In recent years, OD practitioners have also begun to show a more active concern with organizational effectiveness and with using development practices to further the strategy of the organization. This joint concern with both people and performance has thus become the credo of many contemporary OD change agents. The focus has shifted from simple humanistic advocacy to generating data or alternatives that allow organizational members to make informed choices.[16]

SOME SPECIFIC ORGANIZATIONAL DEVELOPMENT STRATEGIES

The organization that seeks to "develop itself" has recourse to a wide variety of specific techniques, and many have been used in combination. Some of these techniques were discussed earlier in the book. For example, work restructuring through systematic job enrichment and Management by Objectives (Chapter 7) are usually classed as OD efforts. In this section we will discuss four additional

OD methods that illustrate the diversity of the practice. *Team building* illustrates how work teams can be fine-tuned to work well together. *Quality circles* reveal how small groups can be used to improve organizational effectiveness. *Survey feedback* shows how OD can be conceived of as an ongoing applied research effort. Finally, *Grid OD* illustrates a structured, long-range approach to system-wide change and development.

Team Building

Team building attempts to increase the effectiveness of work teams by concentrating on interpersonal processes, goal clarification, and role clarification.[17] (What is our team trying to accomplish, and who is responsible for what?) As such, it could facilitate communication and coordination. The term *team* can refer to intact work groups, special task forces, new work units, or people from various parts of an organization who must work together to achieve a common goal.

Team building usually begins with a diagnostic session, often held away from the workplace, in which the team explores its current level of functioning. The team might use several sources of data to accomplish its diagnosis. Some data might be generated through sensitivity training and open-ended discussion sessions. In addition, "hard" data such as attitude survey results and production figures might be used. The goal at this stage is to paint a picture of the current strengths and weaknesses of the team. The ideal outcome of the diagnostic session is a list of needed changes to improve team functioning. Subsequent team-building sessions usually have a decidedly task-oriented slant—How can we actually implement the changes indicated by the diagnosis? Problem solving by subgroups might be used at this stage. Between the diagnostic and follow-up sessions, the change agent might hold confidential interviews with team members to anticipate implementation problems. Throughout, the change agent acts as a catalyst and resource person.

The city government of Tacoma, Washington, assisted by external consultants, has made extensive use of team building to improve communications within and between existing departments.[18] Because the work of the personnel department affected that of all other departments, any errors made by personnel had a high degree of impact and visibility. As a result, personnel had become the scapegoat of the system. Initial team-building sessions concentrated on having department members identify and work out internal communication problems. In addition, clients of the personnel department from other city departments were invited to day-long sessions in which they aired their complaints to personnel and worked out solutions. One result of this was a system by which each client department was assigned to a particular member of the personnel department. This member then served as an ongoing "contact person" to expedite requests from clients.

Tacoma also used team building to improve communication among the top management of its fire department. This was a particular problem because the battalion chiefs were geographically decentralized in various fire stations and because they worked shifts. As a result of team building, it was decided to hold bimonthly meetings of all management staff to facilitate ongoing communication. Those who were off duty when meetings were held were paid overtime to attend.

When team building is used to develop *new* work teams, the preliminary diagnostic session might involve attempts to clarify expected role relationships and additional training to build trust among team members. In subsequent sessions the expected task environment might be simulated with role-playing exercises. One company used this integrated approach to develop the management team of a new plant.[19] In the simulation portion of the development, typical problems encountered in opening a new plant were presented to team members via hypothetical in-basket memos and telephone calls. In role-playing the solutions to these problems, they reached agreement about how they would have to work together on the job and gained a clear understanding of each other's competencies. Plant startups were always problem-laden, but this was the smoothest in the history of the company.

Ideally, team building is a continuing process that involves regular diagnostic sessions and further development exercises as needed. This permits the team to anticipate new problems and to avoid the tendency to regress to less effective predevelopment habits.

Quality Circles

Of all the techniques discussed in this chapter, quality circles represent the most recent addition to the North American OD scene. Also, they are the most common example of the importation of "Japanese management" techniques to our shores. Quality circles began in Japan as part of an effort to rebuild the country's industrial base following World War II. At that time, Japan was widely known as a producer of shoddy, slipshod merchandise, and the Japanese managers were eager to change this reputation. American-developed statistical quality control techniques were embraced with great enthusiasm, and a philosophy gradually developed that all workers were responsible for quality control. Small groups of workers were formed into quality circles (or "quality control circles") throughout an organization and taught the statistical principles of quality control. They were then encouraged to detect and suggest solutions to quality problems in their own domains. This unusual mixture of participative management and industrial engineering has become something of a national movement in Japan.[20]

Faced with the reality of superbly constructed Hondas, Sonys, and Nikons and with the phenomenal productivity growth of Japan, North American firms have shown great interest in the quality circle concept. The North American version of **quality circles** might be described as follows:

> Small groups of people who perform similar work meet voluntarily on a regular basis, usually once a week, to analyze work-related problems and propose solutions to them. QC's are usually led by the supervisor or manager of the work unit in which they are located. Members receive training in problem solving, quality control and group dynamics to help them function well.[21]

As you can see, there are elements of both participative management and team building in the quality circle concept. Circles are encouraged to find problems, devise solutions, and submit solutions for management approval. Despite their name, quality circles have gone well beyond quality problems and also focused on safety, working conditions, productivity, and cost-cutting. For example, quality circles have often proposed how to reduce scrap costs and raw materials waste in manufacturing. To build commitment to the quality circle concept and avoid overt resistance, most programs are voluntary, but the circles typically meet on company time. Despite voluntary membership, quality circles are permanent and ongoing. Usually, a steering committee made up of managers, workers, union representatives, and supervisors who lead circles oversees the program. Individuals are appointed to act as facilitators between the steering committee and the quality circles.[22]

Training and management support are critical to the success of quality circles. Leaders of circles require thorough training in leading group discussions. Leaders and members need a thorough grasp of quality control concepts, problem-analysis techniques, and team-building principles. Managers need a firm grounding in the philosophy of quality circles and need to be committed to seriously considering the suggestions that emanate from quality circles. Establishing quality circles requires substantial effort, and they actually represent something of a structural modification to the organization. Thus, there is much pressure for them to be

Quality circle training at a Pontiac plant. (Gerd Ludwig/ Woodfin Camp & Associates)

successful, and nothing can dampen enthusiasm more than the rejection of good ideas.

One organization that reports considerable success with quality circles is Wedgwood, the esteemed English producer of fine china. Their experience shows that even traditional craftsmanship can be improved with new ideas. Circles have developed good ideas to avoid waste and spoilage. For example, one circle designed a new cart that reduced the risk of unfired pottery knocking together and breaking. Another designed a new brush for painting plates and worked with a brush supplier to have it produced. Yet another circle worked with the local bus company to improve service to the Wedgwood factory, effectively reducing commuting problems for employees.[23]

Later we will review the evidence on the effectiveness of quality circles. For now, it is worth noting that some observers have questioned the general application of quality circles in Western cultures. Some have argued that the Japanese traditions of lifetime employment, company unions, paternalism, and concern with social harmony provide a special environment for the use of quality circles. Western cultures, with their emphasis on individualism and a more adversarial relationship between management and labor, might not provide such a conducive background for quality circles.[24]

Survey Feedback

In bare-bones form, **survey feedback** involves collecting data from organizational members and feeding this data back to them in a series of meetings in which the data is explored and discussed. [25] The purpose of the meetings is to suggest or formulate changes that are suggested by the data. In some respects, survey feedback is similar to team building. However, survey feedback places more emphasis on the collection of valid data and less emphasis on the interpersonal processes of specific work teams. Rather, it tends to focus on the relationship between organizational members and the larger organization.

As its name implies, survey feedback's basic data generally consists of either interviews or questionnaires completed by organizational members. Before this data is collected, a number of critical decisions must be made by the change agent and organizational management. First, who should participate in the survey? Sometimes, especially in large organizations, the survey could be restricted to particular departments, jobs, or organizational levels where problems exist. However, most survey feedback efforts attempt to cover the entire organization. This approach recognizes the systemic nature of organizations and permits a comparison of survey results across various subunits.

Second, should questionnaires or interviews be used to gather data? The key issues here are coverage and cost. It is generally conceded that *all* members of a target group should be surveyed. This procedure builds trust and confidence in survey results. If the number of members is small, the change agent could conduct structured interviews with each person. Otherwise, cost considerations dictate the use of a questionnaire. In practice, this is the most typical data-gathering approach.

Finally, what questions should the survey ask? Two approaches are available. Some change agents use prepackaged, standardized surveys such as the University of Michigan Survey of Organizations.[26] This questionnaire covers areas such as communication and decision-making practices and employee satisfaction. Such questionnaires are usually carefully constructed and permit comparisons with other organizations in which the survey has been conducted. However, there is a real danger that prepackaged surveys might neglect critical areas for specific consideration. In and of itself, this is bad enough, but the apparent lack of relevance of a packaged survey can reduce the care that members take in completing it or reduce trust in the final results. For these reasons, many change agents choose to devise their own custom-tailored surveys. They might begin with a series of interviews to determine potential problem areas. In some cases, a task force of organizational members might also be enlisted to help develop the final version of the survey. Again, the goal is to build relevance, trust, and involvement in the people who will be surveyed. This should guarantee valid data. To increase the involvement of managerial personnel, they might be asked to predict the results of the survey.

Feedback seems to be most effective when it is presented to natural working units in face-to-face meetings. This method rules out presenting only written feedback or feedback that covers only the organization as a whole. In a manufacturing firm, a natural working unit might consist of a department such as production or marketing. In a school district, such units might consist of individual schools. Many change agents prefer that the manager of the working unit conduct the feedback meeting. This demonstrates management commitment and acceptance of the data. The change agent attends such meetings and helps facilitate discussion of the data and plans for change.

An example of survey feedback occurred in a school district. The purpose of the exercise was to stimulate changes that would promote more effective problem solving by the faculty members of individual schools. Teachers completed questionnaires concerning their attitudes toward factors such as administrative practices, workload, students, facilities, and relationships with colleagues. In feedback sessions, teachers in individual schools were able to compare their average responses on individual survey questions with those of teachers in the district as a whole. In addition, the responses were grouped into categories and presented as shown in Exhibit 17–3, which compares the responses of "School Z" with those of the district overall. It was hoped that observed discrepancies would reveal strengths and weaknesses and stimulate the desire for appropriate changes. Although this occurred in certain schools, others were unable or unwilling to institutionalize mechanisms for improved problem solving.[27]

In concluding, let's have a look at IBM's survey feedback program in the You Be the Manager feature.

EXHIBIT

17–3

Survey feedback to one school in a school district.

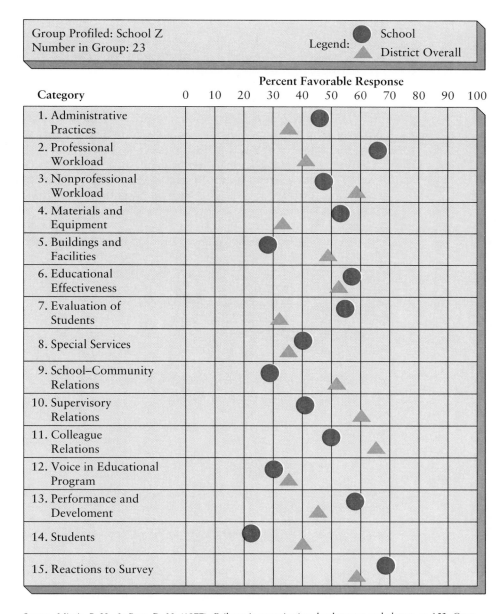

| Group Profiled: School Z | Legend: ● School |
| Number in Group: 23 | ▲ District Overall |

Percent Favorable Response

Category	0	10	20	30	40	50	60	70	80	90	100
1. Administrative Practices				▲	●						
2. Professional Workload					▲			●			
3. Nonprofessional Workload					●		▲				
4. Materials and Equipment				▲		●					
5. Buildings and Facilities			●			▲					
6. Educational Effectiveness						● ▲					
7. Evaluation of Students				▲		●					
8. Special Services				▲	●						
9. School–Community Relations			●			▲					
10. Supervisory Relations				●			▲				
11. Colleague Relations					●		▲				
12. Voice in Educational Program			● ▲								
13. Performance and Develoment				▲		●					
14. Students		●		▲							
15. Reactions to Survey					▲	●					

Source: Mirvis, P. H., & Berg, D. N. (1977). *Failures in organization development and change.* p. 152. Copyright © 1977, by John Wiley and Sons, Inc.

YOU BE THE MANAGER

Employee Surveys at IBM

Like many successful organizations, the IBM Corporation has long used employee surveys to analyze the opinions of its work force as a means of planning and effecting organizational change. Such surveys are particularly important for a firm such as IBM because it employs a diverse global work force. Zeroing in on employees' views and values almost necessitates a formal mechanism such as a periodic survey. However, conventional paper-and-pencil surveys have their limitations when it comes to measuring the opinions of 383,000 employees scattered literally around the globe. The time required to send out and receive back questionnaires is substantial, as is the time required to analyze and feed back the results. These delays can reduce the positive impact of the survey process. Also, the mass administration of surveys might conflict with pressing business for some employees or miss those who are traveling on business at the time. In addition, custom-tailoring some survey questions to special employee groups or local conditions can be extremely complex owing to both size and geographical dispersion.

IBM management was convinced that it could use its own technological base to improve its survey feedback program and avoid some of these problems. What do *you* think?

1. How can IBM use advanced technology to improve its employee survey?
2. What are some advantages of the change that you suggest?

To find out what IBM did, please consult The Manager's Notebook at the end of the chapter.

Source: Adapted from Read, W. H. (1991, January). Gathering opinion on-line. *HRMagazine*, 51–53.

Grid Organization Development

Grid Organization Development is a comprehensive, long-term effort directed toward changing the total organization. It was developed by Robert Blake and Jane Mouton of Scientific Methods, Incorporated.[28] The basic premise of **Grid**

OD is that organizational excellence can be achieved through a *joint* concern with high performance and the maintenance of a psychologically healthy working climate. Ignoring either of these factors at the expense of the other will not promote true excellence.

Grid OD uses a building-block approach that consists of six phases. A large organization might take several years to pass through these phases. Blake and Mouton feel that poor communication and inadequate planning are responsible for most failures to achieve excellence. Thus, the first three Grid phases are oriented toward improving communication, while the latter three are designed to foster careful planning and goal setting:

1. *Grid seminar.* This is a very structured training session designed to encourage individual organizational members to analyze their own management styles. The behavioral theory underlying Grid OD (discussed below) is taught. Top managers usually attend the Grid seminar first.

2. *Teamwork development.* Natural work teams attend seminars designed to extend Grid concepts to improve team functioning. Again, this effort begins at the top and is highly structured.

3. *Intergroup development.* Work teams that must interact with each other attend seminars stressing conflict reduction and improved coordination.

4. *Development of an ideal strategic model.* Top management meets to evaluate the current state of the organization and develop a model for improvement. Key issues include policy, structure, and financial objectives.

5. *Planning and implementation of the ideal model.* Task forces of organizational members with relevant skills are formed to plan and implement the model developed by top executives. Management science techniques are used, and outside experts are brought in if necessary.

6. *Systematic critique.* The results of previous changes are evaluated by using quantitative data, internal evaluation teams, and external independent evaluators. Plans for further OD efforts are based on this critique.

Since the initial Grid Seminar provides the conceptual basis for the whole of Grid OD, it is worth a closer look. These five-day seminars are conducted by line managers in the organization who have received previous training in Grid theory. Blake and Mouton feel that line managers are best at this job because their understanding of day-to-day organizational problems provides them with a high degree of credibility as trainers. In fact, the entire Grid program is conducted with in-house personnel, and the role of external change agents is downplayed. A major purpose of the Grid Seminar is to teach trainees the principles of the **Managerial Grid®** shown in Exhibit 17–4. According to the Grid, leadership is composed of two basic dimensions—concern for production and concern for people. Observe the extreme styles portrayed on the Grid: The 1,1 leader is a "do nothing" person who should exert little influence on subordinates. The 1,9 leader might be portrayed as a "country club" leader who is concerned primarily with easy interpersonal relations. The 9,1 leader is something of a "taskmaster." Finally, the 9,9 leader exhibits high concern for *both* interpersonal relations and the demands of the task. He or she is interested in maintaining high productivity while fostering an open, candid, trusting relationship with subordinates. Grid OD seeks to diffuse a 9,9 philosophy throughout the organization.

Several potential problems of Grid OD are worth noting. First, its prepackaged nature might not suit the development needs of every organization. Second, "concern for production" is very similar to initiating structure, while "concern for people" is very similar to consideration. From Chapter 10, you will recall that being high on both of these dimensions might not always be the optimal leadership strategy. Finally, a large number of changes obviously occur when the full Grid program is implemented. In evaluating the success of Grid OD, it is often

EXHIBIT

17–4

The Managerial Grid.®

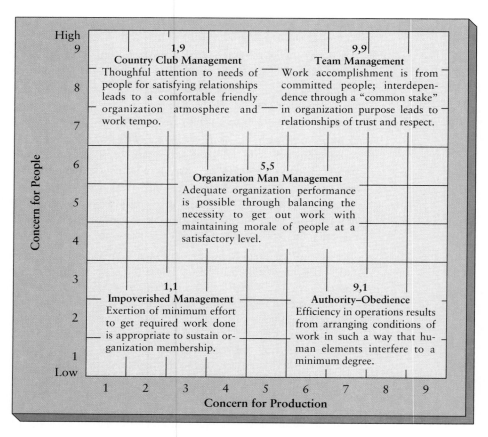

Source: Blake, R. R., & Mouton, J. S. Leadership Dilemmas—Grid Solutions. Copyright © 1985 by Scientific Methods, Inc. Reproduced by permission.

very difficult to determine just which elements of the Grid program were responsible for any favorable outcomes.

DOES ORGANIZATIONAL DEVELOPMENT WORK?

Does it work? That is, do the benefits of OD outweigh the heavy investment of time, effort, and money? The answer to this question is important. OD has been extended from business and industry into more diverse settings, including international relations, domestic politics, health care delivery, schools, universities, and the military.[29] Is such extension justified, or is it an example of faddishness?

At the outset, it should be reemphasized that most OD efforts are *not* carefully evaluated. Political factors and budget limitations might be prime culprits, but the situation is not helped by some OD practitioners who argue that certain OD goals (e.g., making the organization more human) are incompatible with impersonal, scientifically rigorous evaluation.

At the very broadest level, two large-scale reviews of a wide variety of OD techniques (including those discussed in this chapter and job redesign, MBO, and goal setting from Chapter 7) reached the following conclusions:[30]

- Most OD techniques have a positive impact on productivity, job satisfaction, or other work attitudes.
- OD seems to work better for supervisors or managers than for blue-collar workers.
- Changes that use more than one technique seem to have more impact.
- There are great differences across sites in the success of OD interventions.

The last finding is probably due to differences in the skill and seriousness with which OD projects have been undertaken in various organizations.

Turning specifically to the OD techniques covered here, the evidence regarding quality circles can properly be described as mixed.[31] While some studies report clear-cut improvements in factors such as cost reduction or improved employee attitudes, other studies reveal no improvements. One particularly careful study showed initial improvements followed by a return to pre-circle levels.[32] These results are in line with the fact that many firms have instituted and then abandoned quality circles.

Exhibit 17–5, on page 640, illustrates the degree of impact of team building, survey feedback, Grid OD, and eclectic approaches that use a combination of several OD techniques.[33] Process variables include changes in trust, self-awareness, decision making, and leadership. Outcome variables are consequences of process variables such as performance, job satisfaction, profits, and efficiency. As you can see, the OD techniques have a fairly strong impact on both process and outcome variables.

Exhibit 17–6, on page 641, presents similar impact results for a number of specific outcome variables, including work force behavior, monetary criteria, and

EXHIBIT

17–5

Positive changes in outcome and process variables for various organizational development interventions.

Dominant Intervention	Percent Change	
	Process Variables	Outcome Variables
Eclectic approach	52% (5)	52% (5)
Team building	45% (14)	53% (3)
Managerial Grid	43% (4)	68% (3)
Survey feedback	48% (4)	53% (3)

Note: Numbers of studies are in parentheses.

Source: From Porras, J. I., & Berg, P. O. (1978, April). The impact of organization development, *The Academy of Management Review*, Vol. 3, No. 2, p. 259. Reprinted by permission.

productivity. As indicated, improvement was noted in many cases, although it was by no means universal.[34]

Despite these generally encouraging results, research evaluations of the success of OD interventions are often plagued by weak methodologies, leaving the exact impact of the interventions open to question.[35] Some specific problems include the following:

- OD efforts involve a complex series of changes. There is little evidence of exactly which of these changes produce changes in processes and outcomes.
- Novelty effects or the fact that participants receive special treatment might produce short-term gains that really don't persist over time.
- Self-reports of changes in processes after OD might involve unconscious attempts to please the change agent.[36]

For these reasons and others, OD continues to be characterized by both problems and promise. One hopes that promise will overcome problems as organizations try to respond effectively to their increasingly complex and dynamic environments. Speaking of such response, let's turn to innovation.

THE INNOVATION PROCESS

Do you recognize the name Arthur Fry? Probably not. But Arthur Fry is famous in his own way as the inventor of the ubiquitous, sticky Post-its, a top seller among paper office supplies. Fry, a researcher at the innovative 3M Company, developed the product that became Post-its in response to a personal problem—how to keep his place marker from falling out of his church choir hymnal.

EXHIBIT

17–6

The impact of organizational development on specific outcome variables.

Variable	Number of Studies	Percent[a] Change
Work force		
Turnover	7	71
Absenteeism	7	57
Grievances	1	0
Total	11	60[b]
Monetary		
Costs	2	0
Profits	2	100
Sales	1	100
Total	4	60
Productivity		
Efficiency	6	50
Effectiveness	3	33
Quantity	2	50
Total	10	45
Quality	4	50
Overall	15	54

[a] Percentage of variables measured in a category showing significant positive change.

[b] Of 15 variables measured in 11 studies, 60 percent (9) showed significant positive change.

Source: From Nicholas, J. M. (1982, October). The comparative impact of organization development interventions on hard criteria measures. *The Academy of Management Review*, Vol. 7, No. 4, p. 535. Reprinted by permission.

What accounts for the ability of individuals such as Arthur Fry and organizations such as 3M to think up and exploit such innovative ideas? This is the focus of this section of the chapter.

What Is Innovation?

Just what is innovation, anyway? As implied earlier, innovation is a special form of organizational change, a form that in some sense involves newness. Formally, we might define **innovation** as the process of developing and implementing new ideas in an organization. The term *developing* is intentionally broad. It covers everything from the genuine invention of a new idea to recognizing an idea in the environment, importing it to the organization, and giving it a unique application. The essential point is a degree of creativity. Arthur Fry didn't invent glue, and he didn't invent paper, but he did develop a creative way to use them together. Then 3M was creative enough to figure out how to market what might have appeared to less probing minds to be a pretty mundane product.

Innovations can be classified roughly as product (including service) innovations.[37] Product innovations have a direct impact on the cost, quality, style, or availability of a product or service. Thus, they should be very obvious to clients or customers. It is easiest to identify with innovations that result in tangible products, especially everyday consumer products. Thus, we can surely recognize the Polaroid cameras, VCRs, fax machines, and Post-its have been innovative products. Perhaps coming less readily to mind are service innovations such as American Express Travelers Cheques (over one hundred years old), Federal Express door-to-door courier service, and twenty-four hour automated banking. In the story that began the chapter, the Faber Executive Center provided a new service to a new market segment.

Process innovations are new ways of designing products, making products, or delivering services. In many cases, process changes are invisible to customers or clients, although they help the organization to perform more effectively or efficiently. New technology is a process innovation, whether it be new manufacturing technology or a new management information system. New forms of management and work organization, including job enrichment, participation, or quality programs, are also process innovations. As shown in In Focus 17–1, providing products and services faster is a common contemporary process innovation.

Innovation is often conceived of as a stagelike process that begins with idea generation and proceeds to idea implementation. For some kinds of innovations, it is also hoped that the implemented innovation will diffuse to other sites or locations. This applies especially to process innovations that have begun as pilot or demonstration projects:

$$\text{Idea Generation} \rightarrow \text{Idea Implementation} \rightarrow \text{Idea Diffusion}$$

In advance of discussing these stages in the following sections, let's note several interesting themes that underlie the process of innovation. First, the beginning of innovation can be pretty haphazard and chaotic, and the conditions that are required to create new ideas might be very different from the conditions that are required to get these ideas implemented. For example, *thinking up* the Faber Management Center was a very different task from *getting the project realized*. In a related vein, although organizations have to innovate to survive, such innovation might be resisted just like any other organizational change. The result of these tensions is that innovation is frequently a highly political process (Chapter 13).[38] This important point is sometimes overlooked because innovation often involves science and technology, domains that have a connotation of rationality about them. However, both the champions of innovation and the resisters might behave politically to secure or hold onto critical organizational resources.

IN FOCUS 17–1

▼
....

Speed—A Critical Process Innovation

If there is one innovation that seems to be occurring across a wide variety of industries, it is the increasing speed with which products and services are being offered or moved from conception to the marketplace. This innovation is usually a function of both advanced physical technology and changes in management techniques and organizational culture. Computers, flatter structures, fewer "sign-offs" on new ideas, and a sense of urgency on the part of management all play their role. At some companies, such as Honda and Porsche, factory racing teams serve as strong symbols of the speed motif.

At The Limited, fashions can be spirited from design to store in two months, rather than the usual two *seasons* lag. Among other advantages, this means that the firm is much more responsive to fickle swings in trends and taste. At Motorola, electronic pagers are produced two hours after an order is received. It used to take three weeks. Using advanced computer technology, Chrysler is hoping to cut at least a year off its design cycle time, which has been a consistent and critical disadvantage in comparison to the Japanese auto manufacturers. In service industries, customers can sometimes experience the speedup process directly. Many banks are streamlining loan decision processes, and American Express has made a fetish out of fast refunds of lost travelers checks.

Fortune cites a consultant's model that shows that a six-month delay in getting high-technology products to market reduces profits by 33 percent over five years. Being 50 percent over budget cuts profits by only 4 percent. One firm that has taken this message to heart is Northern Telecom, the producer of high-tech communications equipment. After much soul-searching, Northern discovered that *time* was a critical factor in every aspect of its competitive sphere. Thus, it embarked on a strategic change in which speed and customer satisfaction were made the key focus of every aspect of its business, including design, manufacturing, installation, and service. Among other advantages, new product introduction times were reduced by 20 to 50 percent.

Source: Merrills, R. (1989, July-August). How Northern Telecom competes on time. *Harvard Business Review*, 108–114; Dumaine, B. (1989, February 14). How managers can succeed through speed. *Fortune*, 54–59; Staff. (1989, August 7). Chrysler tries to take a year off. *Autoweek*, p. 8.

Generating and Implementing Innovative Ideas

Innovation requires creative ideas, someone to fight for these ideas, good communication, and the proper application of resources and rewards. Let's examine these factors in detail.

Individual Creativity Creative thinking by individuals or small groups is at the core of the innovation process. **Creativity** is usually defined as the production of novel but potentially useful ideas. Thus, creativity is a key aspect of the "developing new ideas" part of our earlier definition of innovation. However, innovation is a broader concept, in that it also involves an attempt to implement new ideas. Not every creative idea gets implemented.

When we see a company such as 3M that is known for its innovations or we see an innovative project completed successfully, as at Faber College, we sometimes forget about the role that individual creativity plays in such innovations. However, organizations that have a consistent reputation for innovation have a talent for selecting, cultivating, and motivating creative individuals. Such creativity can come into play at many "locations" during the process of innovation. Thus, the salesperson who discovers a new market for a product might be just as creative as the scientist who developed the product.

What makes a person creative?[39] For one thing, you can pretty much discount the romantic notion of the naive creative genius. Research shows that creative people tend to have an excellent technical understanding of their domain. That is, they understand its basic practices, procedures, and techniques. Thus, creative chemists will emerge from those who are well trained and up to date in their field. Similarly, creative money managers will be among those who have a truly excellent grasp of finance and economics. Notice, however, that having good skills in one's specialty doesn't mean that creative people are extraordinarily intelligent. Once we get beyond subnormal intelligence, there is no correlation between level of intelligence and creativity.

Most people with good basic skills in their area are still not creative. What sets the creative people apart are additional *creativity-relevant* skills. These include the ability to tolerate uncertainty, withhold early judgment, see things in new ways, and be open to new and diverse experiences. Some of these skills appear to be a product of certain personality characteristics such as curiosity and persistence. Interestingly, creative people tend to be socially skilled but lower than average in need for social approval. They can often interact well with others to learn and discuss new ideas, but they don't see fit to conform just to get others to like them.

Many creativity-related skills can actually be improved by training people to think in divergent ways, withhold early evaluation of ideas, and so on.[40] In addition, some of the methods discussed in Chapter 12 (electronic brainstorming, nominal group, and Delphi techniques) can be used to hone creative skills. Frito-Lay and DuPont are two companies that engage in extensive creativity training.

Source: August 21, 1985, Mankoff/ Reprinted by permission, Los Angeles Times Syndicate.

DOLLAR$ AND NONENE®

© 1985 United Feature Syndicate, Inc.

LEMONADE
25¢

BC MANKOFF

"Intrapreneuring, chief—how about a glass on the house?"

Finally, people can be experts in their field and have creative skills but still not be creative if they lack intrinsic motivation for generating new ideas. Such motivation is most likely to occur when there is genuine interest in and fascination with the task at hand. This isn't to say that extrinsic motivation isn't important in innovation, as we shall see shortly. Rather, it means that creativity itself isn't very susceptible to extrinsic rewards.

Having a lot of potentially creative individuals is no guarantee in itself that an organization will innovate. Let's now turn to some other factors that influence innovation.

Idea Champions Again and again, case studies of successful innovations reveal the presence of one or more **idea champions,** people who see the kernel of an innovative idea and help guide it through to implementation.[41] This role of idea champion is often an informal emergent role, and "guiding" the idea might involve talking it up to peers, selling it to management, garnering resources for its development, or protecting it from political attack by the status quo. Champions often have a real sense of mission about the innovation. Idea champions have frequently been given other labels, some of which depend on the exact context or content of the innovation. For example, in larger organizations, such champions might be labeled *intrapreneurs* or *corporate entrepreneurs* (see the cartoon). In R&D settings, one often hears the term *project champion; product champion* is another familiar moniker. The exact label is less important than the function, which is one of sponsorship and support, often outside routine job duties.

For a modest innovation whose merits are extremely clear, it is possible for the creative person who thinks up the idea to serve as its sole champion and push the idea into practice. In the case of more complex and radical innovations, especially those that demand heavy resource commitment, it is common to see more than one idea champion emerge during the innovation process. For example, a laser scientist might invent a new twist to laser technology and champion the technical idea within her R&D lab. In turn, a product division line manager might hear of the technical innovation and offer to provide sponsorship to develop it into an actual commercial product. This joint emergence of a technical champion and a management champion is typical. Additional idea champions might also emerge. For example, a sales manager in the medical division might lobby to import the innovation from the optics division. At Faber College, Paul Fellows championed the technical concept of the Executive Center, and his chairperson sponsored it to the administration.

What kind of people are idea champions, and what are their tactics? One interesting study examined champions who spearheaded the introduction of expensive, visible new information technologies in their firms (e.g., new management information systems).[42] These "project champions" were compared with nonchampions who had also worked on the same project. The champions tended to be more risk taking and innovative. Also, they exhibited clear signs of transformational leadership (Chapter 10), using charisma, inspiration, and intellectual stimulation to get people to see the potential of the innovation. A wide variety of influence tactics were employed to gain support for the new system. In short, the champions made people truly *want* the innovation despite its disruption of the status quo.

As noted earlier, championing an innovation is usually an informal role. Would it be possible to actually *assign* people to be champions as part of their regular job duties? Just ask Progressive Corporation, a successful Cleveland-based insurance company. Progressive is known for its innovations in specialty vehicle insurance, including selling to risky drivers and insuring recreational vehicles. Several years ago, Progressive switched from a more centralized structure into several decentralized geographical regions. Management was worried that smaller-volume products (such as mobile homes) might be "lost" in the new decentralized structure and lose their innovative edge. To deal with this, they assigned each product a champion to look out for its interests on a total company basis.[43]

Communication Effective communication with the external environment and effective communication within the organization are vital for successful innovation.

The most innovative firms seem to be those that are best at recognizing the relevance of new external information, importing and assimilating this information, and then applying it.[44] Experience shows that the recognition and assimilation are a lot more chaotic and informal than one might imagine. Rather than relying on a formal network of journal articles, technical reports, and internal memoranda, technical personnel are more likely to be exposed to new ideas via informal oral communication networks. In these networks, key personnel function as **gatekeepers** who span the boundary between the organization and the environment, importing new information, translating it for local use, and disseminating it to project members. These people tend to have well-developed communication networks with other professionals outside the organization and with the professionals on their own team or project. Thus, they are in key positions to both receive and transmit new technical information.[45] Also, they are perceived as highly competent and a good source of new ideas. Furthermore, they have an innovative orientation, they read extensively, and they can tolerate ambiguity.[46] It is important to note that gatekeeping is essentially an informal, emergent role, since many gatekeepers are not in supervisory positions. However, organizations can do several things to enhance the external contact of actual or potential gatekeepers. Generous allowances for subscriptions, telephone use, and database access might be helpful. The same applies to travel allowances for seminars, short courses, and professional meetings.

Technical gatekeepers are not the only means of extracting information from the environment. Many successful innovative firms excel at going directly to users, clients, or customers to obtain ideas for product or service innovation. This works against the development of technically sound ideas that nobody wants, and it also provides some real focus for getting ideas implemented quickly. For example, Sony requires new employees in technical areas to do a stint in retail sales, and Raytheon's New Products Center organizes expeditions by technical types to trade shows, manufacturing facilities, and retail outlets.[47] Notice that we are speaking here about truly getting "close to the customer," not simply doing abstract market research on large samples of people. Such research does not have a great track record in prompting innovation; talking directly to users does.

Now that we have covered the importation of information into the organization, what are the requirements of *internal* communication for innovation? At least during the idea generation and early design phase, the more the better. Thus, it is generally true that *organic structures* (Chapter 15) facilitate innovation.[48] Decentralization, informality, and a lack of bureaucracy all foster the exchange of information that innovation requires. To this mixture, add small project teams or business units and a diversity of member backgrounds to stimulate cross-fertilization of ideas. For example, the early project design team for Mazda's new RX-7 had twenty-nine members, thirteen from R&D, six from production, seven from sales marketing, and one each from planning, service, and quality control.[49] There was no room for isolated thinking with that mix! *Fortune* magazine notes a common trend among innovative corporations, including Campbell Soup, 3M, and Apple Computer:

> People in different disciplines are simply not allowed to remain in isolation. Business units are kept small in part to throw engineers, marketers, and finance experts together into the sort of tight groups most often found in start-up companies. Where the interaction fails to

arise naturally, it is engineered: all of these companies require their workers to spend a great deal of time at meetings where information is shared and plans are discussed.[50]

In general, internal communication can be stimulated with in-house training, cross-functional transfers, and varied job assignments.[51] One study even found that the actual physical location of gatekeepers was important to their ability to convey new information to co-workers.[52] This suggests the clustering of offices and the use of common lounge areas as a means of facilitating communication. Equal thought could be given to the design of electronic communication media.

One especially interesting line of research suggests just how important communication is to the performance of research and development project groups.[53] This research found that groups with members who had worked together a short time or a long time engaged in less communication (within the group, within the organization, and externally) than groups that had medium longevity. In turn, performance mirrored communication, the high-communicating medium-longevity groups being the best performers (Exhibit 17–7). Evidently, when groups are new, it takes time for members to decide what information is required and to forge the appropriate communication networks. When groups get "old," they sometimes get comfortable and isolate themselves from critical sources of feedback. It should be emphasized that it is the age of the group that is at issue here, not the age of the workers or their tenure in the organization.

Apple Computer's Macintosh IIsi. Apple fosters innovation through internal communication, making sure that specialists can exchange ideas freely. (Courtesy Apple Computer Inc.)

Although organic structures seem best in the idea generation and design phases of innovation, more mechanistic structures might be better for actually implementing innovations.[54] Thinking up new computer programs is an organic task. Getting these programs reproduced in the thousands and marketed requires more bureaucratic procedures. This transition is important. Although audio and video recording innovations were pioneered in the United States, it was the Japanese who successfully implemented recording products in the marketplace. In part, this

EXHIBIT

17–7

Group longevity, communication, and performance of research and development groups.

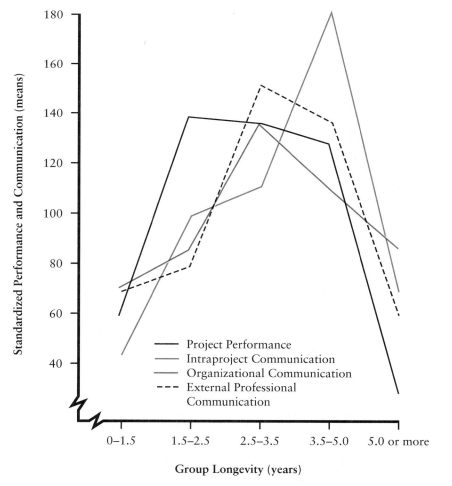

Source: Katz, R. (1982). The effects of group longevity on project communication and performance. *Administrative Science Quarterly, 27,* 81–104, p. 96. Reprinted by permission.

stemmed from a recognition of the different organizational requirements for idea generation versus the implementation of ideas.

Resources and Rewards Despite the romance surrounding the development of innovations on a shoestring using unauthorized "bootlegged" funds, abundant resources greatly enhance the chances of successful innovation.[55] Not only do these resources provide funds in the obvious sense, they also serve as a strong cultural symbol that the organization truly supports innovation. Funds for innovation are seen as an *investment*, not a *cost*. Several observers have noted that such a culture is most likely when the availability of funding is anarchic and multisourced. That is, because innovative ideas often encounter resistance from the status quo under the best of circumstances, innovators should have the opportunity to seek support from more than one source. At 3M, for instance, intrapreneurs can seek support from their own division, from another division, from corporate R&D, or from a new ventures group.[56] (Notice how other idea champions might be cultivated during this process.)

Money is not the only resource that spurs innovation. *Time* can be an even more crucial factor for some innovations. At 3M, tradition dictates that scientists reserve 15 percent of their working time for personal projects. At Chaparral Steel in Midlothian, Texas, supervisors are given "sabbaticals" to work on innovations with customers, suppliers, and universities.[57]

Reward systems must match the culture that is seeded by the resource system. Coming up with new ideas is no easy job, so organizations should avoid punishing failure (see In Focus 17–2). Many false starts with dead ends will be encountered, and innovators need support and constructive criticism, not punishment. A survey of research scientists found that freedom and autonomy were the *most* cited organizational factors leading to creativity.[58] Since intrinsic motivation is necessary for creativity, this suggests rewarding good past performance with enhanced freedom to pursue personal ideas. IBM, for example, has a "fellows program" that provides star performers five years of freedom to work on their own projects. In a related vein, many organizations have wised up about extrinsic rewards and innovation. In the past, it was common for creative scientists and engineers to have to move into management ranks to obtain raises and promotions. Many firms now offer dual career ladders that enable these people to be extrinsically rewarded while still doing actual science or engineering (see Chapter 18).

We have been concerned here mainly with rewarding the people who actually generate innovative ideas. But how about those other champions who sponsor such ideas and push them into the implementation stage? At 3M, bonuses for division managers are contingent on 25 percent of their revenues coming from products that are less than five years old.[59] This stimulates the managers to pay attention when someone drops by with a new idea, and it also stimulates them to turn that new idea into a real product quickly!

Diffusing Innovative Ideas

Many innovations, especially process innovations, begin as limited experiments in one section or division of an organization. This is a cautious and reasonable approach. For example, new automated technology might be introduced for evaluation in one plant of a multiplant company. Similarly, an insurance company might begin a limited exploration of job enrichment by concentrating only on clerical jobs at the head office. If such efforts are judged successful, it seems logical to extend them to other parts of the organization. **Diffusion** is the process by which innovations move across an organization. However, this is not always as easy as it might seem!

Richard Walton of Harvard University has carefully studied the diffusion of eight major process innovations in firms such as Volvo, Alcan, General Foods, Corning Glass, and Shell U.K. Each effort was fairly rigorous and broad-based, generally having the following characteristics:

> The work restructuring approach pursued in the eight cases studied embraces many aspects of work, including the content of the job,

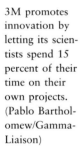

3M promotes innovation by letting its scientists spend 15 percent of their time on their own projects. (Pablo Bartholomew/Gamma-Liaison)

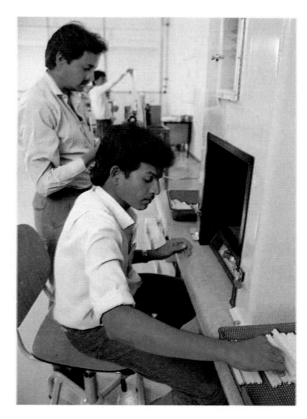

compensation schemes, scope of worker responsibility for supervision and decision making, social structure, status hierarchy, and so on. The design of each element is intended to contribute to an internally consistent work culture—one that *appropriately* enlarges workers' scope for self-management, enhances their opportunity for learning new abilities, strengthens their sense of connectedness with co-

IN FOCUS 17–2

▼
....

Federal Express—Innovation par Excellence

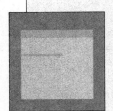

Who says college assignments aren't practical? Don't tell that to Frederick W. Smith, founder and head of Federal Express. The basic plan for Smith's "fly it anywhere, overnight" company was set down in a Yale University economics term paper he wrote in the mid-1960s. The company was incorporated in 1971 and began operations in 1973. Smith's key innovation, of course, was the provision of door-to-door courier service using the company's own fleet of airplanes and trucks. However, the company has a distinguished history of other innovations:

- The spoke-and-hub system, which routes all packages to the company's Memphis superhub for overnight transport to spoke airports.
- One of the first uses of extensive television advertising for what was essentially a business service.
- A grass roots lobbying effort by Federal Express employees to have national air transport laws changed.
- Computerized vans with "super trackers" that enable clients to find out the exact current location of their shipment.
- The establishment of a company weather-forecasting system.

Not all Federal Express innovations have been successful. Its foray into the Zapmail electronic mail service lost millions with the faster-than-expected advent of standard fax machines. However, Smith is adamant that some failure is to be expected and that people need to have the opportunity to fail in order to succeed. Despite the profusion of fax transmission, 70 percent of company revenues come from moving boxes, and Smith is keen for Federal Express to invest in a demonstration project involving the design of a hypersonic jet.

Source: Adapted from Diebold, J. (1990). *The innovators: The discoveries, inventions, and breakthroughs of our time.* Copyright © 1990 by Truman M. Talley, an imprint of Penguin USA. Adapted and reprinted by permission.

workers, increases their identification with the product and manufacturing process, and promotes their sense of dignity and self-worth.[60]

All of the pilot projects that Walton studied were initially judged successful, and each received substantial publicity, a factor that often contributes to increased commitment to further change. Despite this, substantial diffusion occurred in only one of the observed firms—Volvo (see Chapter 7). What accounts for this poor record of diffusion? Walton identified these factors:

- Lack of support and commitment by top management.
- Significant differences between the technology or setting of the pilot project and those of other units in the organization, raising arguments that "it won't work here."
- Attempts to diffuse particular *techniques* rather than *goals* that could be tailored to other situations.
- Management reward systems that concentrate on traditional performance measures while ignoring success at implementing innovation.
- Union resistance to extending the negotiated "exceptions" in the pilot project.
- Fears that pilot projects begun in nonunionized locations could not be implemented in unionized portions of the firm.
- Conflict between the pilot project and the bureaucratic structures in the rest of the firm (e.g., pay policies and staffing requirements).

Because of these problems, Walton raises the depressing spectre of a "diffuse or die" principle. That is, if diffusion does not occur, the pilot project and its leaders become more and more isolated from the mainstream of the organization and less and less able to proceed alone. As noted earlier, innovation can be a highly politicized process.

One classic study suggests that the following factors are critical determinants of the rate of diffusion of a wide variety of innovations:[61]

- *Relative advantage.* Diffusion is more likely when the new idea is perceived as truly better than the one it replaces.
- *Compatibility.* Diffusion is easier when the innovation is compatible with the values, beliefs, needs, and current practices of potential new adopters.
- *Complexity.* Complex innovations that are fairly difficult to comprehend and use are less likely to diffuse.
- *Trialability.* If an innovation can be given a limited trial run, its chances of diffusion will be improved.
- *Observability.* When the consequences of an innovation are more visible, diffusion will be more likely to occur.

In combination, these determinants suggest that there is considerable advantage to thinking about how innovations are "packaged" and "sold" so as to increase their chances of more widespread adoption. Also, they suggest the value of finding strong champions to sponsor the innovation at the new site.

THE MANAGER'S NOTEBOOK

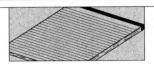

Employee Surveys at IBM

1. IBM instituted an on-line computerized employee survey administered through its organizationwide office information system. Over 90 percent of employees around the world are now surveyed this way. The technology permits "write-in" comments, and they have increased greatly over the pencil-and-paper surveys.

2. The company claims many advantages for the computerized survey. Employees prefer it over the paper-and-pencil mode, in part because they can complete the survey at a time that is convenient for them, exiting the program and returning if they are interrupted for business. Similarly, traveling employees can simply log on and complete the survey wherever they are in the world. Data analysis and survey feedback can be very fast (sometimes taking only a matter of days) because data collection and processing are part of the same system. Finally, it is easy to custom-tailor questions by geographical location or occupational group with the computerized survey.

SUMMARY

- All organizations must change because of forces in the external and internal environments. Although more environmental change usually requires more organizational change, organizations can exhibit too much change as well as too little. Organizations can change goals and strategies, technology, job design, structure, and people. People changes are almost always required to accompany changes in other factors.
- The general change process involves unfreezing current attitudes and behaviors, changing them, and then refreezing the newly acquired attitudes and behaviors. Several key issues or problems must be dealt with during the general change process. One is accurate diagnosis of the current situation. Another is the resistance that might be provoked by unfreezing and change. A third issue is performing an adequate evaluation of the success of the change effort. Many such evaluations are weak or nonexistent.
- Organizational development (OD) is a planned, ongoing effort to change organizations to be more effective and more human. It uses the knowledge of behavioral science to foster a culture of organizational self-examination and readiness for change. A strong emphasis is placed on interpersonal and group processes.
- Four popular OD techniques were discussed. Team building attempts to increase the effectiveness of work teams by concentrating on interpersonal processes, goal clarification, and role clarification. Quality circles involve small groups of workers in solving problems of quality, productivity, and costs. Survey feedback requires organizational members to generate data that is fed back to them as a basis for inducing change. Grid OD is a comprehensive long-term effort to change organizations that uses a systematic series of developmental phases to accomplish its goals. It is grounded in the Managerial Grid®, which emphasizes maximizing concern for productivity and concern for people.
- In many OD attempts that have been adequately evaluated, positive changes in processes and/or outcomes have been observed. Despite this, the careful evaluation of OD programs poses special challenges to researchers.

- Innovation is the process of developing and implementing new ideas in an organization. It can include both new products and new processes. Innovation requires individual creativity and adequate resources and rewards to stimulate and channel that creativity. Also, idea champions who recognize and sponsor creative ideas are critical. Finally, internal and external communication are important for innovation. The role of gatekeepers who import and disseminate technical information is especially noteworthy.

KEY CONCEPTS

Unfreezing	Team building	Innovation
Refreezing	Quality circles	Creativity
Diagnosis	Survey feedback	Idea champions
Change agent	Grid OD	Gatekeepers
Resistance	Managerial Grid®	Diffusion
Organizational development (OD)		

DISCUSSION QUESTIONS

1. Discuss how the introduction of computers has led to changes in organizations. Explain how this change in technology might require changes in job design and people.

2. Describe an example of resistance to change that you have observed. Why did it occur?

3. You have been charged with staffing and organizing an R&D group in a new high-technology firm. What will you do to ensure that the group is innovative?

4. What qualities would the ideal gatekeeper possess to facilitate the communication of technical information in his or her firm?

5. Suppose a job enrichment effort in one plant of a manufacturing firm is judged to be very successful. You are the corporate change agent responsible for the project, and you wish to diffuse it to other plants that have a similar technology. How would you sell the project to other plant managers? What kinds of resistance might you encounter?

6. What personal qualities and skills would be useful for an OD change agent to possess? Describe the relative merits of using an internal staff change agent versus an external consultant.

7. Discuss: The best organizational structure to generate innovative ideas might not be the best structure to implement those ideas.

8. Imagine that the U.S. Marine Corps is forming a special hostage rescue unit to aid American hostages around the world. How could team-building principles be used to enhance the formation and functioning of this unit? What are some limitations to using this approach in the military?

9. Debate this statement: Survey feedback can be a problematic OD technique because it permits people who are affected by organizational policies to generate data that speaks against those policies.

10. Explain why top management commitment is necessary for an organization to proceed through all six phases of Grid OD. Discuss why Grid OD is divided into a number of distinct phases.

EXPERIENTIAL EXERCISE

Trouble at Narrow Rivers

The object of this simulation is to illustrate the phases of diagnosis, development of a change strategy, and implementation of change in an organization setting where absenteeism and turnover is a problem. As you get involved with each of these concepts and wrestle with the critical questions, the complexities and multiple relationships will become evident.

There is no 'right' way to solve the problem. There are many ways to deal with it. Some ways will have more merit than others. Look carefully at the facts of the case and use your empathetic skills to understand some of the unwritten feelings, views and attitudes of the participants.

Narrow Rivers

Narrow Rivers is a private continuing education center/health spa with 350 apartments, a constant population of 535 people who stay from 3 days to several months, and a staff of nearly 200 full and part-time employees. A part-time staff of 40, 2 full-time supervisors and 2 cooks, run the facility for the manager-trainees who attend. Part-timers work 4 hours daily and range in age from 18 to 60.

The employees work in three shifts during the day. Starting times for the help are 6:00 A.M., 10:00 A.M. and 4:00 P.M. One of the cooks starts at 6 A.M. and the second quits at 8:00 P.M. The supervisors are expected to oversee the entire project and fill in where necessary.

Narrow Rivers draws its part-time employees from the surrounding rural area. Seventy percent of the group are women. Most are housewives. The males are an assortment of old and young people partially supported by other jobs. The initial racial composition of the group was 70% white, 12% black, and 18% hispanic.

The Problem

Martin Traynor, the director, has hired you to be a change agent with the organization. There are many sources of irritation at Narrow Rivers due, Traynor believes, to its recent opening just a year ago. There seems to be some understanding of the "opening" problems, but none for food service difficulties. The clients have no patience for the slip-ups in the kitchen/dining area. They harrangue, criticize, send food back, and visit the cook and director frequently. The situation has gotten so bad that the attitudes toward other services in the community are being affected. Educational efforts are hampered; maids and gardeners are being hassled. On some days 20% of the part-time help might be missing. There have been five new cooks hired during the year. All who left found other employment without difficulty.

The food service has been subcontracted to TRISTAR. Narrow Rivers had agreed to a two-year contract with a clause for review after one year. Martin presently is in the process of reviewing that subcontract in light of the difficulties. His attitude is that there is obviously some problem and the TRISTAR has been as diligent as he has been in trying to find a solution. Wages and benefits seem to be in line with the surrounding wage rates, and the people hired seem not to be "the" problem. Troubles are now intensifying as Narrow Rivers and TRISTAR have to go further away to acquire their labor force. Over the year, the racial composition of the employees has changed from that stated earlier to 50% white, 30% black, and 20% hispanic.

_____ 1. Prior to coming to class, your job is to establish an orderly approach for dealing with the problem. Separate your analysis into three sections: diagnosis, change strategy, and implementation. Detail your analysis and provide the rationale for your choice.

_____ 2. Form groups of three to five students in class and take turns presenting your analysis. This is done without critical comment. Clarifying questions are appropriate. (20 minutes)

_____ 3. Develop a common view of the intervention, change strategy and implementation within your group. Analyze the pros and cons of each plan, determining feasibility, and potential resistance. (30 minutes)

_____ 4. Prepare a two-part role play. First, assign one member of your group to be Martin Traynor. The remaining two will be on the consultant team. Prepare in reasonable detail a dialogue between the characters. Martin Traynor *is* dubious about the process and your findings. The remaining member(s) of your group should observe the proceedings and be prepared to discuss the consultants' activities and techniques when the role play is completed.

Source: Adapted from an exercise prepared by H. William Vroman, Tennessee Technological University. From White, D. D., & Vroman, H. W. (1982). *Action in organizations* (2nd ed.). Copyright © 1982 by Allyn and Bacon. Reprinted with permission.

Erehwon Management Consultants, Inc.

Erehwon Management Consultants, Inc. (EMC) is a general consulting firm with offices in six cities, employing about 100 full-time consultants. Until recently, it had exhibited an enviable growth record based on just two "products." The firm's President began to see a slowdown due to both of these products rapidly entering the mature phases of their respective life cycles. In addition, he felt that the pace of work had become too intense and that by gradually bringing down the consultant's workload, it would be advantageous to the firm in retaining less stressed employees.

Cultural Norms Before the Change Program

EMC, like many other firms in the industry, saw its success equated to billable hours and high consultant utilization rates. In other words, the success and even continued existence of EMC depended on, at a minimum, covering the fixed expenses (salary plus overhead and fringes) for its consulting staff. As a result, everyone at EMC watched the weekly "hours billed to clients."

Consultants at all levels were encouraged, usually in indirect ways, to "keep busy" on client efforts and to sell follow-on engagements. At performance review time and at promotion time, it was made explicit that sales and hard work for clients were the keys to personnel career growth at EMC. Partners seemed to be always on the road, calling on potential and current clients, seeking to reach the sales quotas. No organized marketing was done as it implied (to the partners) an unprofessional image.

Source: Buchowicz, B. (1990, Summer). Culture transition and attitude change. *Journal of General Management.* 45–55.

A New Strategy for EMC

The President and the six partners that headed up the offices of EMC met for two days to address his concerns of an impending slowdown and the "quality of life" issue. Since EMC had emphasized sales during its entire existence as a firm and had seen sales success equated with capitalizing on its two existing products, no R&D or new product development efforts had been attempted to date.

To address the slowdown and, at the same time, to enhance the consultant quality of work life, the following strategy was formulated by the group:

- Deemphasize sales and billable hours as measures of consultant performance.
- Set aside approximately five per cent of each consultant's time (i.e., three hours per week) for "R&D" time. Each consultant could use such time for self-improvement of consulting skills, new product idea generation, or researching new industries to which to market existing products.
- Try to schedule consultants so that those who spent extensive time on the road (i.e., on client work) were occasionally "rewarded" with local assignments or officially recognized new product development projects (also not requiring travel).

The Change Program

The President's committee realized that this new strategy represented a substantial departure from the previous approach. However, a sense of urgency seemed to dictate that the new strategy must be put in place without delay.

The head of EMC's largest office, a partner with the firm's best sales record, was given responsibility for designing implementation of the plan. His program centered on the following steps:

- Firm-wide, each consultant would receive a memo from the President stating the new strategy and the need to change.
- In each office, the partner in charge would convene the consultants to explain the new situation and encourage each consultant to develop new product ideas.
- Each office would decide on the travel and "time off" procedures so as to cause minimal disruption to clients.

The President's one-page memo was distributed about two weeks later. It took nearly three months to schedule each of the six offices to have their staff meetings, since clients seemed to continually uncover "major" crises that required consultants on-site.

Consultants' Response

The President's memo surprised and perplexed most of EMC's consultants. In essence, it stated that EMC was evolving into an organization that was willing to invest in its future through its employees. The arguments were vague and the memo seemed to lack the feeling of urgency that had originally motivated the President to act on his concerns. Few if any of the consultants seemed to seriously accept the memo as representing a real change affecting them, at least not in the near future.

The office meetings also seemed to be missing a clear sense of urgency or rationale. In several of these sessions, the partner in charge seemed less than enthusiastic and was even heard to convey that "this is temporary—don't let it affect your *real* work!"

After the meetings were over, life at EMC seemed unchanged. Partners still hustled about, responding to any and all sales leads and consultants were promoted or let go on the basis of their "partnership potential," i.e., the ability to generate business.

Moreover as the expected sales slump began to be felt earlier than anticipated, cold calling and visiting previous clients seemed to become everyone's primary activities. Even some client work in progress was slowed in order to free more staff to make sales calls.

Sales did ultimately resume, albeit spread across a variety of products and markets which lacked any cohesive theme. Partners and consultants never really changed their focus on sales. The "new program" quickly disappeared from the scene.

1. Describe the culture of Erehwon Management Consultants before and after the change effort.
2. Discuss in detail the reasons for the failure of the change effort.
3. Account for the resistance the change effort encountered. After all, the changes seem beneficial to the consultants.
4. Discuss how the techniques of team building and quality circles might have been applied at EMC.
5. Explain the factors that appear to work against "product" innovation at EMC.
6. With hindsight, how might the president have acted differently to achieve his goals?

REFERENCES

1. Katz, D., & Kahn, R. L. (1978). *The social psychology of organizations* (2nd ed.). New York: Wiley.
2. This list relies mostly on Leavitt, H. (1965). Applied organizational changes in industry: Structural, technological, and humanistic approaches. In J. G. March (Ed.), *Handbook of organizations*. Chicago: Rand McNally.
3. Lewin, K. (1951). *Field theory in social science*. New York: Harper & Row.
4. See Levinson, H. (1972). *Organizational diagnosis*. Cambridge, MA: Harvard University Press.
5. The first five reasons are from Kotter, J. P., & Schlesinger, L. A. (1979, March-April). Choosing strategies for change. *Harvard Business Review*, 106–114.
6. Tichy, N. M., & Devanna, M. A. (1986). *The transformational leader*. New York: Wiley.
7. The following relies partly on Kotter & Schlesinger, 1979.
8. For reviews, see Macy, B. A., Peterson, M. F., & Norton, L. W. (1989). A test of participation theory in a work re-design field setting: Degree of participation and comparison site contrasts. *Human Relations, 42*, 1095–1165; Filley, A. C., House, R. J., & Kerr, S. (1976). *Managerial process and organizational behavior* (2nd ed.). Glenview, IL: Scott, Foresman.

9. Lawler, E. E., & Hackman, J. R. (1969). The impact of employee participation in the development of pay incentive plans: A field experiment. *Journal of Applied Psychology, 53*, 467–471.

10. Tichy & Devanna, 1986; Yukl, G. A. (1989). *Leadership in organizations* (2nd ed.). Englewood Cliffs, NJ: Prentice-Hall.

11. Catalanello, R. F., & Kirkpatrick, D. L. (1968). Evaluating training programs—The state of the art. *Training and Development Journal, 22*, 2–9.

12. Goodman, P. S., Bazerman, M., & Conlon, E. (1980). Institutionalization of planned organizational change. *Research in Organizational Behavior, 2*, 215–246.

13. Goodman et al., 1980.

14. For a review of various definitions, see Mapping the territory. In W. L. French, C. H. Bell, Jr., & R. A. Zawacki (Eds.) (1978). *Organization development: Theory, practice, and research*. Dallas: Business Publications.

15. French, W. L., & Bell, C. H., Jr. (1973). *Organization development*. Englewood Cliffs, NJ: Prentice-Hall.

16. Beer, M., & Walton, E. (1990). Developing the competitive organization: Interventions and strategies. *American Psychologist, 45*, 154–161; Beer, M. (1980). *Organization change and development: A systems view*. Glenview, IL: Scott, Foresman.

17. Beer, M. (1976). The technology of organizational development. In M. D. Dunnette (Ed.) *Handbook of industrial, and organizational psychology*. Chicago: Rand McNally. See also Dyer, W. (1987). *Team building: Issues and alternatives* (2nd ed.). Reading, MA: Addison-Wesley.

18. Bell, C. H., Jr., & Rosenzweig, J. (1978). Highlights of an organizational improvement program in a city government. In French et al.

19. Wakeley, J. H., & Shaw, M. E. (1965). Management training: An integrated approach. *Training Directors Journal, 19*, 2–13.

20. Munchus, G., III. (1983). Employer-employee based quality circles in Japan: Human resource policy implications for American firms. *Academy of Management Review, 8*, 255–261; Cole, R. E. (1980). *Work, mobility, and participation: A comparative study of American and Japanese industry*. Berkeley, CA: University of California Press.

21. Marks, M. L. (1986, March). The question of quality circles. *Psychology Today*, 36–46.

22. Crocker, O., Charney, C., & Chiu, S. L. (1984). *Quality circles: A guide to participation and productivity*. Toronto: Methuen; Robinson, A. (1982). *Quality circles: A practical guide*. Aldershot, England: Gower.

23. Fletcher, D. (1984). Keeping going. I: Wedgwood. In M. Robson (Ed.), *Quality circles in action*. Aldershot, England: Gower.

24. See Crocker et al., 1984. See also Ledford, G. E., Jr., Lawler, E. E., III, & Mohrman, S. A. (1988). The quality circle and its variations. In J. P. Campbell & R. J. Campbell (Eds.), *Productivity in organizations*. San Francisco: Jossey-Bass.

25. This description relies upon Beer, 1980; Huse, E. F., & Cummings, T. G. (1985). *Organization development and change* (3rd ed.). St. Paul, MN: West; Nadler, D. A. (1977). *Feedback and organization development: Using data-based methods*. Reading, MA: Addison-Wesley.

26. Taylor, J., & Bowers, D. (1972). *Survey of organizations: A machine-scored standardized questionnaire instrument*. Ann Arbor, MI: Center for Research on Utilization of Scientific Knowledge, Institute for Social Research, University of Michigan.

27. Mohrman, S. A., Mohrman, A. M., Cooke, R. A., & Duncan, R. B. (1977). A survey feedback and problem-solving intervention in a school district: "We'll take the survey but you can keep the feedback." In P. H. Mirvis & D. N. Berg (Eds.), *Failures in organization development and change: Cases and essays for learning*. New York: Wiley.

28. Blake, R. R., & Mouton, J. S. (1964). *The managerial grid*. Houston: Gulf; Blake, R. R., & Mouton, J. S. (1968). *Corporate excellence through grid organization development*. Houston: Gulf.

29. Alderfer, C. P. (1977). Organization development. *Annual Review of Psychology, 28*, 197–223.

30. Neuman, G. A., Edwards, J. E., & Raju, N. S. (1989). Organizational development interventions: A meta-analysis of their effects on satisfaction and other attitudes. *Personnel Psychology, 42*, 461–489; Guzzo, R. A., Jette, R. D., & Katzell, R. A. (1985). The effects of psychologically based intervention programs on worker productivity: A meta-analysis. *Personnel Psychology, 38*, 275–291.

31. Steel, R. P., & Shane, G. S. (1986). Evaluation research on quality circles: Technical and analytical implications. *Human Relations, 39*, 449–468.

32. Griffin, R. W. (1988). Consequences of quality circles in an industrial setting: A longitudinal assessment. *Academy of Management Journal, 31*, 338–358.

33. Porras, J. I., & Berg, P. O. (1978). The impact of organization development. *Academy of Management Review, 3*, 249–264.

34. Nicholas, J. M. (1982). The comparative impact of organization development interventions on hard criteria measures. *Academy of Management Review, 7*, 531–542.

35. Nicholas, J. M., & Katz, M. (1985). Research methods and reporting practices in organization development: A review and some guidelines. *Academy of Management Review, 10,* 737–749.

36. White, S. E., & Mitchell, T. R. (1976). Organization development: A review of research content and research design. *Academy of Management Review, 1,* 57–73.

37. Tushman, M., & Nadler, D. (1986, Spring). Organizing for innovation. *California Management Review,* 74–92.

38. Frost, P. J., & Egri, C. P. (1991). The political process of innovation. *Research in Organizational Behavior, 13,* 229–295.

39. This three-part view of creativity is from Amabile, T. M. (1988). A model of creativity and innovation in organizations. *Research in Organizational Behavior, 10,* 123–167.

40. Basadur, M., Graen, G. B., & Scandura, T. A. (1986). Training effects on attitudes toward divergent thinking among manufacturing engineers. *Journal of Applied Psychology, 71,* 612–617.

41. Galbraith, J. R. (1982, Winter). Designing the innovating organization. *Organizational Dynamics,* 4–25.

42. Howell, J. M., & Higgins, C. A. (1990). Champions of technological innovation. *Administrative Science Quarterly, 35,* 317–341.

43. Orlicke, J. (1985). *The Progressive Corporation (B).* Boston: Harvard Business School.

44. Cohen, W. M., & Levinthal, D. A. (1990). Absorptive capacity: A new perspective on learning and innovation. *Administrative Science Quarterly, 35,* 128–152.

45. Tushman, M. L., & Scanlan, T. J. (1981). Characteristics and external orientations of boundary spanning individuals. *Academy of Management Journal, 24,* 83–98; Tushman, M. L., & Scanlan, T. J. (1981). Boundary spanning individuals: Their role in information transfer and their antecedents. *Academy of Management Journal, 24,* 289–305.

46. Keller, R. T., & Holland, W. E. (1983). Communicators and innovators in research and development organizations. *Academy of Management Journal, 26,* 742–749.

47. Kanter, R. M. (1988). When a thousand flowers bloom: Structural, collective, and social conditions for innovation in organization. *Research in Organizational Behavior, 10,* 169–211.

48. Kanter, 1988; Nord, W. R., & Tucker, S. (1987). *Implementing routine and radical innovations.* Lexington, MA: Lexington Books.

49. Nonaka, I. (1990, Spring). Redundant, overlapping organization: A Japanese approach to managing the innovation process. *California Management Review,* 27–38.

50. Sherman, S. P. (1984, October 15). Eight big masters of innovation. *Fortune,* 66–84, p. 72.

51. Tushman & Scanlan, 1981, pp. 289–305.

52. Keller & Holland, 1983.

53. Katz, R. (1982). The effects of group longevity on project communication and performance. *Administrative Science Quarterly, 27,* 81–104.

54. For a review, see Nord & Tucker, 1987.

55. Kanter, 1988.

56. Galbraith, 1982.

57. Peters, T. (1987). *Thriving on chaos.* New York: Knopf.

58. Amabile, 1988.

59. Galbraith, 1982.

60. Walton, R. E. (1975, Winter). The diffusion of new work structures: Explaining why success didn't take. *Organizational Dynamics,* 3–22, p. 5.

61. Rogers, E. M. (1983). *Diffusion of innovations* (3rd ed.). New York: Free Press.

18

CAREERS

Jan Thompson and Reginald Wilson both graduated from university with bachelor's degrees in business. They wanted to get married and start careers together. Jan was viewed by her many friends as very sociable and "quite an actor," as well as someone who could "sell ice cubes to Alaskans." For her, a marketing major was a natural choice. Because of her good school record, achievements in extracurricular activities, and interpersonal skills, she had a number of job options upon graduation.

Reggie also established a good record while at university. He particularly excelled in accounting and finance because they allowed him to use his numerical abilities, and he thought those fields were "orderly and practical." When a guest speaker in one of his classes noted that people making it to high positions like chief executive officer increasingly had solid accounting backgrounds and a good eye for financial matters, he knew that his finance major and accounting minor were good choices. When he graduated he was happy to have almost as many job options as his socially hyperactive girlfriend.

Planning two careers simultaneously proved trying at times, but in the end, Jan and Reggie were able to get good jobs in not only the same city but the same company. Reggie got a job in the finance department helping to manage the company's investment portfolio. While most of the work during the first year was fairly mundane, he was able to form a good relationship with his boss, who eventually gave him more challenging assignments and even introduced him to the "movers and shakers" in the company. At the end of his third year, a position on the controller's staff in the accounting department opened up. His boss confided that even a junior position on the controller's staff is a "good place to get your ticket punched if you're serious about moving on to bigger and better things." Reggie decided to investigate further and, to his surprise, found that his boss had "greased the skids" well, and he got an acceptable offer in his first meeting with the area manager.

Jan's first job was in marketing. She called herself a rover because she was moved to different areas and projects wherever she was needed. After four years she got a chance to make a regional market test of a new line of hand soap. As product manager, she coordinated the whole show and made numerous price, promotion, and distribution decisions. She even had two subordinates to help with the various duties. After nine months of hard work, the hand soap was a clear success. Jan received plenty of credit and was the natural choice to manage the product line on a national level. This was a big step up the corporate ladder. To everyone's surprise, Jan turned down the promotion. The need to move to the corporate headquarters in another city, with the complications that would cause in Reggie's career, was a factor, but the major reason that she gave to the marketing vice-president was "I'm a marketer, not a manager. I get my kicks from figuring out people's preferences and selling them on the product. The job you're offering has some attractive qualities, but I know the required wrestling with the bureaucracy and digesting all the sales and cost data will do me in!"

Fifteen years later. . . . A number of challenges and changes have been confronted by both Reggie and Jan. Reggie has continued to climb the corporate hierarchy but has moved to a new company. Lack of opportunity seemed to be his main reason for changing. "After ten years and four different positions, I knew that my chances for a high executive position were low. It seems everyone at the top has 'Made in Marketing' stamped on their personnel files. I had accepted a transfer to a marketing job just to pick up this experience, but it was clear that I needed more than a two-year hitch to get by. Even the M.B.A. I picked up in over five years of night classes couldn't compensate for my nonmarketing orientation. It wasn't a company in which I could really trade on my strengths." After this discovery, he looked around and found a general management position with a bank that liked his consumer industry experience and strong financial orientation.

Reggie's consistent and clear career focus is still a bit of a puzzle for Jan. After turning down the product manager's job, she had taken on a number of interesting and challenging marketing assignments. However, at around age thirty she found herself very dissatisfied. She observed that "all of a sudden, the successes at work didn't mean as much as they did before. A big factor was that the company wanted all of me and just wasn't willing to take anything less. Reggie and I had always talked about having a couple of children when the time was right, but for the company there was never a 'right time.' The only option within the company was taking six weeks maternity leave and then jumping back into ten-hour work days with too many travel requirements. It just didn't fit the life I had envisioned for myself, so I quit." Leaving the work force was quite difficult for Jan. As Reggie put it, "When she became pregnant with our second child, it hit her like a ton of bricks. The previous two years as full-time mother and homemaker had been seen as a temporary thing, but with the second child on the way it started to feel like a permanent assignment."

Jan eventually looked around for another job and a company that would be flexible in terms of the level of time commitment required yet provide interesting and challenging assignments. They just were not there! Finally, she discovered that large companies were not the only game in town and that small businesses needed occasional marketing expertise. She now works as a consultant out of her home. She confides, "It's not a perfect situation. The flexibility is great, and I enjoy promoting myself. Unfortunately, the consulting projects I've picked up aren't very challenging and the income is unpredictable, but hopefully this will change."

Organizations need people. Without people, organizations cannot achieve their goals and produce goods or services. In a similar way, people, like Jan and Reggie, need organizations. Without organizations, people would have few opportunities to satisfy their many needs, accomplish their varied goals, and engage in activities that enrich and add meaning to their lives. This mutual dependence on one another is the basis for the topic of this chapter. Careers provide organizations a way to channel people into needed areas and to develop their skills so that they can continue to perform needed organizational functions. If this is done right, employees also gain. Careers can provide chances to have experiences and jobs that offer valued rewards and develop skills, leading to other desirable opportunities and a brighter future. Consider your own case. Why are you in this class and reading this book? For many, it is a chance to develop skills and gain knowledge that will contribute to a successful and satisfying career. At a minimum, this course probably leads to a degree, which in turn will open a few doors. Organizations also have a stake in this process. The supply of graduates that schools produce allows organizations to acquire partially trained and socialized human resources (at what some students consider bargain basement prices!).

However, schooling is only the first step in many people's careers. Most of the interesting action that makes up career processes in people's lives starts after they check out of school and into their first career-oriented job. Accordingly, this chapter will focus on the patterns and consequences of careers in organizations. First, we will define the meaning of the term *career*, and discuss the major ways of conceiving individual career orientation. Then, career and adult life stages that depict changes people tend to go through will be presented. Following this, organizational practices and supervisory behavior associated with effective career management are discussed. The chapter concludes with an approach for students to plan and prepare for their own careers.

WHAT IS A CAREER?

A **career** is a sequence of work activities and positions, and associated attitudes and reactions, experienced over a person's life.[1] Thus, it involves a variety of objective events (e.g., promotions) and self-perceived reactions that occur throughout a lifetime. Three elements are important in fully understanding the meaning of a career. First, a career involves moving on a path over time. This path has two sides. One side is the more or less objective path that employees follow in an organization (sometimes called external careers because they can be seen by external observers).[2] The pattern of placing new graduates in a "contract administrator" position and promoting them into a "senior contract administrator" job and eventually into a "senior contract negotiator" position is an example of the prescribed **external career** in a contracts department in a West Coast aerospace firm. These paths may be orderly, like the three-position contracts sequence, or have major discontinuities of functional, as well as hierarchical-level, position changes in which the duties in one position do not naturally build on the skills developed in the previous job. Frequently, these steps are not planned and seem to emerge over time. The other side of this path is the individual's subjective interpretation of the meaning of various work experiences, sometimes called the **internal career** because it can be known only from the point of view of the actor. Internal careers are the individual's reactions to the objective bench marks of the external career. The criteria that people use to evaluate their progress change over time. For example, being a contract administrator is likely to have a very different meaning to the new graduate at age twenty-two than it will at thirty-two after ten years of no movement. A position that is associated at one point in time with feelings of optimism and a brighter future can later be associated with feelings of being "stuck" or a failure.

The second key element of a career is that it is the interaction of individual and organizational factors. People's reaction to a given job is a function of the fit between the individual's occupational self-concept (i.e., the pattern of needs, aptitudes, and preferences) and types of opportunities, constraints, and demands provided by that job. One person might find the contract administrator job interesting and challenging and a step to a brighter future. Another might find it stifling. Understanding these differences is critical to effectively managing one's own career, as well as helping others, such as subordinates, manage their careers.

The third important element of a career is that it is an occupational identity.[3] What people do in our society is very much a key element in who they are. When we are getting acquainted with someone new, "What do you do?" is often one of the first questions posed. People vary as to how important their occupational self-identity is to their overall identity, but for many it is the primary factor in how they define who they are.

INDIVIDUAL DIFFERENCES IN CAREER ORIENTATION

Fortunately for everyone concerned, people are not all the same. Each of us differs in terms of skills, values, goals, and preferred activities. However, as different as people are from one another, there are also a number of similarities between people. Consider the two people in the story at the beginning of this chapter. Although Jan and Reginald are markedly different in some respects, they are similar in a number of ways to a lot of other people. Useful information on these patterns of similarities and dissimilarities in career orientation would tell us:

- What are the specific ways in which people are similar and/or different from one another?
- How might knowledge of similarities and differences help us to understand how different types of people will react to certain work situations?
- How can the answers to these two questions help individuals to plan more satisfying careers and help organizations to more effectively manage their human resources?

Scientists studying careers have developed a number of insights that help us to answer these questions. Through a number of studies, they have developed ways of categorizing people that capture major patterns of similarities and differences in people's career orientation. As depicted in Exhibit 18–1, **career orientation** is defined in terms of the preferred activities, talents, and attitudes that people have. Different career orientations are consistent with particular task demands and

EXHIBIT 18–1   **Career orientation and its consequences.**

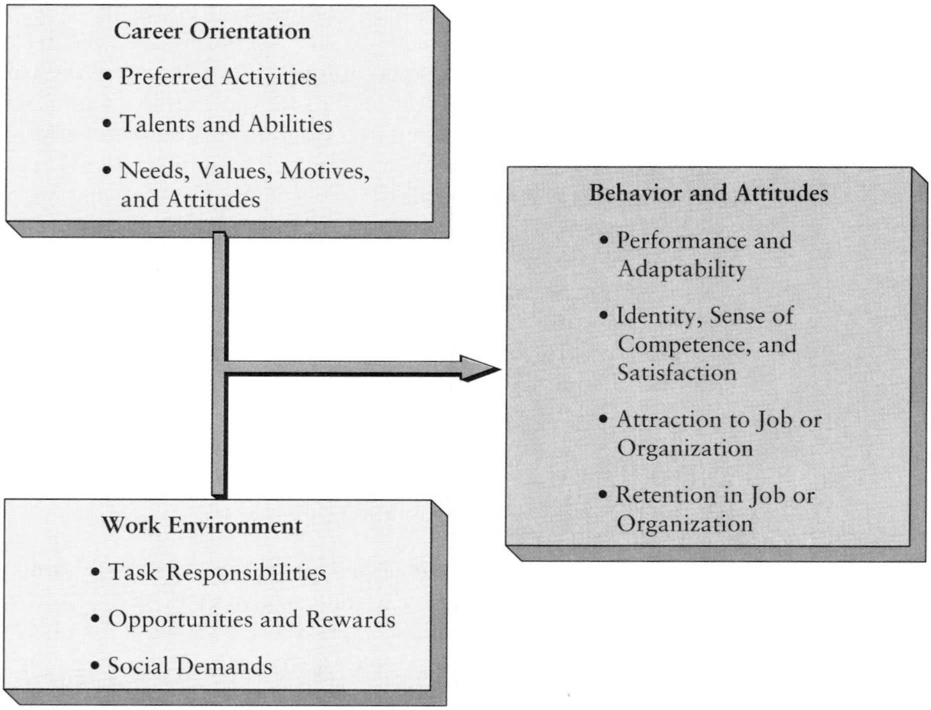

Career Orientation
- Preferred Activities
- Talents and Abilities
- Needs, Values, Motives, and Attitudes

Work Environment
- Task Responsibilities
- Opportunities and Rewards
- Social Demands

Behavior and Attitudes
- Performance and Adaptability
- Identity, Sense of Competence, and Satisfaction
- Attraction to Job or Organization
- Retention in Job or Organization

rewards presented in some work environments. The fit or consistency between one's career orientation and work environment has direct consequences in terms of people's job behavior and attitudes.

Holland's Theory of Career Types

Easily the most researched and best-documented theory of career orientation is John Holland's **theory of career types.**[4] Years of studies have documented that six distinct patterns explain many people's career orientation. These are presented in the hexagonal model in Exhibit 18–2. Some of these orientations or career types are almost the direct opposite of one another, while those adjacent to one another on the hexagonal model are more similar.

EXHIBIT
18–2

Holland's career types.

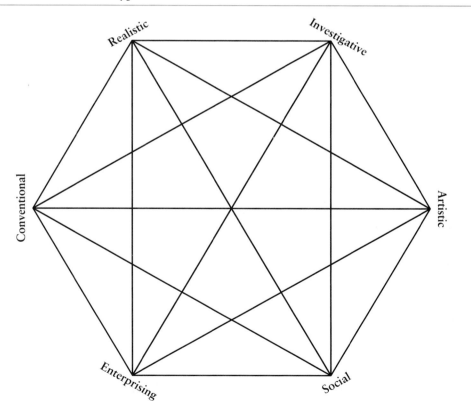

Source: Adapted from Holland, J. L. (1973). *Making vocational choices: A theory of careers.* Englewood Cliffs, NJ: Prentice-Hall, p. 23. Reprinted by permission.

Conventional The conventional orientation is probably the most dominant career type found in business occupations. This type of person prefers rule-regulated, orderly activities that generally include organizing written or numerical information or analyzing this information with an unambiguous set of procedures (e.g., computing financial ratios). These people are typically described as conforming, orderly, efficient, and practical. Less flattering descriptions include unimaginative, inhibited, and inflexible. Reggie, in the opening story, seemed to have a number of these qualities. Accounting and finance jobs, which require the precise organization and evaluation of numerical information in a fairly stable work setting with clear operating procedures, typically fit people with a conventional orientation. The consequence is that they are attracted to, and perform well in, these work environments. Reggie's selection of a finance and accounting emphasis in school and finance and accounting jobs illustrates how career orientation and work environment fit can work.

Artistic The artistic career orientation is the most dissimilar to the conventional type. These people prefer ambiguous and unsystematic activities that entail creating expressive written, spoken, or visual forms. These people are often described as imaginative, intuitive, and independent as well as disorderly, emotional, and impractical. Painting, music, and drama are obvious artistic occupations. The most negative descriptions, like "impractical," are characterizations that the opposite of an artistic type, a conventional career type, is likely to make. Artistic types are, in turn, more likely than other types to return the favor by coming up with pejorative descriptions of conventional-type people, such as unimaginative and inflexible. While business organizations will have far fewer artistic types than conventional types, they could easily be exactly what graphics or advertising departments need.

Realistic The realistic career type prefers activities that require the physical manipulation of objects or tools in a well-ordered work environment with few social demands. These people usually have mechanical abilities and are most likely to be described as genuine, stable, and practical as well as possibly shy, uninsightful, and conforming. This type of person is likely to be at home in semiskilled or crafts positions (e.g., carpenter, mechanic, assembly line worker, plumber) that present consistent task requirements and few social demands, such as negotiating and persuading.

Social The social type is the near opposite of the realistic career orientation. This type of person prefers activities that involve informing, helping, or developing others and has an aversion to well-ordered and systematic work environments. Besides being described as sociable, this person is typically characterized as tactful, friendly, understanding, and helpful. Less positive descriptions (which are most likely to be made by the opposite of this career type, the realistic type) include dominating and manipulative. Clearly, Jan had a number of these qualities and, as a consequence, was attracted to a work situation in which she interacted with, and attempted to understand, other people in a fairly unstructured setting. Nursing and teaching are occupations in which jobs typically fit the social type. Within business firms, marketing, sales, and training and development are areas that often fit the unique needs of this career type.

Enterprising.   The enterprising type is somewhat similar to the social career orientation in that they like to work with people. The main difference is that enterprising types prefer to focus their energies on leading and controlling others (versus helping or understanding) in order to reach specific organizational goals or obtain economic gains. Positive characterizations of these people include self-confident, ambitious, energetic, and talkative. Less flattering descriptions include domineering, power-hungry, and impulsive. Consider Jan again. While she is primarily a social type, the "quite an actor" description, her efforts to successfully launch the new product line, and starting a consulting practice fit the profile of the enterprising type. Perhaps, if the product line manager position that she was offered had involved predominantly interpersonal influence requirements (which fit the enterprising type) and less "digesting" numerical data (which fits the conventional type), Jan would have found it harder to turn down.

Investigative   The investigative is the near-opposite of the enterprising career orientation. People in this category prefer activities that involve observing and analyzing phenomena in order to develop knowledge and understanding. These people are seen as complicated, original, and independent as well as possibly disorderly, impractical, and impulsive, and they have an aversion to repetitious activities and to selling. Science occupations, such as biologist, sociologist, and mathematician, are well suited to this career type. Within business organizations, these people are attracted to research and development positions and staff positions that require complex analyses with little need to persuade and convince others.

Career Choice   Holland's theory is primarily concerned with career choice. It identifies specific types of people and particular types of work environments to which each type will be attracted. There is evidence that people who end up in work environments that are not consistent with their career orientation tend to be dissatisfied and either gradually shift their orientation (i.e., become more like the career type that is congruent with their work environment) or move to a new work situation. One can see an explicit attraction-selection process operating in Jan's and Reggie's early career choices. Each found positions that had work environments (e.g., task duties, rewards, and social demands) that fit each of their distinctly different orientations and chose those jobs over others that they were considering. Being in a congruent work environment also increases the likelihood that they will be satisfied, achieve a sense of competence, and stay with the organization.

At this point, you might be wondering whether all people neatly fit into one of the six career types. The real world is certainly more complicated than this. Many of these complexities are recognized in Holland's theory. He acknowledges that many people are like Jan and seem to be a combination of two, or perhaps three, career types. The combinations that most frequently develop are those which are adjacent to each other on the hexagonal model presented in Exhibit 18–2. Jan's social-enterprising combination is quite consistent with the theory. She was interested in both figuring out people and being involved with them (which is consistent with the social orientation), yet she also enjoyed promoting the new product line and influencing people (which is characteristic of the enterprising type). Another consistent combination is the conventional-enterprising combination, which fits many, but certainly not all, managerial positions. The most unlikely combinations are those involving types that are opposite to each other on the hexagonal model, such as conventional-artistic or investigative-enterprising.

Holland's theory even predicts which people are least likely to be attracted to, or more satisfied in, work environments that seemingly fit their career orientation. Research finds that people with an inconsistent combination of orientations (i.e., those which are opposite one another on the hexagonal model in Exhibit 18–2, such as the artistic-conventional combination) or those with an undifferentiated pattern (i.e., people who see themselves as a little bit like many types and not very dissimilar to any type) are the least likely to be strongly attracted to, or satisfied with, a particular work environment. They are also the ones who are most likely to stay and adjust their career orientation to an initially inconsistent work environment. Those with a less inconsistent or more differentiated combination of characteristics would have a stronger negative reaction to the specific work demands that are incongruent with that orientation and start searching for a better alternative.

Do people use Holland's theory? This theory is the basis for much vocational guidance counseling. Many students, in attempting to figure out what kinds of jobs they want (and what kind of college major they should choose), visit a guidance counselor and are given the Strong Vocational Interest Blank.[5] This instrument compares one's interests to those in a variety of occupations. These occupations are grouped into the six Holland career types. Thus, the test tells you whether you have interests similar to those in occupations in each of the six career type categories. These results are used to guide students into majors and career paths that are consistent with their interests. In summary, the basic thrust of the counseling is to find out what career type you are and then get yourself qualified for jobs that are congruent with the orientation. Doing this increases the chances of finding a career that requires you to use your strengths, fulfills your needs, and puts you into association with people with whom you are likely to have much in common.

Schein's Theory of Career Anchors

A more recent development in the study of careers is Edgar Schein's **theory of career anchors.**[6] Unlike Holland's career types, anchors develop well after childhood and adolescence. Career anchors evolve and develop through the successive new trials and opportunities that one faces in early work experiences. Gradually, as one gains more self-knowledge and a clearer occupational self-concept, a distinct pattern of self-perceived talents, motives, needs, and values emerges. These distinct patterns are called career anchors. The five patterns that have been documented by early research are technical/functional competence, managerial competence, security, autonomy, and creativity. Just as a boat's anchor keeps it from drifting, career anchors keep one centered on certain types of work activities. If people happen to take on inconsistent work assignments, their career anchor acts to pull them back to more consistent activities.

Technical/Functional Competence For people with this anchor the primary factor in their career choices and decisions is the actual content of work. A chance to move to a job that takes them away from their technical or functional area is unattractive. Consider Jan in the opening story. The so-called opportunity to move into general management and away from pure marketing activities was not an opportunity in her eyes. For her, the marketing area and the activities that it required her to do were closely tied to her feelings of competence. Moving would have required her to engage in activities and develop skills that did not fit her basic occupational self-concept. As a result, she told her boss, "I'm a marketer, not a manager." Engaging in marketing activities is consistent with her values and motives and allowed her to use skills and talents in which she had grown confident.

Managerial Competence For people with this career anchor, the ultimate goal is to rise to positions of managerial responsibility. Reggie developed a strong managerial competence anchor early in his career. The position on the controller's staff provided him an opportunity to develop analytical and interpersonal competencies and gain valued exposure while getting his "ticket punched" on the way to his real goal, general management. People with this anchor see their competence tied to three areas: 1) analytical competence with which they can identify and solve problems with incomplete and uncertain information, 2) interpersonal competence through which they can influence others toward the achievement of organizational goals, and 3) emotional competence in dealing with high levels of responsibility and the exercise of power (e.g., firing someone). There appears to be a connection between Holland's enterprising and conventional career types and this anchor. Interpersonal influence competence is consistent with the enterprising orientation, while analytical competence corresponds to some of the characteristics of the conventional type. One potential inconsistency is that the conventional person is attracted to an orderly and stable work environment. Schein often talks about the inherent uncertainty and disorderliness of many managerial work environments. This latter characteristic is most consistent with Holland's social career orientation. Early in Reggie's career, it was unclear whether he would develop adequate interpersonal skills and tolerance for uncertainty and fully fit the characteristics of the managerial competence anchor. Perhaps he took some lessons from Jan along the way.

Security For some people a key factor in career planning and decision making is the development of long-term work life stability and security. A good benefits and retirement package, past employment stability (e.g., few cycles of mass layoffs and rehiring), and clear career paths such as explicit, planned sequences of jobs for employees are some organizational features that are particularly attractive to a person with this anchor. Opportunities to use certain technical skills or promotion prospects may be of some importance if, and only if, they are seen as leading to long-term stability and security.

Autonomy For the autonomy-anchored person, the chance to stay in a technical area, steadily march up a corporate hierarchy, or gain guaranteed-for-life employment would not be a highly valued opportunity. For these people, movement up the organizational ladder could be a trade-off between freedom to pursue their own interests and lifestyle versus status, responsibility, and money. Managerial competence people will want more of the latter, even if it costs them some freedom and constrains their lifestyle. Autonomy-anchored people, however, are more likely to say no to advancement if it means giving up their independence and freedom. The people in this category in Schein's original study were very satisfied. Some found their freedom in consulting roles, while others pursued careers as a freelance writer, a small business proprietor, and a college professor. The size of the organizations they were attracted to was generally small.

Creativity Creativity-anchored people differ from people in the other categories in a specific way. While many of them want some degree of autonomy or to exercise managerial or technical/functional competence, they are unique in their overarching desire to create something that is entirely of their own making. It might be a product or technical process or a company. The creative anchor can find expression in a number of ways. One is through entrepreneurship, which could include starting a new business venture. The second is through "intrapreneurship" from within an established company (Chapter 17). As an intrapreneur, one might carve out a unique role that allows one to try out and develop new ideas. Edwin Land of Polaroid is a prototypical example of this. His role in the organization is to develop innovations. Another possible role is the manager who works on special projects that require such things as developing a new product idea or developing and implementing a new manufacturing process. For creativity-anchored people, inventing something new is a measure of worth and the key to their sense of competence.

Career anchors provide a way to understand and predict how a person (such as Jan or Reggie in the story at the beginning of this chapter) is going to react to a particular work situation. It is important to remember that in the short term, people with very different orientations can find fulfillment in the same job, perhaps working right next to each other. For example, Reggie could conceivably have opted for a marketing position instead of accounting. Thus, for awhile he could have comfortably worked in a position very similar to Jan's. However, over time the differences in the way they evaluate their self-perceived success will reveal very different reactions to similar jobs. Lack of movement or a transfer to another marketing position might be just what Jan wants but might suggest to Reggie that he has been sidetracked and is not succeeding.

Managerial Implications of Career Orientation

The explicit message of both Holland's and Schein's models of career orientation is that the people who run organizations should take into account differences in orientation when managing their human resources. Managerial practices that treat all people the same, which on the surface might seem like the fair thing to do, inevitably treat some of those people in ways that are dissatisfying and detract from organizational effectiveness.

For example, high-level (managerial competence–anchored) managers who create human resource policies and practices sometimes make the mistake of assuming that all reasonable employees basically prefer the same things that they do. As a result, they create reward systems and promotion patterns that conflict with other people's career orientations. Technical/functional competence–anchored people might find that they must leave their technical positions and take on managerial roles in order to have higher levels of compensation, a company-provided car, status, and influence in the company. The lack of a nonmanagerial or technical route to greater prestige and rewards puts nonmanagerial-anchored people in a dilemma. If they choose to stay close to the technical work they love, they will feel a sense of inequity (see Chapters 5 and 6) and might lessen their effort (a key input in equity theory terms) or look for another employer who will treat them in what they consider a fair and just manner. The managerial competence–anchored manager might have a hard time appreciating how an employee who turns down a "good" promotion can feel mistreated! This stems from a lack of understanding of individual differences and the assumption that "people are either similar to me or weird." On the other hand, if the technical/functional competence–anchored person takes the temptation to move to a nontechnical job, the consequence might be some dissatisfaction in spite of the extra rewards and potential poor performance, since the person's orientation does not match task demands. Presenting these types of dilemmas to employees results not only in human costs, but also in organizational costs associated with diminished motivation and a misallocation of human resources.

Treating different people differently not only can be satisfying to those involved, but can help the organization achieve its goals. Doing this requires managers to take some positive steps. These might include:

- Understand and identify key individual difference characteristics that will shape the way in which employees will react to so-called opportunities
- Identify key job and situational factors that are congruent with each of these characteristics
- Develop ways of matching employees to congruent work environment factors

The first two steps have been the focus of the first part of this chapter, while approaches for matching individuals and work situations will be addressed below.

Before turning our attention to those issues, a bias that is present in both Schein's and Holland's theories must be corrected. Both suggest that people are rather static and that once they develop their career orientations, by their middle to late twenties, they stay the same for life. This is clearly not true. Careers, like lives, have a dynamic quality and evolve and change in some predictable ways across adulthood.

CAREER AND ADULT LIFE STAGES

Over the past few years, behavioral scientists have found evidence of specific patterns of change and development throughout the adult years. Theorizing and research have been directed to patterns of change in one's work role (career stages) and more broadly focused patterns of development that include nonwork issues. While no two people go through a career or life in exactly the same fashion, the patterns that scientists have discovered are broadly descriptive of many people's careers and adult years. Awareness of these patterns provides a general "road map" of many issues and demands that a young adult will face over his or her adult years.

Adult Life Stages

Adult life stages have their basis in both biological factors associated with adult aging processes and patterns of social expectations that exist in society. Thus, these are referred to as **biosocial life stages** in that they are the product of both forces. For example, a decline in biological vitality and increased frequency of health problems confront the middle-aged adult with the realization that life is half over and that time, in a very real way, is limited. The sudden emotional realization of this fact of life can lead to a reassessment of prior lifestyle choices and result in rather major changes and reordering of personal priorities (sometimes this stage is called the mid-life crisis). A key social force that influences adult development is **age norms,** which are widely accepted expectations in society about what behavior is appropriate for a person at a given age.[7] People whose behavior does not fit existing age norms find that they are given cues (such as others asking questions like "How come you're not married?" or "Isn't it time to settle down and think about a career?") that put pressure on them to conform.

A number of life-stage theorists have developed theories that, in spite of some differences, are quite consistent with one another. They all generally present the notion that across the adult years there are fairly stable periods that are a time for playing out prior decisions and lifestyle commitments. These stable periods are followed by more dynamic transitional periods during which prior choices are reconsidered and adjustments to various aspects of one's general style of life are explored. Sometimes, but certainly not always, these transitions are fairly traumatic and constitute crises that prompt major changes in people's lives.

One popular view of adult life stages is summarized in Exhibit 18–3.[8] It starts with the "early adult transition," which involves moving from adolescence and the exploration of various work roles and lifestyle choices to settling into a relatively stable period, called "entering adulthood," in which these preliminary choices about one's lifestyle are more fully tested. Toward the end of the twenties comes a period when those earlier choices are reassessed. This "age 30 transition" can be a traumatic time of disillusionment and change (e.g., divorce, major occupational change), but for many people it is more a time of minor adjustments, not revolution. Jan, in the opening story, went through a definite age thirty transition.

■
EXHIBIT
18–3

Levinson's adult life stages.

Approximate Age Range	Life Stage and Major Characteristics
17–22	*Early adult transition.* Leave adolescence, make a preliminary step into the adult world by exploring different lifestyle choices and lessen dependence on parents.
22–28	*Entering adulthood.* Select and test out a specific set of choices of lifestyles and roles.
28–33	*Age 30 transition.* Reassess previous choices, often with a sense of urgency to sort out one's life and make important choices before it is too late; this may be a smooth transition or a painful crisis.
33–40	*Settling down.* Focus on a specific agenda for accomplishing goals and advance, in occupational or nonoccupational terms, to higher levels of status.
40–45	*Mid-life transition.* Reappraise past lifestyle choices and begin to eliminate negative elements and test new choices. Radical changes to major elements (e.g., marriage, occupation) can be the result of a major disillusionment with one's life called the "mid-life crisis."
45–60	*Middle adulthood era.* Carry out lifestyle changes resulting from the mid-life transition. Often people "shift gears" and direct more time into nonwork, leisure activities.
60+	*Late adult transition & late adult era.* Some evidence of a continued pattern of reassessing prior choices and incorporating new values, interests, and behaviors into an altered lifestyle. Little research has been conducted on the specific qualities of these changes.

Source: Adapted from Levinson, D. J., et al. (1978). *The seasons of a man's life.* These stages were identified through an intensive study of forty adult males in a number of occupations. See the text regarding their applicability to women. Copyright © 1978 by Daniel J. Levinson. Reprinted by permission of Alfred A. Knopf, Inc.

She found that events that had previously been satisfying now had less meaning. A combination of social forces, such as friends and family asking her whether she was going to have children and awareness of biological realities that make child-bearing more risky in the middle to late thirties, probably helped to initiate this period of reassessment. Jan made rather dramatic changes in her life (i.e., quitting her job and becoming a full-time homemaker). It appears that Reggie's age thirty transition was very smooth and hardly noticeable.

After the age thirty transition, a more stable "settling down" period begins. A person in this stage often focuses on establishing a stable and secure niche in society and planning and striving to achieve particular goals (such as owning a house in a particular area, having one's own business, making vice-president by a certain age, etc.). In Jan's case it was focusing on her goal of having a family and then adding a limited outside work role. Her going back to paid work was not simply a return to the lifestyle and priorities that she had in her twenties. Her work role in her thirties was important but definitely a secondary element in her overall life. Much of the research on men's life stages paints a very different picture; "making it" on specific work role goals is a central focus in their lives.

Sometimes the relatively stable settling-down stage comes to a rather dramatic conclusion with the onset of the "mid-life transition." In the study that established this theory of life stages, 20 percent of the participants went through a period of minor questioning and adjustments. However, for the remaining 80 percent, this transitional period was a traumatic time in which forgotten values, identities, or fantasies were confronted. The realization of one's biological mortality and a sense of having a limited amount of time are key factors that can be triggered by such events as the death of a friend or parent or a major illness. After the crisis is resolved and ways of giving forgotten identities more expression are determined, the next stable period, "middle adulthood," begins. The research on life stages after this point is quite limited. No doubt that as people live longer and longer, more research on additional life stages will become available.

The life stages shown in Exhibit 18–3 seem to do a reasonable job of explaining Jan and Reggie's somewhat different developmental patterns. However, there has been considerable debate (but not really enough research) about whether such adult life development models apply generally to both men and women. These models, which are usually developed by men studying men, tend to emphasize increasing individualism, autonomy, and work achievement in the first half of adulthood. However, many observers have noted in women an interest in relationships, attachments, and interdependence with others that *could* change both the timing and sequence of adult development stages.[9] In turn, this suggests different but equally viable career patterns for women. For example, it is not uncommon to see women over forty renew a paid career after staying home with children while their husbands are refocusing their own interests on home life.[10]

In summary, adult life stages affect career activity. What is less clear is how similar these stages are for men and women.

Career Stages

Careers are an important aspect of many people's lives. Thus, they are influenced by the evolving pattern of needs, interests, and concerns associated with adult life stages. There are, however, general patterns of developmental changes in work role activities that are distinct from life stages. These are called **career stages**. While everyone's career contains unique demands that dictate highly specific steps to success, there are issues and key tasks that are of general importance to a wide range of people. Exhibit 18–4 summarizes four career stages: exploration, establishment, advancement and maintenance, and late career. Knowing about career stages, like knowing about life stages, provides a map of likely events and concerns that a young adult will face in the future. Having a map increases the likelihood that the journey will be successful.

EXHIBIT

18–4

Career stages.

Approximate Age Ranges	Career Stage and Characteristics
16–28	*Exploration.* Explore various occupational roles and test out an initial occupational identity. Develop skills, establish a social network and mentor relationship, and cope with the emotional demands of early career.
22–42	*Establishment.* Become an individual contributor with a specific area of expertise. Work through work versus nonwork conflicts and develop a plan for achieving career goals.
32–55	*Advancement and maintenance.* Focus on achieving career goals and maintaining organizational progress. Revise career plan in light of progress. Redetermine the relative importance of work and nonwork roles. For many the top position in their career becomes evident, and few promotions are likely. Become a mentor.
55–retirement	*Late career.* Usually the highest position has been reached, and people have started to shift more energy into nonwork pursuits. Their main source of contribution is breadth of knowledge and experience. Mentoring can continue throughout this stage.

Source: Adapted from Hall, D. T. (1976). *Careers in organizations.* Glenview, IL: Scott, Foresman, and Schein, E. (1977). *Career dynamics.* Reading, MA: Addison-Wesley. Note that the ranges identify the ages within which most people enter and complete each stage. The issues and concerns identified with each stage are based on research on technical, professional, and managerial careers and may have less relevance to craft and blue-collar careers.

Exploration   This stage is a time of discovery and choice. People often leave adolescence with a wide range of ideas about what they want to do and, generally, what is possible in the world of jobs and occupations. As they move into the adult world, they must leave behind unrealistic views and settle in on a configuration of roles (i.e., student, wife/husband, occupation) and develop a lifestyle that fits key elements of their identity. This involves leaving one's family of origin and developing a mix of talents, skills, and complementary interests and values that are in demand by society. These choices are broader than establishing one's occupational identity, but often one's choice of work role is the major element.

During the early part of this stage, several trial runs (such as part-time work or summer jobs during college) in different work roles are explored. These set the stage for more focused exploration during one's first "real" job. For many, this is the first job after graduation from high school or college. This job often has an enduring influence on one's career. Successfully coping with three particular tasks seems to increase the likelihood that this influence will be positive. These are:

- Establishing a social network of relationships
- Getting a job that challenges one's skills and abilities
- Coping with the emotional side of work

A social network has two key elements, one's peers and a senior person who will be the person's mentor. Peers can provide information about ways to accomplish job assignments and give feedback about the consequences of different career strategies.[11] This can help to make up for some of the limited experiences of a person in this career stage. Additionally, they can also be a source of friendship and emotional support during times of career or personal crisis. Substantial research has confirmed the importance of finding a mentor early in one's career. A **mentor** is a senior person in the organization who gives a junior person (called an **apprentice** or protégé) special attention. This can include giving advice and creating opportunities. An example of this is present in the opening story. Reggie might never have heard of the opportunity in the accounting department, let alone had someone to put in a good word for him, if he had not developed a special relationship with his supervisor. More on the topic of mentoring will be presented later in the chapter.

A challenging first job can have a lasting impact on people's careers.[12] In one study, a group of young managers was followed for a five- to seven-year period. Their performance at the end of the study, as measured by salary level and performance ratings, was directly tied to the level of challenge in the first job assignment. Those who had easy first assignments, even if more challenging assignments were later added, seemed to be at a distinct disadvantage. Unfortunately, providing an easy first job and then cautiously adding more stretching assignments seems to be the implicit policy of many companies.[13] Successfully completing the first job and getting an early first promotion also have a long-term impact on promotion opportunities ten years later.[14] Jan and Reggie, in the opening story, were both fortunate to land challenging first jobs. Reggie's steady career movement up the corporate hierarchy illustrates the positive consequence of having a challenging first assignment and also getting an early promotion before the others who joined the company at about the same time have been promoted and left him behind.

Dealing with the emotional side of work is also important. A common phenomenon faced by many young people entering the work force is **reality shock.** This is caused by the disparity between unrealistic expectations that people often have and the reality that they confront in their first job (see Chapter 9). The consequence can be strong dissatisfaction until new expectations are developed and more challenging elements are added to the new person's role in the organization. The inherent dependency position associated with being a subordinate can also evoke a negative emotional reaction. This occurs at a time when the person has often only recently left his or her family of origin. The dependencies that one has on his or her bosses can often feel like a return to adolescence. Additionally, people who are just starting out their careers normally feel a little insecure about their untried and untested skills and abilities. Testing those skills and developing more self-confidence require people to cope with the emotional challenges of insecurity. Having a social network can go a long way in helping a person through these difficult times.

Establishment The second major career stage involves establishing oneself as an independent contributor in a fairly specific area of expertise. During the earlier period, people tend to try their hand at many tasks. Establishing a career identity involves setting priorities of skills and interests and focusing on key activities that are central to one's goals and plans. It is generally necessary to move away from a close relationship with a mentor at this time. Dealing with the independence of not having someone to closely check their work can provoke feelings of insecurity unless people have developed some sound skills during the earlier stage. Conflict between work and nonwork roles can also be a problem. For example, people with families might find growing children demanding much more of their time (school plays, recreation programs, etc.) at the very time at which their biological vitality has begun to decline. Role conflict (see Chapter 8) can result when meeting one's career goals also demands an extra investment of time and energy.

Advancement and Maintenance After people establish themselves in a particular occupational role, they often enter a period in which they focus on advancing toward key career objectives such as making partner in an accounting firm or publishing a respected book. This is then followed by a period in which they are concerned with maintaining their status and position. In the early part of this stage, people often feel a sense of urgency to accomplish certain career goals. Final career strategy choices must be made, and unrealistic objectives must be recognized and eliminated. After this, people enter a phase in which they generally stay close to their proven skills and interests. People's main career assets are likely to be breadth of experience and a general knowledge of a variety of areas. Some people take on mentoring responsibilities and find satisfaction in training and developing the next generation. All must confront the fact that there is a younger generation of people who see them as old-timers.

Late Career For a few, late career is a time for continued growth in status and influence within the organization, but for many it is a time when the highest level of responsibility and status has already been reached or is clearly in sight. Signs of aging are obvious in this stage, and some people face serious health problems. Retirement plans and decisions on how to spend postretirement years are made at this point. As one faces pensions and loss of salary financial considerations can be a source of anxiety. People often withdraw energy and time from career pursuits in this stage and become more concerned with nonwork factors.

People in this stage can be a source of wisdom for the organization. At this point, most people move away from a detailed understanding of their technical area and, perhaps, branch into areas in which their broad range of experience and general understanding of a variety of issues can be tapped. Mentoring, which may have begun in the previous stage, can continue throughout this final career stage.

Restructuring and global competition place new demands on managers. Bonnie Stedt, executive vice-president at American Express, works 70-hour weeks. (Rob Kinmonth)

CAREER PLANNING AND DEVELOPMENT: THE ORGANIZATION'S ROLE

Up to this point, the focus of this chapter has been primarily on individuals. Specifically, career orientations, which describe how people differ in terms of motives and interests, and patterns of career change have been presented. Careers, however, involve more than people. Organizations have a large stake in the effective management of people's careers. Organizations can be managed in ways that help people to more successfully meet their own career objectives and, at the same time, contribute to organizational effectiveness.

Historically, more organizations have had an implicit "sink or swim" philosophy about managing human resources. This translates into a "the cream will naturally rise to the top" (or do nothing) approach toward facilitating the career development of employees. While this is still standard practice at a number of organizations, significant changes are taking place. Many organizations are now deeply involved with a variety of career-related programs and actively encourage managers to take their employees' careers seriously. **Career management** activities are programs and systems that are designed to enhance individual **career development** (i.e., development of skills, identification of goals and strategies, and the realization of one's full potential).[15] The more widely used career management practices will be presented first, followed by a discussion of the manager's role in mentoring junior employees.

Career Management Programs

Every couple of months, personnel journals present new and different techniques related to career management. In general, these fit into several basic categories that have been around for some years. Large companies like Sears, IBM, and General Electric might offer a number of such programs.

Performance Appraisal/Career Planning Programs One popular approach is to graft a career planning thrust onto an existing program. Performance evaluation systems that require a yearly appraisal meeting between supervisors and subordinates are a frequent target. For example, a number of business units in General Electric require managers to have their employees complete a self-evaluation that includes assessing career strengths and weaknesses as well as identifying career goals and objectives for the next three years. Managers are instructed to discuss the employee's input either during the regular appraisal session or during a separate meeting. A Management by Objectives (MBO) program (Chapter 7) is also a frequent target for adding on a career thrust. In one study, about 50 percent of the firms surveyed introduced career planning by grafting it on to existing human resource management programs.[16]

Many supervisors probably handle the career-oriented appraisal or MBO meeting skillfully and conclude the session with some specific development suggestions. The basic problem with such programs is that they are solely dependent on the supervisor's skill and motivation. The fact that there is strong evidence that supervisors often do not carry out required yearly performance appraisal does not inspire confidence that merely linking career discussion to the performance appraisal or MBO discussion is the optimal approach to career development.

Formal Career Planning Programs In an effort to avoid such strong dependence upon supervisors, a number of organizations have developed formal programs in which experts give guidance and help employees through a structured sequence of planning steps. The following sequence is typical:

- *Individual identification of needs, goals, and abilities.* This helps the employees to determine some of their key strengths and weaknesses as well as the general types of positions to which they aspire. Sometimes an educational component will be included, and theories on career orientation and stages will be presented.
- *Identification of alternative career options within the organization.* This can include identifying training opportunities (e.g., tuition reimbursement, management development seminars), education and skills required for various jobs, and lower-level jobs that are most likely to prepare a person for specific higher-level jobs (job paths).
- *Establishment of specific career goals.* This should involve both short-term and long-term objectives and can include key future decision points between specific alternatives.
- *Determination of developmental activities needed to attain career goals.* These can include educational activities such as getting an M.B.A. degree or taking on new duties and responsibilities as part of one's current job.

Planning workshops that include, in varying degrees, each of the above steps have been conducted in many organizations. The extensiveness of the program is typically reflected in its length, which varies from a part of a day to one week. However, IBM has included many of these same steps in a computer-assisted program that can be done at the employee's convenience.[17] Perhaps the greatest benefit of these programs is not the identification of specific goals, but rather a proactive, "make opportunities happen" orientation to managing one's career. For an example, pause and consider You Be the Manager.

Developing High-Potential Employees Some types of programs focus on selecting employees with high potential for key jobs (usually managerial positions) and then carefully managing their development. These programs are fairly exclusive, and only a small percentage of employees are designated as high potential, or "high pots." Sometimes high pots are widely known. At the other extreme, this designation is a closely guarded secret, and even the employees who are so designated might not be sure that they have this special status. Sometimes their selection is fairly informal, such as a supervisor's putting in a good word for a subordinate with the personnel/human resources department. In a few cases, the selection is through a formal assessment center. In an assessment center, candidates dem-

YOU BE THE MANAGER

Career Planning at Pittsburgh National Bank

Pittsburgh National Bank (PNB) is located in Pittsburgh, Pennsylvania. Management at PNB gradually became aware that the bank was experiencing employee career development problems. These problems were resulting in unfulfilled career aspirations for individual employees. Also, from the bank's perspective, they were resulting in a less-than-optimal use of human resources.

Several symptoms signaled the need for some kind of a career planning system. For one thing, employees seemed to be applying for every internal job that opened up. This suggested that they were unaware of how their individual skills and talents could be used best at PNB. Also, a personnel department analysis showed that the tuition assistance program's costs were rising without clear evidence of a good return on investment. Evidently, many employees were acquiring outside education that wasn't being used at PNB. Finally, like many organizations, PNB found itself occasionally promoting people into supervisory positions on the basis of their technical competence only to find out that they did not have the skill or interest to manage. It was felt that a career development program would provide such employees with self-insight that would lead them to another career path and thus prevent costly promotion errors.

PNB wanted a career planning program that provided individual feedback to employees but that could be conducted in groups. Conducting the discussions in groups provides an efficient and relatively inexpensive way to provide career planning information. How would *you* design this program?

1. What are some features that you would include in the PNB career planning program?
2. How would you evaluate the success of the career planning program?

To find out what PNB did, see The Manager's Notebook.

Source: Adapted from Sweeney, D. C., Haller, D., & Sale, F., Jr. (1987, August). Individually controlled career counseling. *Training and Development Journal*, 58–61.

onstrate their skill levels in specially designed simulations of key job demands (e.g., group decision making, problem solving, counseling a poor performer) and are rated by multiple observers. Once selected, the development of high pots is usually taken very seriously. They are put into a position that develops key skills and then frequently moved to new positions to maintain optimal challenge and continuous learning. Supervisors frequently spend extra time with these people and give them special developmental assignments. There is usually an emphasis on giving the high pot exposure to various parts of organization. One criticism of this fast-track approach to development is that people are moved too quickly and end up knowing a little bit about everything but lack adequate depth of knowledge in any one area and never stay in one place long enough to really see the results of their efforts. As a consequence, they might not develop the self-confidence necessary for high-level positions.[18]

Career Counseling Some organizations attempt to supplement informal career advisement by having career counselors, typically located in the personnel/human resources department, available to answer employees' career-related questions. An advantage of this approach is that subordinates might not feel free to ask a supervisor about opportunities beyond the current job. Also, specially trained counselors might have more information about the range of career possibilities than the typical supervisor. Additionally, they might have better counseling skills and support material that will aid the employee in identifying career goals and needs. A disadvantage is that the career counselor is not likely to have as good an understanding of the subordinate's strengths and weaknesses as the employee's supervisor. To take better advantage of the supervisor's knowledge of the subordinate, some management development programs emphasize career counseling skills. Besides developing skills, they also provide general information on career alternatives within the company.

Career Information Systems These systems match information on people with information on positions to facilitate selection decisions. Information on people, sometimes referred to as skill inventories, identify job-related skills, abilities, and career goals. Information on positions should identify the skills, abilities, and educational level required to perform job duties. Developing these two types of information requires both a thorough analysis of job demands and sophisticated understanding of human skills and abilities. When a position becomes vacant, the information system generates a list of candidates whose personal characteristics match job requirements. This information is then used by the people making the selection decision in a way that strikes a balance between the twin objectives of selecting a qualified candidate who will perform well in the job and optimizing the employee's long-term development. Some candidates could comfortably carry out the job duties but might not develop in the new position. An ideal decision is one that meets both criteria. Some organizations use a committee to make this decision (sometimes called a selection board) and assign one person the role of emphasizing the employee development objective. This is intended to counterbalance others who might focus on selecting a high performer but ignore developmental issues. A key benefit of developing an information system is that employees who would otherwise be overlooked are at least considered in the earlier phases of the selection process. Without such systems, getting considered can be overly dependent upon employees hearing about a particular opening or having a supervisor or friend nominate them. In other words, such systems take some of the randomness out of career development.

Job Pathing This approach focuses on the types of skills required and developed in various jobs. Initially, an analysis is conducted to identify logical sequences of positions such that skills developed in an initial job provide the basis for further development and successful performance in the next job, and so on.[19] An ideal path is a sequence of positions that channel employees into new positions in which they are qualified to perform yet also challenged and developed by new job demands. These paths can link positions within a given functional area (e.g., marketing) or cross functional boundaries. Additionally, there can be branches and interconnections in the paths that provide multiple routes to higher-level positions. Sometimes the initial analysis can identify problems that can be eliminated only by redesigning jobs. An example is a sequence of jobs in which a later position in a sequence does not adequately go beyond the task demands of earlier positions and adequately challenge employees. An opposite type of problem is a sequence in which a later position requires such a dramatic change in skill requirements that employees moving through the sequence are likely to be overwhelmed. In either case, both current performance and long-term development are likely to be less than optimal. Sears and ARCO are examples of organizations that have used career pathing to further employee career development for a number of years.[20]

Effective Career Management Programs Whatever the exact configuration of programs that an organization selects, research suggests certain guidelines to increase the likelihood of success.[21] These include:

- *Integrate the human resource management system.* Information generated and used for one human resource management activity should be available and, if applicable, utilized in other activities. Assessing people on their creative abilities during the selection process and then ignoring that quality and focusing on such things as consistency and punctuality during their performance evaluation give people contradictory cues that will only hurt career development efforts.
- *Balance long-term developmental needs and short-term productivity maximization.* Both of these objectives are important and will, at times, be in conflict with one another. If management always opts for short-term productivity when the two conflict, employees will quickly figure out what really counts. Doing this requires management to view human resource management expenditures as an investment in the organization's future.

- *Link human resource activities to organizational strategic goals.* Organizational goals cannot be assumed to be constant. Ignoring possible strategic directions and related environmental changes in career development activities can produce a disaster equivalent to producing vacuum tube (1950s technology) specialists for a silicon chip world.

The Manager's Role in Mentoring Employees

The career success of individuals within an organization is obviously influenced by effective supervisor and subordinate relationships. One element of an effective relationship can be the development of an effective mentor-apprentice relationship. While someone other than the junior person's boss can serve as a mentor, often the supervisor is in a unique position to provide mentoring. A number of research efforts have documented the importance of having a mentor to people starting out their career.[22]

Career Functions of Mentoring A mentor provides a number of career-enhancing benefits to the young apprentice.[23] These benefits are made possible by the senior person's experience, knowledge of how the organization works, status, and influence with powerful people in the organization. The career functions of mentoring include:

- *Sponsorship.* The mentor might nominate the apprentice for advantageous transfers and promotions.
- *Exposure and visibility.* The mentor might provide opportunities to work with key people and see other parts of the organization.
- *Coaching and feedback.* The mentor might suggest work strategies and identify strengths and weaknesses in the apprentice's performance.
- *Providing developmental assignments.* Challenging work assignments that the mentor might provide can facilitate the development of key skills and knowledge that are crucial to further advancement.

These career functions are most likely to be provided by a mentor. Peers are infrequently in a position to be able to provide them.

Psychosocial Functions of Mentoring In addition to helping directly with career progress, mentors can provide certain psychosocial functions that are helpful in developing the apprentice's self-confidence, sense of identity, and ability to cope with emotional traumas that can damage a person's effectiveness. These include:

- *Role modeling.* This provides a set of attitudes, values, and behaviors for the junior person to imitate.
- *Acceptance and confirmation.* The mentor can also provide encouragement and support, which can help the apprentice gain confidence.
- *Counseling.* This provides an opportunity to discuss personal concerns and anxieties.

Providing these functions can turn an "all business" relationship, which might be suitable for accomplishing the various career functions, into one that provides for the emotional development of the apprentice.

While all mentors, by definition, provide some subset of the career functions, these psychosocial functions are not necessarily provided by a mentor. A network of close peers can go a long way in providing functions that one's mentor is not providing. People starting out their careers in an organization should be aware of the importance of both of these career and psychosocial functions and should attempt to establish a set of relationships (referred to as a social network) that fulfills them. A mentor relationship is usually a key element in this broader set of relationships.

Benefits to the Mentor   An effective mentor-apprentice relationship also provides a number of benefits for the mentor. In fact, if these benefits are not forthcoming, the mentor is unlikely to be motivated to spend the time and take the risks that mentoring involves. The time requirements of coaching and counseling are fairly obvious. The risk to mentoring is that poor performance by the apprentice will suggest that the mentor has poor judgment or inadequate training and developmental skills. Some of the benefits are task oriented. A good apprentice will typically do a number of mundane tasks. These types of tasks (e.g., copying and collating) must be done accurately. Having a reliable apprentice who will handle these details frees the mentor for other concerns. Other benefits are related to the mentor's career and biosocial life stage. Often, mentors are in the stage of their careers in which promotions start slowing down. Developing an effective subordinate can contribute to the mentor's sense of competence and self-worth. Life-stage theorists have pointed out that at mid-life, people often develop "generativity needs," which can be satisfied only by passing on one's wisdom and experience to the next generation. Effective mentoring will satisfy this need.

Women and Mentors   One factor that inhibits women's career development, relative to that of their male counterparts, is the difficulty women face in establishing an apprentice-mentor relationship with a senior person in the organization.[24] The fact that Reggie (in the opening story) had a mentor and Jan apparently did not illustrates this unfortunate fact of organizational life. The problem goes well beyond the traditional sex-role stereotyping discussed in Chapter 4. It stems from the fact that senior people, who are in the best position to be mentors, are frequently men. A young woman attempting to establish a productive relationship with a senior male associate faces complexities that the male apprentice does not. Part of the problem is caused by the lack of experience many male mentor candidates have in dealing with a woman in some role other than daughter, wife, or lover. Often, a woman's concerns are going to be different from the ones her male mentor experienced at that stage in his career. As a result, the strategies that he models might have limited relevance to the female apprentice. Perhaps the greatest complexity is associated with fears that their relationship will be perceived as involving sexual intimacy. Concerns about appearances and what others will say can make both people uncomfortable and get in the way of a productive relationship. Research has shown that women who do make it to executive positions invariably have had a mentor along the way.[25] Thus, for women with these career aspirations, finding a mentor appears to be a difficult but critical task.

Formal Mentoring Programs Many people have observed that mentors are often unavailable and have argued that organizational reward systems that focus on short-term outcomes tend to discourage mentoring. In an effort to counteract these forces and facilitate subordinate development, a few organizations have implemented formal mentoring programs. For example, the mentoring program at Merrill Lynch is part of its Management Readiness Program for new and prospective managers.[26] Young employees entering this program are assigned to a fairly high-level management volunteer who meets at least monthly with four such employees from different areas in the company. In preparation for this role, the mentors are given general directions, and former mentors are invited in to discuss their experiences. Over the six-month period of the program, the junior people and mentor meet individually and as a group. The most common activities to date include advice about how to get ahead and alternative career paths; tours of key areas (e.g., New York Stock Exchange); and discussions about planning developmental activities, establishing networks, and the structure of the company.

Is a program like this likely to fulfill all of the career and psychosocial functions of mentoring? Definitely not! However, it might provide some of them and would certainly communicate that developmental relationships of this sort are important in the company. A nice side benefit might be that junior people will get to know peers in other areas. This is the start of a social network. Additionally, as a consequence of the program, the formal mentor might be more likely to develop a true mentor relationship with people in his or her own area. Perhaps the program is more of a training ground for mentors than the actual accomplishment of mentoring.

A FOOTNOTE: PLANNING YOUR CAREER

Much of the information presented in this chapter is directly relevant to your own career. The sections on career orientation and career stages provide information that is useful in analyzing your own career needs and interests as well as how they may change in the future. The section on the organization's role provides information that is relevant to managing a career within an organization. Using this information will be greatly facilitated by cycling through the following steps to manage your career:

- *Know yourself.* The criteria for judging your career success are always personal. This first step involves determining what matters most to you. What activities do you like? Would you go crazy in a job in which you often could not talk to other people? How about a job in which talking is all that you do? Figuring out your preferences, needs, values, strengths, and weaknesses is not an easy task. School counselors and self-help books can provide tests and exercises to help. This process requires plenty of time and introspection. Other people (family, friends, or teachers) can provide additional input. This is not something you do once, but something that will need frequent updating.

- *Know your career alternatives.* Successful careers involve achieving good fit between individuals and their work environments. To attain this, one must know about prospective work environments. One can find out plenty of information through reading about various careers. Once a general area is found, more focused reading is in order. Talking with people in particular jobs can provide insights about the social and emotional demands and skills required. People who know their own needs can ask focused questions. Finally, direct experience in related jobs can provide further detail.

- *Establish your career goals and attainment strategy.* Establishing specific long-term goals that take into account both your career orientation and knowledge of alternative work environments provides the target for an attainment strategy. Work and nonwork factors should be considered. This strategy should identify necessary educational activities, early jobs, establishment of social networks, and so on. The younger a person is, the wiser it is to try to build flexibility into the strategy. In other words, select preparatory activities that can serve a variety of goals.

- *Enact your plan and constantly reevaluate.* Nothing ever goes exactly according to plan. Unforeseen opportunities, needs, and constraints will appear. People and their work environments are dynamic. Companies go out of business, recessions happen, a divorce or death can occur, and forgotten interests emerge. A good plan is one that changes with new information. To get this information, one must frequently recycle through the above three steps.

THE MANAGER'S NOTEBOOK

Career Planning at Pittsburgh National Bank

1. Pittsburgh National Bank introduced a voluntary sixteen-hour career planning workshop. Groups of twelve to twenty employees participated on four Saturday mornings, using their own time. Portions of the workshop included self-appraisal using tests and career inventories, matching the self-appraisal with job and career opportunities, and planning and goal setting. To participate, employees needed two years tenure with the bank, a year in their current position, and a satisfactory performance evaluation. Supervisors were informed only about satisfactory completion of the program.

2. To evaluate the success of the career planning program, PNB actually conducted an experiment using the research techniques discussed in Chapter 2. The career histories of several hundred employees who had been through the workshop were compared to those of a control group of employees who had not been through the program. The two groups were matched in terms of tenure, demographics, and performance. Compared to the control group, the workshop group subsequently applied for more posted jobs and received more promotions and transfers. Bank career specialists noted that the workshop participants became more sophisticated and target-oriented in their strategies of applying for internal openings.

SUMMARY

- A career is a sequence of work activities, attitudes, and reactions experienced over a person's lifetime. It involves an objective sequence of positions as well as reactions, attitudes, and an occupational identity that emerge from the fit or interaction between people and their work environments.
- Individual differences are a critical factor in determining the fit between people and their work environments. The two major perspectives on career orientation are Holland's theory of career types and Schein's theory of career anchors. These define the job and situational factors that fit each career orientation and increase the likelihood of an individual's attraction, retention, and sense of competence and satisfaction associated with a given work environment.
- People and their careers are dynamic. As we age, we go through a sequence of biosocial life stages. Over the life course, there appears to be a pattern of transitional periods, during which previous lifestyle choices are reconsidered, followed by stable periods during which previous choices are tested out. Careers also go through a sequence of stages: exploration, establishment, advancement and maintenance, and late career.
- Organizations can facilitate the development of individual careers so that people's short-term productivity and long-term development are enhanced. Organizational practices can range from formalized individual planning workshops to identifying developmental sequences of positions. Effective career-oriented human resource efforts are integrated, balanced, and linked to organizational strategy.
- An effective supervisor-subordinate relationship is crucial to an employee's career development. Research on mentoring identifies key career and psychosocial functions that supervisors and peers can provide. Women face unique problems in forming career-enhancing relationships with mentors.
- Careers should not be left to luck but should be planned. This requires gaining knowledge of one's own needs and motives. Integrating self-understanding with knowledge of the work demands required by various career alternatives should result in identifying specific career goals and an attainment strategy.

KEY CONCEPTS

Career	Theory of career anchors (Schein)	Apprentice
External career	Biosocial life stages	Reality shock
Internal career	Age norms	Career management
Career orientation	Career stages	Career development
Theory of career types (Holland)	Mentor	

DISCUSSION QUESTIONS

1. A career has a number of specific elements. What are these elements?

2. Compare and contrast Holland's career types and Schein's career anchors. Which are quite separate and distinct from one another? Which have some degree of overlap such that people who fit one category of Holland's might also have certain career anchors? What career types and anchors are likely to be negatively related?

3. The father of psychoanalysis, Sigmund Freud, is said to have observed that people are mostly fixed by age six and stay pretty much the same after their early formative years. Is this view consistent or inconsistent with various points presented in this chapter? Identify three different parts of the chapter that back up your answer.

4. Compare and contrast career stages and biosocial life stages. Which life stage is likely to be confronted in which particular career stage?

5. Review the final section on planning your career and discuss how the various career management programs (e.g., career counseling) are likely to either facilitate or ignore various steps in the planning process.

6. Review the formal mentoring program at Merrill Lynch that was presented in the mentoring section and discuss which specific mentoring functions are likely to be fulfilled by the program. What are some difficulties associated with formal mentoring programs?

7. What unique obstacles do women face in their career development? Why should organizations be concerned with these obstacles?

8. Career management effort by organizations requires that they know plenty about their employee's needs, goals, and even nonwork demands (e.g., the need to be home in the evening with children). Isn't this an invasion of privacy? Will employees truthfully provide this information, or will they play a "tell management what they want to hear" game?

EXPERIENTIAL EXERCISE

Managing Careers—You're the Consultant

This exercise requires you to apply your understanding of career management and career development to some real situations. Read through each situation and take the role of a consultant who has been asked for help. For each situation (1) identify conceptual material which appears to be relevant and additional facts you would need to gather to do a thorough analysis, and (2) be ready to present your preliminary assessment and suggest some specific ways to meet the client's needs.

Bad Times at Mobcorp

During your initial contact with Mobcorp the Human Resources Vice-President restated the facts which had emerged from last week's meeting of the top executive group. The basic concern of the executive group is that the turnover of technicians in various engineering categories has continued to grow. A similar labor category in a technically related area of manufacturing is evincing the same trend. Those leaving seem to be predominantly those who have spent several years in their positions and are in the thirty-five to forty-five age category. Management is concerned that younger employees are not ready to take over the duties of these senior technicians and that without experienced people to work with them, they may never be ready. A check of the salaries of the people leaving indicated that their wages were comparable to what other employers in the area were paying. Exit interviews have found that many simply wanted to try something new.

One person put it this way: "Seven years ago when I started, my job was quite exciting. I faced a new challenge every week. I guess the problem is that I've changed and my job hasn't. Every problem I face, I've seen numerous times before. I hate it when people ask me what's new. I sometimes feel like saying that I'm getting older—that's all!"

Career Planning at Educorp

Career planning programs certainly seem to be the thing to do these days. A few of your consulting clients have heard about other companies' efforts and have decided that it is time to test out a program. Your contacts say that the main pressure for this sort of program is from younger people who are not satisfied with letting their careers just happen and want the company to help them manage their own careers. One human resources executive came to the conclusion that "either we do it and give them more information on what the company has to offer, or the best ones will leave." You have come to the conclusion that, with so many clients wanting it, it is time you develop an approach to helping employees plan their careers. You have scheduled a lunch appointment with Fred Emery, Human Resource Vice-President at Educorp, for next week. It is now time to come up with a preliminary design of a career planning program to present to Fred. Also, you need to identify several specific areas in which you will need further information in order to complete the design of the program.

Problems at Stukorp

John Davis, Manufacturing Vice-President at Stukorp, offered you a "free" lunch. You knew from past experience that these lunches are hardly ever free and that there is usually a pressing problem with which the person wants some help. Lunch with Davis was no exception. In between cocktails and coffee, he told you about Dan, the manager of the component reliability section who had spent over twenty-seven years with the company, serving in a number of capacities. Six years ago, he started his present position, and problems are now appearing. At the time of the transfer, the previous vice-president concluded that Dan's managerial competencies would be a real asset and would outweigh his lack of technical experience in the area. The component reliability section had always been staffed with junior people who were very technically qualified but had unknown managerial abilities and interests. Over the last couple of years, some top people had left the area with complaints that Dan did not give them adequate autonomy, tried to get too involved in the details of their work, and made some decisions which any good reliability engineer would know were wrong. Behind his back the employees referred to him as "Deadwood Dan" and considered him to be very defensive to the technically competent people in the department. Recently, Human Resources has had a hard time interesting people in transferring into the department. Morale and performance have been falling. Davis took a sip of coffee and said, "This whole problem is probably the company's fault, so I certainly can't fire him. Besides, he has given twenty-seven years of generally good service to the company. But I don't have any openings elsewhere for him." Davis paused for a few seconds, requested a second cup, and then asked, "Do you have any suggestions on how I should handle this?" He is now waiting for your reply.

Source: Prepared by J. Bruce Prince. Reprinted by permission.

CASE STUDY

Pamela Jones,
Former Banker

Pamela Jones enjoyed banking. She had taken a battery of personal aptitude and interest tests that suggested she might like and do well in either banking or librarianship. Since the job market for librarians was poor, she applied for employment with a large chartered bank, the Bank of Winnipeg, and was quickly accepted.

Her early experiences in banking were almost always challenging and rewarding. She was enrolled in the bank's management development program because of her education (a B.A. in languages and some postgraduate training in business administration), her previous job experience, and her obvious intelligence and drive.

During her first year in the training program, Pamela attended classes on banking procedures and policies, and worked her way through a series of low level positions in her branch. She was repeatedly told by her manager that her work was above average. Similarly, the training officer who worked out of the main office and coordinated the development of junior officers in the program frequently told Pamela that she was "among the best three" of her cohort of twenty trainees.

Although she worked hard and frequently encountered discrimination from senior bank personnel (as well as customers) because of her sex, Pamela developed a deep-seated attachment to banking in general, and to her bank and branch, in particular. She was proud to be a banker and proud to be a member of the Bank of Winnipeg.

After one year in the management development program however, Pamela found she was not learning anything new about banking or the B. of W. She was shuffled from one job to another at her own branch, cycling back over many positions several times to help meet temporary problems caused by absences, overloads, and turnover. Turnover—a rampant problem in banking—amazed Pamela. She couldn't understand, for many months, why so many people started careers "in

Source: Pinder, C. C. (1984). *Work motivation: Theory, issues, and applications*. Glenview, IL: Scott, Foresman.

the service" of banking, only to leave after one or two years.

After her first year, the repeated promises of moving into her own position at another branch started to sound hollow to Pamela. The training officer claimed that there were no openings suitable for her at other branches. On two occasions when openings did occur, the manager of each of the branches in question rejected Pamela, sight unseen, presumably because she hadn't been in banking long enough.

Pamela was not the only unhappy person at her branch. Her immediate supervisor, George Burns, complained that because of the bank's economy drive, vacated customer service positions were left unfilled. As branch accountant, Burns was responsible for day-to-day customer service. As a result, he was unable to perform the duties of his own job. The manager told Burns several times that customer service was critical, but that Burns would have to improve his performance on his own job. Eventually, George Burns left the bank to work for a trust company, earning seventy dollars a month more for work similar to that he had been performing at the B. of W. This left Pamela in the position of having to supervise the same tellers who had trained her, only a few months earlier. Pamela was amazed at all the mistakes the tellers made, but found it difficult to do much to correct their poor work habits. All disciplinary procedures had to be administered with the approval of Head Office.

After several calls to her training officer, Pamela was finally transferred to her first "real" position in her own branch. Still keen and dedicated, Pamela was soon to lose her enthusiasm.

At her new branch, Pamela was made "assistant accountant." Her duties included the supervision of the seven tellers, some customer service and a great deal of paper work. The same economy drive that she had witnessed at her training branch resulted in the failure to replace customer service personnel. Pamela was expected to "pick up the slack" at the front desk, neglecting her own work. Her tellers seldom balanced their own cash, so Pamela stayed late almost every night to find their errors. To save on overtime, the manager sent the tellers home while Pamela stayed late, first to correct the tellers' imbalances, then to finish her own paper work. He told Pamela that as an officer of the bank, she was expected to stay until the work of her subordinates, and her own work, were satisfactorily completed. Pamela realized that most of her counterparts in other B. of W. branches were willing to give this sort of dedication; therefore, so should she. This situation lasted six months with little sign of change in sight.

One day, Pamela learned from a phone conversation with a friend at another branch that she would be transferred to Hope, British Columbia, to fill an opening that had arisen. Pamela's husband was a professional, employed by a large corporation in Vancouver. His company did not have an office in Hope; moreover, his training was very specialized, so that he could probably find employment only in large cities anyway.

Accepting transfers was expected of junior officers who wanted to get ahead. Pamela inquired at Head Office and learned that the rumor was true. Her training officer told her, however, that Pamela could decline the transfer if she wished, but he couldn't say how soon her next promotion opportunity would come about.

Depressed, annoyed, disappointed and frustrated, Pamela quit the bank.

1. Contrast Pamela Jones's external career with her likely conception of her internal career.

2. Compare Pamela's occupational self-concept (her needs, aptitudes, and preferences) with the opportunities, constraints, and demands of the banking jobs she held. In doing this, try to describe her in terms of Holland's theory of career types and Schein's theory of career anchors.

3. In career stage terminology, Pamela was at the *exploration* stage and perhaps into the *establishment* stage during the events described in the case. In terms of career stage concepts, what were some critical events or issues that affected Pamela?

4. Imagine that you are Pamela's mentor during the period described in the case. What advice would you give her?

5. Advise the bank on how to improve its career management system.

REFERENCES

1. Hall, D. T. (1976). *Careers in organizations.* Pacific Palisades, CA: Goodyear.

2. Van Maanen, J., & Schein, E. H. (1977). Career development. In J. R. Hackman & J. L. Suttle (Eds.), *Improving life at work: Behavioral science approaches to organizational change.* Glenview, IL: Scott, Foresman.

3. Van Maanen, J., & Barley, S. R. (1984). Occupational communities: Culture and control in organizations. *Research in Organizational Behavior, 6,* 287–365.

4. Weinrach, S. G. (1984). Determinants of vocational choice: Holland's theory. In D. Brown & L. Brooks (Eds.), *Career choice and development.* San Francisco: Jossey-Bass; Holland, J. L. (1973). *Making vocational choices: A theory of careers.* Englewood Cliffs, NJ: Prentice-Hall.

5. Strong, E. K., Jr., & Campbell, D. P. (1981). *Strong-Campbell interest inventory.* Stanford, CA: Stanford University Press.

6. Schein, E. H. (1975). How "career anchors" hold executives to their career paths. *Personnel, 52,* 11–24; Schein, E. H. (1978). *Career dynamics.* Reading, MA: Addison-Wesley.

7. Neugarten, B. (1968). Adult personality: Toward a psychology of the life cycle. In B. Neugarten (Ed.), *Middle age and aging.* Chicago: University of Chicago Press.

8. Levinson, D. J., Darrow, C. N., Klein, E. B., Levinson, M. H., & McKee, B. (1978). *The seasons of a man's life.* New York: Alfred A. Knopf. For some recent research support, see Ornstein, S., Cron, W. L., & Slocum, J. W., Jr. (1989). Life stage versus career stage: A comparative test of the theories of Levinson and Super. *Journal of Organizational Behavior, 10,* 117–133.

9. For reviews, see Gallos, J. V. (1989). Exploring women's development: Implications for career theory, practice, and research. See also Cytrynbaum, S., & Crites, J. O. (1989). The utility of adult development theory in understanding career adjustment process. Both in M. B. Arthur, D. T. Hall, & B. S. Lawrence (Eds.), *Handbook of career theory.* Cambridge: Cambridge University Press.

10. Bardwick, J. (1980). The seasons of a woman's life. In D. G. McGuigan (Ed.), *Women's lives: New theory, research, and policy.* Ann Arbor, MI: Uni-

versity of Michigan Center for Continuing Education of Women.

11. Kram, K., & Isabella, L. (1985). Mentoring alternatives: The role of peer relationships in career development. *Academy of Management Journal, 28*, 110–132.

12. Berlew, D. T., & Hall, D. T. (1966). The socialization of managers: Effects of expectations of performance. *Administrative Science Quarterly, 11*, 207–223.

13. Hall, D. T., & Lawler, E. E., III, (1969). Unused potential in research and development organizations. *Research Management, 12*, 339–354.

14. Rosenbaum, J. E. (1984). *Career mobility in a corporate hierarchy*. New York: Academic Press. See also Rosenbaum, J. E. (1989). Organization career systems and employee misperceptions. In M. B. Arthur, D. T. Hall, & B. S. Lawrence (Eds.), *Handbook of career theory*. Cambridge: Cambridge University Press.

15. Gutteridge, T. G. (1986). Organizational career development systems: The state of the practice. In D. T. Hall (Ed.), *Career development in organizations*. San Francisco: Jossey-Bass.

16. Walker, J. W., & Gutteridge, T. G. (1979). *Career planning practices*. New York: American Management Association.

17. Minor, F. J. (1986). Computer applications in career development. In D. T. Hall (Ed.), *Career development in organizations*. San Francisco: Jossey-Bass.

18. Thompson, P. H., Baker, R. B., & Smallwood, N.

(1986, Autumn). The derailment of fast-track managers. *Organizational Dynamics*, 41–48.

19. Morrison, R. F., & Hock, R. R. (1986). Career building: Learning from cumulative work experience. In D. T. Hall (Ed.), *Career development in organizations*. San Francisco: Jossey-Bass.

20. Wellbank, H. L., Hall, D. T., Morgan, M. A., & Hamner, W. C. (1978, March-April). Planning job progression for effective career development and human resources management. *Personnel*, 118–129.

21. Von Glinow, M. A., Driver, M. J., Brousseau, K., & Prince, J. B. (1983). The design of a career oriented human resource system. *Academy of Management Review, 8*, 23–32.

22. Dalton, G. W., Thompson, P. H., & Price, R. (1977, Summer). The four stages of professional careers—A new look at performance by professionals. *Organizational Dynamics*, 19–42.

23. Kram, K. (1985). *Mentoring at work*. Glenview, IL: Scott, Foresman.

24. Ragins, B. R. (1989). Barriers to mentoring: The female manager's dilemma. *Human Relations, 42*, 1–22; Noe, R. A. (1988). Women and mentoring: A review and research agenda. *Academy of Management Review, 13*, 65–78.

25. Dennett, D. (1985, November). Risks, mentoring help women to top. *APA Monitor*, p. 26.

26. Farren, C., Gray, J. D., & Kaye, B. (1984, November-December). Mentoring: A boon to career development. *Personnel*, 20–24.

GLOSSARY

Actor-observer effect. A basic difference in attributional perspectives between actors and observers in which actors are generally more likely to attribute their own behavior to situational causes. (4)

Additive tasks. Tasks in which potential performance can be predicted by adding the performances of individual group members together. (8)

Advanced information technology. The generation, aggregation, storage, modification, and speedy transmission of information made possible by the advent of computers and related devices. (16)

Age norms. Widely accepted expectations in society about what behavior is appropriate for a person at a given age. (18)

All-channel communication. A form of communication manifested by the completely free flow of information. (11)

Apprentice. A junior person in an organization who receives special attention and career guidance from a senior person (mentor). (18)

Attitudes. Relatively stable emotional tendencies to respond consistently to some specific object, situation, person, or category of people. (5)

Attribution. The process by which people assign causes or motives to behavior. (4)

Autonomy. The degree to which a job provides freedom and independence in scheduling and performing work. (7)

Beliefs. Assumed facts or statements about the nature of the world that are not evaluative. (5)

Biosocial life stages. Adult life stages that are the product of the aging process and patterns of social expectations that exist in society. (18)

Body language. Nonverbal communication that occurs by means of a sender's bodily motions and facial expressions. (11)

Boundary roles. Organizational positions in which employees are required to interact with members of other organizations or with the public. (14)

Bounded rationality. Limits to rational decision making that include insufficient capacity to acquire and process information, time constraints, and political considerations. (12)

Brainstorming. A technique used to increase the number of creative solutions to a problem by generating a large volume of ideas without evaluation or censure. (12)

Bureaucracy. An organizational structure and management style that emphasizes a strict chain of command; high specialization and centralization; detailed rules, reg-

ulations, and procedures; and selection and promotion based on technical skills. (15)

Burnout. Stress characterized by feelings of emotional exhaustion, depersonalization, and a deteriorating sense of personal accomplishment. (14)

Career. A sequence of work activities and positions and associated attitudes and reactions experienced over a person's life. (18)

Career development. Improvement of skills, identification of goals and strategies, and the realization of one's full potential in a career. (18)

Career management. Programs and systems that are designed to enhance individual career development. (18)

Career orientation. The preferred activities, talents, needs, values, and attitudes that an individual possesses. (18)

Career stages. General patterns of developmental changes in work-role activities, which are distinct from life stages. (18)

Centralization. The extent to which decision-making power is localized in a particular part of an organization. (15)

Central tendency. A tendency for a rater to assign most ratees to a middle-range performance category. (4)

Central trait. Critical or important traits around which people organize their perceptions of others. (4)

Chain of command. The formal lines of authority and reporting relationships designated by an organizational chart. (11)

Change agent. An expert in the application of behavioral science knowledge to organizational diagnosis and change. (17)

Charisma. A leadership quality that commands strong loyalty and devotion from followers. (10)

Coercive power. Power derived from the use of punishment and threat. (13)

Collaboration. A process of interaction characterized by high mutual assistance and low antagonism. (13)

Common sense. Views about organizational behavior developed from everyday experience with behavior, with organizations, and with behavior in organizations. (2)

Communication. The process by which information is exchanged between a sender and a receiver. (11)

Communicators. In attitude change theory, people who attempt to induce attitude change. Effective communicators are perceived as expert, unbiased, and likeable. (5)

Compensation. Applying one's skills in a particular area to make up for failure in another area. (14)

Competition. A process of interaction characterized by low mutual assistance and low antagonism. (13)

Complexity. The extent to which an organization divides labor vertically, horizontally, and geographically. (15)

Compliance. Conformity that occurs as a result of one's desire to acquire rewards and avoid punishment by others. (9)

Compressed workweek. An alternative to traditional working hours wherein the hours worked each week are compressed into fewer days. (7)

Compromise. A conflict resolution strategy in which each party gives up something with the expectation of receiving something else in exchange. (13)

Conflict resolution. A range of strategies for decreasing interpersonal conflict. (13)

Conflict stimulation. A strategy to temporarily increase organizational conflict to encourage changes that benefit the organization. (13)

Conformity. The tendency to act in accordance with the wishes of others. (9)

Conjunctive tasks. Tasks in which potential performance of a group is limited by the performance of its poorest performer. (8)

Consensus cues. In attribution, cues that indicate whether most people engage in a behavior or whether it is unique to a person. (4)

Conservative shift. The tendency for a group to make a more conservative decision than that initially favored by its individual members. (12)

Consideration. Leader behavior that includes being approachable and showing concern for subordinates. (10)

Consistency cues. In attribution, cues that indicate whether or not a person engages in a behavior regularly and consistently. (4)

Context factors. Factors such as pay, supervision, and company policy that are not inherent in the design of a job but that influence responsiveness to job design. (7)

Contingencies. Dependencies that affect relationships between organizational behavior variables. (1)

Continuous versus partial reinforcement. The reinforcement of each and every correct response versus the intermittent reinforcement of correct responses. (3)

Contrast effects. The tendency for interviewers to exaggerate the difference in quality between previously seen applicants and a current applicant. (4)

Control. The ability to affect or manage organizational behavior. One of the primary goals of the field of organizational behavior. (1)

Control group. A group of subjects in an experiment who are not exposed to the independent variable but who

otherwise are as similar as possible to the actual experimental subjects. (2)

Coordination. The process of facilitating timing, communication, and feedback. (15)

Correlational research. A research technique that explores relationships among specific, precisely measured variables without manipulating any of them. (2)

Creativity. The production of novel but potentially useful ideas. (17)

Customer departmentation. An organizational structure that divides members into relatively self-contained units to deliver the organization's products or services to specific customer groups. (15)

Debasement. Experiences designed to humble and test the commitment of new members of a group or organization. (9)

Decision making. The process of developing a commitment to a course of action that involves a choice between alternatives. (12)

Defense mechanisms. Psychological attempts to reduce the anxiety associated with stress. (14)

Delphi technique. A decision-making technique that gathers information from a nominal group of experts who do not interact face to face. (12)

Dependent variable. The variable that the independent variable is expected to affect in experimental research. (2)

Devil's advocate. An individual who challenges weaknesses in plans and strategies in order to improve decision quality. (12)

Diagnosis. Identification of organizational problems and determination of what changes should be implemented. (17)

Differentiation. The tendency for managers in separate functions or departments to differ in terms of goals, time spans, and interpersonal styles. (15)

Diffusion. The process by which innovations move across an organization. (17)

Diffusion of responsibility. The sharing of negative consequences for a bad decision among the members of a decision-making group. (12)

Direct observation. A technique of observational research in which the researcher observes an organizational unit without participation in the activity being observed. (2)

Discrepancy theory. A theory that holds that job satisfaction is a function of the discrepancy between the job outcomes a person wants and the outcomes that are perceived to be obtained. (5)

Disjunctive tasks. Tasks in which potential performance of a group depends on the performance of its best member. (8)

Displacement. Directing feelings of anger at a safe target rather than expressing them where they may be punished. (14)

Dispositional attributions. Attributions that some personality characteristic or trait is responsible for a behavior and that the behavior reflects a person's true motives. (4)

Distinctiveness cues. In attribution, cues that indicate whether a person engages in a behavior in many situations or whether it is distinctive to one situation. (4)

Distributive fairness. A feeling of fairness that stems from receiving an equitable amount of rewards or resources. (5)

Downward communication. Communication that flows from the top of the organization toward the bottom. (11)

Effect dependence. Social dependence and openness to influence due to the rewards or punishments provided by others. (9)

Effective communication. Communication in which the right people receive the right information in a timely manner. (11)

Emergent leadership. Leadership influence exerted by individuals who are not formally appointed leaders. (10)

Employee surveys. Surveys of attitudes and opinions used to enhance upward communication in organizations. (11)

Environmental uncertainty. A situation that exists when events and conditions surrounding an organization are vague, difficult to diagnose, and unpredictable. (16)

Equity theory. A theory of job satisfaction and motivation that asserts that workers compare the inputs they invest in their jobs and the outcomes they receive against the inputs and outcomes of some other relevant person or group. (5)(6)

ERG theory. A need-based theory of motivation that compresses Maslow's hierarchy into three categories—existence, relatedness, and growth needs. (6)

Escalation of commitment. A process in which a decision maker acts as though sunk costs may be recouped, resulting in devoting more and more resources to a failing course of action. (12)

Ethics. Systematic thinking about the moral consequences of decisions. (12)

Exit interviews. Interviews conducted with resigning or dismissed employees in order to gain useful information about problems affecting those who remain employed. (11)

Expectancy. In expectancy theory, the probability that a person can actually achieve a particular first-level outcome. (6)

Expectancy theory. A motivation theory based on the idea that motivation is determined by the outcomes that people expect to occur as a result of their actions on the job. (6)

Experimental research. A research technique in which a variable to be studied is manipulated or changed under controlled conditions and the consequence of this manipulation for some other variable is measured. (2)

Expert power. Power derived from having special expertise that is valued by the organization. (13)

Explanation. The accurate understanding of the causes of organizational behavior. One of the goals of the field of organizational behavior. (1)

External career. An objective path that employees follow in an organization. (18)

External environment. Events and conditions surrounding an organization that influence its activities. (16)

Extinction. Terminating a reinforcer that is maintaining some unwanted behavior to reduce its probability. (3)

Extrinsic motivation. Motivation that stems from the work environment external to a task and is usually applied by someone other than the person being motivated. (6)

Feedback. The degree to which a job provides a worker with clear information about his or her performance. (7)

Fiedler's Contingency Theory. A leadership theory that prescribes the effectiveness of task versus relationship orientation under various degrees of situational favorableness. (10)

Field of organizational behavior. A field that systematically studies the attitudes and behaviors of individuals and groups in organizations. (1)

Filtering. The tendency for a message to be watered down or halted completely at some point during transmission. (11)

Fixed interval schedule. A reinforcement schedule in which some fixed time period occurs between a reinforced response and the availability of the next reinforcement. (3)

Fixed ratio schedule. A reinforcement schedule in which, after a reinforced response, some fixed number of responses must be made before another reinforcement becomes available. (3)

Flat organization. An organizational structure incorporating relatively few levels in its hierarchy of authority. (15)

Flex-time. An alternative to traditional working hours wherein employees work a given number of hours, but the times when they arrive and leave are flexible. (7)

Foot-in-the-door phenomenon. Compliance with minor initial requests is used to prime an individual to be receptive to more demanding requests. (9)

Formalization. The extent to which work roles are highly defined by an organization. (15)

Formal work groups. Groups that are established by an organization to facilitate the achievement of organizational goals. (8)

Functional departmentation. An organizational structure that locates workers with closely related skills and responsibilities in the same department. (15)

Fundamental attribution error. Overemphasizing dispositional explanations at the expense of situational explanations when making attributions about the behavior of others. (4)

Gain-sharing plans. Group incentive plans that are based on measurable cost reductions that are under the control of the work force. (7)

Gatekeepers. Technical personnel who import new information into an organization, translate it for local use, and disseminate it to project members. (17)

Geographic departmentation. An organizational structure that divides members into relatively self-contained units based on specific geographic territories. (15)

Goal setting. A motivation technique that involves establishing specific, challenging, accepted goals and providing feedback about goal accomplishment. (7)

Grapevine. An informal organizational communication network. (11)

Grid OD. A comprehensive, long-term effort directed toward changing a total organization by jointly stressing high performance and the maintenance of a healthy working climate. (17)

Group. Two or more people interacting interdependently to achieve a common goal. (8)

Group cohesiveness. The degree to which a group is attractive to its members. (8)

Groupthink. Extreme conformity in group decision making that is associated with reduced mental efficiency, poor testing of reality, and lax moral judgments. (12)

Growth need strength. The extent to which workers desire to achieve higher order need satisfaction in performing their jobs. (7)

Halo. An observer allows the rating of an individual on one trait or characteristic to color ratings on other traits or characteristics. (4)

Harshness. A bias in which a rater has a tendency to perceive the performance of ratees as especially ineffective. (4)

Hawthorne effect. A favorable response on the part of subjects in an organizational experiment that is due to some factor other than the independent variable being manipulated. (2)

Horizontal communication. Communication that occurs between departments or functional units in an organization, usually as a means of coordinating effort. (11)

House's Path-Goal Theory. A theory that asserts that the effectiveness of various leader behaviors depends upon subordinate characteristics and environmental factors. Based on the idea that the effective leader forms a connection between subordinate goals and organizational goals. (10)

Hybrid departmentation. An organizational structure that combines various elements of functional, product, geographic, or customer departmentation. (15)

Hypothesis. A prediction about the way in which variables are expected to be connected. (2)

Idea champions. People who see the essence of an innovative idea and help to guide it through to implementation. (17)

Identification. Viewing oneself as similar to attractive others; often motivates conformity to norms that they espouse. (9)

Idiosyncrasy credits. The opportunity for high-status group members with a history of conformity to occasionally deviate from group norms. (9)

Ill-structured problems. Decision-making situations in which the existing or desired states are unclear or the method of getting to the desired state is unknown. (12)

Immediate versus delayed reinforcement. Providing reinforcement immediately after a correct response versus waiting some period of time. (3)

Implicit personality theory. Individual expectations about which personality characteristics fit together or correlate with each other. (4)

Independent variable. The variable that a researcher manipulates or changes in experimental research. (2)

Informal groups. Groups that emerge naturally in response to the common interests of organizational members. (8)

Information dependence. Social dependence and openness to influence due to a lack of information. (9)

Information overload. A condition in which a decision maker receives more information than is necessary to make effective decisions. (12)

Information richness. The potential information-carrying capacity of a communication medium. (11)

Initiating structure. Leader behavior that concentrates on group goal attainment. Includes scheduling work and assigning tasks. (10)

Innovation. The process of developing and implementing new ideas in an organization. (17)

Inputs. In equity theory, anything that individuals contribute in their exchange with the organization. (5)

Instrumentality. In expectancy theory, the probability that a particular first-level outcome will be followed by a particular second-level outcome. (6)

Integration. The process of obtaining coordination across differentiated departments. (15)

Integrators. Organizational members who are permanently installed between two departments that are in need of coordination. (15)

Interest groups. Parties or organizations other than direct competitors who have some vested interest in how an organization is managed. (16)

Interlocking directorates. A condition that exists when one person serves as a director on two or more boards of directors. (16)

Internal career. An individual's subjective interpretation of the meaning of various work experiences. (18)

Internalization. Acceptance of the beliefs, values, and attitudes that underlie a norm. (9)

Interpersonal conflict. Antagonism that occurs when one person or organizational subunit frustrates the goal attainment of another. (13)

Inter-role conflict. Role conflict that occurs when a single individual plays several roles simultaneously and the expectations inherent in these several roles are incompatible. (8)

Inter-sender conflict. Role conflict that occurs when two or more role senders differ in their expectations for a role occupant. (8)

Intra-sender conflict. Role conflict that occurs when a single role sender provides incompatible role expectations to a role occupant. (8)

Intrinsic/extrinsic relationship. Concerns the debate about whether or not extrinsic rewards for performance decrease intrinsic motivation. (6)

Intrinsic motivation. Motivation that stems from a direct relationship between a worker and a task and is usually self-applied. (6)

Jargon. Specialized language used by organizational members or professionals to communicate with one another. (11)

Job enrichment. Designing jobs to enhance intrinsic motivation and the quality of working life by increasing their motivating potential via the arrangement of their core characteristics. (7)

Job satisfaction. A collection of attitudes that workers have about their jobs. (5)

Knew-it-all-along effect. The tendency to assume after the fact that one knew what the outcome of a decision would be at the time it was made. (12)

Knowledge of predictor bias. A rater gains knowledge of some factor that may predict the success of a ratee and then rates the person's performance to confirm this prediction. (4)

Leader punishment behavior. Leader behavior that provides subordinates with reprimands or unfavorable task assignments or actively withholds raises, promotions, and other rewards. (10)

Leader reward behavior. Leader behavior that provides subordinates with compliments, tangible benefits, and deserved special treatment. (10)

Leadership. The ability of particular individuals to exert influence over others in an organizational context. (10)

Learning. A relatively permanent change in behavior potential caused by practice or experience. (3)

Least Preferred Co-Worker (LPC). Someone with whom a leader has had a difficult time getting a job done. This concept is used to measure task or relationship orientation in Fiedler's Contingency Theory of leadership. (10)

Legitimate power. Power derived from holding a particular position or job in an organization. (13)

Leniency. A bias in which a rater has a tendency to perceive the performance of ratees as especially good. (4)

Liaison role. A role filled by a person in one department who is assigned as part of his or her job to achieve coordination with another department. (15)

Machiavellianism. A cynical set of beliefs about human nature, morality, and the permissibility of using various tactics to achieve one's ends. (13)

Management by Objectives (MBO). An elaborate, systematic, ongoing management program that is designed to facilitate goal establishment, goal accomplishment, and employee development. (7)

Managerial Grid®. A two-dimensional conception of leadership that involves concern for production and concern for people. (17)

Maslow's hierarchy of needs. A general theory of human motivation that specifies a hierarchy of five sets of needs beginning with the most basic and moving up to the most complex. (6)

Maximization. Decision-making behavior in which the alternative with the greatest expected value is chosen. (12)

Mechanistic structures. Organizational structures that tend toward tallness, narrow spans of control, high specialization, high centralization, and high formalization. (15)

Mentor. A senior person in an organization who gives a junior person (apprentice) special attention and career guidance. (18)

Merit pay plans. Schemes to link pay to performance on white-collar jobs. (7)

Modeling. The process of imitating the behavior of others in learning. (3)

Motivating potential. The degree of enrichment of a job as determined by its skill variety, task identity, task significance, autonomy, and feedback. (7)

Motivation. The extent to which persistent effort is directed toward a goal. (6)

Mum effect. The tendency to avoid communicating unfavorable news to others. (11)

Need for achievement. The need to perform challenging tasks well. (6)

Need for affiliation. The need to establish and maintain friendly, compatible relationships. (6)

Need for power. The need to have strong influence over others. (6)

Need theories. Theories of motivation that attempt to specify the various needs people have and the conditions under which they will be motivated to satisfy these needs in an organizationally useful manner. (6)

Negative reinforcement. Reinforcement that increases or maintains the probability of some behavior by the removal (or prevention) of a stimulus from the situation in question. (3)

Networking. Establishing good relations with key organizational members and/or outsiders in order to accomplish one's goals. (13)

Neutralizers of leadership. Subordinate, task, or organizational characteristics that reduce opportunities for leaders to exercise influence. (10)

Nominal group technique. A technique that is used to make decisions by generating ideas without interaction and then discussing each idea as a group in a structured manner. (12)

Nonprogrammed decision making. Decision making that is tailored to the problem at hand rather than relying on a standardized approach or program. (12)

Nonverbal communication. The transmission of messages by some means other than speech or writing. (11)

Norms. Expectations that members of groups or organizations have regarding the behavior of others. (8)

Observational research. A research technique of finding out about behavior in organizations through observation of the natural activities of people in an organizational setting. (2)

Official goals. General, abstract organizational goals that are usually stated in official organizational documents. (1)

Open door policy. A practice in which any organizational member below a particular manager can communicate directly with him or her without going through the chain of command. (11)

Open system. A system that takes inputs from the external environment, transforms them, and sends them back to the external environment as outputs. (16)

Operant learning. Learning in which one operates on the environment to achieve certain consequences. (3)

Operative goals. Specific goals designed to help achieve the more general official goals of an organization. (1)

Organic structures. Organizational structures that tend toward flatness, wide spans of control, low specialization, low centralization, and low formalization. (15)

Organizational behavior. A domain that includes attitudes and behaviors of individuals and groups in organizations. (1)

Organizational behavior modification. The systematic use of learning principles to influence organizational behavior. (3)

Organizational citizenship behavior. Voluntary, informal behavior that contributes to organizational effectiveness. (5)

Organizational culture. The shared beliefs, values, and assumptions that characterize an organization. (9)

Organizational development (OD). A planned, ongoing effort to change an organization to be more effective and more human. (17)

Organizational politics. The pursuit of self-interest within an organization, whether or not such self-interest corresponds to organizational goals. (13)

Organizational structure. The manner in which an organization divides its labor into specific tasks and achieves coordination among these tasks. (15)

Organizations. Social inventions for accomplishing goals through group effort. (1)

Outcomes. In equity theory, anything that an organization distributes in return for various inputs by employees. (5)

Participant observation. A technique of observational research in which the researcher actively participates in the behavior being studied by becoming a functional member of an organizational unit. (2)

Participative leadership. A form of leadership that involves subordinates in making work-related decisions. (10)

Perception. The process of interpreting the messages of our senses to provide order and meaning to the environment. (4)

Perceptual defense. Instances in which individuals' perceptual systems defend them against unpleasant emotions. (4)

Perfect rationality. An ideal theoretical state in which a decision maker is completely informed, perfectly logical, and concerned only with economic gain. (12)

Performance. The extent to which an organizational member contributes to achieving the objectives of the organization. (6)

"Performance causes satisfaction" hypothesis. A hypothesis that suggests that increased performance will lead to higher job satisfaction. (5)

Person-role conflict. Role conflict that occurs when role demands conflict with the personality or skills of a role occupant. (8)

Persuasion techniques. A series of verbal tactics that are used by communicators to effect attitude change. (5)

Piecerate. A scheme to link pay to performance in which individual workers are paid a certain sum of money for each unit of production completed. (7)

Pooled interdependence. The extent to which a unit is dependent upon the pooled resources generated by the other units in an organization. (16)

Positive reinforcement. Reinforcement that increases or maintains the probability of some behavior by the application or addition of a stimulus to the situation in question. (3)

Power. The capacity to influence others who are in a state of dependence. (13)

Prediction. The accurate anticipation of organizational behavior or the conditions under which it might occur. One of the primary goals of the field of organizational behavior. (1)

Primacy effect. The overreliance on cues encountered early in a relationship in forming impressions of others. (4)

Problem. A perceived gap between an existing state and a desired state. (12)

Problem solving. A conflict resolution strategy that encourages conflicting parties to integrate their needs fully so that both are satisfied. Also, a response to stress directed toward terminating the stressor or reducing its potency. (13) (14)

Procedural fairness. A feeling of fairness that occurs when a just process is used to allocate rewards or other outcomes. (5)

Process theories. Theories of motivation that concentrate on how motivation occurs rather than on details of the human need structure. (6)

Product departmentation. An organizational structure that designates departments on the basis of a particular product, product line, or service. (15)

Program. A standardized approach to solving a problem or making a decision. (12)

Projection. Attributing one's own feelings, ideas, or motives to others (often, to make them seem less negative). (4) (14)

Punishment. Following an unwanted behavior with some unpleasant, aversive stimulus to reduce its probability. (3)

Quality circles. Small groups of people who meet voluntarily on a regular basis to analyze work-related problems. (17)

Quality of working life. The extent to which the work experience is rewarding and fulfilling while precluding stress and other negative personal consequences. (7)

Rationalization. Attributing socially acceptable reasons or motives to one's actions. (14)

Reaction formation. Expressing oneself in a manner that is directly opposite to the way one truly feels, rather than risking negative reactions to one's true position. (14)

Realistic job preview. A recruiting or orientation procedure that counteracts unrealistic job expectations by providing applicants with a balanced, realistic picture of the positive and negative aspects of a job. (9)

Reality shock. The disparity between unrealistic expectations and the reality that people confront in their first job. (18)

Recency effect. The overreliance on cues encountered most recently in forming impressions of others. (4)

Reciprocal interdependence. The extent to which a unit in an organization is dependent upon interplay and feedback from other units in order to perform a task. (16)

Referent power. Power derived from being well-liked by others. (13)

Refreezing. The adoption of newly developed behaviors, attitudes, or structures as the result of a change process. (17)

Reinforcement. The process by which stimuli strengthen behaviors. (3)

Reliability. The degree to which a research measure gives similar results over time or across measurements or observers. (2)

Repression. Preventing threatening ideas from becoming conscious so that a stressor need not be confronted. (14)

Resistance. Overt or covert failure to support a change effort. (17)

Resource dependence. Dependence on the organization's external environment for inputs of resources and markets for outputs. (16)

Restriction of productivity. The artificial limitation of production output due to an informal agreement among workers about what constitutes a fair day's work. (7)

Reward power. Power derived from the ability to provide positive outcomes or prevent negative outcomes. (13)

Risky shift. The tendency for a group to make a riskier decision than that initially favored by its individual members. (12)

Role ambiguity. A condition that exists when the goals of one's job or the methods of performing it are unclear. (8)

Role conflict. A condition that exists when an individual is faced with incompatible role expectations. (8)

Role overload. A condition that occurs when too many tasks must be performed in too short a period of time. (14)

Roles. Positions in a group or organization that have a set of expected behaviors attached to them. (8)

Rumor. An unverified belief that is in general circulation. (11)

"Satisfaction causes performance" hypothesis. A hypothesis that suggests that a more satisfying job will lead to higher job performance. (5)

Satisficing. Decision-making behavior in which alternatives are screened until one that exceeds predetermined criteria is found. (12)

Scientific Management. The use of careful study to determine the optimum degree of specialization and standardization required in a job. (7)

Self-managed work groups. Groups that provide their members with the opportunity to do challenging work under reduced supervision. (8)

Self-management. The process by which organizational members use learning principles to manage their own behavior. (3)

Self-serving bias. The tendency to take responsibility and credit for successful outcomes of behavior and to deny responsibility for failures. (4)

Sequential interdependence. The extent to which a unit in an organization is dependent upon the activity of the unit that preceded it in a sequence. (16)

Similar-to-me effect. A rater gives more favorable performance evaluations to people who are similar to the rater in terms of background or attitudes. (4)

Situational attributions. Attributions that the situation or environment is responsible for some behavior and that a person may have had little control over the behavior. (4)

Skill variety. The degree to which a job requires its incumbent to exercise a variety of skills and talents. (7)

Social-emotional leader. A leader who is particularly concerned with social relationships. Exerts influence by reducing tension, patching up disagreements, settling arguments, and maintaining morale. (10)

Socialization. The process by which a person learns the norms and roles necessary to function in a group or organization. (9)

Social learning. Learning that involves examining the behavior of others, seeing what the consequences are, and thinking about what might happen if one acts the same way. (3)

Span of control. The number of subordinates supervised by a superior. (15)

Status. Rank, social position, or prestige accorded to group or organizational members. (8)

Status symbols. Tangible indicators of rank, social position, or prestige. (8)

Stereotyping. The tendency to attribute certain traits or characteristics to all members of a particular class or category of people. (4)

Strategic alliances. Actively cooperative alliances between legally separate organizations. (16)

Strategic contingencies. Critical factors affecting organizational effectiveness that are controlled by a key subunit. (13)

Strategy. The process by which top executives seek to cope with the constraints and opportunities posed by an organization's environment. (16)

Stress. A psychological reaction to the demands inherent in a stressor that has the potential to make a person feel tense or anxious because the person does not feel capable of coping with these demands. (14)

Stressors. Environmental events or conditions that have the potential to induce tension or anxiety. (14)

Stress reactions. Behavioral, psychological, and physiological consequences of stress. (14)

Strong culture. A condition that exists when the shared beliefs, values, and assumptions that make up an organizational culture are both intense and pervasive across the organization. (9)

Substitutes for leadership. Subordinate, task, or organizational characteristics that take the place of or reduce the need for formal leadership. (10)

Subunit power. Power held by subunits (usually departments or occupational groups) within an organization. (13)

Suggestion systems. Plans designed to enhance upward communication by soliciting ideas for improved work operations from non-managerial employees. (11)

Sunk costs. Permanent losses of resources incurred as the result of a decision. (12)

Superordinate goals. Attractive outcomes for both parties in a conflict that can be achieved only by collaboration. (13)

Survey feedback. Data that is collected from organizational members and then presented in a series of meetings during which the findings are explored and discussed. (17)

Tall organization. An organizational structure incorporating relatively many levels in its hierarchy of authority. (15)

Task force. A temporary group set up to solve coordination problems across departments. (15)

Task identity. The degree to which a job is performed from beginning to end, resulting in a "complete" piece of work. (7)

Task leader. A leader who is particularly concerned with accomplishing the task at hand. Exerts influence by planning, organizing, and dividing labor. (10)

Task significance. The degree to which the performance of a job has a significant impact on other people. (7)

Team building. An intervention that is used to increase the effectiveness of work teams by concentrating on interpersonal problems, goal clarification, and role clarification. (17)

Technological interdependence. The extent to which organizational subunits depend on each other for resources, raw materials, or information. (16)

Technological routineness. The extent to which the transformation of inputs into outputs is characterized by exceptional cases and difficult analysis. (16)

Technology. Activities, equipment, and knowledge that are necessary to turn organizational inputs into desired outputs. (16)

Theory of career anchors (Schein). A theory of career orientation involving distinct patterns of self-perceived talents, motives, needs, and values acquired from work experience: technical/functional competence, managerial competence, security, autonomy, creativity. (18)

Theory of career types (Holland). A theory of career orientation that divides people into six distinct interest patterns: realistic, investigative, artistic, social, enterprising, and conventional. (18)

Theory of cognitive dissonance. A theory that explains attitude changes that occur when certain cognitions are contradictory or inconsistent with each other. (5)

Theory X versus Theory Y. Two distinct views of human nature. Theory X assumes that people generally dislike work, lack ambition, and will avoid responsibility if possible. Theory Y assumes that work is as natural as rest or play and that workers will accept responsibility when self-control can be used to pursue valued objectives. (6)

Traits. Personal characteristics of an individual, including physical characteristics, social background, intellectual ability, personality, task orientation, and social skills. (10)

Transformational leadership. Leadership that inspires a new vision in followers and instills true commitment to a project, a department, or an organization. (10)

Type A behavior pattern. A personality type characterized by aggressiveness, ambition, impatience, competitiveness, and preoccupation with work. (14)

Unfreezing. Recognition that some current state of affairs is inadequate and that change is required. (17)

Upward communication. Communication that flows from the bottom of the organization toward the top. (11)

Valence. In expectancy theory, the expected value of outcomes, that is, the extent to which they are attractive or unattractive to an individual. (6)

Validity. The degree to which a research measure truly measures what it is supposed to measure. (2)

Values. A general tendency to prefer certain states of affairs over others. (5)

Variable interval schedule. A reinforcement schedule in which some variable time period occurs between a reinforced response and the availability of the next reinforcement. (3)

Variable ratio schedule. A reinforcement schedule in which, after a reinforced response, some variable number of responses is necessary before another reinforcement is offered. (3)

Vertical integration. A strategy of formally taking control of sources of supply and distribution. (16)

Wage incentive plans. Schemes used to link pay to performance on production jobs. (7)

Well-structured problems. Decision-making situations in which the existing and desired states are clear and how to get from one state to the other is fairly obvious. (12)

NAME INDEX

SUBJECT INDEX